THE EARLY YEARS

CANADA

LAKE ONTARIO

Birthplace of

LAKE MICHIGAN

Buffalo Manchester **Palmyra**
Canandaigua • Fayette

Church organized 1830

*Joseph tried for
misdemeanor 1826*

MASS.

NEW YORK

Bainbridge

Colesville

CONN.

*First home of Joseph and
Emma. Joseph translates plates*

Harmony

PA.

MICHIGAN

LAKE ERIE

Cleveland
New Portage

Kirtland

*First Mormon
Temple 1836*

• Chicago

Wooster

Richfield

Hiram

*Joseph
tarred and
feathered 1832*

Mansfield

INDIANA

Bucyrus

Bellefontaine

OHIO

Greenfield

WITHDRAWN

Springfield

Scioto River

Ohio River

Paris

Indianapolis

Mad R.

Dayton

Miami River

Greencastle

Cincinnati

Wabash River

NORTH

WEST

KENTUCKY

Ohio River

0   100   200

Scale of miles

JOSEPH SMITH

BOOKS BY DONNA HILL

BIOGRAPHY

Joseph Smith: THE FIRST MORMON
Third Book of Junior Authors
(*with Doris de Montreville*)

FICTION

Catch a Brass Canary

JUVENILES

Not One More Day

NON-FICTION

The Picture File:
A MANUAL
AND A CURRICULUM-RELATED
SUBJECT HEADING LIST

JOSEPH SMITH
The First Mormon

by

Donna Hill

C. 1

DOUBLEDAY & COMPANY, INC.
GARDEN CITY, NEW YORK
1977

ISBN: 0-385-00804-X
Library of Congress Catalog Card Number 73–15345
Copyright © 1977 by DONNA HILL
All Rights Reserved
Printed in the United States of America
First Edition

In memory of my mother
Emma Wirthlin Hill

PREFACE

The life of Joseph Smith was a rousing story of conflict, sacrifice, faith and courage, much of it in raw western country that was not yet fully assimilated into the United States civilization. For that reason a biographer might well be influenced to write for the general reader, and this has been my purpose. However, Joseph's life has much significance for the student of American history, religion and sociology, and I have also tried to take that into account.

From the early days of his church, a great deal of the discussion about Joseph Smith has been whether or not the gold plates from which he claimed to have translated *The Book of Mormon* really existed and whether in fact he had a vision of the Lord telling him that the true church did not then exist on earth. To those questions there can be no answer that will satisfy everyone, and prolonged debate over them has, until lately, diverted attention from the important social and religious forces to which Joseph was responding and to which he contributed.

Early in the nineteenth century, young Joseph and his parents moved to western New York, where they were swept up in the prevailing religious furor. Sect was contending with sect, minister with minister. As Joseph Smith's mother said of a similar situation in her youth, since the churches were all witnesses against one another, a choice from among them was impossible.

To the adolescent Joseph a fundamental question occurred—from what source did these churches receive their authority? In response to his agony of doubts came a vision in which the Lord appeared to him and told him that there was no authority in any of the contending churches. In subsequent visions and revelations, authority was vested in Joseph to establish the true church of Christ in the last dispensation. Thereafter, the young prophet devoted his life to that effort, and to the attempt to provide the kind of society for which his mother and many of their rootless contemporaries expressed the need, one in which all aspects were harmoniously integrated into one authoritarian church. Almost from the outset, Joseph was criticized for trying to solve all of the great religious controversies of his day, but this was in fact his very purpose, to settle divisive questions of doctrine.

Joseph's church was only one of many, including the Seekers, Adventists, Scientists and Campbellites, that were founded after the Revolution in response to the need felt for a religious reform. Like the church established by Joseph, some new movements attempted to restructure society in communal experiments, such as those conducted by the Fourierists, Swedenborgians, Cabet's Icarians, the Spiritualists, Robert Owen's New Harmony, and the Transcendentalists of Brook Farm, or in revisions of familial and sexual mores, such as those made by the Shakers, who renounced sexual intercourse; Josiah Warren's group, who combined free love and spiritualism; and the followers of John Noyes, who practiced communal marriage. Such groups had the difficult task of establishing their unique organization within the larger society, and most eventually failed. Of all, Joseph developed the most extensive following. He had a message that filled a particular need and with it the ability to surround himself with vigorous, talented men and to inspire them to carry out his ideas. His community might have been even more successful during his lifetime if it had not been for certain of his institutions that differed radically from those of the larger society and were interpreted as threatening.

As Joseph saw it, he had the truth, and the truth was for the whole world. His urgent mission was to spread the gospel and to call the faithful to Zion, which he and his people would build as the last refuge against the final onslaughts of Satan before the second advent of Christ. Everywhere he and his followers established a community, however, they were seen as endangering what the older settlers most cherished. Outraged by the Mormons' claim to have the one true religion and by their candid statement that as Saints they would inherit the earth, older settlers grew fearful of Mormon strength and envious of what Mormons achieved by their phenomenal labor, thrift and ingenuity. Joseph soon learned that he could not fulfill his destiny unless he made his people invincible, but his difficulties only increased when he tried to combine spiritual with worldly leadership, adding to his responsibilities as prophet, seer and revelator the duties of real estate agent, city planner, banker, businessman, architectural consultant, journalist, social reformer, lieutenant general of militia and politician. Most of his followers saw nothing improper in this. It seemed only wise and expedient that their prophet, whose inspiration came directly from the Lord, should lead them in all things. To some dissenters within the church, however, and to many neighbors, it appeared that Joseph was violating the sacred American ideals of separation of church and state and democratic distribution of power.

The more powerful Joseph and his people grew, the more they were envied and feared and the more necessary it became for the Mormons to gather strength. A vicious cycle was soon in operation. Insults and harassment of the Mormons progressed to mobbing and assault, assault turned to pillage, confiscation of property, massacre and exile. One city after another, built with great sacrifice and labor, the Mormons were forced to abandon. Finally, only fourteen years after he had established his church, Joseph Smith was assassinated and thousands of his followers were forced out of their beautiful Nauvoo, the show place of Illinois, and driven beyond the boundaries of civilization. In terrible hardship, in the most remarkable migration in American history, they crossed the western plains and established their kingdom of Saints in the Rocky Mountains.

Although state and federal governments had failed to protect them in their rights, the Mormons felt ardently devoted to the Constitution. Like Joseph Smith, most of them had descended from early colonials and patriots who had played a vital role in the founding of the nation. They believed that America was the Lord's chosen land, and they expected eventually to provide the final refuge for their fellow citizens.

Although they were once feared and reviled, the Mormons are now seen by historians, from a longer perspective, as very much a part of the struggling and idealistic young country. Thomas O'Dea, in his *The Mormons,* says he considers them unique, with their own special characteristics, but at the same time typically American. Others agree. William Mulder, in his "The Mormons in American History" (*Utah Historical Quarterly,* January 1959), says that in their colonial origins, their attempts at a utopian community, their emigrations and resettlements, they exemplified the outstanding elements that shaped the larger society. Marvin S. Hill and James B. Allen in *Mormonism and American Culture* say that to describe and discuss the Mormons is to describe and discuss America, its essential drives and some of its basic characteristics and molding forces.

In this work, I have attempted to see Joseph Smith in that context, and as the builder, despite great adversity, of a highly successful community. With my view of him as an inspired spiritual leader who had ordinary human failings, I think he would have been entirely in accord. He himself saw the danger to his followers of holding illusions that he was sanctified, and he repeatedly insisted that he had a man's passions and weaknesses. He was entirely convinced of his mission on earth but thought that the Lord had chosen a weak thing through which to accomplish His work. Joseph's awareness of his failings added a certain poignancy to his high purpose, but at the end he showed the strength of his convictions when he surrendered his life to his enemies to preserve his church.

My intention in this biography has not been to resolve the numerous controversial issues yet remaining in Joseph's history. In Joseph's belief, the workings of his mind in visions and revelations were God's method of communicating with him. Such a belief was common in his day, before the nineteenth-century studies of the subconscious, and it continues to exist in many religious persuasions. I do not attempt a psychological analysis of this or of other aspects of his personality, although in a general way I have tried to understand his feelings, his purpose and his motivation. My aim has been to present the dramatic and human elements of his story, to show the warmth, spirituality and joyousness for which his people loved him, but also his foibles, his implacable will and something of his complexity. In addition I have felt that there could be no meaningful portrayal of the prophet without showing the suffering, sacrifice, courage and conviction of his followers.

As a descendant of Mormon pioneers who crossed the plains in faith and hardship, I cannot deny that my sympathies lie with the Saints. However, I have been as objective as possible within my capabilities, and hold with the late president of the Mormon Church, Joseph Fielding Smith, when he said in his "Libels of Historians" (as quoted in *Dialogue: A Journal of Mormon Thought,* Spring 1972), "No historian has the right to make his prejudices paramount to the facts he should record."

Donna Hill
New York City
January 1976

ACKNOWLEDGMENTS

My debts of gratitude to American libraries and institutions are so numerous that I can offer thanks only in a general way for the uniformly courteous, prompt and efficient replies I have received to my letters of inquiry and to my requests in person for advice and assistance. Of the many I should mention in particular, I want to express my gratitude to the Henry E. Huntington Library, San Marino, California, for the fellowship that my brother Marvin S. Hill and I shared to do research in their Mormon Collection in the summer of 1970. I wish to thank Yale University for the fellowship awarded to my brother, 1972–73, that was of benefit to this work and for their courtesies to me, as well, especially in the use of materials in the William Robertson Coe Collection.

I have been most fortunate in having the use of manuscripts and other materials in the Historical Department of The Church of Jesus Christ of Latter-day Saints, in Salt Lake City. Many of these materials have only recently been made available to scholars, and some have never before been published. Permission to use these materials was obtained for this biography by my brother from the Historical Department when the late Joseph Fielding Smith was Church Historian. To the late President Smith, to Earl Olson, who was then Assistant Church Historian and later Church Archivist, to the present Church Historian, Leonard J. Arrington, to Dean C. Jessee, Senior Historical Associate, and to the other scholars in that Department, I wish to express much gratitude.

I owe thanks to W. Grant McMurray, Director, Library-Archives Services, Reorganized Church of Jesus Christ of Latter Day Saints, for permission to use materials in their collection, and for careful verification of my transcripts.

I am grateful also to the librarians of The New York Public Library for much courteous assistance and to my colleagues at Hunter College Library, the City University of New York, for the interest they have shown in this project, and for the extended loan of some hard-to-find and out-of-print books on American history and religion.

Among other libraries and institutions to which my debt is large are Brigham Young University Library, the Utah State Historical Society, the

Chicago Historical Society, The Stanford University Libraries, Bancroft Library at the University of California at Berkeley, Illinois State Historical Society, Missouri Historical Society, Nauvoo Historical Society, Topsfield Historical Society, the National Archives and the Library of Congress.

I am much indebted also to the recent research and writing of scholars, including James B. Allen, Richard L. Anderson, Leonard J. Arrington, Milton V. Backman, Mauren Ursenbach Beecher, Richard L. Bushman, David Briton Davis, Mario DePillis, Robert Flanders, Klaus Hansen, Keith Huntress, Stanley S. Ivins, Dean C. Jessee, Dallin Oaks, Thomas O'Dea, and to others who have published in such journals as *Brigham Young University Studies; Church History; Dialogue: A Journal of Mormon Thought; Journal of Mormon History; Utah Historical Quarterly;* and *Western Humanities Review.* I have also found much inspiration in the activities of the Mormon History Association, in particular the conference and papers presented in Nauvoo, Illinois, April 1974.

I must acknowledge a debt to the monumental work of the late Mormon historian Brigham H. Roberts, and to the early Saints themselves, for the letters, diaries and memoirs that have made their history come alive for me.

Thanks are due many other individuals, especially to Richard Baltzell and Muriel Fuller, who approached me in 1968 with the proposal that I do this biography, and to my father and my late mother for their encouragement. I wish to thank Marjorie and Darrell Smith, Lila and Marvin S. Hill, Afton Miles and Peter Crawley for the loan of personal materials. I owe many thanks to Mary Ellen Lai for her diligence in deciphering rough drafts, for her indefatigable typing and much other help, and to Laura Lai and David Lai for graciously sharing their mother's attention for that purpose. I am grateful also to Serafine Salemi for typing, to Stanley Miles, Quincy Lai, Frank Giella and Alice Penrose for aid in preparing the manuscript and to Frank W. Penrose for help in organizing my materials.

Particular thanks are due my brother, Marvin S. Hill, associate professor of history at Brigham Young University, for his many suggestions and for the use of his writings and research, especially his dissertation.

CONTENTS

LIST OF ILLUSTRATIONS

CHRONOLOGY

1805 Born in Sharon, Vermont

1820 Receives first vision, in Palmyra, New York

1823 Three visitations of the Angel Moroni

1827 Marries Emma Hale; finds *The Book of Mormon* plates; starts dictating

1829 Joseph Smith and Oliver Cowdery ordain each other to the Aaronic Priesthood

1830 *The Book of Mormon* published; Church of Jesus Christ established

1831 Joseph moves the Church to Kirtland, Ohio; establishes "Zion" in Independence, Jackson County, Missouri. The church membership divides into two main bodies, in Ohio and Missouri.

1833 1200 Saints driven out of Jackson County, settle mostly in Clay County, Missouri

1834 Saints from the eastern states march as Zion's Camp to aid the refugees in Missouri

1835 Twelve Apostles chosen

1836 Kirtland Temple dedicated; Saints in Clay County required to leave; establish new base in Far West, Caldwell County, Missouri

1837 Mission to England founded; establishment and failure of the Kirtland bank

1838 Joseph flees from Kirtland to Caldwell County; the Kirtland Saints follow. Battles in Missouri. Governor Boggs issues order to expel or exterminate the Saints. Joseph imprisoned in Liberty jail; the Saints driven out of Far West and environs; take refuge in Quincy, Illinois.

1839 Joseph escapes from jail; moves with the Saints to Commerce (Nauvoo), Illinois; pleads Mormon cause against Missouri before President Van Buren and the Congress

1840 Nauvoo charters granted by Illinois

1842 Joseph arrested on charge of conspiring to shoot Governor Boggs; released by the Nauvoo Municipal Court; another writ issued; Joseph goes into hiding

1843 Writ on the Boggs charge judged invalid in hearing at Springfield; Joseph arrested again at Dixon, released again by the Nauvoo Municipal Court, non-Mormon populace outraged; revelation on polygamy read to the church High Council

1844 Announces his candidacy for the presidency of the United States; orders destruction of the dissident newspaper, *Nauvoo Expositor;* Joseph and Hyrum assassinated

AUTHOR'S NOTE

In this work, the terms "Saints" and "Mormons" are used interchangeably for members of the church founded by Joseph Smith, while "Gentiles" is used in the sense they gave to the word, meaning everyone else, including the Jews.

The original Mormon was the ancient American of Israelitish descent who gave his name to *The Book of Mormon.* In the belief of Joseph's followers, *The Book of Mormon* was translated by Joseph from plates revealed to him by the heavenly messenger, Moroni, and is Scripture, along with the Bible.

In early days, "Mormon" or "Mormonite" was used derogatively when applied from without the church, and was objectionable to the Saints, but later they adopted it as a nickname. Currently, the name is used only for members of The Church of Jesus Christ of Latter-day Saints who went west with Brigham Young after Joseph's martyrdom and established their headquarters in Salt Lake City, Utah. The Mormons are by far the largest group of Joseph's followers. Others who have also descended from Joseph's original group of Saints, such as the Reorganized Church of Jesus Christ of Latter Day Saints, Independence, Missouri; The Church of Jesus Christ in the United States of America, Monongahela, Pennsylvania; and The Church of Christ (Temple Lot), Independence, Missouri, make it plain that their organizations are entirely distinct from the Mormons and some of their tenets are different.

The grammar, punctuation and spelling of original documents have been retained, but use of "(*sic*)" has been avoided as tiresome, except where its elimination might cause doubts about the original. Some excerpts in this work are from original documents reproduced in secondary sources, and are taken as edited.

In early documents, family and given names are not infrequently spelled in various ways and are here reproduced as found. In the text of this work, however, the most popular form of the name is used, with known variations following in parentheses when the name first appears.

For quotations from the *Doctrine and Covenants,* paragraph numbers are not indicated in the text, but are given in the footnotes.

JOSEPH SMITH

BURIAL OF A MARTYR

The little cortege moved slowly under the parching sun, eight mounted militiamen riding one at each wheel of the two wagons, and a horseman in city clothes, a huge, stocky man of over three hundred pounds, whose left ear and cheek were freshly burned by a musket ball.

Driving the first team was Samuel Harrison Smith, a young man of thirty-six, who looked ill and worn with grief. Grief also marked the plump face of the horseman, Willard Richards, but the other teamster and the sweating militiamen rode impassively. Mile after mile they had traveled in silence, the only sound a clatter of the wagons, the clink of soldiers' accouterments, the buzz of prairie flies and the muffled hoofbeats in the road, which was muddy from days of rain.

It was Friday, June 28, 1844. A cloudy morning had given way to a glaring sun and sweltering heat. The company had been riding since 8 A.M. on that dreary plain in Illinois, from Carthage to the Mormon town of Nauvoo, and it was now nearly two in the afternoon. They had moved as if reluctant to reach their destination.

Each wagon held a ghastly freight—a lidless coffin knocked together from slabs of pine, and a blood-soaked corpse protected from the sun, heat and flies only by prairie brush, and on the first, a ragged Indian blanket. The bodies were those of Samuel's two elder brothers.

Heavy in the coffins, the bodies were of large, strong men in their prime. The one under the blanket was Joseph Smith, thirty-eight, and the other was Hyrum, forty-four. Both were the victims of mob hysteria.

Joseph Smith had lately become a powerful figure in Illinois and a focus of national attention, founder and mayor of Nauvoo, the largest city in the state, lieutenant general of an independent militia of some five thousand well-trained men, "Prophet, Seer and Revelator" of a rapidly growing church which had voiced the expectation of converting all the world, businessman and real estate agent, temple builder, newspaper editor, candidate for the presidency of the United States with able speakers stumping for his religion and his politics in every part of the country, and disrupter, it was claimed, of social and family institutions in his establishment of polygamy and his repeated escapes from legal writ. About two weeks before his death he had defied the sacred American precept of freedom of the press, by demolishing an opposition newspaper called the *Nauvoo Expositor,* on the grounds that it was libelous and a public nuisance.

Some of the citizens of Hancock and neighboring counties could tolerate no more. Impatient with the orderly procedure of the law, or perhaps convinced that the law could not reach Joseph Smith, their fear and hatred had grown to a frenzy. Mobs began to demonstrate. The state militia was called out. Fearful that a civil war was imminent, the governor had rushed to the Hancock County seat at Carthage and called for Joseph and other Mormon leaders to surrender for trial. Under threat that his city would be sacked and his innocent people subjected to a repetition of the pillage, murder and banishment they had suffered in Missouri, Joseph and his brother had given themselves up under promise of the governor's personal protection and were in Carthage jail awaiting trial when a mob in blackface had swept past the guards and killed them.

To Joseph the accusations made in the *Expositor* had seemed just another in a long series of harassments and persecutions he had suffered, which in his own thinking were the manifestation of Satan opposing the work he had been assigned by the Lord, the establishment of the last dispensation in preparation for the second coming of Christ. The more he and his people were harassed, the more he tried to build a social structure of absolute independence and strength as refuge against the onslaughts of Satan. Tragically, the stronger he grew the more threatening he seemed to outsiders, and the more dangerous his own situation became. At last he found himself in an intolerable dilemma, his ideals in conflict with the success of his life's work. In a moment of bad judgment, he and his City Council ordered the destruction of a press that they considered libelous and this provided neighbors with the pretext they had been seeking to rise against him.

The dead men's brother, Samuel, had been working on his farm when he heard of the riots and his brothers' imprisonment. Desperately afraid for their safety, he had saddled a fast horse and dashed for Carthage. On the way some of the mob in blackface recognized him and rode after him. Samuel spurred his horse into the woods, outraced them and escaped when they stopped at the edge of town, not daring to go back to the jail. Samuel had reached Carthage in a state of shock from fright and exhaustion, only to be shown his brothers' mutilated bodies. Samuel would be dead himself within a month, from a fever contracted during that ordeal.

The big horseman riding with the cortege was Willard Richards, who had been with the Smith brothers and another Mormon leader, John Taylor, when the mob attacked. Willard had escaped in a hail of bullets with a mere grazing of his face, but John Taylor was badly wounded and was now lying in a Carthage tavern at the mercy of the townsfolk.

The wagons and their escort had left a scene of panic in Carthage. Soon after the news of the assassination the cry had gone up from house to house, "The Mormons are coming!" Word spread that the Nauvoo Legion would swoop down upon Carthage in revenge for the death of their leaders.

Most of the militia called out to put down the riots had been disbanded earlier and the town was defenseless. County administrators hastily piled official records into a wagon and had them carted away. The townsfolk snatched a few provisions and fled, the women and children in carriages and wagons, the men on horseback or on foot, pulling out in such haste that windows and doors were left open, food on the table and animals abandoned. Tradesmen, housewives, farmers and officials crowded the roads to south and southeast, in the direction opposite from Nauvoo.

On his way back from Nauvoo, where he had cautioned the Mormons to submit to the law, Governor Ford learned to his horror that the Mormon leaders under his protection had been murdered. He pushed on to Carthage and arrived long after nightfall to find the place nearly deserted. Hurrying to the public square, he announced to the few people left that the Mormons would probably burn the town and urged everybody to run for safety. With his entourage, he then put as many miles as he could between himself and Nauvoo, according to J. W. Woods, who was Joseph Smith's attorney. He went by a devious route from Carthage to Crooked Creek to Augusta to Chili without stopping until he reached Quincy. From there he wrote at once to Woods and sent word to Joseph's wife Emma and to Major General Dunham of the Nauvoo Legion that the Mormons would have justice.

Within a few hours, Carthage had become a temporary ghost town, wind-swept and deserted except for a few elderly or sick who could not get away and the family of the tavern keeper, where the wounded Taylor lay a semi-hostage.

Hysteria spread at once throughout the county. People from Warsaw, whose newspaper, the *Warsaw Signal,* had been pouring out vitriol against Joseph Smith, began streaming across the river to Missouri. As far away as the governor's refuge in Quincy, bells were ringing the alarm.

The panic, however, was groundless. The Mormons in Nauvoo were subdued in grief, and frightened themselves. A few families, remembering the destruction, looting and beatings the Mormons had already suffered in Missouri, thought the mob that had killed their leaders would next attack their town and fled across the river to Iowa. Most of the Mormons, however, had remained behind in shock and sorrow. All trade and business activities in Nauvoo had ceased while the people came to hear the counsel of forbearance which the leaders had sent before their martyrdom. Willard Richards too had sent a message ahead, "Be still and know that God reigns."

About two o'clock, the Mormons began to gather by the hundreds in Mulholland Street, which ran through town just south of the half-built temple. Workmen, farmers, housewives, children, businessmen, leaders of the church, members of the City Council, officers and men of the Legion came in growing numbers, but under the direction of the city marshal, the crowds remained orderly. Among them, however, were many recent converts from Ireland and Wales, who began a low moaning, which increased to a keening the like of which had never been heard before in that part of the New World.

The crowds enlarged as the Mormons from outlying farms got to town. About three o'clock the people walked out to meet the cortege, their piercing lamentation preceding them across the plain. The crowd of people turned as the group drew near, surrounded the men and wagons and escorted them back to town to the Mansion House, near the riverbank, where Joseph Smith had lived with his wife Emma, who was pregnant, and their four children.

By now there was a multitude of between eight and ten thousand. Though exhausted by his ride and his ordeal, Willard Richards signaled that he would speak. The people grew quiet instantly, knowing that he had been with the prophet and his brother when they were killed. Richards asked the people mildly to keep the peace. He said that he had pledged his life on their good conduct, and reminded them that another of their leaders lay wounded and helpless in Carthage. The Mormons agreed that they would leave vengeance to God.

The bodies of Joseph and Hyrum were taken into the Mansion House. The doors were closed and the citizens of Nauvoo were asked to go home until morning.

Three men washed the bodies and plugged the wounds with cotton soaked in camphor. Joseph had been shot in the chest, the lower abdomen and the back and Hyrum had been shot in the face at close range. The bodies of the two brothers were made as presentable as possible and lovingly dressed in drawers, fine plain shirts, white neckerchiefs, white cotton stockings and shrouds. At last Joseph's wife Emma and Hyrum's wife Mary and their children were allowed to see them.[1]

The next morning, the bodies were put into coffins lined with white cambric and covered with black velvet studded with brass. A glass lid with brass hinges was put over each face, and the bodies were laid out for viewing in the dining hall.[2]

At eight o'clock the doors were opened. As many as ten thousand people, it was estimated, passed through the house in slow procession, pausing in grief and reverence over the coffins. At five o'clock the doors were closed and the people were asked to leave the dead brothers to their families.

Behind the locked doors, however, hasty and secret preparations began. It was said that before his surrender at Carthage Joseph had given directions to his Council of Twelve Apostles about how he should be buried.[3] The coffins were taken out of the pine boxes and hidden in a tiny bedroom in the northeast corner of the house. Sand and rocks were put in the boxes in place of the bodies and the boxes were nailed shut. At the time appointed for the funeral, the boxes were taken in the hearse to the graveyard and buried in a public ceremony conducted by leaders of the church.

At midnight, under armed guard, the bodies were carried out quietly through the garden to the site of Nauvoo House, then under construction nearby, and buried in the freshly dug basement. The graves were smoothed and obliterated, covered with wood chips and rubbish, to hide the brothers even in death from their enemies, who, it was rumored, were after Joseph's head for the price still on it in Missouri.[4]

Joseph had not been ready to leave this existence for the next, resplendent though he believed the next would be. "I defy all the world and prophesy they will never overthrow me till I get ready," he had said only eight months before.[5] Joseph took great joy in earthly life, in family, children, love and friendship, in dogs and horses, in ceremony and pageantry, in contests and games, parades, banquets, music and dancing, and in all the pleasures of living, which he did not deny himself, despite the complaints of some of his followers who thought an ascetic life would have been more becoming to a prophet of the Lord. At the first alarm, Joseph had taken flight across the river, planning to disappear in the untrackable west. Yet when he realized that the destruction of the Mormon town by frustrated mobs was inevitable if he escaped, he returned and surrendered. "I am going like a lamb to the slaughter," he told a faithful member of his church.[6]

Joseph Smith's followers were shocked, anguished and outraged by his murder. Emily Dow Partridge, one of the prophet's plural wives, said the news hit "like a thunderbolt, crushing the people to earth." John Taylor, who was with the Smiths and Willard Richards and was grievously wounded at the time of the prophet's assassination, thought first of the Mormons' terrible loss. He wrote that soon after the attack, Willard Richards confirmed his worse fears that Joseph was dead. "How lonely was that feeling! How cold, barren and desolate! In the midst of difficulties he was always the first in motion; in critical positions his counsel was always sought. As our Prophet he approached our God, and obtained for us his will; but now our Prophet, our counselor, our general, our leader, was gone . . . for all things pertaining to this world, or the next, he had spoken for the last time on earth."[7]

Yet the Mormons were later to become exalted by their prophet's martyrdom, as though by a crowning achievement. The official announcement by his church said, "He lived great, and he died great in the eyes of God and his people, and like most of the Lord's anointed in ancient times, has sealed his mission and his works with his own blood . . ."[8]

Who could ever doubt him again? The Gentiles (Joseph's name for everybody outside his church), the skeptics and the scornful were outdone. As it evolved, the prophet's martyrdom did not seal his testimony for any but his followers. He remained as puzzling and controversial to the Gentiles after death as he had been during life.

James Gordon Bennett, editor of the *New York Herald,* once made a personal visit to Nauvoo and afterward kept a close watch on Joseph's activities by sending correspondents. He wrote often about the prophet, sometimes with admiration and sometimes with a scarcely veiled sarcasm which Joseph chose to overlook. In his editorial of April 3, 1842, Bennett said:

> This Joseph Smith is undoubtedly one of the greatest characters of the age. He indicates as much talent, originality, and moral courage as Mahomet, Odin, or any of the great spirits that have hitherto produced the revolutions of past ages . . . He believes himself divinely inspired and a worker of miracles. He cures the sick of diseases—so it is said—and although Smith is not aware of the fact, we have been informed by a medical man that his influence over nervous disorders, arises from a powerful magnetic influence . . .[9]

Governor Ford, who is remembered mainly for his failure to protect Joseph and Hyrum from assassination while they were in jail under his personal guarantee of safety, thought Joseph Smith was a unique mixture of talent, knavery and charm. In his *History of Illinois,* published ten years after the prophet's death, he emphasized the trouble Joseph and the Mormons caused his administration. He wrote that Joseph

> . . . had some great natural parts, which fitted him for temporary success, but which were . . . obscured and counteracted by the inherent corruption and vices of his nature . . . It must not be supposed that the pretended Prophet practiced the tricks of a common imposter; that he was a dark and gloomy person, with a long beard, a grave and severe aspect, and a reserved and saintly carriage of his person; on the contrary, he was full of levity, even to boyish romping . . . being

always able to satisfy his followers of the propriety of his conduct . . .[10]

This was the kind of opinion that Ford's Mormon contemporary, Orson
Spencer, would intend to refute when he wrote in a letter of 1842, ". . .
he seems to employ no studied effort to guard himself against misrep-
resentations, but often leaves himself exposed to misconstructions by those
who watch for his faults." Again, Spencer wrote, "No matter what is said
against Joseph Smith, or who, or how many say it, or however *credible* the
witnesses, they are not competant to testify because they have not the gift
of revelation . . . Flesh and blood cannot reveal the spiritual things, but
our Father in heaven. The things of the spirit require the same spirit to
discern them."[11]

Upon those whom he met in person, Mormon and Gentile alike, Joseph
Smith had a remarkable effect. In the rough territories in which he spent
most of his mature life, where glamour was no common commodity, he
was dazzling. One contemporary said of him, "He was one of the grandest
samples of manhood that I ever saw walk or ride at the head of a legion of
men."[12] An early church leader, George Miller, said that the first time he
saw the prophet, he seemed familiar, as if he had always known him.
When George realized that this man was the prophet Joseph Smith, "Indeed my whole frame was in a tremor at the thought, and my heart seemed
as if it were coming up into my mouth."[13]

Jesse, son of the prophet's Uncle Silas, who spent a good deal of time in
the prophet's home after his father died, said of him: "I am unable to fully
describe my sensations when in the presence of this wonderful man . . . I
have never heard any human voice, not even my mother's that was so attractive to me. Even his bitterest enemies, if they had the privilege of hearing him speak, became mollified, and forgot their anger . . . his domestic
animals seemed to love him . . . The dog and the horses rejoiced when
they saw this man . . . his children rejoiced when he was present."[14]

General Moses Wilson, one of the officers who took Joseph for trial in
Missouri, said, "He was a very remarkable man. I carried him into my
house a prisoner in chains, and in less than two hours my wife loved him
better than she did me."[15]

The prophet's wife, Emma, had cause to complain about her husband's
magnetism. A comment that she made years after his death is amusing and
revealing of his charisma. She wrote in a letter to her son Joseph III: "I
do not expect you can do much more in the garden than your Father
could, and I never wanted him to go into the garden to work for if he did
it would not be fifteen minutes before there would be three or four, or
some times a half a dozen men round him and they would tramp the
ground down faster than he could hoe it up."[16]

Some of the prophet's followers turned against him, but their statements often revealed their own disappointed expectations rather than any valid assessment of Joseph's character. Ezra Booth, a convert who became disillusioned early, wrote to one of the faithful, Edward Partridge, in a letter which was published December 6, 1831, in the *Painesville Telegraph,* "Have you not frequently observed in Joseph, a want of that sobriety, prudence, and stability which are some of the most prominent traits of the Christian character. Have you not discovered in him, a spirit of lightness and levity, a temper of mind easily irritated, and an habitual proneness to jesting and joking? Have you not repeatedly proven to your satisfaction that he says he knows things to be so by the spirit when they are not so?"[17]

Some followers of the prophet acknowledged that he might not be perfect but indicated that they did not require his perfection.

Brigham Young spoke of a conversation he had had with a man of another faith who charged Joseph Smith "with everything bad, that he could find language to utter." Brigham, who had not yet met the prophet, replied, "I have never seen him, and do not know his private character. The doctrine he teaches is all I know about the matter, bring anything against that if you can. As to anything else I do not care. If he acts like a devil, he has brought forth a doctrine that will save us, if we will abide it. He may get drunk every day of his life, sleep with his neighbor's wife every night, run horses and gamble, I do not care anything about that, for I never embrace any man in my faith. But the doctrine he has produced will save you and me, and the whole world."[18]

To countless Mormons, no matter what others said about him, Joseph remained the ideal man of God. Daniel Tyler wrote that when Joseph's brother William and several other members of the church rebelled against him in Kirtland, he called them to a meeting. Tyler wrote:

> I perceived a sadness in his countenance and tears trickling down his cheeks . . . he opened the meeting by prayer. Instead however, of facing the audience, he turned his back and bowed upon his knees, facing the wall . . . to hide his sorrow and tears.
>
> I had heard men and women pray—especially the former—from the most ignorant, both as to letters and intellect, to the most larned and eloquent, but never until then had I heard a man address his Maker as though He was present listening as a kind father would listen to the sorrows of a dutiful child . . . [the prayer] was to a considerable extent in behalf of those who accused him of having gone astray and fallen into sin, that the Lord would forgive them and open their eyes that they might see aright . . . There was no ostentation, no raising of the voice as by enthusiasm, but a plain conversational tone, as a man would address a present friend. It appeared to me as though, in case the veil were taken away, I could see the

Lord standing facing His humblest of all servants I had ever seen. Whether this was really the case I cannot say; but one thing I can say, it was the crowning . . . of all the prayers I ever heard.[19]

A conflict between pride and humility was apparent in the prophet. Although he could be magnanimous to enemies, especially when he had the upper hand, friends said Joseph would not let himself be bested by anyone. Newel Knight, who had known Joseph from boyhood and remained his devoted follower, said, "in all his boyish sports and amusements, I never knew any one to gain advantage over him."[20] Yet he kept the good will of his friends.

Another faithful Mormon, Benjamin F. Johnson, recalled that Joseph "would allow no arrogance or undue liberties; criticisms even by his associates were rarely acceptable, and contradictions would rouse in him the lion at once, for by no one of his fellows would he be superceded."[21] A non-Mormon said, "he possessed the most indomitable perseverance . . . and deemed himself born to command, and he did command."[22]

Some of the prophet's intolerance of criticism perhaps reflected the need to sustain his calling. He was painfully conscious that in education and refinement he was not equal to some of his associates. By his own conviction, the Lord had called him in a revelation to demonstrate His wisdom through the weak things of the earth. In things of the spirit or in bodily prowess he was not weak, and of this he often reminded his followers. It is reported that a fight nearly broke out between Joseph and one John McDaniel, not a member of the church, when the latter questioned Joseph's ability to prophesy. "Nobody can slander me!" Joseph cried. "If my brethren cannot protect me I will do so myself."[23]

Besides the hundreds of contradictory opinions about the prophet that make an objective assessment of his character difficult is the fact that in the popular view he often assumed the attributes of a folk hero, and to his name highly imaginative stories were attached. The prophet was fully aware of this and sometimes expressed his annoyance. In Springfield in January 1843, he learned that one of the townsfolk was telling it about that he had seen the prophet in Nauvoo, asked him where he got his gray horse and the prophet replied that it had come from the white cloud then passing across the sky. Joseph wrote, "This is a fair specimen of the ten thousand foolish lies circulated by this generation to bring the truth and its advocates into disrepute."[24]

There has been a great deal of conjecture about whether Joseph Smith was a saint or a charlatan, but little has been known or said about his own deepest searchings of soul. Those who observed him, whether friendly or not, often commented upon his easy pleasant manner and his self-assurance, which seemed to indicate serenity and a lack of introspection. Those who touched upon the possibility of the prophet's introspection usually did so lightly, as did J. B. Newhall, when he wrote, "He is a *jolly* fellow; and according to his view is one of the last persons on earth whom God would have raised up a prophet or priest, he is so diametrically opposite to that which he ought to be, in order to merit the titles or to act in such offices."[25]

The fact that attention has not often been paid to this subject by his biographers may be partly because the prophet left very little about it in his own hand.

Joseph is commonly said to have been deficient in the skills of penmanship and grammar. That he himself felt such a lack has frequently been recorded. As he said to Emma in one of the few letters extant in his own hand, "I hope you will excuse . . . my inability in conveying my ideas in writing."[26] For his voluminous books, revelations, journals and correspondence, he relied almost entirely upon scribes. With the exception of a few letters and notes and parts of two diaries of 1832 and 1835, everything was dictated and to that extent made impersonal. Much of his history, especially after he found less time for it, was not even written at his dictation, but was done by others and put into the first person, as though by Joseph, although in most cases probably under his close supervision. The record from December 21, 1842, through June 27, 1844, was written in this way by Willard Richards, and pages from the journals of others, including some by Joseph's cousin George Albert Smith, were incorporated as though by Joseph.

The fact is, however, that Joseph's supposed deficiency in writing is exaggerated. His spelling was inconsistent, but this was not uncommon in his day even among the well educated. He made errors in punctuation and sometimes in grammar, but his sentence structure was mature, usually correct and at times complex, revealing a logical and subtle mind. His vocabulary far exceeded his orthography. His penmanship was blotchy (probably from lack of practice with pen and ink) and certainly not equal to that of the best-educated people of that time when the art was stressed, but it may well be considered superior in legibility to the average hand of college students of a later period.

Nevertheless, since he felt inadequate, he was reluctant to use his own hand, and did not record much of his self-communing. There are enough accounts of his introspection, however, to indicate that he did deeply probe his own acts and motives. He left indications throughout his life of anxiety over his behavior before the Lord, but never suggested, in anything he said, dictated or wrote in his own hand, that he had any doubt of his calling as the Lord's chosen prophet.

Even when very young, he had worried about his follies, whether he was serious enough in purpose and demeanor. At the outset of his work as a religious leader, he confessed to his mother and later wrote in his journal that he was rebuked by the angel of the Lord for considering how he might turn his findings in the Hill Cumorah to profit. Later in his life there is evidence that he had occasional painful doubts about polygamy.

That Joseph believed that the Lord spoke to him through his mind and that he was afraid he was not always worthy to be the Lord's chosen vessel is evident from the fact that the revelations he received so often contained personal rebukes. Even in a very early revelation, received in 1829 before the church was founded, the Lord severely reprimanded him for allowing himself to be persuaded to let the manuscript of *The Book of Mormon* go out of his hands, saying, "and behold how oft you have transgressed the commandments and the laws of God."[27] Another revelation later that year chastised him, "I command you my servant Joseph to repent and walk more uprightly before me . . ."[28]

A revelation of 1833 said, "verily, I say unto Joseph Smith, Jun. —You have not kept the commandments, and must needs stand rebuked before the Lord."[29]

That perhaps Joseph hoped the Lord was not requiring extraordinary saintliness from him is suggested in his revelation of 1841, "unto this end have I raised you up, that I might show forth my wisdom through the weak things of the earth."[30]

An instance of his painful self-searching but his firm faith is revealed in a letter to Emma early in his career as a religious leader. He was writing to her from an inn in Greenville, Indiana, where he had to remain four weeks with Newel K. Whitney, who had broken his leg while he and Joseph were on their way back from a visit to the Saints in Missouri. No indication is in Joseph's journal that his spirit was then in turmoil, although he noted that he took frequent walks out to a little spot in the woods where there were several fresh graves. Under date of June 6, 1832, he wrote in his own hand:

> Dear Wife . . . I have visited a grove which is just back of the town almost every day where I can be Secluded from the eyes of any mortal and there give vent to all the feelings of my heart in meditation and praiyr I have Called to mind all the past moments of my life and am left to morn and Shed tears of Sorrow for my folly in Sufering the adversary of my Soul to have so much power over me as he has had in times past but God is merciful and has forgiven my Sins and I rejoice that he Sendeth forth the Comferter unto as many as believe and humbleth themselves before him . . . I will try to be contented with my lot knowing that God is my friend in him I shall find comfort I have given my life into his hands I am prepared to go at his Call . . .[31]

Perhaps most poignant is what he said in a meeting on August 27 less than a year before his death, as recorded in his journal while Richards was his scribe. For a man of so flamboyant and compelling a personality, displaying such talent, strength and conviction in his role as God's mouth-piece, it stands as a touching plea before his own soul: "If I have sinned I have sinned outwardly—but surely I have contemplated the things of God."[32]

PART ONE

New England

CHAPTER

1

JOSEPH SMITH'S
ANCESTORS

T he error has been perpetuated by some of Joseph Smith's biographers, who were influenced perhaps by the gossip of his day, that he came from shiftless and irreligious forebears. Careful research reveals this to be entirely untrue, although it is a fact, as Joseph Smith himself said, that his parents were once in "a miserable situation." He said elsewhere that his parents, "being in indigent circumstances were obliged to labour hard for the support of a large family having nine children and . . . it required the exertions of all that were able to render any assistance . . ."[1]

A series of unfortunate circumstances had so reduced them from the economic and social status of their ancestors that when Joseph was born and during his boyhood the Smiths were nearly destitute. Nevertheless, as the writings of Joseph and his mother, Lucy Mack Smith, amply demonstrate, the family had retained the values of their colonial forebears, the respect for education (although they themselves had had little opportunity to go to school), the strict moral conscience, the ethic of hard work, the preoccupation with salvation, and the Yankee independence and pride which are not consonant with the shiftless character that some have endeavored to attach to them. Joseph Smith and his mother always seemed to feel entitled to a higher social standing than they had in his boyhood and to believe themselves entirely justified in the distinction that Joseph later achieved for the family. Part of this came from their conviction of Joseph's importance in God's plan for humankind, but to some extent it probably also derived from the fact that young Joseph and his parents knew that they were from early American families of more than average means and influence.

Joseph's paternal ancestor, Robert Smith, was born in Toppesfield County, Essex, England, and came to Massachusetts in 1638, at the age of about fifteen. He prospered in his new country, married the daughter of Thomas French and had ten children. It was said that he built the third house in Boston to have a cellar. Later he bought 280 acres in Rowley, afterward called Boxford, where it is known that he was active in civic affairs from the fact that his name appears on a petition of 1673 to the General Court requesting denial of certain efforts to "free us from Topsfield and lay us to Rowley."[2] Later he became one of the early residents of Topsfield, a strictly Puritan town whose officials are on record for censuring the use of tobacco on the Lord's day, swearing and dressing frivolously.[3]

At his death in 1693, Robert Smith left an estate valued at 189 pounds, which was considerably larger than the average of his period.[4]

Robert's sixth child, Samuel, born in 1666, was a holder of public office, and was listed in court and town records as "gentleman." History is complicated by the fact that at least three Samuel Smiths lived in Topsfield at that time, two of whom married Curtis sisters. Samuel, son of Robert, married Rebecca Curtis and they had nine children, the third of whom was also named Samuel, born in 1714.

Samuel the second was distinguished in public affairs, served six terms in the state legislature and twelve as a selectman. He was chairman of the Tea Committee at Topsfield in 1773 which sustained the action of the Boston Tea Party, and he was elected to the Ipswich Convention and the First Provincial Congress in Massachusetts in 1774.[5]

Samuel the second married Priscilla Gould, a descendant of Zaccheus Gould, the founder of Topsfield. When she died after bearing him two sons and three daughters, Samuel married her cousin, a woman of the same name, who bore no children but reared those of the first Priscilla, including the prophet Joseph's grandfather Asael (sometimes spelled Asahel), who had been born March 7, 1744, just six months before his mother's death.[6]

The colonists had come to New England in large part to find liberty to practice religion as they saw fit. They were not democratic, however, and once in the new land, they had set up their own rigid system of church and state. As Michael Zuckerman suggests in his *Peaceable Kingdoms,* the Puritans of the seventeenth century thought of the ideal community as one in which the members were in strict accord with uniform convictions.

However, under the demands of a fresh environment, the rise of new generations and the influx of people, New Englanders began to adopt freer attitudes, and with the arrival of diverse religious groups, church became less and less strictly identified with community.

Resentment grew among the colonials against regulation from across the ocean by a nation that had little sympathy for their needs. At last they threw off their allegiance to the King of England and formed an independent nation, with a government based upon the consent of citizens. Consensus remained the basis of the new order, but more by compromise than by uniformity of conviction. Tolerance of differing views gradually became an American ideal.

With political revolt came the further weakening of established religions, in particular the Anglican Church. Some New Englanders chose religious as well as political independence and withdrew from all church affiliation. Meanwhile, as the population increased, New Englanders began to leave the coastal regions for the interior.

Succeeding generations of Joseph Smith's family reflected very well the changing attitudes and conditions of the New World. His earliest ancestors who settled in Massachusetts conformed easily to colonial society and achieved distinction in it. Joseph's paternal grandfather, Asael, who reached his prime during the Revolution, displayed independent political and religious ideas, and although he held a profound faith in a personal God and Savior, he came to oppose established churches, and left his father's community to make a new, freer life in pioneer Vermont.

Asael was the youngest. As a boy, he suffered a burn which injured the cords of his neck so badly that forever afterward one shoulder was high, earning him the name of "Crook Neck." Nevertheless as he grew up he developed a powerful physique, and earned the reputation of being able to subdue two men at once. He married Mary Duty of Windham, New Hampshire, and they lived for their first five years in Topsfield, in Asael's father's house, where their third child, Joseph, the prophet's father, was born, July 12, 1771.[7]

Asael always cherished his own ideas and spoke them freely. One contemporary said "some regarded his sentiments as more distorted than his neck," but a more sympathetic opinion of him is recorded in the Topsfield Historical Society Collections (8:89), "a man of very liberal views . . . which he would not yield to bigotry nor opposition." Asael was credited with refusing to associate closely with denominations because he could not reconcile their teachings with the Scriptures and his own reason. He was, however, a man of warm Christian faith, as his own writings testify, and his first three children, Jesse, Priscilla and Joseph, were baptized in the Congregational church at Topsfield on March 8, 1772. The church minutes of that same day state that Asael and Mary "owned the covenant."[8]

In May 1772, Asael and his family moved to Mary's birthplace, Windham, New Hampshire, and two years later to Dunbarton. In July

1776, Asael enlisted for service in the Revolutionary War with Colonel Joshua Wingate's regiment. From 1779 until 1786 he served as town clerk of Derryfield.

A touching account of the death of Asael's father was given years later by one of Asael's younger sons, John. Asael returned to New Hampshire from Topsfield, and sorrowfully told his children about the death of their grandfather. The old gentleman had jumped up crying that his family would suffer unless he could get to the mill. Asael assured him, "I will take care of the family. Dear sir, do go to bed," and promised that he would also provide for his stepmother. Asael said that the old gentleman then "lay down quietly knowing that I always did as I agreed, and soon after fell asleep and was gathered to his people." John wrote that this promise cost his father a great deal of money and trouble but he never regretted it.[9]

Asael's father died November 14, 1785, at the age of seventy-two, the cause named as apoplexy. His obituary, in the *Salem Gazette* of November 22 that year, said he was so amiable and worthy a character in public and private that it would "render the memory of him ever precious . . . a sincere friend of the liberties of his country and a strenuous advocate for the doctrines of Christianity."[10] He left his land equally divided between his sons Asael and Samuel the third, and a requirement that they must provide a horse to carry their stepmother to meetings on Sunday.

As set forth in his will, Samuel's estate seemed of considerable value, but John wrote that Samuel's public duties had required so much of his time that his personal affairs had suffered. Samuel the third, who had been farming on shares with their father, came to Derryfield to tell Asael that the estate would not cover their father's debts. When Asael learned that Samuel felt unable to assume the obligations, he offered to do it himself, determined that no stain would rest upon their father's reputation.[11]

On March 24, 1786, "Asael Smith of Derryfield . . . cooper" and his wife Mary deeded their land to "Samuel Smith of Topsfield . . . gentleman" for 120 pounds, which was 60 pounds less than Asael had paid for it eight years before. On the same day, for a stipulated 250 pounds, Samuel deeded his half of the Topsfield farm to Asael.[12]

Soon afterward, in April, Asael moved his family back to his father's home, a large and solid two-story colonial farmhouse built in 1690 and acquired by Asael's father sometime after 1755.

Topsfield was about twenty miles north of Boston in the middle of Essex County, a heavily wooded area with rich meadows and excellent farm lands, especially along the banks of the Ipswich River. Flax and wool were produced there for spinning and weaving at home, but corn, which had been introduced by the Indians to the first settlers and was used for food, fodder and bedding, was the largest crop, as it was all along the Atlantic seaboard. Although only a young child at the time, John remembered Topsfield as a pleasant town in a region planted like a garden for miles around.[13]

Times were not as easy as they might have seemed to young John, however. His grandfather Samuel had contracted his debts during inflation and his father Asael was trying to pay them while the economy was still depressed.

Massachusetts had made heavy sacrifices during the Revolution. It had the largest assessment for war expenses, had contributed more soldiers and sailors than any other colony and by this time was under a huge debt. Taxes were heavy, demanding, it was estimated, at least a third of a farmer's income. Prices for farm products fell as much as 50 per cent in the post-Revolutionary period, and showed no tendency to rise until 1792. The paper dollar, which had steadily depreciated since the war, was valued at less than one cent just before Samuel died. Although hard money was scarce, petitions by farmers to be allowed to pay debts in produce were refused. Sale of farms and personal property for debts and taxes became common, and so did imprisonment for debt.

During this trying period, Asael proved himself a man of exceptional ability and character. He struggled for the next five years to pay his father's debts from the little he could save beyond what was required for his wife and ten children. As he had promised, he cared for his stepmother also, although from what John said, there seemed to be little affection between them.

Asael managed some eighty acres, mostly pasture and meadow, with an orchard and about eight acres of hay, grain, potatoes and flax. He kept a few pigs, cattle and sheep. Besides his work on the farm, he continued his trade as a cooper, one of eight in Topsfield at that time, and taught the art to his son Joseph.

Like other farm families of New England in that day, the Smiths were close and interdependent, their house not only a shelter but a place for labor, prayer and education. The children learned to work at an early age in the barnyard, fields and household. Any excess beyond need was hard to accumulate, and the children had to learn diligence and thrift.

Despite his work and worries, Asael kept a sense of fun. Given to writing jingles, he sent one to the selectman of Topsfield with his tax assessment. After pleading the poor quality of his holdings, he ended:

> Three heffers two years old I own,
> One heffer calf that's poorly grone!
> My land is acres Eighty two,
> Which sarch the record youle find true;
> And this is all I have in store;
> I thank you if youle tax no more.[14]

After struggling for five years, Asael decided that his best course was to sell the farm to pay the remaining debts. In 1791, he sold the lands, house and barn to Nathaniel Perkins Averill for a stipulated 270 pounds, which was a third less than the value as listed in their father's estate, this third apparently the widow's allotment. Asael found himself clear of his father's obligations at last, but with very little money left.

Having a family which now numbered eleven children to provide for and their future to consider, Asael and Mary no doubt keenly weighed their situation. It was probably not an easy decision, however. In Topsfield, Asael's family had enjoyed an honored status since the town's earliest days. Society there was firmly regulated by church and town meeting, where affairs of the community were conducted and discipline was dispensed. It was a well-ordered life, close-knit, secure socially if not financially, self-sufficient, harmonious and satisfying, in which labor and virtue were duly rewarded. However, although they had sustained the Smith family honor in Topsfield, Asael and Mary had sacrificed their holdings, and Asael perhaps his franchise, since, like many other towns in New England, Topsfield allowed the vote only to "commoners," Englishmen who espoused the orthodox religion and held a stipulated amount of property. Besides, Asael was not altogether content in the stiff religious climate of this little town where he had suffered criticism for his liberal views. The Smiths decided that the time had come to make a new start elsewhere. The New England way of life had made a deep imprint upon Asael and his family, however, which they would carry with them and bequeath to succeeding generations.

In the spring of 1791, the family rented a good dairy farm in nearby Ipswich to be run by Mary and the younger sons while Asael and the eldest son Jesse set out to look for a home in new country.

John's boyhood memory of Ipswich was of a bustling town doing brisk trade, with an elegant courthouse, two meetinghouses and a jail holding six prisoners who were publicly whipped that summer with a cat-o'-nine-tails. Fruit was plentiful and the salt marsh grasses which grew six to eight inches high made good hay for the cattle. Mary and her children had a pleasant summer while waiting for Asael to return.

Asael and Jesse came back with the news that they had taken title to eighty-three acres in the new state of Vermont, at a cost of twenty-six pounds, about a dollar an acre.

It was decided that the two older sons, Jesse, then twenty-three, and Joseph, twenty, should go ahead to clear the land of the heavy timber and prepare for the family to follow in the spring. John writes that his brothers were not gone very long, however, before Asael found he could not bear the separation. He settled his affairs at once, even selling his crops on the ground, and the family packed up to follow the young men. It was October 1791 when they set off for their journey of a hundred and forty miles to Vermont, which at that time, as John writes, was "a monstrous long tour." Asael's third son, also named Asael, who was then eighteen, drove the family team, and a hired man, Webster, came along with his wagon and three yoke of oxen. On the second or third day out, they met Joseph, who had injured his leg and was traveling home in hopes of rest and recovery, but he turned back with the family.

Their two loads of household goods were heavy and the roads were bad. It took the little caravan fourteen days to pass through New Hampshire. In Vermont their route was even more difficult. Asael and his family had to cut their own path through woods far from any settlement, and even to build bridges for the wagons and teams. At last they came to the little clearing made by Jesse and Joseph and the rough log cabin they had built and covered with the bark of elm trees.

The family's task was hard, breaking virgin forest, felling timber and clearing rocks before they could till the land, and setting up a household which had to be self-sustaining. However, Asael, then forty-six, was in full vigor, and Mary too was strong and capable. They had the help of three grown sons and several sturdy children, and they were all well-schooled in hard work and self-sufficiency.

Vermont had long, severe winters and cool summers, but it abounded in wildlife, deer, rabbits, grouse, ducks and geese. Lakes and streams had excellent trout and other food fish. Plums, cherries, grapes and berries grew wild, as did some medicinal plants, including ginseng, and sugar maples were prevalent. The country seemed to offer the chance for a good life.

There is evidence that Asael continued his trade as cooper, and not long after their arrival, he added two or perhaps three farms to his holdings. Their land, which was in South Tunbridge, on the north Royalton boundary, became known as the Smith settlement. It was set off in school district number thirteen, of which Jesse was appointed trustee.

When the Smiths arrived, Vermont had been a state in the Union for less than eight months and offered plenty of opportunity for energetic men. If Asael had dropped from his father's status in the old community, in the new he soon attained distinction of his own. He served as selectman, grand juror, surveyor of highways, and over the years came to hold nearly every office in Tunbridge.

On January 14, 1796, about four years after his arrival in Vermont, he wrote to his friend, the town clerk of Topsfield, Jacob Perkins Towne, a letter that revealed his belief in the imminent fulfillment of Daniel's prophecy of the restoration of the perfect kingdom, which belief would be shared and elaborated upon by his grandson, the prophet Joseph. Asael saw the American Revolution as the first event in the millennium and the rule of God which was soon to come. As Asael wrote to Towne:

he has conducted us through a glorious revolution, and has Brought us into the promised Land of peace & Liberty, and I Believe that he is about to Bring all the world in the Same Beatitude in His own time & way . . . And I Believe that the Stone is now cut out of the mountain, without hands, spoken of by Daniel, and has Smitten the image upon his feet, By which the iron, the Clay, the Brass, the Silver and the gold, (viz all monrical and Ecliesaistical Terony) will be Broken to peaces, and Becom as the Chaff of the Summer Thrashing flore, the wind Shall carry them all away that there Shall be no place found for them . . .[15]

Of his personal affairs, Asael said in this letter that he expected to move into a new house the following spring, and he planned to start another farm. The new farm was to be worked at halves with his son Joseph.

On the margin of his second page, Asael added the interesting note that he expected his son Joseph to be married in a few days. Joseph would marry Lucy Mack, who was then in Tunbridge visiting her brother.

In 1797, Asael was moderator of a meeting to establish one of the early Universalist Societies in Vermont. He and sixteen others, including his sons Jesse and Joseph, signed a statement of the formation of their society under the state law, declaring that they did not wish to be taxed to support the teacher of any other denomination.[16] The belief of the Universalists, as set forth officially at a convention in New Hampshire in 1803, was in one God, "whose nature is love, revealed in one Lord Jesus Christ, by one Holy Spirit of grace, who will finally restore the whole family of mankind to holiness and happiness."[17]

In many ways, Asael exemplified the New England pioneer, hardy, proud, morally strict, civic-minded but independent. He was pious as well but skeptical of organized faith, and warmly patriarchal. Like many religious dissenters, Asael believed in the right of individual conscience and personal interpretation of the Scriptures, which conviction his grandson Joseph was also to espouse. Especially revealing of Asael's character is a paper he wrote for his wife and children, April 10, 1799, about nine years after their arrival in Vermont. Asael intended his message for his family after his death, but they read and cherished it for many years before that event.

He addressed his paper to "My Dear Selfs," saying that he asked God to care for his wife, and advised her, "Put your whole trust solely in him; He never did, nor never will, forsake any that trust in him." To his children, he testified to his belief in immortality and gave them his deepest thoughts:

Trifel not in this point; the Soul is immortal; you have to Deal with an infinit Majasty; you go upon Life and Death therefore in this point be Serious . . . as to religion, I would not wish to point out aney perticuler forme to you; but first I would wish you to sarch the Scriptures, and consult sound reason . . . and See if they . . . are not Sufficant to Evince to you, that religion is a Necessary theam, then I would wish you to Study the Nature of religion, and See whether it consists in outward formalities; or in the hidden man of the heart, whether you can, by outward formes, rites, and ordinances Save your Selves; or whether there is a Necessity of your having help from aney other hand than your own, if you fiend that you Stand in Need of a Saviour; Christ Saith Look unto me and be ye Saved all ye endes of the Earth. then Look to him . . . but miend that you admit no others as Evidences, but the two that god hath apointed (viz) Scripture & Sound reason. . . . and having gottne this Evidence that god is true, be Still adding to your Evidence and injoy your present assurance; Do all to god as to your father, for his Love is ten thousand times greator toards you, than Ever aney Earthly fathers could to his off-spring. . . .

avoid a malancolly Disposition . . . which will work you to all unthankfulness against god, unlovingness to men, and unnaturalness to your Selves . . .

as for your callings aney honist calling will honour you, if you honour that: it is better to be a rich Cobler than a poor Marchant; a rich farmor than a poor preacher, and Never be Discouraged . . . passivear in the way of well Doing and you may hope for Success for my Self, I . . . Never found aney thing too hard for me in my Calling, but Discoragement and unbileaf . . .

forsake not an old friend, be friendly, and faithful to your friends. . . . as to Your Marriages I Do not think it worth while to Say much about them for I believe god hath created the parsons for Each other . . . But for your Children. make it your cheafest work to bring them up in the ways of Virtue, that they may be usefull in their generations. give them, if posable a good education . . . my Last request & Charge is, that you Will Live together in undivided bond of Love . . . Comfort, counsel, relieve, Succour, help and admonish one another . . . I know, I say, and I am Confident in it, that if you will trust god in his own way, he will make Comfortable provisions for you . . . Bless god that you Live in a Land of Liberty, and bear your Selves Dutifully and conscionably toards the authority under which you Live, See god's providence in the appointment of the federal con-stitution, and hold union and order as a precious Jewel . . .

Sure I am my Saviour Christ is parfect and Never will fail in one circumstance. To him I commit your Souls, bodies, estates, names, carracters, Lives, Deaths and all . . . and wish to Leave to you evry thing that I have in this world but my falts, and them I take with me to the grave . . .[18]

Many of Asael's ideals and attitudes would be echoed later by his grandson, the prophet Joseph. Asael believed, as would his grandson, that religion pertained to the inner man, the "hidden man of the heart," and that truth would be granted to the individual through his own efforts and study of the Scriptures. Asael and Joseph after him espoused the Protestant ethic, believing that perseverance in good works would assure success, and that God would provide for those who trusted in Him.

Asael charged his family to succeed economically, while being mindful of the Lord, perhaps reflecting his sensitivity to his father's economic decline and his own loss of status among his father's neighbors. His grandson would later assume that the righteous would prosper, that worldly comfort and achievement would reward the faithful. Asael was optimistic, maintaining that he never found anything in his calling too hard, except discouragement and disbelief. His grandson was confident that there was no task the Lord assigned to him or to his people that could not be achieved.

Asael revered the Constitution, seeing God's providence in it, and he looked upon the Revolution as the will of God to put an end to monarchy and ecclesiastical tyranny. He expected Christ to return and assume government of the world. With this his grandson would be entirely in accord.

Asael thought of order and union as "precious jewels." Order and union would be Joseph's goals for his followers, in a community based upon shared property. To him this would be more important even than liberty, which he would also prize, but would define in his own terms.

Asael believed that marriage partners were created for each other. He considered the family of the utmost importance, and told his children that he wished them to maintain equality, love and family solidarity. Joseph would see the family as the basis for God's plan of salvation, implemented by sealing for eternity, and by baptisms for dead forebears.

Asael admonished fidelity to friends, and loyalty in friendship would later become very important in Joseph's ethic. That Joseph did, in his grandfather's terms, "avoid a melancholy disposition" was attested to by many who thought a more sober demeanor would have been better suited to his calling.

Asael was to live another thirty-one years, to the sturdy old age of eighty-six. In his last year he read *The Book of Mormon* without glasses, and came to believe that his grandson Joseph would fulfill his conviction that God intended to raise some branch of his family to be of great benefit to mankind.[19] He died on October 30, 1830, at the home of his son Silas, in Stockholm, New York.

Mary lived six years longer, to the age of ninety-three, and in her last days made an arduous journey of five hundred miles to visit her descendants, including great-grandchildren, in Kirtland, Ohio. Happy in that reunion, she died about sunset, May 27, 1836, in the home of the prophet Joseph.

While the religious convictions of Joseph's paternal grandfather, Asael Smith, were apparently lifelong and fervent, though liberal and anti-organizational, those of Joseph's maternal grandfather, Solomon Mack, were by Solomon's own admission non-existent until his old age. Then at last he had an overwhelming conversion, confessed that although unrecognized by him, the hand of God had been upon his entire life, and he devoted the remainder of his days to bearing that testimony.

What the two old gentlemen had in common, as the few extant documents from their own hands make evident, was a belief in the utmost importance of religious education for the young, though Solomon came to this conviction only late in life.

Solomon Mack was the grandson of John Mack, who was born in Inverness, Scotland, from a line of clergymen, and came to New England in 1669, to settle in Salisbury, Massachusetts. Although not John's eldest son, Solomon's father, Ebenezer, born in 1697, inherited his father's large property in Lyme, Connecticut, including his house, barn, orchard and all his lands as well as the rest of his "moveable" estate, and the responsibility of caring for his mother. Ebenezer prospered, made numerous land transactions, married Hannah Huntley and kept his family in good style.

Hannah taught young people for about thirty years. She had "experienced the power of God from an early age with all the good morals of life," as Solomon wrote of her, and when she died in 1796 she rejoiced that she was going to meet her Father in heaven.

Ebenezer had a series of misfortunes. According to Solomon, he became the victim of the greed and dishonesty of others and was unable in the end to keep his five children together. Solomon was bound out to a neighboring farmer in Lyme.

In old age, full of his change of heart, Solomon wrote a narrative of his life and published it at his own expense, forty-eight pages tightly packed with information and at times quite vivid.[20] However, it is hard to read because events are not always in sequence, and the printer did not trouble to correct errors, which appear throughout in spelling, punctuation and typography. Those who like to denigrate his grandson Joseph Smith have suggested that Solomon's book was the work of an indigent and slightly addled old man who put together some tall tales to peddle about the countryside. However, the facts of Solomon's life as he states them, his holdings of land and his military and maritime experiences, are verified by official records which reveal that his claims, rather than exaggerated, were in fact modest. Army records show not only that he served where and when he said he did, but that his unit was cited for valor, which he did not mention. Maritime records prove that he was a shipowner and a sea captain, and county records and deeds establish that at various times he held a sizable amount of property.[21] If Solomon dwells upon grave perils and petty woes, making his story something of a tragicomedy of accidents, illnesses, close calls and failures, it is to reiterate the theme which had become of the utmost importance to him, that though on the surface his life was calamitous, he had nevertheless been under the constant watch of the Lord, blessed and protected in his many hours of danger, and brought to humility in order to learn how futile it was to store up treasures of the world.

Solomon says the devil had great hold on him, and he served the devil well, drinking, swearing and breaking the Sabbath. He scoffed at God, and if he kept any passages from the Bible in mind it was only so that he could call them up for ridicule.

Almost in spite of himself, however, Solomon makes an impression of zest, courage and enterprise, and reveals that he was a hardy adventurer of considerable native ability. He does not name his virtues, but what also becomes apparent is that he was honest, and generous sometimes to the point of personal hardship. In all accounts of the money and property he acquired, there was nothing he did not earn by his own hard labor.

Solomon was born in Lyme, Connecticut, September 15, 1732, according to Lyme vital records, but he thought he was three years younger, and it has been suggested that his master lied to him about his age to keep him longer in bondage. Solomon says he was indentured from the age of four until twenty-one, although it was probably until he was twenty-four, and he was treated not like a member of the family, as expected, but like a slave.

Solomon details his indenture bitterly, though not without justification. He says he was allowed to grow up "like a wild ass's colt" with no sense of obligation to society. He was never given any instruction in religion or even taught to read and write, which was the cause of great hardship to him in later life.

Solomon was correct in believing that he was entitled to an education from his master. The General Assembly Act of November 27, 1703, which remained in force with minor revisions throughout the colonial period, required that apprenticed children be given instruction in religion and a trade and be taught to read and write "as they may be capable." Responsibility for this belonged to the master and violators of the law were subject to fines or a sentence in jail.[22]

Solomon said that his master's wife was afraid he might bring suit against them for this negligence, and took him aside to tell him that he was such a fool "we could not learn you."

Solomon had many accidents as a youth, including a scalding which caused a nearly fatal fever sore on his leg, but even then he says his master never spoke to him of judgment or eternity.

Two months before Solomon reached what he thought was his twenty-first birthday, he quarreled with his master and left, but was persuaded to return and fill out the indenture. Frequently abused, he finally found his indenture papers in his master's custody and burned them.

Solomon enlisted for service in the French and Indian War, was in the battle of Halfway Brook in 1755, escaped injury but his fate, typically anticlimactic, was to come down with a cold which kept him ill for months.

In 1757 he mustered two teams of oxen in the service of the king. After carrying baggage to Fort Edward, he went halfway back to Stillwater in search of stray oxen, alone except for a man who followed him at some twenty rods. Four Indians came out of the woods ahead, armed with tomahawks, scalping knives and guns. Afraid it would be the end of him unless he could outwit them, the unarmed Solomon charged with his staff, shouting, "Rush on, brave boys! We'll have the devils!" When the Indians saw the man in the distance, they thought a troop was coming and fled.

In 1756, Solomon bought a farm in Connecticut and added eight acres to it in 1758, but as always it seemed that his progress was attended by difficulties, both serious and petty, when he contracted smallpox and was swindled out of two teams of oxen.

In 1758 he enlisted again and fought in bloody battles near Lake George. In the attack on Fort Ticonderoga, Solomon helped storm the log walls and saw hundreds killed all around him, but he himself had only a musket ball graze his neck. Later, marching on patrol with his unit in single file, he says the Indians suddenly rose like a cloud and attacked them, bullets and tomahawks flying like hailstones. Half the men were killed, captured or injured, but Solomon was unhurt and even managed to rescue a wounded soldier from the Indians. In that battle, Solomon's unit of volunteers from Connecticut earned a commendation from Major Robert Rogers.[23]

After his discharge, he set up a sutler's shop in Crown Point, Lake Champlain, but his woes continued when his clerk abandoned him, and Solomon, still unable to read, write or keep accounts, lost the value of several years' work. He then chartered a vessel and sold his cargo for a good profit in New York, although he lost money when his vessel was damaged in a gale off Long Island.

On January 4, 1759, after a short acquaintance, Solomon married Lydia Gates, a young schoolteacher and member of the Congregational Church, the eldest child of Daniel Gates of East Haddam, Connecticut, who was a church deacon, a tanner and the owner of a large farm. It might be wondered what Lydia, well-educated and from a well-to-do, religious family, saw in this rough soldier, sailor and former bondsman, who was illiterate, irreverent and rowdy, but perhaps he was a dashing figure to the sheltered girl. She was devoted to him until the end, attended him in sickness and misfortune, endured the lonely years of a seafarer's wife and followed him when he chose to live in the wilderness. Although Solomon does not say

so, it seems likely that it was Lydia who finally taught him to read and
write, perhaps at the same time she taught their children, and it was she,
he admits, who gave him his only instruction in religion. In this she
persisted apparently for years, despite his continuing skepticism.

With a handsome sum, as he called it, of silver and gold accumulated
from his endeavors after he left the army, Solomon bought sixteen hundred acres in Granville, an unsettled area in northern New York, the deed
requiring that he clear some of the land and build a log house. However,
Solomon cut his leg, which disabled him for the whole season. His daughter Lucy added that he paid a man in advance to finish clearing, but the
man absconded and Solomon lost the property.

In 1761, Solomon and Lydia, with their two young sons, Jason and
Stephen, moved to Marlow, New Hampshire, taking one hundred acres in
a wilderness where only four families lived within forty miles. They
remained ten years and had four more children. Lydia assumed the education of the children, along with all her other duties as a pioneer. She called
them to prayer morning and evening and taught them to love one another.
Her daughter Lucy wrote that the habits she instilled in them of gentleness
and reflection were passed to the next generation. Apparently, however,
Lydia was still at that time unable to persuade her husband to religious
views.

In 1767, Solomon was elected game warden, or "deer reeve" as it was
known, and in 1770, he added seventy-six acres to his property in
Marlow. The next year the family moved to nearby Gilsum, where
Solomon and his brother Elisha built the first sawmill, gristmill and bridge.
Here he and Lydia had two more children. The youngest, Lucy, born July
8, 1775, would become mother of the prophet Joseph.

During the Revolution, Solomon enlisted in the American artillery for a
short campaign but took sick, went home and in rapid succession was
crushed by a tree, mangled on a water wheel and then injured so badly by
a blow on the head from a falling tree limb that he was subject thereafter
to blackouts, "fits" as he called them, which were gratuitously explained
by one historian as epilepsy, although there is no evidence and no family
history of that disease.

In March 1779, Solomon and his two adolescent sons, Jason and
Stephen, signed on the *Beaver,* a privateer carrying twelve guns and a crew
of about eighty. Pursued and fired upon by five British privateers, the
Beaver was shattered and her rigging cut away, and she was forced toward
land. Guns on shore drove off the British, but the *Beaver* was no sooner
repaired and under sail than she was engaged by two schooners, two
sloops and two row galleys. Solomon, who was on watch, called up the
sleeping crew and they made shore. In a great exchange of cannon fire, the
Beaver was badly damaged again but when one of the galleys nearly ran

aground, the crew of the *Beaver* killed some forty of the enemy in close combat with small arms. Three or four of the *Beaver*'s crew were killed and several wounded, but Solomon and his sons remained unhurt.

Of this, Solomon wrote, ". . . I thought nothing of futurity, which if I had considered a moment and viewed a watery grave already made, it appears as if I must have shuddered at the thought. My God must have given me some warnings of my danger, but if he did, his calls I would not harken to. The devil had great hold on me, and I served him well. But the Lord was with me—"[24]

About 1784, Solomon heard that a large sum due him was ready in Liverpool, Nova Scotia. He asked Jason to go with him, probably with the plan of investing the money in voyages to fish and trade. Jason agreed, although reluctantly, since he was very much in love and about to be married. One misfortune followed another to keep the two men away from home for four years, a hurricane, a shipwreck on a reef and Solomon's illness, and at last they had to return home empty-handed.

Solomon found Lydia and the children homeless and swindled out of several hundred dollars' worth of property by friends Solomon had trusted. For Jason the news was even worse. A rival had intercepted Jason's letters to his fiancée and, perhaps using a story of one of the shipwrecks, had forged a report that Jason was dead. After waiting four years, his fiancée married the unscrupulous rival shortly before Jason returned. The bride collapsed when she saw her true love, and the heartbroken Jason went to sea again, alone.

At this point, Solomon felt extremely low, he says, in sorrow for his son and for his own life. Now about fifty-six, he felt his best years were gone for nothing and he did not care whether he lived or died.

Nevertheless, he went to work again, trying one thing and another, constructing bridges and dams in Massachusetts with his brother Elisha, and farming in New Hampshire.

In 1799, Solomon and Lydia moved to Tunbridge, Vermont, to be near their second son Stephen, by now a successful businessman, and their daughter Lucy, who had married Joseph Smith in 1796.

In Vermont Solomon managed to acquire some property but he had been injured so often that by now he was a cripple and still subject to blackouts. Again he was reduced to poverty when he went bail for friends and lost everything.

In 1804, Solomon made a down payment on a farm of one hundred acres in Sharon, Vermont, which he soon afterward rented to Lucy and Joseph. Although it turned out to be rocky and barren, Lucy, Joseph and their children remained on it for some two years, and Joseph Jr., the prophet to be, was born there in 1805. When Lucy and Joseph left, Solomon and Lydia returned to the farm and lived there alone until 1811.

In the winter of 1810, when he was seventy-seven, Solomon became so ill with rheumatism that he could not get in and out of bed without the help of Lydia. At last he began to consider his ways. Sleepless and in great distress, he imagined lights and voices, believing that his body and soul were in great danger and death was near. That winter he began reading the Bible and calling upon the Lord for mercy, for deliverance from sin and for understanding. All winter he was ill with rheumatism, but in the spring it began to seem to Solomon that the Lord was with him. One night he prayed that as a token of the Lord's presence, his pains be eased. He slept free of pain and awoke rejoicing at the discovery that Christ would fulfill His promises. He said that the Lord then put such light into his soul that everything appeared new and beautiful. "How I loved my neighbors; how I loved my enemies. I could pray for them; everything appeared delightful."[25] He felt love for all mankind, rich and poor, black and white, and though a cripple who could not get on and off his horse without help, he resolved to spend the rest of his days in the Lord's service.

At this time he began writing his narrative, with the purpose, he said, of teaching others to avoid his mistake of seeking after the world's goods and ignoring God, and especially to admonish those in charge of children to bring them up in fear of the Lord.

In 1811 Solomon sold his interest on the farm in Sharon and perhaps used some of the proceeds to pay for the printing of his book, which was done in nearby Windsor.

Afterward, "Old Captain Mack," as he was called, was often seen in villages and on farms in the back country, riding out sidesaddle on his plodding old horse to peddle his book and testify of his conversion. He became a zealous missionary, especially among the young, and often visited schools to talk to children. To some he became a ridiculous figure, but he was unmovable in his conviction and never abandoned the program he had set for himself in old age.

Solomon and Lydia were especially close to their daughter Lucy and her husband and children and remained close until the Smiths moved to Palmyra, New York, when Joseph Jr. was about ten years old.

From her parents, Lucy no doubt acquired her lifelong conviction that God kept a warm, personal interest in His children, that He would hear and answer prayers, and offer guidance. This conviction her son Joseph would share. Perhaps also from the example of Solomon's life, Joseph was influenced to the belief he later expressed in salvation based upon accumulated works and lifetime fidelity, as opposed to deathbed repentance.

Lydia was riding part of the way to Palmyra with Lucy and her children when the wagon overturned and Lydia was seriously injured. Feeling that her end was near and she would not see her daughter again, Lydia parted with her tearfully, with a last admonition to remember the Lord. Her premonition proved true. About two years later, in 1818, Lydia died as a result of her injuries.

After Lydia's death, Solomon went to live with his son Solomon in Gilsum, and in old age was much reduced in circumstances. In 1819, he had no property subject to taxes except his horse, but no doubt he did not mind. He had long before come to believe that it was foolish to store up wealth.

He had concluded in his narrative, "My friends, when you read this journal, remember your unfortunate friend Solomon Mack, who worried and toiled until an old age to try to lay up treasures in this world, but the Lord would not suffer me to have it. But now I trust I have treasures laid up that no man can take away—but by the goodness of God through the blood of a bleeding Saviour."[26]

Solomon died August 23, 1820, about three weeks before his eighty-eighth birthday, and was buried in Gilsum, where his tombstone records the old mistake in his age, stating that he was eighty-four.

CHAPTER

2

EARLY LIFE
OF JOSEPH'S PARENTS

Lucy Mack, youngest daughter of Solomon and Lydia and mother-to-be of the prophet, was born July 8, 1775, in Gilsum, New Hampshire.

Like her father before her, Lucy wrote an autobiographical narrative in her old age. She accomplished it with the help of scribes when she was seventy-eight and it was published in England in 1853, two years before her death.[1]

Although Lucy's work is more detailed and more literate than her father's, it is, like his, mainly a reminiscence of the workings of God in her life. She calls it *Biographical Sketches of Joseph Smith the Prophet, and his Progenitors for many Generations,* but it is a chatty account of family events and vicissitudes, in particular those in which she herself plays an important role. She presents herself as heroine, perhaps not unjustly. Like her father, she leaves an impression of energy, confidence, ambition and native intelligence. Unlike him, she reveals personal pride and much concern for the social status of her family.

Lucy gives an account of her brothers and sisters, their state of grace and worldly success. Jason, eldest of Solomon and Lydia's eight children, went to sea after his unhappy love affair, became a preacher and later settled in New Brunswick, where he bought a tract of land for the use of thirty families who shared it in a communal experiment. Stephen, the second son, became an enterprising businessman, settling first in Tunbridge, Vermont, and later on the frontier at Detroit, Michigan, where he had several stores, a farm, a tinning business, a sawmill and a flour mill and upon his death left a sizable estate. About her brother Daniel, Lucy had little to say other than that he once saved three men from drowning, and about Solomon she wrote that he spent the whole of his agrarian life in Gilsum, New Hampshire. Her two elder sisters, Lovisa and Lovina, both died of consumption in young womanhood. Of her remaining sister, Lydia, Lucy wrote that she prospered and always remembered the poor.

After the death of Lovina, Lucy mourned so deeply that Stephen was afraid she would become ill, and took her to stay with him in Tunbridge.

Lucy, then about nineteen, says she remained melancholy and wondered if life was worth living, but she read the Bible and prayed diligently, hoping for a change of spirit. She thought that unless she joined a church she would be considered worldly, but she found herself in a dilemma because contending clergymen each pronounced his own church right and all others wrong. Convinced that this made the churches witnesses against one another, she believed that none could be the true church of Christ, thus voicing an opinion shared by many of her period, and one that would be expressed later by her son, the prophet Joseph.

During her visit with her brother, Lucy met Joseph Smith. Joseph was then about twenty-five, and had been living in Vermont with his parents for five years. Like his father Asael, Joseph was a powerful man, six feet two without shoes, muscular and vigorous from his hard pioneer life in the Vermont woods and fields. Though noted as a wrestler, he was described as gentle and kindhearted. Lucy and Joseph were married January 24, 1796.

As Lucy tells it with some zest, her brother Stephen and his business partner each gave her five hundred dollars, which made a substantial sum for that day. Having other means to set up housekeeping, Lucy was able to put this money aside.

Lucy and Joseph visited her parents in New Hampshire, and then settled on the farm in Vermont that Joseph and his father planned to work at halves. It was a handsome farm, Lucy wrote, and the young couple started out hopefully, with every prospect, it would seem, for a happy and comfortable life.

They worked the farm for six years. Here their first two children were born, Alvin, February 11, 1799, and Hyrum, February 9, a year later. For reasons Lucy does not specify, but which might have been that the farm, although "handsome," was stony and unproductive, they put the farm up for rent and moved to Randolph, where they opened a shop. Six months later Lucy was pronounced consumptive, like her two older sisters before her. Told she was about to die, she says she pleaded with the Lord during the night and promised Him her service. She said she heard a voice saying, "Seek, and ye shall find, knock, and it shall be opened unto you. Let your heart be comforted; ye believe in God, believe also in me." Lucy says that by morning she was beginning to recover, and afterward she was occupied only with thoughts of religion, searching for someone to instruct her in the way of salvation.

She went from church to church but could not find any that satisfied her and decided at last to keep the Bible as her guide. Considering it her duty, nevertheless, to be baptized, she sought out a minister who was willing to do it without requiring her to join his congregation.[2]

Among the meetings she attended about 1803 were some held by the Methodists. At first her husband went along at her request, but his father and eldest brother, Jesse, objected strenuously.[3] Asael was particularly upset by what he considered Joseph's capitulation to organized religion and disapproved in particular of the Methodists. Lucy wrote in her preliminary manuscript that Asael came to their door one day and threw Thomas Paine's *Age of Reason* into the house, angrily bidding his son to read it until he believed it.[4]

What perhaps Asael hoped would impress Joseph was Paine's denunciation of creeds and religious superstition. As Asael's devout letter to his family clearly shows, there was much in Paine with which Asael was not in agreement, including Paine's argument that Christ, though admirable, was not the Son of God and that the Scriptures were fraudulent. But he strongly espoused Paine's plea for sound reason and for the right of each man to decide for himself what he should believe.

Lucy says that to keep peace with his father, Joseph stopped going to meetings with her. Distressed, she went to a grove to pray that the true gospel might be presented to her husband. Afterward she had a dream which she interpreted to mean that eventually he would embrace the gospel.

About this time, Joseph learned that ginseng, which grew wild in Vermont, was in great demand in China, where it was believed to be a remedy for impotence and the plague. Joseph made a heavy investment in the herb and went to New York to contract with a ship captain for its transport and sale. A man named Stevens, of Royalton, followed Joseph to New York and arranged to send his son on the same ship to sell their ginseng.

When the ship returned, young Stevens told Joseph that the only thing Joseph realized from his investment was a small chest of tea. Later young Stevens, while drunk, revealed to Lucy's brother Stephen that the transaction had been a swindle. Stephen Mack told Joseph at once, but in the meantime young Stevens fled with all the profits to Canada.

Going over his accounts, Joseph found that he was left with some eighteen hundred dollars in debts. He sold his only remaining property, the farm in Tunbridge, for eight hundred dollars, which Lucy says was little more than half its value. To this Lucy added her wedding present money, which enabled them to pay their debts in full, although like Asael before them, they were left destitute.

Joseph and Lucy moved to Royalton for a few months, then moved to

Sharon, Windsor County, Vermont. Here Joseph rented Solomon Mack's farm in the hills above White River. It was poor land, but Joseph worked hard on it during the summer and during the winter taught school. In addition to Alvin and Hyrum, Lucy and Joseph now had a daughter, Sophronia, born 1803. Two years later, December 23, 1805, Joseph Smith, Junior, was born.

Not long afterward, the family decided that they would not be able to survive on Solomon's unproductive land. For several years they moved from place to place, trying to find a suitable farm or some other means to make a living.

From Sharon, they went back to Tunbridge, where a fourth son, Samuel Harrison, was born March 13, 1807. Soon afterward, they moved a short distance to Royalton, Vermont, where three years later Ephraim was born, also on March 13, though he died after eleven days. Another son, William, was born on the same day the following year, 1811.

In Royalton, Joseph went to the school on Dewey Hill and was taught his letters by Deacon Jonathan Rinney.

In 1811, the family moved to Lebanon, New Hampshire, where their situation at first improved. Lucy says they found good schools for the children. They sent Hyrum to Moore's academy in Hanover, and the others to a common school nearby.

Their troubles were not over, however. In the winter of 1812–13 hundreds of people in that area contracted the dread typhoid fever, which at that time was confused with and often called typhus. It was a horrifying disease, cause and cure unknown, in which the body wasted away in fever, delirium and coma, the skin became mottled and the tongue turned black. Hyrum came home from school with it and each of the Smith children fell ill with it in turn. Sophronia was given up by the doctor and saved, Lucy was convinced, only by the prayers she and Joseph offered at her bedside. This was one of many demonstrations Lucy records of the family's faith in a God Whose interest was personal, and Whose intervention was assured by supplication.

Joseph, then seven years old, was ill with the fever only about two weeks, but the disease left complications. After they thought he had recovered, he developed an agonizing pain in his shoulder. A Dr. Parker whom they called in said it was a sprain, and although Joseph protested that he had not injured his shoulder, the doctor treated him with bone liniment and applications of a hot shovel. The disorder later proved to be a large abscess, which began to heal when it was lanced, but then pain and swelling developed in the boy's leg. Lucy wrote that for two weeks Joseph lay in agony. Hyrum remained by his low bed much of the time day and night bracing Joseph's afflicted leg in his hands to help him endure his suffering. This is the first demonstration on record of the lifelong devotion of Hyrum for his younger brother.

The Smiths called in Dr. Nathan Smith, a well-known surgeon from Dartmouth College at nearby Hanover. The surgeon made an eight-inch incision in Joseph's left leg between knee and ankle, but it relieved the pain only until the wound began to heal.

Again Dr. Smith operated in vain. Later the surgeon and an associate named Perkins returned, accompanied by eleven doctors, who were perhaps medical students from Dartmouth. The surgeons approached Joseph and one of them, probably Dr. Smith, said, "My poor boy, we have come again." The decision had been made to amputate.[5]

Joseph says that young as he was, he utterly refused to have the operation. Lucy insisted that they try to cut out the diseased part of the bone and give the leg another chance to heal.[6]

Joseph consented to what he later called the "experiment" of removing a large part of the bone of his leg. Already at this young age exhibiting a strong will like that of his mother, he would not be bound, as the doctors ordered, nor would he take their brandy. Showing a stout faith in the personal intervention of God in answer to prayer, as his mother had done, Joseph said the Lord would help him.

Lucy put folded sheets under his leg and went several hundred yards from the house to be out of hearing. The brutal operation was performed by boring into the diseased bone on one side where it was affected and then the other and breaking off the pieces of bone with forceps. Joseph's shrieks when the first piece was broken off brought Lucy running back to the house, but the boy shouted for her to go away. After the third piece was removed, she burst into the room again to the horrifying sight of her child pale as a corpse, his leg torn open, lying on a bed soaked with blood. But he was triumphant. His leg was saved.

Joseph's recovery was so slow and he got so thin that his mother could easily carry him. He had to use crutches for about three years, and retained a slight limp for life.

About 1814, when Joseph was well enough to travel, although still on crutches, the family sent him with his Uncle Jesse to Salem, where they hoped the sea air would help him regain his strength.

Life in Salem at that time was rich and colorful. The large houses were handsome and beautifully furnished and even the cottages had charm. Elegant carriages drove through the streets. Six or eight of Salem's merchant vessels were returning every week with riches from all parts of the world— furniture, books and paintings from France, textiles and rugs from India, art objects from Spain and Italy, blue Canton from China. Cooking was exotic, with rare imported herbs, foods, coffee, teas and wine, and the town had a lively social life with an elegance of manners unknown in the backwoods.

It is not recorded how long young Joseph remained with his Uncle Jesse, but to a sensitive boy from a poor family, Salem must have been a heady experience, even if he could do little more than observe. Later he was to show a taste for good food and fine clothes and a yearning for the refinements of life for which there was no precedent in his immediate family background.

Of Joseph's earliest days not much else is known. Existing descriptions of him as a boy and young man are contradictory in many details, and dubious at best, since they were mainly hearsay and recorded some years after he became a figure of controversy. Not much more can be established than that he was a towhead, tall for his age and well built, healthy and agile despite his limp, and capable of a good day's work.

Lucy herself said little about Joseph's boyhood, although she admits to having been questioned often by people who no doubt would have liked to hear sensational stories. She says Joseph was a quiet boy, "remarkably well-disposed," and that he had an entirely normal childhood. Since she was proud of her son and believed implicitly in his mission, this speaks well of her as a sincere and levelheaded woman, who resisted any temptation to present Joseph as exceptional.

By 1814, after a year of family sickness from typhoid fever, the Smiths found their circumstances very low.

They moved to Norwich, Vermont, and began to farm on the property of one Esquire Moredock, perhaps as squatters. Their crops failed the first year but they sustained themselves by selling fruit from the trees on the land. The second year's crops failed and then the third's when a summer of such cold weather occurred that crops were frosted on the ground and a near famine swept the area.

In 1816, Joseph Sr. decided to move to recently settled country in western New York, where he had heard that the soil was rich and easily tilled and wheat grew abundantly. The Smiths called their creditors and debtors together and made arrangements which they thought were satisfactory to all.

Joseph went to Palmyra, Wayne County, New York, in 1816, with Caleb Howard, whom he sent back in a few weeks with a wagon and team for Lucy and the children.

As they were about to set off, however, some of the creditors appeared and made further demands for money. Lucy was outraged, but rather than contest the claims, which would have kept Howard waiting on expense, she gave them what to her was the enormous sum of $150.

Refusing a neighbor's offer to take up a collection for them, the proud Lucy set out with her seven children, ages four to seventeen, the infant Don Carlos, who had been born March 25, and her elderly mother, Lydia, who was going with them as far as Royalton to her son Daniel.

It was on this journey that their wagon was upset and Lydia received the injuries that two years later caused her death.

Caleb Howard soon spent the money Joseph Sr. had given him on drinking and gambling, presumably at inns along the way. He grew careless with the goods and unkind to the children. When the Smiths fell into company with a family named Gates who were traveling in their direction, Lucy and her sons got separated. Joseph says that Howard put him off the Smith wagon to make room for two of the Gates's daughters, whose company he enjoyed, and forced him to walk for miles, despite his lame leg. When his older brothers tried to come to his defense, Howard knocked them down with the butt of his whip. Lucy confirmed Howard's cruelty, saying that the man had neither sympathy nor principles, and was especially hard on Joseph, who was then only ten years old.

Joseph says that when they reached Utica, New York, Howard threw their goods into the street and was about to drive away with the horse and wagon when Lucy grabbed the reins and shouted that Howard was stealing her property. In Lucy's account, her action was more dignified but no less forceful, as she denounced Howard in the barroom before a crowd of people and dismissed him. From then on, Lucy and the older boys managed the wagon and team by themselves.

Having run out of money, they were obliged to barter for their needs with their belongings and even their clothing. They arrived at last in Palmyra with almost nothing left of their effects and two cents in cash.

It has been suggested that Lucy was the greatest influence in Joseph's life.[7] Certainly her strong role in the family cannot be doubted. She set for her children a vivid example of fortitude, integrity, belief in a God Who had a personal interest in His children and would respond to prayer, and faith in prophetic gifts, including her own. Assertive, proud, inclined to self-importance, Lucy's personality made an interesting contrast to that of her husband. Joseph Sr. has been described as having the reputation in Broome County of a typical Yankee peddler, with a smooth tongue and full of stories acquired on his rounds,[8] but this contradicts the usual impressions recorded of him as reticent and in his early life skeptical of established churches, like his father, but deeply religious and in constant expectation of the last days.

By the year 1816 when they moved to Palmyra, Joseph and Lucy had been married for twenty years, had eight children and had buried one, and had lost or been swindled out of all their money and property. They had tried to settle seven times in five different communities, but each of their farming and merchandising ventures had failed. They had not given up hope, however, and moved into the new community with much good will and energy, ready to start a new life.

PART TWO

New York

JOSEPH'S FIRST VISION

The Smiths were penniless when they first came to Palmyra, New York, in 1816, but they were optimistic. The area seemed promising. They were willing and able to work hard.

Palmyra was then a small frontier village of log cabins, wooden huts and a store or two. The population was only about six hundred but hopes were high because it was said that the village would be on a spur of the Erie Canal. The Canal, which Governor De Witt Clinton had at last persuaded the New York Assembly to approve, would connect the Great Lakes with the port of New York, and would open markets to farmers and merchants along its entire route. Work began on the Canal in 1817, just a year after the Smiths arrived.

Lucy says that, reunited, the family held a council and decided to combine their efforts to get a good piece of land. Joseph and his two older sons, Alvin and Hyrum, took whatever odd jobs they could find, gardening, harvesting and well digging, and supplemented their income with fishing and trapping, while Lucy, who was skilled at painting designs on oilcloth, sold enough table covers to buy provisions and to furnish a house. The family posted a sign at their door, "cake and beer shop," and offered among other things, gingerbread, root beer, pies and boiled eggs, and whenever crowds gathered in the village, they peddled cakes from a pushcart.

Every member who was old enough made some contribution. Joseph Jr., although only eleven, hired out on local farms. His younger brother

William later said that the neighbors "knew where they could get a good hand and they were not particular to take any of the other boys before Joseph either."[1]

Lucy says that her husband contracted with a land agent for one hundred acres in Manchester, and within a year they had made nearly all of the first payment. If the Smiths made a down payment under a legal contract, no record of it has been found, but apparently they thought they had claim to the property, and they moved onto the land after two years in Palmyra.

Lucy wrote:

> So that in 2 years from the time we entered Palmyra strangers destitute of friends home or employment. We were able to settle ourselves upon our own land in a a snug comfortable though humble habitation built and neatly furnished by our own industry And if we might judge by any external manifestation we had every reason to believe that we had many Good and affectionate friends for never have I seen more kindness or attention shown to any person or family than we received from those around us Again we began to rejoice in our prosperity and our hearts glowed with gratitude to God for the manifestations of his favor that surrounded us . . .[2]

The land was in the northwest corner of Manchester, its north line the boundary between Manchester in Ontario County and Palmyra in Wayne. Through that same corner ran Crooked Brook, where some of the first converts to Joseph Smith's church would be baptized. The village of Palmyra lay about two miles north of the Smith home.

In Palmyra, Lucy enjoyed some social life. While unconsciously revealing her concern for social status and material welfare, she rather self-righteously made occasion to declaim her basic conviction that spiritual and moral values were supreme. She writes with apparent satisfaction of a day in which she had tea with a circle of ladies of a superior place in local society. The true feelings of others in the little drama are open to conjecture, but Lucy makes herself transparent. She writes:

> the ladies invited were some wealthy merchants wives and the minister's lady we spent the time quite pleasantly each seeming to enjoy those reciprocal feelings which renders the society of our friends delightful to us—when tea was served up we were passing some good-natured remarks upon each other when one lady observed Well I declare Mrs ought not to live in that log house of her's any longer she deserves a better fate and I say she must have a new house. so she should says another for she is so kind to every one She ought to have the best of every thing Ladies said I thank you for your compliments but you are quite mistaken I will show you that I am the

wealthiest woman that sits at this table Well said they now make that appear—Now mark answered I to them I have never prayed for riches of the world as perhaps you have but I have always desired that God would enable me to use enough wisdom and forbearance in my family to get good precepts & examples before my children whose lives I always besaught the Lord to share as also to secure the confidence and affection of my husband that we acting togather in the education and instruction of our children that we might in our old age reap the reward of circumspection joined with parental tenderness viz the Pleasure of seeing our children dignfy their Fathers name by an upright and honorable course of conduct in after life I have been gratified so far in all this and more I have tis true suffered many disagreable disapointments in life with regard to property but I now find myself very comfortably situated to what any of you are what we have has not been obtained at the expense of the comfort of any human being we owe no man we never distressed any man which circumstance almost invariably attends the Mercantile life so I have no reason to envy those who are engaged beside there is none present who have this kind of wealth that have not lately met with a loss of children or othe [sic] friends (which really was the case) and now as for Mrs. the Minister's lady I aske you how many nights of the week you are kept awake with anxiety about your sons who are in habitual attendance on the Grog Shop & gambling house—they all said with a look that showed conviction Mrs. S. you have established the fact . . .[3]

The Smiths continued their hard work. The soil on their property was good, but farming was difficult with the crude methods then in use, oxen hitched to what was called a bull plow made of wrought iron which had to be sharpened frequently by a blacksmith.

William said, "We cleared sixty acres of the heaviest timber I ever saw . . . We also had on it from twelve to fifteen hundred sugar trees, and to gather the sap and make sugar and molasses from that number of trees was no lazy job."[4] Lucy says that their average production of maple sugar per year was one thousand pounds.[5] One season the Smiths won the county prize for production of maple syrup.

Besides their farming, sugar making and other enterprises, the family sold cord wood and vegetables, made and sold baskets and brooms, and continued to peddle cakes whenever they had an opportunity. Joseph Sr. also worked as a cooper, the trade he had learned from Asael. Lucy "doctored" many of their neighbors, but probably in friendship and not for money.

The Smiths did not at first join any church. This was some mark in their disfavor socially, but not a serious one. Although several denominations,

Methodists, Baptists, Quakers and Presbyterians, had come early to Manchester and Palmyra, there were families, as in New England after the Revolution, who had separated from the old-line churches. The strict church requirements of Puritan communities did not prevail.

Nevertheless, like many others, the Smiths had remained intensely religious within the family circle. In 1811, before they had moved to New York, Lucy says that her husband had become much preoccupied with religious thoughts. Like her, he had become subject to dreams, or visions, as Lucy often called them. The Smiths were like many people of that day who, according to the contemporary revivalist and philosopher Lorenzo Dow, believed that dreams were inspired by God.[6]

To Lucy, her husband's visions were so important that she could relate them in detail half a century later. She and her family took their dreams as evidence that they were especially important to God, which perhaps prepared them to accept and support the claims of Joseph Jr. to God's personal manifestations to him and to his special mission on earth.

Lucy says that in the first of seven visions he had, her husband was traveling through a field of dead timber with a spirit who told him this represented the world without religion, but that Joseph would find a box of food that gave wisdom. Joseph was happy, though he was kept from eating the food by horned beasts. Lucy says the dream confirmed her husband's belief that the preachers of their day knew no more than anyone else about the kingdom of God, thereby echoing the conviction of his father, Asael.

Joseph Sr. soon had another vision, in which he was led by the spirit to a tree bearing white fruit. Praising God, Joseph brought his family to share it. Opposite the tree was an immense building in which richly dressed people stood pointing at the Smiths "with the finger of scorn." The spirit told Joseph that the fruit was the love of God and the building was Babylon, which must fall.[7]

Since it is probable that young Joseph heard these visions in the family circle time and again, it is not surprising to find the ideas a part of his lifelong religious orientation. As he was later to see it, richly dressed people in many guises were to persecute him and his church for their beliefs and point "the finger of scorn." The idea that "Babylon must fall" persisted throughout young Joseph's career.

In every account of the Smith family life which we have from their own hands, faith and prayer were predominant. Joseph Jr. said that his parents "spared no pains" in the religious education of their children.

William wrote that their mother was concerned for the welfare of the children both here and hereafter, and tried in every way "to get us engaged in seeking for our soul's salvation, or (as the term was then) in getting religion."

William confessed that as a child he had found so much religious practice irksome. When the boys saw their father reaching for his spectacles, they knew they were in for another religious session. The children were required to sing hymns together on their knees and to listen to prayers morning and night in which their parents poured out their souls to God, as the donor of all blessings, and prayed, apparently at some length, that their children might be saved from sin.[8]

Lucy said years afterward that she had raised her children "in the fear and love of God, and never was there a more obedient family."[9]

In spite of all their hopes, work and prayer, life grew more difficult for the Smiths, as it did for everybody in the area.

Towns had grown and new commercial enterprises were undertaken, based on the general optimism brought on by the Erie Canal, but instead of the prosperity anticipated, depression as an aftermath of the War of 1812 was setting in throughout the nation. Farmers were hit especially hard. In Palmyra in 1818, a bushel of wheat brought only twenty-five cents in trade, and the market continued to decline.

By 1819, some farmers in that region began to put even their best lands up for sale, but buyers were few and many families had to abandon their homesteads. Difficulties would exist in the national economy for several years. William wrote that a great deal of hard labor was needed to supply their family's wants.

Some eleven years after the events, Joseph Jr. said much the same thing, but with an added poignant note about the effect on the children:

> as it required the exertions of all that were able to render any assist-ance for the support of the Family therefore we were deprived of the bennifit of an education suffice it to say I was mearly instructed in reading writing and the ground rules of Arithmatic which constuted my whole literary acquirements.[10]

The Smiths did what they could in that regard, too, however, and according to a neighbor who lived within about a mile, they held school in their own home, studied the Bible, and although they had no teacher, they struggled to educate themselves.[11]

The Smiths, newcomers, found it more difficult to make a living than did established families. Perhaps it was at this point that they began to experience a certain social isolation. In their poor circumstances, and new to that area, without the status their families had held in the communities from which they had migrated, they began to be looked upon by some as of a lower class. Unlike their forebears, who had known hard work but never actual poverty, the Smiths in Palymra were reduced to scratching for a livelihood.

One former resident of Palmyra remarked, some years after the Smiths had left, "I knew the Smiths . . . but they were too lowly to associate with."[12]

For a family of pride, this was a hard burden, especially for Lucy. Joseph Jr. too was made ashamed, and one of his lifelong concerns would be to raise the status of his family.

Later, when the Smiths and their religious claims became more widely known, they would experience outright hostility from some of their neighbors in Palmyra. Many hostile statements, expressed retroactively, collected in interviews and made popular in lectures by Philastus Hurlbut and in published works by E. D. Howe, Pomeroy Tucker, and James Gordon Bennett gave the false impression that the Smiths were always under some social ostracism, and that negative opinion about them was unanimous.

However, as William Smith said, "We never knew we were bad folks until Joseph told his vision. We were considered respectable til then, but at once people began to circulate falsehoods and stories in wonderful ways."[13]

Nevertheless, some of their contemporaries in Palmyra held them in high esteem. In an interview a number of years later, Orlando Saunders was quoted as saying:

> I knew all the Smith family well . . . the old man was a cooper; they have all worked for me many a day; they were very good people; Young Joe (as we called him then), he worked for me, and he was a very good worker; they all were. I did not consider them good managers about business, but they were poor people; the old man had a large family . . . they were the best family in the neighborhood in case of sickness; one was at my house nearly all the time when my father died; I always thought them honest; they were owing me some money when they left here; that is, the old man and Hyrum did, and Martin Harris. One of them came back in about a year and paid me.[14]

John H. Gilbert, who set the type for *The Book of Mormon,* remarked, "Oh, I don't think the Smiths were as bad as people let on for. Now Tucker, in his work, told too many big things; nobody could believe his stories."[15]

Another contemporary, Thomas H. Taylor, a lecturer and lawyer in the area, said:

> I knew them very well; they were very nice men, too; the only trouble was they were ahead of the people; and the people, as in every such case, turned out to abuse them, because they had the manhood to stand up for their own convictions . . . Why! these rascals at one time took Joseph Smith and ducked him in the pond that you see over there, just because he preached what he believed . . . there was something about him they could not understand; some way he knew more than they did, and it made them mad . . . I can take you to a great many old settlers here who will substantiate what I say.[16]

In 1820, young Joseph Smith was approaching his fifteenth year, a fair-haired, strapping youth, a willing farm hand, hardened by work in the fields and woods, his limp by then scarcely noticeable. He was patched and badly shod even in winter, but he had a merry disposition and enjoyed good times when they came his way.

In the opinion of Dr. John Stafford, who lived a mile from the Smiths, Joseph Jr. "was a real clever, jovial boy . . . The old woman had a great deal of faith that their children were going to do something great. Joe was quite illiterate. After they began to have school at their house, he improved greatly."[17]

Joseph's mother said candidly that although he was more inclined to meditation, he was less fond of books than were her other children and not much given to studying the Bible.[18] But he had been exposed to the religious beliefs of his grandparents and was under the influence of the devout atmosphere in his home, hearing the Bible read, singing hymns, listening to the earnest prayers of his parents and to their fervent recounting of visions, and for the previous three years, according to his own statement, he had been thinking deeply about matters of religion.

In a brief autobiography that Joseph wrote some time between July and November 1832, he included the earliest account of his youthful religious experiences that has been discovered. Written on six pages of a ledger book, it was dictated in part to Frederick G. Williams, who was then Joseph's scribe, but a significant part, including the following, was in his own hand:

> about the age of twelve years my mind became seriously imprest with regard to the all important concerns for the welfare of my immortal soul which led me to searching the Scriptures believeing as I was taught, that they contained the word of God . . . from the age of twelve years to fifteen I pondered many things in my heart concerning the situation of the world of mankind the contentions and divions the wickedness and abominations . . . my mind became excedingly distressed for I became convicted of my Sins . . .[19]

Joseph's youthful distress over his moral state was not unusual in the context of his background and times. As one study has shown, children of New England Puritanism were not infrequently tormented by a conviction of their own wickedness and a terror of damnation. It was common among young people who had experienced a religious conversion to confess and renounce previous sin.[20]

As he was approaching his fifteenth birthday, Joseph became disturbed by the fervid religious contentions in the area around his home. Writing of this period again, a few years later, he said that during the second year after his family moved to Manchester, there was "in the place where we lived an unusual excitement on the subject of religion. It commenced with the Methodists, but soon became general among all the sects in that region of the country, indeed the whole district of Country seemed affected . . ." He said that priest contended with priest, convert with convert, and "no small stir and division" were created among the people.[21]

It also seems likely, although he does not mention it, that Joseph was distressed by religious conflict between his parents, his mother's pietistic orientation, which depended upon the evidence of the heart and was characteristic of the revivalists, and his father's rationalism. Joseph Sr., while a believer in God and in the Bible, had acquired Asael's Universalist principles, rejected emotionalism as incompatible with "sound reason" and believed that evangelical churches were corrupt. When Joseph Sr. had decided in Vermont, under the influence of his father and brother, not to join the Methodists as Lucy had requested, she had expressed her deep disappointment, and said, "I prayed to the Lord in behalf of my husband —that the true gospel might be presented to him." For Lucy the churches were all put in doubt since they testified against one another, but she and many like her hoped to find the one definitive, true, authoritarian church.[22]

Lucy had gone from sect to sect searching for that church and continued her quest in Palmyra. That year, 1820, she, Hyrum, Samuel and Sophronia, but not Joseph Sr. or the others, joined the Presbyterian Church, which at that time had the only meetinghouse, a little frame building, in the village of Palmyra.[23]

Many others in that region had expressed religious discontent at that time. Asa Wild, a contemporary itinerant preacher and philosopher of Amsterdam, New York, tried several denominations without finding any that he could accept. Solomon Chamberlain, who was living twenty miles east of Manchester when Joseph was there as a youth, wrote that he got the fear of hell as a young man, repented and wanted to be saved, and began to search for the right church. He said that about that time the Lord showed him in a vision that no people on earth were right, that all churches were corrupt and that except for a few people no one had faith.[24] Later, he joined the Mormon Church. Jesse W. Crosby, who was also to join the Mormons, said that in his sixteenth year he became concerned about religion and attended many churches but was not satisfied, and prayed secretly for divine aid.[25] Another contemporary, Joel Hills Johnson, who joined first the Freewill Baptists and later became a Mormon, also said that as a boy of fifteen and sixteen, his mind was greatly agitated about religious matters. He read the New Testament, felt like a sinner and wondered why there were no baptisms for the remission of sins, and no healing of the sick.[26]

The Reverend William Bacon, in a sermon delivered and published in 1818 at Waterloo, a few miles from the Smith farm, warned members of his congregation who were about to leave for another sect just organized:

"If you embrace wrong doctrines and unite with a corrupt church, you may expect coldness and darkness all your lives."[27]

For that region's relatively sparse population, a number of religious groups were contending for souls. In early Manchester, the Methodists had been established since 1800, although they had no church building there or in Palmyra until 1823. There were two Presbyterian churches in Farmington in 1820, two Baptist churches in towns nearby and three meetinghouses of the Quakers. Nearby also were Freewill Baptists, Episcopalians, Congregationalists and Eastern Christians.

Revivals too were frequent in western New York during the first half of the nineteenth century, so many occurring that the area has been labeled the "burned-over district."[28] Between 1816 and 1821 more revivals were reported in New York than in any previous period. The Presbyterian Church in the minutes to their General Assembly of 1820, held in Philadelphia, expressed "heart-felt" joy for the past year of "genuine religious revival" and named eight very active areas, of which six were in New York.[29] The *Palmyra Register,* which the Smiths read, reported accounts of revivals in the eastern part of the state in the spring and summer of 1820, and in the central and northern parts later that year, which Joseph might well have heard discussed.[30]

After three years of lesser activity, the great climax of religious awakening in New York occurred between 1825 and 1827.

Joseph's statement about the prevalence of revivals in 1820 has been challenged, debated and defended, with the implication that the credibility of his visionary experience must rest upon the incidence of revivals when and where he said they occurred. The evidence is that there was fervent religious activity just as Joseph said, but whether or not it was as intense as in other periods is not so significant as the fact that to the youthful Joseph that activity was of the utmost importance.[31]

Several denominations, including Baptists and Presbyterians, held camp meetings in western New York in the early nineteenth century, but the Methodists conducted more of them than did any other group, and it was the Methodists whom Joseph mentioned in particular. At that time they had a very efficient ministry divided into districts and circuits in Ontario County. Where the church had no meetinghouses, such as in Palmyra and Manchester in 1820, traveling ministers came about every two weeks, and preached in a school or in some settler's cabin, or when weather permitted, under the open sky, in a clearing or a grove in the forest.

The Methodist camp meetings were popular, attended not only by their own, but by members of other churches and even by those who had no affiliation. From two or three hundred to several thousand people would come from miles around, bringing their children and effects in wagons. They pitched tents, built cook fires and prepared to stay for several days, exhilarated by the festivities, which were social, convivial and even somewhat commercial, as well as religious. Children scurried about excitedly. There was music and the chance to see friends and neighbors. On the outskirts of the camp, produce markets would be set up, and grog stands would be erected, sometimes with deleterious effect.

Nevertheless, the meetings were fervently religious, often lasting most of the day and going on into the night. One preacher followed another, and in large meetings, two or three might be speaking at once in different parts of the camp, while counseling, prayer circles and group singing went on simultaneously.

In earlier revival meetings, religious excitement was often expressed in seizures, trances or rolling on the ground, but in this period in western New York, the emotions of participants were more restrained. Conversions were frequent, however. At one meeting held by the Methodists near Palmyra, June 19, 1818, forty conversions and twenty baptisms were reported.[32]

In July of the following summer, at Vienna, a town not far from Manchester which was afterward called Phelps, a conference of about one hundred Methodist ministers was held in a yellow clapboard church scarcely finished and still bare. The ministers afterward held a series of camp meetings nearby and from then until the summer of 1820, religious activities were intense.[33]

Perhaps at first Joseph went to some of these meetings to peddle cakes, since the Smiths sold their wares wherever crowds assembled. Apparently other members of the Smith family attended for religious reasons. Joseph is reported to have told a church member later in life that his mother, one of his brothers and a sister got religion at a revival meeting, and that he wanted to feel what they felt and shout the way the others did, but that he could not.[34]

In another account, often repeated, Joseph caught a "spark of Methodist fire" at a camp meeting "down in the woods, on the Vienna road" and became an "exhorter" in the evening sessions.[35] Joseph himself said that he attended Methodist meetings and considered joining their church.[36]

However, he found it intolerable that so many people should be squabbling about their religious beliefs and, worse, that they should fail to practice what they professed. At the same time, like many adolescents, he was in awe of the mysteries of the universe, and longed to reach some understanding of them.

In the earliest known (1832) account previously mentioned, Joseph told of his distress over the situation, saying that he could not find any denomination that seemed in accord with the gospel of Jesus Christ as set forth in the New Testament, and that he mourned for his own sins and for the sins of the world. Yet he was thrilled with the evidence he saw of a supreme creator. In his own hand, he wrote:

I looked upon the sun the glorious luminary of the earth and also the moon rolling in their magesty through the heavens and also the Stars Shining in their courses and the earth also upon which I stood and the beast of the field and the fowls of heaven and the fish of the waters and also man walking forth upon the face of the earth in magesty and in the strength of beauty whose power and intiligence in governing the things which are so exeding great and marvilous even in the likeness of him who created them and when I considered upon these things my heart exclaimed . . . all all these bear testimony and bespeak an omnipotent and omnipreasant power a being who makith Laws and decreeeth and bindeth all things in their bounds who filleth Eternity— who was and is and will be from all Eternity to Eternity.

In his youthful fervor, he went to the woods to pray for guidance. He said that a pillar of light fell upon him, and that the Lord opened the heavens:

I Saw the Lord and he Spake unto me Saying Joseph my Son thy Sins are forgiven thee . . . be hold I am the Lord of glory I was crucified for the world, that all those who believe on my name may have Eternal life behold the world lieth in Sin at this time and none doeth good no not one they have turned asside from the Gospel and keep not my commandments, they draw near to me with their lips while their hearts are far from me and mine anger is kindling . . . I come quickly as it written of me in the cloud clothed in the glory of my Father and my Soul was filled with love and for many days I could rejoice with great joy and the Lord was with me but could find none that would believe the heavenly vision . . .[37]

Over a period of years, Joseph made several accounts of that experience. The best-known version was written by Joseph in 1838, and is published in the *History of the Church,* and in many other sources.
In this account, Joseph said:

In the midst of this war of words, and tumult of opinions, I often said to myself, what is to be done? Who of all these parties are right . . . I was one day reading the Epistle of James, First Chapter and fifth verse which reads, If any of you lack wisdom, let him ask of God . . ." I reflected on it again and again . . . At length I came to the conclusion that I must either remain in darkness and confusion or else I must do as James directs . . . I retired to the woods to make the attempt . . . immediately I was seized upon by some power which entirely overcame me, and had such astonishing influence over me as to bind my tongue so that I could not speak. Thick darkness gathered around me, and it seemed to me for a time as if I were doomed to sudden destruction . . . just at this moment of great alarm, I saw a pillar of light exactly over my head, above the brightness of the sun, which descended gradually until it fell upon me.

It no sooner appeared than I found myself delivered from the enemy which held me bound. When the light rested upon me I saw two personages, whose brightness and glory defy all description, standing above me in the air. One of them spake unto me calling me by name and said—pointing to the other—"This is my beloved Son, hear him."

My object in going to inquire of the Lord was to know which of all the sects was right . . . I was answered that I must join none of them, for they were all wrong, and the personage who addressed me said that all their creeds were an abomination in His sight; that those professors were all corrupt, that "they draw near to me with their lips but their hearts are far from me; they teach for doctrines the commandments of men: having a form of godliness but they deny the power thereof."[38]

Joseph wrote that he was told many other things which he could not write. When he came to, he found himself lying on his back, looking up into heaven.

Although they differ in details, all the accounts Joseph made of his vision are consistent in the important facts, that his experience occurred in his adolescence, after he had become agitated by sectarian conflict and had prayed for guidance.

The question may be raised why Joseph did not mention the presence of God the Father in his first account. This may not be answerable to the satisfaction of all but one possibility is suggested by the course of his religious development. What he experienced in 1820 was highly personal, the resolution of deeply felt conflicts. At first he might not have seen the implications which his experience would have for others. According to his account in the *History of the Church* he said to his mother after the vision, "I have learned for myself that Presbyterianism is not true." Yet he told her that he did not wish to prevent her from going to any church she pleased.[39] Some years later, however, Joseph's vision was taken as a message of inspiration for converts, and as such required from him the fullest theological implications.

Joseph wrote that a few days after his vision he described it to a Methodist preacher, one of those involved in the current religious excitement, and to his great surprise, the preacher reacted with contempt, told him that visions and revelations had ceased with the apostles, and that his vision had come from the devil. Joseph added, "my telling the story had excited a great deal of prejudice against me among professors of religion, and was the cause of great persecution, which continued to increase; and though I was an obscure boy, only between fourteen and fifteen years of age, my circumstances in life such as to make a boy of no consequence in the world, yet men of high standing would take notice sufficient to excite the public mind against me . . ."[40] Whether or not the scorn to which his youthful exuberance and faith were subjected by the local minister had as much social impact as he thought, the boy himself apparently felt deeply hurt and humiliated, and for years afterward would share his experience only with his family and a very few close friends. He neither included an account of it in the prefatory material published with *The Book of Mormon* nor told it publicly at the time of the organization of the church in 1830. It was not spoken of by missionaries then going out to preach and there was no reference to it in the *Book of Commandments,* published in 1833. Joseph's first known written account was made, as has been mentioned, in 1832, but it was not published. Joseph did not publish an account of his first vision until 1842, when he included it in the opening pages of his history, which he was induced to write, as he said, because of the many false reports about the church then being circulated.[41]

After its publication, the first vision was told by missionaries and soon afterward it became and has remained an important part of missionary presentation and of church doctrine.[42]

It is puzzling why Joseph's claims of such a religious experience in his youth should arouse skepticism and hostility. An intense conversion experience is not uncommon during adolescence and this was recognized in Joseph's day. Joshua Bradley said of revivals in Delaware and Connecticut between 1811 and 1818 that, like most awakenings, the work was mainly among young people.[43] In the numerous revivals led by Charles G. Finney in New York state in the 1820s it was the youth in every community who were most involved. Others, including Jonathan Edwards and James H. Hotchkin, have made similar statements.

Even the more vivid manifestations of religious experience, such as dreams, visions and revelations, were not uncommon in Joseph's day, neither were they generally viewed with scorn. Asa Wild, who claimed to have had many revelations, wrote in 1823 that the Lord "told me that the Millennial state of the world is about to take place," that every denomination had become corrupt and that dreadful judgments would descend upon sinners within seven years. John Samuel Thompson, who lived in Palmyra in the 1820s, said that in a dream he saw Christ come down from heaven in a brightness ten times that of "the meridian Sun" and heard Christ call him to carry the news to mankind that He had come. Other contemporaries, including Charles G. Finney and Elias Smith, claimed to have had visions of Christ before they went into the ministry.

Lorenzo Dow wrote that about 1791 when he was past thirteen, "It pleased God to awaken my mind by a dream of the night," and he saw God sitting upon a throne of ivory overlaid with gold, with Jesus on His right "and angels, and glorified spirits, celebrating praise . . ." When he awoke he realized that what he had seen was a dream, but it was strongly impressed upon his mind that his dream must be from God. He broke away from his evil companions and evil ways, "which some call innocent mirth," and began to read the Bible.[44]

Nevertheless, Joseph's visions, in particular his first, have received the special attention of historians, theologians and psychologists who have called them hallucination, delusion, fabrication, imagination and hoax. Taken out of the context of their period and place, the visions have been thoughtlessly cited as evidence that young Joseph had a psychiatric disorder.

Efforts have been made even in recent times to depict Joseph as an opportunist who either embellished some dimly recalled dream or fabricated the story of his vision later in life and at best eventually convinced himself that he was a prophet of God.[45] Such a conclusion is not supported by the fullest evidence of his life and background. The religious fervor of the times, the then not uncommon reports of dreams and visions, the intense conversions not infrequently experienced by adolescents and the fact that Joseph sustained his testimony ever afterward, lived fully in accordance with it and died a martyr to his conviction suggest that he spoke the truth when he said that in his youth he had the religious experience which was as meaningful to him as he maintained.

VISITATION OF MORONI

After his first vision, Joseph worked as usual in the fields with his father, and the family went on much the same as before, struggling against poverty, trying to improve their living conditions, holding religious services together but divided in their belief as to whether or not joining a denomination was necessary. To this was now added Joseph's continuing humiliation by neighbors, who laughed at his religious claims.

His mother says that one evening about this time Joseph was coming home from an errand and had just passed through the yard when a gunshot blasted across his path. Badly frightened, he dashed into the house. The family ran out to look for the attacker, but he had slipped away in the twilight. The next morning they discovered the imprint under a wagon where he had lain, and found one of their cows, which had been standing in a dark corner opposite the wagon, shot in the neck and head.

Lucy does not suggest any connection between this and the "persecutions" Joseph was enduring; rather she says that the family had no reason to suspect anyone of bad feeling toward the youth. She remained puzzled about the incident until the day of her writing, and so far as is known, Joseph himself never mentioned it.

For the next several years the Smiths farmed during the summer and spent their winter months, beginning each November, in trying to build a new house. By 1822, Lucy says, they had the frame raised and "all the materials necessary." It has been suggested, however, that this might have meant only that the materials were available from the nearest sawmill, probably in exchange for produce or labor.[1]

By 1823, Joseph was six feet tall, a powerful youth of nearly eighteen. He has said that he continued to be much concerned about the welfare of his soul and where he was to find the true church, and by his own account, which his mother corroborated, he was suffering the persecutions of all classes of men, both religious and irreligious, because he had declared that he had seen a vision.

In the *History of the Church*, Joseph says:

> . . . having been forbidden to join any of the religious sects of the day, and being of very tender years, and persecuted by those who ought to have been my friends, and to have treated me kindly, if they supposed me to be deluded to have endeavored in a proper and affectionate manner to have reclaimed me—I was left to all kinds of temptation; and mingling with all kinds of society, I frequently fell into many foolish errors, and displayed the weakness of youth, and the foibles of human nature; which I am sorry to say, led me into divers temptations, offensive in the sight of God. In making this confession, no one need suppose me guilty of any great or malignant sins. A disposition to commit such was never in my nature. But I was guilty of levity, and sometimes associated with jovial company, etc. . . .[2]

Joseph was not specific about his youthful foibles, but there is evidence that they might have included fighting and some drinking. There was no suggestion of dishonesty or of sexual misconduct made by his neighbors, even by those who were manifestly hostile to the Smith family. Several of the neighbors, even the more impartial ones, said that Joseph drank to some extent, "like everybody else" as they put it. One neighbor said, when questioned about this point some years later, "It was customary in those early days for everybody to drink more or less. They would have it at huskings, and in the harvest field, and places of gathering."[3]

Other neighbors said that the Smith boys could be quarrelsome. According to an account given years later, Joseph himself declared that in his youth he had to learn to fight against his will, since his parents had taught their children that quarreling and fighting were "sins that are beastly." Although some of the fighting was perhaps in defense of his religious claims, Joseph said that whenever he laid a hand on someone in anger it gave him sorrow and a feeling of shame.[4] An occasional physical approach to controversy was an aspect of his personality that Joseph would never entirely overcome, however. He himself recorded some of his encounters as a grown man, and a number of them are mentioned in the journals and memoirs of his friends. Benjamin F. Johnson even said of him that refractory brethren were sometimes helped out of the congregation by the prophet's foot.[5]

Although Joseph was not specific about his youthful foibles, he said they were "not consistent with that character which ought to be maintained by one who was called of God as I had been." Elsewhere, however, when his reputation was under attack, Joseph wrote that his "vices and follies" were "a light, and too often vain mind, exhibiting a foolish and trifling conversation. This being all, and the worst that my accusors can substantiate against my moral character."[6]

On September 21, 1823, a Sunday night when the children had been hustled off to bed and the house had grown quiet, Joseph prayed earnestly into the small hours, asking that it be manifested to him how he stood with God. He says he prayed with full confidence that he would receive some divine manifestation as in the past, and in fact it was not long before a light appeared in his room, which increased until it was brighter than at noon. At once:

> a personage appeared at my bedside, standing in the air, for his feet did not touch the floor. He had on a loose robe of most exquisite whiteness . . . his whole person was glorious beyond description . . .
>
> I was afraid; but the fear soon left me. He called me by name, and said unto me that he was a messenger sent from the presence of God to me and that his name was Moroni; that God had a work for me to do; and that my name should be had for good and evil among all nations, kindreds, and tongues . . . He said there was a book deposited, written upon gold plates, giving an account of the former inhabitants of this continent, and the sources from whence they sprang. He also said that the fullness of the everlasting Gospel was contained in it, as delivered by the Saviour to the ancient inhabitants; also that there were two stones in silver bows—and these stones, fastened to a breastplate, constituted what is called the Urim and Thummim— deposited with the plates; and the possession and use of these stones were what constituted "Seers" in ancient or former times; and that God had prepared them for the purpose of translating the book.[7]

The messenger, Moroni, told Joseph that when he was given the plates, the Urim and Thummim and the breastplate, he should show them to no one without permission, or he would be destroyed.[8] While the messenger was talking, Joseph said a vision was opened to his mind and he could see clearly where the plates were deposited.

The light gathered around the messenger until the room was dark again, except for a conduit of light rising to heaven, in which the messenger ascended until he disappeared. Joseph lay marveling at what had occurred when the room grew light again, and the messenger reappeared with the identical message, adding that great judgments of famine, sword and pestilence were coming in the present generation.

Moroni appeared for a third time and repeated what he had said, with the warning that Satan would try to tempt Joseph, because of his family's poverty, to get the plates for money.

Joseph wrote that when he rose as usual and went to the fields, he was too exhausted to work. Lucy's account adds that it was Alvin who first noticed Joseph seemed distracted. Always the conscientious elder brother, he admonished Joseph to keep up his work. Their father, however, saw that Joseph was pale and sent him home to be doctored.

Trying to climb the fence on the edge of the field, Joseph fell unconscious to the ground. The first thing he remembered was being called by Moroni, who stood above him surrounded by light, repeated his message and commanded him to tell it to his father. Lucy says the messenger asked Joseph why he had not already told his father. Joseph confessed that he was afraid his father would not believe him, to which Moroni replied, "He will believe every word you say to him."

Joseph returned to the field. His father listened intently and then assured him that the messenger was from God and told him to do as he was commanded.

Joseph says that he went directly to the place he had been shown in the vision, a hill three or four miles from Palmyra, on the east side of what was then the mail road from Palmyra to Canandaigua, just before Manchester.

On the west side of the hill, near the top, Joseph says he found a large stone, partly buried. Brushing the dirt from the edges, he lifted the stone with a lever and found the plates, the breastplate and the Urim and Thummim, lying in a box made of stones held together with some kind of cement.

He tried to take the objects out of the box, but was forbidden by the messenger, who told him that he was not to have them for another four years. Meanwhile, Joseph was to meet him at the Hill Cumorah, as it came to be known, every year precisely at the same time for further instructions.

In his account of 1832, Joseph said that the angel told him he could not have the plates because he wanted them "to obtain riches."[9] That Joseph was tempted by the thought that the treasure would "raise him above a level with the common earthly fortunes of his fellow men, and relieve his family from want . . ." was attested to in 1834 by his close friend, Oliver Cowdery.[10]

Lucy also says that Joseph thought there might be something he could turn to profit in the stone box, but she dates the incident as a year later when Joseph returned for his appointment with the angel, confident that he had kept the Lord's commandments and expecting to receive the plates. Instead, the angel was displeased with Joseph, Lucy wrote, and caused the plates to disappear.[11]

At this time, Joseph's family was still in difficult circumstances, struggling in poverty to keep their farm. Apparently there was conflict over

religion, since Lucy and several of the children had joined the Presbyterian Church, while Joseph and his father would not.[12] That the situation
distressed Lucy and very likely Joseph as well is suggested by the emphasis
she placed upon the family harmony that resulted after Joseph began to
tell them about his visions. The evening after he first saw the plates, Lucy
says that Joseph told the family what had happened and charged them
never to mention the plates outside the home. The secret kept among the
family members helped to solidify them, gave them a united front against
society and helped induce a certain religious harmony. Lucy wrote that the
family would sit in a circle in the evenings after work to listen to Joseph,
convinced that God was about to reveal something that would give a more
perfect knowledge of the plan of salvation. Significantly, she added, "this
caused us greatly to rejoice, the sweetest union and happiness pervaded
our house, and tranquility reigned in our midst."[13]

In the meantime, the Smiths continued building their house, and were
very likely close to completing it, under the direction of Alvin, who often
said that he wanted to see his parents settled, with a pleasant room to sit
in after their hard labors.

On the morning of November 15, 1823, just two months after Joseph
had visited the Hill Cumorah, Alvin was stricken with bilious colic. Since
their own doctor was away, the Smiths called in a man named Greenwood
who prescribed calomel, a heavy white compound of chloride of mercury
used as a purgative, which Alvin at first refused. When he was finally persuaded to take it, his symptoms grew worse, and he declared that the
calomel was lodged in his stomach and would kill him. He summoned
each member of the family to say goodbye, asking Hyrum and Sophronia
to see that the house was finished for their parents and that they were
cared for in their old age.

Calling Joseph to his bedside, Alvin, who had from the first taken a particular interest in his brother's visions, admonished him to do as he was
commanded and to be sure to get the records. Alvin died just four days
after he was stricken. An autopsy revealed that his own diagnosis was correct, the calomel was lodged in his upper bowel, surrounded by gangrene.

Joseph always spoke of Alvin with great affection and admiration. "He
was . . . the noblest of my father's family," he wrote some years later. "In
him there was no guile."[14] Twenty years after Alvin's death, when Joseph
was visiting his sister Catherine, he told her as an example of Alvin's sense
of justice and his great physical strength that once in Palmyra a ring of
spectators, apparently including Alvin and Joseph, had gathered to watch
two Irishmen fight. When one got the best of the other and was about to
gouge his eyes out, as Joseph told it, "Alvin took him by his collar and
breeches and threw him over the ring . . ."[15]

Alvin was a youth of such singular goodness, according to his mother, that the whole neighborhood mourned his death. One neighbor said that it was he who worked the farm and was the mainstay of the family.[16]

Oddly in contrast with Lucy's account of Alvin's popularity is the statement William made many years later, that the Reverend Benjamin Stockton, presiding elder of the Presbyterian church to which Lucy belonged, intimated that Alvin, who would not attend the church, was going to hell.[17] This infuriated Joseph Sr. and apparently confirmed him in his antipathy to established religions.

Less than a year after Alvin's death, the family heard the shocking rumor that Alvin's grave had been ransacked and his body mutilated. His father opened the grave with the help of friends on September 25, 1824, for the sorrowful job of ascertaining whether or not this was true. That same day, and for the following two weeks, the Smiths paid for a notice in the *Wayne Sentinel* denying that the young man's body had been desecrated and pleading that the rumor-mongers desist.[18]

Whether this was an early manifestation of community hostility to the Smiths, perhaps already in reaction to their religious claims, which got about despite Joseph's cautions to the family, or merely some callous prank, cannot be determined. The two-week run of the notice suggests that the cruel rumor persisted. Though the cost of such a notice was very likely modest, it was some expenditure for a family of little means, and is an indication of their love for Alvin and their continuing family pride. Lucy, who consistently glosses over whatever might seem to diminish the family status, does not mention this incident in her account of Alvin's death.

CHAPTER

3

COURTSHIP,
MONEY-DIGGING,
MARRIAGE

The family's circumstances remained very low, and Joseph went on laboring with his hands, hiring out by the day at whatever work became available. His religious experience did not preclude worldly contacts and endeavors. Among these was the then current fad of treasure hunting, or "money-digging" as it was called. Although at the time Joseph considered money-digging only one of any number of odd jobs he did, the experience would have consequences of great importance in his life.

In October 1825, one Josiah Stowell (sometimes spelled Stowel or Stoal), a well-to-do farmer from South Bainbridge, New York, came to ask young Joseph to help him find a lost silver mine in the Susquehanna Valley. Stowell claimed to have an ancient document describing and locating the mine, which he believed had been opened and later abandoned by the Spaniards, and he had already done some work on the site. In his day, he was only one of many men of character and substance who were convinced that treasures had been buried in various places in the New World, and who spent money and effort in search of them.

Stowell came to the Smiths saying that he had heard young Joseph held certain "keys" by which he could discern things invisible to the naked eye. Although Lucy says that Joseph tried to dissuade him, Stowell was insistent and offered "high" wages, which Joseph described with less enthusiasm as fourteen dollars a month. Since the family was, as always, in need of money, young Joseph and Joseph Sr. agreed to go, along with several neighbors.

The diggers went to board with Isaac and Elizabeth Hale, who lived in Harmony, Pennsylvania, not far from the supposed site of the mine.

The Hales were devout Methodists who had opened their doors to itinerant ministers in the Broome County circuit so often that it was said that Father Hale's house was the preacher's home. Isaac was generous to others as well. A skillful hunter, he would take long trips up the Starucca, a creek branching off the Susquehanna River in wild country noted for fish and game, where he would shoot elk. He would salt the meat and pack it home later, often leaving much of it at the door of some needy family.

Seventh of the nine Hale children was Emma, born July 10, 1804. One contemporary called her a fine girl of good reputation but poor parentage; however, this assessment of the Hale financial situation was no doubt relative, since they had property and were well enough off to be generous and hospitable. Later, when Joseph's mother met the Hales, she was impressed with their style of living, but that too was relative since Lucy was poor by any standard.

Emma was a schoolteacher. Tall, with abundant dark hair, level and impressive hazel eyes and a good singing voice, she had a certain dignified reserve which attracted and perhaps challenged the ebullient young boarder, Joseph Smith.

Joseph too had considerable presence. He was now six feet tall, muscular and like his father, noted as a wrestler, but his face was sensitive, with remarkably blue and compelling eyes under heavy eyelashes, thick blond eyebrows, a high, slanting forehead and light auburn hair. He looked at others directly, with an open and sympathetic interest, and his smile was easy and warm. In later years, Emma was reported to have said of him that no painting could catch his expression, which was always changing in reflection of his thoughts and feelings.

It soon became apparent that Joseph's interest in Emma was reciprocated. Her family disapproved. In fact, as Emma later wrote, they were "bitterly opposed."

Joseph maintained that the Hales objected to him on religious grounds, mainly because he had asserted that he had seen a vision. Isaac said that Joseph was careless, poorly educated and insolent to his father, the last a complaint never raised by Joseph's parents themselves. Isaac was not well disposed toward any of his boarders, for whose digging project he had soon lost sympathy. Some years afterward he said that one of them had skipped out owing him $12.68, although that charge was not made against the Smiths.

Isaac Hale's poor opinion of Joseph was not shared by everyone. Stowell conceived a lasting affection and respect for the young man, and years later expressed faith in Joseph as a prophet and in his church.

Young Joseph, his father and the other hired hands dug for Stowell with the aid of Joseph's special gifts for divining, which according to Isaac included looking into a stone in a hat in which Joseph buried his face. Isaac said that Joseph at first led the diggers to believe an enormous treasure awaited their discovery, but later declared that the enchantment became so strong as they drew near that he could no longer see it.

Joseph and his mother maintained that it was Joseph who finally persuaded Stowell to abandon the project. The diggers stopped about the seventeenth of November, after a month. Joseph and Lucy both said that Joseph's work for Stowell was the source of subsequent stories that Joseph was a money-digger.

When his father and the others returned home, Joseph stayed to work on Stowell's farm. Whenever possible, he rode to Harmony to visit Emma, whether welcomed by her father or not, and he attended school as he could, perhaps reacting to Isaac's comment that he was poorly educated, perhaps encouraged by Isaac's handsome, schoolteaching daughter.

Meanwhile, in Palmyra, Joseph's family had a good crop and were apparently in somewhat better circumstances, since the economy had improved and prices were higher for produce. However, they remained among the poorer families in their area.

The land they occupied was actually in Manchester but just on the border of Palmyra, and the Smiths identified with that village. Lucy and three of her children continued to attend the Presbyterian church there, perhaps for social reasons.

Palmyra was enjoying increased prosperity with the renewed promise of the Erie Canal. The middle section of the Canal, from Utica to Saline, had been finished in 1820, and its eastern section in Albany in 1823. During the preceding years, Palmyra had grown from a pioneer settlement of huts and log cabins to a bustling village with brick houses, a three-story hotel and a tavern. In 1822, an editorial of June 19 in a local newpaper, the *Western Farmer,* said, "the day is fast approaching when in point of business wealth, and respectability . . . [Palmyra] will have but few rivals in the state." By then Palmyra had numerous enterprises, including ten gristmills, seventeen sawmills, six distilleries and an ironworks.

The neighboring village of Manchester was also growing rapidly. A woolen mill which had begun operation in Manchester in 1813 was by the 1820s turning out cloth good enough, it was said, for "Sunday-go-to-meeting" clothes. Manchester, too, expected to benefit greatly from the Canal. Citizens began comparing their town to that of its English namesake, the great center of British manufacturing.

De Witt Clinton, reelected governor in 1825, saw the culmination of his seven years of effort in the grand celebration at the opening of the Canal. He and other officials set out from Albany on October 26 for the journey of 363 miles to New York City, carrying a barrel of water from Lake Erie which the governor emptied into the Atlantic on November 4.

Soon after the Canal was opened, Palmyra could boast several dry goods stores, two millinery shops and even a dancing school. Business was concentrated along the Canal banks where farmers brought their produce for shipment. Soon mule- and horse-drawn barges were passing each way every day, the arrivals announced by the blast of a bugle. They carried as much as seventy-five tons of freight—corn, wheat, oats, hides, lumber and manufactured goods.

The new water route reduced the cost of shipping dramatically, became the most important route west and was of enormous significance in the expansion and economic development of the country.

Although society in Palmyra in 1825 was still fluid and without sharp class distinctions, some families were beginning to feel superior and to have cultural aspirations. Social "bees" with exclusive invitations became popular, and talk was no longer confined to local farming and merchandising but frequently expanded to world affairs. The Smiths, however, apparently remained on the fringes of society.

The basic structure of their new house had been finished some two years before. Recently they had done the finishing touches on it with the help of a hired carpenter named Stoddard, and according to Lucy were now within a few months of the last payment on the farm, although, as has been noted, no evidence has been found that they had a formal contract for it.

Lucy wrote that Stoddard offered them fifteen hundred dollars for the house, but the Smiths declined to sell. Soon afterward, he and two accomplices told the Smiths' agent in Canandaigua that Joseph Sr. and young Joseph had run away and that Hyrum was defacing the farm and cutting down the sugar trees. With this they persuaded the agent to give Stoddard the deed to the property upon immediate payment.

Stoddard offered the deed to the Smiths for a thousand dollars. The Smiths tried desperately to raise the money, but failed. However, they persuaded one Lemuel Durfee to buy the farm, and county records show that he took ownership on December 20, 1825, for $1,135.[1] A Quaker of the Hicksite persuasion, owner of a woods near Palmyra in which the little Quaker church stood, Durfee apparently treated the Smith family with sympathy. He gave them a lease on the house and they would remain in it another three years, until December 30, 1828, when they would move to another house a little farther south.

Whether or not they had made legal arrangements to buy the land, the Smiths were strongly attached to it, and considered their loss a tragedy. How deeply they felt is indicated by Lucy's remark years later that every corner of the house had reminded her of Alvin, to whom she was still grateful for his planning and his handiwork.

In the meantime, Joseph Jr. continued working for Stowell on his farm, going to school and riding to Harmony to court Emma.

Somehow, for some reason unknown, Joseph had made an enemy of Peter Bridgeman, nephew of Mrs. Stowell. Four months after operations stopped in the Stowell mine, Bridgeman made a formal complaint against young Joseph and he was brought to trial in Bainbridge, New York, on March 20, 1826, before Justice of the Peace Albert Neely. Apparently Bridgeman's accusation was that Joseph was a disorderly person and an imposter.

Reports that young Joseph had been a "money-digger" with the aid of a "peep stone" (common parlance for any stone used like a fortuneteller's crystal to hunt for buried treasure) and that he had been brought to trial for such activity have long been in dispute. In recent years, however, these reports have been substantiated by the discovery of what is believed to be Judge Neely's bill of costs for that trial, set at $2.68, in which Joseph Smith is designated as "the glass-looker," and charged with a misdemeanor.[2]

Determining exactly what happened at the trial is difficult, however, because several diverse accounts of it exist but no fully authenticated transcript. Oddly, Joseph is recorded as testifying against himself in at least three of these, but there is no mention of any defense counsel. In one account which purports to be a transcript (published in *Fraser's Magazine* in 1873), certain aspects remain questionable, although the fact that it states the exact amount of Judge Neely's bill of costs gives some support to its validity.[3]

In that account, Joseph said he had a stone which he looked into to search for gold mines, that he had used it in working for Stowell and that he had also used it in Palmyra to find lost property. He said that he had not solicited this business, and lately he had given it up because it made his eyes sore.

Josiah Stowell testified to his belief in Joseph's skill with the stone, and other witnesses described the stone as white and transparent, and said that in it Joseph could see objects at a distance. Another witness, Jonathan Thompson, who professed faith in Joseph's stone, said that Joseph had gone with him and a man named Yeomans one night at Yeomans' request to look for a chest of money. Thompson said that the diggers struck something which was probably the chest, but because of the enchantment, it kept settling away from them.

Another account was written some years after the trial by a Bainbridge doctor, W. D. Purple, who claimed to have been present and to have taken notes at the request of Judge Neely. Since his version names Josiah Stowell as "Isaiah Stowell" and mistakes who brought the charges, it seems probable that some of it at least was based upon memory rather than notes.

According to Purple, Joseph testified that as a boy he had met a girl who owned a glass which she allowed him to look through. Years later he had found a stone of his own that enabled him "to annihilate distance, so gaining one of the attributes of deity." Purple's version of Thompson's testimony was that the diggers had fasted and prayed to break the charm which protected the buried treasure, and that at Stowell's instigation they had sprinkled the blood of a lamb around the spot as "propitiation" to the spirit, but the treasure had eluded them. The most significant thing recorded by Purple was that Joseph Smith, Sr., confessed that he and his son were "mortified that the wonderful power which God had so miraculously given . . . should be used only in search of filthy lucre." The prophet's father's statement indicates that the Smiths believed that Joseph's gift was from the Lord for a serious purpose.[4]

In most known accounts of that trial, Joseph was found guilty, although no sentence was recorded. However, Oliver Cowdery, who was to become Joseph's scribe not long after the trial, wrote in 1835 that it was "some officious person" who had complained of Joseph as disorderly, but since there was no cause for action, he was honorably acquitted.[5] According to A. W. Benton, who published his brief statement in 1831, "the public had him arrested as disorderly person, tried and condemned before a court of justice, but because he was a minor, because they hoped he might reform, he was designedly allowed to escape."[6]

Besides the evidence from this trial, there is testimony from early Mormons that Joseph had searched for treasure, that to some extent he had accepted the myths which often accompanied belief in buried treasure at that time and that a number of his close friends in the church were "money-diggers" and rodsmen.

Brigham Young, Joseph's successor as head of the church, said that Joseph's friend and one of his first converts, Porter Rockwell, was "an eye-witness to some powers of removing the treasures of the earth. He was with certain parties that lived near by where the plates were found that contain the records of the Book of Mormon. There were a great many treasures hid up by the Nephites. Porter was with them one night where there were treasures, and they could find them easy enough, but could not obtain them."[7]

According to Brigham, Joseph said in 1841, "every man who lived on the earth is entitled to a seer stone, and should have one, but they are kept from them in consequence of their wickedness."[8]

Another early convert who was important in Mormon history, Martin Harris, said that after he learned Joseph had found the gold plates, he and two others "took some tools to go to the hill and hunt for some more boxes, or gold or something, and indeed we found a stone box. We got excited about it and dug quite carefully around it, and we were ready to take it up, but behold by some unseen power, it slipped back into the hill."[9]

Martin Harris said elsewhere that Joseph and his father belonged to a company of "money diggers" who worked in Palmyra, Manchester and other areas.

James Colin Brewster, a dissenter from the Mormon Church, published a pamphlet in 1843 in which he said that many Mormons were "money diggers" and that Joseph Smith, Sr., declared in a High Council meeting in Kirtland that "he knew more about money digging than any man alive, had been at it for 30 years."[10]

Perhaps little would have been made of Joseph's money-digging if he had not used a stone in searching for treasure as well as in transcribing the word of God. That Joseph had a seer stone and that he used it in translating most of *The Book of Mormon* and in giving many of his early revelations was attested to by David Whitmer, Martin Harris and other members of the church.

After Joseph became known as a prophet, stories about his money-digging proliferated, and as early as 1830 were used to try to discredit him and his new church. Among the more enthusiastic talebearers was Abner Cole, who published them under the name of Obadiah Dogberry in the Palmyra *Reflector* after Joseph had prevented him from unauthorized printing of parts of *The Book of Mormon*. Philastus Hurlbut, excommunicated from the Mormon Church for misbehavior in 1833, began collecting stories in Palmyra, frequently from people who had had some quarrel with the Smiths, and he allowed his stories to be published by Eber D. Howe in a book called *Mormonism Unvailed*, which was widely read and oddly influential.

The fact was, however, that in New England and in western New York at that time digging for treasure was widespread among respected citizens and churchgoers, who saw no conflict between that and their religious convictions.

Josiah Stowell himself, according to Purple, had been "educated in the spirit of orthodox Puritanism, and was officially connected with the first Presbyterian Church of the town . . . a very industrious exemplary man."[11]

Stowell recognized Joseph's religious convictions and became convinced of his role as a prophet. Some years later, in 1843, when he was ill, he had one of his neighbors, a member of the church named Martha Campbell, write Joseph to ask him to pray in his behalf. Martha wrote, "He says he was never staggered at the foundation of the work for he knew too much concerning it . . . He thinks your prayers would do him good. He needs the milk of the Church. It is his request you should write to him immediately. Do write to him. It would be very consoling to him . . . He gave me strict charge to say to you his faith is good concerning the work of the Lord."[12]

Porter Rockwell's sister, who lived in Manchester and had gone to school with the Smith children, said, "there was considerable digging for money in our neighborhood by men, women and children." She added that Sallie Chase, a Methodist, had a peep stone which she would consult for people who came to her to find anything lost, hidden or stolen.[13]

An article reprinted in the *Wayne Sentinel* at Palmyra, February 16,

1825, from the Windsor, Vermont, *Journal,* said, "respectable men" could be named who "believed in the simplicity and sincerity of their hearts" that treasure could be found in the Green Mountains and who had persevered in digging for years, adding, "Even the frightful stories of money being hid under the surface of the earth, and enchanted by the Devil or Robert Kidd, are received by many a respectable citizen as truths."

In that same issue of the *Sentinel,* it was reported that "a respectable gentleman" in Tunbridge had claimed to discover a gold chest with the help of a vision and a mineral rod. On March 2, 1825, the *Sentinel* carried the account of a wood chopper who said he had found gold in the trunk of a tree near Utica.

The *Lyons Advertizer,* August 29, 1827, quoted a story from the New London *Gazette* about two men from Vermont who caused great excitement in town by announcing that they were going to dig for a box of dollars stolen from a Spanish galleon, the box being buried in mud under six feet of water near the wharf. The men had consulted a woman who used a transparent pebble as a talisman, claiming for it "the power of opening to her view the recesses of the earth."

By 1831, according to the Palmyra *Reflector* of February 1 that year, "the mania of money digging soon began to diffuse itself through many parts of this country; men and women without distinction of age or sex became marvelous wise in the occult sciences, many dreamed and others saw visions disclosing them deep in the bowels of the earth, rich and shining treasures."

Some money-diggers were religious mystics who only incidentally dug for treasure. About the year 1800 members of a religious cult in Wells, Vermont, claimed to be descendants of the tribes of Israel, said they were to inherit the land for miles around, preached that judgment day was imminent, believed in primitive Christianity and in its attendant gifts of healing and at the same time used rods they considered miraculous to search for buried money and find lost articles. Oliver Cowdery's father, it has been said, was one of them.[14]

Oliver himself had what was called a "rod of nature," which Joseph Smith's revelation in the *Book of Commandments* called "the work of God"; he added to Oliver, "whatsoever you shall ask me to tell you by that means, that will I grant you."[15]

After his trial in Bainbridge, Joseph remained for several months longer with Stowell, and continued to pay court to Emma. He did not find himself any more welcome at the Hales' home, however. According to Emma's brother-in-law, Emma's brothers, especially Alva, "vexed" Joseph at every opportunity, though about what is not known—perhaps glasslooking and money-digging. Once, on a fishing trip when the Hale boys teased the usually good-natured Joseph beyond endurance, he threw off his coat and offered to fight them.

Nevertheless, Joseph announced his intention to marry Emma to his parents and received their approval. Sometime in November of that year, 1826, he left Stowell, and went to work for his family's old friend, Joseph Knight, Sr., and remained with him, earning and saving as much money as he could until his marriage. Joseph Knight furnished him with a horse and cutter so that he could visit Emma, and the well-to-do farmer Martin Harris, for whom Joseph had worked as a boy, bought Joseph a new suit of clothes to help him make a good impression before her and her father.

When Joseph presented himself to Isaac and asked for Emma's hand, Isaac refused him. He told Joseph that he was not well enough known to the Hales, and that they could not approve of his business, presumably his money-digging.

There is no statement from Isaac that he objected to Joseph because of his religious claims. This was what Joseph believed, however, and indeed it does not seem likely, since Isaac was strongly attached to the Methodist faith, that he would have approved of Joseph's unorthodox background.

Emma, as Joseph was to learn, had a will of her own, however, and she was of age. Not long afterward, on Sunday morning, January 18, 1827, while Isaac was at church, the Hales' neighbors, W. H. Hine and his wife, saw Joseph riding past their door on an old horse with Emma up behind. They were married that day in South Bainbridge at the house of Squire Tarbill.

Immediately afterward, Joseph and Emma left for Joseph's parents' home, where they were made welcome, and Joseph spent the next season farming with his father.

Emma had eloped with Joseph with nothing but the clothes she was wearing, leaving behind everything else she owned, the rest of her clothing, some furniture and several cows. A few months after her wedding, she wrote to her father to ask if she could have her belongings. Isaac agreed, and in August Joseph set out to get her property. When Joseph and the Hales met again, apparently they made a reconciliation. It was Isaac's story that Joseph promised to give up "glass looking," to bring Emma back to Pennsylvania and to accept Isaac's offer of help in getting started to work. Joseph and Alva were also reconciled and Alva said that he would go to Palmyra later to help Joseph and Emma move back to Harmony.

Not long after Joseph came back to Manchester, according to his mother, he went to town on business for his father, but did not return when expected. His parents grew worried. Several hours late, Joseph came in and fell into a chair, exhausted. When his anxious father questioned him, Joseph said that he had met the angel again as he passed the Hill Cumorah, and was accused by him of neglecting the work of the Lord. It was time, the angel said, for Joseph to bring forth the record.

CHAPTER

4

THE GOLD PLATES

It was about midnight on the twenty-first of September, 1827, according to Lucy, and she was still up working when Emma passed through the room in her bonnet and riding dress. Emma and Joseph went off together, taking the horse and wagon of Joseph Knight, Sr., an old friend of the family's who was then a guest in the house.

Joseph Knight, Sr., wrote about the event several years later. In a narrative extant in his own hand, he recorded that he had been to Rochester on business that September, had returned by way of Palmyra and was there for a few days. He said:

He [Joseph Smith] had talked with me and told me the Conversation he had with the personage which told him if he would Do right according to the will of God he mite obtain [the plates] the 22nt Day of September Next and if not he never would have them . . . So that night we all went to Bed and in the morning I got up and my Horse and Carriage was gone. But after a while he came home and he turned out the Horse. All Come into the house to Brackfirst. But nothing said about where they had bin. After Brackfirst Joseph Cald me into the other Room and he set his foot on the Bed and leaned his head on his hand and says, "Well I am Dissopinted. "Well," says I, "I am sorry." "Well," says he, "I am grateley Dissopinted; it is ten times Better than than I expected." Then he went on to tell the length and width and thickness of the plates, and said he they appear to be

Gold. But he seamed to think more of the glasses or the urim and thummem then he did of the Plates, for, says he, "I can see any thing; they are Marvelus . . ."[1]

In Joseph's account he had gone to his usual meeting place at the Hill Cumorah and had been given the plates, the Urim and Thummim and the breastplate by the heavenly messenger, Moroni, and charged to be responsible for them until the messenger came for them again.

Lucy wrote that Joseph placed something in her hands and said, "See here, I have got a key." In the first edition of her history, Lucy gave a description of the object, which was not included in later editions. She said it was two smooth, three-cornered diamonds set in glass and the glasses set in silver bows, like old-fashioned spectacles. This was the Urim and Thummim, she said. Later Joseph showed her the breastplate wrapped in a muslin handkerchief thin enough to allow the glistening metal to be seen. It was concave-convex, with metal straps for fastening to hips and shoulders, and was made for a man of extraordinary size.[2]

In a sermon William gave years later, he said that Joseph brought the plates home wrapped in an old frock. His father asked, "What, Joseph, can we not see them?" Joseph replied, "No. I was disobedient the first time, but I intend to be faithful this time, for I was forbidden to show them until they are translated." He allowed the family to handle them, however, and according to William it was easy to tell that they were thin sheets of metal that could be riffled like the pages of a book. William said they were a mixture of copper and gold, and much heavier than wood or even stone. He thought they weighed about sixty pounds.[3]

Lucy wrote that two years earlier Joseph Sr. had told their friend Martin Harris in strict confidence about Joseph's visions. Somehow the word had spread. Some of the neighbors later said the plates were a "hoax," but a number of them believed Joseph had found something of value. Years later, in an interview in Palmyra, one of the neighbors, Thomas H. Taylor, who said he knew the Smiths well, was asked if he thought that Joseph ever got plates out of the hill as he maintained. Taylor said, "Yes; I rather think he did. Why not he find something as well as anybody else. Right over here, in Illinois and Ohio, in mounds there, they have discovered copper plates since . . . [the Smiths] were good, honest men, and what is the sense in saying they lied? Now, I never saw the Book of Mormon— don't know anything about it, nor care; and don't know if it was ever translated from the plates . . . but all this don't prove that Smith never got any plates."[4]

It would not have been the only time artifacts were discovered in that region of New York. In the private journal he kept during a visit to the area in 1810, De Witt Clinton, later governor, wrote that copper kettles, wampum and other items had been found in a burying ground near Canandaigua.[5]

Some of the neighbors began to snoop and harass the Smiths with questions. A number grew excited and made outright efforts to get Joseph's find away from him.

Joseph Knight, Sr., wrote, "Now it soon got about that Joseph Smith had found the plates and peopel Come in to see them But he told them that they Could not for he must not shoe them. But many insisted and oferd money and Property to see them. But, for keeping them from the Peopel they persecuted and abused them and they [the Smiths] ware obliged to hide them . . ."[6]

Mary Adeline Noble, wife of Joseph B. Noble, one of Joseph's early converts, said that although he did not see the plates, her father Alva Beman had once helped Joseph hide them when a mob came to search the Smith home.[7]

According to Martin Harris, some of the trouble came from money-diggers. If so, it seems reasonable to suppose they were Joseph's former companions who wanted a share of his treasure.

Lucy wrote that Joseph Sr. learned that ten men, led by a neighbor, Willard Chase, had sent some sixty miles for a conjurer to tell them where "Joe Smith's gold bible," as they called it, was hidden. One night they ransacked the Smith property and tore up the floor of Joseph Sr.'s cooper shop. Later the family learned that Willard's sister Sallie had directed the search with the aid of a piece of green glass through which she claimed to see wonderful things.[8]

Martin Harris, as has been mentioned, was "fired with the hope of discovering a buried treasure" and went digging on the hill. However, he was also impressed by Joseph's account of his visions, having been told about them by Joseph's father, and he was interested in the religious significance which Joseph claimed for his discovery. That the religious aspects of Joseph's discovery were known early is indicated by several contemporary newspapers in the area. On June 26, 1829, the *Wayne Sentinel,* published in Palmyra, wrote of the speculation which had existed "for some time past" about the discovery claimed to have been made "through superhuman means, of an ancient record, of a religious and divine nature and origin." Similar comments were made that year by newspapers in Rochester.[9]

The task before Joseph now, as he said, was to get the records translated with the aid of the Urim and Thummim, and for this he needed to escape from the greedy and curious neighbors.

Martin Harris approached Joseph in town one day and gave him a bag of fifty silver dollars, telling him that it was to be used for the Lord's work. Years afterward Joseph was still speaking of his gratitude to Martin, saying that Martin had provided the means for him to travel to a safe place to begin his translation.

In December, Alva Hale arrived to help Joseph and Emma move to Harmony.

Joseph says he put the plates in a small box which he hid in the bottom of a forty-gallon barrel of beans among their household goods in the wagon. Harmony, 128 miles away, was a four-day wagon journey. It was midwinter when they set out, and Emma was pregnant. That they undertook such an ordeal suggests that Joseph felt the move was much more urgent than a mere compliance with his father-in-law's request to bring Emma back.

When Joseph and Emma arrived and began to unload their goods, Isaac and his family were curious about the box in the bean barrel, although none of them believed that it held gold plates.

Isaac described the box as like those used for ordinary window glass, which would have been about ten by twelve inches. He was allowed to feel its weight but not to look inside, which so angered him that he declared the box had better be taken out of his house because he was determined to see it.

Joseph and Emma moved into a little house on Isaac's property which had been occupied by the Hales' eldest son Jesse and his family, who had gone to Illinois. Some two and a half years later, on August 25, 1830, Isaac and Elizabeth Hale signed a deed transferring the property to Joseph for $200. Apparently Emma had six acres of her own on one corner of Isaac's farm, but it is not known whether this was attached to the land on which Joseph and Emma lived.

The first home of Joseph and Emma was a small frame house of three rooms on a plot of thirteen and a half acres on the Susquehanna, some 450 feet east of the Hales' house. It was said to have had a beautiful maple floor. Doors off the little front entrance led to the attic and to the kitchen-living room, where there was a good fireplace next to a small bedroom. Part of the upstairs was partitioned off into a room with a window facing east and here, according to tradition, Joseph did much of his translating.

In December, as soon as they were settled, Joseph says he began work and continued until the following February. Considering himself a poor writer, Joseph required the help of a scribe, and in early stages he was assisted by Emma, and also, according to Emma, by her brother Reuben.

Emma later said that her husband translated the first part with the Urim and Thummim, but afterward used a small stone, which she described as not exactly black but rather a dark color.

Emma said that she wrote for her husband hour after hour as he dictated, sitting with his face buried in his hat, which had the stone in it. According to Emma, he was not reading from any book or manuscript. Emma wrote:

> No man could have dictated the writing of the manuscript unless he was inspired . . . when returning after meals, or after interruptions, he would at once begin where he had left off, without either seeing the manuscript or having any portion of it read to him. This was a usual thing for him to do. It would have been improbable that a learned man could do this; and for one so ignorant and unlearned as he was, it was simply impossible.[10]

Joseph's explanation of his work was that, "Through the medium of the Urim and Thummim I translated the record by the gift, and power of God."[11]

The young couple had a hard time that winter, but found a faithful friend in Joseph Knight, Sr., who wrote:

> Now he Could not translate But little Being poor and nobody to write for him But his wife and she Could not do much and take care of her house and he Being poor and no means to live But work. His wifes father and familey ware all against him and would not hlp him. He and his wife came up to see me the first of the winter 1828 and told me his Case. But I was not in easy Circumstances and I did not know what it mite amount to and my wife and familey all against me about helping him. But I let him have some little provisions and some few things out of the Store a pair of shoes and three Dollars in money to help him a litle . . .[12]

In January, Knight took Joseph's father and his brother Samuel to see the young couple and at that time gave Joseph a little money to buy paper for his work. In March, since the sleighing was still good, he went to see Joseph again, this time persuading his wife Polly to come along. The young prophet talked to them about his work and his revelations. Knight wrote that from that time Polly began to believe. She would continue in remarkable faith until her death a few years later.

Apparently it had been agreed that as soon as Joseph transcribed some of the characters from the plates, Martin Harris would come to Harmony for the copy and take it to some learned men in the East for their evaluation.

Martin Harris was a neighboring farmer who had hired Joseph as a boy of ten to work in his fields for fifty cents a day. At the time he became interested in Joseph's plates, he was a sturdy man in middle life, with sideburns, chin whiskers and at times a visionary look in his eyes. According to one report, he had been a member of several denominations, including the Quakers, to which his wife belonged, after which he joined in succes-

Joseph Smith. COURTESY ILLINOIS
STATE HISTORICAL LIBRARY.

Hyrum Smith, elder brother of Joseph
and an early leader of the Saints.
COURTESY ILLINOIS STATE
HISTORICAL LIBRARY.

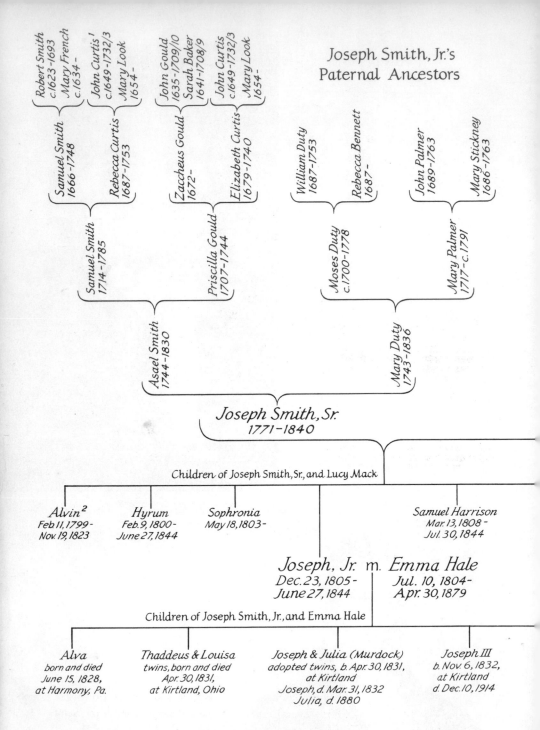

Joseph Smith, Jr.'s
Paternal Ancestors

Robert Smith c.1623-1693
Mary French c.1634-

John Curtis¹ c.1649-1732/3
Mary Look 1654-

John Gould 1635-1709/10
Sarah Baker 1641-1708/9

John Curtis¹ c.1649-1732/3
Mary Look 1654-

William Duty 1687-1753
Rebecca Bennett 1687-

John Palmer 1689-1763
Mary Stickney 1686-1763

Samuel Smith 1666-1748
Rebecca Curtis 1687-1753

Zaccheus Gould 1672-
Elizabeth Curtis 1679-1740

Moses Duty c.1700-1778
Mary Palmer 1717-c.1791

Samuel Smith 1714-1785
Priscilla Gould 1707-1744

Asael Smith 1744-1830

Mary Duty 1743-1836

Joseph Smith, Sr.
1771-1840

Children of Joseph Smith, Sr., and Lucy Mack

Alvin²
Feb 11, 1799 -
Nov. 19, 1823

Hyrum
Feb. 9, 1800 -
June 27, 1844

Sophronia
May 18, 1803 -

Samuel Harrison
Mar. 13, 1808 -
Jul. 30, 1844

Joseph, Jr.   m. Emma Hale
Dec. 23, 1805 -   Jul. 10, 1804 -
June 27, 1844   Apr. 30, 1879

Children of Joseph Smith, Jr., and Emma Hale

Alva
born and died
June 15, 1828,
at Harmony, Pa.

Thaddeus & Louisa
twins, born and died
Apr. 30, 1831,
at Kirtland, Ohio

Joseph & Julia (Murdock)
adopted twins, b. Apr. 30, 1831,
at Kirtland
Joseph, d. Mar. 31, 1832
Julia, d. 1880

Joseph III
b. Nov. 6, 1832,
at Kirtland
d. Dec. 10, 1914

Joseph Smith's family tree.

¹For some time previous to the act of Parliament, 1752, that imposed the Gregorian calendar on Britain and the colonies, events occurring between January 1 and March 25 were recorded as double years, for example: 1732/3.

²Lucy Mack Smith, in her *Biographical Sketches of Joseph Smith the Prophet* . . . (Liverpool, 1853), gives Alvin's death as 1824, and so does Mary Audentia Smith Anderson, *Ancestry and Posterity of Joseph Smith* . . . (Independence, Missouri, 1929). However, Alvin's gravestone gives 1823, and so do later editions of Lucy's work.

Joseph Smith, Jr.'s Maternal Ancestors

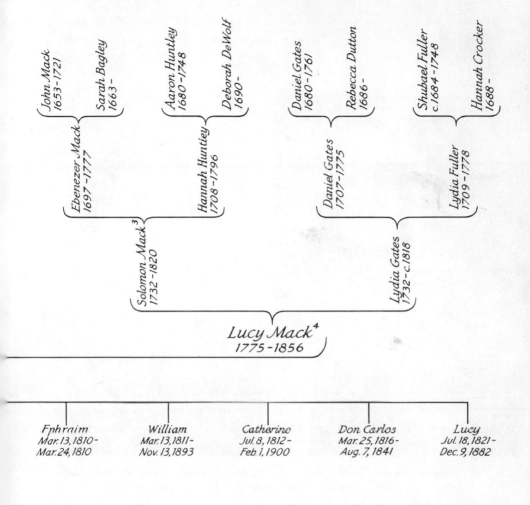

Ephraim Mar. 13, 1810 – Mar. 24, 1810	**William** Mar. 13, 1811 – Nov. 13, 1893	**Catherine** Jul. 8, 1812 – Feb. 1, 1900	**Don Carlos** Mar. 25, 1816 – Aug. 7, 1841	**Lucy** Jul. 18, 1821 – Dec. 9, 1882

Frederick Granger Williams b. June 20, 1836, at Kirtland d. Apr. 13, 1862	**Alexander Hale** b. June 2, 1838, at Far West, Mo. d. Aug. 12, 1909	**Don Carlos** b. June 13, 1840, at Nauvoo, Ill. d. Aug. 15, 1841	**David Hyrum** b. Nov. 17, 1844, at Nauvoo d. Aug. 29, 1904

[3]Lucy and Solomon record his birth date as September 26, 1735, but vital records, Lyme, Connecticut, give it as September 15, 1732. See Richard Lloyd Anderson, *Joseph Smith's New England Heritage* . . . (Salt Lake City, Utah: Deseret Book Co., 1971), p. 162, n. 10.
[4]Lucy records her birth date as July 8, 1776, but town records, Gilsum, New Hampshire, give it as July 8, 1775. See Richard Lloyd Anderson, p. 182, n. 97.

Two views of Emma Hale Smith, who married Joseph in 1827. Portrait *(left)*: COURTESY ILLINOIS STATE HISTORICAL LIBRARY. Photo *(right)*: UTAH STATE HISTORICAL SOCIETY.

sion the Universalists, Restorationists, Baptists and Presbyterians. He was known for his extensive knowledge of the Bible and was able to quote chapter and verse at length.

Martin had married his first cousin, Lucy Harris, or Aunt Dolly, as she was more frequently called, and they had worked together early and late, managing their farm of some 240 acres, growing wheat, and conducting several other prosperous enterprises, including the manufacture of worsted and flannel cloth. Martin was active in community affairs as a commissioner of common school and an overseer of highways, and he was known as an honorable man and an obliging neighbor.

Dolly was piqued at the mystery of the plates. According to Lucy, she was rather deaf and whatever was said that she did not hear distinctly she considered suspicious. She demanded a look at the plates and when this was denied, her annoyance increased. Learning of her husband's plan to go to Harmony to get the transcription, she determined to go with him, but Martin eluded her and made the trip with Hyrum.[13]

Of Martin's trip to Harmony, Joseph said in his journal of 1832:

> because of his faith and his righteous deed [in helping finance Joseph's move to Harmony] the Lord appeared unto him in a vision and shewed unto him his marvilous work which he was about to do and mediately came to Susquehannah and Said the Lord had shown him that he must go to New York City with some of the characters so we proceeded to Coppy some of them and he took his Journey to the Eastern Cittys and to the Learned . . .[14]

How Martin found out where to go for an evaluation of the plates is not known, but there is evidence that he asked for advice. The Reverend John A. Clark, of Palmyra, wrote that Martin called at his home "much in earnest" with characters copied from the plates. Clark implied that Harris looked to make money from the venture, but also said he expected it to resolve many controversial points of doctrine.[15]

Apparently Martin then went to Albany to see Assemblyman Luther Bradish, who had traveled in Egypt and had some knowledge of antiquities.

Of scholars who might have assisted Martin, including Charles Anthon of Columbia College, Edward Robinson and Edward Everett of Harvard and T. D. Woolsey and George Ticknor of Yale, only Anthon was then available. Martin Harris also had the name of a certain scholar usually identified only as "Mitchell" but who, according to one careful study, was very likely Samuel L. Mitchill, a classicist, professor, physician and United States congressman, known as "a chaos of knowledge." Martin evidently got a letter of introduction from him to Anthon.[16]

By 1828, when Martin Harris went to call on him, Anthon had been a teacher of Greek and Latin at Columbia College for some eight years. He was a forty-one-year-old bachelor, known as a crotchety taskmaster, but a brilliant classicist. His revision of Lemprière's *A Classical Dictionary* had gone through six editions, but Anthon would later enlarge and expurgate it, explaining that the earlier scholar's work was "frequently marked by a grossness of allusion" which made it unfit for the young. The Dictionary held references to a number of writings on Egypt, including Champollion's *Précis du Système Hiéroglyphique* . . . , of which Anthon owned a copy.

Anthon was living on campus at Columbia College, at that time in lower Manhattan. When Martin came in he was alone, probably in his study. Unfortunately, because their stories differ, there were no witnesses to what transpired. According to the account in the *History of the Church,* Martin afterward told Joseph Smith that he presented the characters and the translation to the professor, who said that the translation was correct, "more so than any he had before seen translated from the Egyptian." When Harris showed him more characters not yet translated, Anthon pronounced them true "Egyptian, Chaldaic, Assyric, and Arabic," and gave Harris a certificate to that effect. As Harris was leaving the professor asked where he had found the characters. Martin told him they were from plates revealed by an angel of God. Anthon asked to see the certificate he had just written. When Martin handed it back, Anthon tore it up, saying that there was no such thing now as ministering of angels. He offered to translate the plates if they were brought to him. Martin says he told the professor that part of the plates were sealed and he was forbidden to bring them. To this, Anthon replied, "I cannot read a sealed book."[17]

Martin says he then went to "Dr. Mitchell," who agreed with Professor Anthon's verification of the characters and the translation.

Anthon's version of what happened between him and Martin Harris was written in two letters, the first on February 17, 1834, to Eber D. Howe, and the second in 1841 to the Reverend Thomas Winthrop Coit.

Anthon wrote to Howe after he heard from Howe that "vile use" was being made of his name by Mormons who were claiming that Anthon had declared Joseph Smith's characters to be ancient shorthand Egyptian. Anthon told Howe that Harris, whom he described as "a plain and apparently simple-hearted farmer," had come to him with a letter from Dr. Samuel L. "Mitchell," and said that he had been asked to contribute toward publication of the book, and that he intended to sell his farm, but he had come to New York as a precaution to get the opinion of the "learned." Anthon wrote:

> The paper in question was, in fact, a singular scroll. It consisted of all kinds of singular characters, disposed in columns, and had evidently been prepared by some person who had before him at the time a book containing various alphabets; Greek and Hebrew letters, crosses and flourishes, Roman letters inverted or placed sideways . . . and the

whole ended in a rude delineation of a circle . . . evidently copied after the Mexican calendar, given by Humboldt . . . I am thus particular as to the contents of the paper, inasmuch as I have frequently conversed with my friends on the subject since the Mormon excitement began, and well remember that the paper contained any thing else but "Egyptian Hieroglyphics"![18]

This account by Anthon is curious in at least two respects. So far as is known, Martin Harris, at the time he called on Anthon, had not yet considered aiding the prophet to the extent of selling his farm, although Dolly's opposition suggests that he had some contribution in mind. Since by the time Anthon wrote to Howe, Martin had sold his farm, it is conceivable that Anthon had picked up this information in his "frequent conversations" about the Mormons.

It is curious also, as has been observed, that Anthon's description of the characters does not fit the facsimile believed to have been carried by Martin to New York.[19]

Anthon's letter to Coit, an Episcopal clergyman in New Rochelle, was in reply to his statement that Mormon missionaries in his area were "claiming the patronage of Professor Anthon's name." Anthon said Martin "was told" (but he does not say by whom) to come and convince himself there was no risk involved in the project. What he wrote for Martin, Anthon said, was to demonstrate that the characters were a hodgepodge in imitation of various alphabets. Anthon told Coit that some time later, "the countryman" returned and tried to give him a printed copy of the "golden Bible."[20]

Since it should be allowed that Harris and Anthon were both men of integrity, coming to a decision about what actually happened between them is difficult. One suggestion has been made that if Anthon had said at first that the characters were transcribed correctly, Harris, an unsophisticated man, might have understood him to mean translated.[21]

Mitchill and Anthon probably would have been able to verify that the characters were some form of Egyptian, since by the time Harris came to see them a number of works had been published with facsimiles of Egyptian writing. However, very little translating of Egyptian had as yet been done, and it seems highly unlikely that either man could have been certain that the characters were correctly translated.[22]

Whatever actually happened during Martin's visit to New York, the fact remains that he came home convinced that the characters were authentic. As Joseph wrote in his journal of 1832:

He took his journey to the Eastern Cittys and to the Learned Saying read this I pray thee and the learned Said I cannot but if he would bring the plates they would read it but the Lord had forbid it and he returned to me and gave them to me to translate and I said I cannot for I am not learned but the Lord had prepared Spectacles for to read the Book therefore I commenced translating the characters and thus the prophecy of Isaia was fulfilled which is writen in the 29 Chapter concerning the book . . .[23]

The Reverend Clark wrote that Harris said Anthon "thought the characters in which the book was written very remarkable, but he could not decide what language they belonged to."[24] According to John H. Gilbert, Martin came back satisfied that "Joseph was a little smarter than Professor Anthon."[25]

The incident between Harris and Anthon was reported in several newspaper accounts which mainly took a humorous view, and it was mentioned in a book for the first time in E. D. Howe's *Mormonism Unvailed.*[26]

Very likely what helped to persuade Martin to support the project was that he knew, or was reminded by Joseph, of the prophecy of Isaiah 29:11, which reads:

And the vision of all is become unto you as the words of a book that is sealed, which men deliver to one that is learned, saying, Read this, I pray thee, and he saith, I cannot; for it is sealed.

Later, as Joseph continued work on *The Book of Mormon* a parallel appeared in the words of the prophet Nephi, 27:15–18:

But behold it shall come to pass that the Lord God shall say unto him to whom he shall deliver the book: Take these words which are not sealed and deliver them to another, that he may show them unto the learned, saying: Read this, I pray thee. And the learned shall say: Bring hither the books and I will read them . . . And the man shall say: I cannot bring the book for it is sealed . . .

The fate of the transcript of characters which Martin Harris took to New York is not known for certain, although David Whitmer later claimed that it had come into his possession. The transcript owned by Whitmer was given to the Reorganized Church by his heirs in 1903. Lucy maintained that Dolly Harris had a copy made of Martin's transcript.[27] The fate of that copy is also unknown.

Three lines of characters purported to be a reproduction of the transcript Martin took to Anthon appeared in a little unofficial Mormon newspaper published in New York City, called *The Prophet,* issue of December 21, 1844. With the illustration was the heading, "The stick of Joseph taken from the hand of Ephraim," and the statement, "The following is a correct copy of the characters taken from the plates which the Book of Mormon was translated from: the same that was taken to Professor Mitchell, and afterwards to Professor Anthon of New York, by Martin Harris . . ." The source of that illustration was not given but it was probably a black and gold placard of 1844 which bears the same characters and almost identical words. The publisher of that placard is unknown. The only copy extant, which has a statement on the back that it was the property of Hyrum Smith, is now owned by the Historical Department of the Church of Jesus Christ of Latter-day Saints in Salt Lake City.[28]

Over the years various attempts have been made to identify these characters as some form of Egyptian, but nothing definite has been established.

JOSEPH TRANSLATES

While Martin was away, Dolly, a vigorous and strong-willed woman who got about the community on horseback, called on Lucy Smith and told her that she had property and she knew how to take care of it. This suggests that Dolly knew that Martin meant to aid Joseph financially, and she intended to investigate thoroughly before she allowed it. Lucy had quite a lot to say about Martin and Dolly. Lucy's history, along with its evidence of her sincere religious conviction and moral courage, is often like gossip at a tea party, lively, human, self-righteously enjoying other people's foibles and contretemps, while revealing more than a little effort to make the best impression of herself and her family.

When Martin got home from his trip to New York, he settled his affairs in Palmyra as soon as he could, which was sometime in April 1828, and set out for Pennsylvania to act as Joseph's scribe. Lucy says that Dolly insisted upon going with him, and was no sooner in the Smiths' home than she informed Joseph that she had come to see those plates and would not leave until she did. She started at once to ransack every trunk, nook and cupboard. When she could not find the plates in the house, she became convinced that Joseph had buried them, and went outdoors to search despite the cold and the snow still on the ground.

During the two weeks that Dolly remained in Harmony, she spread her view among Joseph's neighbors that he was a "grand imposter" with designs on her property.[1]

Apparently Joseph and Emma bore all this patiently, and Martin went steadily on as Joseph's scribe. The two men worked together hidden away in the little attic room for two months between April and June.

Despite his continuing efforts for Joseph, Martin had periods of doubt, or perhaps of susceptibility to Dolly's influence. He confessed years later to Edward Stevenson, as reported in *The Latter-day Saints' Millennial Star,* 1881, that he once substituted a stone of his own for the seer stone to see if Joseph could detect the difference. Martin was gratified when Joseph exclaimed that all was dark and he could not translate.

When Dolly at last returned to Palmyra, having failed in her purpose to see the plates, she went from house to house asking for storage for such of her furniture, linens and bedding as she could move, to prevent Joseph Smith, she said, from stripping her of everything.

Dolly's fears were not entirely imaginary. After years of laboring with her husband in building up their property, she saw it threatened by a project for the validity of which she could find no assurance, despite her every effort.

Martin remained with the Smiths, writing for Joseph until June 14, by which time they had done a hundred and sixteen pages on foolscap.

Apparently from the outset, Martin had pleaded with Joseph to allow him to show the manuscript to his wife, in the hope of winning her to the cause. Joseph inquired of the Lord if this might be done, but met refusal. At last, after Martin's constant pleading, Joseph received a revelation which gave Martin permission to show the manuscript to his wife and to four others, her sister Abigail Harris Cobb, Martin's brother Preserved and his parents. Martin was bound in solemn covenant to show it to no one else.

Joseph's account of this says:

> . . . he desired to carry them to read to his friends that peradventure he might convince them of the truth therfore I inquired of the Lord and the Lord Said unto me that he must not take them and I spoke unto him (Martin) the word of the Lord and he Said inquire again and I inquired again and also the third time and the Lord Said unto me let him go with them only he shall covenant with me that he will not shew them to only but four persons and he covenented with the Lord that he would do according to the word of the Lord . . .[2]

Martin set out for Palmyra on June 14, with all 116 pages, the only copy of the manuscript so far translated.

On the fifteenth, the day after Martin left, Emma gave birth to her first child. It was a difficult labor, and the baby died the same day. A little headstone was carved with the words, "In memory of An Infant Son of Joseph and Emma Smith June 15 1828" and set up in the little cemetery, which was visible from the window of Joseph's "translation room."

Emma was so ill that for two weeks Joseph was afraid she might die, and put everything else out of mind to care for her. When she began to recover, his thoughts returned to his manuscript and he began to wonder why Martin had been gone so long without sending back any message. According to Lucy, Emma shared his concern, and persuaded him to go to Palmyra and investigate. He took the first stage in growing alarm, and arrived early one morning exhausted, after taking the last twenty miles through the woods on foot.

The Smiths sent for Martin Harris, but it was several hours before he appeared. At last he crept toward the Smith property and perched on their fence, with his hat pulled over his eyes. When he finally came into the house he looked so ghastly that Hyrum asked if he were ill. Martin cried, "Oh, I have lost my soul!"

The wretched Martin confessed that the manuscript had disappeared.

Martin told the horrified Smith family that he had shown the manuscript to his wife and their relatives as permitted, after which Dolly had allowed him to lock it up in her bureau. One day while his wife was out, the voluble Martin told a friend about the manuscript, and the friend no doubt exhibited such skepticism that Martin forgot his covenant. When he went to his wife's bureau, Martin discovered that the key was gone. Impatiently, perhaps angrily, he picked the lock, took out the manuscript and displayed it in triumph to his friend.

Dolly was furious when she discovered the damage to her bureau, and added that to her growing list of grievances.

After he had allowed one unauthorized viewing of the manuscript, Martin began showing it to any friend who happened along. He had apparently not taken it out for some time, however, when the Smiths sent for him, because it was not until then that he discovered the manuscript was missing. He searched the house frantically, but in vain.

Now he stood in guilt and anguish before the injured Smiths. Lucy told about her son's reaction.

"Oh, my God!" Joseph cried. "All is lost . . . What shall I do? I have sinned—it is I who tempted the wrath of God . . ." Weeping and groaning, he began to walk the floor.

Joseph begged Martin to search again, but the dejected Martin told him that there was nowhere else to look. He had even ripped open the beds and pillows.

"Then must I return to my wife with such a tale as this!" Joseph cried. "I dare not do it, lest I should kill her at once. And how shall I appear before the Lord? Of what rebuke am I not worthy . . . ?"[3]

The manuscript was never found, and its disappearance has never been satisfactorily explained. Dolly insisted that she knew nothing about it, but she was not generally believed. Martin and the Smiths thought she had given it to someone in the hope of making a mockery of the prophet's work. According to one resident of Palmyra, Dolly stole the manuscript while Martin was asleep and burned it, keeping her act a secret for years after publication of the book. An acquaintance of the Hales', a Mrs. McKune, maintained that Dolly burned part of the manuscript but kept some of it to show in an effort to discredit Joseph.

Joseph said that Martin "broke the covenent which he made before the Lord and the Lord suffered the writings to fall into the hands of wicked men and Martin was chastened for his transgression . . ."[4]

Joseph returned to Harmony greatly disturbed. The loss of the only copy of his manuscript was a disaster with which he hardly knew how to cope.

In his revelation of July 1828, Joseph also was chastised:

. . . behold how oft you have transgressed the commandments and the laws of God, and have gone on in the persuasions of men . . . you should not have feared man more than God . . . thou art Joseph, and thou wast chosen to do the work of the Lord . . . repent of that which thou has done which is contrary to the commandment which I gave you, and thou art still chosen . . . my work shall go forth, for inasmuch as the knowledge of a Savior has come unto the world, through the testimony of the Jews, even so shall the knowledge of a Savior come unto my people . . . the Lamanites . . . And for this very purpose are these plates preserved . . .[5]

Joseph received another revelation that summer that marked a new step in his developing role as prophet. This was the first of many revelations that he received and put on paper in answer to practical problems, for the conduct of everyday life. This lengthy revelation came in direct response to his agony of mind over the fearful loss of the Lord's work, and it told that the evil men into whose hands the translation had fallen were inspired by Satan to try to discredit him by altering the text. Joseph was shown a means to outwit them. He was not to retranslate the stolen parts but to turn instead to other plates in his possession, which contained an account by Nephi of the same events.[6]

Chagrined and self-reproachful, Joseph did not return immediately to translating. He spent his time at work on his small farm in Harmony.

Meanwhile, word that Joseph was a gifted "prophet, seer and revelator" was spreading.

In the fall of that year, 1828, Joseph Sr. wrote to his father Asael, then living in Stockholm, St. Lawrence County, New York, that young Joseph had received several remarkable visions. Asael's grandson George Albert Smith recorded that Asael was impressed, and said that he had always known God would raise up some branch of the family to be a great benefit to mankind. Asael's eldest son Jesse had nothing but ridicule for his brother Joseph's news. The younger sons Asael, Silas and John, father of George Albert, were also antagonistic at first.

Soon afterward, Joseph Jr. wrote a letter himself, in which, according to George Albert Smith, he "declared that the sword of vengeance of the Almighty hung over this generation and except they repent and obeyed the Gospel, and turned from their wicked ways, humbling themselves before the Lord, it would fall upon the wicked, and sweep them from the earth as with the beacon of destruction."

George Albert, at that time a boy of eleven, says this letter made a deep impression upon him and upon his father, whose comment was that "Joseph wrote like a Prophet."[7]

The summer and fall of 1828 were difficult for Joseph, what with worry over the loss of his manuscript, the death of his newborn son, the illness of his wife, his continued poverty and the sting of being unable to do better for the handsome and intelligent Emma. He was almost dependent upon his father-in-law, who very likely was still looking upon him with scorn and distrust for occupying himself with his seer stone and his Urim and Thummim.

He had not written to his parents for some two months. They began to worry about him and Emma, and about the consequences to Joseph of the loss of his manuscript. They set out to visit. Lucy writes they were relieved to see Joseph's pleasant looks, and to hear that the plates and the Urim and Thummim were safe in a red morocco trunk on Emma's bureau.

On this visit, Joseph's parents met the Hales for the first time. Lucy pronounced them an intelligent and highly respectable family, living in good style. She said that she and her husband passed a very agreeable time with them. Concerned, as always, to make the best impression, Lucy makes no suggestion of disharmony between the Hales and her son.

In February 1829, Joseph received a revelation for his father that a marvelous work was about to come forth among the children of men, and that if Joseph Sr. desired to serve God, he was called. In the same month, young Joseph received a revelation to begin his work again.

Emma had by now recovered from her illness and the initial shock and sorrow over the loss of her first-born. Perhaps welcoming the diversion, she began to write for her husband again, when household chores permitted. According to Lucy, this was not enough help to satisfy Joseph, and he began to pray to the Lord to send him a scribe.

For some time, Martin Harris had been considering supporting the publication of Joseph's book. He was still at times uncertain about it, however, and was constantly berated by his wife, who grew more and more outraged by what she called her husband's "craziness" and predicted that if Martin financed the "golden Bible" he would ruin himself and his family.

Martin decided to ask that there be a witness to the plates, and he went to see Joseph with the request in March 1829.

That same month Joseph received a revelation directed to Martin which answered his wish abundantly. Not one but three witnesses would be allowed, and if Martin would humble himself in prayer and acknowledge his mistakes, he should be one of them, and would say to the people of his generation, "Behold I have seen the things which the Lord hath shown until Joseph Smith, jun., and I know for a surety that they are true, for I have seen them . . . by the power of God and not of man."

With this, Martin was told in effect to stop nagging. "I command you," said the revelation, "my servant Joseph, that you shall say unto him, that he shall do no more, nor trouble me any more concerning this matter."

In the same revelation, Joseph was told to give up translating for a while. "Stop and stand still until I command thee, and I will provide means whereby thou mayest accomplish the thing which I have commanded thee."[8]

Not long afterward young Oliver Cowdery appeared, to become the prophet's diligent and faithful new scribe.

Oliver was a lean young man with a long, narrow head and hollow cheeks, but with a certain tenderness of expression. About a year younger than Joseph, he had been born in Wells, Rutland County, Vermont, the son of one of the followers of Nathaniel Woods, leader of the religious rodsmen whose center was in Wells.

Oliver had lived in New York City for a while and then moved to Palmyra, where he taught in the district school and boarded with local families in turn, as was the custom then to help support teachers.

Oliver had a friend in Palmyra, David Whitmer, a stocky young man of twenty-four. The two had often discussed the popular rumors about Joseph Smith and his gold plates.

When it became Lucy's turn to give room and board to the teacher, Oliver had a chance to question Joseph Sr., who, although he was at first reluctant, eventually gave Oliver the whole story about the plates.

Of a religious and mystical turn himself, Oliver decided to go to Harmony to investigate. On the way, he stopped to see David Whitmer at his parents' home in Fayette and promised to write to him as soon as he had formed an opinion about the young prophet.

Oliver arrived in Harmony on April 5, 1829. He and Joseph talked for two days, during which time Joseph told him that it was "the will of heaven" that Oliver should become his scribe. Oliver began to work for Joseph on April 7.

Although he now had the full-time help of a scribe, Joseph's poverty remained a problem. Hearing that Joseph was in difficulty that spring, the faithful Joseph Knight, Sr., again came to his rescue. Knight wrote:

I bought a Barral of Mackrel and some lined paper for writing . . . nine or ten Bushels of grain and five or six Bushels taters and a pound of tea, and I went Down to see him and they ware in want. Joseph and Oliver ware gone to see if they Could find a place to work for provisions, but found none. They returned home and found me there with provisions, and they ware glad for they ware out. Their familey Consisted of four, Joseph and wife, Oliver and his [Joseph's] Brother Samuel. Then they went to work and had provisions enough to Last till the translation was Done.[9]

As he had promised, Oliver wrote to David Whitmer. He told him that he was convinced Joseph had the record of an ancient people and a revealed knowledge of their truth.

In April, Joseph had a revelation for Oliver through the Urim and Thummim:

be diligent; stand by my servant Joseph, faithfully, in whatsoever difficult circumstances he be for the words sake. Admonish him in his faults and also receive admonition of him. Be patient; be sober; be temperate; . . . Behold I am Jesus Christ, the Son of God . . . Verily, verily, I say unto you, if you desire a further witness, cast your mind upon the night that you cried unto me in your heart, that you might know concerning the truth of these things. Did I not speak peace to your mind concerning the matter? What greater witness can you have than from God? . . .[10]

Oliver confessed to Joseph that he had indeed called upon the Lord while in bed one night at the Smiths' home in Palmyra, and prayed to know the truth about the plates. Oliver said the Lord had manifested to him that what he had heard was true, but Oliver had divulged that secret to no one.

Oliver claimed some prophetic and divining powers of his own, and had brought with him a "rod of nature," perhaps acquired while he was among his father's religious group in Vermont, who believed that certain rods had spiritual properties and could be used in divining.

Joseph was anxious to finish his translation, and if some of the work could be done by an assistant, he would be grateful. In his first revelation for Oliver, Joseph said, "And behold, I grant unto you a gift, if you desire of me, to translate, even as my servant Joseph . . ."

Oliver was told something about the process of translating:

. . . you shall receive a knowledge concerning the engravings of old records, which are ancient, which contain those parts of my scripture of which has been spoken by the manifestation of my Spirit.

Yea, behold, I will tell you in your mind and in your heart, by the Holy Ghost, which shall come upon you and which shall dwell in your heart.

Now behold, this is the spirit of revelation . . .

Ask that you may know the mysteries of God, and that you may translate and receive knowledge from all those ancient records . . . and according to your faith shall it be done unto you.[11]

With this encouragement, Oliver sat down to translate, but he soon had to confess that nothing came to him. Another revelation, received by Joseph for Oliver, told him:

you have not understood; you have supposed that I would give it unto you, when you took no thought save it was to ask me. But behold, I say unto you, that you must study it out in your mind; then you must ask me if it be right, and if it is right I will cause that your bosom shall burn within you . . .

From Joseph's own words, it is apparent that he believed his inner voice was the way God had chosen to communicate with him. Joseph had a faith in his spiritual gifts, but he was also a practical man, and recognized that his translating required thought and organization, as did his revelations, which were always meaningful and relevant to the circumstances and the people involved. Oliver, who had not understood the necessity for his own participation in the process of translating, sat blankly waiting for the Lord to fill his mind, and was baffled and disappointed when he was unable to work with the "keys" presented to him in Joseph's revelation.

Oliver was excused for the present from further attempts: "it is not expedient that you should translate now." However, he was told to continue to write for Joseph.[12]

After considering for some time the question of authority for baptism, the two young men went into the woods on May 15, 1829, to pray to the Lord for enlightenment on that subject.

In the prophet's account, while he and Oliver were praying, a messenger from heaven descended upon them in a cloud of light, and laid his hands upon them, saying, "Upon you my fellow servants, in the name of Messiah I confer the Priesthood of Aaron, which holds the keys of the ministering of angels, and of the Gospel of repentance, and of baptism by immersion for the remission of sins . . ."[13]

The *History of the Church* records that this messenger was John the Baptist, acting under the direction of Peter, James and John, who held the keys of the Melchizedek, or higher, Priesthood, which would later be conferred upon Joseph and Oliver. The messenger directed Joseph to baptize Oliver and he in turn to baptize Joseph, after which they were to confer the Aaronic, or lesser, Priesthood upon each other. Immediately after they came out of the water, the Holy Ghost fell upon them and they stood and prophesied many things. "We were filled with the Holy Ghost, and rejoiced in the God of our salvation."[14]

Oliver Cowdery also wrote of this experience some five years later in 1834. He said that he and Joseph had gone to a secluded spot to pray, and that:

On a sudden, as from the midst of eternity, the voice of the Redeemer spake peace to us, while the vail was parted and the angel of God came down clothed with glory, and delivered the anxiously looked for message, and the keys of the gospel of repentance! What joy! what wonder! what amazement! While the world were racked and distracted—while millions were groping as the blind for the wall, and while all men were resting upon uncertainty . . . our eyes beheld—our ears heard, as in the "blaze of day," yes, more—above the glitter of the May sun-beam, which then shed its brilliancy over the face of nature! Then his voice, though mild, pierced to the center, and his words, "I am thy fellow-servant," dispelled every fear . . . what joy filled our hearts . . . when we received under his hand the holy priesthood, as he said, "upon you my fellow servants, in the name of Messiah I confer this priesthood and this authority, which shall remain upon earth . . ." The assurance that we were in the presence of an angel; the certainty that we heard the voice of Jesus, and the truth unsullied as it flowed from a pure personage, dictated by the will of God, is to me, past description, and I shall ever look upon this expression of the Savior's goodness with wonder and thanksgiving . . .[15]

There is no direct account of the restoration of the Melchizedek Priesthood in Joseph's history or in other contemporary works, but there are several references to it and the event has been deduced by one historian as having occurred within the next fifteen months, or some time between May 15, 1829, and August 1830.[16]

For the time being, Joseph says, he and Oliver did not reveal the restoration of the priesthood because a spirit of persecution had been manifested in the neighborhood.

Joseph began to feel an obligation to discuss the gospel with more of his friends, acquaintances and family. He talked with his younger brother, Samuel Harrison Smith, who was then in Harmony on a visit, but Samuel was not easily convinced. However, when he was advised to go to the woods and pray for guidance, he did so and was persuaded of the truth of Joseph's mission.

Samuel was baptized soon afterward and would remain faithful to the end of his short life. He would be one of the eight witnesses to *The Book of Mormon,* one of the early missionaries in the church, and would become an unspectacular martyr for the faith not long after the murder of his elder brothers, Joseph and Hyrum.

Soon after Samuel's baptism, Hyrum came to Pennsylvania, and Joseph received a revelation for him saying that "a great and marvelous work is about to come forth" and that he should "seek to bring forth and establish the cause of Zion."

Joseph's circle of converts and supporters was growing, and some of them were already manifesting exceptional devotion. Joseph Knight, Sr., the old friend of the Smith family for whom Joseph had worked as a farm hand in his youth, came several times with his son Joseph Jr. from their home in Colesville, New York, with a wagonload of provisions for the young prophet so that he would not have to interrupt his work. Joseph Knight, Jr., who had worked closely with young Joseph Smith on his father's farm, said his father considered Joseph the best hand he ever had, and "a boy of truth." Joseph Smith had told them about his vision, and they had believed him, although the two older Knight boys, Nahum and Newel, had not.[17]

The provisions were a great help to Joseph and Emma, who always remembered that kindness. Joseph had a revelation for Joseph Knight, Sr., at the time of his first visit to Harmony, which instructed him, too, to keep the Lord's commandments and to help establish the cause of Zion. The Knight family were soon to become devoted members of Joseph's church.

Joseph had a great deal of further assistance from the family of David Whitmer.

David came to Harmony early in June with a wagon and team to take Joseph to his father's house in Fayette, a distance of some 135 miles, where Joseph would have free board and room and the aid of David's brothers to take his dictation. David added what was probably to Joseph an irresistible appeal, that the people of the neighborhood were eager to hear more about his work.

Joseph met David Whitmer for the first time when he came for him with the Whitmer wagon. Oliver went to Fayette with them and continued helping Joseph with the book until it was finished, while Emma stayed behind to take care of the home in Harmony.

David's parents, Peter Whitmer, Sr., and Mary, had come originally from Pennsylvania and had moved to Fayette early in the nineteenth century. They had eight children, three of whom, David, John and Peter Whitmer, Jr., soon became Joseph's friends and zealous aides.

At Fayette Joseph's work went fast but apparently not all in an easy flow of inspiration. David Whitmer said that Joseph confessed to him that sometimes his mind was too much on earthly things and he would be unable to translate until he went out to pray.[18]

As David had said he would, Joseph found the people of Seneca County friendly and interested in the "strange matters which now began to be noised abroad." Many neighbors opened their doors to him and called in their friends to hear him preach. A number became convinced that he was speaking the truth, and some, Joseph said, were willing to obey the gospel.

The Whitmer brothers and Hyrum Smith were soon baptized and from that time on the number of converts increased rapidly.

THE MANUSCRIPT
PUBLISHED

Joseph had not forgotten his revelation that there were to be three witnesses to the plates, and neither had his friend Martin Harris.

When Martin came to Fayette from Palmyra that June 1829, he, Oliver Cowdery and David Whitmer urged Joseph to seek a revelation in their behalf. The friends heard what they had hoped to hear, that they would be the ones to see the plates. ". . . and ye shall testify that you have seen them, even as my servant Joseph Smith, Jun., has seen them, for it is by my power that he has seen them, and it is because he had faith."[1]

One morning soon afterward, at the conclusion of the usual Whitmer family service of Scripture-reading, singing and prayer, Joseph rose from his knees and told Martin that if he would humble himself and obtain forgiveness for his sins, which referred to his carelessness with the first part of the manuscript, he would see the plates that day with David and Oliver.

The four men walked out to the woods near the Whitmer farm, and after sitting on a log to talk for a while, they began to pray, Joseph first and the others in turn. When their prayers had no result, they renewed their efforts, but in vain. At last Martin rose, saying that he felt responsible for their failure since he could not summon sufficient faith. He withdrew and the others prayed again. As David Whitmer told it later:

> All at once a light came down from above us and encircled us for quite a little distance around; and the angel stood before us. He was dressed in white, and spoke and called me by name and said "Blessed

is he that keepeth His commandments" . . . A table was set before us and on it the records were placed . . . While we were viewing them the voice of God spoke out of heaven saying that the Book was true and the translation correct.[2]

Joseph then went to look for Martin Harris, and found him not far away in fervent prayer. At Martin's request, the prophet joined him in pleading with the Lord. At last Martin cried, "'Tis enough; Mine eyes have beheld!" He jumped up praising God and rejoicing.[3]

According to the prophet's mother, who was there with her husband on a visit, the men returned to the Whitmer home between three and four in the afternoon. Lucy recalled that Joseph threw himself down beside her and exclaimed, "You do not know how happy I am." His friends had seen the plates, he said, and an angel who had testified to them. Since others could now bear witness, he could no longer be accused of deceiving. He felt relieved of a great burden.[4]

Martin came in, almost overcome with joy, Lucy wrote, and testified vigorously to his experience. So did Oliver and David. The witnesses signed a testimony saying that they knew that the plates had been translated "by the gift and power of God, for his voice hath declared it unto us." They continued:

wherefore we know of a surety that the work is true. And we also testify that we have seen the engravings which are upon the plates; and they have been shown unto us by the power of God, and not of man. And we declare with words of soberness, that an angel of God came down from heaven, and he brought and laid before our eyes, that we beheld and saw the plates, and the engravings thereon; and we know that it is by the grace of God the Father, and our Lord Jesus Christ, that we beheld and bear record that these things are true. And it is marvelous in our eyes . . .

Soon afterward, Joseph called eight more witnesses, his father, his brothers Hyrum and Samuel, the Whitmer brothers—Christian, Jacob, John and Peter Whitmer, Jr.—and Hiram Page, who was the Whitmers' brother-in-law. Lucy said this occurred when Joseph came to Palmyra with the Whitmers and Hiram Page to make arrangements for publication of his book. The eight men saw the plates in Manchester, near the Smith home, in the woods where some of the family sometimes went alone to pray in private.

According to the testimony signed by the eight brethren, Joseph showed the plates to them himself. They said that the plates had the appearance of gold, adding:

. . . and as many of the leaves as the said Smith has translated we did handle with our hands; and we also saw the engravings thereon, all of

which has the appearance of ancient work, and of curious workman-
ship. And this we bear record with words of soberness, that the said
Smith has shown unto us, for we have seen and hefted, and know of a
surety that the said Smith has got the plates of which we have spoken.
And we give our names unto the world, to witness unto the world that
which we have seen. And we lie not, God bearing witness of it.

Joseph published the two testimonies in the first edition of *The Book of
Mormon,* and they have been included in every edition since.

Among additional statements by the witnesses was that of John
Whitmer, who said in 1836:

I desire to testify to all that will come to the knowledge of this address; that I have most assuredly seen the plates from whence the
Book of Mormon is translated and that I have handled these plates,
and know of a surety that Joseph Smith, Jr. has translated the book of
Mormon by the gift and power of God, and in this thing the wisdom
of the wise most assuredly has perished.[5]

In 1847, Hiram Page said:

To say my mind was so treacherous that I have forgotten what I saw,
to say that a man of Joseph's ability, who at that time did not know
how to pronounce the word Nephi, could write a book of six hundred
pages, as correct as the book of Mormon without supernatural power
. . . it would be treating the God of heaven with contempt, to deny
these testimonies . . .[6]

The testimonies published in *The Book of Mormon,* especially that of
the three witnesses, have been the subject of long debate, and remain one
of the many intriguing aspects of the early Mormon Church which have
never been explained to the satisfaction of all.

The Mormon belief has always been in the objective reality of the experience as described. Mormons have emphasized the fact that although the
three witnesses left the church after 1837, none ever denied his testimony.
Some critics not of Mormon belief have tried to cast doubt upon the truth-
fulness of the witnesses, or to suggest that they were deceived by Joseph in
some way, or that they succumbed to his powers of suggestion, or that
Joseph had made their ability to see the plates a test of each man's personal faith. Some have suggested that the testimonies were written by
Joseph and signed by the witnesses merely because Joseph said they were
true. One early historian asked why Smith should call in the angels to convince the world that he had the plates, when all he had to do was exhibit
them to the public.[7] Governor Ford of Illinois wrote that some of the eight
witnesses (the second group) later told him that they could not see any
plates in the box Joseph showed them, but Joseph had them pray for two

hours, reprimanding them as sinners of little faith, which measures achieved the desired result.[8]

Although they were interviewed by both friendly and hostile investigators many times afterward, none of the three first witnesses ever told anybody that Joseph had subjected them to undue pressure. From their own statements, it is apparent that whatever the three witnesses saw, they saw without coercion, although it has been said that one of the witnesses declared their view of the plates was with "spiritual eyes." Martin Harris was quoted to this effect by a number of people, including Reuben Harmon, John Gilbert and the Reverend Jesse Townsend, all from Palmyra. A Mormon elder named Stephen Burnett, who had left the church, wrote to a Brother Johnson that Martin Harris made what was to Burnett a devastating confession. Burnett wrote, "When I came to hear Martin Harris state in public that he never saw the plates with his natural eyes only in vision or imagination, neither Oliver nor David . . . the last pedestal gave way, in my view our foundations were snapped."[9]

Burnett added, however, that Martin said afterward, in a meeting in the Kirtland temple on March 25, that he was sorry for any man who rejected *The Book of Mormon* for he knew it was true, and that more than once he had hefted the plates in a box with only a tablecloth or handkerchief over them.

George Albert Smith, the grandson of Asael, wrote of that meeting in the temple to Josiah Fleming, saying that Martin "bore testimony of its truth and said all would [be] damned that rejected it."[10] George Albert apparently found nothing to alarm his faith in what Martin Harris had said previously and he became one of the strong leaders of the church.

Although he made great personal sacrifices for the church, Martin's fervent conviction alternated with periods of wracking doubt. Following their disagreement over *The Book of Mormon,* Martin and Dolly separated, after which, according to one early historian, neighbors who had looked upon Martin "charitably" began to consider him "utterly infatuated and crazy."[11] Later Martin married a Mormon woman of unswerving faith and had a second family by her, but they all left him to go west with the pioneers under Brigham Young.

In Kirtland, from about 1838 to 1844, Martin affiliated with various groups which had withdrawn from the Mormon Church, and for a time he belonged to an entirely different sect.

In 1870, broken in health, impoverished and anxious to see his Mormon family, he made the journey to Utah. At a church meeting in the tabernacle in Salt Lake City, he reaffirmed his certainty of the truth of *The Book of Mormon.* Martin enjoyed popularity in his later life. He spoke on many occasions, saying that he had seen the plates as clearly as he could see his hand. He reaffirmed the reality of his experience at every opportunity, until his death in 1875 at the age of ninety-two.

Martin Harris's doubts and convictions were always on a rather naive level. Oliver Cowdery, however, was a more complicated personality. His many letters written between 1831 and 1848 reveal that he was sensitive, intelligent and courageous in dissent.[12] Oliver left the church in 1838, after a fiery quarrel with leaders of the church. He stoutly opposed some of Joseph's policies, decried plural marriage and said also that he would not be controlled by ecclesiastical power in temporal concerns. After leaving the church, Oliver moved to Tiffin, Ohio, where he practiced law, and apparently for a time became a Methodist. In 1848, he was rebaptized into the Mormon Church at Council Bluffs and evidently planned to join the Saints in Utah when his death intervened. Among his last statements was an affirmation that he had seen and handled the plates, and that he had received the priesthood from divine authority.[13]

David Whitmer became disillusioned with Joseph, and although he professed love for him until the end, he believed that Joseph lost his powers of prophecy when he gave up his seer stone, and thereafter led the church astray. David left the church in June 1838, in fear for his life from the secret band of Danites, which was one segment of Joseph's followers that David abhorred and denounced. However, none of the witnesses was interviewed more frequently or held to his testimony more doggedly than he, and his long life made him a favorite of newspaper feature writers well past 1880.

In 1887, after his eighty-second year, David published his convictions in a fervently worded pamphlet called *An Address to All Believers in Christ* in which he said that Joseph had drifted into error in establishing polygamy as well as in other ways, but only the weak in faith would be deterred on that account from embracing the truth. He concluded, "God has given to this generation the Book of Mormon, and how plain and simple is the doctrine of Christ set forth therein."[14] He continued to affirm that belief until he died.

It is apparent that however others might judge their experience, or attempt to explain it away, it was real to the three witnesses. The closest scrutiny of their testimonies can leave no doubt that their faith in *The Book of Mormon* was based upon what they believed to be a direct manifestation from God. Their lives were changed thereafter in accordance with that belief, and they held to their conviction in spite of their disappointment in the way Joseph Smith's church developed. All three died reaffirming their testimony. However Joseph Smith might fail in their eyes, it was as a man, subject to the weakness of the flesh. They were utterly and irrevocably convinced that God had chosen him to bring to light *The Book of Mormon* as a witness for Christ in the New World, and to establish the last dispensation.

In March of 1830, when he had the signed testimonies of eleven witnesses, Joseph began to make rigorous efforts to get his book printed.

After investigating several possibilities, he chose Egbert B. Grandin, publisher of the *Wayne Sentinel,* in Palmyra. Grandin, however, required a guarantee of $3,000 before he would begin setting type.

Although Martin Harris had agreed to finance the project, when he was called upon for the cash, he was reluctant, or perhaps he was intimidated by his wife. He did try to raise a loan, however. With a letter of recommendation from the minister of the Presbyterian church in Palmyra, he made application to borrow $1,300 from the bank in Geneva, New York. The banker was impressed with Martin's business reputation, but when he learned the purpose of the loan, he refused it.

According to David Whitmer, Hyrum became impatient with Martin for failing to sell his farm outright, and urged Joseph to look elsewhere for the money. Hyrum also said that he had heard Joseph might sell the copyright of his book in Canada. Urged by his friends, Joseph sought council through revelation, and received word which was written down, according to Whitmer, but never printed, that Hiram Page and Oliver Cowdery were to travel to Canada and sell the copyright in Toronto.

The delegates set off, full of confidence in their mission. In Canada, to their consternation, they found no one with any interest in buying Joseph's copyright. For the first time in the young prophet's life, a revelation failed.

Joseph was in the Whitmer home, according to David, when Hiram Page and Oliver Cowdery returned. Also present were David's brothers Jacob and John, and they and the delegates were all greatly troubled by the outcome of the mission. They turned to the prophet for an explanation. Joseph inquired of the Lord through his stone, David said, and received the statement that "some revelations are of God, some are of man, and some are of the devil." David Whitmer and Hiram Page both believed the mission to Canada had failed because Joseph's friends insisted that he provide a revelation to solve their dilemma. Later David expressed his interpretation of that event: "When a man enquired of the Lord concerning a matter, if he is deceived by his own carnal desires, and is in error, he will receive an answer according to his erring heart, but it will not be a revelation from the Lord." In David's opinion, that experience offered a lesson from which they all should have profited.[15] Some of the prophet's later revelations were to become the subjects of heated controversy within and without the church, but the majority of his followers accepted his pronouncements as from the Lord, when Joseph so proclaimed them.

On August 5, 1829, Martin Harris mortgaged his farm for $3,000 and pledged to pay the full amount to Grandin within eighteen months, giving Grandin authorization to sell the farm in default of payment. Grandin began printing.

On August 29, 1829, well before any of the book came off the press, the *Palmyra Freeman* called it "the greatest piece of superstition that has come to our knowledge." Aware of the continuing hostility of his neighbors, and remembering the loss of the first part of his manuscript, Joseph took elaborate precautions for the safety of his work before its publication. He had Oliver copy the whole manuscript for the printer's use, keeping the original locked away and watched over night and day by the Smith family. Oliver's copy was delivered to the printer under guard a few pages at a time, no more than would be used in one day's work. The manuscript which was used by the printer and covered with his marks, about five hundred pages of unruled foolscap closely written in ink on both sides, was cherished by Oliver Cowdery until his approaching death, when he bequeathed it to David Whitmer.[16]

In spite of all Joseph's efforts, however, Abner Cole, a former justice of the peace, town gossip and self-appointed censor who wrote under the name of Obadiah Dogberry, managed to get part of the work, some said with Grandin's complicity, and began to set it up in type on Grandin's press.

One Sunday, according to Lucy, Hyrum surprised Cole in Grandin's office up to his elbows in printer's ink, and asked him why he was working so hard on the Lord's day. Lucy wrote that Hyrum saw a prospectus of Cole's weekly and was shocked to discover that it carried a blatant advertisement that parts of *The Book of Mormon* would be printed in it so that subscribers could avoid buying the book. Cole would not be persuaded to desist in his piracy, and managed to publish some of *The Book of Mormon* in the Palmyra *Reflector* with the comment "priestcraft is short-lived" before Joseph could make a trip from Harmony to give him a forceful reminder of the laws of copyright.[17]

Stephen S. Harding, afterward governor of Utah Territory, came home to Palmyra from college as a young man that summer of 1829 and was fascinated by the stir about *The Book of Mormon,* especially when he learned that it was being published by the Joe Smith he remembered as a long-legged, tow-headed boy three years older than himself whom he used to see fishing in the pond at Durfee's gristmill on Mud Creek. Harding went to find the prophet at Grandin's print shop, and was interested to see that he had grown into a tall, rather pale and beardless young man, his hair turned to a light auburn. According to Harding, the prophet had little to say, but his companion, Martin Harris, said a lot.

Harding expressed interest in reading *The Book of Mormon,* but this was not allowed in its unpublished form. However, he was invited to the Smith home to hear some of it read by Oliver Cowdery.

Harding said that "the old lady," meaning Lucy, at that time only fifty-three but very likely aged by hard work, gave him a good supper of brown bread, milk and heaps of fresh raspberries, brought in by two girls, perhaps Catherine and Lucy, the prophet's younger sisters.

The Smiths had only one light, a tallow candle in a tin candlestick, by which Oliver read until it began to sputter. All of the family then went to bed except the prophet's mother, who sat up and talked to young Harding about dreams.[18]

The people of Palmyra became more and more agitated about the printing of Joseph's book. Editors of local newspapers soon began making negative comments for what they claimed were rational or religious reasons.

In Palmyra, a mass meeting was held at which pledges were made not to buy the book when it appeared and to discourage its purchase by others.

These resolutions were made known to Grandin without delay. He became so alarmed that although his contract with Martin Harris had almost a year left to run, he suspended publication and demanded payment in full. Joseph returned to Palmyra again and urged Martin to make the payment, but Dolly was so strongly opposed that Martin could not be persuaded. In March 1830, Joseph received a revelation for Martin:

> I command you to repent—repent, lest I smite you by the rod of my mouth, and by my wrath, and by my anger, and your sufferings be sore—how sore you know not, how exquisite you know not, yea, how hard to bear you know not . . .
>
> And again, I command thee that thou shalt not covet thine own property, but impart it freely to the printing of the Book of Mormon, which contains the truth and the word of God . . .
>
> Impart a portion of thy property, yea, even part of thy lands, and all save the support of thy family.
>
> Pay the debt thou hast contracted with the printer. Release thyself from bondage.
>
> Pray always, and I will pour out my Spirit upon you, and great shall be your blessing—yea, even more than if you should obtain treasures of earth and corruptibleness to the extent thereof.
>
> Behold, canst thou read this without rejoicing and lifting up thy heart for gladness?[19]

Martin Harris sold part of his farm to a neighbor and paid the printer.

Five thousand copies of the book, bound in leather, came off the press that month. It was advertised for sale March 26, 1830.[20]

Martin set out to make up his investment by his own efforts. The previous January 16, Joseph Smith, Sr., had given him a signed statement that he would have equal rights with him and his friends to sell the book until the cost of the printing was repaid. Immediately after it was published, Martin was seen every day on the streets of Palmyra, dressed in a suit of gray homespun and a large stiff hat, with books under his arm, trying to sell them to friends and neighbors for $1.25 a copy.[21]

He was not able to sell many copies. The best he could say about the financial aspects of his investment was that Joseph ultimately repaid him all the money he had advanced.

CHAPTER

7

THE BOOK OF MORMON

The Book of Mormon, nearly six hundred pages of small print in the first edition, contains the chronicles of three groups of immigrants to the New World, most of it concerning a period from about 600 B.C. to A.D. 421. It is in fifteen main divisions, or books, each named after its principal author, and is based upon three sets of plates, or engraved records, the Plates of Nephi (which are of two kinds, larger plates of secular history and smaller sacred records), the Plates of Mormon, an abridgment of the Plates of Nephi made by Mormon with his comments and a continuation by his son, Moroni (who became the angel Moroni), and the Plates of Ether, abridged by Moroni, a history of the Jaredites, who came to the new land when the people were dispersed after the destruction of the Tower of Babel. Other records to which frequent reference is made in *The Book of Mormon* are the Brass Plates of Laban, which contain the ancient Hebrew Scriptures.

Most of *The Book of Mormon* is about the descendants of Lehi, who left Jerusalem with his family in 600 B.C., following God's warning about His pending scourge of the wicked. Lehi and his family built a ship and came to Central or South America, bringing with them the Plates of Laban. Their posterity were soon divided into the righteous light-skinned Nephites and the rebellious dark-skinned Lamanites. Interspersed with accounts of their wars and contentions are the admonitions and teachings of various prophets on numerous subjects such as the nature of man, the fall and the atonement.

The Book of Mormon confirmed that the new land was a land of promise for the descendants of the tribes of Israel (2 Nephi 1:5): "We have obtained a land of promise, a land which is above all other lands; a land which the Lord God hath covenanted with me should be a land for the inheritance of my seed . . . forever and also all those who should be led out of other countries by the hand of the Lord."

But the people must keep the Lord's commandments, Nephi warns, or they would be smitten and scattered. A nation dwindling in faith is told that the time for repentance is brief.

A prophecy of 1 Nephi 22:23 denounces sectarianism and the corruption of churches, "for the time speedily shall come, that all churches which are built up to get gain, and all those who are built up to get power over the flesh, and those who are built up to become popular in the eyes of the world . . . are they who need fear, and tremble, and quake; they are those who must be brought low in the dust . . ."

A warning is given in 2 Nephi 27:20 against the Gentiles who in their pride build many churches in which they "put down the power and the miracles of God, and preach up unto themselves their own wisdom and their own learning . . . and there are many churches built up which cause envyings, and strifes, and malice."

The Book of Mormon was to reconcile religious controversy and settle all disputes over biblical interpretation. As the prophet Lehi said to his son Joseph (2 Nephi 3:12), referring to *The Book of Mormon* and the Bible, "the fruit of thy loins shall write; and the fruit of the loins of Judah shall write; and [these works] . . . shall grow together, unto the confounding of false doctrines and laying down of contentions, and establishing peace among the fruit of thy loins, and bringing them to the knowledge of their fathers in the latter days, and also the knowledge of my covenants, saith the Lord."

In addition, *The Book of Mormon* is another witness for Christ, as in 1 Nephi 13:40: "These last records, which thou has seen among the Gentiles, shall establish the truth of the first . . . and shall make known the plain and precious things which have been taken away from them; and shall make known to all kindreds, tongues, and people, that the Lamb of God is the Son of the Eternal Father, and the Savior of the world; and that all men must come unto him, or they cannot be saved."

About five hundred years after Lehi and his family immigrated to the new land, King Mosiah recommends to his people (29 Mosiah 25–26) that they relinquish the monarchy and choose judges to lead them according to the law and the voice of the majority. The people elect their high priest Alma to be their first chief judge as well, in this way establishing religious and political leadership in one person.

Some 130 years later, the resurrected Christ appears to the Nephites, inhabitants of the new land, His "other sheep," and ministers to them and gives them His message, which includes a reiteration of the Sermon on the Mount (3 Nephi 12).

Jesus warns the wicked of God's vengeance, but adds (3 Nephi 21:22–25), "if they will repent, and hearken unto my words, and harden not their hearts, I will establish my church among them, and they shall come in unto the covenant and be numbered among this the remnant of Jacob, unto whom I have given this land for their inheritance; And they shall assist my people . . . that they may build a city, which shall be called the New Jerusalem. And then shall they assist my people that they may be gathered in . . . And then shall the power of heaven come down among them; and I also will be in the midst."

The ideal society is set forth as existing among the people for some two hundred years after Christ's visit. It is a theocracy, in which all, Nephites and Lamanites alike, are members of the one true church. Peace and harmony prevail, all things are held in common so that no poor, no bondsmen, no thieves or murderers exist among them, strife and religious contention are unknown, "and surely there could not be a happier people among all the people who had been created by the hand of God" (4 Nephi 16).

But they are unable to maintain this level of righteousness. A war between the Nephites and the Lamanites eventually leaves a single Nephite survivor, Moroni, who buries the records of his people with their message for a later generation in the Hill Cumorah.

The Book of Mormon is not easy to read, and from its unpopular reception in some areas, it did not seem likely at first to reach a large audience. However, when ardent young missionaries began to carry the book about the countryside and to urge its prayerful consideration it soon aroused interest.

Alexander Campbell, founder of the Campbellite Church, who was annoyed when some of his followers deserted him for the Mormon faith, considered the book a fraud, and said it had anachronistic ideas on democratic government and the rights of man derived from the United States. As has been suggested, Campbell overlooked the fact that the form of government extolled in the book was more theocratic than republican.[1] Campbell was correct, however, when he said that the book was concerned with the very issues in religion which were then being intensely debated. He said that the author reproduced:

> every error and almost every truth discussed in New York for the last ten years. He decides all the great controversies—infant baptism, ordination, the trinity, regeneration, repentance, justification, the fall of man, the atonement, transubstantiation, fasting, penance, church government, religious experience, the call of the ministry, the general res-

urrection, eternal punishment, who may baptize, and even the question of free masonry, republican government; and the rights of man.

It seemed to Campbell that Joseph Smith "infallibly decides by his authority every question."[2]

This authority was exactly the basis for much of the appeal of *The Book of Mormon*. That the church founded on that book answered the urgent need of many who like the members of Joseph's family were distressed by sectarian conflict and were looking for an authoritarian revival of the primitive Christian church is demonstrated by the frequency with which converts spoke of the disruption to their faith caused by numerous and contending sects. Notable among these were men who later became vigorous leaders in Joseph's church, among whom were Oliver Cowdery, Brigham Young, Wilford Woodruff, Amasa Lyman and Lorenzo Snow. Hosea Stout, a convert to Mormonism who had been a Methodist, wrote that he discovered a hostile spirit between the Methodists and the Cumberlands, and that "It threw me much in the back Grounds to hear preachers slander each other because of small differences of opinion in 'non-essentials' so called."[3]

Joseph Smith's uncle John, in moving from New York State to live near his nephew and others who believed in *The Book of Mormon,* wrote that he was glad to leave that land of confusion. John's son George Albert had been troubled even as a boy by the numbers of different religions and had asked his father for an explanation of their origin. Some of the earliest Mormon converts had not previously joined any religious group, but had remained "seekers" awaiting restoration of the primitive church of Christ, which would offer the gifts of healing and prophecy. Many converts wrote that they had accepted the admonition to read *The Book of Mormon* prayerfully, asking the Lord to manifest to them whether or not it was true, and this was what led them into the Mormon Church.

Jared Carter, from Chenango, Broome County, New York, was traveling on business when he heard of *The Book of Mormon* from a man who opposed it so violently that Jared became fascinated. He got a copy, read it prayerfully and was so moved that he could not keep his mind on his business. He was baptized soon afterward, in February 1831, by Hyrum Smith and that summer he too became a missionary. Among those he met on his mission was Zerah Pulsipher, who stated that if the true church existed on earth he had not yet found it. Zerah read *The Book of Mormon* twice, heard Jared's testimony about the plates and the founding of the church and became convinced.[4]

Parley P. Pratt, who was later to become an apostle of the church, read *The Book of Mormon* with intense excitement, forgetting to eat and sleep, and declared, "As I read, the spirit of the Lord was upon me, and I knew and comprehended that the book was true, as plainly and manifestly as a man comprehends and knows that he exists."[5]

Newel Knight's studies of the Bible had convinced him that a great falling away from the true church had occurred. He read *The Book of Mormon* avidly, and listened to the young prophet, whom he felt spoke plainly and honestly. Newel became convinced that *The Book of Mormon* was a completion of the word of God, a restoration and a fulfillment of the gospel.[6]

Anson Call heard Mormon elders in Ohio in 1833, and though he disliked what they said, he found himself unable to dispute it. He decided that before he met them again, his knowledge of the Bible and *The Book of Mormon* would equal theirs. He spent six months in prayer and study, and became convinced that what the young elders had told him was true.[7]

Many early Mormons were from rural areas, but when missionaries began to labor in the large cities, they made converts there as well. Whether urban or rural, however, most converts had a history of social mobility, economic insecurity, dissatisfaction with contending sects and hope for a millennium in which discord and hardship would be eliminated and status in the Lord's kingdom would depend upon spiritual rather than material values.

Although Alexander Campbell was antagonistic toward *The Book of Mormon,* he came close to understanding the reason for its impact, whereas others who reviewed it usually failed to grasp its religious and sociological significance. Critics most frequently busied themselves with speculations about its origin or with searching for flaws. *The Unitarian* of January 1, 1834, said, "Coming, as Lehi and his family are represented to have done, from Jerusalem, there would be some traces of Jewish manners and customs among the people. But . . . we see no account of sacrifices and of national festivals . . . The exhortations are strongly tinctured with the doctrines of modern Orthodoxy."

In a rather lengthy review of some ten pages, the author made much of grammatical errors and of the number of paragraphs beginning with "and it came to pass," and added that if *The Book of Mormon* were read critically, it would be seen that unlike the Bible, the geographical references in it could not be identified and the customs and controversies of the people were presented as nearly the same before and after the appearance of the Savior. He did, however, make a limited attempt to understand the spread of the Mormon faith, and allowed that there was "some degree of plausibility, both in the course pursued by the preachers, and in the contents of the book itself." He expounded his belief, with examples, that the book was "adapted to the known prejudices of a portion of the community."[8]

Somewhat later, February 13, 1841, a generally sympathetic article with a fair grasp of Mormon uniqueness appeared "From the New Yorker" on page one of the *Iowa Territorial Gazette and Advertizer*. Taking a distinctly opposite view from that of *The Unitarian*, the article said that the work:

> is remarkly [*sic*] free from any allusions that might betray a knowledge of the present practical or social state of the world . . . It is difficult to imagine a more difficult literary task than to write what may be termed a continuation of the Scriptures, that should . . . fill up many chasms that now seem to exist, and thus receive and lend confirmation . . . To establish a plausibly-sustained theory, that the aborigines of our Continent are descendents of Israel without committing himself by any assertion or description that could be contradicted, shows a degree of talent and research that in an uneducated youth of twenty is almost a miracle of itself.

The writer, while professing astonishment and calling the work "almost a miracle," apparently believed that Joseph Smith was its author. Others who could neither accept Joseph as author nor his statement that the work was a translation from ancient records unearthed under the direction of the angel Moroni tried to advance various theories about the origin of the book.

Some three years after the book was published, Philastus Hurlbut (variously spelled Hurlburt, Hulbert, Hurlbert, etc.), a disgruntled Mormon convert excommunicated from the church in June 1833 for "unChristian conduct with women," heard that one John Spaulding said that *The Book of Mormon* resembled a novel written in 1812 by his brother Solomon, a minister and amateur archaeologist who had died in 1816. Intrigued, Hurlbut went to interview John, his wife and their neighbors, who maintained that, although it had been twenty years since they had heard Solomon read his novel aloud, they remembered it well enough to say that it had remarkable similarities to *The Book of Mormon*. Hurlbut got permission from Solomon's widow to examine her husband's papers, and found the manuscript, but to his disappointment, it was similar to *The Book of Mormon* in only superficial ways. Calling itself a translation of ancient scrolls found in a cave, it was a slim adventure story about pre-Christian immigrants to America. In florid eighteenth-century prose, full of romantic clichés, it was entirely different in style from *The Book of Mormon*, and it had no religious import. It could not be set forth as the original.

Despite the widow Spaulding's statement that her husband had written only one such story, Hurlbut insisted that there must be another manuscript. He tried to prove that Sidney Rigdon, who had known the publisher to whom Spaulding offered his novel, had somehow used the manuscript as a basis for *The Book of Mormon*. The allegation was accepted by a surprising number of people in the nineteenth century including Alexander Campbell, who had believed that Joseph Smith was the author of the book until Sidney Rigdon, his co-founder of the Campbellite Church, joined the Mormons.

Scholars have since concluded that the similarities between the books were mere coincidence and that the accusation of plagiarism was motivated by animosity. Rigdon himself, an intelligent and accomplished man who never showed an inclination to relinquish his due, vigorously maintained throughout his life that he had no part in the production of *The Book of Mormon* and never saw it until it was published.

Other theories were also put forth. In 1904, one writer, Charles W. Brown, quoted a statement that those who knew the family best put no credence in the Spaulding theory, but believed that *The Book of Mormon* was "a production of" the Smiths, aided by Oliver Cowdery.[9] That Cowdery had a part in it is not tenable, however, because he had met the prophet after the work was well advanced. Only part of the manuscript is in his hand, as Joseph's scribe. Cowdery himself said that although he tried, he was unable to produce a single sentence under inspiration.

In the early twentieth century, one scholar offered internal evidence that the book must have been written by a man of Joseph's generation in that region of New York soon after 1826, which seemed to him sufficient proof that the book was by Joseph Smith.[10]

A more recent historian has suggested that Joseph took his theme from Ethan Smith, a Congregationalist minister from Vermont (no relation to the prophet's family so far as is known) whose *View of the Hebrews,* first published in 1823, proposed that the American Indians were descendants of the lost tribes of Israel.[11] In 1842 Joseph Smith mentioned Ethan Smith's work in *Times and Seasons* in the context of a corroboration of *The Book of Mormon,* but there is no evidence that he had an earlier acquaintance with it. It may be, however, that Joseph was previously aware of the idea of the Jewish origin of the Indians, since there was a great deal of popular speculation on that subject well before his time.[12]

Joseph himself described *The Book of Mormon* as "coming forth out of the treasure of the heart . . . bringing forth out of the heart, things new and old."[13] His attitude toward it was manifested in what he told the Twelve Apostles, that "The Book of Mormon was the most correct of any book on earth, and the keystone of our religion, and a man would get nearer to God by abiding by its precepts than by any other book."[14]

The Mormons were not disturbed by controversies over the origins of *The Book of Mormon.* An article in the *Gospel Reflector* of 1841 said, "we are not astonished that the Book of Mormon has become a stumbling-block to so many; and the fact that the learned, the wise of this world, and the professors of religion, are our vilest persecutors, and most inveterate enemies, does not discourage us, when we consider that Christ himself was a rock of offence to the Jews."[15]

To the converts, Joseph's church was not only based upon *The Book of Mormon* but the book was its reason for having come into existence. One early writer, a non-Mormon, said that at church meetings held in the home of Joseph Smith, Sr., there was no preaching, singing or praying, but the time was spent in reading *The Book of Mormon*.[16] That *The Book of Mormon* was read at meetings is likely true, but it may be doubted that there was no praying, and sermons and hymns were soon well established in the church services. However, Joseph's followers were identified with the book from the outset, and it was not long before they became known by the nickname of "Mormons," or "Mormonites."

The Book of Mormon confirmed what converts already believed, that American society with its religious conflicts and materialistic orientation was doomed unless it could be reformed. To the gratification of those who were so weary of controversy, the teachings of the new church, as based upon the Bible, *The Book of Mormon* and the revelations of the prophet Joseph Smith, provided authoritative, clear and certain outline for salvation.

THE EARLY CHURCH

The Church of Christ, as it was first called, had a quiet beginning.[1] On April 6, 1830, eleven days after *The Book of Mormon* was put on sale in the Palmyra bookstore, Joseph held a meeting at the home of Peter Whitmer, Sr., with some friends and sympathetic neighbors and the few who had already been baptized. A service of prayer, confirmations, blessings and the Lord's Supper was held, and the business of organizing under the law was conducted, with Joseph, Hyrum and Samuel Smith, David and Peter Whitmer, Jr., and Oliver Cowdery sustained as elders.

Several more members were baptized in Seneca Lake, among whom were Martin Harris and Orrin Porter Rockwell, Joseph's devoted young friend and neighbor, who was to become his personal bodyguard and right-hand man. Baptized also, to the prophet's great joy, were his parents. To witness the baptism of his father, who had for so long resisted joining any organized church, and to realize that he had reconciled his parents' religious conflict was no doubt a supreme experience for Joseph. His mother wrote that Joseph stood on the shore to watch his father's baptism, and when he came out of the water, Joseph took his hand and exclaimed with tears of happiness, "Oh, my God! Have I lived to see my own father baptized into the true church of Jesus Christ!"[2]

Of that occasion, Joseph Knight, Sr., wrote:

> There was one thing I will mention that evening that old Brother Smith and Martin Harris was Baptised. Joseph was fild with the Spir-

rit to a grate Degree to see his Father and Mr Harris that he had Bin with so much he Bast out with greaf and Joy and seamed as tho the world Could not hold him. He went out into the Lot and appeard to want to git out of site of every Body and would sob and Crie and seamed to Be so full that he could not live. Oliver and I went after him and Came to him and after a while he came in. But he was the most wrot upon that I ever saw any man. But his joy seemed to Be full. I think he saw the grate work he had Begun and was Desirus to Carry it out.[3]

Although participating in the service that day with apparent joy, David Whitmer later reported misgivings about one aspect of the new church organization. Shortly before the meeting, some members of the group had expressed the belief that the church should have a leader, and had begged Joseph to inquire about it of the Lord. Just after the meeting, Joseph had a revelation that informed the members that a record should be kept in which he should be called:

a seer, a translator, a prophet, an apostle of Jesus Christ, an elder of the church through the will of God the Father, and the grace of your Lord Jesus Christ, Being inspired of the Holy Ghost to lay the foundation thereof, and to built it up unto the most holy faith . . . Wherefore, meaning the church, thou shalt give heed unto all his words and commandments which he shall give unto you as he receiveth them, walking in all holiness before me; For his word ye shall receive, as if from mine own mouth, in patience and faith.[4]

David later wrote that the members began to receive Joseph's words as if from God's own mouth, and to look upon him as their lawgiver. In this he believed they made a mistake.[5] The elders were young, David would recall, and so was their prophet, and they all loved him. Apparently they saw no risk in the assumption of so much power by one man. There was no hint of dissension at the time and no one foresaw objections from the outside. Joseph himself believed it right for him as prophet to control the church, and although he would be challenged many times in the course of his career, he would never relinquish his dominant position. Rather he extended his influence and made his role more powerful with every passing year until his death.

To Joseph, the charge later made against him of acting in matters that should be of no concern to a prophet of God made no sense. Religion was to him a matter of total commitment and every aspect of life was a part of the Lord's plan. He felt himself to be chosen of the Lord to reveal the true gospel in the latter days and he was keenly aware of his responsibility. He was anxious for salvation not only for himself, his family and his followers, but for his country, and for the world. God's plan was meant for all. For those who rejected it, there was nothing ahead but disaster. Time was short; the millennium was fast approaching. Zion, the refuge for the righteous, must be built. The message must be carried as fast as possible to everyone who would listen.

On Sunday, April 11, Oliver Cowdery gave the first public discourse of the church at the home of the ever-hospitable Whitmers. Joseph wrote that a large crowd attended, and five more of the Whitmer family were baptized, along with Hiram Page, Katharine Whitmer's husband. A few days later, Oliver baptized another seven.

Not long after the organization of the church, Joseph's father and brothers were ordained and sent out on missions to preach. Samuel, twenty-two, and other missionaries were sent off without purse or scrip to spread the word wherever an audience could be gathered. In that first year after the church was organized, sixteen missionaries were sent out, and fifty-eight were sent the following year.[6]

In August 1830, Joseph Sr. with his son Don Carlos, who was then only fourteen, went on a mission to northern New York State and Canada. On the way, Joseph visited his parents, brothers and sisters, in St. Lawrence County, but had a mixed reception and was the cause of family disruption. According to the account of his brother John, their elder brother Jesse told Joseph that if he said one word about *The Book of Mormon* he would be thrown out of his house. Jesse offered to enforce his threat with his broadax, if necessary.

Jesse had already heard about *The Book of Mormon* and had formed a violently negative opinion. On June 17, 1829, he had written to Hyrum, addressing his letter "once as I thot my promising Nephew," and went on to say he considered "the whole pretended discovery, not a very deep, but a very clear and foolish deception, or a great wickedness, unpardonable, unless you are shielded by your ignorance."[7]

At the home of Joseph's brother Silas, where his parents were staying, Joseph received a more cordial reception. Asael showed a great interest in Joseph Sr.'s message, but Jesse burst in and told Joseph to "shut up his head," saying he would not have his father's mind corrupted. Joseph tried to reason with Jesse mildly, but to no effect. Silas finally asked Jesse to leave.

Joseph talked to the others in the family for more than a week, however, and eventually they were all converted, according to Joseph Jr., except Jesse and one sister, Susanna. Asael died before the end of the year, and although he had not been baptized into the church he expressed a firm belief in Joseph's teachings.

Through the fervent activities of the missionaries, it was not long before three little branches of the church were founded, in Fayette, Manchester and Colesville.

Those of his neighbors whom Joseph and his missionaries failed to convert did not remain indifferent. Activities of the Mormons became a matter for the local gossips, at tea parties, in the taverns and even among the clergy. If at first people were entertained by speculations about the origin of *The Book of Mormon,* they soon became resentful of the missionaries' teachings that other churches were the tools of Satan, that destruction of the unregenerate was imminent and that the Church of Christ was the only way to salvation. At first amused and scornful, they later became resentful as they watched the spread of Joseph's influence. The rougher elements began to display open hostility. William Smith later wrote that mobs would gather at meetings of the Saints and pelt them with sticks and mud.

Opposition to Joseph's teachings was raised by leaders in some of the more powerful churches.

Not long after the Church of Christ was organized, Joseph went to Colesville to visit his old friends, the Knight family. While there, he held several meetings in the neighborhood, which drew much attention. Among those who attended regularly was Joseph Knight's son, Newel, and his wife Sally.

About Joseph, Newel wrote:

> It was evident to me that great things were about to be accomplished through him—that the Lord was about to use him as an instrument in His hands to bring to pass the great and mighty work of the last days. This chosen instrument told us of God's manifestations to him, of the discovery and the receiving of the plates from which the Book of Mormon was translated, of his persecutions for the gospel's sake . . . So honest and plain were all his statements that there was no room for any misgivings with me on the subject.[8]

At Joseph's meetings in Colesville, however, Newel could not bring himself to take a turn at praying in public. When Joseph urged him, Newel replied that he would rather pray by himself. Alone in the woods he suffered pangs of conscience and began to feel so bad in mind and body that he stumbled home, alarming Sally. He asked her to go for the prophet. By the time Joseph arrived, Newel was thrashing about in great distress, his face and limbs distorted. Eight or nine neighbors and relatives who had heard about the strange seizure had gathered helplessly to watch. When Newel pleaded with Joseph to cast the devil out of him, Joseph took his hand and commanded the devil to depart in the name of Jesus Christ. Newel said that he saw the devil leave his body at once and disappear.

The seizure stopped, but Newel was so weak that he had to be put to bed. He declared ecstatically that visions of heaven opened to him. Most of those present were so impressed that they joined the church. Joseph declared this the first miracle performed in the church, not by him, but by the Lord.[9]

The news quickly spread through the area.

Newel went to Fayette after Joseph returned and was baptized there by David Whitmer in May.

On June 9, 1830, the church held its first conference, attended by the total membership, which was by then twenty-seven, and a number of visitors. Newel Knight said that his heart was filled with love and glory, that he had a vision of the Lord Jesus Christ on the right hand of the majesty on high and was given to understand, to his unspeakable joy, that he would eventually be admitted to the divine presence.

Not long after the conference, Joseph, Emma, Oliver and two of the Whitmer brothers, John and David, went on another visit to Joseph Knight in Colesville, where a number of people were waiting to be baptized. Joseph appointed a meeting for the next Sunday, and on Saturday afternoon the brethren went out to build a dam across a nearby stream to form a baptismal font. During the night a mob tore down the dam, incited, Joseph said, by certain preachers in the area.

It is not known whether the Reverend John Sherer of the Presbyterian Church, the most influential church in Colesville, was among those instigators, but he had been agitating against the Mormons in another direct and very personal way. A few days before the incident of the dam, he had called at the home of Newel and Sally Knight to see Sally's young sister, Emily Coburn, who was there on a visit. The Reverend Sherer, who considered Emily one of his flock, had come to try to discourage her interest in the new church. Failing that, he told her that one of her brothers was waiting outside to take her home. Emily went out with him but discovered that her brother was not there and turned back. The Reverend Sherer took Emily by the arm to force her along, but Sally came running to her sister's rescue, and when the two women proved to be more than he could cope with, the pastor slunk away in chagrin.

Against the Reverend Sherer's advice, Emily attended the meeting with her sister that Sunday. Among the congregation were some who had helped tear down the dam, and as soon as the service ended they raised their voices against the little church. In the midst of the hubbub, the Reverend Sherer appeared. Not idle in the interval, he had managed to persuade Emily's elderly father to give him power of attorney, and with that he forced Emily to leave with him. All his efforts proved in vain, however, for soon afterward Emily Coburn was baptized and confirmed into the Church of Christ.[10]

Writing of the incident the following November to the authorities of the American Home Missionary Society, Sherer lamented the loss of Emily, and added that a number of people in Colesville professed belief in *The Book of Mormon* and about twenty had joined the church. He complained that the new sect called themselves the only Church of Christ, maintaining that all who did not accept their doctrines had only the form of Godliness, without the power.[11] In this Sherer voiced the basic complaint of the clergy against the "Mormonites" and one of the reasons that the Saints were to find difficulty with their neighbors wherever they tried to settle.

Very early that Monday morning, the members went out to repair their dam and perform their ceremonies, hoping to finish before anyone interfered. Oliver baptized thirteen, including Emma, the prophet's wife, and Joseph Knight, Sr., and his wife, Polly. But the word had spread and a mob collected with surprising rapidity and began yelling taunts. During Joseph Knight's baptism, hecklers stood in a row along the banks, guffawing and demanding to know if the elders had been washing sheep.

Not content with that, some fifty men followed Joseph and his friends to Joseph Knight's house and surrounded it, shouting threats. Joseph and the others left for Newel's house, but the men followed and continued their abuse.

That evening, when the newly baptized members met with Joseph for their confirmation, a constable appeared to arrest Joseph and take him for trial at South Bainbridge on a charge of being disorderly in "preaching" *The Book of Mormon.* The constable told Joseph that the men who had obtained the warrant were lying in wait for him, but the officer was determined that they should not get him, because the prophet was not the kind of man he had been led to expect. The two men had not gone far when their wagon was surrounded by a jeering crowd, who seemed to expect their victim to be surrendered. Instead, the constable whipped up his horses, the men were taken by surprise and Joseph and the officer escaped.

At South Bainbridge, the constable found lodgings for Joseph in the upper room of a tavern and gave him the bed, while he himself slept with his feet against the door and a loaded musket at his side.

Joseph Knight, Sr., engaged two men for Joseph's defense, James Davidson and John Reid, respected and intelligent farmers who knew the law although they were not lawyers. Reid, who was to remain Joseph Smith's lifelong friend without accepting his religion, spoke years later in a public address in Nauvoo (May 17, 1844) about the persecutions that had followed the young prophet "when his cheeks blossomed with the beauty of youth and his eyes sparked with innocence."[12]

Because of his efforts on the prophet's behalf, Joseph Knight, a sober and honest man who had in the past been respected and loved by his neighbors, was raided by a mob that night and a great deal of mischief was done to his property. Some of his wagons were overturned, others were sunk in the stream and rails were piled up against the doors of his house.

Joseph's trial began about ten in the morning before Justice of the Peace Joseph Chamberlain, with two determined prosecutors named Seymour and Burch and a large assembly of excited spectators, many of whom expressed aloud their views that Joseph was guilty of everything gossip maintained.

Among the many witnesses called against the prophet was his old friend

Josiah Stowell, whom the prosecution tried to coerce into corroborating the popular story that Joseph said an angel had authorized him to appropriate one of Josiah's horses. Josiah stoutly denied the story, declaring that Joseph had bought the horse as would any other man. When asked if he had been paid, Josiah said, "That is not your business."

Pressed, Josiah said he had Joseph's note, which was as good as pay as far as he was concerned. He declared that he knew Joseph to be an honest man and if asked would give him another horse that moment on the same terms.

Stowell's two daughters, with whom Joseph had kept company before his marriage, were called in the hope they would smirch Joseph's character, but to the disappointment of the prosecution as well as the audience, they had only the best to say of what his conduct had been in public and in private.

The trial was prolonged until midnight, as long as possible, Joseph wrote, to allow time for another warrant to be brought from the neighboring county. Meanwhile, the prisoner was given nothing to eat or drink the whole day.

When it was recognized as inevitable, Joseph was acquitted, but he had no sooner stepped out of court than he was arrested again. The new constable at once began a course of insults and abuse. Although he knew Joseph was hungry and exhausted, he hustled him away and gave him a hard ride fifteen miles to Broome County. He took Joseph to a tavern where rough men spat upon him and mocked him, crying, "Prophesy, prophesy!" This Joseph bore meekly, later writing that the men behaved like those who had crucified Christ.

When Joseph asked for food, he was given crusts and water. When he went to bed at last, the constable made Joseph lie next to the wall, while he lay beside him with one arm holding him fast to prevent his escape.

Joseph's second trial was held at Colesville. Reid and Davidson, who had followed from South Bainbridge, defended him again. Three justices presided, men of obvious bias, and the same prosecutors, Seymour and Burch, appeared, calling some of the same witnesses, who swore such palpable lies and contradicted themselves so frequently that the court was obliged to reject most of the testimony.

Newel Knight was called and sworn, and questioned by Seymour, a zealous Presbyterian.

"Did the prisoner, Joseph Smith, Jr., cast the devil out of you?"

"No, sir."

"Why, haven't you had the devil cast out of you?"

Newel replied that he had, and admitted upon close examination that Joseph had had some hand in it, but he was firm that it was the work of the Lord. Newel was asked to tell the court what the devil looked like. When told he need not reply to that, Newel said he would if the lawyer himself would answer one question. This agreed, Newel asked, "Do you, Mr. Seymour, understand the things of the spirit?"

"No, I do not pretend to such big things."

"Well, then, it would be of no use to tell you what the devil looked like, for it was a spiritual sight . . . and of course you would not understand it . . ."

Laughter filled the courtroom and the lawyer dropped his head, abashed.

The prosecution, John Reid said, sent out for more witnesses, as many drunks and derelicts as could be found, who repeated malicious local stories until two o'clock in the morning, after which there were two more hours of argument in court.

Seymour's long and vitriolic summation revived the old gossip, including stories about Joseph as a money-digger, but Joseph's defense countered the points against him so ably that it became obvious the purpose of the trial was to persecute rather than to serve justice. Reid said that despite all efforts against Joseph, he "came out like the three children from the fiery furnace, without the smell of fire upon his garments." The three justices could render no decision except acquittal, but they harangued Joseph before the court to please the prosecution and the audience.[13]

The purpose of causing Joseph such hardship was candidly admitted by A. W. Benton, a young Presbyterian of South Bainbridge who obtained the first warrant for Joseph's arrest. In a letter to the *Evangelical Magazine and Gospel Advocate,* Benton wrote that Joseph was brought to trial "in order to check the progress of the delusion, and open the eyes and understanding of those who blindly followed him." Benton described the South Bainbridge trial but said nothing about his own part in it. His interpretation of what the trial revealed was that "the Book of Mormon was brought to light by the same magic power by which he pretended to . . . discover hidden treasure."[14] That Joseph's accusers had little concern for justice is demonstrated by the fact that Cyrus McMaster, another member of the Presbyterian Church who helped to instigate the trial, told Joseph that he "considered him guilty without judge or jury."[15]

Reid felt that Joseph's subsequent escape from some three hundred angry citizens was a work of the Lord. The arresting constable had a change of heart, apologized to Joseph and led him safely out a private way to avoid a tar and feather party.

To escape from the mob, Joseph traveled until daybreak without stopping for food, though he had eaten nothing but crusts for two days. He rode to the house of his sister-in-law where Emma was waiting for him, and they went on together to Harmony.

Joseph claimed that he returned home in "good spirits." Yet the experience left him bewildered. He and his friends felt the irony of being persecuted for their faith in a country in which the Constitution guarantees to every man the right to worship God according to his own conscience. It was the first of many disappointments Joseph was to suffer in the failure, as he saw it, of the law to protect his constitutional rights.

It never occurred to Joseph and his followers that their teachings had given gross offense. How could the word of God be offensive? They had the truth and they merely wanted to share it. Any opposition must be inspired by the devil to frustrate the work of the Lord.

During this period, Emma had seen her hopes for happiness dwindle. In the three years of her married life, she had been shuttled from one house to another, frequently left alone, displaced in her young husband's affections by his overwhelming involvement with his work, his church and his youthful disciples. She had lost her first child and had so far been deprived of every expectation for a stable home, children and a husband who would steadily provide for her. She had suffered humiliation, poverty and strife within her own family on Joseph's account. No doubt the harassment her husband had suffered lately made her misery acute and it would have been understandable if she had begun to question the value of what he was doing.

In July 1830, Joseph received a revelation for her, which recognized her unhappiness but commanded her to sustain the work. "Murmur not because of the things which thou has not seen, for they are withheld from thee and from the world, which is wisdom in me . . ." Her calling, Emma was told, was to provide "comfort unto my servant, Joseph . . . in his afflictions, with consoling words, in the spirit of meekness." She was also to continue as Joseph's scribe, releasing Oliver Cowdery to be sent "whithersoever I will." She was told her sins were forgiven, pronounced "an elect lady" and promised an opportunity to "expound scriptures, and to exhort the church." She was also appointed to make a selection of hymns for use in meetings.[16] She need not worry, the revelation said, for her husband would "support thee from the church."

It seems that Emma was gratified, for she accepted confirmation soon afterward. The ordinance was performed in her home at Harmony, in the presence of Joseph, Newel and Sally Knight who had come to visit, and John Whitmer, who was at that time living with the Smiths and helping Joseph arrange and copy his revelations.

As Newel told it, Joseph went out to get some wine for the sacrament but on the way he was met by a heavenly messenger and given a commandment that wine and strong drink were not to be bought from their enemies. The Saints were to use only wine newly made by themselves.

The five then prepared their own wine and took the sacrament, and the two women were confirmed. Newel wrote that they spent the evening in a glorious manner, "the spirit of the Lord poured out upon us."[17]

It was probably because of Emma's anxiety about their security that Joseph bought thirteen acres in Harmony that month for $200, apparently with the intention of farming again. Lucy says, however, that almost at once Joseph received a revelation to move to Waterloo. He sent for Newel Knight to come with his wagon and team, locked up his house with the furniture in it, and he and Emma went to Fayette to accept once more the hospitality of the Whitmer family before they moved to Waterloo. Joseph and Emma had left Harmony and her father's family circle forever.

The reasons for this final break remain uncertain. There was of course Isaac's disapproval of Joseph, which Isaac afterward claimed had existed from the outset, although during the interval when Joseph and Emma lived on Isaac's land, Joseph and his father-in-law seem to have been reconciled. Whatever occurred to reopen the old antagonism is not known, although Joseph says in his history that a certain Methodist minister told Isaac and his family some falsehoods about Joseph of "the most shameful nature."[18] What these accusations were has never been established. Isaac was apparently convinced by them and so furious that he would no longer countenance Joseph's teachings or even defend his reputation among the neighbors.

Besides the difficulties with his father-in-law, Joseph had encountered mockery among the villagers in Harmony, though nothing to the extent of the harassment at South Bainbridge and Colesville. According to one account, a certain lay preacher named Nathaniel G. Lewis asked Joseph if the seer stone could be used by anyone to translate. When Joseph assured him that it could, Lewis asked to borrow it. Joseph was greatly annoyed.

No doubt Joseph wanted above all to be in a community where his religious views were accepted and where he was respected. He wanted the same for his loved ones, it seems, since at this time Lucy says Joseph had a revelation that his brother Hyrum and his father were in danger. Hyrum was directed to move at once with his family to Colesville, while Joseph Sr. was to go ahead of his wife and family and prepare a place for them in Waterloo.

If the young prophet thought he could avoid adversity by moving, he was mistaken. In September, troubles arose for them all, and for Joseph a problem which he hardly expected, in the rebellion of some of his most faithful followers.

CONVERSION
OF SIDNEY RIGDON

The troubles that awaited Joseph in Fayette were foreshadowed by a letter he had received from Oliver Cowdery not long before he moved to Waterloo. To Joseph's intense indignation, Oliver had written that he had discovered an error in the commandment Joseph had given which said that those who witnessed before the church that they had repented and had manifested by their works that they had received the spirit of Christ "unto the remission of their sins" should be received by baptism into the church. To this Oliver apparently protested that Joseph had assumed the capacity to forgive sins. Oliver had written to the prophet, "I command you in the name of God to erase those words, that no priestcraft be among us!"[1]

Joseph replied at once asking upon what authority Oliver had ordered him to alter a revelation from Almighty God.

When Joseph went to see Oliver at the Whitmer farm, he found that the Whitmer family had accepted Oliver's opinion. After great perseverance, Joseph convinced Christian Whitmer that his revelation was consistent with Scripture, and with Christian's help, managed at last to persuade the Whitmers and Oliver to that view.

Other problems had also arisen among the members at Fayette. When Joseph had abandoned the seer stone after finishing his translation and had announced that henceforth the elders should rely upon the Holy Ghost, some of the brethren, notably David Whitmer, had protested. In David's belief, Joseph was mistaken about some of his subsequent revelations when he thought them to be from the Lord.[2] Most of Joseph's other followers did not object to his giving up the seer stone.

Arriving in Fayette with Emma at the end of August, Joseph heard news that was even more shocking. Hiram Page had been giving revelations to the brethren about the government of the church and the building up of Zion, which he claimed to be receiving through a stone of his own. Hiram's revelations had already accumulated to a sizable collection of papers, and some of the Saints were giving them serious consideration.

When Newel Knight came to Fayette in September for the second church conference, he found Joseph in great perplexity and distress over the situation. Newel said they knelt together and spent most of the night in prayer for guidance.

A few days later, just before conference, Joseph had a revelation for Oliver saying that no one was to receive commandments and revelations in the church except Joseph Smith.

> and thou shalt be obedient . . . And thou shalt not command him who is at thy head, and at the head of the church; For I have given him the keys of the mysteries, and the revelations which are sealed, until I shall appoint unto them another in his stead.[3]

Oliver was told that after the conference he was to go forth and preach to the Lamanites, *The Book of Mormon* name for the Indians, but in the meantime he must help to settle the difficulties in the church by telling Hiram Page that Satan had deceived him and that what he had written with the aid of his stone was not from the Lord.

Joseph had another revelation before the conference that month saying that the Saints were to be "gathered in unto one place upon the face of this land . . . For I will reveal myself from heaven with power and great glory."[4] The millennium was coming soon, when the wicked would be destroyed. An earlier revelation had said that it was not yet revealed where Zion was to be built, but it would be on the borders by the Lamanites.[5]

The commandment to gather immediately was to have profound social, economic and political consequences for the little church. The urgent necessity for gathering was perhaps reinforced in Joseph's mind by his realization that as soon as the Saints were out of his sight and influence, they began to lose their community of spirit. Already David Whitmer and Oliver Cowdery had shown they were not content under Joseph's leadership and neither were some others who had once belonged to the anti-mission movement, which opposed a hired and authoritarian ministry.

By the time the conference opened on September 26, 1830, the church had grown to sixty-two members, a sizable community that could become difficult for the young prophet to manage. The membership at once revealed its discontents, and the conference became a stormy affair. Oliver rose to protest against Joseph's claim to receive commandments for the whole church. Joseph countered by denouncing Hiram Page's revelation, which he said contradicted the New Testament and the latest word of God received by him, their prophet.

Hiram and his adherents were adamant, however, and the danger of a schism in the church became apparent. No matter the cost, Joseph felt that the church must hold together. Deciding to risk all, he demanded a vote of confidence from the congregation.

Put to that test, the members, including Hiram Page himself, renounced Hiram's stone and revelations, and sustained Joseph as their prophet.

According to Newel Knight, Joseph's behavior at that conference was "wonderful to witness . . . for truly God gave unto him great wisdom and power, and . . . none who saw him administer righteousness under such trying circumstance could doubt that the Lord was with him." Apparently the congregation came to that conclusion also, because for the remainder of the three-day session harmony prevailed. Members were confirmed, men were ordained to the priesthood and church business was smoothly transacted. Newel wrote that before that memorable conference closed, three other revelations (mostly calling brethren to preach the gospel) were received from God by their prophet "and we were made to rejoice exceedingly . . ."[6]

Soon after the conference, Hyrum Smith and his wife and family left their home and went to Colesville, in obedience to the revelation Joseph had given them, as previously mentioned. There they moved in with Newel and Sally Knight. Hyrum spent most of his time preaching in the villages nearby and made several converts, notably Emer, a brother of Martin Harris's, who proved to be an able member of the church. Joseph Sr., however, did not have a chance to move at once, as Joseph's revelation had directed.

As Lucy tells it, the morning after Hyrum and his family left, a Quaker called at the Smith home and demanded payment from Joseph Sr. for a note of fourteen dollars, which he had bought from Joseph's creditor. Joseph Sr. offered him all he had, which was six dollars, with a promise for the remainder, and Lucy was willing to give him her gold beads, but the man said that unless Joseph paid the whole debt at once he would go to jail. He did, however, offer an alternative: If Joseph would renounce and burn his copies of *The Book of Mormon,* the debt would be forgiven. This Joseph Sr. refused, and he was taken into custody by a constable who was standing by.

Lucy was left alone except for her youngest daughter, age nine. That night a band of rowdies appeared asking for Hyrum. Told he had left town, they began to appropriate Lucy's store of corn on pretext that it was for a debt, and threatened to plunder and wreck the house. At that moment, however, William, a tall and powerful youth of nineteen, came home unexpectedly. He charged among the invaders brandishing a great handspike and shouting "I'll be the death of every one of you!" He sent them flying out of the house.

Joseph Sr. was kept in a cell four days until Samuel returned home and got him released to the prison yard. There he worked in the cooper's shop while he served a sentence of thirty days. No matter his circumstances, the prophet's father was mindful of his convictions, preached every Sunday during his confinement and converted two men, whom he baptized after his release.

Joseph wrote that during the conference that September some of the brethren expressed a great desire to carry the gospel to the Lamanites in the west, "knowing that the purposes of God were great respecting that people, and hoping that the time had come when the promises of the Almighty [in *The Book of Mormon*] in regard to them were about to be accomplished . . ."[7]

The western migrations of the Indians during this period were of great interest to the Mormons. White settlers who had been clamoring for more and more Indian lands in the eastern and southern areas of the country found a ready sympathy in President Andrew Jackson during his terms in office, 1829–37. Legislation was passed to move the Indians off their lands to a supposedly permanent home west of the Mississippi. Between 1829 and 1837 some ninety-four treaties for that purpose were negotiated by the federal government with various Indian tribes, despite debates in Congress instigated by a minority who rightly foresaw enormous injustice to the Indians and the death of thousands from starvation and disease as they were forced out of their homes by the army and marched to the wilderness. To the Mormons and others who considered the Indians to be descendants of the tribes of Israel, the migrations were a manifestation of the gathering of the Israelites, which was to precede the millennium. Soon after the conference of September 1830, Joseph received a revelation that Parley P. Pratt, Ziba Peterson and Peter Whitmer, Jr., were to accompany Oliver Cowdery on his mission to the Indians. Feeling a need to take the message of *The Book of Mormon* to Indians without delay, the four missionaries began to prepare at once for their difficult assignment. On that mission, one of the missionaries, Parley Parker Pratt, was to convert a new member who would be of great importance to the church.

Parley, who was only twenty-three, had been baptized just a month before by Oliver Cowdery and at once ordained an elder. Born April 12, 1807, in Burlington, New York, a descendant of early settlers in Connecticut, Parley was a burly young man close to six feet tall, with deep eyes and a strong, set jaw. He had known hard work on a farm and few opportunities for an education, but he had shown a religious nature from early youth and had joined the Baptist Church. In 1827 he had married Thankful Halsey, a widow ten years his senior, and they had moved to the wilderness west of Cleveland, Ohio. About eighteen months later, when the

Campbellite preacher Sidney Rigdon came to that area, Parley was converted by him to the Campbellite faith. He sold his farm and set out with his wife to visit his relatives in New York before embarking on a mission. Along the way, Parley heard about *The Book of Mormon.* Sending Thankful ahead to her parents in Canaan, he went to Palmyra to investigate and decided that he had found the true religion. He went on to the home of his relatives to preach, but the only convert he made there was his nineteen-year-old brother, Orson. A slight youth with a sensitive face and large, gentle eyes, Orson was later to become one of the leading intellectuals in the church.

Parley and Orson went to Fayette for the conference of the church that September and there met Joseph Smith, whom they both loved on sight. Parley had eagerly accepted his assignment to preach the gospel to the Indians.

The four missionaries, all in their twenties, were going to need all of their youthful vigor and enthusiasm. They set off in rough clothes made for them by Emma and some of the sisters, carrying their poor equipment on pack mules, but they had high hopes and a sense of urgency. The plan was that they would precede the whole church west, where the gathering was soon to occur in Zion, the exact location of which was as yet undetermined.

The Cattaraugus Indians at Buffalo, where they made their first stop, received them courteously. When the missionaries discovered that some of the tribe could read English, they gave them two copies of *The Book of Mormon* and pushed on.

The missionaries continued westward, preaching in villages along the way to white men and Indians alike, wherever they could get a hearing.

Their most important stop proved to be near Parley's former home in Ohio, and their most important convert a white man, Parley's former colleague, Sidney Rigdon.

Sidney was at that time a rather portly and handsome man of thirty-seven, taller than the average, with the assurance that comes from years of leadership. Born in Pennsylvania, February 19, 1793, the youngest of four children, he had been kept at work on the farm in spite of his wish to go to school. Sidney borrowed books which he read until late at night by the light of hickory bark thrown on the fire, and so became a thorough Bible scholar and proficient in history and English grammar. At twenty-six, he left to study theology under a Baptist minister, taking a license to preach, although he had reservations about some Baptist doctrines, in particular the fate of unbaptized infants. He traveled about the country as a preacher and earned a reputation for eloquence.

In 1820 he married Phebe Brooks and in 1824 he left the ministry to work for two years as a journeyman tanner for his wife's brother. During this period he met Alexander Campbell and Walter Scott, with whom he often held discussions about religious reformation, and with them attracted a following which became the sect called Disciples, or Campbellites. In 1826, Rigdon went to Bainbridge, Ohio, as a preacher, and the next year he was invited to Mentor. There and in nearby Kirtland, despite some opposition, he developed a sizable church.

Asked by his congregation what he was going to charge them, Rigdon answered that the apostles had taken nothing and neither would he. The congregation said they wanted to give him something in return for the gospel which he had given them, and undertook to build a house for him on a small farm on the edge of the village.

Among his followers, Rigdon established a little communal society like that of the early Christians, but Alexander Campbell objected. When he found that his ideas could not be reconciled with theirs, Rigdon broke with the Campbellites at their conference in August 1830, and was independent of that affiliation when the young Mormon missionaries arrived at his home in Mentor.

Sidney's son John wrote that the missionaries handed his father a copy of *The Book of Mormon* in the presence of Phebe and their ten-year-old daughter Athalia. John's mother and sister afterward told him that Parley said, "Brother Rigdon, here is a book which is a revelation from God," and added the history of its origin and translation. Sidney replied, "You need not argue the case with me. I have one bible which I claim to have some knowledge [of] and which I believe to be a revelation from God. But as to this book, I have some doubts, but you can leave it with me when you go away in the morning and I will read it, and when you come again I will tell you what I think about it."

To this the young missionaries agreed, but asked if they might preach in Rigdon's church that night.

Rigdon hesitated a moment but said he supposed it would do no harm. A sizable congregation assembled to hear Parley and Oliver give their message, after which Parley told Sidney that he would be pleased to hear his comments. Sidney rose and advised his congregation to consider the matter carefully, saying, "Brethren, we have listened to strange doctrines tonight but we are commanded to prove all things and to hold fast to that which is good." He invited the young missionaries to spend the night at his home.

In the morning the missionaries left a copy of *The Book of Mormon* with Sidney, and told him that they were going to Kirtland, which was about five miles away, and would return in two or three weeks.

John wrote that as soon as the missionaries had gone his father started to read the book. "He got so engaged in it that it was hard for him to quit long enough to eat his meals. He read it both day and night. At last he had read it through and pondered and thought over it."[8]

Meanwhile, the young missionaries were spreading their message in

Kirtland, at that time a busy little town not far from Cleveland, with a population of about two thousand people whose most important business was trading with trappers from nearby Lake Erie. The missionaries made their views well known in the area and attracted considerable attention.

The Ohio *Painesville Telegraph* of November and December that year carried several stories about them, reporting that Oliver Cowdery predicted the destruction of the world within a few years, that he expected to found a city of refuge, that he proclaimed that he and his associates were the only ones on earth qualified to administer in the name of Jesus and that they were going to gather and convert the Indians, who were the lost tribes of Israel. An article in December quoted Parley as saying that when the Mormons went among the tribes great miracles would be wrought, as in the day of Pentecost.

Sidney spent a fortnight studying *The Book of Mormon*. Fascinated, he discovered that the book affirmed his own beliefs in a literal gathering and an imminent millennium.

When the missionaries returned to Mentor, Sidney questioned them about the prophet. Learning that Joseph Smith was not yet twenty-five years old and had had but a meager education, Sidney was convinced that such a youth could not have written the book. John wrote that his father was fully satisfied it was a revelation from God.

The missionaries told Sidney that they were going to baptize some converts the following week in Kirtland. They invited Sidney and Phebe to witness the ceremony. The Rigdons did more; they too were baptized.

John wrote that when his parents got back to Mentor, Sidney's congregation was furious, saying that he was throwing away a promising future as a divine "to follow a fool of a boy." To this Sidney replied that he was convinced the Mormon doctrine was true and he was going to preach it, no matter the consequences. The congregation refused to allow Sidney and his family to move into the house they had built for him.[9]

Sidney and Phebe moved their family to nearby Hiram and with about twenty other converts formed a little branch of the church.

Parley Pratt and the missionaries continued west, adding to their company a new convert, Frederick G. Williams, a middle-aged physician (then forty-three) who left his farm and medical practice to accompany the young men on their arduous mission.

They spent several days with the Wyandot tribe near Sandusky, Ohio, but the tribe was too busy to give much attention, since they expected soon to have to move west.

Early in 1831, the missionaries began to cross the vast prairie. By now they were walking and carrying their own packs, the mules left behind for lack of fodder. Often they went through snow and howling winds, meeting no one from morning until night.

Without means to make a fire, the missionaries ate corn bread and raw pork, which were sometimes frozen so hard that they could only gnaw at the edges. After a journey of fifteen hundred miles mostly on foot, they reached Independence, Missouri, the western frontier of the country.

It was decided that two of the missionaries would remain in town to find work while Oliver, Parley and a third would go on to the Delaware Indians across the border. Chief Anderson, the old Sachem or Great-grandfather of the ten tribes of the Delawares, received the men cordially in his own tent and offered them a dish of beans and corn and the use of one spoon for all. However, he informed them through an interpreter that he never allowed missionaries to preach to his people. Changing his mind when told that the book the missionaries offered explained the origins of his people, the chief called a council of some forty tribal leaders to listen to a sermon by Oliver Cowdery. Afterward, the chief agreed that his people should hear more. The missionaries remained several days and distributed copies of *The Book of Mormon* to those who could read it.[10]

At first the missionaries had high hopes for their work among the Lamanites. Oliver wrote to Joseph April 8, 1831, from Missouri:

> God of hosts has not forsaken the earth but is in very word about to redeem his ancient covenant people & lead them with the fulness of the Gentiles to springs yea fountains of living waters to his holy hill of zion . . . the principl chief says he believes every word of the Book & there are many now in the Nation who believes & we understand there are many among the Shawnees who also believe & we trust that when the Lord Shall open our way we shall have glorious time for truly my brethren my heart sorrows for them for they are cast out & dispersed and know not the God in whom they should trust.

Oliver added, however, that the agent for the Indians was very strict with them "and we think some what strenuous respecting our having liberty to visit our brethren the Lamanites," but Parley was going to General Clark, Superintendent of Indian Affairs west of the Mississippi, to see what could be arranged.[11] Apparently their hopes from Clark were not realized.

Parley later said that the tribe was just becoming excited about their message when Indian agents and other missionary groups who were envious of their success had the Mormons ordered out of Indian territory as disturbers of the peace.

According to one historian, there was a regulation forbidding white men to enter Indian territories to trade or for any other purpose.

In any case, Oliver and Parley returned to Jackson County, and there labored among the white settlers.

Although they were unable to do more at that time, the Mormons did not abandon their dream of preaching to, and gathering, the Indians. William Phelps, in writing to Oliver Cowdery in 1835, made a good summary of the Mormon view that the Indians were the children of Israel and must hear the gospel:

> Our government has already gathered many of the scattered remnants of tribes, and located them west of the Missouri to be nationalized and civilized . . . I rejoice to see the great work prosper. The Indians are the people of the Lord; they are of the tribes of Israel; the blood of Joseph, with a small mixture of the royal blood of Judah, and the hour is nigh when they will come flocking into the kingdom of God, like doves to their windows.[12]

Sidney Rigdon was anxious to see the young prophet, founder of the church which he had espoused so suddenly and with such enthusiasm. In December 1830, he set out for New York with Edward Partridge, a prosperous hatter of Rigdon's age, a gentle and unassuming man who was later to reveal surprising moral strength, and whom Joseph would call "a pattern of piety and one of the Lord's great men."

According to his daughter Emily, Edward was not as ready at first to believe as was his wife, who had been baptized almost at once by Parley Pratt. Edward had told the missionaries that he thought they were imposters and Oliver Cowdery replied that he was thankful there was a God in heaven who knew the hearts of all men. Perhaps impressed by that, Edward read *The Book of Mormon* after they had gone and decided to accompany Sidney Rigdon to see the prophet in person.[13]

Joseph welcomed the two men joyfully, and baptized Edward himself, on December 11, in Seneca Lake. He had revelations for them both, telling Rigdon at length that he would do great things, and Edward that he was called to preach the gospel "with the voice of a trump."[14]

David Whitmer recognized Sidney Rigdon's talents and education, but his praise had an edge of resentment. He said that Sidney "soon worked himself deep into Brother Joseph's affections, and had more influence over him than any other man living. He was Brother Joseph's private counsellor, and his most intimate friend and brother for some time after they met. Brother Joseph rejoiced, believing that the Lord had sent to him this great and mighty man . . . to help him in the work."[15] David said that they all rejoiced in Sidney Rigdon at first, but the enthusiasm of some members was dampened when they learned that he was urging Joseph to return with him to Kirtland.

On January 2, 1831, Joseph had a revelation directing the whole church, then comprising about sixty members, to move to Ohio. The news was not well received by all. To David Whitmer, the son of a prosperous farmer, the suggestion of leaving could not have been welcome, although it was not until some years later that he expressed his belief that the principle of the gathering was hasty and unwise.[16] Joseph had to labor for several weeks to persuade his flock that they must migrate. His revelation described the land that awaited them as flowing with milk and honey, but some were not convinced and a few suggested that Joseph had invented the revelation to have his way with the people. In the end, however, most of the members were persuaded that migration was the will of the Lord.

To Emma the prospect of moving must have seemed grim. Already, in her first four years of marriage, she had been compelled to move seven times. She was in delicate health, having just recovered from an illness of four weeks, and she was pregnant. The journey to Ohio was three hundred miles, and Joseph wanted to go at once, in the middle of winter. Joseph prevailed, however, and at the end of January 1831, he and Emma, with Sidney Rigdon and Edward Partridge, set out for Kirtland in a sleigh which they obtained from Joseph Knight. Members of the church were instructed to dispose of their property as best they could, even at a sacrifice, and prepare to follow their prophet in the spring.

PART THREE

Ohio

THE CHURCH
IN TWO MAIN
SETTLEMENTS

Joseph and his party, riding in Joseph Knight's sleigh, reached Kirtland, Ohio, at the beginning of February 1831. According to James Henry Rollins, then a boy about fourteen, Joseph and Emma went to his neighbor, Sidney Gilbert, looking for a place to stay. However, none of the rooms in Gilbert's house was to Emma's liking, James said, and they went elsewhere.

They were taken into the home of Newel K. Whitney, Sidney Gilbert's partner in a general store on Main Street. Like the several other families upon whom Joseph and Emma were dependent during their early marriage, the Whitneys considered it a privilege and a blessing to have the prophet and his wife in their house. They kept Joseph and Emma for several weeks and became their devoted friends.

The Whitneys were recent converts to the church. Elizabeth Ann Whitney said that she and her husband, both former Campbellites, had prayed to know how they might obtain the Holy Ghost. They heard a voice from heaven telling them that the word of the Lord was coming. Soon afterward Parley Pratt and the other missionaries had arrived in Kirtland and converted them.

Joseph was happy to discover that the membership of the church in Kirtland had grown to about one hundred. This was nearly twice the size of his following in New York. However, he was very soon to experience the difficulties of building and directing the kind of community he wanted. In Ohio he would try through his continuing revelations to draw church

.....ne into a coherent whole, to provide his followers with an understanding of the universality of God's plan and of the concept of eternal progress, and to publish his revelations to make them accessible and comprehensible to all. He was soon to learn, however, that many of his followers, like most of humankind, were mindful of the present world, covetous, envious and incapable of tolerating much disappointment. Even though they accepted his plan as the way to perfection, they could not practice it completely. Joseph would learn the hard fact necessary to the leader of any community, however idealistic, that its most urgent problems are not moral and spiritual, but economic.

The dissension and challenge to his authority that he had already met in New York were mild compared to what he would encounter in Ohio. Joseph's patience would grow thin and he would become accustomed to making strong denunciations. He would encounter furious opposition and be subjected for the first time to extreme violence.

Although Joseph found able men to assume responsibility for the material welfare of his followers so that he would be free to enlarge his role as their prophet, he did not relinquish ultimate authority in the church. He undertook strict regulation of every aspect of his followers' lives, without regard to the possible dangers of such a course.

Joseph soon discovered that all was not to his liking in Kirtland. He found that he had competition from a sister Hubble, who was winning some of his followers with claims to be a prophetess of the Lord and was issuing commandments, laws and revelations of her own. As he had in Fayette, Joseph received a revelation for the Kirtland church which announced, "this ye shall know assuredly—that there is none other appointed unto you to receive commandments and revelations . . ."[1]

Joseph also found that "strange notions" existed among some members of the Kirtland church, and that during meetings there were exhibitions of the kind of popular revivalist phenomena, trances, fits and contortions, that he had never countenanced. He gave the Kirtland Saints an ultimatum, that God had sent him there, and the devil would have to leave, or he would.

When Parley Pratt returned from his mission to Missouri several months later, Joseph sent him and a companion on a tour of the branches of the church to root out "false spirits."

Among Joseph's constant problems was poverty, both his own and that of a great many converts. On February 4, 1831, he had a revelation for the Kirtland Saints which said that a house should be built for their prophet, in which he could live and continue his work. Isaac Morley put up a cabin for Joseph and Emma on his land.

Joseph had a full appreciation of worldly luxuries and joys, but he believed that they should be shared in a spirit of brotherly love and that none of the brethren should be deprived while others were in comfort. It was obvious, however, that sharing would not be accomplished without planning and spiritual encouragement.

On the ninth, he had a lengthy revelation establishing the Law of Consecration, an outline for a communal society that would have important consequences in the early church.[2]

Kirtland already had the small communal group known as "the family" established by Sidney Rigdon. Living in a row of log houses on Isaac Morley's farm, the members had attempted to hold all things in common, but by the time Joseph arrived, their community had begun to disintegrate. According to John Whitmer, the members were appropriating each other's personal belongings and had begun to quarrel.

In the plan presented by Joseph, land and goods belonging to the Saints would be consecrated to the Lord. Forms were to be signed deeding property to the church, relinquishing all control of it and agreeing that it could not be reclaimed even if the owner should apostatize. Sufficient property for each family's needs would be returned as a "stewardship," and all surplus would be held and administered by a bishop to further the work of the Lord.

The bishop was not only to assign stewardships according to need, determine surplus and oversee church lands, buildings, crops, cattle and goods, but was also to purchase more land for the church and its members, provide for the elderly and infirm, build churches and schools, and supervise the development of new commercial enterprises. Such a program would seem an impossible burden for one man, but the church had good fortune in the first bishop whom Joseph appointed, Edward Partridge, an honest, indefatigable, patient, much-beleaguered man who did his utmost to assure justice for all.

In April, Joseph resumed his new work, which he called a "translation" of the Scriptures, although from his description of procedure, he obviously meant a revision by inspiration.[3]

Emma and Joseph were living in the little house built for them by Isaac Morley when Emma's pregnancy came to term. Emma was still in delicate health, not having fully recovered from her illness and the arduous midwinter journey from New York. On April 30, she gave birth to twins, a boy and a girl, but to her great sorrow they lived only three hours. She had the help of the kindhearted Morley daughters, who kept house for her and nursed her, but nothing could ease her anguish over the fact that she had lost all three of the children so far born to her and Joseph. It happened that John Murdock's wife had twins on the same day as Emma but she died nine days later. Emma gladly took the babies, a girl named Julia and a boy named Joseph, to raise as her own.

Meanwhile, the Saints in New York were preparing to follow their prophet to Kirtland. Newel Knight spent most of his time that spring visiting the Saints in Colesville and helping to arrange their affairs, so that they could travel in a body. Their efforts met continual harassment by their neighbors.

Lucy led a party of eighty (by her count) to Buffalo by the Erie Canal, where they planned to meet the Colesville Saints and continue together to Kirtland. Her group had a very different leave-taking from their community, apparently, than had the Saints from Colesville. Lucy said neighbors came from all over the area to tell them goodbye and to pray for their safe voyage. One man brought a gift of seventeen dollars.

Although the Saints were faithful and courageous, they were human also, as Lucy amply reveals. She wrote that with their unanimous approval she took charge of the company for their five-day Canal boat trip and supplied the needy with food, although she was annoyed that some had spent their money on clothes and expected others to provide for them. Lucy admonished the flirtations of younger sisters with strangers on board, appeased grumbling and bickering adults, helped with sick babies and disciplined excited children. She led the Saints in prayers and started them singing hymns, to the pleasure of the captain and others on board.

The two groups of Saints met in Buffalo, intending to take passage together on a boat for Fairport, Ohio, on Lake Erie, about ten miles from Kirtland, but cold winds blew from the lake and so clogged the harbor with ice that they were delayed for nearly two weeks.

As it happened, Lucy found the boat that had belonged to her brother Jason. After Jason's death the boat had been bought by his captain, who could not honor her enough, Lucy said, when he learned her identity.

Stormy weather continued after they put out and made nearly the whole group of Saints seasick, but at last they arrived in Kirtland, with great rejoicing. Joseph's parents were taken in by the Morley family for their first two weeks.

James Henry Rollins wrote that he saw Joseph's parents at a meeting at Isaac Morley's the day after they arrived. All were exhausted and the prophet's younger brother, Don Carlos, who was then fifteen, fell asleep in his chair, but after several had spoken he rose and bore as strong a testimony as James had ever heard. He and the young James became fast friends. Of Joseph's other brothers, James said Samuel was a man of few words, but hard-working. Apparently James liked William, who often took him out on shooting expeditions along the river.

It was decided that the Saints from New York would remain together and be known as the Colesville Branch. Many were now in financial straits and dependent upon the church, having followed Joseph's commandment to sell their property at a loss if necessary, or abandon it. The Colesville Saints were settled in Thompson, a village not far from Kirtland, under the leadership of Newel Knight. Two Ohio converts, Ezra Thayre and Leman Copley, were persuaded to share their lands with the newcomers, and a contract for a thousand acres was agreed upon at half value. Bishop Par-

tridge appointed lots according to need under the new Law of Consecration, and it was with these Saints from Colesville that the law was first
fully put into effect. The Colesville Saints settled to work with a will, got
their houses in order and began to sow crops.

In June, at Kirtland, Joseph held the first general conference in Ohio,
during which, according to church documentation, the most important
event was Joseph's announcement of the ordination of several High
Priests.

The church was growing and attracting attention. By this time, Joseph
had developed into a preacher of some ability, with a naturally powerful
voice and an easy, entertaining manner. Parley Pratt said he had seen him
keep an audience laughing and weeping for hours in cold, rain or glaring
sun. Visitors to Kirtland were frequent, coming from all over the state to
see the young prophet and hear his astonishing claims. Some came to
laugh and scorn or be amazed, but others had an honest interest in his
message.

One day a Methodist preacher named Ezra Booth arrived bringing a
party that included a well-to-do farmer from Hiram named John Johnson
and his wife, whose arm was partially paralyzed from rheumatism and
could not be raised above her head. The visitors had been talking with
Joseph about various aspects of theology, including spiritual gifts, when
one said, "Here is Mrs. Johnson with a lame arm; has God given any
power to a man now on the earth to cure her?"

A few minutes later, after the conversation had turned to another subject, Joseph went up to Mrs. Johnson, took her by the hand and astonished everyone present by saying with calm assurance, "Woman, in the
name of the Lord Jesus Christ I command thee to be whole." The
witnesses were astounded when Mrs. Johnson at once raised her arm.
Home the next day, she did her washing without any pain.

The incident so amazed and convinced the group that Ezra Booth and
the whole Johnson family, including several grown sons and daughters,
joined the church.

Others were converted to the church for rather bizarre reasons. In June,
Simonds Ryder, a well-known Campbellite preacher, joined because he
read of an earthquake in Peking, China, which he claimed to have heard
predicted by a Mormon girl six weeks earlier. The newspapers at that time
were making sensational copy of the Mormons, including such incidents as
this, and Joseph was angered by their numerous false or exaggerated reports.

He was also getting unfortunate publicity beyond the local papers. That
summer of 1831, an ambitious newspaperman, James Gordon Bennett,
made a tour with Martin Van Buren, then U. S. Secretary of State, to investigate public opinion in upstate New York. There Bennett heard gossip
about the departed Mormons and used it as the basis for two articles about

the new church and its founder, which were published in a leading newspaper in the east, the *Morning Courier and New York Enquirer,* on August 31 and September 1, 1831. As one scholar has recently pointed out, his misinformed and sensational stories popularized an impression that the Saints were irreligious and ludicrous. In this Bennett was partly responsible for the scornful attitude toward the origins of the Mormons that prevailed during the nineteenth century, and he even influenced some historians in the twentieth century.[4]

Their bad publicity notwithstanding, Joseph and the Saints in Kirtland continued in their endeavors to prepare for the millennium.

Although Joseph's revelations had made further references to Zion, none had as yet disclosed its location. In May, when Parley Pratt had returned to Kirtland exhausted but fervent, having walked most of the way from Missouri, he gave vivid details about Jackson County, near the Missouri border. Oliver Cowdery, who was still in Missouri, had written that he believed many people there were earnestly seeking the truth.

The area did not at first seem attractive, however. The missionaries had been ordered out of Indian territory, and their efforts with white settlers had had little success. But the need for a chosen land was pressing. Converts were unwilling to settle down or buy land anywhere until the site for Zion was made known.

In June 1831, Joseph had a revelation directing him to go to Missouri with Sidney Rigdon, Edward Partridge and Martin Harris. Other elders, including John Murdock and Hyrum Smith, Lyman Wight and John Corrill, Isaac Morley and Ezra Booth, Parley P. Pratt and his brother Orson, were commanded to set out two by two for the same destination, taking different routes and preaching along the way.

While preparations were being made for the journey, a man who would subsequently have an important role in the church, William Wine Phelps, arrived from New York with his wife Sally and their children. Born February 17, 1792, and now approaching forty, William was a man of experience and ability, who had edited a partisan newspaper and was once a candidate for the office of lieutenant governor of New York. William told Joseph that he had come to do the will of the Lord. Joseph had a revelation for him that said he must first be baptized and ordained, and then accompany the group to Missouri and work there with Oliver Cowdery in printing books for the church.

Other events that month were not so felicitous. Newel Knight came to the prophet as an emissary from the Colesville Saints in Thompson to say that the community was in difficulty. Leman Copley, who had been turned out of the church for bad conduct, had withdrawn from the covenant, and he and Thayre had told the Saints they must leave their land under penalty of the law. Furthermore Copley was demanding sixty dollars from each family as damages to his property, on grounds that they had made alterations to his houses and planted crops on his ground.

Joseph had a revelation for the Colesville Saints that they were to choose a leader and move in all haste to Missouri. Under the leadership of Newel Knight, the little group which had already undergone so much for the faith began at once to uproot and make preparations for another exodus, this time much farther and more difficult, a journey of 824 miles to the western frontier.

On June 19, 1831, Joseph and his companions began the tedious journey west—by wagon, canal boat and stage to Cincinnati, by steamer to Louisville and by another steamer to St. Louis. There Joseph left the rest of his party and with several of his hardier companions, including Martin Harris, William Phelps and Edward Partridge, undertook to walk the remaining 250 miles of sparsely settled prairie under a burning July sun.

When they arrived at last, Joseph confessed to considerable disappointment. Compared to what he called the "highly cultivated society" he had left behind, Joseph found the Missourians "lean in intellect and degraded," living in a great wilderness, a century behind the times.[5]

Missouri had been a state in the Union only ten years. Its frontiers were wild and had few white settlers. The census of 1830 had shown only 2,823 in Jackson County, and some neighboring counties were even smaller. Just the year before Joseph arrived, the first white settler in Daviess County had built his cabin on what had recently been Indian territory. The vast regions beyond the western border, occupied by Indians, were still largely unexplored by whites.

Everything was different from what the Saints had been accustomed to in the east. Blacks, of whom there were a large proportion, as well as Indians were little known to the Saints and the white settlers seemed strange in their backwoods dress, manners and speech. They said, "I reckon" and "a right smart chance." Instead of "carrying" things they would "tote" them on their heads, and they did not say "bucket" or "pail" but "piggin." Clothes were not "washed" but "battled" on a smooth board with strong soap. Small children were carried straddling one hip of their mothers, and in warm weather boys up to ten years of age were dressed in nothing but a shirt. Everybody, including the women and children, wore skins, since few had means and energy to make homespun clothing even for Sunday best. Money was scarce and store goods, including calico at twenty-five cents a yard, was too expensive.

The cabins were crude, with mud chimneys and dirt floors; windows, without glass, were covered in cold weather by a slab of wood or a blanket. Food was corn and wild game cooked on the hearth or over a campfire outside the cabin door.

Independence, on a rise about three miles south of the Missouri River, was no more than a rough settlement, a point of departure for explorers, trappers and traders. It had only a few log cabins, a schoolhouse, a brick courthouse and three stores.

On their first Sunday, William Phelps preached to a little gathering of Indians, Negroes and indigent white settlers. Two converts were baptized.

Although his first impressions of the area were bleak, Joseph took a prophetic view of the situation. He could see an advantageous site for the town on the edge of a great sweep of territory extending to the Rocky Mountains. Though the land was unlike the east, he saw and described its beauty, the rolling prairies blooming with flowers as far as the eye could see and the luxuriant trees of many kinds including oak, hickory, black walnut and cherry that grew in woods from one to three miles wide following the course of rivers and streams.

As a farmer's son, he recognized that the soil was fertile and announced that it would yield wheat, corn, cotton and many other crops in abundance. The cattle, although inferior to breeds in the east, almost raised themselves on the open range. Wild turkeys, geese and ducks were plentiful, and so were buffalo, elk and deer. What was lacking, mills, industries, schools and the refinements of society, could soon be instituted by the Saints themselves.

That month Joseph had a revelation that this was the promised land. Independence was to be the center of Zion, with the site for the all-important temple nearby. The Saints were commanded to purchase land, Sidney Gilbert to establish a store and William W. Phelps and Oliver Cowdery to set up a printing office, with press and type to be bought in Cincinnati. The Colesville Saints were told again to come to Zion as soon as possible.

This the faithful Colesville Saints accomplished almost at once, arriving in July. Joseph settled them in Kaw township, twelve miles west of Independence, between Independence and the Indian border. Though a wilderness at that time, it was a propitious site that later became Kansas City.

Sidney Rigdon consecrated the land for the gathering of the Saints and Joseph helped to lay the first log for the first house. The following month a site just west of Independence was dedicated for the temple and the cornerstones were laid in a solemn ceremony.

The Saints held frequent house "raisings." After the logs were hauled and prepared the Mormon men in the area would turn out and help put up the building. Families took pride in their houses, which were neatly constructed, with hewn logs and corners made smooth. As soon as the Saints had finished their cabins they put up a log schoolhouse.

On August 8, Joseph had the sad duty of speaking at the funeral of the first member of the church to die in Zion. This was Polly Knight, the wife of his old and faithful friend, Joseph Knight, Sr. She had been ill during the long trek west from Ohio with the Colesville Saints, and her family had so despaired for her life during their journey that her son Newel thought they would soon have to bury her and had left the boat to buy lumber for her coffin. She refused to forgo the arduous journey, however, and in a touching example of faith and courage, had asked of the Lord only that she live long enough to set foot on the promised land.

Of her burial, her husband wrote succinctly, but he revealed much heartache in his new pioneer life:

> She was Burried in the woods a spot Chosen out By our selves. I was along By where she was Burried a few Days after and I found the hogs had Began to root whare she was Burried. I Being verry unwell But I took my ax the nex Day and went and Bilt a pen round it. It was the Last I done for her.[6]

Not all of the Saints were happy to be in the promised land. Edward Partridge thought the soil was poor. Sidney Rigdon wanted to return to Ohio as soon as possible. Most bitterly disappointed was Ezra Booth, although he contained his feelings at the time.

On August 8, Joseph had a revelation directing him to go back to Kirtland. This he did immediately, with Sidney Ridgon and Oliver Cowdery. William Phelps and others were assigned to travel home in pairs and preach the gospel along the way. Edward Partridge was left behind as Bishop of Zion.

Joseph's followers were now in two settlements, one in Independence and the other in Kirtland, with more than eight hundred miles of poor roads and uncertain mails between them. Nevertheless, communications were maintained remarkably well. A common faith and a sense of community prevailed, although the Saints in Independence were greatly disappointed that the prophet should choose to leave the promised land and return to Kirtland.

In Missouri, where as pioneers the Saints had more work and trouble than goods to share, the Law of Consecration at first functioned well. Edward Partridge did not allow his misgivings about the choice of land to interfere with the performance of his duties as bishop, and despite his personal hardship, he remained fair and conscientious.

His daughter Emily wrote that he had bought a house in Kirtland shortly after his conversion, but had never lived in it. His wife Lydia had found it hard enough when Edward left for Missouri with the prophet, but when she had the news that he was to stay, she felt her real trials had begun. The younger children were just recovering from measles and the eldest was still very sick with fever and a congestion of the lungs. Edward wrote to Lydia from Missouri August 5, 1831, expressing great anxiety over the fact that Lydia and the children would have to break up their home and make the hazardous journey without his help. He wanted to return but felt that he must not, because of his responsibilities in the Lord's work. "And as I am occasionally chastened I sometimes feel as though I must fall. Not to give up the cause, but fear my station is above what I can perform to the acceptance of my Heavenly Father. I hope you and I may so conduct ourselves as at last to land our souls in the haven of eternal rest."[7]

Edward sold the family property in Kirtland at a great sacrifice, for which his friends pronounced him insane, and the next season Lydia moved to Missouri in the company of William Phelps and Sidney Gilbert.

Edward rented a log cabin for his family from Lilburn W. Boggs, who later became governor of the state and the Saints' implacable enemy. When winter came and accommodations grew even more scarce, the Partridge family took in a widow with four children, which made twelve or thirteen people crowding around one fireside. As soon as he could, Edward built a log cabin of one small room with attic and cellar near the temple lot, half a mile from Independence.

Edward's children found the new life very strange, hard and sometimes terrifying. Emily wrote of one day in school when the door and windows were suddenly filled with Indian faces and Indian eyes could be seen in every crack between the logs where the chinking had fallen out. The teacher bravely went to talk to the chief, while the pupils, who were not yet used to Indians, were as white as mice.

In Ohio, where the Saints were less equal in worldly goods, the more fortunate were reluctant to share with poor newcomers, despite the presence of the prophet to encourage and chastise them, and the Law of Consecration did not function as well as in Missouri.

On December 4, 1831, Joseph had a revelation naming Newel K. Whitney bishop in Kirtland, to be keeper of the Kirtland storehouse and responsible for church funds and members in that area. The revelation also said that the new bishop was:

> To take an account of the elders as before has been commanded, and to administer to their wants, who shall pay for that which they receive, inasmuch as they have wherewith to pay . . . And he who hath not wherewith to pay, an account shall be taken and handed over to the bishop of Zion, who shall pay the debt out of that which the Lord shall put into his hands.[8]

With this, the long-suffering Edward Partridge, as Bishop of Zion, was made responsible for the debts of the Saints in Ohio.

Joseph was relieved now of the temporal and financial affairs of his community. With Emma and their two adopted children, he moved to Hiram, thirty miles southeast of Kirtland, to live with John Johnson, who with his wife and family had been converted the previous winter after the cure of Mrs. Johnson's rheumatic arm. A well-to-do farmer of fifty-two, honest, sensible and goodhearted, he offered Joseph the security and leisure he needed to finish his revision of the Bible. With Sidney Rigdon as scribe, Joseph hoped also to revise his revelations, which the members at conference in Hiram on November 1 decided would be published by the press in Zion as the *Book of Commandments*.

CHAPTER

2

TAR AND FEATHERS

During the first two years Joseph was in Ohio, he gave some forty-nine revelations, including many admonitions and announcements of importance to the growing church. In these revelations, the prophet named new leaders, sent elders out in pairs to preach, reiterated the moral law, denied false spirits, renewed proclamations of the second advent of Jesus, elaborated theology, established the Law of Consecration, announced the seat of Zion, appointed Saints to emigrate, consecrated the land, chose the temple site and made assignments of grave responsibility to certain members of the priesthood. The church was governed by Joseph's revelations, from small mundane tasks to large ideological precepts, and the lives of the Saints were directed from the plain garments they were to wear and the conduct of their daily lives to precepts of the utmost importance to their progress through eternity.

Revelations were usually given in response to an inquiry through prayer, in conformity with the admonitions, "ask and ye shall receive"; "Seek and ye shall find." Joseph preceded many of his revelations with the statement, "I inquired of the Lord and received for answer the following."

Joseph's revelations, composed in the idiom of the King James Bible, were often repetitious, sometimes caustic, usually vivid and forceful, and always direct and immediately relevant. By contrast, Sidney Rigdon's writing, as revealed in several of his letters and in his epistle from Kirtland to the Saints, August 30, 1831, was at times disorganized and vague. Though Rigdon was an effective preacher, his words on paper often seem a tiresome harangue. A comparison of the styles of these two men makes it apparent how much Joseph's revelations were indebted to inspiration, however that may be defined, in religious terms or in those of spontaneity and intensity of feeling.

Not only what he said but the sight of their prophet under inspiration was awesome to the Saints. Anson Call wrote that when Joseph was seeing a vision, his face became a living brilliant white. Joseph's complexion was described by others as transparent, and when he was excited it seemed to be illuminated.

Parley Pratt said that in giving revelations, Joseph spoke each sentence slowly and distinctly, with a pause between them long enough to allow the words to be taken down. There was never any hesitation, never any reviewing or reading back, never any revision or correction during his dictation.

According to Zebedee Coltrin, once when one of Joseph's revelations was given in the presence of several elders, some of them undertook to correct his grammar. Joseph rebuked them, saying that every word of that revelation had been dictated by Jesus Christ.[1]

Before publication, however, the revelations were revised by Joseph, Oliver and Sidney as a committee. A number, including William McLellin, thought this should not have been done.

Like other followers of Joseph Smith, McLellin tried to write a revelation. But on the day of his attempt, in November 1831, several elders witnessed his failure, and Joseph announced that it was "an awful responsibility to write in the name of the Lord." The elders then bore testimony to the truth of Joseph's revelations, saying that the Lord had "borne witness to our souls, through the Holy Ghost . . . that these commandments were given by inspiration of God." Among the ten elders who signed the statement, which might have been intended for publication in the *Book of Commandments* but which was not used, was the apparently humbled William McLellin.[2]

In the last of four special conferences held from November 1 through 12 at John Johnson's, it was agreed that the revelations were "the foundation of the church in these last days, and a benefit to the world . . . showing the riches of eternity within the compass of those who are willing to live by every word that proceedeth out of the mouth of God." The conference voted as a body that they prized the revelations "to be worth to the Church the riches of the whole earth, speaking temporally."[3]

The revelations were ready by November 15, 1831, and Oliver Cowdery, with John Whitmer as companion and guard, was sent to Independence with the copy, for publication as the *Book of Commandments*.

In Independence, according to the *History of the Church*, the revelations were reviewed once again on Joseph's order by Phelps, Cowdery and John Whitmer, who prepared such "as shall be deemed proper for publication." In his letter to Phelps of July 31, 1832, however, Joseph warned Phelps to take care "not to alter the sense of any of them, for he that adds to or diminishes the prophecies must come under the condemnation written therein."[4]

During the time Joseph and Sidney were working on the revision of the New Testament, they shared an important revelation. Joseph wrote that it was on February 16, 1832, after they had been working on St. John's Gospel, that he and Rigdon saw what he described as "a vision of the glories."

According to Philo Dibble, the heavens opened to Joseph and Sidney in the presence of about twelve elders in John Johnson's house in Hiram. Philo was there, and though he did not see the vision, he said he "saw the glory and felt the power."

For about an hour the witnesses sat speechless and enthralled, while Joseph and Sidney described the progress of their experience. Joseph would say at intervals, "What do I see?" and relate what he was seeing. Rigdon would respond, "I see the same." Rigdon would then tell what he was seeing and Joseph would say in turn, "I see the same." Neither Joseph nor Sidney moved during the whole event. Joseph sat calmly and firmly, but Sidney was limp and pale. At the end, Joseph commented wryly, "Sidney is not used to it as I am."[5]

Joseph wrote, "Now this caused us to marvel, for it was given unto us of the spirit . . . the Lord touched the eyes of our understanding and they were opened, and the glory of the Lord shone round about. And we beheld the glory of the Son, on the right hand of the Father, and received his fulness; And saw the holy angels and them who are sanctified before his throne, worshiping God, and the Lamb . . . and this is the testimony last of all, which we give of him: That he Lives!"[6]

Joseph wrote that during their study of the Scriptures, it had appeared evident to him that if God rewarded everyone according to his deeds, heaven must include more than one kingdom. Perhaps he was inspired after reading Paul's first letter to the Corinthians 15:41 and the verse following, "There is one glory of the sun, and another glory of the moon, and another glory of the stars; for one star differeth from another star in glory. So also is the resurrection of the dead."

In a revelation that followed the vision he shared with Sidney Rigdon, Joseph announced three degrees of glory. The highest glory was the celestial, like the glory of the sun, and reserved for those who had received the testimony of Jesus, were baptized and had kept His commandments. The second, terrestrial glory, was like the moon compared to the sun, and was for those who died without the law, but received it after death. The third, telestial glory, was like the stars compared to the moon, and was for those who had never received the gospel of Christ.

Speaking of his revelation Joseph said, "Nothing could be more pleasing to the Saints upon the order of the Kingdom of the Lord, than the light which burst upon the world through the foregoing vision."

The prophet's own joy in it is evident from his description: "The sublimity of the ideas; the purity of the language; the scope for action; the continued duration for completion, in order that the heirs of salvation may confess the Lord and bow the knee; the rewards for faithfulness, and the punishments for sins, are so much beyond the narrowmindedness of men, that every honest man is constrained to exclaim: 'It came from God.' "[7]

In a revelation of March 1832, Joseph affirmed the necessity for the establishment and regulation of the storehouse for the poor, adding, "That you may be equal in the bonds of heavenly things, yea, and earthly things also . . . For if ye are not equal in earthly things ye cannot be equal in obtaining heavenly things . . ."

He advised the Saints to earn a place in the celestial world by obeying the Lord's commandments, adding, "ye are little children, and ye have not as yet understood how great blessings the Father hath in his own hands and prepared for you . . . The kingdom is yours and the blessings thereof are yours, and the riches of eternity are yours. And he who receiveth all things with thankfulness shall be made glorious; and the things of this earth shall be added unto him, even an hundred fold, yea, more."[8]

In that same revelation, for reasons unexplained, Joseph assigned special names for certain leaders of the church and for himself. Joseph was Gazelam, or at times, Enoch; Newel K. Whitney was Ahashdah; and Sidney Rigdon, Pelagoram.

That month, to the satisfaction of the Saints, William Phelps issued his prospectus for Zion's newspaper, *The Evening and the Morning Star,* in which he announced the purpose of giving news of the gospel, publishing revelations and heralding the return of Israel to the favor of God.

Despite the growth and development of the church and the glories Joseph promised the faithful, not all of his followers were happy. Some were beginning to complain about the church and the Law of Consecration and a few had apostatized. Among these were four of the sons of Joseph's host, John Johnson. Olmstead Johnson was chastised by Joseph for rebellion, and Eli, Edward and John Johnson, Jr., had openly left the church, charging that Joseph was trying to get their father's property.

Simonds Ryder apostatized because he received a message signed by Sidney Rigdon and Joseph Smith saying that it was the will of the Lord made known by the spirit that he was called to preach, but the message spelled his last name with an "i" instead of a "y." Ryder said that if the spirit could make a mistake in spelling his name, it could also make a mistake in calling him to the ministry. He and Ezra Booth compared views of the church to the increase of their discontent.

At the conference of September 6, 1831, it was voted that Ezra Booth be barred from preaching as an elder in the church. However, he refused to be silenced. Though not the first to leave the church, Ezra was the first to publish against it. A man of some talent and education, Booth wrote nine letters which were published in the *Ohio Star* at Ravenna, and through them he became the most influential apostate of his time.

It was the prophet's contention that Ezra Booth was embittered by the hardships he had suffered in Missouri and by the failure of his hope that the Savior would grant him "power to smite men and make them believe."

As Booth stated them, his objections were more definite. Joseph's prophecies had failed, he said, and worse, Joseph and Sidney had "twisted" the prophecies to justify themselves. Booth said that Joseph had told them they would find a large church in Missouri, whereas there were only four women, and that when Partridge accused Joseph of telling the elders things that were not so, Joseph replied, "It will be so." When Partridge protested that the land around Independence was inferior to other areas, Joseph was furious, and had a revelation chastising Partridge for "unbelief and blindness of heart."

In Booth's opinion, Joseph and Sidney intended to found a community in Independence which they could rule as despots.

Booth also protested against Mormon dealings with the Indians in Missouri, charging that the Mormon store traded in Indian goods to give the elders contact with the Indians. Some elders were to marry Indians, he said, and one had been freed for that purpose from a wife who opposed the church. Worse, according to Booth, the Mormons were teaching the Indians that they were to go among the white people as a lion among the beasts of the forest, which "treadeth down and teareth the pieces, and no man can deliver."

Booth declared that some of the prophet's followers were too zealous, in particular Sidney Rigdon, whom he quoted as saying that Joseph's "weakness and wickedness can form no reasonable objection to his revelations."

Perhaps Booth objected most of all, fervent Methodist preacher that he had been, to Joseph's statement that the Bible was defective in its present form. To Booth, Joseph's efforts to revise the Scriptures constituted gross infidelity.

Ezra Booth's letters were widely read in Ohio and roused a good deal of feeling against the Saints among their formerly tolerant neighbors. Non-Mormons in Hiram were particularly incensed against this handsome young prophet who had come among them, as they thought, so sanctimoniously.

That December, Joseph had a revelation directing him and Sidney to go about the countryside preaching and holding meetings to allay the spreading animosity. This they did until about the middle of January, when they returned to their work in Hiram believing that they had removed most of the ill feeling toward the church and its leaders.

On the night of March 24, Joseph and Emma went to bed early on the Johnson farm. They were very tired from caring for their adopted twins, now about eleven months old, who had been ill for some time with measles. Emma took Julia, while Joseph fell asleep on the trundle bed holding Joseph. Later that night, Simonds Ryder at the head of a gang of forty or fifty whiskey-goaded men, including some of the Johnson boys, crept up to the house and tapped on the window gently, to see if anyone was awake. Emma heard the tapping but was not alarmed until a few moments later when the door burst open. Joseph was awakened by Emma's screams, and found himself going out the door in the rough hands of a dozen swearing men who clutched him by the hair, shirt and drawers. Joseph struggled desperately, managed to free one leg and sent a man sprawling out on the doorstep. Swearing by God they would kill him if he did not submit, the men choked Joseph until he lost consciousness and dragged him out into the cold night. They carried him to a meadow where they tore off his clothes, leaving only his collar, and beat him brutally. One pounced upon him like a mad cat and scratched his naked body until the blood ran, crying, "God damn ye, that's how the Holy Ghost falls on folks!"

Another tried to force a vial of something Joseph believed to be poison down his throat, but Joseph cracked it in his jaws, breaking a tooth. For years afterward he had a slight whistle in his speech, until the tooth was repaired in Nauvoo.

The men smeared Joseph with hot tar, forced the tar paddle into his mouth and covered him with pillow feathers.

When at last they left him, he got to his feet, pulled the tar away from his lips so that he could breathe more easily and staggered home.

Emma came to the door and seeing her husband's naked body in the poor light, took the tar for blood and went faint. Friends who had gathered to the house threw a blanket around Joseph and took him in. Mrs. Johnson got lard to spread on the tar and she and the others worked all night to scrape the tar off Joseph's lacerated body.

The mob had also gone after Sidney Rigdon and dragged him by the heels over the rough, frozen ground, injuring his head so badly that he was knocked unconscious. They covered him with tar and feathers nevertheless and left him for dead. Sometime later his wife found him wandering in a stupor. For several days afterward he was delirious, calling for a razor to kill his wife and Joseph Smith. It may be that the excessive zeal Sidney later began to exhibit, especially in Far West, was a result, in part, from that injury to his head.

One of the assailants later made a comment upon the difference in personality between Joseph and Sidney. When Sidney was attacked he said to his assailants that he presumed they were gentlemen, perhaps in this hoping to dissuade them from their purpose, but Joseph fought them until he was overpowered.

The leader of the mob, Simonds Ryder, said afterward that Joseph and Sidney had not been assaulted because of their beliefs. He said that the people of Hiram were liberal about religion and had not been averse to Mormon teaching. What had infuriated the attackers, according to Ryder, were some documents they had found which revealed to new converts "the horrid fact that a plot was laid to take their property from them and place it under the control of Smith." (If true, this might have been their interpretation of the Law of Consecration.) A company was formed of outraged men from Shalersville and Garrettsville, as well as Hiram.[9]

According to one historian, it was said that besides fearing for his father's property, Eli Johnson was furious because he suspected Joseph of being intimate with his sister, Nancy Marinda Johnson, and he was screaming for Joseph's castration. Eli's brother Luke, who was not one of the mob, wrote that Joseph's night clothes were torn off for that purpose, but at the last moment, seeing Joseph naked and stretched helpless on a plank, the doctor, a respected man named Dennison, refused to perform the mutilation.[10]

There had been innuendo, notably by Ezra Booth, that Joseph had indulged in sexual irregularities but no direct accusation other than the one reportedly made by Eli. Years after Joseph's death, Nancy Johnson was sealed to him in eternal marriage in a Mormon temple ceremony, with consent of her husband, Orson Hyde.[11]

There is some possibility that Nancy was a plural wife of Joseph's. Although he said nothing about his brother's accusation against Joseph in regard to Nancy, another of Johnson's sons, Lyman, told Orson Pratt, his missionary companion, that Joseph had made known to him as early as 1831, while he was living on the Johnson farm, that God had revealed to him that plural marriage was a correct principle but that the time had not yet come to teach and practice it in the church.[12] Joseph B. Noble also said that the prophet told him that the doctrine was revealed to him during the time he was translating the Scriptures.

On the Sunday morning following the assault, Joseph, who was scheduled to preach, went to meeting, although he was sick and exhausted.

In the congregation were several men from the mob, including Simonds Ryder and Felatiah Allen, who had provided the attackers with a barrel of whiskey to goad their actions. They had expected to hear that the prophet would not speak that day, but to their chagrin, Joseph made a quiet entrance and preached his sermon, as planned. He made no reference to events of the previous night, but allowed the account of how he had received his lacerations and bruises to be told afterward by the neighbors who had come to his aid. That day, he baptized three new members into the church.

Joseph and Sidney were not the only victims of that night's work. The Smiths' adopted baby Joseph Murdock, already sick with measles, caught cold from exposure when the mob raided the house, and he died within a few days.

Sidney Rigdon and his family moved to Kirtland shortly after the assault, and then, still fearing the mob, moved on to Chardon.

Joseph sent Emma to live with the Whitney family in Kirtland while he and Sidney Rigdon, with Newel K. Whitney and Peter Whitmer, started out April 1 on another trip to the Missouri frontier, where discontent had arisen among the Saints.

Lucy wrote that when Joseph and Newel left for Missouri, Newel invited Emma to stay with his wife, Elizabeth Ann, while he was away. Emma had been shuttled around, dependent upon the charity of friends quite often, and to a proud woman, this could be mortifying. However, she no doubt recalled the warm hospitality she and Joseph had received from the Whitneys when they had first arrived in Kirtland, and probably agreed readily enough. Apparently no one had told Elizabeth Ann, however, and when Emma presented herself, a maiden aunt who was then living with the Whitneys was angered, and said that if Emma moved in she would move out. Elizabeth Ann asked Emma to leave. Lucy wrote that in order to maintain good feelings, Emma said nothing about the humiliating encounter, and Lucy herself did not learn of it until years afterward.

During Joseph's absence, Emma concealed her hurt and moved in with various other members of the church in turn, including her mother-in-law. Of Emma at this time, Lucy wrote, "she was not Idle for she labored faithfully for the interest of those with whom she staid cheering them by her lively and spirited conversation . . ."[13]

Meanwhile, in Missouri, the Saints had grown disgruntled partly because they had been told by Joseph's revelation of December 4, 1831, that Zion would be responsible for Kirtland's debts. Life in Zion was not easy. Daily necessities were still hard to obtain, and they lived mainly on beef and coarse bread made from corn. They had had a hard time adjusting to life on the frontier. Newel Knight said the Saints had arduous and unfamiliar work in providing every necessity for themselves in a wilderness where very little could be bought in the stores. The Saints had labored in good cheer, however, and stoutly claimed that they had passed their first winter in tolerable comfort. Their hearts were united and their church meetings well attended. But it did not seem fair that the debts raised in Kirtland, where there was much more wealth, should be made the responsibility of the overworked pioneers in Zion.

Nevertheless, they welcomed the prophet gladly. Joseph called a general council of the church in Independence on April 26, 1832, at which he was sustained as president of the High Priesthood, the office to which he had been ordained in Ohio the previous January, and he "received the right hand of fellowship on behalf of the church" from Edward Partridge.

In a revelation given by Joseph that day, Newel K. Whitney, Sidney Rigdon, Joseph Smith, Oliver Cowdery and Martin Harris were assigned:

. . . in your several stewardships—To manage the affairs of the poor and all things pertaining to the bishopric both in the land of Zion and in the land of Shinehah [Kirtland]; . . . And you are to be equal, or in other words, you are to have equal claims on the properties, for the benefit of managing the concerns of your stewardships.[14]

The minutes of the meeting recorded that "all differences settled, and the hearts of all were united together in love."

On the twenty-eighth and twenty-ninth, Joseph went to visit his ever-faithful Colesville branch in Kaw township, and as always was received by them with great joy.

Assured that harmony was restored in Zion, Joseph, Sidney and Newel Whitney started back for Kirtland on May 6. As they were approaching New Albany, Ohio, in a stagecoach, the horses bolted. Newel leaped out of the coach, but caught his foot in the wheel and broke his leg and foot in several places. The athletic Joseph leaped out after him safely.

They sent Sidney ahead to Kirtland, while Newel put up at a public house in Greenville, Indiana, for four weeks, with Joseph caring for him. Apparently Joseph did this so well that the doctor who attended Newel said it was a pity they had no Mormon in their town, since Mormons could set broken bones or do anything else.

During their stay, Joseph suffered from poisoning of some kind, and vomited so violently that he dislocated his jaw. He had Newel lay hands upon his head in the name of the Lord, and it was Joseph's testimony that he was healed from that moment.

It was during this brief semi-isolation that Joseph confessed a sense of remorse and some agony of spirit in the letter that he wrote to Emma on June 6. The nature of what was troubling him, and whether early or recent, remains open to conjecture, but that he did not consider it trifling is apparent from his tone and from the fact that he gave it daily thought. As he told Emma, he had gone out almost every day to a little grove to pray and meditate, and had "Shed tears of Sorrow for my folly in Sufering the adversary of my Soul to have so much power over me as he has had in times past." He added, however, that he felt his sins had been forgiven by God, and that he had entrusted his life to God's hands.[15]

Soon after this, according to church account, Joseph gave evidence of his prowess as a seer. Although Newel had not stepped out of bed for four weeks, Joseph announced to him one day that if he would agree to start the next morning, they would take a wagon to the river and at once find a ferry to carry them across where a hack would be waiting. The hack would take them to the landing where they could board a boat and be traveling up the river before ten o'clock. It all transpired just as Joseph predicted, and they reached home speedily and safely in a very short time.

Later in June, the first edition of *The Evening and the Morning Star* was issued in Zion, and the Saints took great pride in it as the westernmost publication in the United States.

Despite Joseph's efforts, troubles were not over in Zion. By now about three hundred Saints were there, with new converts arriving daily. Of the newcomers, only about half could be persuaded to join in the Law of Consecration, and those almost invariably the poorer. Furthermore, although the rules of the Law were that members who apostatized must forfeit their property, the Saints in Missouri discovered that they could defy the church with impunity because the courts in Missouri upheld their rights. Phelps began denouncing slackers in his newspapers, as well as any Saints who tried to better themselves independently by working for their Gentile neighbors. Joseph soon sent a message that unless converts shared in the Law, they were not to be admitted to the church.

With the July issue of *The Evening and the Morning Star* Phelps began to discuss the disadvantages of the wilderness, to declare that the land so far cultivated could barely sustain those already on it and to warn the Saints not to come to Zion without a prior consultation with their bishop in Ohio.

By this time, the troubles of the Saints in Zion were not merely internal. As the Saints grew in numbers, strength and influence, the older settlers began to look upon them with apprehension and hostility, finding cause to complain first about the Mormon attitude toward the Indians. To the old settlers, the Indians were savages and a threat to safety and property. They were dismayed by the thousands of Shawnee and other tribes evicted from their lands in Ohio, Illinois and Kentucky who were now moving through Missouri toward the great plains to which they had been banished by Andrew Jackson's decree. The settlers protested in vain against the practice most of the tribes had of camping for a night or two outside the village of Indpendence before crossing the Missouri border. The Mormons, however, encouraged and befriended the Indians, rejoicing and broadcasting their belief that the migrations were a manifestation of the gathering tribes of Israel.

Throughout the remainder of 1832, Phelps published accounts of the Indian migrations as a manifestation of the second advent of Christ, which he predicted would occur within nine years. In his exuberance, Phelps sometimes enlarged upon official church news, and his articles often unintentionally fanned the anger of old settlers. Before the end of another year, the settlers would break into open hostility, with disastrous results for the church.

PROGRESS
AND PERIL IN KIRTLAND

In the fall of 1832, Joseph settled Emma, who was pregnant, and their adopted daughter Julia in the Kirtland house owned by Newel K. Whitney and Algernon Gilbert, formerly used as their store. Asking Hyrum to look out for them, Joseph made a hurried trip to Albany, New York City and Boston with Newel to negotiate loans and buy goods for Joseph's new endeavor in behalf of the church, a general store.

In New York, Newel, a competent businessman, spent hours every day examining and ordering merchandise, which Joseph acknowledged was a tedious job that required good judgment and thorough knowledge. While waiting for him, Joseph explored the city, which he was seeing for the first time.

On October 13 he wrote to Emma expressing his astonishment at the "great and wonderful" buildings; "the language of my heart is like this," he wrote; "can the great God of all the Earth maker of all things magnificent and splendid be displeased with man for all these great inventions sought out by them my answer is no it can not be   Seeing these works are calculated to mak men comfortable wise and happy therefore not for the works can the Lord be displeased only against man is the anger of the Lord kindled because they give him not the glory therefore their iniquities shall be visited upon their heads and their works shall be burned up with unquenchable fire . . ."

He found the iniquity of the people printed in nearly every face and nothing but their dress made them look beautiful. Yet when he reflected upon that great city which seemed "like Nineveh," he said he was filled with compassion. "Oh how long Oh Lord shall this order of things exist and darkness cover the Earth and gross darkness cover the people . . ."

After seeing as much as he could stand, he would go back to his room to meditate and calm his mind and think about home, wife and daughter Julia.

He added, "I hope God will give you strength that you may not faint I pray God to soften the hearts of those around you to be kind to you and take the burden from your shoulders as much as posable and not afflict you I feel for you for I know you State and that others do not but you must comfort yourself knowing that God is your friend in heaven and that you have one true and living friend on Earth your Husband."[1]

Joseph wrote that there were about a hundred boarders where they were staying, and sometimes more, from all parts of the world. The one who impressed him most was a beautiful young gentleman from Jersey who told him that he had been seized by cholera but spared by the Lord for some wise purpose. Joseph took the opportunity to open a long discourse with him and they talked until late at night. When the young man's boat left the next day, he and Joseph parted with much reluctance.

Joseph and Newel negotiated for $20,000 worth of goods in a very short time, and returned to Kirtland, arriving home on November 6, 1832, just after Emma gave birth to a son. Emma had very hard labor, but the child survived, and was named Joseph Smith III. It was an occasion of great joy for Emma and Joseph and the whole community.

The general store in Kirtland for which Joseph and Newel had bought the supplies was Joseph's first business venture for the church. Later it was described as modest and poorly furnished and a failure from the start because Joseph could not refuse goods to anybody who came in with a tale of hardship. Joseph was "a first rate fellow" with everybody as long as he did not ask them to pay, and the store was soon depleted without return.[2]

With the needs of his community constantly in mind, Joseph also tried to run a sawmill and a tannery, but these were not successful either, no doubt for the same reason.

Two days after the birth of his son, while Joseph was out in the woods near his parents' house chopping and hauling wood with his brothers, three new converts to the church arrived to see him. From Mendon, near Rochester, New York, they had been traveling by horse and wagon since September, stopping along the way to visit and preach to friends. The new arrivals were to be of enormous importance in the church—Heber C. Kimball and two brothers, Joseph and Brigham Young.

Brigham, born June 1, 1801, in Vermont, was a heavy-set and powerful young man of thirty-one, by trade a carpenter, painter, glazier. He had moved to Mendon in 1829, and there had read a copy of *The Book of Mormon* left at the home of his brother Phineas by the prophet's brother,

Samuel H. Smith. Converted to the church by elders passing through the area, Brigham had traveled to Canada and there converted his elder brother Joseph, at that time a Methodist preacher. Just two months before his visit to the prophet, Brigham's wife had died, leaving him with two little girls. He and the children had been taken in by the Kimball family.

Joseph Smith and Brigham Young took an immediate liking to one another. Brigham wrote later, "My joy was full at the privilege of shaking the hand of the Prophet of God, and receiving the sure testimony, by the spirit of prophecy, that he was all that any man could believe him to be as a true prophet."[3]

They returned to Joseph's parents' house and in the evening held a meeting with a few of the Saints. Called upon by Joseph to preach, Brigham spoke in tongues. When they rose from their knees, the Saints immediately crowded around Joseph to ask his opinion of what had happened, some expecting him to condemn the manifestation. "No," Joseph said. "It is of God."[4] In his history, Joseph added that it was the first time he had heard that gift among the brethren.

This was the introduction of tongues among the Saints in Kirtland, although tongues had been heard in Mendon and in branches of the church in Pennsylvania. According to John Whitmer the gift of tongues afterward became quite general among the Saints in Ohio.

Brigham Young became Joseph's devoted friend and disciple. Years later, after he had become president of the Utah church, Brigham said, "From the first time I saw the Prophet Joseph I never lost a word that came from him concerning the kingdom. And this is the key of knowledge that I have to-day, that I did harken to the words of Joseph, and treasured them up in my heart, laid them away, asking my Father in the name of his Son Jesus to bring them to my mind when needed."[5]

While in New York, Joseph had heard much discussion about world affairs and also about events in his own country, in particular the current protest of South Carolina against the tariff imposed by Congress in 1828 and 1832. Shortly after Joseph's return to Ohio, the Nullification Convention met in Charleston and issued a declaration that those tariffs were void in the state of South Carolina.

It was propounded by Calhoun that the Union was a compact of sovereign states, that federal regulations were limited by the Constitution and that within their own territory the people of any state could suspend a federal law that they decided was unconstitutional. The assumption was that even if the majority of states accepted a federal law, a state that rejected it had the option to withdraw from the Union.

On these grounds, South Carolina rejected the federal tariffs and threatened to secede if attempts were made to enforce them. Determined to save the Union, President Andrew Jackson issued a proclamation refuting nullification and declaring the Union paramount. He called in the army and navy to march against the rebellious state if necessary. A fear of civil war spread across the nation. Agreement was reached, however, before an armed confrontation occurred, and the Union was, for the time, held supreme.

On Christmas Day, 1832, Joseph had a revelation, perhaps his most famous, which included what has since been called his "Civil War" prophecy:

Verily thus saith the Lord concerning the wars that will shortly come to pass, beginning at the rebellion of South Carolina, which will eventually terminate in the death and misery of many souls; And the time will come that war will be poured out upon all nations, beginning at this place. For behold, the Southern States will call on other nations, even the nation of Great Britain, as it is called, and they shall also call upon other nations . . . and then war shall be poured out upon all nations. And it shall come to pass, after many days, slaves shall rise up against their masters . . . and thus, with the sword and by bloodshed the inhabitants of the earth shall mourn; and with famine, and plague, and earthquake, and the thunder of heaven, and the fierce and vivid lightning also, shall the inhabitants of the earth be made to feel the wrath, and indignation, and chastening hand of an Almighty God, until the consumption decreed hath made a full end of all nations . . . Wherefore, stand ye in holy places, and be not moved, until the day of the Lord come; for behold, it cometh quickly, saith the Lord. Amen.[6]

On the twenty-seventh, he received a lengthy revelation that he called "the Olive Leaf" about the ministrations of the comforter, incidents relating to the Lord's coming, and the functions of the school of the prophets.

On January 23 with the elders assembled in conference, Joseph introduced the ordinance of the washing of feet, at which he wrapped himself in a towel and washed and dried the feet of each in turn. Before washing his father's feet, he asked of him a father's blessing. Joseph warned that if any should sin willfully thereafter, they would be "given over unto the buffetings of Satan until the day of redemption."

Joseph, meanwhile, had kept on with his laborious revision of the New Testament. It was finished at last in January 1833, and on February 2, he sealed it and said it was not to be opened until it reached Zion for publication.[7]

Joseph intended to have the revised New Testament issued in one volume with *The Book of Mormon,* but the press in Zion was overthrown before the work was done, and he found no other opportunity to publish it.[8]

In February, Joseph gave his most famous revelation pertaining to the daily lives of the Saints. He wrote that it was sent:

. . . not by commandment or constraint, but by revelation and the word of wisdom, showing forth the order and will of God in the temporal salvation of all saints in the last days—Given for a principle with promise, adapted to the capacity of the weak and the weakest of all saints . . . inasmuch as any man drinketh wine or strong drink among you, behold it is not good, neither meet in the sight of your Father, only in assembling yourselves together to offer up your sacraments before him. And, behold, this should be wine, yea, pure wine of the grape of the vine, of your own make. And, again, strong drinks are not for the belly, but for the washing of your bodies. And again, tobacco is not for the body, neither for the belly, and is not good for man, but is an herb for bruises and all sick cattle, to be used with judgment and skill. And again, hot drinks are not for the body or belly.

Herbs, all grains and fruit in season were commended, but flesh of beasts and fowls was to be used sparingly. "And all saints who remember to keep and do these sayings, walking in obedience to the commandments, shall receive health in their navel and marrow to their bones . . . And shall run and not be weary, and shall walk and not faint . . ."[9]

The revelation was presented mildly and with due consideration for the weakness of humankind. Later, in a meeting of the High Council in February 1834, after a discussion among the brethren, Joseph announced the decision that disobedience to the "Word of Wisdom" was grounds for dismissal from church office. Adherence to the Word of Wisdom soon became a token of good standing in the church for all members.

In March, again with the needs of his community in mind and with an eye to its growth, Joseph had the church buy three farms in Kirtland. One property known as the French farm was bought for its brickmaking facilities, and Frederick G. Williams was appointed to hire men and superintend the yard.

For a short while, things went well for Joseph and the church. As a result of Joseph's strong missonary program, the Saints in Kirtland and in Zion were growing rapidly in numbers. Land speculation, which was at this time beginning throughout the country, had not yet affected his plans. Despite frequent problems, Joseph was still optimistic about the Law of Consecration and had hopes that it would solve the economic difficulties of his community. His personal affairs were good. He now had a house of his own and a well-run farm of a hundred and forty acres. Emma and their little family, the baby Joseph and the adopted daughter Julia, were contented.

On May 25, 1833, Joseph reported with joy that his Uncle John Smith arrived in Kirtland. The first of Joseph Sr.'s relatives to join the church, John had been baptized in 1832 and had begun at once to preach. His former friends had called him crazy and, as his son George Albert wrote later, in every neighborhood where he spoke ministers of other faiths followed him and made slanderous remarks about him and the Saints. John had sold his farm and fitted out two covered wagons, an innovation in his area, and he and his wife Clarissa, daughter Caroline and two sons John and George Albert had traveled five hundred miles to Kirtland. Not far from the site of the future Kirtland Temple, they bought a small farm of twenty-seven acres and employed Brigham Young to lay the floor of their cabin.

On June 1, Joseph had a revelation describing in detail the temple to be built for the work of the Lord. It would be sixty-five feet long by fifty-five feet wide, and would have two courts, a lower for sacrament meetings, and a higher for the school of the prophets.

Hyrum Smith, Jared Carter and Reynolds Cahoon, who were appointed to obtain subscriptions, sent out a circular at once and work was soon started.

On June 5, George Albert Smith, then fifteen years old, had the honor and the thrill of hauling the first load of stone for the temple. Hyrum Smith and Reynolds Cahoon, not confining their efforts to fund-raising, began digging a trench for the walls and finished it not long afterward with their own hands. The cornerstone was laid on July 23, 1833.

In Joseph's eyes it was not fitting for the temple of the Lord to be anything less than the best the Saints could produce. "Shall we, brethren, build a house for our God of logs?"

Joseph was able to fire the Saints with enthusiasm and they undertook astonishing tasks for so poor and small a community. His hard-pressed followers would labor and sacrifice their time, money and means for three years before they could finish their temple.

Joseph also designed the city of Zion as one square mile blocked out in plots of ten acres, each subdivided into half-acre lots. He provided in detail for from fifteen to twenty thousand inhabitants, the houses to be brick and stone set in gardens and groves well back from broad streets. Squares in the middle of the city would be reserved for public buildings, schools, a storehouse and offices for the presidency and the lesser priesthood. Farms and stables were to be laid out on the periphery of the town.

In Joseph's plan, as soon as the city was completed another was to be established on the same pattern, and so his community would grow and the world would be filled up in the last days.

Joseph also described the temple he hoped to build in Zion. Of hewn stone and brick, it was to be eighty-seven feet long and sixty-five feet wide, considerably larger than the one in progress in Kirtland.

Before their temple in Kirtland could be finished, or Joseph's plans developed, a variety of troubles would befall the Saints.

Some of their troubles were caused by the ex-convert Philastus Hurlbut, who began trying to establish that *The Book of Mormon* was the work of Solomon Spaulding and to raise hostilities against the church and dissension among the members.

Joseph E. Johnson, who had known Hurlbut well during the year he had boarded with Johnson's mother, described him as a handsome, well-built man of some ambition, but poorly educated and rather pompous. According to Johnson, Hurlbut made no secret of his hope to get a good church position and to marry into the family of one of the leaders. Given the title "doctor" by his parents in the old folklore tradition that as a seventh son he had supernatural powers, Hurlbut had also tried to set himself up in the community as a physician.

Hurlbut, who had been excluded by the Methodists for immoralities, had visited Joseph in his home one day in March 1833, and Joseph had talked to him at length about *The Book of Mormon*. He was ordained five days later by Sidney Rigdon, but disfellowshipped from the church in June for "unChristian conduct with women" (afterward more clearly described as using obscene language to a young member) while he was on a church mission in the east.

Hurlbut appealed his excommunication on the grounds that he had been absent from the proceedings. Allowed a hearing, he confessed, and was forgiven and restored. Only two days later, however, he was called in again when two brethren accused him of boasting that he had "deceived Joseph Smith's God." This was more than the council could tolerate, and Hurlbut, to his great indignation, was cut off from the church.

Hurlbut declared himself an enemy of the Mormons from that day. After the interview he held with Solomon Spaulding's brother and his wife and neighbors, as described earlier, Hurlbut began to hope that he could prove *The Book of Mormon* false. He went to Palmyra in the fall of 1833 in search of evidence against Joseph Smith. In two months of diligent work he could not find anything to substantiate the theory that *The Book of Mormon* was written by Solomon Spaulding, but he did find about one hundred residents of Palmyra and Manchester who were willing for one reason or another to make derogatory statements about the Smiths. Hurlbut eagerly collected their signed affidavits.

One neighbor of the Smiths', Peter Ingersoll, maintained that Joseph had told him he had no gold plates but made his family believe in them by exhibiting a bundle of sand tied up in his smock. Another neighbor, William Stafford, said of the Smiths that "a great part of their time was devoted to digging for money." According to Willard Chase, Joseph and his brother Alvin were helping him dig a well in 1822 when they found a peculiar stone for which Joseph afterward claimed special powers. Joseph Capon declared that Joseph Smith, Jr., "pretended to find the Gold Plates" in a "scheme" to relieve his family of pecuniary embarrassment, and that Joseph Sr. called the book a speculation which would place his family "above the generality of mankind." A statement signed by fifty-one residents of Palmyra said of the Smiths, "we consider them destitute of that moral character, which ought to entitle them to the confidence of any community."[10]

Hurlbut took his affidavits on a lecture tour through the regions in Ohio where the Saints were living and even brazenly showed them in Kirtland. He raised such a storm of hostility against the Mormons that they became frightened for their lives. Heber C. Kimball said that the Saints stood guard for nights on end, not even daring to take off their clothes. Young George Albert Smith spent much of his time that fall and winter on watch over Sidney Rigdon's house. Joseph too had constant protection. Most of the brethren armed themselves, but a few left the church, maintaining that they did not believe it was right to shed blood, even in self-defense.

More threatening to Joseph's community than any new violence from neighbors was the disillusionment spreading among some of the Saints themselves. To combat this, Joseph read Hurlbut's affidavits at meetings and denounced them as the work of Satan.

Rigdon meanwhile undertook a vigorous campaign against Hurlbut, making some charges which were unjustified. Enraged, Hurlbut made a public threat on Joseph's life. Joseph brought out a complaint. Hurlbut was tried on April 12, 1834, convicted and held on a two-hundred-dollar bond to keep the peace for six months.

Hurlbut found his prestige and credibility much reduced, but managed to sell his affidavits to the editor of the *Painesville Telegraph,* Eber D. Howe, for five hundred dollars. Howe published them later that year in his *Mormonism Unvailed.*

Howe's book, which was the first widely known work against the Mormons, influenced several generations of historians. The Saints always considered it perjured testimony and a work effected by Satan.

Years afterward, William H. Kelley, a member of the Reorganized Church, went to Palmyra to interview some of those who had given affidavits to Hurlbut and to make further inquiries about the reputation of the Smith family among non-Mormons and some of their professed enemies. He found a number of people who spoke favorably of the Smiths and some who did not, but nothing so deleterious as what had been elicited by Hurlbut. Despite Kelley's protests of impartiality, his survey, which was published in the newspaper of the Reorganized Church, *The Saints Herald,* June 1, 1881, also had indications of predisposition, although not to the extent revealed by Hurlbut. Neither interviewer was sophisticated in techniques of polling opinion and in the main each received what he was looking for. Nevertheless, Kelley's survey offers a substantial refutation of Hurlbut's vindictive work.

In the meantime, in 1833, the Saints in Zion were in far deeper trouble with their neighbors than Hurlbut could cause them in his worst efforts.

CONFLICT IN ZION

Until shortly before the Saints moved to the Missouri frontier it probably would have been an ideal environment for a new faith. Few settlers were there and among them was no strong orthodoxy that might be expected to protest religious innovations. The settlers were mainly hunters and trappers, hardy and independent people of meager education who wanted little more than plenty of open land with abundant game from which to make their living.

Soon after 1830, however, Andrew Jackson established the Indian border, which prevented white men from moving west to new lands. As their population grew, the early settlers in Missouri became resentful of new families encroaching upon the diminishing free space. When the Mormons moved in they met the ready resentment of Missourians against any newcomers, but in addition they soon roused a particular animosity because of their beliefs and activities.

The Mormon proclamations that the Indians would be united in strength and restored to their rights angered the frontiersmen, who saw these as an open incitement to Indian rebellion.

Also intolerable to the old settlers who wanted to keep Missouri a slave state was the fact that the Mormons, who were mainly from New England, did not have slaves. As early as 1832, the old settlers accused the Mormons of sowing dissension among their Blacks.

Neither did the frontiersmen like the evident purpose of the Mormons, who were busily laying out farms, building good houses, setting up mills and establishing industries, to make a permanent community in what had been wide, free country. Settlements were growing rapidly, and by the summer of 1833, over a thousand Mormons were in Jackson County. It seemed to the frontiersmen that the newcomers, whom they saw as fanatics who believed they could perform miracles and see angels, would soon be electing all the county officers and would next control the territory. Worse, they had heard rumors that the Mormons maintained that the land was to be theirs for an inheritance, and the old settlers feared this meant the Mormons intended to have it all without price.

From the earliest days of the church, the Saints had had the peculiar capacity to rouse the enmity of their neighbors. Failing to see that they had a part in what occurred, they themselves always thought it the work of Satan to frustrate God's purpose in the new dispensation. Nothing they had encountered so far, however, prepared them for the barbarism of the frontiersmen in Missouri.

To the Mormons, it probably seemed part of Satan's plan that violent opposition to them was encouraged by members of rival churches. In the summer of 1833 one Reverend Pixley from the eastern Missionary Society and a Reverend Finis Ewing of the Cumberland Presbyterians began to make inflammatory outcry. Reverend Pixley wrote to newspapers in the east as well as in the west, made speeches to both whites and Indians, and produced a tract against the Mormons which he carried from cabin to cabin. Reverend Ewing wrote, "The Mormons are the common enemies of mankind and ought to be destroyed."[1]

All that summer, the Mormons were harassed by their neighbors. Bishop Partridge's daughter, Emily, then about nine years old, later wrote in her memoirs that the neighbors would ride into Mormon settlements at night, shouting abuses, breaking windows and shooting into the houses. Edward Partridge had a large haystack in his back yard, which a mob set on fire, making a tremendous blaze. At night families would gather in the Partridge cabin for protection. The women and children would go upstairs, while the men stayed in the room below, praying together out loud, although not in unison. The children heard so much about the mob that the word became a "perfect terror" to them, and they would often cry out in their sleep, "The mob is coming!"[2]

That year, a few free Black members of the church tried to emigrate to Zion as their white brethren were doing. They found themselves confused and hampered, however, by certain laws in Missouri, one of which forbade the entry of free Blacks without a certificate of citizenship from another state, a law which was in fact designed to keep them out. To prevent misunderstanding among church members outside of Missouri about the rights of Blacks to emigrate to that state, Phelps published the statute in *The Evening and the Morning Star* of July 1833. Knowing the explosive feelings of the frontiersmen, he added what he thought was a mollifying sentence or two: "As to slaves, we have nothing to say; in connection with the wonderful events of this age much is doing toward abolishing slavery, and colonizing the blacks in Africa."

To the frontiersmen, this seemed the final outrage. A great body of them met and produced a manifesto which catalogued all their grievances, declaring the Mormons to be "deluded fanatics" or knaves, guilty of blasphemy in claiming revelations direct from heaven, especially that God had given them this country for an inheritance. Until now, the manifesto said, the Mormons had been tolerated in the hope their pretensions would pass away, but Phelps's article invited free Negroes from other states to join the church and settle in Missouri. This, they said, would:

> Inflict on our society an injury that they knew would be to us entirely insupportable, and one of the surest means of driving us from the country . . . the introduction of such a caste among us would corrupt our blacks, and instigate them to bloodshed . . . we believe it a duty we owe to ourselves, our wives, and children, to the cause of public morals, to remove them from among us.

The frontiersmen agreed that the Saints should be given "timely warning," should receive compensation for property they could not take, and if they refused to leave the region in peace "as they had found it," the settlers would use whatever means proved necessary to get rid of them, "peaceably if we can, forceably if we must." Several hundred men signed the manifesto, including such community leaders as Samuel C. Owens the county clerk, and his deputy, Russell Hicks, and Samuel D. Lucas, judge of the court. The manifesto announced a mass meeting to be held in the courthouse in Independence on July 20, 1833, to decide the next action.

The manifesto was circulated widely among the old settlers.

At once Phelps published and distributed an extra edition of his paper. He protested that his previous issue had been misunderstood. "Our intention was not only to stop free people of color from emigrating to this state, but to prevent them from being admitted as members of the Church."[3] In this he was stating what was by no means church policy, but his own attempt to ease the threatening situation.

Despite Phelps's efforts, the mass meeting was held as planned on July 20 and attended by several hundred very excited old settlers who decreed that no more Mormons would be admitted into Jackson County, that those already there must leave, that the Mormon press, storehouse and shops must close at once; and that Mormons who chose not to comply should ask those of their brethren who had the gift of prophecy what would result.

What started as a meeting soon turned into a raging mob. About three hundred men poured out of the courthouse and descended upon the office of *The Evening and the Morning Star*. They threw William Phelps and his furnishings into the street, expelled a family living in the building, dumped the press, paper and type out the second-floor wndow and destroyed as much as they could find of the *Book of Commandments,* which was then in progress.

The mob whipped some of the elders while the women and children ran off in terror to the nearby woods and fields. Then they went in search of Bishop Partridge.

Emily and her sister were on their way to the spring for water when they saw the mob approach and surround their house. The girls remained in terror at the spring until the men disappeared with their father. They were sure, from the threats they heard, that he was going to be killed.

In the complaint he later filed with the Jackson County Court, Edward Partridge wrote that George Simpson and two others burst into his house while he was sitting with his wife, who was still feeble from childbirth, and forced him outside. He was taken to the public square by about fifty men, including Samuel D. Lucas, who was to become the Saints' determined enemy. A crowd of some three hundred people had gathered near the courthouse. One of the mob, Russell Hicks, told Partridge that his word was the law of the county, and that Edward must agree to leave or face the consequences. Edward answered that he was not aware of having injured anyone and would not agree to leave, and that if he had to suffer for his religion, it was no more than others had done. The mob shouted him down, jeering, "Call upon your Jesus!" Others yelled for quiet so that they could hear what the Mormon was saying.

The men threw Edward on the ground and kicked and struck him violently. Hicks began stripping off Edward's clothes, but his protests against being naked in the street roused some interference and he was allowed to keep his shirt and pantaloons. The mobbers smeared him with tar from head to foot and covered him with feathers. Edward bore this abuse so meekly that the anger of the mob began to subside. Many grew solemn and at last in silence they allowed him to get up and start for home with the help of one of the young brethren.

Charles Allen was also stripped and tarred and feathered that day by the mob when he refused the choice they offered him of leaving the county or denying *The Book of Mormon.*

Emily Partridge was looking out the window, worrying about her father, when she saw two men coming toward the cabin. One was a young man she knew, carrying a hat, coat and vest. The other she took for an Indian of such terrifying appearance that she fled upstairs. When the men came straight to the door and into the house, she realized that the man in feathers was her father, so thickly covered with tar that nothing was free except his face and the palms of his hands. Neighbors hung up blankets around the fireplace to screen him and began to pull off the feathers and scrape the tar.

While his friends removed the tar, which apparently had been mixed with some kind of acid and was eating into his flesh, the bishop said that he was proud to have been persecuted for the truth.

On the following Tuesday the mob returned, this time armed with rifles and knives, bearing a red flag in token of blood. They threatened to whip church leaders to death and to turn slaves loose on the Mormon community to raze the houses and burn the crops. At this six Mormon leaders, William Phelps, Edward Partridge, Isaac Morley, Sidney Gilbert, John Whitmer and John Corrill, offered themselves as ransom, to the death if necessary, if the mob would allow the rest to stay and live in peace. According to Edward Partridge, one of the mob replied that every man should die for himself.

The Mormons finally promised that the leaders, their families and half of the Saints would leave Jackson County by the first of January, and the rest by the first of April, that the newspaper and the store would be discontinued and that no more Saints would come to the area.

A witness to this action was Lilburn W. Boggs, a resident of Independence and lieutenant governor of the state, who was to play a large part in Mormon history. Born in Kentucky in 1792, Boggs had moved to Missouri Territory in 1816, worked as a bank cashier in St. Louis and then as a "circuit riding merchant." In 1826, after marrying his second wife, a granddaughter of Daniel Boone, he had moved to Independence, served as state senator and then as lieutenant governor, while continuing as a merchant when the General Assembly was not in session. Hardly a disinterested party in the Mormon difficulties, Boggs had contended with certain Mormons for land in Jackson County, and in fact owned tracts of land from Independence to Livingston County. He had no wish to see the growing strength of a group opposed to slavery. To the Saints he said, "You now know what our Jackson boys can do, and you must leave the country."[4]

An agreement in writing was made between the Mormons and men of the mob, and was signed by, among others, Richard Simpson and Samuel D. Lucas, two men of the tar and feather party.

Simpson and other signatories of the agreement sent a notice to the *Western Monitor* which was published August 2, giving an almost entirely false account of what had happened and declaring that an agreement had been made with the Saints in an orderly manner and "no blood spilled, nor any blows afflicted."

Oliver Cowdery took the appalling news to Joseph in Kirtland. Lucy wrote that Joseph was overwhelmed with grief, that he sobbed aloud, exclaiming that he wished he had been with the brethren to share their fate, and cried, "Oh, my God, what shall I do in such a trial as this?"[5]

He had a revelation for the Saints on August 6, enjoining Christian patience in their persecution, and admonishing them to support the constitutional law of the land. He suggested that those who were under the greatest duress should leave, while the rest bear all until hostilities should cease. He sent Orson Hyde and John Gould to aid and counsel the Saints in Independence, and with the word, according to William McLellin, that "The Lord would justify them to stand in their own defense—sword in hand."[6]

In September, William Phelps and Orson Hyde were sent to Jefferson City with a petition to Governor Daniel Dunklin. Signed by Partridge and nearly every member of the church in Jackson County, the petition stated their case and asked for troops to protect their rights.

On October 1, Joseph sent Oliver Cowdery to New York with eight hundred dollars to buy another printing press to be set up in Kirtland, where it was decided that *The Evening and the Morning Star* (its title shortened to *The Evening and Morning Star*) would be published until it could be returned to Zion.

On October 5, the prophet and Sidney Rigdon set off on a missionary tour to Canada. During their absence, Governor Dunklin replied to the Mormon petition, but offered little hope. Although he expressed sympathy, the governor's only advice to the Mormons was to sue in the local courts.

The Saints in Independence approached a well-known law firm, the members of which included Alexander Doniphan and David Atchison, two men who were to play an active part in Joseph's history. The firm agreed to act for the Mormons for a thousand dollars, a very large fee for that day, which the lawyers justified by saying that the case would deprive them of other practice in that area. This the Mormons apparently did not think unfair, and a note for that amount was signed by Edward Partridge and William Phelps and endorsed by Gilbert and Whitney.

Word spread immediately that the Mormons intended to sue for their rights. The next night, October 31, a party of some fifty frontiersmen, many armed with guns, attacked a little community of ten cabins isolated west of Big Blue River. They broke down doors, tore off roofs, smashed furniture, beat and stoned the men and drove the women and the screaming, terrified children off into the woods, where they remained exposed to the cold all night.

On the following nights mobs terrorized the whole area, striking one settlement after another. Sidney Gilbert's house was partly pulled down. Parley Pratt was struck on the head with a rifle butt while trying to guard Newel Knight's mill. Other men were whipped, women and children were chased from their homes, Gilbert and Whitney's store was broken into and the goods scattered in the street. One non-Mormon, Richard McCarty, caught in the act of throwing a brick into the store, was taken before the justice of the peace, who refused to issue a warrant against him. Later McCarty got out a warrant for false arrest against William McLellin, John Corrill, Sidney Gilbert, Isaac Morley and others who had accused him, and the Mormons were arrested and thrown in jail. Neither in this incident

nor in any that followed was there evidence that any of the Saints had broken the law.[7]

On November 4, David Whitmer led thirty mounted Mormons, seventeen of whom had guns, in a patrol of the beleaguered areas and encountered a group of marauders who shot at them. When the Mormons answered fire, the mob retreated at once, leaving some of their horses in
David Whitmer's cornfield and two of their men dead on the ground. In
that exchange several others were wounded on both sides, including
Philo Dibble, who received a ghastly wound in the abdomen, but survived,
and Andrew Barber, who died the next day, the first immediate martyr
among the Saints.

That night runners went out in every direction among the old settlers
spreading the alarm that the Mormons had taken Independence. The old
settlers threatened to kill their Mormon prisoners and sent out a plea for
the militia.

Distressed by these events, about one hundred Mormons under the
leadership of Lyman Wight assembled the next day just west of Independence to consider what to do. They were met by Colonel Thomas
Pitcher, one of the signers of the anti-Mormon manifesto, and a company
of men, some of whom had helped to destroy the Mormon press. Announcing themselves as militia from Lieutenant Governor Boggs, the company demanded the Mormon arms on pretext of ensuring the peace. Boggs
himself appeared and urged the Mormons to cooperate, assuring them that
the mob would also be required to surrender arms. Seeing a number of the
mob in the so-called militia, the Mormons were suspicious, but to show
their good faith they agreed to the terms and gave up their weapons.

News spread fast that the Saints were now unarmed. That night mobs
fell upon every Mormon community in turn, wrecked, burned or pillaged
more than two hundred houses, dispersed stock, whipped the men and
drove the old, young, sick and helpless from their homes. Twelve hundred
people were forced out that night into a rising November gale.

By Thursday November 7, the shores of the Missouri River were lined
with people and their hastily collected boxes, chests and provisions. The
ferrymen worked continuously taking people and goods across. By nightfall, the riverbanks were turned into a great camp. In a pouring rain hundreds of people huddled under improvised tents near campfires while
others wandered from group to group looking for missing loved ones.

The next day, with the number of refugees increasing constantly, the
men felled small cottonwood trees to make temporary shelters, and the
riverbank began to look like a village of wigwams.

The Colesville Saints kept together as always and made a little settlement of temporary shacks on the Missouri bottoms.

Some of the Mormons, including Parley Pratt, his wife and the Partridge
family, went to Clay County, where they were kindly received and allowed

to move into any empty shacks and hovels they could find. Two other counties nearby turned Mormons away. Partridge and John Corrill found a log stable, cleaned it as well as they could and moved their two families, a total of fifteen people, into the one room. They hung blankets up a few feet back of the large fireplace to keep in as much warmth as possible, but it was still so cold, Emily wrote, that her father's ink froze in his inkwell as he tried to keep up his correspondence.

The elders who had been imprisoned escaped and sent the governor an affidavit about the treatment of the Mormons during that week.

About two o'clock on the morning of November 13, the Saints camping on the riverbanks were roused by a glorious sight in the heavens. Thousands upon thousands of brilliant meteors were streaking head on toward the earth, in the most amazing display ever recorded until that time. The swarm of meteors seemed to radiate from a point in the heavens and moved very fast, bursting on fire as they encountered the atmosphere and often leaving a green trail which lasted several seconds. As the night passed, their numbers increased until toward dawn, according to one observer, they seemed almost half the frequency of snowflakes.

The phenomenon was seen with amazement throughout the country, and many religious groups who believed in the imminent millennium accepted it as the fulfillment of the word of God that stars would fall to herald the advent of Christ. Bells were tolled and many prepared for the end. The Mormons camping out of doors hailed the sight joyfully, with cries of hallelujah. To them it seemed of special import, occurring as it had immediately after their persecution by the enemies of their faith.

Joseph, who had returned to Kirtland from his mission to Canada on November 4, was awakened at four on the morning of the thirteenth by an elder who called him to see the meteors.

In the small diary he was keeping at that time the prophet wrote:

> I arose and beheld to my great joy the stars fall from heaven; yea, they fell like hail stones, a literal fulfillment of the word of God as recorded in the holy scriptures and a sure sign that the coming of Christ is close at hand. O how marvellous are thy works, O Lord and I thank thee for thy mercy unto me thy servant. O Lord save me in thy kingdom for Christ sake. Amen.[8]

Joseph did not hear the latest news about the Saints' tragic situation until December 5, when a letter arrived from William Phelps. About that same time he received an account Orson Hyde had sent to the *Missouri Republican*. There were some discrepancies in these reports, probably because all of the facts had not yet been ascertained. Joseph wrote immediately to the Saints in care of Bishop Partridge in Clay County expressing his concern, but said that it was difficult to advise them, because he was not certain about what had actually happened. He assured the Saints that they were in God's hands, but added "they who will live godly in Christ Jesus, shall suffer persecution; and before their robes are made white in the blood of the Lamb, it is to be expected . . . they will pass through great tribulation."⁹

He urged any Saints who had not surrendered their arms to remain on their property and defend it until the last. He advised them to collect specific data about the actions of the mob and to use every lawful means to gain redress. It would be impossible, he added, for Kirtland to come to their aid in any material way.

A few days later he again wrote expressing sympathy but said that some individuals must have forsaken the covenant and "walked in disobedience."

On December 15, William Phelps wrote the prophet a pathetic letter, revealing the patience, humility and bewilderment of the Saints who had remained faithful under their great trials. He said:

> The condition of the scattered Saints is lamentable and affords a gloomy prospect. No regular order can be enforced . . . We are in Clay, Ray, Lafayette, Jackson, Van Buren and other counties; and cannot hear from one another oftener than we do from you. I know it was right that we should be driven out of the land of Zion, that the rebellious might be sent away. But, brethren, if the Lord will, I should like to know what the honest in heart shall do? Our clothes are worn out; we want the necessaries of life, and shall we lease, buy, or otherwise obtain land where we are, to till, that we may raise enough to eat? Such is the common language of the honest, for they want to do the will of God. I am sensible that we shall not be able to live again in Zion, till God or the President rules out the mob . . . The mob swear if we come we shall die! If, from what has been done in Zion, we, or the most of us, have got to be persecuted from city to city . . . we want to know it; for there are those among us that would rather earn eternal life on such conditions than lose it; but we hope for better things and shall wait patiently for the word of the Lord . . .¹⁰

Joseph gave a lengthy revelation on the sixteenth mingling chastisement, comfort and assurance that Zion would stand:

> I, the Lord, have suffered the affliction to come upon them . . . in consequence of their transgressions . . . there were jarrings, and contentions, and envyings and strifes and lustful and covetous desires among them . . . notwithstanding their sins, my bowels are filled with compassion towards them. I will not utterly cast them off . . . I have sworn . . . that I would let fall the sword of mine indignation in behalf of my people . . . Mine indignation is soon to be poured out . . . And they that have been scattered shall be gathered . . . They that

remain and are pure in heart, shall return, and come to their inheritances . . . there is none other place appointed than that which I have appointed; neither shall there be any other place appointed . . . for the work of gathering my saints.[11]

On February 27, 1834, William Phelps reported to Kirtland what he called the "farcical" efforts of the officers of Missouri to enforce the law in behalf of the Saints. About twelve of the brethren, including Bishop Partridge, were subpoenaed as witnesses in behalf of the state and taken to Jackson County under the protection of the "Liberty Blues," some fifty armed militia under Captain Atchison, for the prosecution of some members of the mob who had driven the Mormons out of the county. The company had no sooner arrived than the court, intimidated by the immediate gathering of many more of the old mob, dismissed the witnesses and the militia.

William Phelps entered legal proceedings against Samuel D. Lucas and others for the loss of his press and the damage to his property. The defense pleaded not guilty on the grounds that the house belonged to one James H. Flournoy, that the press was merely moved to another location and that no unnecessary damage was done.

Edward Partridge charged Samuel D. Lucas and others with assault, saying he was "greatly hurt, bruised and wounded" and that his "reputation and standing in society" were also injured. Court was held on February 24, 1834, in Independence, and to all charges the defendants pleaded separately that they were not guilty and that their attack upon Partridge was in self-defense. One defendant, John M. Walker, said that in defending himself he did "necessarily and unavoidably a little beat, bruise, wound and ill treat the said Edward Partridge, and rend, tear, damage and spoil the wearing apparel, and unavoidably did besmear the said Edward with a little pitch, tar and feathers." The manner of Edward's alleged attack upon some six defendants before a large crowd was not documented.[12]

No legal redress was ever attained by the Mormons for their injuries and loss of property in Jackson County.

Every attempt of the Saints in succeeding weeks to return to their homes met violence. The burning of houses and haystacks continued, and the mob, who had formerly used whips, began to use clubs.

Made aware that the Saints had been deprived of their arms without sufficient provocation, the governor sent a direct order to Colonel Pitcher for their return, but by this time the arms had been dispersed among the mob, who insolently refused to surrender them, and they were never retrieved.

It began to seem to some of the Saints in Missouri that they had no recourse but to recover their rights for themselves.

CHAPTER

5

THE SAINTS RECRUITED

In February 1834, Parley Pratt and Lyman Wight came to Kirtland in great agitation to see the prophet in behalf of the Mormon refugees in Clay County. They reported that Governor Daniel Dunklin had investigated the mob action in Zion, arrested Colonel Pitcher for disarming the Mormons, offered to send the militia to escort the Saints back to their homes and suggested that the Saints organize and apply for public arms. The Mormons, however, felt that the governor's offers were meaningless because he had indicated that he could not maintain a guard after the Mormons were reinstated, and no matter how well they were armed, the Saints in Missouri would be hopelessly outnumbered. Parley Pratt and Lyman Wight had come to ask the prophet for an army to march to Missouri to restore the Mormons' rights and save Zion.

Joseph had a revelation February 24 which approved this plan:

Behold, I say unto you, the redemption of Zion must needs come by power; Therefore I will raise up unto my people a man, who shall lead them like as Moses led the children of Israel . . . Mine angels shall go up before you.[1]

The revelation said that Parley Pratt and Lyman Wight should not return to their brethren until they had raised a company of five hundred men to go to Zion, but added that since men did not always do the will of the Lord, three hundred or one hundred would suffice.

Meanwhile, on April 10, the Saints in Missouri sent a petition to President Jackson reiterating their grievances. They declared that no impartial investigation could be made in their own territory because the magistrates were among the offenders, and added that the powers of the governor seemed inadequate to effect justice. They asked the President to call out the federal troops to protect their rights, mentioning that the outrages against them had been committed within thirty miles of the United States military post at Fort Leavenworth on the Missouri River.

On the same day the Saints wrote to Governor Dunklin telling him about their petition and asking him to write to the President on their behalf. Dunklin replied that he would have to see the petition before he could support it but he believed the Mormons were asking for more than the President had power to do.

This, in fact, was the view taken by the President. In his behalf, the War Department replied to the Mormons on May 2, 1834:

> The offenses of which you complain are violations of the state . . . and not of the laws of the United States. The powers of the President under the constitution and laws to direct the employment of a military force . . . extend only to proceedings under the laws of the United States.[2]

To the Saints, this seemed to reaffirm that they must defend their rights for themselves.

After a recruiting campaign of two months, however, they raised fewer than two hundred volunteers and some $500—about $200 from Kirtland and $251.60 from members in the east. In the record book Joseph was keeping in his own hand at that time, he made notes about the money received from the Saints for Zion's Camp, and it came in very small but willing amounts from the impoverished Saints, about $5 per donation, and from one sister, apparently straining to the utmost, $7.60.

In a printed brochure of May 10, 1834, Sidney Rigdon and Oliver Cowdery wrote that the volunteers were "sufficiently strong in the strength of the Lord," but that they would like to see "the propriety of more numbers"; that if ten men were to go the mob would be inclined to attack, thinking they could overpower them, but if many went the mob would run away or stop their acts of aggression. They added that if the Mormons quietly submitted to abuse no one embracing the gospel would be safe in any part of the country.[3]

Joseph and the brethren made ready to go. A little more than half were to leave from Kirtland under Joseph Smith and the rest from Pontiac, Michigan, where volunteers had gathered under the leadership of Hyrum Smith and Lyman Wight. On April 19, Sidney Rigdon was set apart to preside over the church in the prophet's absence. Only a few of the brethren would be left in Kirtland with him—Oliver Cowdery, several men working on the temple and the old and infirm.

On Sunday, May 4, in Kirtland, Joseph preached under the shade of the partly raised schoolhouse. He bore testimony of the truth of the work and admonished the Saints to be faithful and patient and to obey God's commandments. To the soldiers of Zion's Camp, as the little army came to be called, he said that those who lived as they should would return safely, but those who did not would be visited by God's wrath.

According to the *Painesville Telegraph* of May 9, 1834, Joseph also told the troops that he himself was ready for martyrdom.

William McLellin thought that raising an army was a mistake, and that the ardor of the men of Zion's Camp was not altogether religious. In expressing his opinion sometime later, he wrote:

> But O! fatal day for the Church! Her ministers, yea, her GREAT ONES, caught the fire of war in their bones . . . Their hearts beat high for distinction and for glory. Their faith now, instead of being fixed in the God of Daniel for the deliverance of Zion, is centered in their own all powerful arms . . . A different spirit had seized almost the whole ranks of the Church, from what had hitherto propelled them onward.[4]

To others, however, this was not a military adventure, nor merely an endeavor to regain their rights; it was a crusade to recover Zion, their holy city, their refuge against the holocaust before the millennium. As Oliver Cowdery wrote just before Zion's Camp began the march:

> . . . it is of little consequence to proclaim the everlasting gospel of men, and warn them to flee to Zion for refuge, when there is no Zion, but that which is in possession of the wicked. Lo, Zion must be redeemed, and then the Saints can have a place to flee for safety.[5]

On Sunday night, their last before leaving Kirtland, members of the Camp packed their gear. Among the eager recruits making ready were two of Joseph's young cousins, both then about seventeen, George Albert Smith, the son of Joseph's Uncle John, and Jesse Smith, the son of Joseph's Uncle Jesse, who had expressed antagonistic feelings about *The Book of Mormon.* Young Jesse, who had left his home in upstate New York, had arrived in Kirtland only a short time before and announced his intention of joining the Camp. Knowing his father's feelings about the church and suspecting that he would object strenuously to Jesse's plan, Joseph's mother attempted to dissuade the youth, but in vain. George Albert, who suffered from a chronic inflammation of the eyes, could not see well, but he said with obvious pride that he had been selected to go by Joseph Smith himself. George Albert's father gave him a musket called a queen's arm, a pair of pantaloons made of striped bed ticking, two cotton shirts, a straw hat, a cloth coat and vest, a blanket and a pair of new

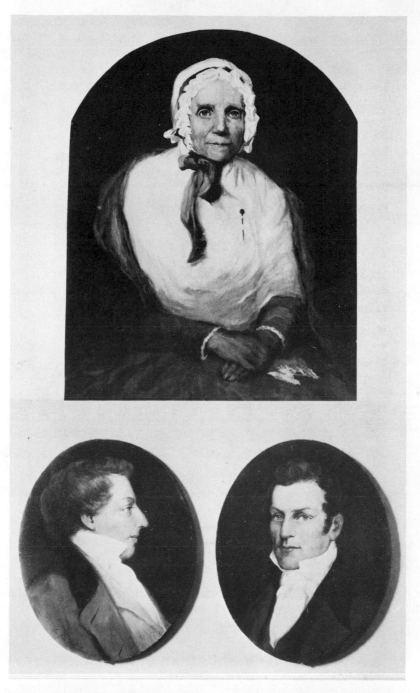

Lucy Mack Smith, with her sons Joseph (*left*) and Hyrum (*right*). UTAH STATE HISTORICAL SOCIETY.

The three witnesses to *The Book of Mormon: (clockwise)* Oliver Cowdery, Martin Harris and David Whitmer. UTAH STATE HISTORICAL SOCIETY.

Parley Pratt, an early convert and one
of the original apostles of the church.
UTAH STATE HISTORICAL SOCIETY.

Orson Pratt. Converted by his brother
Parley, he also became an original
apostle and early leader of the church.
. UTAH STATE HISTORICAL SOCIETY.

The Mormon temple at Kirtland, Ohio. COURTESY OF THE LIBRARY OF CONGRESS.

Meteoric shower of November 13, 1883.

boots, and his mother packed up a knapsack for him made of apron check.

On Monday morning, May 5, the army set out, most of them on foot, armed with whatever they could find, muskets, pistols and swords, and taking twenty wagonloads of clothing and provisions for the relief of the Saints in Missouri. Two companies of sharpshooters rode on the flanks.

The men were organized into companies of twelve, under captains of their own choice, and assigned duties to cook, tend horses and wagons or set up tents. With them went eleven wives of the soldiers and seven children. Parley Pratt was to continue as recruiting officer with the job of raising additional men, arms, stores and money along the way.[6]

Captain of one company was Brigham Young, who had provided himself with a gun, bayonet, dirk, ax and, perhaps in case of extremity, some farm tools.

Best armed in the camp was Joseph Smith, who carried an excellent sword, a rifle and a brace of silver-mounted, brass-barreled horse pistols that had been captured from a British officer in the War of 1812. Fearing that spies intended to take the prophet's life if they could identify him, the men called him Squire Cook. Joseph often changed his place in the ranks, and for additional protection, Samuel Baker gave him a great bulldog, which soon became devoted to the prophet and was constantly by his side. However, the dog could not well distinguish friends from foes and before long was hated by most of the men in camp.

The brethren traveled twenty-seven miles the first day. George Albert's new boots soon blistered his feet, but to his great relief, Joseph gave him a pair of his own. George Albert was chosen to be in Joseph's mess, and slept in Joseph's tent at his feet. After a long day's march, he had to bring water, make a fire and run errands for their cook, Zebedee Coltrin. The men bought flour and meal and baked their own bread. Their food was generally good but sometimes scanty.

The army arrived at New Portage on May 6, and there the brethren consecrated all their money into a common fund.

The plan was to travel ostensibly as settlers, and to separate at towns and pass through individually, avoiding questions. The fact that they were an armed body of men traveling with very few women and children made this subterfuge unlikely, and despite all precautions, they roused a great deal of curiosity. Occasionally townsfolk followed the company for some distance asking questions, which the Mormons would answer politely and vaguely, saying that they were from the east and going west, and that they had no particular leader but took turns being in charge. When they passed through Dayton, Ohio, on May 16, a whole delegation came out to make inquiries.

George Albert Smith said that the curious would usually approach him as the greenest-looking member of the camp. Though large, George Albert looked very young and usually fell to the rear, cutting a sorry figure in his bed-ticking pantaloons, which had soon become ragged, and his battered straw hat, which he had accidentally sat upon in the tent. He seemed so artless that the prophet delegated him to answer questions as they passed through the towns. George Albert wrote that he had many amusing conversations with the inquisitive, and though he tried to speak to them courteously, he did not think they learned much from him.

Once or twice men tried to steal the Camp's horses. Guards were posted at night and vigilance was maintained at all times.

The army did not abandon religious discipline for the military, however. Every evening and again at 4 A.M., in answer to a trumpet blast, the men knelt in their tents for prayers.

When strangers turned up at their Sunday services in camp, the Mormons preached diversionary sermons to give the impression that they were Baptists, Methodists, Campbellites or some other denomination.

After Sunday meeting on May 18, when they were camped in Indiana, Joseph sat in his tent to write to Emma, telling her that William, Jesse and George were in good health, humble and determined to be faithful, and that all the Kirtland brethren were well and could not fail.

However, the trek was a thousand miles, and would take forty grueling days. To avoid being observed the men often took muddy side roads through heavy woods and each day could make only twenty-five to forty miles. It was hot, and the untrained soldiers soon grew weary of the march. They began to say that the Lord did not require such a tiresome journey.

Sylvester Smith one day refused to share his bread with Parley Pratt, who had to go without. Joseph chastised Sylvester, telling him to beware of the Lord's wrath. The next morning every horse in camp was sick. This Joseph proclaimed was God's admonition, and advised the men to humble themselves. The only horse which failed to recover belonged to Sylvester Smith.

On May 26, the army passed through Paris and came to a stretch of prairie of sixteen miles. The prairie was a great curiosity to the easterners, who were astonished at the deceptive distances, and chased a deer across the plains for some time before they realized it was out of reach. The prairie added to their problems. The heat grew intense and the only water they could find had to be strained of live "wigglers" before it could be drunk. They had to guard against rattlesnakes.

The Camp was detained at Decatur township while one of the brethren bought a horse. As a diversion, Joseph separated the men into three sections for a sham battle. He sent two parties off into the woods to execute an attack on the camp. To his satisfaction a number of the captains showed more military skill than he had expected and the spirits of all were raised. Heber C. Kimball became overenthusiastic, however, and grasped the sword blade of an opponent during a charge and had the skin cut off the palm of his hand.

The improvement in morale did not last after hardships increased on the road. Wagons got stuck in the mire and had to be pulled out with ropes. The heat became oppressive, provisions dwindled, water ran out, bread went sour, the bacon and cheese became infested with maggots, some men got colic and all of them endured blisters and bleeding feet. Tempers grew short and quarrels more frequent.

To add to their troubles, the horses bloated from eating dry corn and prairie grass. The men doctored them with tobacco, copperas and cayenne pepper stirred into whiskey when available, which concoction they called "18×24" and declared that it would cure a sick horse in a few minutes. Nevertheless, or perhaps in consequence, not all of the horses survived.

According to George Albert Smith, some members of the Camp were always willing and never murmured. Among them he mentioned Samuel Baker, a former soldier who had given Joseph the watchdog, and who taught George Albert useful lessons in military discipline. Now almost eighty years old, Baker walked the whole journey, refusing lifts offered by the teamsters, saying, "God commanded me to go to Zion, and go signifies to walk, not to ride."

George Albert said this was considered a rather stern interpretation by some of the young men, who were not above resting for a mile or two in a luggage wagon when the opportunity came.

To George Albert, however, most remarkable for humility and forbearance was the prophet himself. Constantly at Joseph's side, and probably in a better position to observe him than anyone else in the camp, George Albert said that Joseph took his full share of the fatigues of the journey, suffering blisters and bloody feet with the rest, but during the entire trip he never uttered a complaint, while most of the men came to him to grumble over everything, and "even a dog could not bark at some men without their murmuring at Joseph." George Albert wrote, ". . . many of us were careless, thoughtless, heedless, foolish or devilish, and yet we did not know it. Joseph had to bear with us and tutor us like children."[7]

It was his habit to provide for the men before himself, to do so with good humor and to persuade the members of his company to do the same.

Even so, the others were often ungrateful. In one town, Joseph bought twenty-five gallons of honey and a dozen cured hams. Since there were not enough hams for everyone, Joseph's company agreed to eat mush and honey for supper. They had scarcely finished their inadequate meal when six hams were flung down at the tent door with the outraged cry that the men did not eat stinking meat. The hams were a little damaged on the outside, but Joseph called his cook to fry them and his company satisfied their hunger for the first time in two days.

More and more concerned about the fractious spirits of some of the men, Joseph called them together at noon on June 3 and told them that the Lord had revealed to him that a scourge would come upon the Camp unless the men repented. Heber C. Kimball afterward recalled this prediction, and in his view this was what did take place, "to the sorrow of the brethren."[8]

The army reached the banks of the Mississippi on June 4. At the point of their crossing, the river was a mile and a half in width, and with only one ferry operating, it took two days to get all of the men to the other side. While some were crossing, others augmented the store by hunting and fishing. One of the brethren in Sylvester Smith's company used the time to make a fife out of a stick of sweet elder. Sylvester's company was the last to cross. He marched his men smartly into camp single file to a tune on the fife, but this so excited Joseph's watchdog that it barked at the men as though they were the enemy. Sylvester shouted at the prophet in a rage.

The next morning Joseph heard further complaints about the dog. According to the account George Albert Smith wrote in his journal for June 6, Joseph told the men he would give them a sample of the spirit of the Camp, saying, "If a dog bites me, I will kill him. If any man insults me, I will kill him. If any man injures me I will injure him. And this spirit keeps up division and blood shed throughout the world."

At this Sylvester Smith came up and said, "If that dog bites me I will kill him."

By this time, apparently even Joseph's patience was giving out, and he answered, "If you kill that dog I will whip you." He added "in the name of the Lord," that if Sylvester did not get rid of his wicked spirit, the day would come when a dog would gnaw his flesh. "You are prophesying lies in the name of the Lord!" Sylvester cried. Others reported that there would have been a fight between Sylvester and Joseph if the brethren had not intervened. Brigham Young later said that Joseph turned to the men and asked them if they were not ashamed of such a spirit, adding, "I am."[9]

On June 7, the company camped in a woods near Salt River, Missouri, where members of a little branch of the church gave them every help. The army remained there until June 12, washing, mending and baking, repairing their firearms and shoeing their horses. Here on June 8 Hyrum and Lyman Wight joined Joseph with the volunteers who had marched from Michigan. With those who had joined along the way, the Camp now numbered 205 men and 25 baggage wagons. Joseph took great pleasure in the company, and said they were delightful to see, young men and a group of fourteen older men called the Silver Greys, who took meals with Joseph.

At this point, Joseph was acknowledged commander in chief of the army, and chose twenty men as his lifeguard, with his brother Hyrum as captain and George Albert as armor-bearer.

George Albert enjoyed his new duties, which relieved him of some of his work for the cook. He went with Joseph nearly everywhere, carried his arms and kept them clean, polished and loaded.

Lyman Wight, who was made general of the camp, second in command under Joseph, marched the men out to the prairie, inspected their firelocks, ordered target practice and drilled them for half a day. The brethren were also taught swordsmanship by a convert from Ireland who had served more than twenty years in the British dragoons. The men of Zion's Camp began to feel more like soldiers and some were looking forward to combat.

DISASTER
IN ZION'S CAMP

J oseph's contention that spies were watching the Camp was perhaps true, for a man from Ohio sent the postmaster of Independence, Missouri, a letter which was printed in the *Missouri Intelligencer and Boon's Lick Advertiser* June 7, 1834, saying that the Mormon army had "every kind of instrument of destruction from scalping knives to double-barrelled rifles." The letter gave an exaggerated count of their numbers as between two and six hundred men and said that a dissenter had informed him that they were trying to enlist the aid of the Indians in their "holy war" against Jackson County.

On June 14, John Corrill wrote to the editor of *The Evening and Morning Star* about rumors in Jackson County that the Mormon refugees were coming back as a mob. The whole county was raised in alarm by men riding in every direction, crying, "The Mormons are coming—they are now crossing the river—they are coming to kill, destroy!" Terrified women and children were hiding in the woods while two or three hundred men, armed with the confiscated Mormon guns, were banding against the Mormons and setting up guards at ferry landings from one end of the county to the other. For fear that Mormons would return to their property, they set fire to houses and destroyed fences. Corrill wrote that he was at a loss to understand the alarm, because the Saints were attending to their own affairs and had no thought of trying to come back at that time, and never any thought of returning as a mob.[1]

Soon it was told throughout Missouri that an army from Ohio, including hired men, was marching upon the state and that they carried a flag with "peace" on one side and "war or blood" on the other. Horror stories were spread that the Mormons intended to slay the women and children. One citizen in Liberty wrote to a friend that Joseph Smith and five hundred well-armed young men were camped within a mile and that citizens from Jackson and neighboring counties were ready to do battle.[2]

Sentiment in the state was not entirely against the Mormons. The editor of the *Missouri Intelligencer and Boon's Lick Advertiser* wrote on June 21 that the people of Jackson County would now probably reap the bitter fruits of their lawless acts. Since the courts in that county were virtually closed to them, the Mormons were taking the only course they probably could to obtain redress. The editor said he regretted that the people of Jackson had forgotten their duty to the government, adding, "it is doubtful whether in this contest they have the sympathies or even the respect of a large portion of the state."

Nevertheless by the middle of June most of western Missouri was taking up arms to oppose the Mormons.

Knowing this, the refugee Saints in Clay County began trying in desperate haste to replace the weapons taken from them by the state militia. They set up an armory and manufactured swords, knives, rifle stocks and pistols. The women molded bullets.

With both sides arming, it appeared to all that a war was imminent.

Until this time, Governor Dunklin had given the Saints reason to believe he would support their cause. He had repeatedly said that he would call out the militia to escort them back to their land whenever they were ready to return, although he had warned that he could not leave the militia there to protect them once they were home. On June 6, 1834, he had written to Colonel J. Thornton, "A more clear and indisputable right does not exist, than that of the Mormon people, who were expelled from their homes in Jackson County, to return and live on their lands." He had added that his course as the chief executive of the state was plain. Already, however, his growing anxiety was evident. In the same letter, he wrote:

Rumor says that both parties are preparing themselves with cannon. That would be illegal . . . I am told that the people of Jackson County expect assistance from the adjoining counties, to oppose the Mormons in taking or keeping possession of their lands. I should regret it extremely if any should be so imprudent as to do so . . . The citizens of Jackson county have a right to arm themselves and parade for military duty in their own county . . . but if citizens march there in arms from other counties without order from the commander-in-chief . . . it would produce a very different state of things. Indeed, the Mormons have no right to march to Jackson county in arms, unless by order or permission of the commander-in-chief; men must not "levy war" in taking possession of their rights, any more than others should in opposing them in taking possession . . . The character of the state has been injured in consequence of this unfortunate affair; and I sincerely hope it may not be disgraced by it in the end.[3]

Joseph sent Orson Hyde and Parley Pratt to Jefferson City to ask the governor to fulfill his promise to reinstate the Mormons. By the time the messengers arrived, Dunklin's alarm about the possibility of civil war had overcome his resolve to serve justice, and he told the elders that he could not reinstate the Mormons "on the ground of impracticability." Dunklin was now basing his hope for their cause upon his application for a federal arsenal for Jackson County, which should, he thought, make federal troops available to help protect the Mormons. He was also considering dividing the county into areas for Mormons and non-Mormons.

Hyde and Pratt rejoined Zion's Camp on June 15 and gave the prophet the governor's decision. Despite their bitter disappointment, Joseph and his men remained confident in the help of the Lord. They marched ahead twelve miles and crossed the Chariton River at its mouth. Here to the prophet's joy, Bishop Edward Partridge visited the Camp bringing welcome news from Clay County that despite their danger and hardship, unity and good feeling prevailed among the refugees.

The next day, June 16, some of the Mormon refugees and some citizens of Clay County, in all about eight hundred people, met at the courthouse in Liberty, Clay County, where a deputation from the old residents in Jackson County came to make an offer. Implying that Mormons and non-Mormons could not live together peacefully in their territory, the old residents presented a proposal to buy all the Mormon land and improvements at double value. The value was to be determined by three men approved by both parties, with the aid of twelve Mormons. The old settlers were to pay within thirty days, and the Mormons were to agree never to return to Jackson County. As an alternative, the old settlers offered their property on the same terms.

Hot speeches were made by anti-Mormons, including one of the Jackson County delegation, Samuel C. Owens. The Reverend Riley cried that the Mormons had been in Clay County long enough, and "they must either clear out or be cleared out." Judge John F. Ryland, who had called the meeting, tried to mediate. He admonished the old settlers to obey the laws and told the Mormons that the whole upper country was hostile toward them, and that if they should retake Independence, hundreds from adjoining counties would swoop down upon them in revenge. The moderator of the meeting, Turnham, raised a plea for reason, saying, "Let us honor our country and not disgrace it like Jackson County. For God's sake don't disfranchise or drive away the Mormons. They are better citizens than many of the old inhabitants."

Alexander Doniphan exclaimed, "That's a fact . . . I love to hear that they have brethren coming to their assistance. Greater love can no man show, than he who lays down his life for his brethren."

This raised a hubbub. Some shouted to adjourn the meeting, others to continue. Someone at the door bawled, "A man stabbed!" The mob rushed out in hope to see a Mormon killed, it was said, but one Missourian had dirked another, and the meeting broke up.

The *Missouri Intelligencer and Boon's Lick Advertiser* of June 28 called the meeting "unsuccessful" and said it was feared the next news would be war.

The offer made by the delegation from Jackson County seemed fair on the surface, but it was in fact a mockery. Most Mormon property had been destroyed, while that of the old settlers was extensive and obviously beyond the Mormons' means. In any case, the Saints could not promise to relinquish Zion. Nevertheless, they agreed to lay the matter before their brethren, saying that peace was their desire, and promised to try to persuade the men of Zion's Camp to stay out of Jackson County until an answer was given.

Some of the Jackson County settlers had no patience with arbitration, however. Samuel C. Owens, James Campbell and fifteen others set out for Independence, where they intended to raise troops against Joseph Smith. Campbell swore that eagles and turkey buzzards would eat his flesh before two days had passed if he did not "fix Joe Smith and his army so that their skins will not hold shucks."

At dusk on June 17, Owens, Campbell and ten of their men started for home across the Missouri River at Everett's Ferry. Their boat capsized in midstream and the party was swept overboard. Campbell disappeared. Three weeks later his body was found lodged on a pile of driftwood some five miles downstream, his bones picked by buzzards and wild animals, which left him, as Joseph later wrote, "a horrible example of God's vengeance." Five others were also drowned. Samuel Owens survived after being swept four miles downstream, losing his clothes and crawling out at last on an island. An account in the *Missouri Intelligencer and Boon's Lick Advertiser* of June 28 reported that some of the committee members returning from their meeting at Liberty had drowned, and the survivors blamed the Mormons. Another page in the same issue carried Owens' account of the event, in which he said he believed that something had been done to their boat. Joseph and the members of Zion's Camp, however, saw it as the work of the Lord for their protection.

Joseph wrote in his journal that the men of Zion's Camp crossed the Wakenda River at noon on the seventeenth. Soon afterward, Joseph was informed that an opposing force had gathered on the Missouri River and intended to attack the Camp. Despite the care of weapons, the drills, and the sham battles the prophet had ordered and enjoyed, he did not want his army involved in actual combat. He loved his men and abhorred blood-shed. His real expectation was that the mere display of strength, with the Lord's help, would allow him to conduct the refugees to their homes in safety.

Now, to avoid a surprise attack, he ordered the men to pack wood and water and march on into a stretch of prairie, where there were no trees to conceal an enemy ambush. Some murmured against the order, and Lyman Wight opposed it outright, preferring to camp in the pleasant grove by the river. Sylvester Smith sided with Lyman, and posted himself in the road, shouting at passing comrades, "Are you following your general, or some other man?" Twenty of them turned back, but the rest went on with Joseph and spent a dreary night with bad water and insufficient wood for fires to cook their dinner. The next morning, Lyman Wight and his men rejoined the main body. When Joseph reprimanded them, Lyman became contrite, but Sylvester furiously accused the prophet of lying again in the name of the Lord.

Zion's Camp pushed on and two days later, June 19, they passed through Richmond in Ray County, where they were warned again that enemies were lying in wait for them. They continued, however, to the border of Clay County, determined to cross over and meet with the refugee brethren. That night they camped on a slight elevation between Little Fishing and Big Fishing rivers.

About two hundred men from Jackson County had in fact assembled and made arrangements to cross the Missouri, above the mouth of Fishing River, into Clay County, where they were to meet some sixty more from Richmond and combine forces against Zion's Camp.

However, a series of anticlimaxes ensued. Zion's Camp and their enemies were never to meet in actual combat. That night a scow crossed with a vanguard of about forty men from Jackson County, but it had just started back for a second load when a great squall blew up. The scow could scarcely make the Jackson County shore before dark. A tremendous thunderstorm followed, with lightning and heavy winds. A cold pouring rain and hailstones as large as hens' eggs drove the men on the Jackson County side under their wagons or to whatever cover they could find. The vanguard had no shelter all night and suffered the relentless pounding of hail, which cut limbs from the trees and beat crops to the ground.

At Zion's Camp, tents were blown down and beds were afloat, but there was no hail. The Saints found a comfortable refuge in a nearby Baptist meetinghouse.

The next morning, the vanguard of Missourians rowed back across the river. Their ammunition was soaked and some of their horses had been frightened off by the storm. It was reported that one of their number was killed by lightning. Joseph saw the storm as the Lord's further protection against his enemies, and even the enemies began to believe it. One declared that if that was the way God fought for the Mormons, they might as well give up. The men set out for home in Independence.

The next day, Joseph and the Camp moved about five miles out again to prairie land.

On June 22, the sheriff of Clay County came to the Camp at the request of Judge John F. Ryland to present the views of the people of Jackson and Clay and to hear what the Mormons intended to do. The sheriff brought the proposal made by the delegates from Jackson County at the riotous assembly at Liberty on June 16. It was in effect an ultimatum that the Mormons sell their land in Jackson County or buy out their enemies, and that they must stay out of Jackson County during negotiations.

To this Joseph replied that it was not the intention of his men to commit hostilities against persons or property, and that the arms they bore were for self-defense, the need for which had been so fully demonstrated in Jackson County.

He made a counteroffer that the Saints would buy the property of anti-Mormons for a sum to be agreed upon by the proposed twelve-man panel, but that the damages they had suffered must be deducted from that amount. He said that the Mormons would pay within a year and would stay out of Jackson County until the debt was settled.

That afternoon, Joseph read a revelation to his army which said that the Saints had not been obedient in sharing with the poor and afflicted, and that Zion could not be built unless it was based upon the principles of the celestial kingdom. The people must be chastened and the elders must wait "for a little season" for the redemption of Zion. The revelation continued, "I do not require at their hands to fight the battles of Zion; for, as I said in a former commandment, even so will I fulfil—I will fight your battles. Behold, the destroyer I have sent forth to destroy and lay waste mine enemies; and not many years hence they shall not be left to pollute mine heritage . . ."

However, the revelation added, "inasmuch as there are those who have hearkened unto my words, I have prepared a blessing and an endowment for them, if they continue faithful. I have heard their prayers, and will accept their offering; and it is expedient in me that they should be brought thus far for a trial of their faith."

The Saints were to sue for peace, buy all the land they could in Jackson County and wait until the Lord's army could become great before they regained their lost property. Those of Zion's Camp who had families would remain in Missouri only a little longer. "Verily I say unto you, it is expedient in me that the first elders of my church should receive their endowment from on high in my house, which I have commanded to be built unto my name in the land of Kirtland."[4]

According to one account, Joseph consoled the men by promising that "within three years they should march to Jackson County and that there should not be a dog to open his mouth against them."[5]

To some of the men, in particular the volatile Lyman Wight, this seemed capitulation. According to Nathan Tanner, some said they would rather die than return without a fight. Drawing their swords, they discharged their anger on a patch of brush and mowed it down like grass. George Albert Smith said that a few men apostatized because they were denied combat.

On June 23, the company went on toward Liberty, Clay County, within five miles of which they were met by David Atchison and a party who advised them not to continue because non-Mormons there were so enraged against them. The company turned aside, crossed a patch of prairie and camped on the bank of Rush Creek, in a field belonging to one of the brethren.

Joseph, William, Jesse, George Albert Smith and several others went to stay at Sidney Gilbert's home about three quarters of a mile from the camp.

On June 20 Joseph had reported that three of the brethren were sick with cholera. On the night of June 24, cholera broke out among others in the camp so suddenly that men standing guard were struck down with their guns in their hands. Moans and cries filled the tents.

Early on the twenty-fifth, most of the healthy members of the Camp were separated into small groups and sent to stay with Saints in the area. That day, Joseph wrote to Thornton, Doniphan and Atchison to say that he wished to adopt every measure to assure peace and would disband Zion's Camp.

In less than a week, sixty-eight members of Zion's Camp were stricken with cholera. Measures to help them were crude. As a remedy for the cramping and vomiting, the victim was dipped in cold water and given doses of whiskey thickened with flour.

Young James Henry Rollins, who had a pony, was kept busy riding to Liberty for medicine and carrying messages from the prophet to Edward Partridge, Isaac Morley and other church leaders.

Men began to die. It was impossible to get coffins. The dead were rolled in their blankets, taken at night on a horse sled and buried on the bank of a stream about half a mile away.

Joseph Bates Noble, who was among the most active in caring for the sick and helping to bury the dead, had an agonizing siege of cramps that lasted about forty hours. William and Hyrum came down with it, and so did Joseph.

Sidney Gilbert died on the twenty-ninth. Four others in his house also died.

James Henry Rollins said that he, George Albert Smith and Jesse Smith were out in the road trying to get a ball out of a pistol which had gotten wet at Fishing River. They were joking and laughing when Jesse said, "We had not ought to be out here making so much noise, while there are so many of our brethren sick and dying in the house."

Soon afterward, Jesse himself fell sick while he and his cousin George Albert were helping to bury one of the victims. Jesse was tended by his cousin for some thirty hours and then George Albert too was stricken.

Jesse Smith, "that noble boy," as his friend James Henry Rollins called him, grew worse. Joseph and others worked over him, administering warm medicines and massaging him, but he died on July 1, lying on the floor in the Gilbert house. The brethren wrapped his body in his bedclothes and buried him with others during a thunderstorm in a shallow grave in the mud.

Joseph took the death of his young cousin very hard, especially, James Henry Rollins thought, because he had probably been entrusted with the boy's care by his parents. No doubt Joseph's awareness of his Uncle Jesse's antipathy toward him and the church augmented his grief.[6]

George Albert too was heartbroken. He told Joseph that it would have been better if he had died, since Jesse had a good education, good eyesight and many other attributes George thought he himself lacked that would have been of use to the church. Joseph replied, "You do not know the mind of the Lord in these things."[7]

In total, Joseph lost fourteen of the brethren from cholera, and his sorrow over them was deep.

On July 3, Joseph authorized Lyman Wight to discharge Zion's Camp and send the members home. The Camp's small common fund was divided among them, each receiving only $1.14.

That day also Joseph organized a High Council in Zion for whatever important business could not be handled by the bishop and his council. David Whitmer was named president, William Phelps and John Whitmer assistants, and twelve councilors were appointed. On the seventh, the brethren were ordained. Benjamin Winchester wrote that David Whitmer was ordained by Joseph to be his successor in case Joseph met with an accident.[8] As William McLellin told it, Joseph said that if he should be taken, David was to head the church, to be prophet, seer and revelator.[9] This has not been accepted as official, however, by most of Joseph's followers.

Soon afterward, Joseph set out for Kirtland in a wagon with Hyrum and several of the brethren.

Some of the Saints were bitter. McLellin later wrote, "Thousands of dollars by this wild expedition had been swallowed up, valuable lives lost, much human suffering endured, and many, very many privations undergone, as well as months of precious time spent worse than in vain . . ."[10]

To Joseph, who often showed the enthusiasm and the imagination of a child at play, Zion's Camp, for all its serious purpose, was very likely a high adventure, at least at first, when the reality of bloodshed was remote. He loved the life outdoors, the campfires, the long palavers in the tents, the fun of organizing troops, the excitement of drills, maneuvers and sham battles. No doubt even the suspicion of spies, the threats of danger and the games of subterfuge were thrilling. The grumbling of his soldiers was a puzzle at first; why couldn't they enjoy it all as much as he did? But it must be said for him that unlike a child, when the fun began to wear thin, when he suffered blistered feet, fatigue, thirst and hunger like the rest, and the tempers of his men grew short, he saw the venture through with courage and good grace. He persisted until the cause was hopeless, when to his shock and horror, his comrades were struck down by sickness and death.

Joseph's affection for the men of Zion's Camp and his grief for those who had died under his command were profound. Brigham's brother, Joseph Young, wrote that the following year, on February 8, the prophet called him and Brigham to the bedroom of his house in Kirtland and told them of a vision he had had. As Joseph Young recorded it, "He said, 'Brethren, I have seen those men who died of the cholera in our camp; and the Lord knows, if I get a mansion as bright as theirs, I ask no more.' At this relation he wept, and for some time could not speak." Joseph Young added that when the prophet recovered, he asked Brigham to call the brethren to a conference at which he would appoint the Twelve, who would carry the gospel to foreign nations.[11]

Zion's Camp has sometimes been presented as a grave mistake on Joseph's part. To members of the Camp who had expected to fight the enemy from Jackson County hand to hand, to rout them with the Lord's help and restore the refugees to their lands, the effort was a blatant failure. However, the ordeal of Zion's Camp brought some unexpected benefits to the Saints. The faithful were welded into a devoted band of brethren whose loyalties to the church, to Joseph and to each other would withstand many future trials and remain lifelong. From among them the subsequent leaders of the church were chosen. The skills learned in moving a large body of people with their wagons, goods and teams through a wide stretch of the country, over barren plains, across swollen rivers, in conditions of summer heat and violent storms, solving problems of food, shelter, discipline and morale, were invaluable for the great migrations from Missouri to Illinois and from Illinois to the Rocky Mountains which lay ahead for the Saints under Brigham Young. Of Zion's Camp, Brigham is reported to have said, "I would not exchange the *experience* gained in that expedition for all the wealth of Geauga County."[12]

LIFE IN KIRTLAND

Whan Joseph got back to Kirtland from Missouri early in August 1834, after a hot and tedious journey, he was surprised to learn that many of the Saints were worried and waiting for an account of what had happened to their men. Roger Orton, who had left the little army when cholera broke out, had traveled as fast as horses could carry him, reaching Kirtland in fifteen days, and had told the Saints that the dread disease was killing all the brethren in Zion's Camp.

The men began to arrive soon after Joseph. They had traveled singly or in small groups as best they could with very little money, most of them weak from fatigue, exposure and the devastations of disease. George Albert Smith, though a large, strong youth, was tormented by ague for six months after his return.

Some were bitter about what they considered to be the failure of the mission and the waste of time. Later that year, in December, a number sued the prophet for back pay for their military service. A few apostatized.

Sylvester Smith was not content merely to complain; he brought the prophet up before the church leaders on charges which Joseph described as "black as the author of lies himself." Among other things, Sylvester called him king, usurper, abuser of men and false prophet. Worse, he accused Joseph of prophesying lies in the name of the Lord and of taking money consecrated to the Camp.

On August 11, in a six-hour meeting of High Priests and elders, Joseph justified the public rebukes he had given Sylvester, explained his distribution of Camp money and property and established his innocence to the satisfaction of the assembly. Sylvester then asked forgiveness for accusing Joseph of prophesying lies, and this was accepted as a partial confession.

A council under Newel K. Whitney decided that Sylvester's confession and a statement exonerating Joseph should be published in *The Evening and Morning Star*. Sylvester objected and was then voted guilty of a misdemeanor. Finally, in October, Sylvester sent a retraction to the *Messenger and Advocate*.[1]

Sylvester's quarrel with the prophet was apparently resolved to Joseph's satisfaction, because Sylvester was soon appointed to an important new office, and later he served as Joseph's scribe. In triumph Joseph was never vindictive.

Meanwhile, one of the results of the expulsion from Jackson County was the dissolution of the Law of Consecration among the Saints in Zion. In Ohio the Law of Consecration was abolished by the Kirtland council on April 10, 1834, just a few weeks before Zion's Camp began the long march. Making a just distribution of community holdings was difficult, but Joseph's revelation of April 23 assigned church property as stewardships to various leaders. Sidney Rigdon was given charge of the tannery, Oliver Cowdery and Frederick G. Williams the printing office, Newel K. Whitney the store and Joseph the temple lot. These and other leaders received the lots on which they were living and other property was to be sold.

In the same revelation Joseph was allowed "this privilege for once" of mortgaging properties that had belonged to the church under the Law so that the Saints could be "delivered out of bondage."[2]

Sidney Rigdon was reluctant to abandon the Law of Consecration, since a communal society had always been his particular ideal. Joseph was to make only one more effort, in 1838, to reinstate the Law, but again it would fail. Nevertheless, tradition has remained among the Saints that the Law of Consecration is the will of the Lord, and will be reestablished when the Saints prove worthy.

During the next two years a number of petty troubles beset Joseph and the Saints—quarrels, recriminations and trials before the church council, some of which resulted in reprimands or disfellowships. The wrongs the Saints had suffered in Missouri were not redressed, but were followed by more wrongs there and harassment in Kirtland. However, it was always Joseph's fervent endeavor to keep his community devout, cohesive in spirit, well provided for, educated and obedient to the decrees and revelations he gave as prophet of the Lord. Under his determined leadership, the Saints in Kirtland worked hard and remained devoted and optimistic. They built houses, developed farms and industries and worked on the temple with great enthusiasm and self-sacrifice. They set up another newspaper, the *Latter-day Saints' Messenger and Advocate,* to replace *The Evening and Morning Star,* which was discontinued after the few numbers issued in

Kirtland. Joseph established new offices and functions in the priesthood and a foreign ministry, consistent with his conviction that the church as the new and last dispensation of the gospel of Christ was intended for all peoples of the earth.

During the winter of 1834–35, the Saints worked on a building to house their printing office and a school for the elders, where they could attend lectures on theology and prepare to serve missions for the church.

Early in the year 1835, under Joseph's direction, twelve apostles were chosen by the three witnesses to *The Book of Mormon* and ordained "to go to all nations, kindreds, tongues and people." They were Brigham Young, Heber C. Kimball, Luke S. and Lyman E. Johnson, Orson Hyde, William E. McLellin, David W. Patten, Orson and Parley P. Pratt, John F. Boynton, Thomas B. Marsh and William Smith. The brethren were told they were to receive their endowments in the temple, after which they were to prepare their minds to bid a long farewell to Kirtland.

Joseph made other changes and ordinations, also. He changed his own title from "first elder" to "president" and made Oliver Cowdery assistant president, in acknowledgment that he had remained second elder all the while his duties had been in publishing for the church.

He also ordained the first Quorum of Seventy, who were selected from the members of Zion's Camp, and organized the chosen into seven groups of ten, each group under a president. Among the first quorum were Joseph B. Noble and George Albert Smith, and among the presidents, Joseph Young and Sylvester Smith.

The church now had five governing bodies, all of equal authority according to revelation—the presidency, the Twelve Apostles, the Seventies, and the High Councils of Kirtland and Zion. When the Apostles began to exert the most influence, despite protest from the other authorities, Joseph had a revelation on March 28, 1835, which established the president as supreme over the church, to be seer, revelator, translator and prophet. The Apostles were designated as a traveling High Council under the president's direction. The revelation named specific duties of each holder of the two branches of the priesthood, the Melchizedek and the lesser Aaronic.

Joseph Smith, Sr., was appointed patriarch of the church, with the duty and privilege of giving patriarchal blessings, at a slight compensation and expenses. Sidney Rigdon was made first counselor to Joseph, and Hyrum, second. Don Carlos Smith, the prophet's youngest brother, was made president of the High Priests.

On March 12, Joseph proposed to the Apostles that they take their first mission to the eastern states. They decided to start early in May, and to hold conferences in the several branches of the church which now existed in New York, Canada, Vermont, Massachusetts, New Hampshire and Maine.

Harmony existed in Kirtland for a while that spring. William Phelps, who arrived from Missouri in the middle of the month, wrote to his wife on May 26 that there was a great deal of "sameness" among the Saints in Kirtland. "They keep the word of wisdom, drink cold water, and don't even mention tea and coffee; they pray night and morning."[3]

That summer, however, criticism of the prophet was made by some church members and discord arose among the leaders. Rumors began to spread about Joseph and the seventeen-year-old girl, Fannie Alger, whom he and Emma had taken into their home. The word "polygamy" was whispered. Memoirs of several members of the church mentioned the situation, sometimes defensively, sometimes with indignation.

Questioned years afterward about Joseph Smith's early practice of polygamy, Benjamin F. Johnson, a faithful Mormon all of his long life, said he scarcely knew how to answer wisely, because sometimes it was better to withhold the truth. However, Benjamin admitted that during this period he had learned from his sister's husband, Lyman R. Sherman, one of the presidents of the first Quorum of Seventy, that Joseph had told him that the ancient practice was to be restored in the church.

Benjamin was about Fannie's age, knew her as a very nice and lovely young woman, and said that he was "partial to her," as everyone seemed to be. He heard whispers even at that time that Joseph loved her, and Warren Parrish told him later that he and Oliver Cowdery both knew that Joseph had had Fannie as a wife, because the two had been watched and found together. Benjamin said that he realized later that Joseph's polygamy was one cause of disruption and apostasy in Kirtland, although it was rarely discussed in public.

Benjamin wrote, "Without doubt in mind, Fanny Alger was, at Kirtland, the Prophet's first plural wife, in which, by right of his calling he was justified of the Lord (see D. & C. Sec. 132:59–60) while Oliver Cowdery, J. Carter, W. Parrish, or others, were not justified in their criticisms upon the doings of the Prophet, or in their becoming a 'law unto themselves,' thru which they lost the light of their calling and were left in darkness."[4]

Oliver Cowdery was more than merely critical. He denounced Joseph in a letter to Warren Cowdery, his brother, January 21, 1838, calling Joseph's relationship with Fannie a "dirty, nasty, filthy affair," and despite pressures from Joseph, he would never retract his statement.[5]

According to Benjamin Winchester, who later left the church, there was scandal involving Joseph Smith and two or three families. He said that Joseph announced to a congregation in the temple that since he was empowered to establish the kingdom of God, church members had no right to question what he did. Winchester said this caused great excitement and a number left the church that summer, in 1836.[6]

Others thought the opportunity had come for them to practice polygamy also. Benjamin Johnson wrote that Lyman R. Sherman said of Jared

Carter that "as he had built himself another house, he wanted another wife," but Joseph would not permit it.[7]

Fannie Alger, who eventually moved to Indiana, never either confirmed or denied her relationship with Joseph Smith, even to her brother after the prophet's death. Years later, however, her brother was introduced in the St. George Temple by Heber C. Kimball as "the brother of the prophet's first plural wife."[8]

In August 1835, while Joseph was on a visit to Michigan, William Phelps prepared a statement of church policy on marriage. "Inasmuch as this Church of Christ has been reproached with the crime of fornication and polygamy, we declare that we believe that one man should have one wife, and one woman but one husband, except in case of death, when either is at liberty to marry again." All legal contracts of marriage made before baptism into the church were to be held sacred and fulfilled, the statement said. That month, the article was approved unanimously at a general assembly of the priesthood and the church and was accepted for inclusion in the *Doctrine and Covenants*.[9] The Statement remained in every edition of the *Doctrine and Covenants* until 1876.[10]

Later asked about the validity of this statement, Lorenzo Snow said that any violator at that time would have been cut off from the church. "It would have been adultery under the laws of the church and under the laws of the State, too."[11]

There are records of church enforcement of the law. About two years after its adoption, Uriah and Lydia Ann Hawkins were tried before the High Council for "unlawful matrimony" and disfellowshipped. At the time, the president of the council protested a "baneful tendency of countenancing such practices in our midst."[12]

Exceptions did occur, however. When Newel Knight was called back to Kirtland from Missouri after his wife Sally died there in childbirth, he met and fell in love with an attractive convert named Lydia Goldthwait. Although Lydia returned his feelings, there seemed an insuperable difficulty for the couple in the fact that she had a husband who would neither release her nor join the church. The prophet sympathized with the predicament of his faithful friend, and on November 24, 1835, he performed a ceremony for him and Lydia. Newel recorded in his journal with some pride that this was the prophet's first ceremony, and added that Joseph said at the time that many things about the ancient institution of marriage were yet to be revealed.

The prophet also wrote of that occasion. Emma went with him to the Knight home, where a large company had assembled. After prayers, Joseph asked the bride and groom to rise and join hands. He told them that marriage was instituted of heaven in the garden of Eden and should be solemnized by the everlasting priesthood. In a service which he said was original with him, Joseph asked if they did covenant to be each other's companion through life and discharge the duties of husband and wife in every respect. To this they assented, and he pronounced them husband and wife in the name of God, with the blessing the Lord had conferred upon Adam and Eve, to multiply, and the addition of long life and prosperity. The following April, Newel and Lydia left to make a new home in Clay County, Missouri.[13]

Although the Mormons had been forbidden to perform marriages by the Geauga County Court on the grounds that they were not regularly ordained ministers, Joseph performed another marriage ceremony in December 1835, three on January 17, 1836, and another on the twentieth. Not long afterward he devised a certificate which said, "I hereby certify, that, agreeable to the rules and regulations of the Church of Jesus Christ of Latter-day Saints, on matrimony, Mr._____and Miss_____, both of this place, were joined in marriage, on_____." To this were added place and Joseph's signature and title as presiding officer of the church.[14]

On March 20, Joseph had a number of elders' licenses to marry made at the printing office and sent them to the court of Medina County to circumvent the Geauga County ban.

The question of polygamy was to remain in limbo, officially denied even after Joseph's announcement of it as a revelation of church doctrine on July 12, 1843, until publicly acknowledged as a tenet of the church by Brigham Young after the Saints migrated to the Rocky Mountains.

During this period in Kirtland Joseph reiterated for the Saints the importance of education, and got the enthusiastic participation of men, women and children in going to school.

On November 3, 1835, Joseph opened the Kirtland School of the Elders with a dedication in the name of the Lord and a comment, as he said, on the "great necessity of our rightly improving our time and reining up our minds to the sense of the great object that lies before us, viz—the glorious endowment that God has in store for the faithful."[15]

That evening he preached in the schoolhouse to a large gathering. Afterward he reported regularly that he attended school and with the others made rapid progress in studies.

The Kirtland School had two divisions, theology and academic subjects. Theology was taught to the elders of the church. Academic subjects, including penmanship, arithmetic, English grammar and geography, were taught under William McLellin's direction to about one hundred students, male and female, young and old.

At the same time, Joseph and his close friends began the intensive study of Hebrew. Very likely what helped to promote their interest in Hebrew was a visit made by Joseph, Oliver Cowdery and other brethren on November 2, the day before the opening of the Kirtland School, to nearby Willoughby College. Willoughby was a new institution of which the dean was John C. Bennett, a man of talent and duplicity, who was later to play a brief but fateful role among the Mormons in Nauvoo. The brethren went to the college that day to hear a lecture in physics by Dr. Daniel Peixotto, who was a Jew. Impressed with Dr. Peixotto, Joseph made him an offer, probably on the spot, to teach Hebrew in the Kirtland School. Although Peixotto did not accept the offer, the brethren's interest in Hebrew was excited.

Oliver Cowdery went to New York later that month to make arrangements to buy a book bindery, and came back with a number of Hebrew books for the Kirtland School. He gave Joseph a Hebrew Bible, lexicon and grammar, a Greek lexicon and an English dictionary. Always eager to add to his knowledge, Joseph wrote with obvious pleasure that he spent the next day at home examining his books and studying the Hebrew alphabet, and that evening he met with the members of Hebrew class, who decided they must have a Jew to teach them, even if they had to send for somebody from New York.

Not long afterward, Joseph found Joshua Seixas, a highly competent young professor about his own age, teaching at the seminary in Hudson, Ohio. Seixas, who was from a distinguished family of American Jews of Portuguese-English descent, had prepared himself to teach Hebrew by studying Aramaic, Syriac and Arabic. He had already devoted several years to a manual on Hebrew, in the hope, as he said, of promoting that best of all studies, the Bible. For a short time he had taught Hebrew at Oberlin, where Lorenzo Snow, later to become fifth president of the Mormon Church, had been one of his students.

The brethren eagerly studied Hebrew for some time before their teacher arrived. Joseph too, despite his many church responsibilities, studied Hebrew whenever he had a spare moment, with friends or by himself at home, in his office or at council meetings, and even while he was ill with a severe cold.

Professor Seixas arrived on January 26, 1836. He and Joseph at once set up a schedule of two one-hour classes per day, five days a week for seven weeks, for which Seixas was to receive $320. Classes began that same day, and Joseph wrote that he was very much pleased with the professor's first lesson.

So many, both men and women, wanted to study Hebrew that by the end of February the conscientious professor was teaching four classes a day. The shortage of books became acute and the students had to take a Bible apart and share it.

Their handicaps notwithstanding, the class Joseph attended began translating from the Hebrew Bible in less than three weeks. Joseph noted with pleasure that the professor called them "the most forward class he ever instructed for the same length of time."

Joseph soon recorded that his "soul delighted in reading the word of the

Lord in the original." He acknowledged the hand of the Lord in the acquisition of his new skill:

> It seems as if the Lord opens our minds in a marvelous manner, to understand His word in the original language; and my prayer is that God will speedily endow us with a knowledge of all languages and tongues that His servants may go forth for the last time the better prepared to bind up the law, and seal up the testimony.

Joseph would have liked to convert the young professor to the Mormon faith. He invited him home for a discussion, and when the professor listened attentively Joseph said he believed that the Lord was striving with him. Joseph considered him "a chosen vessel unto the Lord to do His people good" and was tempted, he confessed, to prophesy upon his head. Since the professor did not respond further, it seems likely that his attention was from courtesy and his silence from a wish to avoid theological controversy.

On February 19, the professor invited nine outstanding students from the first class, including Joseph Smith, to meet with him in special sessions.

At the end of seven weeks, the professor agreed to extend his term to ten, and went home to get his wife and household goods.

Classes continued even during the week of the temple dedication in March, but on March 29, Joseph wrote that he attended the last day of the Hebrew lectures, which was one week short of the agreed time. Two days later, Orson Hyde wrote Seixas a letter of thanks, with no mention of what seems the sudden termination of the classes. With that the conscientious young professor disappeared from Mormon history.[16]

All the while Joseph was studying Hebrew, he was busily at work with another ancient language, Egyptian. In July 1835, four months before the opening of the Kirtland School, Joseph had had a visit from one Michael H. Chandler, who brought with him four mummies and several scrolls of papyri discovered in Egypt in 1831 by his uncle, the French explorer Antonio Sebolo.

At that time, little was known about Egyptian hieroglyphics. Although Champollion had worked out the principles for deciphering hieroglyphics with the aid of the Rosetta stone and had published several works on that subject, his Egyptian grammar would not be published until 1836 and his Egyptian dictionary until 1841. Chandler's hopes of finding someone who could translate his scrolls were dim. Told at the Customs House in New York that nobody in that city could do it, Chandler was pleased to learn of the prophet Joseph Smith's claim to have found and translated plates with similar characters. He found Joseph and the Saints in Kirtland readily interested in the scrolls and mummies. Since he had been disappointed that his uncle had not left him any jewels or other Egyptian treasures,

Chandler was glad to turn a little profit from his inheritance, and sold his scrolls and mummies to the Saints.

Joseph started to work on the scrolls immediately. In his journal for July 1835 he wrote:

> . . . with W. W. Phelps and Oliver Cowdery as scribes, I commenced the translation of some of the characters or hieroglyphics, and much to our joy found that one of the rolls contained the writing of Abraham, another the writings of Joseph of Egypt, etc.—a more full account of which will appear in its place, as I proceed to examine or unfold them. Truly we can say, the Lord is beginning to reveal the abundance of peace and truth.[17]

Later, Joseph rented a room at John Johnson's inn in which to exhibit the mummies and scrolls. Afterward they were shown in an upper room of the temple. They aroused a great deal of interest, but, as always in reports about the Mormons, the truth was mixed with wild rumor. A false story spread that Joseph was trying to attract the gullible with a claim that the mummies were the bodies of Abraham and Joseph of Egypt.

For the rest of the month of July, as Joseph wrote, he was "continually engaged in translating an alphabet to the Book of Abraham and arranging a grammar of the Egyptian language as practiced by the ancients." Apparently he did not use them, however, but conducted his translation of the Egyptian scrolls in his familiar way, which was described as by revelation.[18]

If Joseph received any advice from Seixas about translating the scrolls, he did not mention it. That he had at least one conference with the professor about them is known, however, from his statement of January 30, "Mr. Seixas, our Hebrew teacher, examined the record, and pronounced it to be the original beyond doubt."[19]

Joseph's translation of the scrolls was published in Nauvoo about seven years later in *The Pearl of Great Price; a Selection from the Revelations, Translations, and Narrations of Joseph Smith.* In it with other writings were *The Book of Moses,* "As revealed to Joseph Smith the Prophet, in June, 1830" and *The Book of Abraham,* with the foreword note, "A translation of some ancient Records, that have fallen into our hand from the catacombs of Egypt—The writings of Abraham while he was in Egypt . . . written by his own hand, upon papyrus." In his *Book,* Abraham says that in Chaldea his fathers had turned to the worship of heathen gods and to human sacrifice, but that he protested against the heathen worship and insisted upon his hereditary right of appointment as a High Priest. The Pharaoh of Egypt, though a righteous man, was a descendant of Ham, of the blood of the Canaanites, and for that reason he could not hold the priesthood. An attempt was made to offer Abraham as a sacrifice but he was saved when the Lord destroyed the altar, the priest and the heathen gods and caused great mourning in Chaldea and at the court of the Pharaoh.

Joseph's scrolls remained in the possession of the church for some years after his death. When eventually they disappeared, it was thought that they had been destroyed in the Great Chicago Fire in 1871, but later some of them were discovered in the Metropolitan Museum of New York, where they were recognized by a professor from Utah in 1968 and acquired about a year later by the Mormon Church.

What identified the scrolls as some of those Joseph had worked on were the illustrations, in particular that which Joseph called Facsimile Number 1. The original of this is partly demolished, but in Joseph's reproduction the missing parts were added. The original has been described by one scholar as a well-known scene from the Osiris mysteries in which the jackal-headed god, Anubis, is ministering to the dead Osiris on a bier.[20]

A preliminary study by current Egyptologists indicates that the papyri are writings—spells, religious texts and illustrations, mainly from the Book of the Dead—which were usually buried with a deceased by custom in Egypt from ancient times until the beginning of the Christian era. According to that study, the fragments are comparatively recent, some having been made after 500 and some after 300 B.C.[21]

One suggestion has been made that if examination of these scrolls establishes that *The Book of Abraham* can no longer be considered a direct translation from the Egyptian, the evidence may indicate that it was the "product of a highly intuitive mind stimulated at least in part by an earlier work of revising the creation accounts of the authorized version of the Bible, 1830–1833."[22]

In another opinion, "The problem of Joseph Smith as an inspired prophet never enters into the discussion at all, since that lies entirely beyond the province of scholarship . . . Today nobody claims that Joseph Smith got his information through ordinary scholarly channels."[23]

The evidence so far accumulated suggests that Joseph Smith had no need of the Egyptian papyri to produce *The Book of Abraham,* but he found them stimulating. Feeling in direct communion with the Lord, through the workings of his mind, he believed that he had done a translation.

The Utah church accepts *The Pearl of Great Price,* including *The Book of Abraham,* as Scripture, while other followers of Joseph Smith, among whom are the Reorganized Church and The Church of Christ (Temple Lot), do not.

CHAPTER

8

PROGRESS IN KIRTLAND; PROBLEMS IN CLAY

Joseph and the Saints in Kirtland had a happy winter and spring that year, 1835–36. By the end of November, winter had set in with a blast and snow fell heavily. It was a season for snug fires, jolly company and rewarding study. Joseph attended several weddings and officiated at several others, enjoying the festivities, where cake was served, and sometimes, as he wrote, "our hearts were made glad with the fruit of the vine. This is according to the pattern set by our Savior Himself, and we feel disposed to patronize all the institutions of heaven."[1] Parties and feasts were frequent, and Joseph was "much blessed with company" at home. Meeting with the choir, he noted and praised the singers' progress. Many visitors came from out of town to see the mummies and papyri, some from as far away as New York. Joseph enjoyed the out of doors, also, and frequently noted in his journal that the weather was perfect for sleighing.

Work was progressing on the Saints' beloved temple. Among poor and well-to-do families alike, stories have been proudly told through the generations of money given, hours of labor devoted, gold rings and jewelry sacrificed, and even household china and glassware broken and turned into stucco, which gave the outer walls of the temple a unique glitter. On January 8, Joseph reported that the plastering and hard-finishing outside the temple were completed. The following month the lower room was ready for painting, and Brigham Young left the Hebrew class to supervise the work. The sisters of the church made white canvas curtains, which they called veils, hung so that they could be lowered to divide the main hall into four sections.

The temple was completed in March 1836. The Saints felt they had reason to be proud of their labor and their sacrifice, for they had built the most impressive structure in that part of the country. The long-awaited dedication ceremonies were scheduled for Sunday, March 27.

The Saints began assembling at seven on that morning, two hours before services were to start. Joseph, Sidney Rigdon and Oliver Cowdery seated about a thousand, as many as could be made comfortable, and another thousand greatly disappointed people were left milling about, crowding the doors. Joseph recommended that they hold a meeting in the schoolhouse, which they did, but many were still left out.

Stewards collected $963 in donations, a great sum from the people at that time.

At nine o'clock services began. Sidney Rigdon read psalms, the choir sang, there were prayers and hymns and then Sidney spoke for two and a half hours in what his son John said was considered one of the great efforts of his life. Taking the text, "whatsoever ye shall bind on earth shall be bound in heaven," he reviewed the tribulations of the Saints in building their temple, and said that many large houses existed on the earth for the worship of God, but only this was built by divine revelation.

He then called upon the several quorums and the congregation to signify their acceptance of Joseph as prophet and seer by rising, which they did unanimously. After more hymns, Joseph asked the quorums and congregation to acknowledge the presidency and the other leaders of the church. He then gave the dedicatory prayer.

Don Carlos Smith blessed the bread and wine and it was passed by the elders. Testimonies followed and many spiritual manifestations were reported. David Whitmer and Frederick G. Williams both recorded that they saw angels mingle with those present. Brigham Young spoke in tongues. The people were then blessed by the prophet and dismissed. The rapt congregation had sat without a break for seven hours.

That evening, Joseph met with the quorums. Many spoke in tongues, others prophesied, some said they saw visions. When George Albert Smith stood to give testimony, a noise like a mighty rushing wind filled the temple, and all the congregation rose simultaneously. Joseph reported that he beheld the temple filled with angels.

People of the neighborhood came running at the strange sounds and said they saw a light like a pillar of fire resting upon the temple.

On Tuesday, March 29, Joseph held an all-night meeting with the presidents and their counselors, and on Wednesday at 8 A.M. three hundred brethren came to attend the ordinance of washing feet. The brethren fasted all day, performed their ordinances and at seven in the evening had bread and wine, ordered by the prophet.

Joseph told the brethren that all necessary ceremonies were now performed, and they were ready to go forth and build up the kingdom of God. He left the temple at nine since he had another service to attend in the morning, but the brethren remained all night.

The next day, Thursday, the thirty-first, Joseph and Sidney Rigdon repeated the dedication ceremonies for those who had missed the first service.

On the following Sunday, services were held with a full congregation. After the Lord's Supper, Joseph and Oliver Cowdery went behind the veils and bowed together in silent prayer. Joseph recorded that a vision was opened for them:

We saw the Lord standing upon the breastwork of the pulpit, before us; and under his feet was a paved work of pure gold, in color like amber. His eyes were as a flame of fire; the hair of his head was white like the pure snow; his countenance shone above the brightness of the sun; and his voice was as the sound of the rushing of great waters, even the voice of Jehovah, saying: I am the first and the last; I am he who liveth, I am he who was slain; I am your advocate with the Father. Behold, your sins are forgiven you; you are clean before me; therefore, lift up your heads and rejoice. Let the hearts of your brethren rejoice, and let the hearts of all my people rejoice, who have, with their might, built this house to my name. For behold, I have accepted this house, and my name shall be here; and I will manifest myself to my people in mercy in this house . . . Yea the hearts of thousands and tens of thousands shall greatly rejoice in consequence of the blessings which shall be poured out . . .

In the same revelation, Joseph wrote that Moses, Elias and Elijah appeared and bestowed upon them the keys of their dispensations, Moses the keys of the gathering of Israel and Elias the dispensation of the Gospel of Abraham. Elijah opened the doors of salvation for the dead and said that the great and dreadful day of the Lord was near.[2]

On Monday, April 4, the elders of the church began leaving Kirtland to spread the gospel.

In May, Silas Smith, Joseph's uncle, and others of the Smith family moved to Kirtland. To his delight, the prophet learned that his grandmother, Mary Duty Smith, widow of Asael, was on her way and had already reached Fairport. Joseph and Hyrum went at once in a carriage to bring her home. Although ninety-three years old, she had been determined to see her descendants before she died, and had made the difficult journey of five hundred miles in good cheer. Every one of her descendants whom she had ever seen she recognized, and she was happy to meet her great-grandchildren. She was particularly pleased to see Joseph, and said she

was convinced that he was the prophet whom her husband Asael had long
ago predicted would be raised up in their family.

After a short but happy visit with her descendants, Mary Duty Smith
died in her sleep about sunset on May 27. She was buried in the cemetery
near the temple with her family in attendance. Sidney Rigdon delivered
her funeral address. Although Mary Duty Smith had never been baptized
into the church because of the continued opposition of her eldest son,
Jesse, her daughter-in-law Lucy wrote that she died firm in the faith.

She died just a few weeks before the happy occasion of the birth of
Emma and Joseph's second son, Frederick, on June 20, 1836.

Meanwhile, the Saints in Missouri were not faring so well, and all their
efforts to regain their rights seemed in vain.

Petitions to restore them to their property in Missouri had been
collected from all parts of the country and mailed from Kirtland to Governor Dunklin on December 10. They made such a large package that the
postage, as Joseph noted with some pride, cost five dollars. However, the
governor had replied the following January 22, 1836, that while his sympathies remained with the Saints, he felt, as before, that their only remedy
was through the courts. Dunklin added that the Secretary of War had done
nothing about his request for a depot of arms on the Missouri River near
the western boundary, which he had hoped would give the Mormons some
protection if they should return. It began to seem to the Saints in Missouri
that they had little hope for redress from the state.

In June, William Phelps reported that he and Edward Partridge had
been out on two expeditions to explore the regions of Missouri called "Far
West" as a possible home for the Saints kept out of Jackson County. A
"sort of road" went part way toward Busby Fork, but after that the
brethren had to cross stark prairie, with scrubby timber, deep ravines and
creeks to reach Ray County.

Shoal Creek had some fair mill sites, Phelps wrote, but he was doubtful
about the prairies, which stretched to the horizon and made him feel like a
sailor in mid-ocean. "What the design of our heavenly Father was, or is, as
to these vast prairies of the Far West, I know no further than we have revelation," he wrote. "The Book of Mormon terms them, the land of desolation."

They were not without beauty in his eyes, and put him in awe of the
Lord's work. "The pinks variegate these widespread lawns, without the
hand of man to aid them, and the bees of a thousand groves banquet on
the flowers, unobserved, and sip the honey-dews of heaven." The timber,
however, was insufficient to support a large population, and in any case,
nearly every patch of woods to the northern state line already had someone in it, Phelps had been told. Although he found these back settlers honorable and generous and said of them, "you are in most instances welcome
to the best they have,"[3] the region did not seem suitable for the Saints.

However, as matters developed, it soon proved more hospitable than where they were in Clay County.

The Mormons were finding their presence more and more irksome to the old settlers in Clay County, who had at first been so sympathetic and generous to them in their miserable flight from Jackson County. John Corrill said that the Mormons' enemies in Jackson County tried to incite the people of Clay to drive the Mormons out. Whether true or not, the citizens of Clay were beginning to consider that the Mormons had outstayed their welcome.

Anderson Wilson, who with his two brothers had migrated about 1834 to Clay County from North Carolina but who considered himself one of the old settlers, wrote home on July 4, 1836, voicing the general complaint against the Mormons. They were coming in in great numbers, he said, swarming over the country, living in the woods, in wagons, tents, bark houses and cabins, and in one area four miles long, a rider would not be out of sight of a Mormon "den" the whole route. Wilson wrote that letters from Ohio indicated that the Mormons intended to outnumber the old settlers and rule the county, to buy land at exorbitant prices, offering for example $1,000 for a tract of eighty acres which had sold the year before for $250. Once the Mormons were established, Wilson said, no one but members of their faith would want the land and it could be had at their own price.

Wilson and others especially feared the possibility of Mormon political power. Wilson wrote:

you may See Just where we are we are [sic] to Submit to a mormon government or trample under foot the laws of our Contry . . . To go away was Just to give up all for if emigration once Begun none could buy our land but mormons and they would have it at their own price So we were resolved what to do. We thought of petitioning the governor but He was Sworn. We thought of fleeing. There was no place to flee to. We thought of fiting. This was Cruel to fight a people who had not Broke the law & in this way we became excited. I never Saw as much excitement in my life . . .[4]

Wilson said that on June 24 men were working on the public road, according to the county custom that each man give a specified amount of time, when a number of Mormons came along. The men became angry at the thought that they were building the roads for these invaders, who would finally drive them out. They proposed a meeting, and held one in the schoolhouse four days later, on June 28, which many citizens attended. Resolutions were made to rid the county of the Mormons.

Wilson was sorry to report that several outrages occurred against the Mormons that night. Six of the old settlers went to a Mormon town and after a skirmish pulled a Mormon out and gave him a hundred lashes. It was feared the Mormon would die.

That night the old settlers were alarmed to hear that thirty-five wagons and three hundred more Mormons were headed for their county, and were already within twenty-five miles.

The old settlers rallied a hundred volunteers and the next morning rode out with rifles to meet the Mormons on the road. They announced that the Mormons were not welcome and would proceed at their own risk. The wagons turned back at once, with the old settlers close on their rear.

That same day, June 29, 1836, a mass meeting was held in Liberty, which Wilson attended as a representative of his township, Fishing River.

Among the committee of nine that drew up the report for that meeting were David R. Atchison and A. W. Doniphan, who had already been involved for some time with the Mormon difficulties in Missouri. Their report said:

We cannot conceal from ourselves the fact that at this moment the clouds of civil war are rolling up their fearful masses, and hanging over our devoted country. Solemn, dark and terrible. This painful state of things has been produced mainly by the rapid and increasing emigration of that people commonly called Mormons . . . They always declared that they looked not upon this county as their home, but as a temporary asylum; and that, whenever, a respectable portion of the citizens of this county should request it, they would promptly leave us in peace as they found us.

That period has now arrived . . . Their rapid emigration, their large purchases, and offers to purchase lands, the remarks of the ignorant and imprudent portion of them, that this country is destined by heaven to be theirs are received and looked upon, by a large portion of this community, as strong and convincing proofs that they intend to make this county their permanent home . . .

The report protested that the Mormons were not compatible with their neighbors because they were from the east, with different customs and speech. They were opposed to slavery in a time when abolition was a hot issue in every slaveholding region. The Mormons maintained contact with the Indian tribes on Missouri frontiers and announced that the Indians and Mormons would jointly inherit the land. The report added, not unreasonably, "We do not vouch for the correctness of these statements; but whether they are true or false, their effect has been the same in exciting our community."

The committee asked that the Mormons put an immediate stop to their immigration and recommended the territory of Wisconsin, where vast unsettled tracts could be had, where slavery was prohibited, and the few settlers already there were from the north and east, like the Mormons. In the view of the committee, the tenets of the Mormons were so different from other churches of the times that they always had and always would excite prejudice. They confessed that they could not claim the least right, under the law, to banish the Mormons, but suggested that, if the Mormons had any gratitude for the assistance they had received in their "hour of darkness," they would not remain when to do so was sure to result in war, "ruin, woe, and desolation." They wrote:

> We, therefore, in a spirit of frank and friendly kindness, . . . request them to leave us, when their crops are gathered, their business settled, and they have made every suitable preparation to remove. Those who have forty acres of land, we are willing should remain until they can dispose of it without loss, if it should require years.[5]

To this William Phelps and the Saints in Clay County replied July 1 that they were grateful for the help given them by the Clay County citizens. They denied having claim to Clay County or any other except that of the right to purchase land with money as the laws allowed to any citizens. They said they had taken no part either for or against slavery; but were opposed to abolitionists and considered that men had a right to hold slaves or not, according to law. They also denied communication with the Indians, and held themselves as ready as other people to defend their country against any barbarous attack.

The Mormons agreed, however, that for the sake of friendship and peace they would go away.

Upon receipt of this message, the old settlers appointed a committee of representatives from each township to take up a subscription to help indigent Mormons leave their county.

Anderson Wilson said that further meetings were held July 1 and 2 and volunteer companies totaling five hundred men were formed in the townships ready to drive the Mormons out if necessary. "By this you may see what abomination the mormons is held in the Mo.," he added. In defending their principles at all hazards, as Wilson put it, he claimed they possessed "the spirit of '76" and spoke admiringly of a smooth-faced lad who would not leave his company although he had had nothing to eat since the day before except three biscuits, and of a man, crippled since youth, who marched with his crutch under one arm and his rifle under the other.

Wilson's comment on the decision to take up a subscription for the Mormons was, "I have understood today that they want us to bear their Expenses away or Some of them wont go & if this is the Case it wont Cost us much as high as powder & lead Sells here and these are the only expenses we will pay . . ."[6]

Joseph and the brethren in Kirtland were indignant at the news, and wrote the Saints in Missouri on July 25 that they did not consider the fault to be with them, but they concurred in the decision to leave. They wrote, "be not the first aggressors. Give no occasion, and if the people will let you, dispose of your property, settle your affairs, and go in peace. You have thus far had an asylum, and now seek another, as God may direct." Joseph advised stopping short of Wisconsin, however, if it was possible to do so in peace. "Be wise; let prudence dictate all your counsels; preserve peace with all men, if possible; stand by the Constitution of your country; observe its principles; and above all, show yourselves men of God, worthy citizens, and we doubt not, the community, ere long, will do you justice . . ."[7]

Joseph wrote to Atchison, Doniphan and the committee at Liberty saying that he admired their candor and respected their wish to prevent bloodshed, but in justice he must exonerate the Saints from the "foul charge" made against them and the effort to deprive them of their constitutional rights. It was unjust and untrue to say that the Mormons intended to usurp the country; nothing in their religion warranted that accusation, on the contrary, their religion required strict obedience to the law, and rather than fight in Jackson County they had given up their rights and were still awaiting legal redress. "Should Providence order that we rise not as others before us to respectability and esteem, but be trodden down by the ruthless force of extermination, posterity will do us justice when our persecutors are equally low in the dust with ourselves, to hand down to succeeding generations the virtuous acts and forbearance of a people who sacrificed their reputation for their religion; and their earthly fortunes and happiness to preserve peace . . ."[8]

In response to a new appeal, Governor Dunklin wrote to the Mormons in Missouri, July 18, that he deeply deplored the treatment they had received, but he also made a statement tantamount to a confession that the situation was beyond his abilities. In what seems a blatant denial of minority rights, he wrote:

> Public sentiment may become paramount to law; and when one man or society of men become so obnoxious to that sentiment as to determine the people to be rid of him or them it is useless to run counter to it . . . Your neighbors accuse your people of holding illicit communication with the Indians, and of being opposed to slavery. You deny . . . whether true or false, the consequences will be the same . . . in this Republic the *vox populi* is the *vox Dei*.[9]

The area just northeast of Clay County that Phelps and Partridge had already scouted seemed the best hope for the Saints. They began at once to pack up and move again. The few and isolated settlers there, who probably had little knowledge of the newcomers and their troublesome ideas, made no objection. Mormons bought or laid claim to large tracts and began at once to lay out farms and build new communities. By October 1836, they had a sizable gathering at Shoal Creek, and in December they

petitioned for an act of incorporation for a new county to be named Caldwell.

The Mormons' petition was strongly supported by their friend in the
state legislature, Alexander Doniphan, but it was opposed by the new governor, Lilburn W. Boggs, successor to Daniel Dunklin, who had resigned
in September, shortly before the end of his term. Despite Boggs, the petition was granted almost at once, but Doniphan reported to the Mormons
that because of Boggs, they would have less territory than he had hoped.

The area above Ray County was sectioned into Caldwell County, where
it was supposed that the Mormons would confine themselves, and Daviess
County, adjacent to Caldwell on the north, which some understood would
be reserved for non-Mormons.

Most of the prior settlers in Daviess County had been there only since
early 1834. The first settlers had built their homes in the woods, ignoring
the prairies, because, as it was said, they had always cleared land to establish a farm, and did not realize what good soil for crops the prairie would
have. In the spring of 1834, the prairie was first broken for use in planting
on a tract just three quarters of a mile southwest of what became the little
settlement of Gallatin.

Until one Robert P. Peniston established a corn mill, in a place later
called Millport, the people had to go to Liberty in Clay County to get meal,
or else to pound their corn in a hole burned in a log. The new mill was
considered a marvelous advance to the community and soon changed the
whole area. A general store opened nearby, strongly built but crude in
service, with boxes for counters, and offering only the basics, salt, coffee,
tea, yarns, bar iron for horseshoes, powder and lead, cottons, jeans, boots
and whiskey, which was considered a staple. Until that time, the settlers
had to go to one of the towns along the Mississippi River for supplies.
When a grocery store opened and then a blacksmith shop, the basis was
laid for Millport, the first town in Daviess County, which became a center
for the settlers for miles around. Gallatin also developed, and soon had a
dram shop and a boardinghouse.

Indians in the area were peaceful, living mainly on a government an-
nuity which included an allotment of powder and lead. Before the stores
were instituted, Indians and pioneers had an odd reversal of usual trading
procedures. The Indians would trade their powder and lead to pioneers for
skins, which the Indians would then sell to whites in the settlements along
the riverbanks.[10]

Among the Mormons in Caldwell County the community developed
much faster. At Far West, the county seat, log and frame houses, schools
and shops sprang up and a thriving little community was formed almost at
once. Mormons began to gather from all parts of Missouri to occupy the
land for fifteen or twenty miles around the town. The few non-Mormons
who had already settled in Caldwell made no protest at first that the new-

comers controlled the elections and that most of the county officers (including judges, magistrates and the county clerk) and all officers of the militia were Mormons. The relations between the Mormons and their neighbors started out amicably, and the Mormons hoped that they had found a resting place at last.

THE ANTI-BANKING
COMPANY

With every passing year the Saints in Kirtland found themselves in greater financial difficulty. In undertaking the Lord's commandments through Joseph their prophet to proselytize, build a temple, provide for the unfortunate and prepare for the gathering, the church had assumed obligations far beyond its resources, which were contributions from members who were mostly poor. Old debts for the now dissolved Law of Consecration were pressing, money was due for merchandise obtained in the east on credit, and for the temple. The church had been buying land in Kirtland at high prices, and in addition, the Saints in Missouri desperately needed money for land to make a new start after their expulsion from Zion.

Joseph had tried to better the Kirtland economy in a number of business ventures—a general store, printing press, sawmill and tannery—but had only incurred more liabilities.

In the fall of 1836, he and the other leaders of the church began to consider pooling their resources and establishing a bank in Kirtland. It would, they thought, enable the Saints to pay their debts, give them and their neighbors a needed medium of exchange and improve the economy in Kirtland by keeping capital in the area and providing an incentive to business.

Their possibilities were two: a state-chartered bank, or a stock association with limited power to issue notes. The brethren decided upon an institution to be called the Kirtland Safety Society Bank, and on November 2 drew up articles of agreement. Oliver Cowdery went immediately to Philadelphia to have plates made for printing bank notes and Orson Hyde went to Columbus to petition the legislature of Ohio for a charter.

In setting up their bank, the Mormons were following a common procedure in that period. Conservative banking did not meet the new needs for capital at that time when the national economy was expanding with the growth of industrialization, improved transportation and the rise in population. Capital was needed especially in the west, where labor and raw materials were abundant and opportunities seemed unlimited. After 1832, when President Jackson vetoed renewing the charter of the Bank of the United States and shifted government deposits to favored state institutions, the central controls were off and a great rise in private and state banking occurred. Only 3 commercial banks had existed in the country in 1790, but there were 788 by 1837.[1] Between 1830 and 1837, the circulation of bank notes more than doubled.[2] The federal government accepted bank notes for public lands, which was a tacit encouragement to land speculation. In the laxity of regulations a belief was current that anyone who wished could establish a bank or a stock company. Amateur banking was especially dangerous where it was most frequently practiced, in rural areas and on the frontiers, where long-term loans were needed on little security.

The motive of some who set up banks was to make a quick profit. Sometimes a group of debtors formed a bank and printed their own notes simply to relieve themselves of obligations. Occasional offices were opened in remote places said to be known only to the beasts, with access to them for the redemption of notes so difficult that they became known as "wildcat banks," and were little better than counterfeiting operations.

Many banks, however, like the bank the Mormons hoped to establish in Kirtland, were sincere if overeager efforts to bring about prosperity.

Not all of the Mormons favored the idea. William McLellin said that Joseph and the other church leaders did not wait for a charter, but "seemed to think that everything must bow at their nod—thus violating the laws of the land . . ." Although McLellin, who left the church in 1836, might have misquoted them, he said that the three witnesses to *The Book of Mormon* warned Joseph against "this evil course" but only managed to rouse his anger.[3]

Sidney Rigdon's son John said that his father was opposed to the bank because it had no charter and he believed it would be illegal, but Joseph did not agree, and persuaded Sidney to participate.[4]

In any event, Oliver came back to Kirtland with handsome and expensive plates, while Orson returned empty-handed. To the Mormons the denial of their petition seemed an act of religious discrimination, but their rejection was only one of a number made by the legislature, which was alarmed at the current proliferation of private banks in Ohio and the rising inflation.

A meeting of the Kirtland Safety Society was called on January 2, 1837, to annul the old agreement and adopt a new. The brethren drew up a pre-amble, in which 188 subscribers announced their intention to improve their affairs in agriculture, mechanical arts and merchandising by forming the Kirtland Safety Society Anti-Banking Company. Capital stock would be not less then $4 million, to be divided into shares of $50 each, increasable to any amount at the discretion of the company's thirty-two managers.[5] Sidney Rigdon as president and Joseph Smith as treasurer were to sign the company's promissory notes.

The plan of the bank was to issue notes to landowners in return for mortgages which would become the basis for more notes, a structure which was weak but not uncommon at the time. Subscriptions to the capi-tal stock were mostly paid for in Kirtland lots, estimated during the cur-rent inflation at five or six times normal value. The whole capital stock of the bank was land within an area of two square miles of Kirtland.[6]

The company reportedly printed $200,000 in bills on their new plates. Rather than send the plates back to Philadelphia for an expensive job of reengraving, the leaders took the bills to the printing office in Kirtland and had them stamped to suit the new institution by adding "anti" before and "ing" after the word "bank" on each bill.

Oliver Cowdery said that in the beginning the bank vaults held a fair amount of cash since specie and bills from specie-paying banks had been drawn out of circulation in Kirtland to form the bank's base.

In the Kirtland Safety Society stock ledger, Sidney Rigdon's name is the first entry, dated October 18, 1836, with the notation that he paid $12 for 2,000 shares of stock. The following month he added another 1,000 shares. Sidney, Joseph Smith and two others held 3,000 shares each, which made them the largest stockholders. Of the 69,636 shares subscribed in the ledger, a total of 48,000 were owned by thirty individuals, of whom eight were relatives of Joseph Smith, holding in toto about one sixth of the stock.

The ledger indicates that although the face value of shares was $50, more than 95 per cent of shareholders bought them at 26¼ cents per share, often on credit. That price could have been meant as the first payment on installment, since some of the accounts were so noted, but many shareholders never paid further amounts. Joseph Smith and a few others paid a higher rate than 26¼ per share, and some paid less. A few paid twice that amount, or 52½ cents, and the highest payment was made by Joseph Fielding about three weeks before the final entry was posted, when he bought shares at over four times the prevailing rate. No one paid face value. When it was reported later that stock values dropped to 12½ cents per share, the actual loss was much less than face value indicated. This puts an entirely different light on the losses afterward claimed by shareholders.

Stock might not have actually been issued, since no specimens have been found. It is not known if bank notes were distributed for sub-scriptions, although it is possible that they were put in circulation that way.

Although the bank failed technically in February 1837, business ap-parently continued after that date, since entries were made in the ledger regularly until July 2, when the last entry was posted.[7]

In connection with the bank's articles of agreement, Joseph published a notice in the January *Messenger and Advocate* inviting the brethren from abroad to take stock in the Safety Society. Saints in Canada as well as in the United States invested in the bank, and so did non-Mormons.

Wilford Woodruff recorded that he visited the bank on January 6 and saw the first money issued by the treasurer. He said that he heard Joseph say he had received the word of the Lord that morning about the Kirtland Safety Society, and if the Saints would heed His commandments, all would go well. Wilford wrote, "May the Lord bless Brother Joseph with all the Saints & support the above named institution & protect it so that . . . the Kirtland Safety Society shall become the greatest of all institutions on EARTH."[8]

The Kirtland notes were not acceptable for the money Joseph owed in the east. John Rigdon said because the bank had no charter, Joseph's creditors in New York, Pittsburgh and Cleveland refused to take them in payment. However, Joseph used them for local debts. Among the Saints, the Kirtland bills were said to be "as safe as gold." Wilford Woodruff wrote that now every face was cheerful. The bank, the market and the temple were tokens of a city in prosperity.

Kirtland was like a boom town, however. Its growth in population had been sudden, by now about two thousand Saints, and there were few buildings of substance in the community other than the temple. Most were hastily put up frame houses of board or clapboard. The prophet's house also was small and unpretentious. Nevertheless, some of the Saints now began to think they were rich.

According to John Whitmer, "the whole church partook of the spirit of speculation . . . they were lifted up in pride, and lusted after forbidden things of God."[9]

The unsophisticated thought that owning shares in the stock company had made their fortune, since an investment of only $52.50 for two hun-dred shares would have face value of $10,000. Oliver Cowdery wrote that men who were not thought to be worth fifty dollars began to buy goods to the amount of thousands. Many families ran up great bills for clothing and merchandise. Prices rose outrageously. Tailors charged from fifty cents to a dollar for cutting out a coat and nine dollars for making it. Milliners asked fifty cents for the plainest silk bonnet.

Although in Kirtland at this time many honorable people hoped their bank would improve the economy and enable them to pay their debts, others saw it as a chance to profiteer. Some collected notes at a discount and took them to Joseph demanding redemption in specie at par. Joseph honored the bills as long as he could, but on January 27, only a few weeks after the bank opened, the *Painesville Telegraph* carried notice that the Kirtland bank would not redeem any more notes except with land. Some Saints and their neighbors began trading off their Kirtland bills as fast as possible.

In February 1837, a writ was sworn against Joseph for illegal banking. Brought to court March 24, he pleaded that the state law which the Kirtland bank was accused of defying had not been in force when the bank was organized, but the decision went against him, and he was fined a thousand dollars plus costs. Later he appealed, but his appeal was never ruled upon.

The Kirtland bank was only one that would founder in 1837. When paper money from the new state and private banks had begun flooding the United States treasury, President Jackson had issued the Specie Circular of July 1836, decreeing that the federal government would accept nothing but gold and silver in the sale of public lands. People started hoarding coins, which gradually disappeared from circulation. Bank notes began to go for a discount and some became worthless. A great many banks failed, the exact number never ascertained. Of eighty-nine state banks that were holding over 49 million public deposits and some 26 million individual deposits on November 1, 1836, all but six suspended operations within a year.[10] Losses to the public were enormous and untold. During the great financial crash which occurred that year, 1837, the situation was particularly bad in Ohio. Every bank except one stopped redeeming notes.[11]

Although the Kirtland bank failed technically in February, hope remained, and the bank went on issuing notes for another four months.

On April 6, Joseph spoke to the Saints in assembly, reviewing the church history of poverty and persecution, the debts and the large contracts for land entered into for the Lord's work. He said, "but our brethren from abroad have only to come with their money . . . and every brother that will take hold and help secure and discharge those contracts that have been made, shall be rich."[12]

Despite his difficulties, Joseph had not surrendered his dream for Kirtland. Joseph spoke to the Saints for three hours that day, and described Kirtland as he had seen it in a vision. Wilford Woodruff wrote in his journal that "it was great marvelous & glorious the city extended to the east, west, north & south, Steam boats will come puffing into the city our Goods will be carried upon railroads from Kirtland to many places & probably to Zion. Houses of worship would be reared unto the most high beautiful streets was to be made for the Saints to walk in Kings of the earth would come to behold the glory thereof . . ."[13]

Sidney Rigdon followed Joseph with a plea of his own. "Prey not one upon another, brethren, and for the time being say not, Pay me what thou owest; but contribute all in your power to discharge the great debts that now hang over the church."[14]

That January, Willard Richards had written to his sister, "There is an equality here which exists among no other people; not that they have all things common, but one is not made a king because he is worth 16 more than his neighbor. Is he a righteous man? is the question,— It is not to be expected that a people, coming from the four winds, will be exactly agreed upon all points. No! but there is one thing in which the people see *eye to eye—the gospel.*" He added perhaps wryly, "& should the eyes of any one become dim he can get his vision polished by the prophets as in the days of old." To be a Mormon, he wrote, is "to *believe & practice every known or revealed truth in relation to every being & thing.* This I prepare to do consequently I am a 'Mormon.' "[15]

Now, however, the atmosphere in Kirtland was changing. On Sunday, only a few days after his vision of the future Kirtland and his plea for help, Joseph rose in Sunday meeting, and according to Wilford Woodruff:

> like the lion of the tribe of Judah he poured out his soul in the midst of the Congregation of the Saints but who can find the language to write his words & teachings as with an iron pen in a stock that they may stand for future generation to look upon. A fountain of knowledge rolled from his mouth to the people which was the word of God Even in the name of God he proclaimed that severe judgment awaited those characters that professed to be his friends & friends to humanity & the Kirtland Safety Society But had turned tritors [sic] & opposed the currency.

In Wilford's opinion, Joseph was entirely in the right. "There is not a greater man than Joseph standing in this generation," he wrote in his journal that day. "The gentiles look upon him & he is to them like bed of gold conceled from human view. they know not his principle, his spirit, his wisdom, virtue, phylanthropy, nor his calling. His mind like Enochs swells wide as eternity nothing short of a God can comprehend his soul."[16]

In May, Wilford said grievances were voiced in the streets and in the secret chambers, and some in high places rose against the prophet.

Parley P. Pratt wrote that during the summer of 1837, after his return from Canada, he found that many of the Saints had apostatized. He said that he himself was "overcome by the same spirit in a great measure, and it seemed as if the very powers of darkness which war against the Saints were let loose upon me." Apparently Parley quarreled with Joseph over real estate Joseph had sold him at a price Parley considered highly inflated and it seems Parley threatened the prophet with legal action. Parley was brought up before the High Council for an investigation of whether or not his behavior was worthy of his calling, but the council members could not reach an agreement, and the meeting broke up in confusion.[17]

Parley and Joseph were reconciled, although how was not revealed. Parley wrote, "I went to Brother Joseph Smith in tears, and, with a broken and contrite spirit, confessed wherein I had erred in spirit, murmured, or done or said amiss. He frankly forgave me, prayed for me and blessed me."[18] Soon afterward, Parley asked to be sent east on a mission.

Complaints against the prophet continued. In May, he wrote, "The enemy abroad and apostates in our midst united in their schemes . . . and many became disaffected toward me as though I were the sole cause of those very evils I was most strenuously striving against, and which were actually brought upon us by the brethren not giving heed to my counsel."[19]

Nevertheless, when Joseph spoke in his own defense in the temple on May 28, Wilford Woodruff recorded that he convinced many that he would stand and his enemies fall.

Meanwhile, despite their temporal problems, many of the Saints had not forgotten their spiritual purpose in the church. Wilford Woodruff was elated to be a part of what he believed was the Lord's great work in the final days. On April 2, the eve of his temple endowments, which would take several days and include twenty-four sleepless hours of fasting and prayer, he had written in his journal that he had been contemplating the rise and decline of nations from the days of Adam until 1837 years after Christ, when in the fulfillment of ancient prophecy Israel would be established "by a Theocratic government." He wrote, "As this hath began in my days & I am called to act a part in the work by being placed with the first Seventy Elders of Israel to become a special witness of Jesus Christ to all Nations I need much faith, fortitude, holiness & wisdom. May the Lord enable me not to seek honour from man but God & be faithful . . . and do honour to the Holy Priesthood . . ."[20]

Joseph too in all his troubles had not lost sight of the Lord's commandment to spread the gospel. He wrote that "In this state of things . . . God revealed to me that something new must be done for the salvation of His Church."[21] Heber C. Kimball said that on Sunday, June 4, 1837, the prophet came to him in the temple where he was seated before the sacrament table, and told him quietly, "Brother Heber, the Spirit of the Lord has whispered to me: Let my servant Heber go to England and proclaim my Gospel, and open the door of salvation to that nation."

To Heber, the thought was overpowering. As a stutterer, he felt entirely unfit for that assignment. He wrote:

The idea of being appointed to such an important mission was almost more than I could bear up under. I felt my weakness and was nearly ready to sink under it, but the moment I understood the will of my heavenly Father, I felt a determination to go at all hazards, believing that he would support me by his almighty power, and although my family were dear to me, and I should have to leave them almost destitute, I felt that the cause of truth the gospel of Christ, outweighed every other consideration. At this time many faltered in their faith, some of the twelve were in rebellion against the prophet of God. John Boynton said to me, if you are such a d——d fool as to go at the call of the fallen prophet, I will not help you a dime . . . Lyman E. Johnson said he did not want me to go on my mission, but if I was determined to go, he would help me all he could; he took his cloak from off his back and put it on mine . . . Hyrum, seeing the condition of the church, when he talked about my mission wept like a little child; he was continually blessing and encouraging me, and pouring out his soul in prophesies upon my head; he said go and you shall prosper as not many have prospered.[22]

Orson Hyde offered to accompany him. Willard Richards said he would go also, and so did several others, including a number from Canada who wanted to carry the gospel to their friends in England. Joseph's instruction to the missionaries was to adhere to the first principles of the gospel and remain silent about the rest until the work should be fully established. For Vilate Kimball and other wives of the early missionaries, their departure was a great sacrifice and trial of faith. Most were left in poverty, without any support from their husbands, to a life of drudgery and loneliness. Often their only means of livelihood for themselves and their small children was cooking, sewing, cleaning and washing for others. They did at times have help from the church but it was not always adequate. Vilate did not labor this point, however. She wrote:

> At length the day for the departure of my husband arrived. It was June 13th, 1837 . . . at nine o'clock in the morning of this never-to-be-forgotten day, Heber bade adieu to his brethren and friends and started without purse or scrip to preach the gospel in a foreign land. He was accompanied by myself and children, and some of the brethren and sisters, to Fairport. Sister Mary Fielding, who became afterwards the wife of Hyrum Smith, gave him five dollars, with which Heber paid the passage of himself and Brother Hyde to Buffalo.[23]

The missionaries set sail for England on July 1, 1837.

Meanwhile, the situation in Kirtland grew worse. In June, Sidney Rigdon was taken to court on a charge of "making spurious money." Joseph was charged by Grandison Newel with conspiracy to take his life, a charge which Wilford Woodruff said was made out of spite. The faithful Wilford rode some eighteen miles to Painesville with Joseph and other officials to attend court. Although the case was later dismissed, the publicity was bad for the church and for the Mormons' financial affairs.

On June 17, 1837, in a suit brought by a local tradesman against a customer for tendering Kirtland bills, Oliver Cowdery, as justice of the peace, rendered the decision, "It is considered that said bills are not lawful tender," and awarded the plaintiff the amount due of $10.53 plus costs.[24]

In July Joseph was arrested several times for debt and acquitted at least three times. The *Messenger and Advocate* that month published a statement that a man "may be a celebrated divine, and be no mechanic and no financier, and be as liable to fail in the management of a bank as he would in constructing a balloon . . . We are not prepared in our feelings to censure any man."

Early in July, Joseph and Sidney Rigdon resigned from the bank, and were succeeded by Warren Parrish, Joseph's scribe, and Frederick G. Williams.

Stark accusations soon rose against Parrish as cashier. George Albert Smith said that Parrish and others withdrew thousands of dollars from the vault without Joseph's knowledge and sent agents among the Saints to buy cattle, horses, wagons and even farms. According to George Albert Smith, when the brethren put money in the bank, Parrish would take it out again to buy more, and he continued this practice until he was discovered.[25] Benjamin Johnson wrote that in a deliberate effort to dishonor Joseph Smith, Parrish and Williams signed and issued a great many bank notes and sent runners out with them to cheat the unsuspecting. Johnson added that the disgrace was in fact attached to the prophet rather than the perpetrators, who apostatized.[26] According to Benjamin Winchester, Parrish might have printed $25,000 or more in notes during a time when the bank should have cut off its issue.[27] Later, in the *Elders' Journal* of August 1838 Joseph accused Parrish of absconding with $25,000. However, the stock ledger records that only slightly over $20,000 was paid into the bank. According to one study of it, the ledger has some irregularities but no evidence of dishonesty by Parrish or any other person.[28] It has been suggested that if the bank held as much as $25,000 while Parrish was in office, it could only have been in its own notes. If the bank had had that much in specie, it would have been saved long before Parrish supposedly absconded with the money.[29]

Joseph left on a missionary tour of Canada in mid-July 1837, and returned five weeks later. According to Nathan Tanner, before Joseph got back to the bank, Warren Parrish had issued so many bank notes at twenty-five cents on the dollar that the bank could not redeem them.[30] Many brethren still had such confidence in the bank that they sold everything to help redeem the paper. Tanner himself sold his last team and wagon, his last cow and the watch out of his pocket.

In August, the *Messenger and Advocate* carried Joseph's warning that the bills of the Kirtland Safety Society were not valid in Kirtland.

The bank notes became worthless. While the face value of notes was sometimes large, in reality holders never lost much. Some did lose property, however, and the price of everything declined. Much bitterness followed among the Saints, more apostasy and a great deal of criticism of Joseph in and outside the church.

Warren Parrish resigned as cashier, no doubt angry over the accusations against him, and began making some accusations of his own against Joseph as his predecessor. He said, "I have been astonished to hear him declare that we had $60,000 in specie in our vaults and $600,000 at our command, when we had not to exceed $6,000 and could not command more, also that we had $10,000 in bills in circulation when he as cashier of the institution knew that there was at least $150,000."[31]

Several years later Newel K. Whitney told his brother that Parrish had scratched his and Newel's names off the bank Book of Constitution and had written others over them. Whitney said he thought a better way would be for Parrish and the books to be kept out of court. His fear was that the courts in Ohio might compel stockholders to redeem Kirtland bank notes. This Newel thought would be unjust, and added that most of what had been done was under "religious influence, which thousands can testify in any court."[32]

By now the division in the church was serious.

Even the three witnesses to *The Book of Mormon,* David Whitmer, Oliver Cowdery and Martin Harris, began to speak against the prophet. Lucy said that secret meetings were held at David Whitmer's house every Thursday by the group, which circulated a paper among the Saints to gain followers. According to Lucy, a large proportion of the Saints were in favor of "the new party."[33]

At conference on Sunday, September 3, Sidney Rigdon asked the Saints if they still looked upon Joseph Smith as their president. Put to the direct question, the Saints then present sustained him unanimously.

Soon afterward, Joseph announced that Oliver Cowdery, David Whitmer, John Whitmer, William W. Phelps and others were in transgression, and would lose their standing unless they humbled themselves and made satisfaction.

After a decision made in conference, on the seventeenth of September 1837, Newel K. Whitney, as bishop in Kirtland, and his counselors sent a message the next day to all the Saints, reminding them of "the very flattering prospects of the prosperity of the cause of God in our land, and also of the peculiar condition of the city of Kirtland, which is a kind of first fruits of the cities which the Lord has begun to build unto Himself in these last days," and of the "fact well known" that the Saints in Kirtland had had to sustain grave afflictions and carry a great burden to secure the foundation for the kingdom of God. The message was sent in appeal to the philanthropy of all the Saints, and said:

It is the fixed purpose of our God, and has been so from the beginning, as appears by the testimony of the ancient Prophets, that the great work of the last days was to be accomplished by the tithing of His Saints . . . Let every man and woman give heed the very instant that they embrace the Gospel . . . gather up your gold and your silver and all the means you have and send on to the Saints who are engaged in this great work of building the Zion of God, that there may be a place of refuge for you and your children in the day of God's vengeance . . .[34]

About the middle of October, Joseph and Sidney Rigdon went to Far West, met with church leaders there, announced that a reorganization of the church had taken place in Kirtland and received their sustaining vote.

The prophet was away from Kirtland a great deal that year, perhaps to avoid the many lawsuits pressing him. Each time he returned he found his community at odds, and each time he tried to reestablish unity. At last, however, when he got back from another trip to Far West about the middle of December, he found the situation beyond his control. Warren Parrish, John Boynton, Luke Johnson and others had united to renounce him and his followers as heretics, and to claim the old standards for themselves, under the name of the Church of Christ.

Joseph called a meeting in the temple of all groups. He made a forceful speech in his own behalf, and was supported by Sidney Rigdon, who, though ailing, spoke in his old fiery manner, accusing the dissenters of counterfeiting, theft and adultery. The congregation listened until Rigdon left the temple exhausted, and then they broke out in a clamor of protests and accusations. Joseph at last demanded the excommunication of leaders of the opposition. The Kirtland church was divided into factions led by Joseph and Sidney on one side and the Cowderys and John and David Whitmer on the other. Each group made bitter accusations against the other, including the charge of issuing bogus money.

On the morning of December 22, Brigham Young was hounded out of Kirtland by a mob of dissenters for declaring in public that Joseph was a prophet of the Most High God and was not in transgression.

Other Saints left for Missouri to escape lawsuits. Some of the dissenters also went to Missouri, including David and John Whitmer and Oliver Cowdery.

At the end of December, the prophet's parents and others of his family set out for Far West. They walked much of the distance and endured illness and many hardships. Their daughter Catherine's baby was born in a rude hut they found along the way.

On January 1, 1838, John Smith wrote to his son George Albert, who was then in Virginia on a mission, that the prospects in Kirtland were dim. The family had not received anything on any of the notes they held from the time George had left until the previous Tuesday, when they got a few bushels of buckwheat. John added, "but we have been fed by the hand of the Lord every day."

He also wrote, "The spiritual condition at this time is gloomy also." The High Council had cut off twenty-eight dissenters the previous week, including Cyrus Smalling, Martin Harris, Luke Johnson, John Boynton and Warren Parrish. Altogether between forty and fifty had been cut off from the church since George Albert left. John wrote that the church had "taken a mighty pruning," but would soon rise "in the greatness of her strength."[35]

When Joseph heard that a warrant was out for his arrest on a charge of fraud made by Grandison Newell, he decided that the time had come to leave Kirtland "to escape mob violence, which was about to burst upon us under the color of legal process."[36] About ten o'clock on the night of January 12, 1838, he and Sidney Rigdon rode off for Missouri on the fastest horses they could find. According to a contemporary newspaper account, Joseph and Sidney prophesied before leaving that the town would be destroyed.[37]

Business stopped in Kirtland and money grew more and more scarce. The Saints began to leave the town. Nathan Tanner's father, who had put up money for the church, lost everything including his farms, and he and his family left Kirtland in an old turnpike cart pulled by a broken-down stage horse. The cart collapsed and his daughter died and had to be buried on the road before they reached Far West.

The office of the printing press, which had been attached to the judgment held by Newell, was sold at auction to a dissenter. John Smith said the "black legs" who bought it were highly pleased, drank a quantity of strong drink and then, because of carelessness or in some way unknown, the office caught fire and burned with everything in it, including copies of *The Book of Mormon*.[38] Joseph himself later said in the *Elders' Journal* that a "gang of a baser sort burned our property at Kirtland, the printing office."[39] Warren Parrish believed, however, that the press was burned at Joseph's instigation to quell dissenting opinion and to fulfill his own prophecy.[40] The most specific statement came from Benjamin F. Johnson, who wrote that the printing office, which the dissenters thought to use for their organization to oppose the prophet, was in fact set on fire and destroyed by a member of the church High Council, Lyman R. Sherman.[41]

John Smith wrote to his son George Albert in Virginia that the faithful were going west, and suggested that if any Saints there wanted land in Kirtland, now was the time to buy because property was as much below par as it had been above par the previous winter. Cattle, horses and wagons could be traded for land. Don Carlos added to John's letter that the dissenters "pretend the Church has gone astray . . . the prophet also has transgressed, (according to their idea of things) and finally after summing the whole matter up he was a liar from the begining, and yet (say they) the Book of Mormon is true, the revelations that came throu him are from god, &c and many other things that are full as consistent; O the folly of this generation! and the weakness of the heads . . ."[42]

George Albert Smith returned to Kirtland, and wrote from there to Josiah Fleming on March 29, 1838, that Parrish and his friends had launched a lengthy argument about *The Book of Mormon.* ". . . one of them told me tha Moses was a rascal and the prophets were Tyrants Jesus Christ a Despot and Paul was a base Lier and all Religion a fudge." According to George Albert, Parrish said that he agreed.

George Albert added, however, that Martin Harris had testified to the truth of *The Book of Mormon* and declared that everyone who refused it would be damned.[43]

Families of those who remained faithful to Joseph, for the most part the poorer Saints, worked desperately to pay their debts, dispose of their property, get wagons and teams and prepare to follow their prophet. On July 6, 1838, the Kirtland Camp, a wagon train more than a mile long, moved slowly out along the old Chillicothe road and headed for Missouri.

Some members faithful to Joseph stayed in Kirtland, held regular services and carried on a missionary program. Kirtland remained the center of several splinter groups as well, including the Church of Christ, led by William McLellin, who tried in vain to get David Whitmer to assume leadership. But the real life of Kirtland had left with the wagon train. Gradually the town dwindled and was at last swallowed up in the expanding metropolis of Cleveland.[44]

Joseph remained concerned about the debts and problems in Kirtland for years afterward. On May 4, 1841, he wrote from Nauvoo to Oliver Granger, whom he had appointed to serve as his agent in Kirtland, "I am very anscious indeed to have the matters which concern the First Presidency settled as soon as possible, for until they are I have to labor under a load that is intolerable to bear . . ." He said, "The house and store encumbered by the debts for the 'Plates' are now at liberty that debt having been settled." (This probably refers to the plates made for the bank notes.) He asked Granger to see that the judgment in the circuit court on the temple mortgage was satisfied and instructed him to keep the keys of the temple until he received further instructions.[45]

PART FOUR

Missouri

CHAPTER

1

MORE TROUBLE
IN MISSOURI

Joseph and Sidney rode hard the night of their escape from Kirtland, January 12, 1838, and did not stop until they reached Norton, where they met their families, Sidney's family arriving in a lumber wagon.

On the seventeenth they pushed on. As Joseph passed through towns where runners had disposed of Kirtland bills, he was accosted by angry citizens, and in some places served with writs, but he always managed to escape, often by hiding in the back of his wagon.

In Dublin, Joseph met Brigham Young and other Saints traveling west. Joseph was destitute of money by this time and proposed to take a job chopping wood, but Brigham told him to rest and the money would be supplied. Soon afterward, a Brother Tomlinson sold his farm in that area, after having tried for a long time in vain, and Brigham told him that it was the hand of the Lord to serve Joseph's wants. Tomlinson readily gave Joseph three hundred dollars.

Shortly thereafter Joseph and Sidney decided to split the party, each to lead a group of Saints by a different route.

Joseph wrote that his group had a trying journey. Such crowds were around each campfire that the women had a hard time doing their cooking. It was especially difficult for Emma, whose pregnancy was well advanced. The Saints pushed on, however, and arrived in Far West, Missouri, on March 14, 1838.

A great throng of their brethren came out to welcome them with cheers and singing. Joseph and Emma were taken into the home of George W.

Harris and his wife Lucinda. On June 2, Emma's third son, Alexander Hale, was born.

Sidney Rigdon's party was delayed by a blizzard, and arrived three weeks after Joseph's on a bright morning in April. Joseph had heard they were coming in, and met them as they entered the village with tears in his eyes, thanking God for their journey's end with all the warmth that was so characteristic of him and that so endeared him to his followers. He asked Sidney at once if he would preach the following Sunday. Sidney did so in the large schoolhouse which the Saints had built just outside the village. He preached for two hours to a crowded room, with many leaning in through the open windows.

Far West and its environs now had about fifteen hundred Saints, a large proportion of them women and children. The conduct of their leaders, William Phelps, John Whitmer, Edward Partridge and John Corrill, had gained the first Mormon settlers an honorable reputation among their neighbors, and merchants had not hesitated to give them credit. By the time Joseph arrived, Far West had six stores, all doing good business, and nearly every Mormon family had a farm. The town had been laid out in Joseph's plan of wide streets and neat squares. In one year the Saints had built 150 houses and improved the whole county. Many of the buildings were poor, board shanties put up to serve the newly immigrated population, but it had been remarked that no other people of the same number could have built a town like Far West so fast and accomplished so much in agriculture. One of the first buildings the Saints had erected was their schoolhouse, which they used for meetings, and they had already dug the foundation for their temple in the middle of the main square. Sidney Rigdon soon had the best house in the area, built of double logs on the main square, and it was there that the Saints had their "endowment room," in which to conduct temple ceremonies until the temple could be completed.

Within eighteen months after the first settlement, Caldwell County, of which Far West was the county seat, was filled to capacity and the Saints were spreading into the adjoining counties, Ray, Daviess and Carroll.

Joseph began surveying and laying claim to large tracts of land for thousands of acres around Far West. In March 1838, he sent John Corrill, Edward Partridge and Isaac Morley to buy government land around the upper Missouri, but the Mormons who had been buying land on credit, as was the common practice on the frontier, now found themselves greatly handicapped by Jackson's decrees that only gold and silver would be accepted for government lands.

On one of the exploring trips that Joseph made in the company of Sidney Rigdon, Edward Partridge and a number of others, the brethren came to a spectacularly beautiful spot in Daviess County, on high ground overlooking the Grand River and miles of rolling prairie on which the wild flowers of spring were blooming. Here they found the remains of what appeared to be an altar. The brethren had called the place "Spring Hill," but Joseph said, "by the mouth of the Lord it was named Adam-ondi-Ahman, because, said He, it is the place where Adam shall come to visit his people, or the Ancient of Days shall sit, as spoken of by Daniel the Prophet."[1]

Here the Saints founded a little town and gave it the name Adam-ondi-Ahman.

Beautiful though much of this new territory was, with vast tracts of land which seemed ideal for Mormon expansion, the area could not claim a peaceful history. The issue of slavery was hot. Lynchings had occurred and a Black man accused of murder had been burned to death. One courageous newspaper editor named Elijah Lovejoy had protested the court's tolerance of that example of mob rule, but this had only brought about his own exile to Illinois. There he was murdered in 1837, not long before Joseph arrived in Missouri.

Although at first their neighbors seemed friendly and peaceful, as the Mormons grew in numbers and began to show strength, their neighbors took notice of their peculiarities, the fact that they did not own slaves and held strange beliefs. The more the Mormons spread over the free territory, the more indication their neighbors gave of suspicion and dislike. The Mormons began to consider ways to protect themselves from the kind of persecutions they had already suffered.

John Whitmer said that the "secret combinations" and "Gadianton bands" whose members were bound by oaths had begun in Kirtland at the time the bank was established and the church had been "lifted up in pride, and lusted after forbidden things of God." He maintained that Joseph and Sidney had brought the "new organizations" with them to Far West.[2] Whether this was the case or not, the Saints in Far West felt the need for strength. According to Joseph, Sampson Avard came to him with a plan for military companies of tens and fifties, each under a captain, every man sworn to secrecy and brotherhood, to be called up by passwords when needed to protect the Saints, defend the presidency or keep watch on dissenters. An organization was formed along those lines, except that the secret was not well kept. Rumors spread through Far West about the band, which was known by various names, including the Brothers of Gideon, the Daughters of Zion and the Sons of Dan, but most often the members were known simply as Danites, which name soon became a dreaded household word.

It was said that protection of the Saints was not the only function of the band. Joseph wrote in his journal that Avard assembled his captains and told them that it would soon be their "privilege" to take their men out to raid the Gentiles for spoils. He quoted Avard as saying:

. . . for it is written, the riches of the Gentiles shall be consecrated to my people, the house of Israel; and thus you will waste away the Gentiles by robbing and plundering them of their property, and in this way we will build up the kingdom of God . . . If any of us should be recognized, who can harm us? for we will stand by each other and defend one another in all things. If our enemies swear against us, we can swear also.

The captains, Joseph wrote, were confounded, but Avard went on:

Why do you startle at this, brethren? As the Lord liveth, I would swear to a lie to clear any of you; and if this would not do, I would put them or him under the sand as Moses did the Egyptian . . . and who can stand against us? And if any one of us transgress, we will deal with him amongst ourselves. And if any one of this Danite society reveals any of these things, I will put him where the dogs *cannot bite him.*

Joseph wrote that the officers were shocked and protested that such acts would violate the law and were contrary to the doctrines of Christ and the church. Avard replied that he cared nothing for the law, that a new dispensation had arrived in which the kingdom of God was to put down all other kingdoms, and the Lord's laws would prevail.

When Avard's proposal was rejected, he said that he had received his authority from no one less than Sidney Rigdon, but that he would drop the subject.[3] Later he maintained that he was in close contact with the presidency, "receiving instructions from them as to the teachings of the Danite band, and I continually informed them of my teachings."[4] Apostles Orson Hyde and Thomas B. Marsh revealed in later testimony that they knew what the Danites were doing.[5] However, John Corrill said that the first presidency was not much involved with the organization at first, although they did attend meetings occasionally, and that many of the Danites themselves did not know the real purpose of their leaders. Corrill called Avard "as grand a villain as his wit and ability would admit of."[6] Lyman Wight said that Avard intended to seize control of the church.[7]

According to Joseph, when the presidency heard Avard's scheme, they cut him off from the church, after which he went about in an angry whispering campaign against church leaders and tried to make friends with the Saints' enemies.

Joseph maintained that Avard's Danites were not the same companies of ten and fifty organized by the brethren for self-defense and to help families in distress by harvesting, chopping firewood and distributing food. He said that the Danites were dissolved almost before they began.[8]

Other evidence suggests that the Danites did have an existence of some months. Avard was leader of the Danites from June until November 1838, and he left the church after his testimony at the Richmond hearing in November 1838, some four months before his actual excommunication, which was March 17, 1839.

It is possible, perhaps probable, that Joseph did not realize Avard's full program at the time, but he did know of the band, and according to report, attended at least one of their meetings and spoke to the members. He told them the Lord willed that they should take up arms in self-defense, but added, "We wish to do nothing unlawful. If the people of the world will but let us alone, we will preach the gospel and live in peace."[9]

It was Avard who decreed that revolt against the presidency was an unforgivable crime in the church. He frightened and controlled his men by saying that they must support the presidency in everything, right or wrong, and that if he met anyone cursing the presidency, he could curse right along with him, and give him brandy, and after a while get him into the brush "when I will into his guts in a minute and put him under the sod."[10]

Some of the dissenters in Far West had preceded the prophet from Kirtland. Oliver Cowdery, David and John Whitmer and Lyman Johnson had found refuge some twenty-five miles from Far West in the home of William McLellin, who had left the church in 1836, fearing, as he said, that the course of its leaders would end in disaster.

In January of that year, William Phelps, David Whitmer and Oliver Cowdery had denied the accusation that they had broken the law of God in selling their Jackson County land and said that if they were deprived of such rights, they would sell their possessions in Far West also and move out. They refused, they said, to be controlled by ecclesiastical power in matters that were temporal.

The holdings of the dissenters in Far West were considerable and their resistance to Joseph's wish to reestablish the Law of Consecration was troublesome to leaders of the church. Oliver Cowdery offered to take the issue to the courts, but this idea was not favored by Sidney Rigdon, who was afraid a court decision would go to the dissenters.

On Sunday, June 17, 1838, Sidney spoke for more than an hour, before a large congregation in what came to be known as his "salt sermon." Reed Peck said that Rigdon took his text from Matthew 5:13, "Ye are the salt of the earth," and tried to establish that when Saints lose their faith, it is the duty of their brethren to trample them under foot. According to Peck, he called the opposition liars, counterfeiters and swindlers, and accused them of planning to kill him and Joseph Smith. He challenged the people to rise and rid themselves of the dissenters, concluding, "if the county cannot be freed from them any other way, I will assist to trample them down or to erect a gallows on the square of Far West and hang them up as they did the gamblers at Vicksburg, and it would be an act at which the angels would smile with approbation."

When the crowd responded angrily, Joseph added his own counsel, according to Peck, "I don't want the brethren to act unlawfully; but I will tell them one thing, Judas was a traitor, and instead of hanging himself was hung by Peter."[11]

Great excitement followed, but it was the opinion of Reed Peck that the threats were a mere farce which Sidney and Joseph hoped would frighten the dissenters into leaving without further opposition. When they refused to be intimidated, Sidney composed a letter of some length accusing them of counterfeiting, of rabble-rousing in Ray and Clay counties and of threatening to find flaws in the titles of those who had bought city lots. He got the signatures of eighty-three leaders of the church, including that of Hyrum Smith, and sent the letter to the dissenters with word that they and their families had three days in which to leave.

Oliver Cowdery, John and David Whitmer and Lyman Johnson took the threatening letter to a lawyer in Clay County. Meanwhile, writs of attachment had been sworn against the dissenters for their property, including even their furniture. John Whitmer wrote that on their way back from Clay County, he and the others met their families stumbling along, ejected from their homes, and left with nothing but their blankets and their clothes. He said they had been turned out by the Danites and ordered never to return to the county.

William Phelps, John Corrill and others who spoke against that action fell under the suspicion of church leaders.

On the Sunday following the flight of the dissenters, Sidney Rigdon, peculiarly forgetful of the Saints' outrage at their own painful expulsion from communities which did not want them, preached that a Republican society had the right to eject dissenters.

Soon afterward, on July 8, Joseph gave a revelation that, in effect, the old Law of Consecration was to be revived. The Saints were required to turn over their surplus property to the bishop for the use of the church, after which the Saints were to pay an annual tithing of all their interest. The church income was to be used by the bishop for building up Zion, supporting the presidency and erecting the temple in Far West.

According to Reed Peck, Sidney Rigdon announced that all who did not consecrate their property would be turned over to the Danites, "and sent bounding over the prairies."[12]

Joseph was disappointed to see no great haste in complying with the act of consecration. According to Reed Peck, John Corrill said openly that he had no faith in the revelation that decreed it. In the presence of several people, Joseph shouted at him, "If you tell about the streets again that you do not believe this or that revelation, I will walk on your neck, sir!" He told Corrill that unless he changed his ways, he would never be admitted to the kingdom of heaven. "I will stand at the entrance and oppose you myself," Joseph cried, "and will keep you out if I have to take a fisty cuff in doing it." Corrill answered nonchalantly, "I may possibly get there first."[13]

Soon Joseph offered an alternative plan in which instead of title, the church would take a lease on property for from ten to ninety-nine years without interest. Four corporations were formed of farmers, shopkeepers, laborers and mechanics to use the land, machinery and strength of the Saints for the good of all.

Some members of the church approved, believing that the plan would make the church independent of their enemies, give full employment to the Saints at pay of one dollar per day and guarantee the needs of every family.

On the Fourth of July, 1838, several thousand Mormons and Gentiles gathered at Far West to celebrate the day and to witness the laying of the cornerstone for the temple in the main square of town. A company of militia and a martial band with a bass drum and two small drums led a procession around the square, and came to a halt by the temple foundation. John Rigdon felt that they made quite a showing for a small town. A liberty pole was put up bearing the eagle and the Stars and Stripes, and the temple cornerstone was laid. A stand had been erected, and places on it were taken by dignitaries of the church, including Joseph Smith, Hyrum and Sidney Rigdon, and several non-Mormon guests, men who were outstanding in the state.

Sidney Rigdon was the principal speaker, and he started out with the usual Fourth of July oration, followed by a description of the temple to be built on that spot. In his closing remarks, however, excitement took hold of him and he launched a tirade about the persecutions of the Saints.

> We have not only, when smitten on one cheek, turned the other, but we have done it again, and again, until we are wearied of being smitten, and tired of being trampled upon . . . that mob that comes on us to disturb us, it shall be between us and them a war of extermination; for we will follow them til the last drop of their blood is spilled, or else they will have to exterminate us; for we will carry the seat of war to their own houses and their own families, and one party or the other shall be utterly destroyed. Remember then, all men! We will never be the aggressors; we will infringe on the rights of no people, but shall stand for our own until death . . . Neither will we indulge . . . vexatious law suits . . . We this day then proclaim ourselves free, with a purpose and a determination that never can be broken—No, never! No, never! NO NEVER!!![14]

Ebenezer Robinson said that Rigdon was not entirely responsible for those views, but that they had been prepared beforehand and "understood" by the presidency. Sidney had been chosen to deliver them because of his talent as an orator. Later, when the Mormons put Rigdon on trial in Nauvoo, the speech was attributed to him alone. At the end of the speech, Joseph shouted, "Hosannah!", which was taken up by the crowd. The

Missouri guests caught the enthusiasm and began to cry, "Hurrah!", but soon saw that they were not in accord with what the rest were shouting and gave it up.[15]

Not all of the Saints were pleased with the speech, however. Sidney's son John said that in his opinion, the last remarks should not have been made. Luman Andros Shurtliff wrote that the oration made him gloomy the rest of the day. Among Missourians, the speech raised anxiety and a lasting resentment.

The Liberty press published the speech with Joseph's permission, and copies were distributed as pamphlets. Newspapers throughout Missouri took note of it and published angry editorials in rebuttal.

Perhaps as a result of Sidney Rigdon's proclamation that the Saints would not "indulge . . . vexatious law suits," complaints went around among old settlers that the courts in Caldwell County were closed, no debts could be collected and justices and constables refused or neglected their duties. One old settler said, "if this is not a manifestation to prevent the force of law, we do not know what is."[16]

Missourians became resentful also that Mormons had moved into Daviess County, believing that it was understood the Mormons would confine themselves to Caldwell.

Ephraim Owens, in a memorial he later wrote to Congress, December 20, 1838, said that he was present in June 1836 when the Mormons were turned out of Clay County. He wrote that it was stipulated that the Mormons should settle north of Ray County, and from a wasteland they soon transformed it into a garden. Their great numbers quickly filled up the habitable part of that county, however, and they began spreading out to settle on Grand River, in Daviess County, about twenty-five miles from Far West. Ephraim, who was among the first to move there, wrote that at the time old settlers made no objection whatsoever to the Mormons and said they were convinced that reports of the Mormons' bad character were false. When Mormons became active in politics, however, some earlier settlers began to resent them.[17]

Several months before elections for the state legislature, William P. Peniston, colonel of militia in Daviess County and Whig candidate, went from house to house with Adam Black and warned the Mormons to get out of the county. As election day approached and other candidates came to the Mormon community making promises, Peniston tried another tack. He told Lyman Wight that he had been wrong about the Saints, and now believed them to be "first rate citizens."[18] According to Ephraim Owens, he even attended Mormon meetings. When it became apparent to him that most Mormons, who were Democrats, favored his opponent Judge Warren, who had befriended them from the outset and had even provided the needy with corn and bacon, Peniston determined that he would keep the Mormons away from the polls.

Only a few Mormons were eligible to vote in Daviess County but those few were determined to exercise their rights. Equally determined to stop them, Peniston rallied old Missourians to the polls in Gallatin before they opened on election day, August 6.

Gallatin, the county seat of Daviess, was a village of only about ten houses, three of them saloons, which on that day did a very good business.

When eight Mormon elders arrived to vote, they found forty or fifty Missourians already there. Peniston jumped on a whiskey barrel and bellowed out against the Mormons, calling them horse thieves, liars and counterfeiters. A man named Richard Weldon shouted that the Mormons had no right to vote, "no more than the damned negroes," and struck Elder Samuel Brown over the head. A melee broke out.

Another Mormon elder, John Butler, wrote that he recalled the Danite oath that the brethren were to protect one another. He said, "It made me feel indignant to see from four to a dozen mobbers on a man and all damning 'em and G——damning the 'Mormon'." He seized an oak heart from a pile of lumber and jumped into the fray.

"When I got in reach," Butler continued, "I commenced to call out loud for peace and at the same time making my stick move to my own utter astonishment, tapping them as I thought light, but they fell as dead men . . ."

The brawl lasted only a few minutes, but thirty men got bloody heads. The Mormons went to the polls, voted, jumped on their horses and rode off without delay.[19]

Joseph Smith was told that two of the brethren had been left dead on the ground at Gallatin. Immediately he and Sidney Rigdon called a retinue of armed Mormons and rode to see Lyman Wight, from whom they learned that the report was false.

Four or five of the brethren, Avard and Wight among them, went to lodge a protest with Adam Black, who had just been elected county judge. They got no satisfaction from him and were confirmed in their suspicion that he was the leader of an anti-Mormon mob. Black grew angry, denied any connection with the mob and sent for Joseph Smith. Some said that Joseph asked Black to sign an affidavit. John Taylor said the affidavit was Black's idea, and he drew it up and signed it with no one but himself responsible for its grammar and syntax. The affidavit said:

I Adam Black a justice of the peace of Davis county do here by sertify to the People, caled mormin that he is bound to suport the consticution of this State & the united State & he is not attached to eny mob nor willnt attach his self to eny such people and so long as they will not molst me I will not molest them. Adam Black, J. P., This the 8th day of august, 1838.[20]

Peniston swore before Judge Austin A. King that the Mormons had besieged Black's house, threatened his life and intended to drive old citizens out of the county and take their land. On Peniston's affidavit, a sheriff went to Far West to bring Joseph and Lyman Wight to trial.

Wight defied the sheriff, saying he could not be taken into custody despite the whole of Missouri. When the story was published in newspapers throughout the state, irate citizens met in Daviess and Carroll and sent pleas to nearby counties for aid against the Mormons. Governor Boggs sent Joseph's former lawyer, General David R. Atchison, to the scene with four hundred men of the state militia. Joseph went to Atchison and asked him how to prevent the further action of Missourians. Atchison told the prophet to submit to trial, and Joseph duly appeared September 7 before Judge King at a farmhouse just inside Mormon territory. The trial established that Adam Black had misrepresented Mormon intentions and the prophet was released on bond of five hundred dollars to keep the peace.

The citizens of Daviess County were not satisfied with this turn of events and many left their farms to join the militia on camp grounds. In September the *Jeffersonian Republican* said:

> Our ploughshares have been turned into swords in this quarter, and the Mormon War is the all-engrossing topic of conversation. Even politics is submerged in the deafening sound of the drum and the din of arms.[21]

Some newspapers tried to keep a fair assessment of the situation. On September 22, 1838, the *Daily Commercial Bulletin* of St. Louis reprinted an article from the *Western Star,* saying that both sides were to blame for the trouble in Caldwell, but that the Mormons had violated their agreement to confine themselves to Caldwell and had spread to Daviess, Clinton, Carroll and Livingston counties, where older inhabitants were afraid that they would soon be governed by Joseph Smith's revelations. On September 27 a rebuttal said that the Mormons were not the aggressors, but were merely retaliating. What right had anyone to require that kind of agreement? the article asked, and added that any agreement to remain in Caldwell could not be held binding.

Nevertheless, hostilities against the Mormons spread rapidly. Mobs surrounded De Witt, a pleasant little town in Carroll County on the Missouri River, which had become predominantly Mormon within the last year or so after George Hinkle and other Mormons saw its potential as a port for the shipment of goods to Far West. Mormons traveling by river began to disembark there, many people passed through by land and De Witt had soon prospered.

Zadoc Judd, a Mormon convert from Canada who had come to De Witt that year, had found it a beautiful place, with broad acres of rich soil covered with grass and plenty of timber nearby, on a lovely spot where the river was half a mile wide. He decided to stay, because help was needed in the growing town. He cut wild hay for winter feed and felled logs for houses. Soon after his arrival, however, the mobs had begun to gather. The Mormons put up a barricade of wagons and stood guard. Shots were exchanged and the mob demanded that the Mormons evacuate the town.[22]

When Joseph Smith learned of the situation in De Witt, he gathered a company of volunteers, traveled along back roads, got past the mob and into town. There he found the situation desperate, with the Saints very low in supplies. He sent an urgent message to the governor asking for the state militia to protect them.

At the same time General Samuel Lucas, enemy of the Mormons since Jackson County days and now commanding state troops at Boonville, wrote to the governor that a fight at De Witt would "create excitement in the whole upper Missouri, and those base and degraded beings will be exterminated from the face of the earth. If one of the citizens of Carroll should be killed, before five days I believe that there will be from four to five thousand volunteers in the field against the Mormons, and nothing but their blood will satisfy them."[23]

At the height of the Mormons' distress the messenger Joseph had sent to the governor returned with the word that "the quarrel was between the Mormons and the mob" and the Mormons might "fight it out."[24]

According to Zadoc Judd, the situation was very trying to some of the Saints. They believed it was wrong to fight, and it almost "rocked their faith in the Gospel" to have to take up arms. Some pretended to be ill and kept to their wagons, but the rougher element wanted to go out and do battle with the mob, and "so we find it in our day," Zadoc wrote, "some are willing to die for their religion but not willing to live it."[25]

Reduced to making terms with their enemies, the Mormons were required to abandon De Witt and leave everything behind. The refugees were on the road four or five days to Far West, and many were without food most of that time. Several died of hunger and exposure and were buried by the wayside.

At Far West, which was itself under siege, they found little comfort. There was not enough housing for the floods of refugees, and many had to live in their wagons, in tents or in whatever shelter they could make with poles and brush. Some had nothing but a blanket to huddle under in the open fields. Children cried constantly from cold, hunger and exhaustion, while pregnant women, the sick and the old were left without care.[26]

Zadoc Judd said that the refugees had to remain that way for several weeks. They had little to eat except corn meal, which they boiled and grated, and Missouri pumpkins made into johnnycake, which gave Zadoc diarrhea whenever he ate it. When snow began to fall, the misery was intense.

The prophet was afire with indignation at these further wrongs the Saints were suffering. On Monday, October 15, he called the brethren to assembly on the public square of Far West and addressed them:

We have applied to the governor and he will do nothing for us. The militia of the county will do nothing. All are mob; the governor is mob, the militia is mob, and the whole state is mob . . . I am determined that we will not give another foot, and I care not how many come against us . . . God will send us angels to our deliverance and we can conquer ten thousand as easily as ten!

If the elders had to live off the land, said the prophet, they would be justified, for they were at war.[27]

Sidney Rigdon then demanded that all able-bodied men join the force. When a third of those present opposed the expedition, Rigdon said any man who refused to fight would be thrown on his horse with pitchforks and forced to the front, his property confiscated to the army.[28]

George Hinkle, in command of a hundred men, marched to Adam-ondi-Ahman to join Lyman Wight there and establish a base. Joseph described this action as a company of Caldwell County militia under Lieutenant Colonel George M. Hinkle, agreeable to the orders of General Doniphan, with the object of protecting Adam-ondi-Ahman from the mobs. Joseph, who had property there, went with them. He wrote that while he was there several Mormon houses were burned by the mob, and cattle, hogs and horses driven off. Those in outlying districts, including many women and children, fled into town.

On the seventeenth and eighteenth there was a snowstorm. At eleven o'clock one night, Agnes, the wife of Don Carlos, the prophet's younger brother who was then on a mission in the south, came stumbling in with her two babies, after having walked three miles through snow and wading the Grand River in icy water to her waist. Hearing that her goods had been confiscated and her house burned down, Lyman Wight, who had led the Mormons at De Witt, went to General H. G. Parks of the Ray County militia, and demanded furiously, "How long must we suffer this violence?"

General Parks told him to go with a company of armed men and disperse the mobs wherever he found them around Adam-ondi-Ahman.[29]

On October 18, Lyman Wight and David Patten marched to Gallatin with forty men. They burned a store belonging to Jacob Stollings to the ground and carried the goods to Adam-ondi-Ahman to be consecrated to the Lord.[30] The elders raided and burned houses at Millport and Grindstone Fork, and carried off food, cattle and household goods for the bishop's storehouse. Hearing that the Mormons were coming, the mob left Millport and took a cannon they owned to the Methodist campground, some twenty-five miles away. David Patten and his hundred men rode there at once to look for the cannon. While the elders were searching the camp, a boy noticed a sow rooting in the highway, and saw that the animal had uncovered the butt of the cannon. He called out to the men, who hoisted the cannon, a six-pounder, onto a cart and hauled it with sacks of powder and balls, to Adam-ondi-Ahman. It was placed on the heights of

Daviess with much rejoicing, and, as Parley Pratt said, "uttered its voice in favor of liberty and law, and told the sad tale for some twenty miles around, that the robbers had lost their God of war."[31]

One Mormon wrote to his father in October:

> Far West is headquarters for the Mormon war. The armies of Israel are seen from my door every day . . . The word of the Lord is for the saints to gather to Zion in haste for the perplexities of the nations have commenced . . . Now father, come to Zion, and fight for the religion of Jesus, many a hoary head is seen with their armour about them bold to defend their master's cause . . . the Prophet now goes before his people as in times of old. Bro. Joseph has unsheathed his sword & in the name of Jesus declares that it shall not be sheathed again until he can go into any county or state in safety and peace.[32]

The prophet raised a flag in Far West and declared that it would fly on the square to proclaim "free toleration to all religions, and to all people that would flock to it." One elder said that Joseph believed thousands would come and help him carry on the war. Another said Joseph intended to take the state, the country and after that the world. Another expected to fight "until the blood shall come up to the horsebridles."[33]

Word spread that the Mormons were striking back and that the whole state would be laid waste. Astonishment and terror seized the old settlers. Hearing a rumor that the elders were coming to burn the village of Buncombe, citizens organized a militia under Samuel Bogard (sometimes spelled Bogart), who rode without waiting for authorization and drove Mormons out of their homes in the southern part of Caldwell County.[34]

Told this was mob action, David Patten, known among the Mormons as Captain Fear-Naught (or Fear-Not), assembled a company of about seventy elders on the night of October 25 and rode toward Crooked River, about twenty-five miles from Far West, where he had heard Bogard and his men could be found. On the way he pressed into service a youth of about eighteen named Patrick O'Banion, who was not a Mormon, to show them where Bogard was camped. The Mormons dismounted, left their horses in a grove and approached the river. A sentinel called, "Who comes there!" The Mormons later said that the Missourians fired without waiting for a reply. David Patten was shot through the body. Beside him young Patrick fell down, shot in the back, and Gideon Carter was shot through the neck.

The Missourians fled across the river. One was shot as he tried to scramble away and his body tumbled down the bank. The Mormons rode into the camp, confiscated horses, arms and blankets left by the Missourians, took up the bodies of Patten and O'Banion and started back to Far West. In the confusion, Gideon Carter was not missed and it was not discovered until later that he too had been killed.[35]

According to the Missourians, Patten and his men attacked between midnight and daybreak. When the guard cried, "Who comes there!" he fired a warning shot and retreated toward camp. The Mormons charged the camp so suddenly that there was little resistance.[36]

The elders stopped at a Mormon house and sent for David Patten's wife, who got there just before he died. Young O'Banion was taken to Sidney Rigdon's home in Far West, where he lingered, dying in agony for two days. His parents, who were not Mormons, came for his body and carried it away.

In the presence of mourners at David Patten's bier, Joseph said, "There lies a man that has done just as he said he would—he has laid down his life for his friends."[37]

The Saints gave their dead a military burial. Joseph, Hyrum and Sidney rode on horseback at the head of the procession, followed by the martial band. The bodies were taken to a little burying ground outside the city.

In what came to be known as the battle of Crooked River, it was reported throughout the state that the Mormons had annihilated Bogard's militia.

In the state capitol at Jefferson City, a distance that was a hard ride from Caldwell County, Governor Lilburn Boggs had been getting more and more alarming reports, the reliability of which, apparently, he did not investigate. He was told that citizens in the western area were in great fear, that fourteen thousand Mormons were in arms, and that it was presumed they had allies among the Indians beyond the Platte. When he heard about the battle of Crooked River, he issued an order immediately, on October 27, to General Clark. His order was to become infamous in Mormon history:

> I have received . . . information of the most appalling character, which changes the whole face of things, and places the Mormons in the attitude of open and avowed defiance of the laws, and of having made open war upon the people of this state. Your orders are, therefore, to hasten your operations . . . The Mormons must be treated as enemies and must be exterminated or driven from the state, if necessary for the public good.[38]

Hearing throughout the state of their governor's "extermination order," excited Missourians by the thousands took up their guns and went out in open season against the Mormons.

THE FALL OF FAR WEST

About four o'clock on October 30, 1838, a pleasant, sunny Tuesday, children were playing on the banks of Shoal Creek at the little Mormon community of Haun's Mill. The men were gathering crops and the women were working in their tents or cabins.

The village was small, composed only of a gristmill, a sawmill, a blacksmith shop, eight or ten cabins and behind the blacksmith shop some tents put up for temporary shelter. It was a little oasis among the Gentiles, where Mormons sometimes camped overnight on their way west. The Mormons had worked hard here and did not want to abandon their settlement for better protection elsewhere, even though the prophet had warned them about the danger of remaining.

In the village that day were Amanda Smith, her husband Warren and their six children, who were passing through from Ohio.

There also temporarily was a young man named Oliver Cox, foster brother of James Henry Rollins's wife. Oliver had left home not long before despite the tears and pleading of his sisters. "Never mind, girls," Oliver had told them. "If I die, I will have my boots on, and I will not be shot in the back." Oliver's boots were new, and apparently he was wearing them with pride.[1]

At Haun's Mill that afternoon, with no warning, a great party of armed men came galloping up to the peaceful scene. Their commander, Nehemia Comstock, had promised peace to the Mormons at Haun's Mill only the day before, but when he heard of the governor's extermination order, he promptly led his men against the Mormons. The raiders numbered 240 men, among whom were community leaders including a member of the state legislature and a clerk of Livingston County.

Alarmed at their hostile appearance, one of the Mormons swung his hat and cried for peace. The answer was a blast of gunfire from the leader and a shout to his men, "Shoot everything wearing breeches, and shoot to kill!"[2]

Then came a barrage of rifle shots.

The Mormon men called for the women and children to run to the woods. Some of the men also ran for the woods. Others took off their hats and cried "Quarter!" until they were shot down.

Several made a dash for whatever weapons they could find. A few men and boys fled for cover to the blacksmith shop, which was a poor choice, because the logs were loosely put together, with large cracks between them. The raiders charged the shop and aimed through the cracks, shooting the people inside like animals in a pen.

Heedless of whether or not their targets wore breeches, as their leader had commanded, the raiders fired at the women and children as they tried to escape to the woods. One young woman was shot through the hand. Amanda Smith gathered her girls but looked around in vain for her boys. With the mob on every side except toward the brook, she ran down the bank, crossed the millpond on a board and scrambled with her children up the hill, bullets whistling past and cutting down the bushes all around. One child was wounded at her mother's side and fell over a log. Her dress hung across the log, and the raiders, thinking it was the girl's body, took aim and kept firing. Amanda testified that twenty bullets were later cut out of that log. Joseph Young, Brigham's brother, escaped harm by running, but others were not so fortunate. Isaac Laney, also running for his life, survived eleven bullets in his body—his legs, arms, hips and back were pierced and a rib was broken.[3]

Hiding with her terrified children, Amanda Smith witnessed some of the horror. She said the raiders were howling like demons as they plundered cabins and wagons, ran off the horses and prowled around putting more shots into inert bodies.

The few Mormons who had squirrel guns and shotguns returned fire but were overpowered, and when they tried to flee, Missourians hacked them down with their homemade swords. One Mormon, himself shot through the lungs, reported that he saw a Missourian named Rogers order Thomas McBride, an old man and Revolutionary War veteran who had valiantly gone for his gun, to surrender. When McBride handed over his gun, Rogers shot him with it, then drew out his corn cutter and hacked the old man to bloody pieces.

When the raiders rode off and the survivors were at last sure they would not return, they began to creep back. Amanda said it was sunset. The dogs were howling over their dead masters; the cattle were bellowing at the scent of blood; a dozen widows and thirty or forty fatherless children mingled their crying with the groans of the wounded.

Fifteen people were dead, two were dying and thirteen were wounded. Amanda found her husband Warren's dead body on the ground. Among the nine murdered in the blacksmith shop, she found her ten-year-old son, Sardius. He had tried to hide under the bellows, but was dragged out by a mobber, who, according to his own boast later, blew off the top of the child's head at close range with his rifle. Amanda's other son, Alma, seven years old, lay nearby, badly wounded in the hip. He had escaped only by pretending to be dead. Another boy, nine years of age, had seen shot three times and died later.

Young Oliver Cox had been shot in the stomach and his new boots dragged off his body.

The survivors, mostly women and children, hastily threw the dead, including Oliver Cox, Warren Smith and little Sardius, down the shaft of an abandoned well. They gathered their wounded, and those who had horses fled from the settlement. Since Amanda's horses had been run off or stolen, she, her wounded son Alma and her other surviving children had to remain in Haun's Mill with a few others, in constant terror of the mob's return.

Of the raiders, only three were wounded. One man had his thumb shot off. None was killed. The raiders had fired more than sixteen hundred shots at the helpless victims at Haun's Mill.[4]

The Saints at Far West were shocked, outraged and stricken with grief at the news. Haun's Mill became a symbol of all they had suffered from their oppressors.

Joseph Smith wrote, "Thus are the cries of the widows and the fatherless ascending to heaven. How long, O Lord, wilt thou not avenge the blood of the Saints?"[5]

That same day, October 30, men rode into Far West to tell Joseph and the Saints that a multitude was coming to slaughter them. Soon afterward the Mormons saw the militia marching over the hill and across the prairie, bayonets glittering the setting sun. More than two thousand strong, the troops advanced and halted in a large grove at Goose Creek.

Terrified, the people of Far West prepared to defend themselves. To make a breastworks on the edge of town facing the militia, they tore down log cabins, turned over wagons and piled up timber. The women began frantically gathering their valuables, ready to take flight if a battle occurred in the morning.

Sidney Rigdon's son John said that he saw Joseph Smith in front of Sidney's house loading a gun, surrounded by forty or fifty badly frightened men. Joseph sent the men to get their guns, then led them down within half a mile of the Missourians to try to ascertain whether or not they intended to attack in the night. John Rigdon, his brother and several other boys trailed along.

Joseph drew his men into line and watched the Missourians for some time, at last deciding that the militia were too busy making camp to attack.

John said that his father came running up and angrily ordered him and his brother home, saying they could get killed there.[6]

A militiaman bearing a white flag came up with a fearful message for the Saints—the troops were standing by for the governor's orders to destroy Far West. In command arbitrarily, after outracing others to the scene, was the dreaded General Samuel D. Lucas.[7]

The Mormons worked all night strengthening their barricade, but John Corrill said it was about as much protection as a common fence. Much had been written, Corrill said, about the Mormon "fort," but this was all they had.

Corrill said that in the night both armies were alarmed, each afraid of attack from the other.[8]

In the main square, Sidney Rigdon's two-story house, built of double logs, was crowded with women and children sitting packed in all night as tightly as possible on the floor of the upper story.

James Henry Rollins, one of those on guard most of that dark, rainy night, said that their captain told him he was going to get something to eat and would be back soon, but he never returned. He buried his sword and did not appear among the Saints again.[9]

Not all of the Mormons were afraid, however. Luman Shurtliff said that though the Saints were small in numbers, he felt confident that "the Lord [would] work our escape with our lives, and the Kingdom of God roll on."[10]

Not all of the Missourians were afraid, either. That night some of them laid waste the Mormons' outlying fields, trampled the growing corn and killed livestock for sport. Mary Horne, a young convert of about twenty who had moved to Far West with her husband two years earlier, said that hideously painted and drunken men armed with knives and guns destroyed property and killed chickens, sheep and cattle.[11]

Lucas's militia surrounded the city and let no one out. A few Mormons who tried to gather corn for their families were turned back by gunfire. One Brother Carey, who had arrived in Far West with his wife and small children only a few hours before the siege, was bashed in the head by the breech of a trooper's gun, and was left bleeding and dying on the ground for several hours, his wife not permitted to help him. John Corrill said the slain man had been accused of burning his attacker's house, but the house later proved to be intact. The trooper was never brought to trial for the murder.[12]

The next morning at sunrise, October 31, the Mormon men were called to their posts at the barricade. Soon afterward, Joseph learned of the governor's "extermination order." He heard that Major General Clark was coming to command that operation with another army of six thousand men.

Nevertheless, the Mormons stood their ground that day. Lucas's militia came up to the barricade but stopped when they saw the armed defense. Joseph told his men to be as calm as a summer morning, a favorite phrase of his. He ordered them to present arms and each to pick his target and hold sight on him but not to fire until commanded. The Mormons marched forward and the Missourians withdrew.

The Missourians came up and retreated three times, according to John Rigdon. The fourth time they carried a flag of truce hitched to a gun. With them were General Lucas and about 250 men. The general demanded the Mormon arms and their leaders as hostages, promising to treat the hostages kindly. Seymour Brownson replied that he would tell the Mormon leaders about the offer, and ran immediately to consult Joseph.

Accounts of what happened are varied. According to Reed Peck, he and George Hinkle were sent by Joseph Smith to General Doniphan to sue for peace, and were talking with him when General Lucas rode up and demanded the surrender of the Mormon leaders.

James Henry Rollins, who was at the breastworks that morning, said a considerable fuss was made by Colonel Hinkle to find a white flag. Finally one of the men tore off his shirt flap and tied it on a stick. Rollins says he carried the flag and he and Chauncey Higbee were sent out to confer with the Missourians, who were very "saucy" to them and asked many questions.

In another version John Corrill said that Joseph sent him, Reed Peck and Colonel Hinkle out with a white flag to parley with the generals. Joseph seemed greatly alarmed and told Corrill to beg like a dog for peace, saying that he would rather go to prison for twenty years or be killed himself than have the people exterminated.

Corrill said that not only was Lucas out of the bounds of his division but that the governor's orders were to General John B. Clark, and Lucas had no authority to make demands. The Mormons were so vastly outnumbered, however, that they had to submit.[13]

In the *History of the Church,* Joseph says that Colonel Hinkle went to meet the flag of truce and secretly agreed that the church leaders were to be tried and punished, that the property of the Saints would be appropriated to pay for damages and that the Saints would surrender all arms and, under protection of the militia, leave the state.

Joseph wrote that during the day, the militia was reinforced by the arrival of fifteen hundred men, and that news of the destruction of Mormon property came in from every quarter.

Toward evening, Joseph continued, Hinkle told him that officers of the militia wanted an interview with him and other leaders of the church to see if terms could be reached without carrying out the extermination order. Joseph said he immediately agreed to talk with them, believing it to be the only alternative to having the town sacked. He went out with Sidney Rigdon, Parley P. Pratt and others to the camp of the militia, but Joseph says he never offered to surrender. Joseph and the others were taken prisoner and treated with the utmost contempt.

Accounts agree that Joseph and the other leaders went out to the militia voluntarily and were held captive. Parley Pratt said that General Lucas rode up without speaking a word to the Mormons and ordered his guard to take them. The brethren were surrounded and marched into camp while unruly troops under Cornelius Gilliam, savage-looking men dressed and painted like Indians, whooped and shrieked around them.

The triumphant shrieking could be heard all over Far West. Zadoc Judd said it was loud, long and ferocious, worse than any human noise he had ever heard.[14]

A drumhead court-martial was convened at once, and according to one report, lasted all night. The Mormons were not permitted to attend.[15]

Joseph and the others were kept out on the open ground that night in the rain, while their guards carried on a tirade of abuse. Parley Pratt says they taunted the prophet with such remarks as "Come, Mr. Smith, show us an angel." "Give us one of your revelations." "There is one of your brethren here in camp whom we took prisoner yesterday in his own house, and knocked his brains out with his own rifle . . . he lays speechless and dying; speak the word and heal him, and then we will all believe." They boasted of having raped Mormon women and girls.[16]

Word reached the brethren that the court-martial had sentenced them to be shot the next morning by General Doniphan in the public square at Far West. The prisoners knelt together in prayer, asking the Lord that their lives be spared. The Saints never forgot what followed. When Major General Lucas sent orders to Doniphan to execute the prisoners, Doniphan denounced and defied him. This was a rare, perhaps unique, instance in which an American military officer refused on moral grounds to carry out the command of a superior without being called to account. The following communications between the two officers are in Caldwell County records:

"To Brigadier-General Doniphan: Sir: You will take Joseph Smith and the other prisoners into the public square of Far West and shoot them at 9 o'clock tomorrow morning. Samuel D. Lucas, Major-General Commanding."

To this, Doniphan promptly replied, "It is cold-blooded murder. I will not obey your order. My brigade shall march for Liberty tomorrow morning, at 8 o'clock; and if you execute these men, I will hold you responsible before an earthly tribunal, so help me God. A. W. Doniphan, Brigadier-General."

At sunrise, Doniphan came to the Mormon prisoners and said, "You have been sentenced to be shot this morning, but I'll be damned if I will have any of the honor of it, or any of the disgrace."[17]

Doniphan and his brigade marched off. Great excitement broke out in camp. The prisoners overheard whispering among the officers about whether or not the execution would be carried out.

The next day the men of Far West were ordered to give up their arms to the militia, who were drawn up in a hollow square outside the barricade. The Saints came out in military formation, with their band playing Washington's death march, and formally surrendered their arms. When young James Henry Rollins saw two men he knew from the Jackson County mob jump their horses over the barricade, he threw his drum from his shoulder and ran after them. He found them in town before Burk's tavern, with two women, one of whom was his aunt. James says he spoke to the women severely for talking to the enemy that had come to destroy the Saints. "Why, Henry," said one of the men, "we will not hurt them. We did not come to destroy the women, but wanted the men to be subject to the law." Nevertheless, the two men went riding over the town while the brethren were surrendering their arms.[18]

Mary Horne said that the troops burst into houses, confiscated whatever they pleased and taunted and intimidated the women. As she stood in her doorway, several men rode up and one said, "Bid your prophet good-bye. You will not see him again till you see him in hell." To Mary, whose descriptions of the prophet indicate that she greatly revered him, this apparently came as a great shock.[19]

The troops ransacked Joseph's house, pushed Emma and her children out into the street and carried away most of their property. Hyrum Smith, though ill, was taken at bayonet point to the camp and thrown in with Joseph and the other prisoners. A table was brought to the public square and the people were called out and forced to sign away their possessions.

There was pillage and destruction throughout the town, and an allegation of the gang rape of several women, although some believed this might have been based merely on the boasting and taunting of the soldiers. John Corrill said he doubted that there had been any rapes, although there had been insults. He added that whenever such offenses were reported, the officers set guards to prevent further trouble.[20]

However, in the memorial sent to Congress by the City Council of Nauvoo in 1843, formal complaint was made that Missourians dragged women from their houses and "bound them upon benches used for public worship, where they in great numbers ravished them in the most brutal manner."[21]

Some plundering was done by soldiers on the excuse that they were collecting for debts or reclaiming property that Mormons had stolen. Much corn and fodder was taken for the militia upon promise of officers that the state would reimburse the owners, but payment was never made.

General Lucas sent a report to Governor Boggs on November 2. Of his officers and men, whom he numbered at 2,500 against the Mormons' 600, Lucas said he wished to express his gratification at their "good conduct and gallant bravery . . . not knowing but that the charge would be sounded every moment for surrounding the town." There was no noise or confusion among them, he said, "nothing but an eager anxiety upon the countenance of every man to get at the work. When the hostages were received the troops, with some slight exceptions, marched back in profound silence."

Lucas said that on November 1 the Mormons marched out under Colonel Hinkle and grounded their arms before his troops, artillery and cannon. Hinkle rode up and delivered his pistols and sword to Lucas. The Mormons were marched back to town under guard.

To gratify the army and to let the Mormons see their forces, Lucas says he paraded his men through the main streets of the town and then back to headquarters. He ordered a brigade to Adam-ondi-Ahman to disarm the Mormons there, and closed his report with an account of his command to General Wilson to take the prisoners to his headquarters in Independence to await orders.[22]

Lucas made no mention of the pillage and cruelty of some of his men, of his own drumhead court-martial or of the valiant defiance of his subordinate, General Doniphan, which forestalled the execution of the Mormon leaders. There was never any investigation of Doniphan's defiance or any disciplinary action against him.

On November 2, in a drenching rain, Joseph, Hyrum, Parley Pratt and the other Mormon leaders were taken to the public square, where covered wagons were standing ready to carry them to Independence. After much pleading, they were permitted to go to their homes under heavy guard to collect clothing and say a brief goodbye to their families.

Joseph found his wife and children in tears, believing he had been shot. His request to see them alone for a few minutes was denied. Who could realize his feelings, he wrote, to be torn away from them, to leave them among "monsters in the shape of men," not knowing if their needs would be supplied. Joseph said that his little boy was clinging to him when a trooper thrust the child away with his sword, saying, "God damn you get away you little rascal or I will run you through."[23]

Parley Pratt found his wife sick with fever, with her three-month-old baby at her breast and her little daughter of five standing helplessly by. At the foot of the same bed lay a woman in labor, who had been driven from her house. Hyrum Smith's wife was also pregnant and near confinement.

The prisoners were taken back to the square and loaded into two covered wagons for the sixty-mile journey to Independence, as Lucas had commanded, where he expected to have his orders for their execution carried out.

The prophet's mother was told that her sons were about to be taken away to be shot. She and her teen-aged daughter Lucy rushed out but could not get within four hundred yards of the wagons until a sympathetic man pushed a way for them through the crowd of soldiers. They only managed to grasp the hands Joseph and Hyrum squeezed through the wagon canvas before the wagons moved out.[24]

When General Clark arrived a few days after Joseph and the others were taken away, the Saints asked to see him but were refused. They then prepared a memorial to Clark, unable to believe he was acquainted with all the facts of their case.

Instead of responding to their statement, Clark took fifty-six more men prisoner and on November 6 gave the Saints a memorable speech in which he outlined the terms of truce, named the conditions already met and announced a fourth, which was the Saints' immediate departure from the state. Clark added, "whatever may be your feelings concerning this, or whatever your innocence, it is nothing to me." He said he concurred fully with the terms made by General Lucas and intended to see them carried out. His orders from the governor had been to exterminate the Mormons, he said, and if they had not cooperated thus far they would by now have all been destroyed and their houses in ashes.

"You are indebted to my clemency," he said. ". . . As for your leaders, do not think—do not imagine for a moment—do not let it enter your minds that they will be delivered, or that you will see their faces again, for their fate is fixed—their die is cast—their doom is sealed."[25]

IN JAIL AT LIBERTY

Joseph Smith, the other prisoners and their guards were two days on the road to Independence, Jackson County. On the morning of November 3, 1838, as the prisoners moved along, Joseph said to them in a confident voice, "Be of good cheer, brethren; the word of the Lord came to me last night that . . . whatever we may suffer during this captivity, not one of our lives shall be taken."

General Moses Wilson, who was in charge of the prisoners, told the brethren that hints had been made by some of the officers and troops that they would hang Joseph and the others on the first tree they came to, but Wilson added, "I'll be damn'd if anybody shall hurt you. We just intend to exhibit you in Independence, let the people look at you, and see what a damn'd set of fine fellows you are." He added that he meant to keep them from "that G—d damn'd old bigot of a Gen. Clark and his troops, from down country, who are so stuffed with lies and prejudice that they would shoot you down in a moment."[1]

At one of their halts before they reached Independence, a woman came up asking the troops which one was "the Lord whom the 'Mormons' worshipped." When Joseph was pointed out to her, she asked him if he professed to be the Lord and Savior, to which he replied that he was nothing but a man and a minister, sent by Jesus Christ to preach the gospel. This so surprised the woman, Joseph wrote, that she asked about Mormon doctrine, and she, her companions and the soldiers standing by listened in amazement to Joseph's discourse. The woman left praying God would deliver Joseph Smith and the Mormons.[2]

The company reached Independence about noon on Sunday, November 4, where despite a pouring rain they were met by a multitude of spectators. Their arrival was heralded by a triumphant blast of bugles from the soldiers' camp, Hyrum said, and the prisoners were paraded like a caravan of elephants.

Joseph saw no indignity in their reception, however. That day he wrote to Emma that he was well and all were in good spirits. They were treated courteously, he said, and arrived in the middle of a splendid parade. Instead of being sent to jail, they had been provided with a good house, although elsewhere he said the house was vacant and they had to sleep on the floor. He was worried about his family and his people, however, and wrote:

> I have great anxiety about you, and my lovely children, my heart morns and bleeds for the brotheren, and sisters, and for the slain of the people of God . . . what God may do for us I do not know but I hope for the best always in all circumstances although I go unto death, I will trust in God . . .
>
> Oh Emma for God sake do not forsake me nor the truth but remember me, if I do not meet you again in this life may God grant that we may may we meet in heaven, I cannot express my feelings, my heart is full, Farewell Oh my kind and affectionate Emma I am yours forever your Huband and true friend.[3]

After a day or two the prisoners were taken to a comfortable tavern to eat and sleep, although they were required to pay their own bills, which were exorbitant. They were allowed to walk about freely and to preach, and Joseph said he believed that he was able to dispel a great deal of prejudice. Peter Burnett, a lawyer who was there at the time, recalled how quickly Joseph changed the attitude of some of his enemies. Although Burnett thought Joseph's views were "strange and striking," he said that his manner was "so earnest, and apparently so candid, that you could not but be interested. There was a kind, familiar look about him that pleased you . . . [he had] the capacity for discussing a subject in different aspects and for proposing many views, even of ordinary matters." Burnett saw him "out among the crowds, conversing freely with everyone, and seeming to be perfectly at ease. In the short space of five days he had managed so to mollify his enemies that he could go unprotected among them without the slightest danger."[4]

It was while Joseph was General Wilson's prisoner that he said of the prophet, "He was a very remarkable man. I carried him into my house a prisoner in chains, and in less than two hours my wife loved him better than she did me."[5]

However, it seemed that General Wilson was not wholeheartedly committed to the prophet's welfare. As Joseph wrote later, Captain Bogard had stolen his valuable horse, with a saddle and bridle worth two hundred dollars, and sold them to Wilson. When Joseph complained to Wilson, he had Wilson's word "as an officer and a gentleman" that the horse and saddle would be returned to him, but they never were.[6]

The leniency they had in Independence did not last for long, however. Within a few days, orders came from General Clark that the prisoners were to be taken to Richmond, Ray County. When they arrived in Richmond on the evening of November 9, Joseph, Hyrum, Sidney and four others were taken to an old log house under guard. One Colonel Price came in with padlocks and two chains, saying that he had orders from General Clark to put them on the prisoners. The windows were nailed shut, the brethren were searched and deprived of their pocketknives and one of the guards chained Joseph and the others together by their legs. Sidney Rigdon was ill and delirious with fever, but he was kept chained to the others and required with them to sleep on the floor. They were allowed no chance to make themselves comfortable, and were required to eat their food with their fingers. They were kept under the charge of Colonel Price, who allowed them to be grossly insulted and abused by the men of the guard.

According to Hyrum, it was reported to the prisoners that General Clark went so far as to name a squad for their execution, but protest was made that he had no right to subject civilians to martial law. Hyrum said that Clark sent to Fort Leavenworth for the military code of laws and locked himself up with them for several days, but at last he announced that the Mormons would be delivered to civil authorities for trial.[7]

Clark admitted to Governor Boggs that he had detained officers for the purpose of holding a court-martial if necessary, and added:

> I this day made out charges against the prisoners, and called on Judge King to try them as a committing court; and I am now busily engaged in procuring witnesses and submitting facts. There being no civil officers in Caldwell, I have to use the military to get witnesses from there, which I do without reserve. The most of the prisoners here I consider guilty of *treason;* and I believe will be convicted; and the only difficulty in law is, can they be tried in any county but Caldwell? If not, they cannot be there indicted, until a change of population. In the event the latter view is taken by the civil courts, I suggest the propriety of trying Jo Smith and those leaders taken by General Lucas, by a court martial, for mutiny. This I am in favor of only as *dernier resort.* I would have taken this course with Smith at any rate; but it

being doubtful whether a court martial has jurisdiction or not in the present case—that is, whether these people are to be treated as in time of war, and the mutineers as having mutinied in time of war— and I would here ask you to forward to me the attorney-general's opinion on this point. It will not do to allow these leaders to return to their treasonable work again, on account of their not being indicted in Caldwell. They have committed *treason, murder, arson, burglary, robbery, larceny, and perjury.*[8]

On November 12, Joseph had another opportunity to write to Emma. He said:

. . . there has been things that were unbeknown to us, and altogether beyond our controul, that might seem to the mob to be a pretext, for them to persacute us, but on examination, I think that the authorities will discover our inocence, and set us free, but if this blessing cannot be obtained, I have this consolation that I am an innocent man, let what will befall me, I received your letter which I read over and over again, it was a sweet morsal to me, Oh God grant that I may have the privaliege of seeing once more my lovely Family . . . Brother Robison is chained next to me he has a true heart and a firm mind, Brother Whight, is next, Br. Rigdon, next, Hyram, next, Parely, next, Amasa, next and thus we are bound together in chains as well as the cords of everlasting love, we are in good spirits and rejoice that we are counted worthy to be persicuted for christ Sake, . . .[9]

Joseph told her that lawyers Rees and Doniphan, both able men, would plead their cause, and he was sure that if justice could be done the prisoners would be freed.

He did not tell Emma about some of the other dreadful aspects of their situation, but Parley Pratt gave further details, and spoke also of the moral strength Joseph exhibited under their ordeal. Parley said that Sidney Rigdon's daughter, wife of George W. Robinson, although a delicate woman, had come to Richmond with her baby to care for her father during his illness. One night, despite the presence of the woman and child, guards were laughing and exchanging raucous and obscene stories and jokes about rape, robbery and murder committed by soldiers against the Saints at Far West. Kept awake in horror and disgust, Parley sensed that Joseph and the others were awake as well. Parley wrote that Joseph suddenly rose in his chains, "roaring as the lion," rebuked the guards in the name of Christ as "fiends of the infernal pit" and commanded that they stop such talk "or you or I die *this instant!*" Although chained, Joseph stood "erect in terrible majesty," and looked upon the armed but shrinking men, who begged his pardon, and thereafter remained silent until they were relieved of duty.[10]

Clark delivered Joseph and the others to the civil authorities, their chains were removed, and they were taken with the other brethren, some fifty in all, to the courthouse on the morning of November 13 for a preliminary hearing for treason, murder, arson and the sundry other charges. The prisoners were appalled to learn that the presiding judge was Austin A. King, who had publicly denounced the Danites and had already condemned the Mormons in the *Jeffersonian Republican* on November 3, 1838, and again in the *Missouri Argus* on November 8. In the *Missouri Argus* he had said, "Until lately, I thought the Mormons were disposed to act only on the defensive; but their recent conduct shows that they are the aggressors, that they intend to take the law into their own hands . . . the Mormons expect to settle the affair at the point of the sword . . . I can assure you that either with or without authority, something will shortly have to be done."

According to Hyrum, King and District Attorney Birch, who was prosecuting, had both sat on the court-martial when the Mormons were sentenced to be shot.[11]

Although no one denied that King knew the law, he was said to be unpopular with younger colleagues, who considered him a humorless man and a religious zealot.[12] In this hearing, his object was plain from the start, to see the Mormon leaders brought to trial for treason against the state.

Representative Scott of the Missouri legislature later called King "the most unfit man I know" to have presided in the case, and expressed the wish that the legislature had the power to remove him "from the station he disgraces."[13] The editor of the *Missouri Republican* said that regardless of politics, King's conduct was "almost universally condemned."[14]

For two weeks witnesses for the state were called. None, Representative Scott said, was put under oath. Sampson Avard, called first, had previously told Oliver Olney that if Olney wished to save himself from the court and the mob he must "swear hard" against the leaders of the church, and that was what he meant to do or they would take his life. Other Mormons testified under the same duress, including John Corrill, George Hinkle, Reed Peck, John Whitmer and Orson Hyde. William W. Phelps later wrote that his testimony against the Danites had also been given under fear for his life.[15]

After denouncing the Danites, Orson Hyde suffered tortures of conscience for months, until he was reinstated in the church. Wilford Woodruff later wrote in his journal that the "horrors of hell has rolled o'er his soul, even to the wasting of his flesh, and he has now humbled himself in the dust, desiring to return to the church."[16]

Sampson Avard, who did not return to the church and was later excommunicated, in March 1839, testified that the Danites had secret oaths of brotherhood to defend each other, right or wrong, till death. He described their efforts to put down dissension and their raids on the non-Mormons.

The others testified that the church was a temporal kingdom, with the purpose of filling the earth and subduing all other kingdoms.

Judge King concentrated much of his questioning on Mormon views of the prophecies of Daniel 2:44, "And in the days of these kings shall the God of heaven set up a kingdom, which . . . shall break in pieces and consume all these kingdoms, and it shall stand forever," and again, Daniel 7:27, "And the kingdom and dominion, and the greatness of the kingdom under the whole heaven, shall be given to the people of the saints of the most High . . ."

Parley Pratt wrote that when the judge was told that the Mormons believed those prophecies, he turned to the clerk of the court and said, "Write that down; it is a strong point for treason." One of the lawyers for the defense countered, "Judge, you had better make the Bible treason." The judge made no reply.[17]

At last ordered to produce their own witnesses, the Mormons handed in forty names. Judge King made out subpoenas and sent Bogard with fifty soldiers to Far West. He brought in the witnesses, but they were immediately thrown into jail. They were not allowed to see the defendants and few were permitted to testify.

According to Hyrum, Judge King then turned to Joseph and the defendants and said, "Gentlemen, you must get your witnesses. We are not going to hold the court open on expense much longer for you."

Twenty more names were turned in, Hyrum said, and Bogard set off again, but the Mormons had by this time heard what was happening and did not let themselves be found. Hyrum said Bogard returned with only one man, and he too was jailed.[18]

Finally the Mormons' lawyers, Alexander Doniphan and Amos Rees, advised them not to bring in any more witnesses; so many had been thrown in jail or chased out of the county that they were afraid none would be left for the trial. It was apparently Doniphan's belief that the witnesses would make no impression on King in any case. He said that if a cohort of angels were to come down and declare the Mormons innocent, it would make no difference to King, who was determined from the beginning to have the Mormons in prison.[19]

In the later published *Senate Document 189*, thirty-nine witnesses were quoted for the state, and only seven for the defense. Three of these were women (including Nancy Rigdon, Sidney's daughter), who merely testified that certain Mormon leaders were at home at the time of particular Danite raids.

Nevertheless, at the conclusion of the hearing most of the prisoners were set free for lack of substantial evidence. Others were charged with arson, burglary, robbery and larceny and were released on bail. On November 28, six of the brethren, including Joseph, Hyrum and Sidney Rigdon, were remanded by King to Liberty jail to await trial on charges of treason and murder. Parley Pratt, Morris Phelps and three others were sent to Richmond jail for trial on the same charges.

The state legislature, embarrassed over the hearing's violation of legal procedure, debated whether to publish the transcript. It was published eventually with apology, and only because the Mormons had effectively used newspapers and pamphlets to make known their cruel expulsion from Missouri.[20] Soon afterward, as described below, the state legislature considered, but decided against, a thorough investigation of the events in Daviess County. The editor of the *Missouri Republican* published the debates of the legislature in detail, expressing regret that this would likely be the only hearing the people of the state would have.[21]

Meanwhile, a non-Mormon named M. Arthur wrote to the representatives of Clay County on November 29 in protest against the treatment given the Saints in Caldwell County:

> These demons are now constantly strolling up and down Caldwell county, in small companies armed, insulting the women in any way and every way, and plundering the poor devils of all the means of subsistence (scanty as it was) left them, and driving off their horses, cattle, hogs, etc. and rifling their houses and farms of everything therein, taking beds, bedding, wardrobes, and such things as they see they want, leaving the poor Mormons in a starving and naked condition . . . They [the Mormons] are entirely willing to leave our state, so soon as this inclement season is over; and a number have already left, and are leaving daily . . . Now, sirs, I do not want by any means to dictate to you the course to be pursued, but one fact I will merely suggest . . . the propriety of the legislature's placing a guard to patrol on the lines of Caldwell county, say, of about twenty-five men . . . rendering that protection necessary to the Mormons. Should this course not be approved of, I would recommend the restoration of their arms for their own protection. One or the other of these suggestions is certainly due the Mormons from the state.[22]

There is no record of any action being taken on Mr. Arthur's suggestions to the legislature.

On December 18, 1838, the report to the state legislature of the joint committee appointed to investigate the Mormon situation merely set forth their reasons for stating that it was not expedient at that time to investigate.[23] The next day John Corrill read a petition to the legislature sent by the Mormons, signed by Edward Partridge, Heber C. Kimball, John Taylor, Brigham Young and others, setting forth the history of the persecution of the Mormons in Missouri from their expulsion from Jackson County to their treatment in De Witt, Haun's Mill and Far West, and recounting the death, destruction and looting they had suffered. Members of the legislature sat transfixed during the reading, in tense and absolute silence, but as soon as Corrill had finished the house broke into a roaring debate. A member from Jackson County jumped up with face inflamed, and cried there was not one word of truth in the petition and it should never have been read on the floor. Others vehemently agreed, adding verbal abuse of the Mormons. An elderly member suggested that since there was such an effort to suppress the petition it must be true. Several demanded an immediate investigation, crying that the honor of the state was destroyed. One went so far as to say if matters were not rectified, he would leave the state.

Nevertheless, very little more than hot debate occurred in the legislature.[24]

On December 24, 1838, the *Missouri Republican* (p. 2) gave details of the charges and countercharges in the debate before the legislature. The editor added: "this may be the only hearing we'll have of the injustices done to Mormons whose only offense may have been that they inhabited fair lands that others coveted. We think it is certain no investigation except a one sided one will ever be made, for right of petition was denied."

Meanwhile the Saints were abandoned largely to their own devices. A committee was formed to search out the needy. Brigham Young, who had been made president of the Twelve Apostles after Thomas B. Marsh left the church in October that year, proposed that the Saints pledge to devote all their means to assist the less fortunate among them, and in two days got the signatures of 380 subscribers to that plan.

Families were leaving as best they could. Emma and her children went with the help of Stephen Markham on February 6, and on the fourteenth, Joseph's parents left. In February and March, about 130 families moved out and camped on the banks of the Mississippi to wait for the ice to dissolve so that they could cross. Most had very little food and some had only what shelter they could improvise from bedcovers.

Meanwhile Joseph, Hyrum and the others were kept in Liberty jail awaiting trial.

On February 25, the suffering Sidney Rigdon was ordered released on a writ of habeas corpus by one of the county judges, Judge Turnham, but remanded to jail because it was considered too dangerous to let him go while public opinion was still so violently opposed to the prisoners' release. However, Sheriff Hadley and the jailer, Samuel Tillery, allowed him to steal out in the night with a warning to be out of the state as fast as possible. Although he was discovered and pursued by armed men, Rigdon made it safely to Quincy, Illinois.

Petitions of habeas corpus were twice refused the other prisoners and once made a travesty when they were taken out for only a few hours.

Judge Turnham's comment was that the Mormons were innocent, that the action against them was persecution, Jackson County reenacted, out of fear that the Mormons would become too numerous in the region.

Jailer Tillery told the prisoners that the governor was now thoroughly ashamed of the whole affair and would set the prisoners free if he dared. However, they were kept in Liberty jail for some six months under loathsome conditions.

When legal efforts failed, the prisoners made at least two attempts to escape. Once they cut through the heavy timbers of the jail and were within a few moments of escaping when they were caught, but they had made a fine breach which cost the county a round sum, as Joseph wrote with some satisfaction. He said that the sheriff and the jailer both sympathized with their attempt.

Some members of the prisoners' families and others of the faithful were able to visit the jail from time to time, and they brought what comforts they could, clothing, boots and food. The sisters handed cakes and pies in at the windows. The home cooking was greatly appreciated because the prison fare was so coarse and disgusting that the men could eat it only in extremity.

Joseph was especially touched by the efforts of the Saints, destitute as they were themselves, to relieve the prisoners' distress, and wrote that he had seen them thrust away and abused by the guards when they came trying to bring some relief or cheer. "Their attention and affection to me, while in prison, will ever be remembered by me," Joseph said.[25]

One of his visitors, Prescindia Huntington Buell, who came with her father and Heber C. Kimball in February 1839, wrote that there was a heavy guard outside and inside the jail, watching visitors closely for fear they would smuggle in tools or weapons. She said that she could not describe her feelings "on seeing that man of God there confined in such a trying time for the Saints when his counsel was so much needed. And we are obliged to leave them in that horrid prison, surrounded by a wicked mob."

Joseph wrote to her March 15:

I was glad to see you. No tongue can tell what inexpressible joy it gives a man to see the face of one who has been a friend, after having been inclosed in the walls of a prison for five months. It seems to me my heart will always be more tender after this than ever it was before.

My heart bleeds continually when I contemplate the distress of the Church. O that I could be with them; I would not shrink at toil and hardship to render them comfort and consolation. I want the blessing once more to lift my voice in the midst of the Saints. I would pour out my soul to God for their instruction. It has been the plan of the devil to hamper and distress me from the beginning, to keep me from explaining myself to them, and I never had the opportunity to give them the plan that God has revealed to me . . .

Beloved sister, we see that perilous times have truly come . . . Do not let our hearts faint when these things come upon us, for they must come or the word cannot be fulfilled . . . Do not have any feeling of enmity towards any son or daughter of Adam. I believe I shall be let out of their hands some way or other, and shall see good days . . . I have no fears; I shall stand unto death, God being my helper. I wanted to communicate something, and I wrote this. Write to us if you can.[26]

Many writers, including the Mormon historian Brigham H. Roberts, maintain that the prophet's hardships in jail sweetened his personality and strengthened his spiritual qualities.

From prison, Joseph wrote to his people long letters of consolation, advice and thanks for their faithfulness. He recommended that their affairs be conducted by a conference of authorities, with minutes forwarded to him. He also suggested that the Saints collect evidence of abuse and warned against secret bands like that formed by Avard. He combined the practical with the inspirational at some length:

And now beloved brethren, we say unto you that inasmuch as God hath said He would have a tried people, that He would purge them as gold, now we think that this time He has chosen His own crucible, wherein we have been tried; and we think if we get through with any degree of safety and shall have kept the faith that it will be a sign to this generation, altogether sufficient to leave them without excuse; and we think also, it will be a trial of our faith equal to that of Abraham, and that the ancients will not have whereof to boast over us in the day of judgment . . .

He wrote to reaffirm his beliefs:

we say, that the Constitution of the United States is a glorious standard; it is founded in the wisdom of God . . . We, brethren, are deprived of the protection of its glorious principles, by the cruelty of the cruel, . . . [who] forget that the "Mormons," as well as the Presbyterians, and those of every other class and description, have equal rights to partake of the fruits of the great tree of our national liberty. But notwithstanding, we see what we see, and feel what we feel, and know what we know . . . we will hold on until death. We say that God is true; that the Constitution of the United States is true; that the Bible is true, that the Book of Mormon is true, that the Book of Covenants is true; that Christ is true; that the ministering angels sent forth from God are true; and that we know that we have an house not made with hands eternal in the heavens, whose builder and maker is God . . .[27]

In his own wretched condition, Joseph was solicitous for the welfare of his wife and children, and anxious that they neither forget him nor be influenced in their opinion of him because of his term in prison. To Emma on March 21, 1839, he wrote:

> Affectionate Wife . . . I would ask if Judge Cleaveland will be kind enough to let you and the children tarry there untill can learn something further concerning my fate I will reward him well if he will and see that you do not suffer for anything I shall have a little money left when I come my Dear Emma I very well know your toils and simpathise with you if God will spare my life once more to have the privilege of taking care of you I will ease your care and indeavour to comfort your heart . . . try to tain time and write to me a long letter and tell me all you can and even if old major is alive yet and what those little pratlers say that cling around you neck do you tell them I am in prison that their lives might be saved . . . God ruleth all things after the council of his own will my trust is in him . . .

In a postscript he added:

> if you lack for mony or for bread do let me know as soon as possible my nerve trembeles from long confinement but if you feel as I do you dont care for the imperfections of my writings for my part a word of consolation from any sourse is cordialy received by me I feel like Joseph in Egyept doth my friends yet live if they live do they remember me, have they regard for me if so let me know it in time of trouble my Dear Emma do you think that my being cast into prison by the mob renders me less worthy of your friendship no I do not think so . . .[28]

Emma and their eldest son, six-year-old Joseph III, came to visit the prophet in jail twice before she and the children left for Illinois to stay with the Cleveland family. At their final meeting, Joseph gave his son a formal blessing which the boy never forgot.[29]

At last, in April 1839, the prisoners were told they would be taken to Daviess County for trial before the grand jury, but that the defense hoped to obtain a change of venue to Boone County.

Joseph wrote to Emma on April 4:

> I believe it is now about five months and six days since I have been under the GRIMACE, of a guard night and day, and within the walls grates and screeking of iron doors, of a lonesome dark durty prison . . . This night we expect; is the last night we shall try our weary Joints and bones on our dirty straw couches in these walls . . . We lean on the arm of Jehovah, and none else, for our deliverance, and if he dont do it, it will not be done, you may be assured, for there is a great thirsting for our blood, in this State; not because we are guilty of any thing: but because they say these men will give an account of

what has been done to them; the wrongs they have sustained if it is known, it will ruin the State. So the mob party have sworn, to have our lives, at all hasards, but God will disappoint them we trust, We shall be moved from this at any rate and we are glad of it let what will become of us we cannot get in a worse hole then this is . . . My Dear Emma I think of you and the children continualy . . . I want you should not let those little fellows forgit me, tell them Father loves them with a perfect love . . . don't be Fractious to them, but listen to their wants, tell them Father says they must be good children, and mind their mother, My Dear Emma there is great responsibility resting upon you . . . to form their young and tender minds, that they begin in right pathes . . . I suppose you see the need of my council, and help, but a combination of things have conspired to place me where I am, and I know it is not my fault . . . remember that he who is my enemy, is yours also, and never give up an old tried friend, who was waded through all manner of toil, for your sake, and throw him away because fools may tell you he has some FAULTS . . .[30]

On April 6, Joseph and the others were taken to Daviess County under guard, a two-day journey they found very tedious, weakened as they were from their long confinement. Their trial before the grand jury began on April 9, but after several days, the change of venue was obtained for Boone County.

On April 15 the prisoners were loaded into a wagon and sent off with four guards and a sheriff. After they had traveled a day and a half the sheriff showed them the mittimus, which was made without date or signature. He said he had been told not to show it and never to reach Boone. As Hyrum later wrote, the sheriff said, "I'll take a good drink of grog and go to bed. And you may do as you have a mind to." Three of the guards drank whiskey and honey supplied at the Mormons' expense and went to sleep, while the fourth helped the Mormons saddle the horses. The prisoners took off at once for Quincy, Illinois, where many of the Saints from Far West had taken refuge.[31]

Meanwhile, in Far West, only a few widows and old people remained, besides the committee still trying to help evacuees. That month, April, bands of Missourians rode into town twice, threatened the Mormons and did much further damage to property. On April 20, the mob drove the last of the Saints out of Far West, many of the old and feeble helping the sick to go on foot.

At a little past midnight on April 26, some elders and the Twelve Apostles, among whom were Brigham Young, Heber C. Kimball and Orson Pratt, rode into the ruined and deserted Far West and held a meeting, their purpose being to fulfill Joseph's revelation of the previous July 8, which his enemies had mocked as impossible. After some business in which thirty-one members of the church were excommunicated for causes not named, the brethren witnessed the master workman roll up a large stone to the southeast corner of the main square, in symbol of laying the temple foundation. To fill the places of apostles who had left the church, they ordained Wilford Woodruff and George Albert Smith. After prayers and hymns, the master workman rolled the stone aside, to await the time when the Lord would make it possible to finish the work. The brethren stole away, riding some thirty miles that night before they made camp.[32]

William Phelps, who was temporarily disillusioned, saw that effort as folly. He wrote from Far West to his wife Sally in St. Louis, "One of the least of all forcible tricks of the Mormons, was performed on the morning of the 26th of April, in Secret darkness about three o'clock in the Morning. Probably Seven Shepherd and eight principal men, from Quincy (Ill.) and else where assembled on the big house cellar, and laid *one* huge stone, in addition to those already there, to fulfil the revelation given the 26th of April one year ago. I think they strained at a camel and Swallowed a gnat." Of Far West after the exodus, he wrote:

> The inhabitants are gone, The sound of the hammer, and the hustle of business have ceased; The grass is growing in the streets, or where they were: The fences have disappeared, and nothing but empty houses, and the moaning of the Spring breeze, tell what was in Zion (so revealed).
> My love of it has vanished . . .
> The people that have been staying and trading here this winter past, now the mormons have gone, show visible signs of discontent. I think myself they are quite lonesome . . .[33]

Gradually the town of Far West fell into decay and within a few decades no traces were left of the old Mormon settlement.

Later, Hyrum testified that some twelve or fourteen thousand Mormons had been driven from Missouri, some three or four hundred men, women and children murdered, and the Mormons deprived of more than two hundred thousand dollars' worth of land, most of it entered and paid for at the United States land office in Missouri.[34]

Joseph said he spent about fifty thousand dollars in lawyers' fees in Missouri, for which, with a few honorable exceptions (no doubt including Doniphan), he received very little, since most of the lawyers were too afraid of the mob to do much for him.

In his journal, he wrote several paragraphs in praise of the Saints and their conduct under their wrongs and sufferings:

> their courage in defending their brethren from the ravages of the mobs; their attachment to the cause of truth, under circumstances the most trying and distressing which humanity can possibly endure; their

love to each other; their readiness to afford assistance to me and my brethren who were confined in a dungeon; their sacrifices in leaving Missouri, and assisting the poor widows and orphans, and securing them houses in a more hospitable land; all conspire to raise them in the estimation of all good and virtuous men, and has secured them the favor and approbation of Jehovah, and a name as imperishable as eternity. And their virtuous deeds and heroic actions, while in defense of truth and their brethren, will be fresh and blooming when the names of their oppressors shall be either entirely forgotten or only remembered for their barbarity and cuelty.[35]

PART FIVE

Illinois

A NEW START
IN ILLINOIS

In the winter of 1838–39, when the refugee Saints began to stagger into Illinois after traveling on foot or in dilapidated carts and wagons for 150 miles across the width of Missouri, the whole population of Quincy, Illinois, received them with sympathy and indignation.

Quincy, in Adams County, about the middle of the western border of the state, was then the largest town in that area of the upper Mississippi River. It had some sixteen hundred inhabitants, among whom were numbered Governor Thomas Carlin and other men of importance in the state government. Thomas Carlin and his wife Rebecca were personally concerned for the welfare of the refugees and it was said that Rebecca Carlin was moved to tears when she heard of the hardships they had suffered.

The *Quincy Argus* of March 16 wrote, "we know of no language sufficiently for the expression of our shame and abhorrence of her [Missouri's] recent conduct."

The citizens of Quincy began at once to hold public meetings to denounce the "border ruffians" of western Missouri and to take up collections of clothing, money and provisions for the destitute.

They treated the Mormons not only with sympathy but with respect, offered them jobs, took them into their homes. However, Quincy could not hold all of the refugees, who were about five thousand in number and more than three times the town's population. When Ebenezer Robinson arrived about the first of February, after walking the whole distance in bitter cold and snow, he found the town already crowded with indigent Mormons and work very scarce. The Mormons soon began to occupy the countryside for several miles around.

Actually this was not the Mormon's first introduction to Illinois. Mormons had lived in that state since shortly after the church was organized, and as early as 1832 a little branch had been established in Fulton County, east of Hancock.[1] However, the Mormons had not as yet been identified there as a powerful social entity.

Thomas Carlin, a man of medium height and sandy hair, with a long nose in a thin face, was said to be entirely average not only in appearance but in intellect, although he was considered honest and of good intentions. When he was elected the preceding year, Illinois was already in grave difficulty because of overly ambitious plans for internal improvements. Carlin's immediate predecessor, Joseph Duncan, had given a farewell admonition to the legislature to relinquish the projects that had raised the state debt from less than a quarter of a million to well over six and a half million dollars in four years. Carlin, however, had taken the opposite view from the outset. In his inaugural address, he had recalled the successful internal projects of Pennsylvania and other states and added that for the credit and the character of Illinois, their own great plans should not be renounced. Under his leadership, the state was committed to another term of disastrous fiscal policy, and in the meanwhile, not one canal or railroad had been completed.

No doubt a good part of the welcome given the Mormons in Illinois was because the state was greatly in need of citizens and taxpayers. Politicians were also eager to attract the Mormons, since excitement was already high over the presidential elections of 1840, and the vote was permissible in Illinois after a residence of only six months.

Governor Carlin told Sidney Rigdon that the Mormons would find permanent protection in his state. He had shown his friendliness toward the Saints while Joseph was still in jail, and according to Sidney Rigdon, in his letter to the prophet of April 10, 1839, he promised his support in the plan to ask all governors to protest to Congress that Missouri's treatment of the Mormons was unconstitutional.

At the time the Mormons began moving to Illinois in a body, the northwestern part of the state was only sparsely settled. The great prairie between the Mississippi and the Illinois rivers had only recently been organized into counties and towns. Most of the inhabitants lived under primitive conditions, in log cabins or rudely built wooden houses, not unlike the frontier regions that the Saints had left in Missouri.

The Mississippi River and its tributaries, including the Illinois and the Sangamon, made commerce and travel easy from north to south in the state. Transportation on land in this area was difficult, however.

Wide tires were needed on the wagons to keep them from sinking in the mud of the trails. Horses were easily stuck in the mire. Pioneers soon learned that oxen could get through because their split hooves spread in the mud and made a large hole without suction. For the same reason, oxen were used for breaking the prairie sod.

However, it was a land of wild abundance. One pioneer who had moved to Illinois in 1831 described it as teeming with quail, wild ducks, geese, turkeys, flocks of thousands of prairie chickens, and deer that ate the growing corn and fruit trees. Pigeons flew south in the autumn in great dark clouds and broke the branches of the trees on which they settled. There were also foxes, timber wolves, wildcats and bears.

According to Thomas Gregg, a contemporary journalist, various sects were already in the border regions when the Mormons arrived, and got along amiably, often sharing the same poor building for their meetings. At the same time, however, lawlessness was prevalent throughout the area. Thomas Ford, who would succeed Carlin as governor, wrote that not infrequently the people had to defend their claims by force. Some privately owned property was occupied by squatters who despoiled the land of trees in defiance of the law. Finding no legal redress, the owners employed preachers to give sermons about the sins of "hooking" timber. Worse, bands of outlaws roamed, especially in the northern areas, and seemed irrepressible.

The Saints, however, were happy at the refuge they had found in Illinois, and eagerly awaited the arrival of their prophet.

On the morning of April 22, 1839, Dimick Huntington, brother of Prescindia, rode into Quincy at Emma Smith's request in the hope of news from Missouri. Among the passengers who got off the Quincy ferry when it docked at 8 A.M., Dimick saw a pale, gaunt figure in ragged trousers and badly worn boots, with the collar of his cloak turned up and the brim of his wide black hat pulled down. Dimick was within a few feet before he recognized the man. "My God, is it you, Brother Joseph!" he cried. Joseph raised his hand and said, "Hush!"

Dimick told Joseph that Emma and the children were five miles to the east at the home of Judge John Cleveland and his wife. Joseph asked Dimick to take him there at once, postponing a visit to his parents who were then in Quincy because he did not want to distress them by his wretched appearance.

Dimick said that Joseph did not realize that the people of Quincy were friendly. Afraid of being arrested again, he insisted that they take the back streets. Even so, a number of men recognized the prophet. When they arrived at the house where Emma was staying she saw him as he was dismounting and met him halfway to the gate.[2]

Wilford Woodruff, who visited Joseph and Emma on May 3, said that Joseph was "frank, open and familiar as usual" and Emma was truly happy.

In Quincy, Joseph learned that the Saints had been diligently preparing a case against Missouri, writing their letters of complaint to neighboring governors and to the President requesting an investigation.

Joseph's immediate concern, however, was to find a place of their own for the Saints. In this search he welcomed the aid of one Isaac Galland, of Commerce, Hancock County, just to the north of Adams County.

Joseph had a talent for finding men of energy and ability to help him in the planning, growth and governing of his church. Most of those he chose were men of honor and conviction, and though some, such as the Whitmers and Oliver Cowdery, had earned his bitter denunciation for turning against him, they had done so because of disagreement with the prophet and with the way his church was developing.

In Illinois, however, Joseph met two men of an entirely different character whom he accepted in full fellowship and trust but who proved to be adventurers embracing the gospel as a means of furthering their personal ambition. Yet at the outset they gave Joseph and the church extensive help, and it would be several years before Joseph recognized their perfidy.

The first was Isaac Galland, a former Indian agent and a candidate for the state legislature in 1834, who had earlier, according to Governor Ford, admitted in public speeches that he had no pretentions to integrity. He had been known as a thief, counterfeiter and member of the Massac gang of outlaws.

In the fall of 1838, the Mormon elder Israel Barlow had met Isaac Galland in Illinois, and had told him that the Saints had been expelled from Missouri and were in desperate need of land. In February 1839, Galland had written letters to Barlow and to David W. Rogers to tell them and the church that cabins were available where he was living on the Mississippi and farms could be rented on the Half Breed Lands across the river in Iowa. He would be pleased, Galland wrote, to show the territory to Sidney Rigdon or other church leaders. In apparent candor and sympathy, Galland said he felt he was assuming a great responsibility, but wished to be governed by wisdom and discretion, adding:

> The little knowledge which I have as yet of the doctrine, order or practice of the Church, leaves me under the necessity of acting in all this matter as a stranger, though, as I sincerely hope, as a friend, for such, I assure you I feel myself to be, both towards you collectively, as a people, and individually as sufferers.[3]

The following month, David Rogers and Israel Barlow had gone to explore the town of Commerce and regions nearby. They reported that Galland owned the houses in Commerce and had rights to sell some 20,000 acres of the Half Breed Reservation.

On March 25, Joseph had written a lengthy letter to the Saints from Liberty jail:

It still seems to bear heavily on our minds that the Church would do well to secure to themselves the contract of the land which is proposed to them by Mr. Isaac Galland, and to cultivate the friendly feelings of that gentleman, inasmuch as he shall prove himself to be a man of honor and a friend to humanity . . . We really think that Mr. Galland's letter breathes that kind of spirit, if we may judge correctly.[4]

The town which interested the Mormons was Commerce, some fifty miles up the river from Quincy. One of the first villages settled in the county, it had been mapped as a town in 1834 by two eastern land speculators and remapped soon afterward as Commerce City, but it had never attracted settlers and had remained a dreary little outpost on the frontier. By 1839, it had only six or eight houses, a store and a post office.

Half a mile below the village was a farm owned by Hugh White, which was considered a good piece of property, and on a rise to the east, the farm of Daniel H. Wells.[5]

Directly across the river in Iowa territory was the village of Montrose, comprised of two or three buildings, the office of the New York Half-Breed Land Company and the barracks of Fort Des Moines, erected in 1834 during the Black Hawk War. Recently evacuated by the United States Dragoons, the fort's twelve block buildings were now occupied by forty or fifty pioneer families.

About fifteen miles below Commerce was Warsaw, which had about three hundred residents. Carthage, the county seat, in the center of Hancock on a broad prairie, had even fewer and other scattered villages held only a few families each. The population of the whole county was 5,000, and of the state about 465,000.

The site of Commerce, on a broad curve in the Mississippi River at the head of the Des Moines rapids, was among the most beautiful in that region. From the heights of the town, stretches of the river dotted with little islands could be seen to north and south, and just beyond, in Iowa, the beautiful bluffs and prairies of the Half Breed Indian Reservation.

The reservation, a tract of 119,000 acres covering about a third of Lee County and extending for some twenty miles along the river, had been involved in a great deal of speculation and litigation. In 1824, it had been reserved by treaty for the use of the "half breeds of the Sac and Fox Nation of Indians," which was understood to mean it was held, as were other Indian lands, by possession, with the United States keeping a reversionary interest. Ten years later in June 1834, Congress relinquished reversionary interest and authorized the "half breeds" to transfer their land by sale, devise or descent. Congress muddled the affair, however, by failing to name individual owners. As a result, some 160 claims were made, quite a few of which were spurious. In 1836, a company from New York began to make extensive purchases of these lands with the aid of five trustees, one of whom was Isaac Galland. Galland was thought to know the region well, but it was said that the company soon lost confidence in him. In the winter of 1837–38, legislation was passed for the partition of the tract but it was soon repealed, and subsequent attempts to adjust titles so increased the confusion that the situation was for a while abandoned.[6]

About the first of April 1839, Sidney Rigdon and his family, along with his daughter Athalia and her husband, George Robinson, had moved from Quincy to Big Neck Prairie, about fifty miles from Commerce, where they rented a farm and prepared to raise crops. Soon afterward, however, Sidney called on Isaac Galland and was apparently impressed with his property, a two-story stone house with a porch. Standing near the riverbank behind a fine grove of locust trees, it was a place of comfort and some style for that primitive area. Sidney bought the place on the spot and did not go back to Big Neck Prairie. He wrote to George Robinson to say that Galland was willing to give immediate possession. Robinson turned the farm over to one of the brethren in the church and moved the family to Commerce.

When Joseph Smith arrived in Commerce, he found that, although offering beautiful views, most of the territory was a wilderness, thick with trees and underbrush. The land was so marshy that it was impossible to get through with a team, and even very hard for a man on foot. The prophet decided, however, that with the Lord's blessing, the Saints could make it habitable. Perhaps it was his hope also that an undesirable place would rouse no envy of the neighbors and might ensure the isolation and safety of his church.

On May 1, 1839, Joseph acquired Hugh White's farm of about 135 acres for $5,000, and he also bought land west of White's place from Galland for $9,000.[7] Before the middle of May, Joseph and Emma moved to the White farm and settled in a small log house on the riverbank, where members of the church soon began to assemble for meetings. Early in June, the first house built by a Mormon in Commerce, a log cabin some thirty rods from that of the prophet, was put up by Theodore Turley.

Joseph and Hyrum laid out the land in Commerce in village lots and offered them for sale to immigrating Mormons, reserving the bluff overlooking the river for the temple site.

Jesse Crosby, who got one of the first lots in Commerce, helped lay out some of the streets by cutting down timber and heavy brush interwoven with grapevines.

The family of Lorenzo Brown arrived in May 1839, not long after the prophet, and had to live in their wagons at first, but they planted a hundred acres of corn in sandy soil and were delighted to discover that it grew without cultivation.

The woods around Commerce were soon cleared by incoming Mormons and pretty little farms were fenced off on the outskirts of town.

Galland began selling tracts of the Indian lands to the Mormons, giving them "warranty deeds" which conveyed no clear title. Soon he had deeded thousands of acres to them in this way, some in exchange for valuable property in the east. Since it was common knowledge, the Mormons must have realized the titles were not clear. The Burlington *Iowa Patriot,* June 6, 1839, had a chatty news item about the transactions, showing no suspicion of swindle, and but casual feelings toward the newcomers:

> We understand that the Mormons have bought up many of the Half Breed claims, and that a gentleman, well acquainted with the subject is attempting to secure for them all the genuine claims, to this beautiful tract of country. If this can be done, the Mormons can partition it among themselves and a great amount of litigation may thus be avoided. We understand that many of the Mormons are now taking farms on this tract, and that Rigdon has bought the beautiful residence of Dr. Galland, opposite Montrose.

Joseph wrote that on June 24, 1839, the church bought the town of Nashville, Lee County, Iowa Territory, with twenty thousand acres of adjacent land.[8]

On July 3, 1839, Joseph baptized Isaac Galland, confirmed him at the water's edge and two hours later ordained him to the office of elder. Although it was the frank opinion of the *Hawk-Eye and Iowa Patriot* expressed in October 1841, that Galland joined the church the better to operate his schemes, no lack of confidence in him was yet shown by his new brethren.

Mormons gave the town of Commerce a new name, Nauvoo, from the Hebrew, meaning "beautiful" or "beautiful plantation." The choice is usually credited to Joseph Smith, although John Rigdon said it was suggested by Sidney Rigdon's son-in-law, George W. Robinson, who he said "was quite a Hebrew scholar."[9]

On April 21, 1840, the name of the post office was officially changed from Commerce to Nauvoo.

Although the land was beautiful and seemed promising and the Mormons went to work with their usual energy, they soon met new trouble. For years before the Mormons moved in, it was realized that the area was, in the words of early settler Jesse Crosby, "sickly." Jesse wrote, "Our enemies had been known to say that we would die all of us if we attempted to settle there."[10] A great many Saints did die before Nauvoo began to take shape as a town, and many more were seriously ill. On both sides of the river, people, especially those living in wagons and tents, came down with malaria, which they called "swamp fever" or "ague."[11]

Sidney Rigdon and his family became ill soon after they took over their new house, and Sidney's mother, who was eighty-one, died. Joseph Smith, Sr., also took sick and lay seriously ill all summer. Lorenzo Brown was sick for ten months before he finally quit shaking, and said he felt the effects of his illness for over a year.

Joseph and Emma filled their house with the sick and even put up a tent in their yard for the overflow. Emma nursed them with her own herbs and medicines so devotedly that she won the hearts of all the Saints.

That summer Joseph also came down with a violent attack of the fever. Benjamin Johnson said that Joseph's care fell to him. He tended the prophet night and day for nearly two weeks, giving him his only food, gruel, and his only treatment, a flush of the colon with warm water, mixed with myrrh or a little salt and soda.

Benjamin said that after his seizure, Joseph rose like a lion and administered to the sick in his own house and yard and many more who were living in tents along the riverbank. He called for a skiff and crossed the river to visit the sick who were in the old military barracks in Montrose, among whom were several of the Twelve Apostles, including Brigham Young.

Joseph crossed back and forth frequently to visit the afflicted. Several of the brethren, including Heber C. Kimball and Wilford Woodruff, recorded instances of his healing the sick through their faith. Joseph was often accompanied by Wilford Woodruff, who had moved to Montrose with his family not long before. Wilford wrote that July 22 in particular was a day in which the power of the Lord was demonstrated. Joseph went among the sick, took them by the hand and commanded them in the name of Jesus Christ to rise and be whole. One of them was Elder Elijah Fordham of Montrose, who was believed to be dying. Wilford wrote:

> Brother Fordham was unable to speak, his eyes were set in his head like glass, and he seemed entirely unconscious of all around him. Joseph held his hand and looked into his eyes in silence for a length of time. A change in the countenance of Brother Fordham was soon perceptible to all present. His sight returned, and upon Joseph asking him if he knew him, he, in a low whisper, answered "Yes." Joseph asked him if he had faith to be healed. He answered, "I fear it is too late; if you had come sooner I think I would have been healed." The Prophet said "Do you believe in Jesus Christ?" He answered in a feeble voice, "I do." Joseph then stood erect, still holding his hand in silence several moments; Then he spoke in a very loud voice, saying, "Brother Fordham, I command you, in the name of Jesus Christ, to arise from this bed and be made whole." His voice was like the voice of God, and not of man. It seemed as though the house shook to its very foundations. Brother Fordham arose from his bed, and was immediately made whole. His feet were bound in poultices which he

kicked off; then putting on his clothes he ate a bowl of bread and milk and followed the Prophet into the street.[12]

Wilford told of other healings by faith as well. He said it was a time of rejoicing among the Saints.

Many of the faithful died, however, and Joseph lost a number of close friends and members of his family.

Meanwhile, ever since their return from Far West where they had gone to lay the cornerstone of the temple in symbolic fulfillment of Joseph's prophecy, the Twelve Apostles had been preparing to go on their appointed mission to Europe.

Wilford Woodruff wrote in his journal of July 2, 1839, "This was an interesting day." Joseph and his council crossed the river to Montrose to spend the day with the Twelve. The whole company dined at the Woodruff home, and afterward all went to Brigham Young's house for a meeting. The presidency laid their hands on the heads of the Twelve, including Wilford Woodruff and George Albert Smith, to bless them, and also on some of the women, who were to be blessed in the absence of their husbands. Wilford cherished the promise that if they were faithful, the brethren would convert many souls and would return to their families. Hyrum gave the apostles the counsel that it was best to speak only of repentance and to preach only the first principles of the gospel, which was as much as this generation could endure. Wilford wrote that Joseph then "presented some precious things of the kingdom unto us in the power of the Holy Ghost; yea precious principles that ought to be engraven upon our hearts & practiced in our lives." He advised the Twelve to exercise mercy and be ready to forgive a brother at the first intimation of repentance, or better yet, even before. The Twelve were advised to be humble, not to exalt themselves or to try to excel one another, to credit God in all they did, to be honest, open and frank in all intercourse, and never to betray the revelations of God. "But whatever you do," Joseph added, "do not betray your friend."[13]

On August 7, Wilford wrote in his journal what must have been the feeling of every one of the Twelve, that it was no small trial of faith to leave his family and his all and start without purse or scrip on a mission of four thousand miles to preach in foreign nations. Wilford was, besides, still suffering from ague. "Yet I do this freely for Christ sake trusting in him . . ." Wilford wrote. "May the Lord give me grace according to my day & a safe return to my family . . ."[14]

Meanwhile, the Saints were working to establish their community. Soon after his arrival in Illinois, Joseph had sent several brethren back to Far West by night to dig up the press, which had prudently been buried in someone's yard on the night General Lucas laid siege to the town. Hauled to Nauvoo, the press was set up in the damp cellar of a warehouse on the riverbank, and there Joseph's younger brother, Don Carlos, and his friend, a young convert from Canada named Robert B. Thompson, cleaned the mud off the type and got out a prospectus for a new newspaper, to be called *Times and Seasons*. Though a young and vigorous man, six feet four and unusually strong, Don Carlos soon took sick with chills and fever in that dank place, and so did Thompson.

The press was moved out of the warehouse and the first issue was brought out at last in November 1839 by Ebenezer Robinson, who was himself so sick that he had to direct the work from his bed. The paper published a series of articles on the persecutions of the Saints in Missouri, which did much to rouse the initial sympathy of their new neighbors in Illinois.

Though beset by the many problems of clearing the land, planting crops, building a new town in raw, difficult country, struggling against poverty, want and sickness, Joseph had not forgotten the grievances of his people against the state of Missouri.

By early fall that year, 1839, the Saints had made hundreds of affidavits about their wrongs. On October 29, taking the affidavits with a lengthy petition addressed to Congress and letters for President Van Buren from such prominent men as Governors Robert Lucas of Iowa Territory, Wilson Shannon of Ohio and Carlin of Illinois, Joseph set out for Washington. With him in a two-horse carriage went Sidney Rigdon, Orrin Porter Rockwell and Elias Higbee.

Perhaps Joseph's hopes for a sympathetic ear from President Van Buren were high. The Mormons had already expressed their faith in him in the election of October 1836, where he had carried their vote in Kirtland. The *Missouri Republican* of December 3, 1836 (p. 2), had recorded that Van Buren's agent had promised the Mormons that if Van Buren were elected their lands in Missouri would be restored.

Delays and stops to preach along the way would lengthen their arduous journey to nearly a month. They were gone only two days when Sidney Rigdon fell ill and they asked Dr. Robert Foster to ride along to care for him. After several days in Springfield they set out again over bad roads which apparently made Sidney very uncomfortable. On November 9, Joseph wrote to Emma to say that they would have to go on ahead of Sidney, and added a loving note about his concern for the family, especially little Frederick, who had been ill when he left. Apparently depressed, he said, "it will be a long and lonesome time during my absence from you and nothing but a sense of humanity could have urged me on to so great a sacrafice but shall I see so many perish and not seek redress no I will try this once in the name of the Lord."[15]

Joseph left Sidney, the doctor and Porter Rockwell to follow at their leisure in the carriage while he and Elias Higbee went on in the stagecoach to keep their appointments in Washington.

On November 27, in a mountainous region not far from the capital, the driver pulled up at a public house and went in for a grog, leaving the passengers to wait in the coach. The unattended horses bolted and ran down the hill. Joseph kept the passengers in their seats and prevented one terrified woman from tossing her baby through the window. Opening the coach door, he climbed out of the dangerously rocking, jouncing vehicle, crawled into the driver's seat and after two or three miles, managed to rein in the horses. No one was injured. The excited passengers could not praise Joseph enough. Joseph wrote that congressmen who happened to be on board considered proposing him on the floor for a reward by public act, but dropped the subject when they learned he was the Mormon prophet.[16]

Joseph and Elias reached Washington on November 28. Having left Nauvoo with very little money, they spent most of their first day looking for a cheap boardinghouse.

On Friday morning, November 29, Joseph and Elias went to the President's mansion, which Joseph described in his letter of December 5 to Hyrum and the church High Council as a very large and splendid palace, decorated with all the fineries of the world. Presenting themselves at the door they asked to see the President, and in those uncomplicated days were immediately conducted to an upper apartment where the President received them in his parlor and accepted their letters of introduction.

It was perhaps naïve of Joseph to appeal to the federal authorities. He underestimated or ignored the difficult issue of States' rights just then before the leaders of the nation, to which his complaints could only add complication. At the same time, since it was an election year, the legislative bodies were afraid of alienating their constituencies.

After reading the first letter Joseph handed to him, the President looked up with a slight frown. "What can I do? I can do nothing for you!" he said. "If I do anything, I shall come in contact with the whole state of Missouri."[17]

Joseph refused to be intimidated, however, and demanded the Saints' constitutional rights. Before he and Elias left, they managed to elicit some expression of sympathy from the President for the sufferings of the Saints and his promise to reconsider his position. He asked a question or two about the Mormon religion, in particular how it differed from others. Joseph said that the difference lay in the mode of baptism and in the gift of the Holy Ghost by the laying on of hands. The prophet wrote later that he felt all other considerations were contained in the gift of the Holy Ghost and that it was unnecessary to exchange many words with the President on that subject.

Joseph and Elias spent the next several days in delivering their letters of introduction to various representatives and in trying to get their case presented before the House. The prophet wrote that he found the gentlemen from Illinois worthy men, who treated him and Elias kindly and promised to do all in their power, but Joseph understood that they, as well as the Mormons, had to deal with the prejudices and bigotry of the people.

His most pleasing interview was with Judge Richard M. Young, senator from Illinois, who offered the brethren financial aid for their expenses, which Joseph gratefully accepted. In a postscript to his letter to Hyrum of December 5, Joseph added that although Congress had been in session for four days, the House was not yet organized because some seats were contested in the New Jersey delegation. He wrote:

> there is a great deal of wind blown off on the occasion on each day. There is such an itching disposition to display their oratory on the most trivial occasions, and so much etiquette, bowing and scraping, twisting and turning, to make a display of their witticism, that it seems to us rather a display of folly and show, more than substance and gravity, such as becomes a great nation like ours. (However, there are some exceptions).[18]

On December 7, Joseph and Elias met with the Illinois delegation in one of the committee rooms of the Capitol. Representative Robinson took a stand against presenting the Mormon claims to the United States on grounds that it was the business of the state. Joseph countered with a demand for the Saints' constitutional rights, charging that they had been denied by the Missouri government.

Judge Young spoke in the Mormons' favor and promised to seek the opinion of other lawyers in the Senate. Ultimately the delegation decided that Judge Young would present the plea to the Senate, although no action could be taken until the House was organized.

Staggered to hear that the Mormons were demanding $2 million in damages, the congressmen from Missouri began to build a fast defense, mostly based upon the transcript of Joseph's hearing at Richmond.

In the interval, Joseph traveled to Philadelphia by railroad on December 21, and spent several days with the Saints there, and did some preaching from house to house. On the thirtieth he went for a few days to New Jersey, then back to Philadelphia until the end of January. Sidney Rigdon had reached Philadelphia by this time, but again had to stop, not well enough to go on to Washington.

On February 5, Joseph preached in Washington before a large audience which included some members of Congress, who confessed they were curious to hear the doctrine of the Mormon prophet from his own lips. One of those present, a newspaper reporter named Mathew L. Davis, wrote to his wife the following day:

> He is not an educated man; but he is a plain, sensible, strong minded man. Everything he says, is said in a manner to leave an impression

that he is sincere. There is no levity, no fanaticism, no want of dignity in his deportment. He is apparently from forty to forty-five years of age, rather above the middle stature, and what you ladies would call a very good looking man. In his garb there are no peculiarities; his dress being that of a plain, unpretending citizen. He is by profession a farmer, but is evidently well read.

He commenced by saying, that he knew the prejudices which were abroad in the world against him, but requested us to pay no respect to [them] . . . He said, "I will state to you our belief, so far as time will permit" "I believe," said he, "that there is a God, possessing all the attributes ascribed to Him by all Christians by all denominations; that He reigns over all things in heaven and on earth . . ."

Davis reported that the prophet professed belief in the sacred Bible and said that in it the Mormon faith was to be found. Davis continued:

Towards the close of his address, he remarked that he had been represented as pretending to be a Savior, a worker of miracles, etc. All this was false . . . He was but a man, he said; a plain, untutored man; seeking what he should do to be saved. He performed no miracles. He did not pretend to possess any such power . . . The Mormon Bible, he said, was communicated to him, *direct from heaven*. If there was such a thing on earth, as the author of it, then he (Smith) was the author; but the idea that he wished to impress was, that he had penned it as dictated by God.

During the prophet's address of more than two hours, there was nothing, said Davis, to impair the morals of society, but much that would "soften the asperities of man towards man . . . There was no violence, no fury, no denunciation. His religion appears to be a religion of meekness . . . *I have changed my opinion of the Mormons*. They are an injured and much-abused people."[19]

Soon afterward, Joseph decided that his presence in Washington did nothing to further the Mormons' plea. He was particularly dismayed at the reception given him by Van Buren, who had said, "Gentlemen, your cause is just, but I can do nothing for you." Joseph was bewildered and enraged by such a candid remark from the President, which he felt revealed a lack of justice and righteousness. "I found him such a man as I could not conscientiously support at the head of our noble Republic."[20]

After an equally unsatisfactory interview with John C. Calhoun, Joseph left on the train for Ohio with Porter Rockwell and Dr. Foster. Elias Higbee remained alone in Washington to continue the Mormons' suit.

Joseph reached Nauvoo after a wearisome journey through rain, snow and mud, although he said he had many precious moments among the Saints along the way. He took every opportunity to proclaim the iniquity and insolence of Martin Van Buren, saying, "My heart faints within me when I see, by the visions of the Almighty, the end of this nation, if she continues to disregard the cries and petitions of her virtuous citizens, as she has done and is now doing." More succinctly, he was quoted as saying that Van Buren was "not as fit as my dog for the chair of state."[21]

Elias Higbee defended the Mormons' cause at a series of meetings and debates held during February 1840, but on March 4, the Senate Judiciary Committee on the Case of the Saints versus Missouri reported that in their unanimous opinion, interposition by the federal government was not justified, that the allegations referred to the citizens of Missouri within their own territory, and it was from them that the petitioners must seek relief.

On March 24, Higbee wrote to Joseph that the Senate had passed a resolution on the twenty-third that the committee be discharged and that the Mormons might withdraw their papers. Their business in Washington was finished.

Unfortunately, Joseph's charges before Congress against Missouri in behalf of the Saints only increased Missouri's enmity. Governor Boggs was infuriated by what he considered the insult to the honor of his state, and whereas before he had been content merely to be rid of the Mormons, henceforth he would make every effort to recapture Joseph and bring him back for trial.

Meanwhile, the Saints turned their energies to the building of Nauvoo and the kingdom of the Lord.

THE RISE OF NAUVOO

When Joseph got back to Illinois from Washington in March 1840, more troubles were waiting for him.

During his absence, there had been a wave of crime along the banks of the Mississippi, where thieves, pirates, counterfeiters and outlaws of every description found good hideouts. It was also true that a few demoralized Mormon refugees from Missouri who were angered at what they had suffered in that state were trying to recoup some of their losses by raiding the property of Missourians on the other side of the river. Rumor had it that the presidency of the church did not consider robbing the Gentiles of Missouri a sin, at any rate up to the amount of Mormon losses in that state. Apparently the story spread to such an extent that eventually Hyrum made a sworn statement that such behavior was against the teachings of the church. Meanwhile, the Missourians were blaming every incident of theft, however remote, upon the Mormons.[1]

A sense of humor was not lacking in that rough area, however, despite the mounting tensions. John Smith wrote that a man had been seen walking on the waters of the river and the non-Mormons declared that it was probably some Mormon going across to steal something.[2]

On July 7, 1840, a party of Missourians from Tully crossed the Mississippi to search for property that had been stolen. Finding a cache of goods on the riverbank near Nauvoo, they blamed the Mormons and took four Mormons captive. Back in Tully, they beat the Mormons into confessing the theft.

Without investigating the matter, Joseph charged the men from Missouri with entrapment and complained to Governor Carlin, who made a strong protest to Governor Boggs. As it turned out, to the embarrassment of Governor Carlin and the Saints, the quantity of goods proved entirely too large to have been put there as a trap for the innocent. One of the captured Mormons, Alanson Brown, was found guilty. Unfortunately, this left Governor Carlin sorely disappointed in the Mormons.[3]

Sickness also continued among the Saints, and many died, including members of Joseph's own family.

Soon after Joseph's parents had arrived in Illinois, Joseph had built a little house for them near his own. Here Lucy says they would have been happy except that her husband, who had been ill during their trip from Quincy, grew worse. He remained ill during the first months of their arrival, and during the summer heat of 1840, he rapidly declined.

On Saturday, September 12, he suffered a ruptured blood vessel internally and began to vomit blood. The next day he called his family to the bedside. Lucy writes that he said to her:

> . . . you are the mother of as great a family as ever lived upon the earth. The world loves its own, but it does not love us. It hates us because we are not of the world; therefore, all their malice is poured out upon us, and they seek to take away our lives. When I look upon my children, and realize, that although they were raised up to do the Lord's work, yet they must pass through scenes of trouble and affliction as long as they live upon the earth; and I dread to leave them surrounded by enemies.

To each of his children in turn, the patriarch gave a blessing. To Hyrum, he passed his patriarchal powers. To Joseph, he said, "You are called . . . to do the work of the Lord. Hold out faithful, and you shall be blessed, and your children after you. You shall even live to finish your work."

Lucy writes that Joseph cried out, weeping, "Oh, father, shall I?"

His father said, "You shall live to lay out the plan of all the work which God has given you to do. This is my dying blessing on your head in the name of Jesus."

Exhausted, Joseph Sr. paused after his efforts, then said in a tone of surprise, "I can see and hear as well as ever I could."

On Monday, September 14, he announced that he would live seven or eight minutes. He straightened himself, laid his hands together and died so easily and calmly that his family could not at first believe he had stopped breathing.[4] At his death he was sixty-nine years old, six feet two and remarkably straight, although wasted from his normal two hundred pounds by long illness, suffering and exposure.

The whole church turned out to hear a long eulogy read at his funeral the next day by Robert B. Thompson, Hyrum's brother-in-law and collaborator of Don Carlos on the *Times and Seasons*. Thompson said:

> The occasion which has brought us together this day, is one of no ordinary importance: for not only has a single family to mourn and sorrow on account of the death of the individual, whose funeral obsequies we this day celebrate; but a whole society; yes, thousands will this day have to say, *a Father in Israel is gone.*[5]

Joseph felt the loss of his father deeply. He wrote, "He was the first person who received my testimony after I had seen the angel, and exhorted me to be faithful and diligent to the message."[6] From that time on he had given his son his constant support and friendship.

The Smith family suffered many losses from the swamp fever. The prophet's Uncle Silas would soon die. Not long afterward, Joseph's sister-in-law Mary, wife of Samuel, would also die. Don Carlos, Joseph's talented and handsome younger brother, would die August 7, 1841, followed in a week by his infant namesake, Joseph's youngest son. On August 27 would come the death of Robert B. Thompson. A month after that, Hyrum's second son, Hyrum, would die at the age of seven.

Despite their heartache, illness and privation the Saints continued their work. Under Joseph's determined leadership, they bent all of their energies to building their new community. Like all of their previous enterprises, Nauvoo developed rapidly. Houses were built, shops opened for business, craftsmen, blacksmiths, tanners, coopers, tailors and milliners plied their skills. The Saints discovered beautiful building material, limestone nearly as white as marble, almost at their feet, and opened a quarry at once. The *Times and Seasons* was soon a flourishing little monthly. Postal activities in Nauvoo soon increased to such an extent that the postmaster at the county seat in Carthage wrote to Washington to ask that mail, which was delivered on horseback beween Carthage and Nauvoo, be exchanged twice a week, but Washington replied that the expense, which would be raised by $150, was beyond the government's means.

The missionaries abroad were making a large contribution to the population of Nauvoo. Wilford Woodruff, George Albert Smith and the other members of the Twelve had received a joyful welcome in Liverpool from the little branch of twenty-eight converts built up by their predecessors.

Besides preaching the gospel, the missionaries propounded the glories of the New World. Disturbed by the condition of the laboring classes in England, by their slums, poverty and unemployment, the missionaries set forth the economic as well as the spiritual advantages of gathering with the Saints in America, and spoke of the rich tracts of land available to all. To many laborers and craftsmen who had never owned land, the appeal was strong.

Most immigrants came to Nauvoo with mingled hope, faith and anxiety, leaving family, friends and country forever to make a new life in a new homeland. In the eyes of church leaders, how immigrants described Nauvoo in writing back to England became a measure of their faith. Some said they found Nauvoo all they had expected, but others wrote that they were keenly disappointed. The *Millennial Star,* newspaper which the missionaries began in Liverpool in May 1840, printed the letters of the pleased and enthusiastic. Those who expressed disillusionment were said to have fallen from the faith.

That some converts thought the missionaries made exaggerated claims for Nauvoo is apparent from the opinion of James Greenhalgh, a cotton spinner, who was converted in 1839. Greenhalgh said that the Mormons maintained that conditions in the manufacturing districts would get worse in all countries, and spoke of Nauvoo as a haven. He left Liverpool with 270 other converts, but when he arrived in Nauvoo he found no job and no place to stay. Rents were high, log houses four or five dollars a week, wood was expensive, land near the temple grounds was $800 to $1,200 an acre. The people, who rarely had wheat bread, ate Indian corn meal and pickled pork which they got for wages. Provisions, even at Joseph's store, were more expensive than in New Orleans. Greenhalgh was disappointed in the rising temple, which he said had been represented as more beautiful than that of Jerusalem, but he thought it had the look of one of England's common stone Sunday schools.[7]

One convert, Edwin Bottomly, no doubt made an accurate assessment of certain immigrants when he wrote to his father, "Some people form expectations of this country before they come which would be impossible to realize . . . fish in every pool . . . fruit on every tree and that wild fowl will come to them to be shot, furnished houses on every plot of land they want to purchase and that they will have nothing to do but sit them down in ease and plenty when they get here. I must say there is plenty of Fruit and fish and fowl but they are the same in this country as in any other, *no catch no eat.*"[8]

Not only were there material difficulties in Nauvoo but spiritual as well. Joseph warned converts to keep their expectations realistic. "We would wish the Saints to understand that, when they come here, they must not expect perfection, or that all will be harmony, peace, and love . . . there are persons, not only from different states, but from different nations, who, although they feel a great attachment to the cause of truth, have their prejudices of education . . . Again, there are many that creep in unawares, and endeavor to sow discord, strife and animosity in our midst . . ."[9]

Nevertheless, converts were made by the hundreds in England and in Wales, although not in London, which Heber C. Kimball thought was full of sin and about to suffer God's punishment. The British press commented on this strange new sect that was luring away so many English, noting that converts were usually skilled workers and tradesmen of high moral character.

To help converts reach the new land, the church set up an immigration office under the direction of Brigham Young. The office chartered ships and organized supplies so effectively that passage and provisions could be had to New Orleans for less than five pounds. The system became well known, drew comment in the House of Commons, and non-members of the church began asking to emigrate to America with the Mormons.

With the influx of converts from abroad, and the energy of its citizens, Nauvoo was growing at a phenomenal rate and attracting much attention in Illinois.

Joseph's personal fame was increasing and so was his self-assurance. One convert, Howard Coray, who came to Nauvoo in 1840 and was asked soon after to serve as Joseph's clerk, said of him:

the Prophet had a great many callers or visitors, and he received them in his office, where I was clerking—persons of almost all professions —Doctors, Lawyers Priests and people seemed anxious to get a good look at what was then considered something very wonderful: a man who should dare to call himself a prophet, announce himself as a seer and ambassador of the Lord. Not only were they anxious to see, but also to ask hard questions, in order to ascertain his depth. Well, what did I discover: This, verily, that he was always equal to the occasion, and perfectly master of the situation, and, possessed the power to make every body realize his superiority . . .[10]

Among those who were watching Nauvoo with intense interest was John Cook Bennett.

Bennett, who was about the same age as the prophet, was short and slender, with sharp, black eyes, and black hair handsomely touched by gray. A man of proven ability, intelligent and well-educated, with an attractive vitality, he won the admiration of men as well as women.

Born in Fairhaven, Massachusetts, August 4, 1804, he had moved with his parents to Ohio in 1808. He attended Athens state university and studied medicine in Marietta under the well-known Dr. Samuel Hildreth, and later practiced in Ohio and states nearby. Bennett was interested also in education, and participated in the founding of institutions in West Virginia, Indiana and Ohio. At Willoughby he organized the medical school and was the first dean and professor of gynecology and children's diseases. He was a licensed preacher in Ohio for a time, also had military training, and there is evidence that he served as a surgeon in the Black Hawk War. In 1838 he moved to Illinois, was appointed brigadier general of the Illinois Invincible Dragoons, and in 1840 was made quartermaster general of Illinois by Governor Carlin.

Bennett had first become aware of the Saints in Kirtland when he was teaching at nearby Willoughby College and later, at the expulsion of the Saints from Missouri, had written to Joseph offering his help.

At the outset, there seems to have been little Bennett could have seen to his advantage in a connection with the Mormons, destitute refugees that they were, and it has been suggested that he might have genuinely felt the indignation he expressed to Joseph at the treatment they received from the Missourians. The Mormons did not accept his help, however, perhaps, as has been suggested, because they were still hopeful of having their wrongs redressed by the state and the nation.

When the Mormons reached Nauvoo, Bennett wrote to Joseph again offering his services. Joseph answered honestly that although he had no doubt Bennett could be of great help to the Saints, it might neither exalt him nor bring him riches if he devoted his time and efforts to the cause of truth and a suffering people. Joseph added:

> yet by so doing you may rely on the approval of Jehovah . . . Therefore, my general invitation is, let all who will come, come and partake of the poverty of Nauvoo, freely. I should be disposed to give you a special invitation to come as early as possible, believing you will be of great service to us. However, you must make your own arrangements according to your circumstances.[11]

Bennett then made an offer to the Saints which was hardly admissible of refusal. He told Joseph that he had made a particular study of the fever endemic to that area and he was sure he could help make Nauvoo as wholesome as it was beautiful.

At their first opportunity, Joseph and Bennett rode over the territory on horseback to examine its condition. Bennett told Joseph that the remaining marshes were the source of the disease. Most of the marshes had been drained by this time, but Joseph at once put men to work to finish. In answer to Joseph's questions about the cause of the disease, Bennett said it was a poison generated by plant decomposition in hot, moist regions, and seemed to cling to fogs near the earth. He advised the Saints to live on the second floor of their houses. Effective against the disease, he said, was the drug quinine, of which he happened to have a supply.

Soon afterward, in the summer of 1840, Bennett was baptized into the Mormon Church and quickly became the prophet's close associate. Although he did not replace Sidney Rigdon, who remained ill, as Joseph's first counselor, Bennett assumed many of his responsibilities.

Joseph had a revelation which said, "I have seen the work which he hath done, which I accept, if he continue, and will crown him with blessings and great glory."[12]

Bennett soon offered another great service to the Saints. He could help them get the state legislature to approve their charter for the city of Nauvoo. At the same time, they could apply for a charter for a university and for a city militia, for which they could establish their own regulations, appoint their own officers and receive an allotment of state arms.

Bennett, whose influence was considerable at the capital, offered to submit the necessary petition to the legislature at Springfield, which he cannily suggested be done after elections when the Mormons had demonstrated their strength at the polls.

While officially Mormons could vote as they chose, Joseph had publicly and frequently expressed his opinion against the Democrats, who had put Van Buren in the White House and had elected Governor Boggs in Missouri. The Saints had been duly influenced and in the election of August 1840 voted almost as a bloc for the Whigs, except for one Democrat, James H. Ralston, who had befriended the prophet, and was chosen by the Saints instead of a little-known Whig lawyer named Abraham Lincoln.

As soon as both parties began to show some desire to court Mormon favor, Bennett brought up the petition for the Nauvoo charters, which included the charter for the city government, as well as the charters for the militia and the university.

In presenting the bill before the legislature at Springfield, Bennett emphasized the persecutions the Saints had endured in Missouri, the tragedy at Haun's Mill and the disasters in Far West, but said little about the provisions of the Nauvoo city charter.

Joseph wrote that the Nauvoo city charter was "my own plan and device. I concocted it for the salvation of the Church, and on principles so broad, that every honest man might dwell secure under its protective influence without distinction of sect or party."[13]

The powers of the Nauvoo city charter have become almost legendary, and in fact they did permit great autonomy within the city. The City Council (mayor, four aldermen and nine councilmen) could pass any ordinances which did not conflict with the federal and state constitutions. The council also acted as municipal court, and was empowered to organize the Nauvoo Legion (its members exempt from all other military duty) to be at the mayor's disposal to enforce city laws and ordinances, as well as on call by the governor for the public defense. The mayor was a figure of supreme power. As a member of the City Council, he helped to make the local laws, and as head of the municipal court, he gave them legal interpretation. To enforce the laws, he would have the military body under his command.[14]

Joseph Smith's interpretation of the powers of the Nauvoo city charter later gave rise to great protest, but in fact, the charter itself was not unusual. It was very much like the Springfield charter, which had been granted the year before, and some of the laws were identical.[15] The Nauvoo city charter was only one of forty-seven acts of incorporation (eight of which were city charters) passed by that assembly.[16] Supported by Stephen A. Douglas, who was then Secretary of State, and by many others, it was passed in both houses without so much as a complete reading, and was signed by Governor Carlin on December 16, 1840, to go into effect on the first Monday in February 1841.

Bennett wrote a letter to the *Times and Seasons* December 16, 1840, to announce passage of the act, saying that Lincoln "had the magnanimity" to vote for the act, even though the Mormons had withdrawn their support from his candidacy, and had come up after its passage to offer congratulations.

On Saturday afternoon, January 2, 1841, citizens of Nauvoo gathered at the store owned by the converts from Canada, William and Wilson Law, to hear Bennett announce the election of city officers. Only one candidate was put forth for the office of mayor, and that was Bennett, whose election was a mere formality to sustain him in office.

His inaugural address, given February 3, was short but remarkably far-sighted. The new mayor proposed some immediate action for the public weal, namely that the city use its powers to suppress rather than tax the tippling houses, that the university be organized at once upon strictly utilitarian lines, that the Legion be established, that a board of health be appointed and that the lowlands bordering the Mississippi be drained and the timber removed. He also recommended the construction of a wing dam in the Mississippi near the head of Main Street in Nauvoo and the excavation of a ship canal from there to a grand reservoir about two miles east. The canal would afford a harbor for steamboats and water power for machinery for mills and for manufacturing. He suggested the appointment of an agent to negotiate with eastern capitalists on behalf of the city so that the project could be started at once. He envisioned the future Nauvoo as a great commercial city.[17]

It was not long before Bennett was also made chancellor of the university, president of the Nauvoo Agricultural and Manufacturing Association and major general of the Nauvoo Legion, which commission was second only to that of Joseph Smith.

To serve with Bennett as chancellor of the university, the City Council elected twenty-three regents, some of whom were not members of the church. The chancellor and regents at once chose James Kelley, a graduate of Trinity College, Dublin, as president, and appointed Orson Pratt professor of mathematics and English literature; Orson Spencer, a graduate of Union College and the Baptist Theological Seminary, professor of languages; Sidney Rigdon professor of church history and belles-lettres; and Gustavis Hills professor of music. A committee including Daniel H. Wells was assigned to choose a site and draw plans for the university, which was done, although no buildings were erected.

It seems that President Kelley was never active in office, and little is known of him other than that he had a reputation in Nauvoo as a learned man. However, professors Pratt, Spencer and Hills conducted their courses of study during 1841–1842, charging five dollars per quarter for tuition. The development of the university was curtailed when the Mormons' final difficulties began in Nauvoo, but the organization was taken with the Saints who moved west, where it was established as the University of Deseret, with Orson Spencer as chancellor.[18]

Until their dam could be built, the Saints planned to make a port on the Mississippi River just above Warsaw, which was fifteen miles south of Nauvoo. From this port, connections to Nauvoo would be greatly facilitated. Joseph prophesied that Nauvoo would become the biggest city in the west.

As trustee-in-trust for the church, Joseph controlled land sales to the Saints, and later he also became registrar of deeds, which meant that no property could be sold or bought in Nauvoo outside of his jurisdiction. Prices of city lots in Nauvoo were fixed by him at an average of five hundred dollars, with lots free to those who were invalids from the Missouri persecutions.

By early 1841, Nauvoo had developed into a remarkable community with two sawmills, a steam flour mill, a foundry, a tool factory, dozens of shops, schools, bridges, paved streets, and cultivated fields, gardens and orchards, and a cooperative farm on the outskirts of town worked by brethren who had no land of their own. In answer to a revelation of January that year, 1841, the Saints were planning a hotel which would accommodate the city's ever-increasing number of guests and would also provide a suite of rooms in perpetuity for Joseph and his family. In February 1841, the Nauvoo Agricultural and Manufacturing Association, with a capital stock of $100,000, was approved by Governor Carlin for incorporation. On April 6, work was begun on the Saints' most important project, their new temple, which was to be 83 by 128 feet and nearly 60 feet high, built of the beautiful white limestone from their own quarry.

Nauvoo was fast becoming the show place of western Illinois.

For some time, however, the Mormons' neighbors had been uneasy about Joseph Smith's power. A visitor to the city in April of the year before had been particularly impressed by the prophet's influence over his people, and later made a shrewd observation about the source of that influence. He wrote:

A number of principle men of the place soon collected apparently anxious to hear the words which fell from his lips. His bearing towards them was like one who had authority, and the deference which they paid him convinced us that his dominion was deeply seated in the empire of their consciences.

When the visitor spoke of the prophet's potential political power, Joseph is reported to have said, "and our influence as far as it goes, we intend to use." The visitor's article closed with a comment which might well have been alarming to readers in Illinois:

. . . [his] mysterious and awful claims to divine inspiration make his voice to believers like the voice of God, trained to sacrifice their individuality; to utter one cry, and to think and act in crowds . . . these remarkable sectories must necessarily hold in their hands a fearful balance of political power. In the midst of contending parties, a single hand might turn their influence, with tremendous effect, to which ever side presented the most potent attraction; and should they ever become disposed to exert their influence for evil, which may Heaven prevent, they would surround our institutions with an element of danger, more dreaded than an armed and hundred eyed police.[19]

The citizens of Warsaw, in particular, were jealous of Nauvoo's increasing assumption of trade and political power in that area. In 1841, one Rev. B. F. Morris, a pioneer Presbyterian missionary in Hancock County and a resident of Warsaw, wrote:

This deluded, fanatical, and ignorant sect is about to be poured upon us by thousands . . . and thus like the locusts of Egypt consume every green thing in the land and wither away so far as they can every vestige of godliness . . . In view of this prospective state of things nearly all of the old citizens are anxious to sell their property and many of them will no doubt move away. There is not only in this village but all through the country a strong disinclination to live near the Mormons.[20]

In particular, neighbors were anxiously watching the growing strength of the Mormon militia.

Within six months of receiving their charter, the Nauvoo Legion counted nearly fifteen hundred men, and by the end of the first year, February 1842, it would have two thousand men in twenty-six companies of cavalry and infantry, with discipline, drill and uniforms patterned, so far as possible, after the United States Army.[21] In addition, there was a boys' corps of five hundred, of which the prophet's son, Joseph III, was a member. The boys drilled with wooden swords and carried a banner with the slogan: "Our fathers we respect; our mothers we'll protect." The prophet organized their parades and drills, and no doubt enjoyed them as much as the boys did. It must have occurred to many, however, that this youthful recreation would later result in important gains for the militia.[22]

As with the boys' corps, there was a fanciful element in the Legion, and more than a little fun.

The Legion was top-heavy with officers, some rather unlikely, including heralds and armor-bearers. Ostrich plumes in brilliant colors designating rank were added to the officers' hats. The officers were usually well turned out, but the troops were motley, because the demand for uniforms was so great and other work was so pressing that it was difficult to have uniforms made in less than a year.

Joseph took pleasure in his commission as lieutenant general, obtained by petition from Governor Carlin, and despite the fact that his status would not have been recognized outside his own militia, he could not resist mentioning that he outranked every other officer in the United States. He had a handsome uniform, based upon the United States Army dress uniform, a blue coat with epaulettes, high boots and a hat topped with ostrich feathers, and he carried a beautiful sword. Joseph's military regalia was modest, however, compared with that of his second-in-command, Major General John C. Bennett, who wore a marvel of gold braid, buttons and frogs, oak leaves and tassels.

The Legion would be composed of two cohorts, one of foot and one of mounted troops, each commanded by a brigadier general. A number of the officers had already held commissions in the Hancock County Militia, including Joseph's young brother, Don Carlos. Like the usual state militia, the Nauvoo Legion drilled partly for recreation and display. Joseph led the colorful parades, riding on one of his handsome horses and flanked by his personal bodyguard of twelve men in white uniforms. With their stirring music and well-executed drills, the Mormon exhibitions soon became the largest and most exciting in the area, and attracted Mormons and non-Mormons from miles around, many arriving on Mississippi River excursion boats.

Despite their enjoyment, it was apparent that the men of the Legion were in deadly earnest. Their regulations were strict. Every citizen of Nauvoo unless exempt by law was required to participate, and absence from musters and parades was punishable by fines of up to twenty-five dollars.

Bennett, as quartermaster general of Illinois, was able to get three cannons for the Legion, and about two hundred and fifty stand of personal arms. The Nauvoo troops had rifles, which made them the envy of older state militiamen, who still bore muskets. The prophet said he felt proud to be associated with a body of men who "in point of discipline, uniforms, appearance and a knowledge of military tactics are the pride of Illinois, one of its strongest defenses, and a great bulwark of the western country."[23]

With such a history of outrage against them, and with no assurance either of redress or of future protection even by the federal government, the Mormons supported their militia with understandable enthusiasm. The Legion represented their security, their hope to retain the beautiful new city they were building despite hardship, illness and poverty. Although the nation had failed to sustain them in their rights, the Saints still held faith in that tenet of the Constitution which allowed them to protect themselves.

Unfortunately, the sight of the Legion's drills and parades did not merely entertain the Mormons' neighbors, but it inspired their jealousy, and what was more dangerous, their fear. Although Joseph saw his troops as "the bulwark of the western country" and in fact numbered non-Mormons among the officers and men, many people from surrounding towns saw them not so much as a defensive measure as a menace.

On the surface, it might be hard to understand the resentment shown the Legion, since it was in the honored American tradition of a civilian militia. Unlike the professional European soldier who fought on foreign soil, the American militiaman had defended his own property since colonial times, and it was an army of civilians that had won the American Revolution.[24] The Constitution of the new republic had recognized this long tradition in stating that "a well regulated militia, being necessary to the security of a free state, the right of the people to keep and bear arms shall not be infringed."

Unfortunately, however, Joseph Smith was quoted as saying that if people continued to molest the Saints they would establish their religion by the sword, and he himself would become a second Mahomet.[25] The facts were that although Joseph took delight in military drill, held the highest office in the Legion and made belligerent speeches on more than one occasion, he was not actively in command of the troops, and was to call them out as militia only once. It was Bennett who organized and trained the men, and Bennett had a small opinion of Joseph's military skill. He was later to say, "Joseph Smith, the Lieutenant-General, is a military novice of the first water and magnitude, scarcely knowing the difference between a general and a corporal—if it only has the *ral* as the suffix, Joe is therewith content."[26]

But the Mormons' neighbors felt threatened by the Legion. One non-Mormon who lived near Nauvoo said of the Saints in a letter of 1841:

> . . . they must and will take the world. And if they cannot do it by preaching they will by the force of arms they therefore incorporate militerry tacticks with their religion it is said they train Saturday and are well disciplined . . . it is said they take the liberty to tell the people that they now come with the Bible in their hands but ere long they will come with the sword also by their side.[27]

The writer's opinion of the temper of the times is more accurate than his spelling, for, true or not, it is what the Gentiles believed, and as noted in another context by the astute citizens of Clay County, Missouri, the effect on the Mormons' neighbors was the same.

What had begun only a little over two years before as a friendly and auspicious relationship between the Mormons and their new neighbors was changing, as had been the pattern so often in the past, to antagonism, and a series of events began to move with what seemed implacable force toward a tragic conclusion to the young prophet's career.

CHAPTER

3

NAUVOO FLOURISHES

Between 1841 and 1843 the prophet would see many of his cherished hopes fulfilled, his city grow and prosper, his church and doctrine develop and his influence spread. However, he would also suffer personal hardship, financial and legal difficulties, and notoriety on a scale he had not before experienced, becoming nearly the talk of the nation because of one vicious and determined enemy and one opportunistic newspaperman, as it happened, both by the name of Bennett. At the same time, a complex series of interrelated events, including the growing hostilities of neighbors and certain factors in the prophet's own personality, would, as if inevitably, lead him closer to his doom.

The spring of 1841 seemed propitious enough, however. Joseph and the Mormons loved celebrations, and on April 6, having reason to rejoice in the eleventh anniversary of the church and in laying the cornerstones for their new temple, they did so in their typical exuberant manner. The fourteen companies of the Nauvoo Legion were joined for the occasion by two companies of volunteers from Ohio to make a very impressive drill and parade, with a brilliant display of uniforms, artillery and cannon fire, and music from the military band. Joseph Smith, resplendent in full dress, was presented with a national flag of silk by the ladies of Nauvoo. By noon a multitude had assembled on the temple grounds, where Joseph, officers, architects and guests took the stand for a ceremony of hymns, prayers, choir singing and an oration by Sidney Rigdon. After the principal cornerstone was laid, Joseph gave a feast of excellent Mormon cooking to his friends and guests.

Among those who sat by Joseph's side on the stand and later ate his turkey dinner was a non-Mormon guest from the neighboring town of Warsaw, Thomas Coke Sharp, editor of the *Warsaw Signal*.

Sharp was a fiery and ambitious young man, not yet twenty-three years old, who had come to Quincy from Pennsylvania in August of the previous year to practice law, but finding his hearing deficiency a handicap in that profession, he had turned to journalism. In November he had bought a little Warsaw newspaper called *The Western World,* renamed it *Warsaw Signal* and was eagerly involved in county affairs.[1]

While Sharp was watching the Mormons, one of them was watching him, a Norton Jacobs who had been assigned to hold Sharp's horse during the ceremonies. Norton wrote in his journal that he was certain Sharp conceived an animosity toward the Saints that day, out of envy.[2] Joseph, offering fellowship to all, apparently did not observe anything unusual in his guest, but the prophet's brother William noticed him, and recorded that after Sharp returned to Warsaw he opened a tirade against the Mormons evidently without cause.[3] Seemingly from that day he became Joseph's implacable enemy. He turned his hatred upon all of the Mormons as well, and upon any who showed an inclination to be friendly toward them, or even impartial. Any who were not openly anti-Mormon he began to call "Jack Mormons," and the nickname became popular.

To Joseph, the day was highly gratifying, and he took particular pride in the fact that no obscenity, profanity or drunkenness was shown in that enormous crowd. "Can the same be said of a similar assemblage in any other city in the Union?" he wrote. "Thank God that the intoxicating beverage, the bane of humanity in these last days, is becoming a stranger in Nauvoo."[4]

In succeeding weeks, Joseph had reason to be pleased with the progress of the church. Besides one in Nauvoo, church conferences were held in Philadelphia, where Hyrum presided, and in New York City. In Manchester, England, the Council of Twelve assembled as a quorum for the first time in conference in a foreign land, and heard statistics read that the church now had nearly six thousand members in twenty-eight cities throughout England, Ireland and Wales, not counting nearly eight hundred converts who had recently emigrated from those areas to Nauvoo.[5]

Joseph's season of content was short, however. Lilburn W. Boggs, governor of Missouri, had been infuriated by Joseph's complaints against his state before Congress. No longer satisfied merely to have banished the Mormons, he wanted Joseph back to stand trial under the old accusations of treason made after Far West. That spring, 1841, he made an attempt to extradite Joseph from Illinois.[6]

On June 4, 1841, while in Quincy on business, Joseph called upon Governor Carlin at his home, where he was treated with every courtesy. As soon as he left, however, Carlin sent a posse after him, led by a constable and a sheriff from Illinois and an officer from Missouri, an act that seemed so despicable to the Mormons that they withdrew their support from Carlin for the rest of his term.

Arrested and taken back to Quincy, Joseph was given an appointment for a hearing in nearby Monmouth, Judge Stephen A. Douglas to preside. In Monmouth on the appointed day, Joseph and his friends were met by crowds of hostile people who made such trouble pressing against the windows of the house where Joseph was retained that he had to be kept upstairs even for meals.

On Wednesday, June 9, the hearing began before a crowded courtroom. After listening to a passionate speech by one of Joseph's six attorneys, O. H. Browning, who pleaded that Joseph not be surrendered to a people who had savagely driven hundreds of his followers out of their homes into the dread of winter, Judge Douglas delivered the decision that the writ, having once been returned to the executive by the sheriff of Hancock County, was dead. He said that he would not decide the question as to whether or not the evidence in the case was admissible, since there was no precedent, and, in his opinion, important considerations were involved relating to the future conduct of the states.[7]

Joseph was released before noon and he and his company went home in triumph, to meet the acclamation of the Saints.

This was far from the end of the prophet's troubles with Missouri, but in the meantime other matters required his attention.

Early that summer, 1841, Brigham Young and others of the Twelve including Orson Pratt, Wilford Woodruff, George Albert Smith, John Taylor and Willard Richards, returned to Nauvoo after highly successful missionary service in England. In less than two years they had made several thousand converts, of whom no less than 2,749 would immigrate to Nauvoo in 1841 and 1842. They had organized the mission into branches and districts and ordained many new members of the priesthood. Besides initiating the *Millennial Star,* they had published two thousand hymnals and five thousand copies of *The Book of Mormon.*[8]

Parley P. Pratt remained behind to preside and Orson Hyde to preach the gospel in the east and dedicate Jerusalem to a return of the Jews.

It was decided that the Twelve would manage the business affairs of the church, assisting Joseph Smith, who remained sole trustee-in-trust. Under the leadership of Brigham Young, their president, the Twelve would also continue to direct the immigration of converts who poured into Nauvoo not only from the British Isles but from the eastern United States and Canada.

The Mormons' need for land increased. Among the arrangements Joseph had made to provide land was a contract for about five hundred acres in the center of Nauvoo, bought in August 1839 from Horace R. Hotchkiss and partners, New Haven, Connecticut, through Isaac Galland as agent. Joseph had agreed with Hotchkiss to pay the debt and interest with lands acquired from converts in the east, who would receive land in and near Nauvoo in exchange. It was an ingenious arrangement and should have been of benefit to all, except that Galland was less interested in helping the Saints than in what he could do for himself. The price of the land was outrageous for a piece of swamp that nobody else would have. According to one historian the cost to the Mormons was not $53,000, as usually quoted, but with interest amounted to $114,500, which made the price of city lots necessarily high.[9] The Saints liked the location, however, and were willing to work hard to make their new city a beautiful and wholesome place. By August of 1841, the interest on the Hotchkiss debt amounted to $6,000, an enormous sum for a people who had been driven destitute from Missouri and who had other debts, including some still outstanding from Kirtland days.

In an effort to raise money for the interest, and to cover the cost of lots given to those who had been made widows and orphans in Missouri, in particular at Haun's Mill, Joseph tried to sell some land in Nauvoo at a slight increase over the original cost, for which he found himself accused of lining his own pockets.

In the summer of 1841, Joseph sent Isaac Galland and Hyrum to arrange for the transfer of deeds to the Hotchkiss firm. To Joseph's surprise, Hotchkiss wrote to him on July 24 protesting that Galland had left New York without paying the interest due, which made him and his partners feel they "had much reason to be dissatisfied at this silence and apparent neglect."

Joseph replied in anger, on August 25, thinking that Hotchkiss meant to harass him, "I presume you are no stranger to the part of the city plat we bought of you being a deathly sickly hole" and said the Mormons had been unable to realize any profit from it. "And now to be goaded by you, for a breach of good faith . . . seems to me to be almost beyond endurance."[10] (Only two weeks before, on August 7, Joseph had lost his youngest brother, Don Carlos, from the swamp fever.)

In a postscript, however, Joseph wrote that he had just learned that Hyrum had had to leave the east because he was ill, but that Galland had nearly enough to liquidate the amount due and was supposed to have done so long before.[11]

On October 9, Joseph wrote the firm again to say that Galland had not yet returned to Nauvoo. "Why he has not done according to my instructions, God only knows . . . He has a considerable amount of money in his hands, which was to have been paid to you, as we intended." Unwilling to believe that his friend had betrayed his trust, Joseph added, "He is on his way, for aught we know and is retarded in his journey by some misfortune or other. He may return, however, as yet, and give a just and honorable account of himself."[12]

Joseph asked for a little further indulgence until spring, and promised that he would never cease until the matter was adjusted to their satisfaction.

Some weeks later Joseph discovered that Galland was in Keokuk, Iowa, across the river, about fifteen miles south of Nauvoo. He wrote to him on January 17, 1842, asking him either to call within a few days, or to send all the funds he could. The next day Galland sent an insolent reply. "On the receipt of the above note I am at a loss to determine whether you intend it as an absolute dun or as an appeal to my liberality to advance funds for your relief," adding that he did not have five dollars to advance, and that as for coming to Nauvoo, "I have long desired to come there and shall certainly do so as soon as I can so arrange the matters which I am now engaged in . . ."[13]

On the eighteenth, Joseph revoked Galland's power of attorney to act for the church, and wrote him the next day protesting that although he had had no returns from Galland, he had been obliged to cash notes Galland had given for lands in the east. He asked Galland to come to Nauvoo as soon as possible for settlement. This, apparently, Galland ignored.

Joseph sent his most able and aggressive assistant, Brigham Young, with James Ivins for a conference with Galland, and on January 27, Joseph recorded that they returned with a favorable report, bringing a letter of attorney and other papers Galland had received from Joseph and the church. On February 2, Joseph himself spent the day with Galland and reached some conclusion to their current difficulties. It developed, however, that the perfidious Galland had harmed the Saints even further. It was established in the courts that many of his claims to Half Breed Lands he had sold the Saints were invalid, and that in reality his interest was only a small undivided portion of the reservation. Nearly 250 families who had invested all their means and their best labor in building up farms and homesteads on Galland's Half Breed Lands had to vacate and lost everything.

Galland later had only occasional contact with Joseph and the Saints. He spent his last years in Iowa and eventually died there a pauper.

Meanwhile, to help provide for the needs of his growing city, Joseph had a country store built not far from his home, and evidently intended to manage it without relinquishing his other responsibilities. On December 22, 1841, he noted in his diary that thirteen wagons came up from Warsaw, bringing sugar, molasses, glass, salt, coffee, tea and other provisions ordered from St. Louis. With obvious satisfaction, Joseph described his new enterprise. It was spacious for a country store, and painted by an English convert; the counters, drawers and pillars, as Joseph wrote, made "a very respectable representation of oak, mahogany and marble for a backwoods establishment." The ground floor had shelves and drawers for stock with a counting room at the back and stairs to cellar and second story. Upstairs was a large room where the Masons and other groups could meet. There also Joseph had a private office, in which he received revelations, did translating and kept his sacred writings. It was a pleasant, quiet retreat from the bustle of the town, with a window to the south overlooking the Mississippi, the passing boats and the opposite shore, and Joseph pronounced it "altogether a place the Lord is pleased to bless."

Joseph opened his "Red Brick Store" as it came to be known, on January 5, and to his delight it was filled at once with customers. He stood behind the counter all day, dealing out goods as steadily as any clerk to those who had gone without a Christmas dinner for want of sugar, molasses and raisins. It was work in which Joseph said he pleased himself as well as the Saints.

During this time, he was coming to rather dubious national attention through the efforts of the New York newspaperman James Gordon Bennett, a lanky, lantern-jawed Scot who was not highly regarded in all circles because of his practice of making personal, acrimonious attacks on individuals and his policy of emphasizing whatever sensational news would sell his papers. The *New York Herald,* which he had started in a cellar in 1835 as a small penny sheet, had become a great commercial enterprise of national influence. Bennett had visited Nauvoo, thought the Mormons provided good copy and periodically thereafter published stories about Joseph Smith and the Mormons and reprinted articles from the *Times and Seasons.*

On November 18, 1841, apparently in all sincerity, he had written:

> The Mormon movement is one of the most curious of the present age. It is inexplicable on the ordinary principles of philosophy. It is the beginning of a new dispensation, or it is nothing. There can be no mistake in Joseph Smith. He is a master spirit—and his ambition is to found a religious empire that will reach the uttermost ends of the earth. He has given the world a new Bible—and he is now busily engaged in founding a new kingdom of the faithful . . . At this moment they have Apostles in England, France, and Germany, besides a deputation on the road to the Holy Land.

Following his editorial Bennett had printed an article signed by eight of the Twelve which summarized the recent church conference, announced the church contract with Hotchkiss to buy five hundred acres in Nauvoo and reported on the progress of the temple.

Joseph was at first gratified by Bennett's attention, and in turn reprinted the most favorable parts of the *Herald* stories in the *Times and Seasons.* In December 1841, he presented a resolution to the City Council that they extend Bennett an expression of gratitude for giving the Mormons a fair hearing, and that they recommend that the people of Nauvoo subscribe to his paper. However, Bennett's attitude toward the prophet vacillated between seemingly open admiration and sly derision. On January 10, 1842, Bennett wrote:

The Mormons, under the guidance of their great prophet and seer, the famous Joe Smith, are organizing a religious empire in the far west that will astonish the world in these latter days. Civil, religious, military, judicial, social, moral, advertising, commercial organization, are all embraced within the comprehension of their new system—or their new revelation fresh from God himself, in their own enthusiastic language. The astonishing mixture of worldly prudence and religious enthusiasm . . . of civilized reason with ancient ideas of religious observance and military organization, is without a parallel in the history of nations since the time of Mahomet . . . In two years the Holy City of God, Nauvoo, has risen from a few houses to possess 10,000 souls, besides much cattle, all animated by the same spirit . . .

James Gordon Bennett would continue for months in similar vein, and at last a correspondent of Joseph's, James Arlington Bennet, attorney, author and proprietor of Arlington House, an educational institution on Long Island, would write to him on February 20, 1843:

You will see by the NYork Herald that Bennett continues to make sport of you . . . . his sole object in publishing your articles from the Times & Seasons was as he assured me to get up a subscription list for his paper at Nauvoo as well as the excitement this produced here . . . . You would add to your independence & respectability to cast him off . . .[14]

Though his friends might take offense at James Gordon Bennett's continuing discourse, Joseph apparently was neither as disturbed by it as they were nor as duped and flattered as has often been assumed. He wrote to James Arlington Bennet soon after receiving his letter:

As to James Gordon Bennett . . . Your relation of his intentions in extracting from the Times and Seasons, is all in course; the great object was too glaring upon the face of it to be mistaken aside from the folly, vanity and hotch potch, which spotted his comments, in the Herald. . . . the promise is that God will bring every man into judgment with every secret thing whether it be good or whether it be evil.[15]

Although Joseph could discount them, James Gordon Bennett's articles that winter of 1841–42 were perhaps influencing the Mormons' neighbors unfavorable. The *Sangamo Journal* of January 21, 1842, said:

Now as long as Mr. Smith keeps near sanctuary and prophecies of religion he is guiltless of offence, but when he enters upon the duties of a civil office of the state, and as a Lieutenant General, speaks to his friends, whom he KNOWS AS A PROPHET *he can command* . . . he becomes a dangerous man, and must look to the consequences. If he would take a friendly advice . . . let him stick to interpretation and prophecy,—for we do assure him upon an honest belief, that his situation in Illinois is far more dangerous than ever it was in Missouri, if he undertakes to take Mohamet's part.

Actually, however, Joseph was involved in many other kinds of endeavors. He was giving sermons as usual, attending sessions of the City Council, managing his store, serving as trustee-in-trust for the church, conducting sales of lands and city lots, holding sessions with the Twelve Apostles, attending baptisms, visiting the sick and dictating his journal and a large correspondence. At the same time, he was editor of the *Times and Seasons,* and was working on a new edition of *The Book of Mormon,* correcting errors which he said had escaped notice in the sterotype plates of the first edition, and he was busy with his scribe, Willard Richards, preparing the Bible, the hymnbook and the *Doctrine and Covenants* for the press. He was also at work on *The Book of Abraham,* which he published in the *Times and Seasons* in two numbers, March 1 and March 15. In March, he participated in the installation of the Nauvoo Lodge of Free Masons and counseled the sisters in their organization of The Female Relief Society of Nauvoo, the purpose of which was to help the sick and needy.

A man of astonishing energy, Joseph was also overseeing the work on the temple and raising means for its completion.

The previous November 15, 1841, the Twelve had sent a letter to the Saints abroad, saying that the first great object before the church was building the temple and Nauvoo House, an inn much needed for Nauvoo's increasing visitors.

soon the kings and the queens, the princes and the nobles, the rich and the honorable of the earth will come up hither to visit the Temple of our God . . . such, as well as the Saints, should have a comfortable house for boarding and lodging when they come hither . . .[16]

Joseph made the temple a vast community-welding enterprise, involving the work, substance, money, faith and enthusiasm of all.

That fall he had sent a number of the brethren up to pine country in Wisconsin Territory to get lumber. During the winter he had a hundred hands quarrying rock and "multitudes" hauling rock and doing other labor. He encouraged some to give a tenth of their time to work on the temple and others a tenth of their income. The people responded heartily. Scores of families took in one or two temple laborers to board with them and sisters who could do nothing more were knitting socks and mittens for use of the workmen in cold weather. The prophet asked the Saints from miles around to participate, to lend their wagons and to send provisions, clothing and hay.

Members of the little branch of the church in Andover, Ohio, sent a letter with their donation saying they only had a little to give at present but hoped to send more later. Their carefully listed contribution was typical, a testimony of the hardship, faith and sacrifice of the Saints. With names of the donors, they sent twenty dollars in cash, thirteen and a half yards of cloth, a skein of yarn, a quilt, three skins, two pairs of boots and a pair of shoes, some socks and mittens, and twenty-five pounds of apples.[17]

Joseph wrote that the Saints were blessed with means to raise their temple and they looked forward to its completion as an event of great importance to the church and to the world.

Of utmost significance were the ordinances to be performed in the temple, and some were so urgent that they were not to await its completion.

While building was going on, an elaborate temporary baptismal font was set up in the basement, dedicated by Brigham Young on November 8, 1841, and put into use November 21. The font was a source of pride to the prophet, who described it in detail as resting upon twelve oxen, carved of pine planks glued together, for which the model was the most beautiful young steer that could be found.

The font was used for the urgent temple ordinance of baptism for the dead. About this ordinance Joseph wrote, "what has become of our fathers? Will they all be damned for not obeying the Gospel, when they never heard it? Certainly not. But they will possess the same privilege that we here enjoy, through the medium of the everlasting priesthood, which not only administers on earth, but also in heaven." In citing authority for the baptisms, Joseph quoted Paul: "Else what shall they do which are baptized for the dead, if the dead rise not at all? Why are they then baptized for the dead?" (1 Cor. 15:29). Joseph continued, "And now as the great purposes of God are hastening to their accomplishment, and the things spoken of in the Prophets are fulfilling, as the kingdom of God is established on the earth, and the ancient order of things restored, the Lord has manifested to us this day and privilege, and we are commanded to be baptized for our dead."[18]

Joseph rejoiced in the temple building and looked to the future generations to recognize its value. He wrote:

The building up of Zion is a cause that has interested the people of God every age . . . but they died without the sight; we are the favored people that God has made choice to bring about the Latter day glory . . . our children will rise up and call us blessed; and generations yet unborn will dwell with peculiar delight upon the scenes that

we have passed through . . . the all but insurmountable difficulties
that we have overcome in laying the foundation of a work that
brought about the glory and blessing which they will realize . . .[19]

The prophet's view of the city and people of Nauvoo was not without
basis. The Mormons had endured much for their faith and were willing to
endure to the end. Although far from austere, enjoying music, banquets,
dancing, singing, parades, ball games and boat rides on the Mississippi in
all of which they were led enthusiastically by their prophet, they were a
morally strict people, believing in church and home as centers of a chaste
and temperate life. There were no public saloons in the Mormon city, although for a short while, until Emma protested, Porter Rockwell ran a bar
in the Mansion House after it became a hotel. A brothel erected brazenly
near the temple grounds the previous year by a young man who pretended
to be running a grocery store (a grocery store that was oddly covered with
graffiti) was soon closed by the City Council and torn down. Some non-
Mormons lived in Nauvoo, but with the notable exception of brigands who
had used the town as a convenient hideout by the river, most of the townsfolk adopted the Mormon standards. For a while, Nauvoo was a city of remarkable harmony of spirit and enterprise.

THE FRIEND
TURNED ENEMY

For Joseph Smith, the year 1842 would prove exasperating and dangerous, mainly because his former friend, the gifted and unscrupulous John
Cook Bennett, would turn against him viciously and would try to blacken
his reputation, undermine his church, add to his financial problems and
subject him again to his old enemies in Missouri.

By the spring of 1842, disquieting rumors had already been in circulation in Nauvoo for several months about the flamboyant little Dr. Bennett
who had risen so suddenly to a spectacular place among the Saints. Besides acting as first counselor to the prophet while Sidney Rigdon was ill,
Bennett had become mayor of Nauvoo, chancellor of the university and
president of the Nauvoo Agricultural and Manfacturing Association. He
held the rank of major general in the Nauvoo Legion and directed its organization and training. After only eighteen months in Nauvoo he had become second in power to no one but the prophet himself.

The fact was, however, that Joseph had known for some time that Bennett had come to the Saints in a false guise. Among other deceits, he had
represented himself to the women as a bachelor. While on his mission in
Pittsburgh in 1841, Hyrum had discovered that Bennett had a wife and
children in Ohio, although they had left him after charging him with cruelty. When Joseph had confronted him that July, Bennett had confessed
and made a dramatic show of swallowing poison. He recovered, and al
though his recovery was not without suspicion, since as a doctor he might
well have concocted an innocuous dose for himself, his gesture was taken

as evidence of genuine remorse and he was allowed to remain in full fellowship in the church.

However, while mouthing the religious and moral beliefs of the Saints, he secretly found it not at all necessary to renounce the life of a profligate. One aspect of his new religion was a particular source of temptation, and he did not mind how he distorted or perverted it for his own gratification.

Before this time, Joseph had taken several wives in the new convenant of plural marriage. Although polygamy was still denied in public in the realization that the Gentiles and most of the Saints were not yet prepared for such a radical change in the social structure, several high leaders in the church, Joseph's most loyal friends, had been taught what was to be included in the restoration of the ancient order, and some were already participating. Every attempt was made to keep plural marriages secret, but enough rumors were in circulation to make what Bennett told the sisters not altogether incredible. Bennett used his enormous prestige in Nauvoo and the fact that he was thought to be Joseph's closest friend to try to persuade the Mormon women of his choice that the prophet had sanctioned his "spiritual wifery."

Joseph soon began to hear of Bennett's scandalous interpretation of the plural marriage covenants. Perhaps he also began to fear that Bennett was not satisfied to have risen so high so fast to second place but might covet his role as head of the Mormon society. Whether or not he had evidence, Joseph suspected that Bennett planned some harm to him during the Nauvoo Legion's annual parade and celebration on May 7, 1842.

In the sham battle that followed the parade Bennett had suggested that Joseph lead the first cohort, and when Joseph refused, he asked him to take a place in the rear of the cavalry without his life guards, a position that Joseph and his staff considered extremely vulnerable. Joseph chose his own position and kept the captain of his life guards close at his side. In his journal for that day, Joseph wrote that unless he was mistaken, Bennett would soon reveal his true feelings.[1]

Hyrum began an investigation of the rumors about Bennett and gathered testimony that he had tried to seduce a number of women by telling them that it was "perfectly right" if kept secret, that it was one of the mysteries of God to be revealed when the people were strong enough, and that if necessary, he would give them medicine to produce abortion. One witness, a woman whom Bennett had attended during illness, testified that Bennett told her that he wanted to marry her and "clear out with her," that he wished her husband were dead and begged her permission "to give him medicine to that effect."

According to a statement Hyrum made sometime later, Bennett turned up on May 17, 1842, during a recess of the Masonic Lodge meeting held in the store and approached him, weeping and begging to be spared public exposure. When Joseph crossed the yard from his house, on his way to the store, Bennett dashed up and snatched his hand, pleading to be forgiven. Joseph cried, "Doctor! Why are you using my name to carry on your hellish wickedness?" He demanded to know if he had ever taught Bennett such behavior. According to Hyrum, Bennett denied it vehemently and when Joseph asked if he would sign an affidavit to that effect, Bennett eagerly agreed. He went into the office at once with Hyrum and wrote a statement that Joseph had never taught him anything contrary to the laws of God or man, and swore to it before Alderman Daniel H. Wells.[2]

On that same day, May 17, Joseph wrote a note to James Sloan:

Bro. James Sloan.
You will be so good as to permit Gen. Bennett to withdraw his Name from the Church Record, if he desires to do so, and this with the best of feelings towards you and General Bennett.

Joseph Smith.

Sloan drew up a notice to that effect, which Joseph signed and gave to Bennett.[3]

Bennett resigned at once as mayor of Nauvoo, giving as his reason "circumstances of a personal nature."[4]

Two days later, at a special session of the City Council before a house full of spectators, Bennett's resignation as mayor was accepted and Joseph was elected in his place, with Hyrum as vice-mayor. Joseph then pressed Bennett to tell whether or not he had anything against him. Bennett said, "I do not. In all my intercourse with General Smith, in public and in private, he has been strictly virtuous."[5]

Bennett appeared before the Masons on May 26 and acknowledged his licentious conduct, wept like a child and begged to be spared. Joseph wrote that Bennett feigned contrition so well, or perhaps actually felt it so deeply for the moment, that Joseph himself pleaded for him and the brothers extended a further indulgence.

To their chagrin, the Masons soon learned that Bennett, whom they had accepted on his word that he was a member in good standing, had been expelled from his former lodge in Ohio for "rascally conduct." On June 16, the master of the Nauvoo Lodge published a notice warning all members of the brotherhood against him.[6]

On June 23, Joseph made public an edict of excommunication which he said had been written May 11. He published an account of Bennett's actions, which he addressed to the church and "to all the honorable part of the community."[7] By that time Bennett was putting it about that the church was not worthy of his society. He maintained that his excommunication had come after he had withdrawn from the church, that Orson Pratt had refused to sign the edict because he knew nothing against Bennett and that the names of Lyman Wight, William Smith, and John E.

Page, who were all more than a thousand miles from Nauvoo at the time, were forged.[8]

According to Hyrum, Bennett left town swearing to "drink the heart's blood" of his enemies.[9]

He lost no time in reaching the public with his version of what had occurred.

On July 8, 1842, the *Sangamo Journal* in Springfield published an extra with the news of Bennett's excommunication and a notice that he would "reveal conditions" in Nauvoo in a series of letters to the editor. In those letters, which appeared regularly through July until the end of September, Bennett put himself in the role of victim. His story about what had occurred on May 17 was that Joseph had taken him alone to a room in the Nauvoo Lodge, locked the door, pulled out a pistol and said that for the peace of his family, he must go before the City Council and exonerate Joseph from any part of the spiritual wife doctrine, and threatened if he refused to make "cat fish bait" out of him, or turn him over to the Danites. Bennett said he then signed his affidavit before Alderman Wells and made the required statement before the City Council.

In rebuttal, Hyrum said that Bennett could not have had any such private interview with Joseph in the lodge room on the seventeenth because the lodge had convened all that day and Hyrum had the keys.

Bennett tried to present Joseph as an absolute charlatan, accused him of lasciviousness under pretense of religion and of instituting hierarchies of women prostitutes.

Some of Bennett's stories had direct repercussions among the saints. Bennett named women to whom he said Joseph had made improper advances, including Sarah Pratt while her husband Orson was on his mission to England. In his letter dated July 2 to the *Sangamo Journal,* Bennett said that soon after they met, Joseph had told him about his designs on "that amiable and accomplished lady."

Bennett also claimed to have had the confidence of Sarah Pratt. Like many missionaries' wives who were left without support, Sarah had done cooking, sewing and washing to keep herself and her children, and Bennett had taken meals with her. According to Bennett, Sarah confided to him that Joseph had told her the Lord had given her to him as one of his spiritual wives but she had replied that she did not believe in such revelations, and would never break her marriage covenant with Orson. Bennett said that Joseph warned her not to repeat what had happened, but Sarah told her husband when he came home. Orson faced Joseph, but Joseph denied everything and tried to blacken Sarah's reputation.

Considering Bennett's character and his vendetta against the prophet, it is not likely that his story about Joseph and Sarah is entirely reliable. However, it seems that something occurred between Joseph and Sarah that made her indignant, since some years later she told an interviewer that he had made "propositions" to her that enraged her and that she had refused the aid she was supposed to receive from the church while Orson was on his mission.[10]

In any event, the story Orson heard from Sarah or Bennett or both apparently so upset him that for a time he was irrational.

Joseph records that on August 29, 1842, Orson disappeared from Nauvoo and that most of the city turned out in search of him. Orson was found on the riverbank after an attempt to destroy himself.[11]

For a while Sarah and Orson withdrew from the church, but later, according to his brother Parley's great-granddaughter, Parley persuaded Orson that it was better to overlook the matter and keep harmony in the church.[12] Orson never wanted to lose the priesthood or his standing as a member of the Twelve. On January 20, 1843, the Quorum of the Twelve met at the home of Brigham Young in Orson's presence, to reconsider his case. On that same day Orson and Sarah were rebaptized in the river and Orson was restored as an apostle.[13] Orson afterward wrote to a cousin, "J. C. Bennett has published lies concerning myself & family & the people with which I am connected. His book I have read with the greatest disgust No candid honest man can or will believe it."[14]

John C. Bennett also accused Joseph of trying to seduce Nancy Rigdon, nineteen-year-old daughter of Sidney Rigdon, and of attempting to dishonor Martha Brotherton.

That Joseph attempted to persuade Nancy to marry him was recorded by others besides Bennett, including Nancy's brother John. John said that until that incident the Rigdons had been unaware of polygamy in the church. Sidney was profoundly shocked and upset by ensuing gossip among the neighbors. According to John, Joseph denied having proposed to Nancy, but Sidney later got an admission from him that it was true.[15]

Bennett took his story about Martha Brotherton from her own account, which was published in the St. Louis Bulletin, July 15, 1842, and widely reprinted in Illinois and throughout the east. Martha, an eighteen-year-old convert from England, said that Brigham Young had tried to convince her to become his plural wife without the knowledge of her parents, and that he was supported in his suit by Joseph Smith. Martha and her parents left Nauvoo.

In addition to the disturbance among the Saints, Bennett's letters caused an enormous sensation in the state. Besides his lurid and imaginative descriptions of licentious behavior among the Mormons in Nauvoo there were statements that fanned already existing anxieties among the Mormons' neighbors about Nauvoo's growing militarism. Bennett accused Joseph of planning to establish himself at the head of an independent empire by the strength of the Nauvoo Legion, which Bennett claimed had thirty cannon and an enormous collection of small arms acquired from the state. He accused Legion members of having taken the oath of the Danites to defend the prophet right or wrong.

Fears increased when other papers took up the rumors. The *Hawk-Eye and Iowa Patriot* wrote July 28, 1842, "We understand that almost every town of note has in it one of Joe's secret emissaries or Danites. They know each other by signs, and are sworn to protect their leaders. So look out."

Many newspapers reprinted Bennett's letters, no doubt for the stimulus they gave to circulation, even though they often repudiated their credibility. The widely read *New York Herald* printed the letters but later, when they were published in book form, denounced them as "obscene and licentious."

Joseph made an explicit countercharge against Bennett in the *Quincy Whig,* July 9, detailing his scandalous conduct. A friend and admirer of the Mormons in New York, James Arlington Bennet, wrote to Joseph on September 1, 1842, that he wished Joseph had not bothered to respond, because so much said on both sides made the public think no better of either party.[16] This counsel was given too late, however. By July 16, the editor of the *Whig* wrote that he was beginning to believe that Nauvoo must be a den of iniquity.

Bennett's accusations caused the Saints anxiety and embarrassment even at some distance from Nauvoo. Lorenzo D. Wasson, Emma Smith's nephew, who was serving a mission in Philadelphia, wrote to his uncle and aunt on July 30, 1842, saying that the Saints in his area were contending against the slanders, but that the faith of some was failing. Lorenzo offered his services and sent an affirmation of his belief in the prophet. He recalled an event which had occurred before he left for his mission:

I was reading in your chamber last summer—yourself and Bennett came into the lower room, and I heard you give J. C. Bennett a tremendous flagellation for practicing iniquity under the base pretext of authority from the heads of the Church—if you recollect I came down just before you were through talking. There are many things I can inform you of, if necessary, in relation to Bennett and his prostitutes. I am satisfied of your virtue and integrity. I have been with you to visit the sick, and time and again to houses where you had business of importance, you requested me to do so—many times I knew not why, but I am satisfied it was that you might not be censured by those that were watching you with a jealous eye, and I now solemnly protest before God and men, I never saw a thing unvirtuous in your conduct.[17]

From Pittsburgh, John E. Page wrote to Joseph, on August 8, 1842, "The disclosures of Bennett has done much to injure the cause of the kingdom . . . It becomes you and Brothers young and kimball to show yourselves men of the God of Israel this once to put down the slanders of

Bennett and Martha Brotherton . . . Please, Dear Brethren, do quickly and do it well . . ."[18]

A week later, on August 15, he wrote again, mentioning the "high anxieties of the public mind," and said, "we elders abroad in the world are the sufferers on us beat the winds storms and rain because the foundation of the Church is Apostles and prophets but thank God we are able yet—yet we ar anxeous that the Authorities should furnish as much means for argument as posible."[19]

Meanwhile, not only was Bennett's vicious campaign against Joseph Smith disrupting his church, but it was having serious repercussions in Illinois state politics, in the gubernatorial elections of 1842.

CHAPTER

5

THE PROPHET IN HIDING

By the time gubernatorial elections of 1842 were to be held, the Mormons had become a formidable political force in Illinois, and state politicians were greatly concerned about the Mormon vote.

In 1832 and the years intervening, enormous excitement had prevailed in national and state politics. Much discontent had been aroused in some circles by Andrew Jackson's stand on the tariff, his resistance to local improvements at federal expense and his veto of the charter of the second Bank of the United States on the ground that it favored large enterprise over farmers and small businessmen. A coalition of Jackson's opponents had formed a new party, taking their name, as they said, from the Whigs in English and American history who had opposed tyranny. The new Whigs attracted many powerful merchants and manufacturers who favored legislation that would promote business, commerce and urban growth. Although the Whigs found less support in the recently settled areas of the west and among immigrants and the urban poor, they soon became a serious threat to the Democrats. Political competition increased and campaigning assumed a professionalism across the country that had usually been known only in the great cities of the east. A network of party newspapers developed and promoted fervent local and national rivalries.

The Whigs, however, had not raised enough strength to defeat the Democrats in the election of 1836. Jackson's choice, Martin Van Buren, succeeded him and tried to follow his policies, including that of minimal federal interference with states, a policy Joseph Smith had considered so inimical when he had made his complaint to Van Buren against Missouri.

To broaden their appeal in the election of 1840, the Whigs ran a "log cabin and hard cider" campaign, publicizing their candidate, the aristocratic Virginian William Henry Harrison, as "Old Tippecanoe," frontiersman and Indian fighter.

In Illinois that summer of 1840, the Democrats and Whigs were about equal in strength, and before the elections, which were then under the old system held in August, the state had been pervaded by a great excitement. It was believed that the Mormons had generally favored the Democrats until Joseph's trip to Washington, when he had been so gravely disappointed by Van Buren. Now it was thought that most Mormons in Illinois had turned their support to the Whigs. When it began to be rumored that the Mormons would determine the elections in the county and perhaps in the state, Joseph Smith found himself very popular with both parties. According to Thomas Gregg, a non-Mormon journalist of Warsaw, it was "wonderful" how many politicians had business at Nauvoo. He wrote, "and while there, of course, duty and curiosity both required that they should call on the prophet, laugh at his rough jokes, listen to his anathemas against Governor Boggs and the Missouri mob, and his boasts of the up-building of Zion, while partaking of his hospitable entertainment at his Mansion House hotel. Altogether, his hotel was among the best stopping places in the city, and their bills were always paid liberally and willingly."[1]

The Whigs held many rallies across the country and in Illinois, including one in Carthage that had the active participation of Mormons.

Nationwide, the Whig ballyhoo raised 50 per cent more votes than the preceding election and put Harrison in office. He lived to hold that office for only one month, however, and was succeeded by his running mate, John Tyler, another States' rights advocate, who greatly disappointed his party by repeatedly vetoing the proposals that his fellow party member, Henry Clay, put through Congress. With the Whigs at such odds, it seemed to voters that little was accomplished and they began to return their favor to the Democrats. Nevertheless, and despite the fact that Whig newspapers had carried anti-Mormon stories, the Whigs thought that they still held the Mormon vote.

When campaigning began in 1841 for the gubernatorial elections of 1842, announcement was made by the Democrats that their candidate for governor was Adam W. Snyder, who as chairman of the state senate Judiciary Committee had promoted the Nauvoo charters. On December 20, 1841, Joseph Smith sent a statement to the *Times and Seasons* entitled, "The Prophet on the Attitude of the Saints in Politics," in which he said, "We care not a fig for Whig or Democrat; they are both alike to us, but we shall go for our friends, our tried friends, and the cause of human liberty, which is the cause of God. We are aware that 'divide and conquer' is the watchword of many, but with us it cannot be done . . . We voted for General Harrison because we loved him . . . but this is no reason why we should always be governored by his friends." He declared that the Democratic candidates had served the Mormons and the Mormons would serve them.[2]

The Whigs were furious and took every opportunity to castigate the Mormons. Recalling Joseph Smith's statement, the *Alton Telegraph and Democratic Review* of June 4, 1842, protested the fact that Joseph had signed it as lieutenant general of the Legion, and accused him of "commanding" his followers how to vote. This, the editor said, was "too bold a stride toward despotism."

Earlier that year, while he was still a member of the church in good standing, John C. Bennett had written a series of articles for the *Times and Seasons* on the military strength of the Legion, signed "Joab, General in Israel" which had caused the church nearly as much difficulty as the diatribes he had written as an excommunicate. Proclaiming that the Legion was now strong enough to right any wrong, he had written "The blood of murdered Mormons cries aloud for help, and the restoration of the inheritance of the Saints."[3] To the Mormons' neighbors this seemed an outrageous threat, which was made altogether credible by the sight of the efficient Mormon army at drill.

Concern about Mormon militarism became nationwide when an officer of the United States artillery published an article in the *New York Herald* of May 17, 1842, describing the Legion as a fearful host, led by ambitious and talented officers, fired by religious zeal and soon likely to be twenty or even fifty thousand strong. The officer said Bennett had plans for the fortification of Nauvoo which would equal those of Vauban. "The time will come when this gathering host of religious fanatics will make this country shake to its centre. A western empire is certain!"

The Mormon political strength supported by their military powers seemed a fearful thing.

The Whig candidate for governor, Joseph Duncan, announced that he favored recalling the public arms given to the Nauvoo Legion and requiring Mormons to train with the state militia. He also promised that if elected he would see that the Nauvoo charters were repealed. Courageous enough to act on his convictions, Duncan had angered the Democrats when he had left their ranks after they had put him in office both as a young state senator and later as governor of the state, 1834–38. He had withdrawn from the Democrats out of conviction that he could no longer sustain their views, and now out of conviction, as a Whig, he campaigned relentlessly against the Nauvoo city charter and the Nauvoo Legion. It was said he expected to win the election because of his stand on those issues alone.

Whig newspapers continued to fan the public fears about Joseph Smith's powers.

On July 2, the *Alton Telegraph and Democratic Review* wrote: "The people throughout the State have become justly alarmed at the assumption on the part of the Mormons through their spiritual head, 'Joe Smith' to decide who shall and who shall not be elected in this state." The editor advised that the people vote against all candidates who courted Mormon favor. On July 9, the paper reported that some of the southern cities had pledged enough votes for Duncan to balance the Mormon bloc. "Good," wrote the editor; "this is the right spirit; and if carried out, will save Illinois from political Mormonism."

On July 8, the *Sangamo Journal,* a very influential Whig paper, reprinted a statement from the *New York Herald* that the Mormons could already dictate to Illinois and might soon spread their influence to Congress and decide the presidency.

In Warsaw, where fear and hatred of the Mormons exceeded party loyalties, Thomas Sharp, editor of the *Warsaw Signal,* with other leading citizens including Thomas Gregg, had begun campaigning quite early for an anti-Mormon coalition of Whigs and Democrats, and for months they sustained a passionate tirade in the *Warsaw Signal* against Joseph Smith.

In retaliation the prophet's younger brother William started a little newspaper of his own called *The Wasp* and in his first issue, April 16, he stung Thomas Sharp as a "complete Jackass of an editor." A feud was launched between the two papers and continued until *The Wasp* ceased publication the following year.

With the growing anti-Mormon feeling, the Democrats began to fear that support from the Mormons would cause a rush of votes for the opposition. When their candidate, Adam Snyder, died suddenly, the party took the opportunity to choose a successor from northern Illinois who claimed no experience whatsoever with the Mormons. This was Justice of the State Supreme Court Thomas Ford, a slight, thin-faced man of forty-two, who made an unprepossessing public appearance but who was an educated man with a resolute faith in the law.

Ford himself said he was nominated not because of his importance in the party but because none of the leaders was likely to be elected, and they thought that he had no more than ordinary ambition, and they could govern through him.

The *Alton Telegraph and Democratic Review* of July 6, 1842, tried to accuse the Democrats of withholding Ford as a candidate until the Mormons approved. The editor wrote: "If Judge Ford is elected, will he not owe his election entirely to Joe Smith's wishes . . . and the result will be that Illinois will be under Mormon rule and control."

Ford, however, did not court Mormon favor. He made much of the fact that he knew nothing whatsoever about them, and said he had no idea whether they meant to vote for him or Duncan.

Meanwhile, the charges John C. Bennett was currently making against Joseph Smith and the Mormons were put to use in the political arena. On July 15, the *Illinois State Register* accused Duncan of paying for the reprinting of thousands of copies of Bennett's "immoral statements" to use as propaganda. It was suspected by some that Duncan had encouraged Bennett to make his disclosures, or at any rate to continue them, so as to weaken the candidate favored by the Mormons. The Whigs themselves suggested this in the *Alton Telegraph and Democratic Review* of July 23, just a week before election day:

> The rational of all parties rejoice at the disclosures of the Mormon impositions of Joe Smith. Who, we would ask, has been the means of bearding this lion in his den? We answer, Gen. Joseph Duncan . . . But for his moral firmness and intrepidity, Joe Smith would undiscovered still have been perfecting his plot to destroy the State of Illinois and the liberty of her citizens . . .

Despite all efforts by the Whigs, however, Thomas Ford was elected. He had nearly unanimous support in Nauvoo but never gave the Mormons credit for their part in his election, and in fact insisted that the Mormons had been more hindrance than help. He always maintained that he had been put into office because of his stand on the desperate issues of the state's economy.

There is no question that Illinois was in a deplorable condition when Ford took office. The state had borrowed itself out of credit, the people were unwilling and unable to pay taxes, the treasury owed $313,000 for ordinary government expenses and had no cash even for stamps. In addition, a debt of nearly $14 million hung over the state for canals, railroads and other projects undertaken by Ford's predecessor. Ford said that the confusion of counsel was equaled by the confusion of public affairs.[4]

Ford was a modest man, whose misfortune it was to inherit grave fiscal difficulties and to be caught in a tragic conflict between irreconcilable factions in his state, the Mormons and their neighbors.

The repeal of the Nauvoo charter had been a furious issue during the campaign, but apparently a less partial view was taken after elections were over, when a report made to the legislature stated that:

> the powers and privileges sought to be granted by that act however impolitic they may be, are so strikingly similar to the powers and privileges embraced in the charters of the city [sic] of Chicago, Quincy, and Springfield, that the committee can find no cause for the highly exasperated feeling against the last legislature for granting this act of incorporation.[5]

Nevertheless, when Ford took office on December 8, 1842, newspapers reported his succinct remark, "These charters are objectionable on many counts." As it later developed, however, if he had had the support of the legislature, Ford's aim would have been to reform rather than to repeal the charters.

Although Ford was never to have the full support of his party in the legislature, he was not without personal admirers. A contemporary wrote that a Senator Davis was asked by some worried holders of Illinois state bonds to investigate. Arriving in Springfield, Davis inquired after the governor's mansion, but in following directions, he could find only a small, half-story cottage. When he knocked to ask for further information a woman in a checkered apron told him that this was the governor's house and that he was out back sawing wood. Astonished, the senator found Ford working on a hickory log with a dull saw, persisting until he cut it through. The governor took him to the statehouse and showed him the books, which he kept himself, and assured him that Illinois would pay every penny of its debts. The senator concluded that any state that had elected such an example of simplicity and economy would not repudiate its obligations.[6]

During the election campaign, John C. Bennett had furthered his efforts against Joseph by trying to enlist the law to extradite him to Missouri in connection with an attempt on the life of the Mormons' old enemy, Lilburn W. Boggs.

After his term as governor of Missouri, Boggs had opened a store in Independence and had become a candidate for the state senate. On the rainy Friday evening of May 6, 1842, he was reading a newspaper in his study while at his feet were two of the ten children he had by his second wife. To this quiet scene a man had crept up, raised a revolving six-shooter called a pepperbox to the window and fired point-blank at the back of Boggs's head. The assailant dropped his weapon in a puddle and escaped.

Boggs was wounded by four balls—two lodged in the left lobe of his brain, one in the muscles of his neck, and a fourth passed through his neck and out through the roof of his mouth. It was thought surprising that he did not die instantly.[7] Bullets penetrated the wall beyond him, but the two children, a daughter of six and a baby in a cradle, were unharmed.

Since Boggs's administration as governor had been controversial and he was currently running for office, it was at first believed that he had been shot by a political enemy. A man named Tompkins was charged with the crime but soon absolved.[8] Shortly afterward, rumors began to spread that a stranger had been seen around Boggs's house for several days before the attack, and that the stranger was a Mormon. Suspicion fell upon Porter Rockwell, who had recently brought his pregnant wife to Independence to be with her parents for the birth of their child.

Porter was known to have been utterly devoted to Joseph Smith since his boyhood. Born in Massachusetts, in 1813, he had moved with his family to New York state, where they became friends of the Smiths in Palmyra and were among the first to be converted to the church. As a youth, Porter had broken a leg which had remained slightly underdeveloped and caused a slight limp. Short and seemingly shy, or at least taciturn, with small hands, a round face and a rather shrill voice, he appeared much younger than his twenty-nine years, and was still referred to as "the boy" by the prophet. His appearance and his air of innocence lent a certain fascination to the renown he had acquired as a savage fighter and a former Danite. The rumors about him and the fear which his name excited were probably exaggerated, but perhaps the undersized Porter took some compensatory satisfaction in them. He was pleased to be kept constantly at the prophet's side and to serve him as one of his bodyguard, to drive his carriage, run his errands, cut his hair or blacken his boots. It was said that he would do anything the prophet commanded.

In Independence, Boggs's son William, who had reported that the pistol used against his father was stolen from their own store, revised his first opinion that Negroes had taken it, and said he believed it had been taken by Rockwell.

Rockwell left Independence at once and returned to Nauvoo, apparently just two hours ahead of pursuers.

Boggs was so seriously injured that reports gave out either that he was dead or that he was sure to die soon. In Nauvoo, *The Wasp,* May 28, 1842, published a letter signed "Vortex" which expressed indignation that an article in the Keokuk *Hawk Eye* had ascribed the attack on Boggs to some Mormon. "Vortex" continued: "Boggs is undoubtedly killed according to report, but who did the Noble Deed remains to be found out." On the same page was William Smith's editorial comment, "We admit the foregoing communication to please our correspondent, not that we have any faith that any one has killed Governor Boggs. The last account we have received is that he's still living and likely to live."

John C. Bennett charged *The Wasp* with the statement made by "Vortex" and began at once to exploit the situation. He said that Joseph had made a public prophecy in 1841 that Boggs would die violently within the year, and that he had privately offered five hundred dollars to any man who would do the job. Trying to build a further case, Bennett said that one or two months before the assassination attempt, when Porter left Nauvoo, his destination was unknown to most people in town, although Joseph had said Porter had "gone to fulfill prophecy." Bennett also charged that upon his return to Nauvoo, Rockwell displayed sudden affluence, jingling gold in his pockets and riding about in an elegant carriage. To Bennett's mind this was sufficient evidence that Rockwell had attacked Boggs at Joseph's instigation.[9] According to Joseph, Porter used the carriage only for bringing visitors from the steamboat landing to the temple.

After Bennett's accusations, Joseph wrote at once to the *Warsaw Signal* denying the prophecy which Bennett had attributed to him and protesting that he had no part in the attempt on Boggs.

Bennett admitted that Rockwell sought him out, denied his charges and offered to whip him, saying, "I never did an act in my life that I was ashamed of, and I do not fear to go anywhere that I have ever been, for I have done nothing criminal."[10] Nevertheless, Bennett was determined to incriminate him and Joseph Smith.

According to the *Alton Telegraph and Democratic Review* of July 30, Bennett, not content with accusations, went to the new governor of Missouri, Thomas Reynolds, carrying affidavits from a number of "the most respectable men" in and around Nauvoo that Joseph Smith was the "sole cause and instigator" of the attempt to kill Boggs.

Despite his serious injuries, Boggs clung stubbornly to life, and by July 20, 1842, with the people clamoring for his assailant, he was well enough to swear out an affidavit against Joseph. Governor Reynolds was reported to have asked for Joseph's extradition on the grounds that he was a fugitive from justice. Joseph himself believed that Boggs had made an oath before a judge who had issued the requisition himself and that Governor Reynolds was not actually involved. In any case, Governor Carlin of Illinois, who was serving out his term until the newly elected Governor Ford took office in December, signed an order on August 2 for Joseph's arrest and surrender to the agent from Missouri.

Sheriffs came to Nauvoo on August 8 and arrested the prophet and Porter Rockwell. Taken before the municipal court of Nauvoo, Joseph pleaded that he had not been out of the state of Illinois in the last two years. Both men were released by the Nauvoo court on writs of habeas corpus.[11]

That same day, the Nauvoo City Council passed an ordinance giving the local courts authority to judge the validity of every writ served upon a citizen of Nauvoo, although whether or not they expected their ordinance to hold is debatable.[12]

The frustrated sheriffs returned to Carlin without their prisoners. Sent back to Nauvoo to try again, they learned that Rockwell had escaped to Philadelphia and Joseph Smith had disappeared. The sheriffs reported to Carlin that the Mormons seemed very cooperative, but the prophet was nowhere to be found.

Much indignation was expressed in Illinois and Missouri, and in particular by both governors, that the Nauvoo local court had defied the state in releasing the two men.

Carlin offered a reward of $200 for the arrest of Joseph or Porter Rockwell. Later Governor Reynolds made an offer of $300 for each, while according to some reports the reward was $1,300.[13]

Meanwhile, stories were told that Joseph had fled to England or to

Europe and more specifically, that on a certain Saturday night he was seen on a steamboat going up the river toward Canada.

The sheriffs were not convinced, however, that Joseph had left his own territory, and continued for some time to make surprise raids on the town. Joseph was in fact still there hiding out, and he remained in hiding for the next four months, moving from one secret place to another, to a farm on the outskirts of Nauvoo, to the home of a friend in town, sometimes camping on an island in the Mississippi, and coming back intermittently to a secret vault under his own house. He was frequently seen traveling after dark on the river in a skiff, but never by the sheriffs.

There were elements of adventure in this hiding out which the prophet's boyish side must have enjoyed—signal fires, clandestine meetings after dark, diversionary tactics, midnight travels on the river by skiff, secret orders carried by Emma to the new major general of the Legion, Wilson Law, to come to the rescue if necessary, regardless of life or death. In his journal at this time Joseph included vivid lamentations about his plight, which perhaps heightened his sense of the drama, but he usually reported that his health and spirits were good. He had frequent visits from friends and relatives bringing comforts, and from the devoted Emma, who came often, despite the fact that she was watched, followed and harassed by the sheriffs.

In his journal Joseph wrote praises of his parents and his brothers and in particular of Emma, and of his joy in the faithfulness of his friends. He said, "These I have met in prosperity, and they were my friends; and now I meet them in adversity, and they are still my warmer friends. These love the God that I serve; they love the truths that I promulgate; they love those virtuous, and those holy doctrines that I cherish in my bosom with the warmest feelings of my heart, and with the zeal which cannot be denied . . . They shall not want a friend while I live."[14]

This was a promise that Joseph would keep, even though at the last it was to cost his life.

Having heard that the state militia might be called out to search Nauvoo, Joseph considered fleeing north to the pine woods country. On August 16 he wrote detailed instructions to Emma to send him his horse, saddlebags and a valise with shirts, and to load household furniture, writing materials and books, clothing and supplies on a boat to be manned by twenty or thirty of the best men. They would take off from Prairie du Chien, he wrote, "and from thence we will wend our way like larks up the Mississippi, until the towering mountains and rocks shall remind us of the places of our nativity, and shall look like safety and home; and then we will bid defiance to the world, to Carlin, Boggs, Bennett, and all their whorish whores and motly clan that follow in their wake, Missouri not excepted, and until the damnation of hell rolls upon them, by the voice, and dread thunders, and trump of the eternal God . . ."[15]

Emma replied to Joseph that same day, in her matter-of-fact manner, "I am ready to go with you if you are obliged to leave" and added that she would make the best arrangements possible, and Hyrum would come too.[16] This was perhaps only a flight of fancy on Joseph's part, or else the militia was less of a threat than anticipated. In any case, Emma never had to prepare for such an escape.

However, a day or two later, Emma came to Edward Sayer's farm, where Joseph was staying, to warn him that that retreat had been discovered. She and a friend helped him move at once to Carlos Granger's home, a mile northeast of town, just behind Hyrum's property, where Joseph was made welcome and given a room of his own.

On the night of August 18, as soon as he was settled and alone, Joseph wrote to Newel K. and Elizabeth Ann Whitney and their seventeen-year-old daughter, Sarah Ann, whom Joseph had married on July 27, two weeks before he had gone into hiding. The ceremony had been performed by Newel after Joseph's revelation to him that it should be done and what words should be used.[17] Perhaps thinking that if he had to go to the pine country, he would not see his young bride soon again, Joseph asked the three of them to come to him that night. He wrote:

I take this opportunity to communicate some of my feelings, privetely at this time, which I want you three Eternaly to keep in your own bosams, for my feelings are So Strong for you Since what has passed lately between us, that the time of my absence from you Seems So long, and dreary, that it Seems as if I could not live long in this way . . . I know it is the will of God that you should comfort me now in this time of affliction.

He gave them instructions to be cautious. Newel was to walk a little ahead and knock at the window in the southeast corner of the house, next to the cornfield.

"Burn this letter as Soon as you read it," he wrote, "Keep all locked up in your breasts, my life depends upon it." He said also that they should find out when Emma comes "then you cannot be safe . . . I think Emma wont come to night if She dont dont fail to come to night."[18] This last was probably added because Emma was not then and never would become fully reconciled to Joseph's plural wives.

Joseph did not mention this meeting in his journal, but Newel was among the friends whom he praised highly for faithfulness during that time. Among his journal entries for August, he wrote, "Let the blessings of the Eternal also be crowned upon his head. How warm that heart! how anxious that soul for the welfare of one who has been cast out, and hated of almost all men. Brother Whitney, thou knowest not how strong those ties are that bind my soul and heart to thee."[19]

Joseph also spent some time hiding out at John Taylor's father's house, on the Henderson River. John's brother William, who was then nineteen, wrote that he remembered the night of September 2, when Joseph, John and two others appeared at the door very late, having followed a roundabout course. Later, Joseph sent the others back to Nauvoo for news. While waiting for them to return, Joseph spent three days with William in the woods, walking, shooting squirrels, or "doing anything we could to amuse ourselves," an experience which William, and apparently Joseph also, enjoyed very much. William said to him, "Brother Joseph, don't you get frightened when all those hounding wolves are after you?" Joseph replied, "No, I am not afraid; the Lord said he would protect me, and I have full confidence in his word."[20]

If Joseph enjoyed the experience of camping out, and perhaps an exhilarating sense of being persecuted for the Lord's sake, he was also giving serious thought to the Saints and their salvation. During his two-week stay at the Taylors', William Clayton came to take dictation for him, and on September 6 he wrote an Epistle to the Church, later published in the *Doctrine and Covenants* as Section 128, in which he said:

> I now resume the subject of the baptism for the dead, as that subject seems to occupy my mind, and press itself upon my feelings the strongest, since I have been pursued by my enemies.

He detailed carefully how the records of baptisms for the dead should be kept, adding:

> You may think this order of things to be very particular; but let me tell you that it is only to answer the will of God . . . for the salvation of the dead who should die without a knowledge of the gospel . . . John the Revelator was contemplating this very subject in relation to the dead, when he declared, as you will find recorded in Revelation 20:12—*And I saw the dead, small and great, stand before God; and the books were opened; and another book was opened, which is the book of life; and the dead were judged out of those things which were written in the books, according to their works* . . . The nature of this ordinance [baptism for the dead] consists in the power of the priesthood, by the revelation of Jesus Christ, wherein it is granted that whatsoever you bind on earth shall be bound in heaven . . . whatsoever you record on earth shall be recorded in heaven . . . for out of the books shall our dead be judged . . . And now, my dearly beloved brethren and sisters, let me assure you that these principles . . . cannot be lightly passed over . . . For their salvation is necessary and essential to our salvation, as Paul says concerning the fathers—that they without us cannot be made perfect—neither can we without our dead be made perfect . . . for it is necessary in the ushering in of the dispensation of the fulness of times . . . Now, what do we hear in

the gospel which we have received? A voice of gladness! A voice of mercy from heaven; and a voice of truth out of the earth; glad tidings for the dead; a voice of gladness for the living and the dead; glad tidings of great joy . . . Behold, the great day of the Lord is at hand . . .[21]

Emma wrote to Carlin in her husband's behalf, but he answered her on September 7 that the act of the Nauvoo court was a gross and intolerable usurpation of power. The governor exhanged several letters with Emma, and expressed surprise and admiration of the judgment and talent she manifested, but he was not persuaded to change his point of view about her husband.[22]

Newspapers of the area continued to remind Carlin of his failure to capture the prophet, asking what had become of his authority. One taunted him that there was no hope of taking Joseph in his own territory, where it seemed he could defy the laws of the state at will.[23]

At the end of September 1842, Emma took sick with fever. Joseph was with her as much of the time as he dared to be, and was greatly worried, fearing at one point that she would die. On October 5 she was baptized twice in the river, and Joseph said evidently this did her much good. In the night she grew worse, but a day or two later she began to improve, and by the twentieth she was up and about again. Her improvement was slow, however, and she had frequent relapses.

Joseph would remain in hiding about four months, until December 1842, and in the meantime, John C. Bennett found still another way to harass and injure him.

CHAPTER

6

TWO AFFAIRS
IN SPRINGFIELD

Along with his other charges against Joseph Smith in his letters of 1842 to the *Sangamo Journal* John C. Bennett accused him of fraud in the attempt he made that year to take out bankruptcy.

Despite Joseph's struggles against his personal financial difficulties and those of the church, debts had become so oppressive by 1842 that Joseph and other leaders began to consider the National Bankruptcy Act, effective as of February 1, 1842, as a solution to their difficulties.

On April 14, Joseph had asked a lawyer from Quincy to come to Nauvoo, as he said, "to investigate the principles of insolvency" on his behalf. Apparently troubled by the idea of going into bankruptcy, Joseph recorded in his history for that day: "The justice or injustice of such a principle in law, I leave for them who made it, the United States. Suffice it to say, the law was as good for the Saints as for the Gentiles, and whether I would or not, I was forced into the measure by having been robbed, mobbed, plundered and wasted of all my property, time after time, in various places, by the very ones who made the law, namely, the people of the United States . . ."[1]

On April 18, Joseph had gone to Carthage with his brothers Hyrum and Samuel "to testify to their list of insolvency" before the clerk of the county commissioners' court, and on July 15, the *Sangamo Journal* reported that petitions of bankruptcy had been entered by them, and by Sidney Rigdon and several other Mormon leaders, with notice added that creditors should appear before the district court in Springfield on October 1 to show cause, if any, why the petitioners should not receive a final discharge from their debts.[2]

Among other debts was a promissory note for $4,866.38 due the government, which Joseph, Hyrum and other church leaders had signed on September 1, 1840, and for which the United States had won a judgment against them in June 1842.

The note was in payment for a steamboat bought from the federal government by the Mormon businessman Peter Haws. It was signed first by Haws and then by Henry W. Miller, George Miller, and Joseph and Hyrum Smith, the last four, as later documents revealed, merely as sureties. A second note in the same amount, probably for part interest in the boat, was signed by Charles Street and Marvin Street, obligors, and Robert F. Smith, surety. When the boat was wrecked within a few weeks, the pilots, presumed culpable, fled, and the signers of the second note refused to pay the balance due on grounds that they had been offered damaged goods. Peter Haws apparently disappeared and Joseph and the others were unable to pay the first note when it came due the next spring.[3]

Justin Butterfield, then United States Attorney for Illinois, wrote to Solicitor of the Treasury C. B. Penrose that the judgment would be lost if Joseph and Hyrum took out bankruptcy, since all other signatories to the note were insolvent. What was more, Butterfield wrote, John C. Bennett, in the third of his letters to the *Sangamo Journal,* July 15, 1842, had accused Joseph Smith of fraud in cloaking property so as to benefit from the bankruptcy act, and had substantiated his charge with details. Butterfield asked for authorization to investigate. In writing to Penrose, Butterfield did not repeat Bennett's charges specifically, but he enclosed the newspaper that had printed Bennett's letter.[4]

Among the accusations of fraud Bennett made against Joseph was that on April 18, 1842, the very day of his appearance in Carthage to declare his assets before the court, Joseph had recorded in the county deed book a transfer of some 230 city lots in Nauvoo, amounting to almost three hundred acres, from himself and Emma to himself as trustee-in-trust for the church. The transfer was recorded as having occurred on October 5, 1841, which date, Bennett charged, was fictitious.

As historians have suggested, this transfer was made and recorded in the Nauvoo Registry of Deeds at the end of the semi-annual conference of the church when land problems had been under discussion and the apostles had been pressing Joseph to have properties held by him and others in behalf of the church deeded to himself as trustee-in-trust. At the outset in Nauvoo, church affairs had been managed by Joseph and other leaders without distinction from their private affairs, one important instance being the arrangement made by Joseph, Hyrum and Sidney Rigdon with Hotchkiss to buy land on their personal credit for the settlement of the Saints. It was soon realized, however, that church business should be kept separate, and on January 30, 1841, Joseph was made sole trustee-in-trust for the church, apparently without the understanding that Illinois law ("An Act Concerning Religious Societies," February 6, 1835) did not permit religious organizations to hold more than ten acres. When the apostles returned from England in the summer of 1841, it was decided that all deeds held by others in behalf of the church should be transferred to Joseph as trustee-in-trust. Among the most important of these was probably the deed held by Joseph and Emma for lots in Nauvoo, as described above. It seems not unlikely that when Joseph decided to enter a plea for personal bankruptcy, he saw the need to enter the transaction in the Hancock County registry. The date on the deed as acknowledged by Ebenezer Robinson, Justice of the Peace in Nauvoo, was in fact October 5, 1841.[5]

Nevertheless, after his personal investigation in Nauvoo and Springfield, Butterfield reported to Penrose that Joseph had transferred more than enough real estate to cover the government's judgment against the church. Butterfield said he had filed his objections to the bankruptcy of Joseph and Hyrum on October 1, 1842, and a hearing was set for December 15, at which he expected to prevent the Smith brothers from obtaining their discharge.[6]

Butterfield objected to Joseph's discharge on several grounds, saying that he had made improper transfers of property and had concealed assets in order to benefit from the bankruptcy act. However, none of the allegations was established, and evidence suggests that Joseph had not even known of the bankruptcy law at the time the transfers were made.[7]

An inventory of property, signed by Joseph Smith, which was itself undated but was mailed to Nauvoo from Springfield postmarked August 7, lists money owed to Joseph by Isaac Galland, Oliver Granger and others, the debt he and the other brethren owed to the United States government which was then under Butterfield's attention, and but a meager collection of household goods and personal property. The inventory tabulates sixty-nine blocks in Nauvoo (all but eight containing three or more city lots) in which Joseph had an undivided third interest.

At this time, Joseph was still hiding out to avoid capture and extradition to Missouri on the charge of conspiring to murder ex-governor Boggs. Whether he himself appeared before the district court in Springfield on October 1 is questionable. Still hiding out when the hearing occurred on December 15, it seems he did not attend, since in his journal he noted that his delegates continued his plea in Springfield. He wrote, "On the 16th, Brother Hyrum received his discharge in case of bankruptcy; every arrangement was made with Mr. Butterfield, whereby I was equally entitled to a discharge, but was put off with a plea that he must write to the office in Washington before it could be granted."[8]

In his letter to Penrose of December 17, Butterfield said that he had received an offer to secure payment of the judgment against Joseph and the other leaders of the church. The offer, made by the church High Council including Hyrum Smith, Willard Richards and six others, was to give the United States a bond payable in four annual installments and to secure payment by a mortgage on real estate. Penrose replied that if the brethren would pay a third of the debt in cash and the remainder as proposed, Butterfield might withdraw his opposition to Joseph's bankruptcy.

However, it seems that as late as May 25, 1843, Butterfield had not received this counterproposal, since on that date he wrote again to inquire if the Mormons' offer was acceptable. Apparently no further action was taken for about a year. After the death of Joseph in 1844, legal actions continued for more than ten years, but the charge against him of fraud instigated by Bennett was never substantiated. The courts finally ruled that property in excess of ten acres that Joseph held as trustee-in-trust for the church was subject to a lien, and three foreclosure sales were held. The case was concluded July 17, 1852, and most of the proceeds ($11,-148.35) went to the government as payment in full plus interest on the 1842 steamboat judgment, and the rest went for lawyers' fees and to Emma as dower interest.[9]

Meanwhile that fall, John C. Bennett was lecturing in New York, trying to turn his "exposé" of Joseph Smith to profit and looking for someone to publish his letters as a book. Apparently for a while he aroused the interest of James Gordon Bennett. However, John M. Bernhisel, who was then bishop of the New York branch of the church, wrote to Joseph on October 1, 1842, that the newspaperman had finally rejected the idea because the author wanted to use engravings which were considered to be as obscene as those in the worst French books imported and he was afraid the author would get into trouble.[10]

John C. Bennett did find a publisher in Boston, however, and brought his book out before the end of the year under title of *The History of the Saints; or an Exposé of Joe Smith and the Mormons*. An engraved portrait appeared as frontispiece along with the caption, "Gen. John C. Bennett, Doctor of Medicine." An intense-looking man with a small, twisted mouth and sharp eyes under a close cap of dark hair, he shows himself in full dress uniform with right hand slipped through the buttons of his jacket, in a Napoleon-like posture which apparently was not mere coincidence.

In his book he claimed never to have believed in Mormon doctrines, but to have joined to expose them, and to have found a parallel in Napoleon, who, he said, "for the furtherance of the views of the French government upon Egypt and the East, had nominally adopted the Moslem creed." Bennett felt his object was superior, however, since Napoleon merely wished to promote the French government, while he, Bennett, wished to save that of the United States.[11]

To the indignation of the Saints, Bennett took his lecture on a cross-country tour. In Alton, he had broadsides made up announcing that he would lecture in the courthouse to gentlemen only, admission twelve cents.[12] Even the unconscionable Galland was angered when he heard Bennett in St. Louis, and wrote to Joseph that the doctor had misrepresented everything within Galland's knowledge. Bennett had castigated the legislature of Illinois for passing the Nauvoo charters and giving arms to the Nauvoo Legion, but he did not reveal that he himself had worked for passage of the charters and that as quartermaster general of Illinois, he had delivered the munitions.[13]

Bennett continued in every way he could invent to injure Joseph and the Saints. According to James Arlington Bennet he even drew up and distributed false commissions in the Nauvoo Legion.[14]

Meanwhile, still in hiding, Joseph was kept abreast of Bennett's campaigns against him. James Arlington Bennet wrote Joseph September 1 that in his opinion, based upon what John Cook Bennett himself had said, there was no evidence that an honest jury could find against him in the Boggs case. Nevertheless, Bennet said the feelings of the people in Missouri were so intense that Joseph should stay out of reach.[15]

Joseph was still in hiding when Ford assumed office as governor. Hearing that Justin Butterfield believed he could not be held on a requisition from Missouri for a crime committed there while he was in Illinois, Joseph at once sent Sidney Rigdon and several other church leaders to petition the new governor to rescind the requisition. Ford replied that he sympathized but hesitated to interfere with the official act of his predecessor. Butterfield wrote to the prophet supporting the governor's position and recommending that Joseph stand trial in Springfield, assuring him that the judges of the state Supreme Court held unanimously that he would be entitled to a discharge under habeas corpus. Joseph also had a fatherly note addressed "My Son," from Judge James Adams, advising him to come before the court without delay.[16]

On December 27, with a hundred dollars borrowed for expenses, Joseph started for Springfield in the custody of Wilson Law. Hyrum and a number of other Mormon leaders accompanied them. It was a difficult three-day journey through heavy snow and the men and horses could make only twenty or thirty miles at a time. The first night they stayed at Joseph's brother Samuel's farm in Plymouth, where the wife and children of their brother William (who was away, having been elected as a representative to the state legislature) were also living.

The party arrived in Springfield about two on the afternoon of December 30, and saw Justin Butterfield to attend to the preliminaries. Joseph's trial was set for Wednesday, January 4, 1843. In the interval, he called upon the new governor and saw officials of the state and members of the church in their homes, was invited to dinner and met generals, senators and judges, some of whom expressed pleasure and surprise at the young prophet's manner and appearance. When he wished, Joseph could be elegant, often wearing a black broadcloth suit with a wide white cravat in the fashion of the period, and a beaver hat. Said one of the company that day, "We had reason to think the Mormons were a peculiar people . . . having horns or something of the kind; but I find they look like other people; indeed, I think Mr. Smith a very good-looking man."[17]

Asked about the difference between "the Saints and sectarians," Joseph told Butterfield and others that the latter were "all circumscribed by some peculiar creed, which deprived its members the privilege of believing anything not contained therein, whereas the Latter-day Saints have no creed, but are ready to believe all true principles that exist, as they are made manifest from time to time."[18]

The Mormons were given the use of the Representatives Hall on Sunday, New Year's Day, where Orson Hyde preached at services attended by many of the state officials.

When Joseph's case was called on Wednesday, January 4, Judge Pope came to the bench accompanied by several ladies on both sides. If this was a waggish reference to the prophet's legendary propensities, no offense was taken. Butterfield adroitly turned the situation to the defendant's favor, winning the crowd with his opening: "It is a momentous occasion in my life to appear before the Pope, in defense of a prophet of God, in the presence of all these angels," with bows in all appropriate directions.[19]

Butterfield's defense was that Boggs's affidavit did not show that Smith was charged with any crime committed in Missouri, and that the executive had no jurisdiction to transport Joseph to Missouri unless he had fled from that state.

Next day according to Willard Richards the room was crowded with "a very respectable class of society" who seemed decidedly in favor of acquittal.[20]

Again taking his seat in the company of six ladies, Judge Pope gave a lengthy opinion which sustained the position of the defense and revealed his serious attitude despite his seeming facetiousness in having ladies beside him on the bench. He said:

> The importance of this case, and the consequences which may flow from an erroneous precedent, affecting the lives and liberties of our citizens, have impelled the court to bestow upon it the most anxious consideration . . . This case presents the important question arising under the Constitution and laws of the United States, whether a citizen of the state of Illinois can be transported from his own state to the state of Missouri, to be tried for a crime, which, if he ever committed, was committed in the state of Illinois . . .

Pope read the affidavit, which said that Governor Boggs had reason to believe that Joseph Smith was accessory before the fact of his intended murder. He stated that the defendant had affidavits proving that he was not in Missouri on the date Boggs was shot, and continued:

> As it is not charged that the crime was committed by Smith in Missouri, the governor of Illinois could not cause him to be removed to that state, unless it can be maintained that the state of Missouri can entertain jurisdiction of crimes committed in other states . . . It is the duty of the state of Illinois to make it criminal in one of its citizens to aid, abet, counsel or advise any person to commit a crime in her sister state. Any one violating the law would be amenable to the laws of Illinois . . . Those of Missouri could have no agency in his conviction and punishment . . .

Pope found the affidavit faulty on other counts as well, one of which was that Boggs did not give the facts of the case, but presented only his opinion that Joseph Smith was guilty. The judge said, "Mr. Boggs' opinion, then, is not authority," and closed with, "Let an order be entered that Smith be discharged from his arrest."[21]

Joseph got copies of the court's proceedings and on Friday took them to Governor Ford for his certification. Ford took the occasion to advise the prophet to "refrain from all political electioneering," to which Joseph replied that the Mormons were driven to voting in unison by persecution and not by his influence.[22]

Joseph and his party left for Nauvoo on Saturday morning, traveling again through snow and mud in such cold weather that the horses were white with frost. Now, however, their spirits were exuberant. Wilson Law and Willard Richards composed a Jubilee Song, which they wrote down and sang that evening in a long celebration.

A week after his return, Joseph and Emma gave a large party at which Joseph distributed cards printed with the Jubilee Song and another song written by Eliza R. Snow, in which the company joined with great feeling. Dinner was served to more than seventy, including the Smith household. It was a very cheerful company, Joseph wrote, attended by Brigham Young, out for the first time after a severe illness. While serving their friends with their own hands, Joseph and Emma announced that it was their fifteenth wedding anniversary.

Meanwhile, Porter Rockwell had been hiding in Philadelphia, lonely, out of work and miserable. By March he found his exile intolerable and took the steamboat for Nauvoo but rashly got off in St. Louis, where he was recognized, arrested, accused of attacking Boggs at Joseph's instigation and thrown into the local jail.

In distress at the news about Porter, Joseph borrowed a hundred dollars for his defense and wrote by special messenger to Justin Butterfield asking him to take the case, with the assistance, if Joseph could arrange it, of James Arlington Bennet of New York. "Rockwell is innocent," he wrote, "and must be defended." He added that he was ready to testify that he had never "instigated P.P.R. to murder Boggs" and that his only knowledge of the affair was from public accounts.[23] Joseph's efforts to enlist the help of Butterfield and Bennet did not materialize.

Butterfield replied to Joseph on March 27 that he was sorry Porter had had the bad fortune or imprudence to fall into the hands of the Missourians, that the case was difficult and he expected it to cause the Mormons trouble. He offered regrets that he could not help, but advised Joseph in some detail, suggesting that he find a respected lawyer in the area and also that he investigate John C. Bennett's past, to be able to impugn his character as a witness.[24]

In the first week of his arrest, Rockwell was shuttled from jail to jail in St. Louis, Jefferson City and finally Independence, where he and his guard arrived at night to find a mob clamoring to hang him at once. After several days in irons, Porter was tried before a justice of the peace in a brawling courtroom. He was found not guilty of any crime but was committed for his own safety, as he was told, and taken back to jail in hobbles.

Waiting in vain for some weeks to be released, Porter at last attempted to escape. Caught, he was charged with breaking jail. The Mormon's old defender, Alexander Doniphan, got a change of venue for him and he was transported to Liberty jail. As time passed and no action was taken, Porter tried again to escape, this time through a stovepipe hole which lacerated his flesh. Finally, after nine months, he would be convicted of breaking out of jail in Independence, and given a sentence of five minutes. After walking for twelve days, he would arrive in Nauvoo and go straight to the Mansion House, an apparition in dirty rags, with bleeding feet, shaggy hair and a long prison beard, shocking guests at the prophet's Christmas party of 1843, until recognized, to the prophet's great joy.

Although officially cleared of the attack on Boggs, rumor was persistent that Porter Rockwell might not have been innocent. That the rumors derived from Porter's reputation as a fighter and a former Danite and from hints of his own based only on bravado is not altogether improbable. Perhaps, once safely out of jail, he enjoyed the whispers that he was the would-be assassin of the oppressor of his idol, Joseph Smith.

THE PROPHET KIDNAPPED

Meanwhile, although at that time Porter Rockwell was still in jail, June of 1843 started out happily for the prophet and the church. The community was growing rapidly, business in Nauvoo was expanding with shops and commercial buildings going up on all sides. Solid structures of brick or timber had replaced many log cabins and temporary shelters; farms and gardens were well laid out. On June 1, the City Council passed an ordinance to establish a ferry across the Mississippi at Nauvoo. Converts were still pouring in and the missionary program was expanded ambitiously with elders appointed to Russia and the Society Islands. The temple, rising tier upon tier, had already assumed an imposing appearance.

On June 2, Joseph became the delighted half owner of the steamship *Maid of Iowa* and the next day organized an excursion to Quincy for his family and friends, with a band on board to provide music.

In the second week of June, however, Joseph's fortunes seemed to decline. His longtime and faithful friend Judge Elias Higbee, who had gone with him to Washington to plead the Mormons' case against Missouri, died suddenly of a fever. That same day, Emma, who had suffered from poor health a great deal in Nauvoo, again became violently ill, and John C. Bennett renewed his agitations to have the prophet arrested.

At Bennett's instigation, one of Joseph's enemies from Jackson County, Missouri, wrote to Governor Ford on June 10 to say that the circuit court of Daviess County had issued an indictment against Joseph on the old charge of treason, and that papers would soon be coming from Governor Reynolds asking for delivery of the prophet to the agent from Missouri.

On June 13, perhaps thinking that Emma needed a change, Joseph took her and the children north to visit Emma's sister, Mrs. Wasson, and her family, who lived near Dixon, in Lee County. It was a journey of several days.

They had been gone less than a week when Hyrum received a message by express from Judge James Adams in Springfield that Governor Ford had told him he was obliged to issue a writ against Joseph on requisition of the governor of Missouri, effective June 17. At once Hyrum sent William Clayton and Stephen Markham to warn the prophet. Setting out on horseback that same night, Sunday, June 18, the men were determined to save their beloved prophet. Riding furiously night and day, stopping only to snatch a meal now and then and two or three hours of sleep, they covered 212 miles in sixty-six hours and reached Wasson's on the afternoon of June 21. Learning that Joseph had just left for a visit to the nearby town of Dixon, the elders followed, although they and their horses were near collapse.

When they overtook him, Joseph told them that he had no fear. "I shall find friends, and Missourians cannot hurt me, I tell you in the name of Israel's God."[1]

Nevertheless, he agreed to turn back. He canceled an appointment to preach in Dixon on the twenty-third and sent William Clayton there for news.

About halfway to Dixon, Clayton passed the two officers assigned to arrest the prophet, Joseph H. Reynolds, sheriff of Jackson County, Missouri, and Constable Harmon T. Wilson, of Carthage, Illinois, but the men were disguised and Clayton did not recognize them. Representing themselves in Dixon as Mormon elders looking for the prophet, the two officers had hired a wagon and team to carry them to Wasson's.

They arrived about two that afternoon, when the family was at dinner. Knocking at the door, they announced that they were Mormon elders, and asked for the prophet.

Joseph's account of what followed differs from that of the officers. Joseph said that he was crossing the yard on his way to the barn when Wilson discovered him. The men overtook him and pressed their cocked pistols against his body.

"What is the meaning of all this?" the prophet demanded.

Reynolds cried, "I'll show you the meaning, by God; and if you stir one inch, I'll shoot you, God damn you."

Joseph told them to shoot; he had endured so much oppression that he was tired of life. However, he said he would not resist if they had any legal process. The men made no attempt to serve papers, but ordered him to go to their wagon.

At this point Stephen Markham dashed out of the house and tried to intervene. The men shouted at Markham to stop or they would kill him. Turning their pistols on the prophet again, they forced him into the wagon.

Markham seized the horses by the bits. When the officers threatened again to shoot him, Markham cried, "No law on earth requires a sheriff to take a prisoner without his clothes!" He stubbornly and courageously held the horses until Emma came running out of the house with her husband's hat and coat.

Joseph shouted to Markham to ride to Dixon and tell the sheriff that he was kidnapped.

The officers whipped up their horses and rode the whole eight miles to town with their pistols bruising the prophet's sides.[2]

Constable Wilson's story, as reported many years later by Thomas Gregg, anti-Mormon journalist of Warsaw, was that he and Reynolds asked at Wasson's for the prophet and had posted themselves to wait when Wilson spotted Joseph running off through the field toward the woods. Before Wilson could overtake him, the prophet disappeared. Baffled, but sure that Joseph could not have made the woods, Wilson stopped at an abandoned cabin and well, near which some washing was spread to dry over tall weeds. Sticking out under a blanket was a pair of boots. Wilson pounced on the blanket and uncovered the prophet, who surrendered.[3]

However the arrest may have been effected, non-Mormon testimony later affirmed that Joseph's charge that the officers denied him his rights was true. The citizens of Dixon in particular were outraged at what they witnessed. While at Dixon waiting for fresh horses, the officers locked Joseph in the room of a tavern and allowed no one to see him. Joseph threw open the window and in the powerful voice he had developed from years of preaching to thousands in the open air, he cried out to a passer-by that he was held prisoner. Two lawyers from Quincy tried in turn to see him but had the door slammed in their faces. This caused some excitement in the town. The owner of the hotel and his friends gathered at the door to demand justice for the prisoner and at last the two lawyers were admitted to hear Joseph's complaints.[4] They sent at once for the master in chancery and for Cyrus H. Walker, a prominent Illinois lawyer who happened to be in the area campaigning for election to Congress.

Meanwhile, Joseph sent William Clayton back by steamer to Nauvoo to ask Hyrum for help. Stephen Markham turned the tables on Reynolds and Wilson by making complaints before a justice of the peace that they had threatened his life and that of the prophet, and that Wilson had turned Joseph over to Reynolds, who meant to carry him illegally to Missouri. The officers were put under arrest by the constable of Lee County.

The next day, the master in chancery issued a writ of habeas corpus returnable before the judge at Ottawa, which was served at once on Reynolds and Wilson.

Cyrus Walker arrived for a conference with the prophet, but said that unless the prophet could assure him of his vote, he would not be able to take time from electioneering to act as his counsel. Anxious for the help of this man who was considered the best criminal lawyer in that area, Joseph agreed at once. Walker was delighted, and said to Markham immediately afterward, "I am now sure of my election, as Joseph Smith has promised me his vote."[5]

Released on bail and temporarily chastened, the officers took Joseph on the first writ of habeas corpus toward Ottawa, as far as Pawpaw Grove.

When Emma learned that the prophet was no longer in Dixon, she and the children went back to Nauvoo.

In Pawpaw Grove, Joseph was again kept in a hotel room and allowed no visitors. The news spread quickly through town and by early next day a crowd gathered demanding to see the prophet and to hear him preach. Sheriff Reynolds tried to disperse the people, but an old, lame citizen banged his great walking stick on the floor and shouted at the sheriff, "Stand off, you puke!" He added that Pawpaw Grove had a committee that would sit on the officers case and allow no appeal.

Joseph spoke to the people for an hour and a half on the subject of their choice, which was his view of God's law on marriage, and afterward wrote that his freedom commenced from that hour.[6]

Later, the citizens of Nauvoo voted to send the citizens of Dixon, Pawpaw Grove and Lee County their "warmest" thanks "for the firm patriotism" displayed in their support of the prophet against Wilson and Reynolds.[7]

In Pawpaw Grove Joseph's party learned that the judge at Ottawa was out of town. They returned to Dixon for another writ, worded at Markham's request as returnable before the nearest tribunal.

Joseph, his lawyers and friends, the officers and a number of others from the area who went along, apparently out of curiosity, made plans to travel to Quincy, about 260 miles, to go before Judge Stephen A. Douglas. Joseph hired a stagecoach and the party started out on the morning of June 26, for the journey of several days.

Word reached Hyrum on Sunday, June 25, that Joseph had been captured by men trying to take him to Missouri. Hyrum made a public announcement to the brethren assembled on the green and called for volunteers to ride out, find the prophet and make sure that his captors did not infringe upon his rights. More than three hundred men responded, from among whom a number were called to form search parties. Captain Dan Jones took about seventy-five men with him on the steamboat *Maid of Iowa* to search boats up the Illinois River as far as Peoria, on the possibility that the prophet was a captive on one of them. Some 175 armed men rode out that night under General Wilson Law and his brother William. Divided into squads, they took different routes to hunt for the prophet and his captors, riding frantically, whipping and spurring their horses. Some of the men forced whiskey down their animals' throats to keep them going.

Two days later, the first squad found Joseph's party. Joseph wrote that he was unable to repress his tears. "I am not going to Missouri this time!" he cried. "These are my boys!"

Wilson and William Law, with some sixty of the volunteers, reached Joseph on the twenty-ninth. The Law brothers jumped from their horses and hugged and kissed the prophet for joy.

That day, Joseph pointed out to his lawyers that Nauvoo and not Quincy was the nearest place where a writ of habeas corpus could be heard. Over the protests of Reynolds and Wilson, the party changed course for Nauvoo. Surrounded by Joseph's men, riding toward Joseph's city, Reynolds and Wilson began to shake with fear, but Joseph promised them better treatment than they had given him in Dixon, and he kept his word.

It was a peculiar company. Joseph was the prisoner of Reynolds and Wilson, while Reynolds and Wilson were prisoners of Sheriff Campbell of Lee County, who had delivered them all into the hands of Stephen Markham, with the whole party under guard by Joseph's friends so that none could escape.

Joseph sent a message ahead to Nauvoo that he would reach the city about noon on June 30. Emma, Hyrum and a train of carriages started out to meet him, accompanied by the Nauvoo brass band. Lorin Walker, a young man whom Joseph and Emma had taken into their home as a youth, went out ahead with one of the prophet's favorite horses, Old Charley. The volunteers decorated their bridles with flowers from the prairie.

Joseph mounted Old Charley and rode into town triumphantly, with Emma at his side, the stagecoach, carriages and horsemen following, colors flying and the band playing "Hail, Columbia." Guns and cannons fired a welcome as they approached the city. Crowds of cheering people lined the streets and followed the prophet to his house. One man present said that Joseph climbed on a well curb and holding to an upright with one hand and swinging his hat with the other, he shouted, "I am thankful to the God of Israel who has delivered me out of the hands of the Missourians once more." Many wept with joy. The crowds refused to disperse until Joseph blessed them and promised to speak to them later in the grove near the temple.

About one o'clock, fifty of the prophet's friends sat down to dinner served by Emma. The two anxious officers were placed at the head of the table.

The hearing was set for the following morning and Joseph was given permission to address the people.

Some ten thousand assembled in the grove at five o'clock to hear their prophet tell the thrilling story of his capture and rescue. He was in a jubilant mood:

> I discovered what the emotions of the people were on my arrival in this city, and . . . I meet you with a heart full of gratitude to Almighty God, and I presume you all feel the same. I am well—I am hearty . . . I feel strong as a giant. I pulled sticks with the men coming along, and I pulled up with one hand the strongest man that could be found . . .
>
> There has been great excitement in the country since Joseph H. Reynolds and Harmon T. Wilson took me, but I have been cool and dispassionate through the whole . . . They took me unlawfully, treated me rigorously, strove to deprive me of my rights, and would have run with me into Missouri to have been murdered, if Providence had not interposed. But now they are in my hands; and I have taken them into my house, set them at the head of my table, and placed before them the best which my house afforded . . . But before I will bear this unhallowed persecution any longer—before I will be dragged away again among my enemies for trial, I will spill the last drop of blood in my veins, and will see all my enemies in hell! To bear it any longer would be a sin, and I will not bear it any longer. Shall we bear it any longer?

Joseph's journal reported that here one universal "No!" ran through the vast assembly, like a loud peal of thunder. In speaking of the Nauvoo city charter, Joseph said:

> I wish you to know and publish that we have all power; and if any man from this time forth says anything to the contrary, cast it in his teeth . . . The municipal court has all the power to issue and determine writs of habeas corpus within the limits of this city that the legislature can confer. This city has all the power that the state courts have, and was given by the same authority—the legislature.[8]

At the end of his speech, Joseph introduced Cyrus Walker, who told the people that from what he had seen of the Nauvoo city charter, he believed that it did include the power to try writs of habeas corpus.

On Saturday, July 1, after hearing a great deal of testimony about Joseph's ordeal as well as the Mormons' history of grievances against Missouri, the court discharged Joseph for want of substance in the warrant for his arrest and upon the merits of the case.

The action by the court had far more serious ramifications than the prophet's dismissal, which, whatever the legal aspects, was undoubtedly just. The point at question was the assumption of the municipal court that they had the power to invalidate a process served by the state. In assuring the Mormons that their municipal court had such power, Cyrus Walker and his opponent in the coming election, Joseph P. Hoge, who soon expressed agreement with that opinion, managed to please the Mormons, but in fact did them a grave disservice. Governor Ford was highly indignant, saying that the two lawyers must have known better, and he was as scornful of Hoge, a member of his own party, as he was of Walker for debasing their professional integrity to curry political favor.

Not long afterward, on December 8 of that year, the Nauvoo City Council attempted an even further extension of their powers by passing an ordinance that any officer guilty of bringing a writ for Joseph's arrest based upon the Missouri charges would be subject to a life sentence in the Nauvoo jail. No pardon would be allowed even by the governor himself, unless it was approved by the Nauvoo mayor, who was, of course, the prophet. On December 12, the council passed another ordinance requiring every warrant issued in Nauvoo to carry the mayor's signature. These ordinances caused great resentment in the state. The Mormons tried to keep them in effect for only two months, however, and repealed them on February 12, 1844.[9]

Anti-Mormons accused Joseph of having himself taken from his arresting officers by a body of armed men, and were outraged by what they considered his placing himself above the law. They held to that view, despite the statement of four citizens of Lee County that after Wilson and Reynolds were arrested, they were not disarmed until they reached Pawpaw Grove and that their arms were restored on the way to Nauvoo. The four citizens testified also that the Mormons who came out to ride with Joseph were not visibly armed and made no threat of force.[10] In the view of Joseph, the Mormons and their friends, his arrest was a lawless kidnapping. To Joseph it seemed part of the relentless persecution of Missourians, from whom he did not expect either justice or mercy.

On July 2, 1843, following Joseph's hearing, word reached the Mormons that Reynolds and Wilson, who had left Nauvoo after dinner at Emma's table, were importuning the governor to raise the militia to help them take the prophet. At once the citizens of Nauvoo sent a petition to Ford in Joseph's behalf and Cyrus Walker went in person to Ford to protest against his calling the militia to arrest Joseph, adding a plea of his own that Ford not issue any further demands for the prophet's extradition on the old charges.

Ford said that he did not intend to act until he had made an investigation. Afterward he wrote that he had no wish to become involved in the contest between Hoge and Walker for Mormon favor.

Ford had always maintained that the Mormons were not justified in their view of the powers held by the Nauvoo charters. He had attempted without success to persuade the legislature to take action about the charters, but he had failed for lack of support from his own party, whose members still had their eyes on the Mormon vote.

During the celebration of July 4, when Nauvoo was crowded with visitors, Joseph took the opportunity to make a public statement about Mormon politics.

It was a beautiful day, with a clear and pleasant sky. Always ready to enjoy Mormon activities in Nauvoo, the liveliest town in the state, neighbors came from miles around. Besides those who rode in across the prairies, about a thousand arrived in the afternoon on three steamers from St. Louis, Quincy and Burlington, and at least on that occasion a friendly atmosphere prevailed. Each boat was welcomed by the firing of cannon and music from the Nauvoo band, and visitors were escorted to seats of honor.

By the time Joseph rose to speak, in the afternoon, some fifteen thousand people had assembled. He told them:

> some say all the Latter-day Saints vote together, and vote as I say. But I never tell any man how to vote or whom to vote for . . . Joseph Duncan said if the people would elect him he would exterminate the Mormons, and take away their charters. As to Mr. Ford, he made no such threats, but manifested a spirit in his speeches to give every man his rights; hence the members of the Church universally voted for Mr. Ford and he was elected governor. But he was issued writs against me the first time the Missourians made a demand for me, and this is the second one he has issued for me, which has caused me much trouble and expense.[11]

Joseph went on to give an account of his capture by Reynolds and Wilson and their unlawful behavior. Wilford Woodruff, who recorded Joseph's speech that day, added, "the multitude gave good attention and much prejudice seemed to be removed."[12]

When Ford's agent, a Mr. Brayman, arrived on July 7, 1843, Joseph had several clerks sit up all night to copy the records of his hearing, which included lengthy testimony about the expulsion of the Saints from Missouri. To these Joseph and others added further affidavits.

Meanwhile, campaigning for the congressional election continued. Democrats made as much use as they could of the pending Ford decision about whether or not to call out militia to aid in the arrest of the prophet, trying to convince the Mormons that the militia would be sent against them if they voted for the Whigs. The Mormons in Nauvoo sent Backenstos, a Democrat, to Springfield to learn what Ford's attitude was toward them.

Backenstos had not yet returned to Nauvoo when, a week before election day, Hyrum came out for Joseph Hoge, the Democratic candidate, in exchange, rumor said, for Hoge's promise to support Hyrum for a seat in the next legislature. William Law opposed Hyrum vigorously, saying that he believed Hyrum's motive was personal ambition. The *Nauvoo Neighbor* also announced support of Hoge, and advocated unanimity at the polls, saying that without it the Mormons would disenfranchise each other and lose their political power. Joseph, meanwhile, was saying nothing.

Backenstos came back from Springfield only a day or two before elections, claiming that he had received assurance of favor in the capital in return for the Mormon vote for the Democrats. Ford himself later said that he was in St. Louis at the time of Backenstos' visit, and that the assurance was given by a prominent Democrat in Springfield without his knowledge. From Springfield, Backenstos brought a letter for Joseph from Ford's agent, Brayman, marked confidential and dated July 29.

Brayman wrote:

I was surprised, on my arrival at Nauvoo, to find prevailing among your people, so much apprehension, and so general an impression that the Executive of Illinois was actuated by feelings of hostility towards them . . . You will recollect, that I then assured you that the Governor was influenced by no unkind feelings or improper motives in the matter—that he acted (and with *reluctance* too) in obedience to a Sacred constitutional obligation, which he could not without dishonor disobey. I *know* his *feelings* towards you, and again repeat, that no official act of his administration has been performed with so much pain and reluctance. He is a man of integrity and firmness as well as of a kind disposition and a cool judgement and while he will not suffer a single citizen of Illinois to suffer wrong, he will enforce the laws with a firm hand . . .

Brayman told Joseph the result of his investigation, as reported to Ford:

neither you or your people were guilty of any violence, or disorderly, or unlawful conduct whatever; but that throughout the whole of the unpleasant scene connected with your arrest, and the ill treatment which you received, your and their conduct was that of peaceful, law-abiding and good citizens . . .

Brayman said that Reynolds had returned the writ to Ford, that it was now dead and no further action would be called for until a new requisition was made from the governor of Missouri. It was Brayman's opinion that after Ford had read all of the affidavits he had carried to him, he would no doubt write to the governor of Missouri and end all future demands. Brayman went on:

The idea that Gov Ford ever intended to *Call* out the *Militia* is so perfectly absurd, that no one, but a half crazy politician, whose only hope of success depended on his Efforts to inflame your people against the Executive, would have resorted to it. . . . I believe it has been said that Gov. Ford *delays* acting on this matter, for the purpose of *"holding* a *rod over* you," to influence the votes of your people in the coming Election.

To this I say that throughout this whole matter, he has nobly disregarded *political* considerations. . . . His decision in your case will be precisely the same whether he makes it before the Election, or whether you vote for one or the other of the political parties. . . .[13]

Brayman added that these were his views based on what he knew of the governor and, while not speaking for him, he had every confidence results would be as he indicated.

Ford had in fact written to Reynolds on July 26 that the militia would not be called out. His decision was based, he insisted, upon the fact that Joseph had been discharged under "color of the law." He said it would be a dangerous precedent for a governor whenever he supposed a court to have exceeded its powers to call out militia to reverse its decision.[14] Ford later wrote that for this he suffered much abuse. It was characteristic of Ford, an intelligent and conscientious man in a nearly lawless frontier, to bring his experience as a judge to his problems and to try to follow the requirements of the law, as well as to consider the long-term effects of his decisions. For this he was not always given due respect, even by his own party, who had hoped, as Ford himself said, to put him in office merely as a figurehead.[15]

In Ford's opinion, the assurances of favor from the Democrats that Backenstos brought back from Springfield without his knowledge produced a total change in the minds of the Mormon leaders.[16]

Apparently Joseph considered himself in difficulty, since he had promised the Whig Cyrus Walker his vote, and Walker had interpreted that promise as meaning the vote of all the Mormons. It seems that Joseph had not relieved him of that expectation.

At a meeting of several thousand people on Saturday, two days before elections, Hyrum made an announcement that God had revealed to him that the Mormons must support Hoge. William Law protested vigorously that there could be no such thing, since Joseph was voting for Walker. The Mormons waited in a grave dilemma for their prophet's statement.[17]

Joseph made no announcement until Sunday, August 6, the day before elections. Willard Richards recorded that he said:

I have not come to tell you to vote this way, that way or the other . . . The Lord has not given me Revelation. I have not asked the Lord for it   in relation to Mr. Walker. he is the whig candidate a high minded man. Mr. Walker has not hung on to my coat tail to gain his election as some have said . . . before Mr. Walker came to Nauvoo rumor came up that he might become a candidate for congress. says I he is an old friend I will vote for him. —when Mr Walker came to my house, I voluntarily told him I was going to vote for him. When I dictated to him the laws of Nauvoo, he received them on my testimony . . . When I was arested Walker made Reynolds come to me & beg my pardon for abuse he gave me . . . [Walker] withdrew all claims to your vote & influence if it will be detrimental to your interest as a people.

Bro Hyrum tells me this morning that he has had a testimony that it will be better for this people to vote for hoge, & I never knew Hiram say he had a revelation & it failed. Never told Bro Law to tell my private feelings. (Let God speak and all men hold their piece.) And I utterly forbid these political demagogues from using my name hereafter forever. —It is my settled feeling that if Gov Ford erred in granting a writ against me it is of the head and not of the heart. and I authorize all men to say that I am a personal friend of gov Ford.[18]

According to Ford, Hoge received some three thousand votes in Nauvoo the next day, but he won the election by a majority of only six or eight hundred.[19] To the Whigs, the fact that the Mormons had put Hoge in office seemed an outrageous betrayal, and it became a source of bitter resentment.

At the outset of the year the Mormons' neighbors had seemed quite friendly. The citizens of Lee County in particular not only showed an interest in the prophet and his teachings but rallied to his defense when his rights were put in jeopardy in their county. Nauvoo had had many visitors, especially on festive days, and a friendly atmosphere had prevailed. After the events in Lee County, when, as some saw it, Joseph's men rode out to protect him against officers of the law, and after the hearing at Nauvoo, in which the municipal court put aside a state process, more and more neighbors began to express resentment against the Saints. When the results of the election were made known, many people became angry. According to Ford, from that time on the Whigs and some Democrats too grew determined to drive the Mormons out of Illinois.[20] Unexpectedly, a pretext to rise in arms against Joseph Smith would be given to them within a year, by some of Joseph's own followers who became violently opposed to certain of his actions, perhaps beginning with, or at any rate brought to a head by, polygamy, which Joseph had been denying in public but practicing in private for some time.

CHAPTER

8

THE ROOTS
OF
CELESTIAL MARRIAGE

On Saturday, August 12, 1843, about six weeks after Joseph's triumphal return from Dixon, two separate events occurred which, although not at that time connected, were both further precursors of his downfall. Oddly enough, Joseph did not take part in person in either event, being, as he said in his journal, ill and at home.

On that day, the Mormon doctor Robert D. Foster rode to the county seat at Carthage to be sworn in as the new school commissioner, and there he met some fifteen armed men who were angry over the election results and over Joseph's recent defiance, as they saw it, of the law. They tried to intimidate the court to prevent Foster from taking oath of office. In this the men were not successful, but they swore to destroy Joseph Smith's political strength and to keep the Mormons out of office and to that end announced a mass rally of citizens of Hancock County for the following Saturday. A series of violent anti-Mormon rallies would follow and would eventually rouse men to arms throughout that part of the state.

On that same day, the other event that was to have serious repercussions for Joseph Smith occurred in Nauvoo, where the church High Council met in Hyrum Smith's office and heard the prophet's official revelation that polygamy was to be a "new and everlasting covenant" among the Saints. This caused an immediate rift in the council which was a forerunner of fatal opposition to Joseph within the church.

According to the *History of the Church*, Joseph had received the revelation on polygamy exactly one month earlier, on July 12, in the presence of his brother Hyrum and his clerk, William Clayton.[1] By this time, Joseph had married several women, some of whom were the daughters or sisters of leaders of the church who had also been taught the principles of celestial marriage. Emma knew that Joseph had taken plural wives and had in fact given her reluctant consent to at least two of them, but she was not content. Although she believed in her husband as a prophet of the Lord and conscientiously tried to sustain him, she sometimes had doubts that his will and the will of the Lord were necessarily always identical.

According to William Clayton, he and Hyrum were with Joseph in the office that day when Hyrum suggested that Emma would be convinced if she saw the revelation in writing and thereafter Joseph would have peace. "You don't know Emma as I do," Joseph replied with a smile, but he sent Clayton for paper to take his dictation.[2]

The revelation covers some six and a half pages in the *Doctrine and Covenants*, Section 132. Characteristically, it was received after Joseph had sought guidance from the Lord. The revelation states that a new and everlasting covenant was revealed in response to Joseph's inquiry about why the Lord had justified Abraham, Isaac and Jacob, Moses, David and Solomon in having many wives and concubines, adding, "and if ye abide not that covenant, then are ye damned." Covenants not made by "him who is anointed," that is, by Joseph Smith, were of no efficacy "in and after the resurrection," and marriages would not be in force after death. Those who were sealed in marriage by Joseph were to be told that they would come forth in the first resurrection and inherit thrones, kingdoms, powers and dominions.

The revelation said that Abraham had received a promise in regard to his posterity, among whom Joseph was numbered. In accordance with God's command, Sarah had given Hagar to Abraham as a wife. From her sprang many people, and Abraham's concubines bore him many children, and this was considered righteous, because it was God's law. Now God was restoring all things, through Joseph Smith, and whatever Joseph bound on earth in the name of the Lord was to be bound in heaven.

The revelation continued:

And again, as pertaining to the law of the Priesthood, If any man espouse a virgin, and desire to espouse another, and the first give her consent, and if he espouse the second, and they are virgins, and have vowed to no other man, then is he justified; he cannot commit adultery . . . and if he have ten virgins given unto him by this law, he cannot commit adultery . . . But if one or either of the ten virgins, after she is espoused, shall be with another man, she has committed adultery, and shall be destroyed; for they are given unto him to multiply and replenish the earth.

The revelation added that if a man holding the priesthood taught his wife this law, she must "believe and administer unto him, or she shall be destroyed . . ."

The revelation contained a tacit admission that polygamy was already in practice, saying directly to Emma:

. . . let mine handmaid, Emma Smith, receive all those that have been given unto my servant Joseph, and who are virtuous and pure before me . . . But if she will not abide this commandment, she shall be destroyed, saith the Lord . . . But if she will not [sic] abide this commandment, then shall my servant Joseph do all things for her, even as he hath said; and I will bless him, and multiply him, and give unto him an hundredfold in this world, of fathers and mothers, brothers and sisters, houses and lands, wives and children, and crowns of eternal lives in the eternal worlds. And again, verily I say, let mine handmaid forgive my servant Joseph his trespasses; and then shall she be forgiven her trespasses, wherein she has trespassed against me; and I, the Lord thy God, will bless her, and multiply her, and make her heart to rejoice.[3]

We have no direct comment from Emma from the period when she first heard the revelation. It is not known if her feelings were exacerbated by the irony of the blessings that were to accrue to Joseph upon her compliance with polygamy. Joseph's comments about Emma in his journal for those two days are brief. He merely indicated that Hyrum took the revelation to Emma and he directed William Clayton to make out deeds of certain lots of land to her and the children. The next day, July 13, Joseph says no more about his wife than, "I was in conversation with Emma most of the day."[4]

Others, however, were quite explicit about her reactions. As William Clayton told it, Hyrum came back abashed after showing her the revelation and reported that she was angry and bitter and had given him the most severe chastisement of his life. Joseph said, "I told you you did not know Emma as well as I did," and put the revelation in his pocket.[5]

William Law, who said that Emma used to complain to him about Joseph's behavior whenever they met on the street, also reported that Emma was angered by the revelation, but she told him that it said she must submit or be destroyed. She added, "Well, I guess I will have to submit."[6]

Newel K. Whitney made a copy of the revelation that day, with Joseph's permission, and the next day another copy was made by Joseph C. Kingsbury. A few days later, Joseph reported to the brethren that Emma had begged him so urgently to destroy the revelation that he had allowed her to do so, but that he knew it by heart and could repeat it if necessary.[7] As Brigham Young later told the story:

> Emma took that revelation, supposing she had all there was . . . went to the fireplace and put it in, and put the candle under it and burnt it, and she thought that was the end of it, and she will be damned as sure as she is a living woman.[8]

Emma's version of the incident, as reported years afterward by William McLellin from the long conversation he had with her in 1847, was that one night after she and Joseph had gone to bed, he told her that polygamy would ruin the church. He wanted her to get up and burn the revelation, but she refused to touch it, even with tongs. McLellin said she added that he got out of bed, put the revelation in the fire and burned it.[9]

Whether or not the revelation was burned, or by whom, had little effect, however, because the copies existed and the revelation was read to the church High Council as has been indicated, on that eventful day, August 12.

At least two of the council members present, David Fullmer and Thomas Grover, wrote accounts of that meeting. Apparently it started calmly enough, but during its course someone said he believed there must be something to the rumors about polygamy and asked for the truth. Hyrum went across the road to his house and returned with a copy of the revelation and read it to the group. According to Thomas Grover, Hyrum added, "Now, you that believe this revelation and go forth and obey the same shall be saved, and you that reject it shall be damned."

Some of the brethren were astounded. Three voiced immediate and bitter opposition. These were William Marks, the president of the High Council, Austin A. Cowles, whose daughter Elvira, treasurer of the Relief Society, had married Joseph in polygamy the previous year, and Leonard Soby. The three brethren raised such a clamor that they soon divided the council into polygamous and anti-polygamist factions.[10]

In succeeding months, the opposition would grow and new grievances would be added against the prophet. Thomas Grover, who was one of Joseph's life guard as well as a High Council member, wrote that from then on the prophet's life was always in danger. The prophet's loyal followers thought of the dissenters as infamous. Helen Mar Kimball Whitney wrote:

> it was through the treachery of men and women professing righteousness who, under the cloak of religion, proved themselves too corrupt to live within this celestial law of matrimony, and who, because Joseph rebuked them for their iniquities, turned against him, that he and his brother Hyrum were brought to a speedy death.[11]

John C. Bennett, early follower of
Joseph Smith and later his enemy.

An implacable enemy of Joseph Smith
and the Mormons, Lilburn W. Boggs,
Missouri governor. MISSOURI
HISTORICAL SOCIETY.

Colonel A. W. Doniphan, who refused
to obey his superiors' orders to
execute Joseph Smith and other
Mormon leaders in Missouri.
COURTESY OF THE LIBRARY OF
CONGRESS.

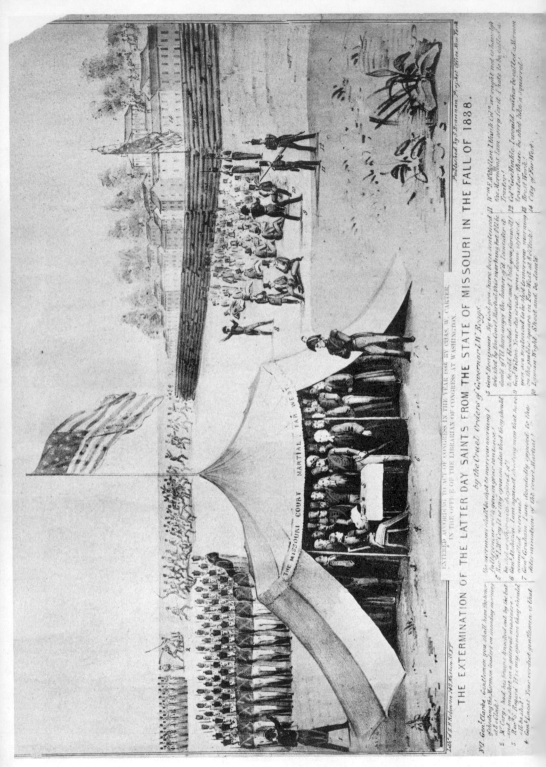

The extermination of the Latter-day Saints from Missouri, fall 1838. COURTESY OF THE LIBRARY OF CONGRESS.

Nauvoo, Illinois, in its heyday. U. S. BUREAU OF PUBLIC ROADS.

The Nauvoo Homestead. U. S. BUREAU OF PUBLIC ROADS.

The persecution and expulsion of the Mormons. U. S. OFFICE OF WAR INFORMATION.

This was the opinion of one faithful Mormon who was not in possession of all the facts, but there is an element of truth in her statement, since complaints of disillusioned Mormons would provide Joseph's enemies with the excuse they wanted to bring about his downfall.

Although the revelation was read to the council for the first time on August 12, 1843, plural marriage was no sudden innovation. Some of the brethren present were already practicing it. In the short history of the church it had had a long development, although just when the prophet first began to consider it important in God's plan of salvation is difficult to establish.

In the belief of the Reorganized Church, whose members were among those who seceded from the larger body of Mormons after the death of Joseph Smith, it was Brigham Young who established plural marriage, and that tenet was neither taught nor practiced by Joseph Smith. The Reorganized Church maintains that polygamy is clearly condemned in *The Book of Mormon,* in Jacob 2:23–25, which says:

David and Solomon truly had many wives and concubines, which thing was abominable before me, saith the Lord . . . Wherefore, I the Lord God will not suffer that this people shall do like unto them of old . . . there shall not any man among you have save it be one wife; and concubines he shall have none . . . Behold, ye have done greater iniquities than the Lamanites, our brethren. Ye have broken the hearts of your tender wives, and lost the confidence of your children, because of your bad examples before them; and the sobbings of their hearts ascend up to God against you.

The polygamists considered this to mean that it was abuse of the practice, rather than the practice itself, that roused the Lord's condemnation and as evidence cited verse 30 in the same book and chapter:

For if I will, saith the Lord of Hosts, raise up seed unto me, I will command my people; otherwise they shall hearken unto these things.

Having faith in continuing revelation, the Mormons declared that a commandment to one generation would not necessarily be intended for another. One set of commandments was given in the dispensation of Moses and another in the dispensation of Jesus Christ. The dispensation of the latter days, as Joseph Smith said, "differs from either yet includes both."[12] The Saints believed that change could occur in the will of the Lord, as revealed by their prophet.

That Joseph very early considered marriage important in God's plan is apparent in his revelation of March 1831, which commanded Leman Copley, a former Shaker, to go with Parley Pratt and Sidney Rigdon to preach to the celibate Shakers in their village near Kirtland.

The revelation said:

whoso forbiddeth to marry is not ordained of God, for marriage is ordained of God unto man.

Wherefore, it is lawful that he should have one wife, and they twain shall be one flesh, and all this that the earth might answer the end of its creation.[13]

The reference to one wife in this revelation is of interest because there has been testimony that polygamy was revealed to Joseph in that same year, 1831.

William Phelps wrote to Brigham Young some years after the event that on Sunday, July 17, 1831, while in Missouri, Joseph gave a revelation foretelling that the white brethren would take Indian wives in polygamy. At the time, the seven elders were beyond the boundary, west of Jackson County, and had united there in prayer. According to Phelps, the revelation was not recorded because they had no pen and ink, but he maintained that he remembered it in substance, and that it said, "verily I say unto you, that the wisdom of man in his fallen state knoweth not the purposes and the privileges of my Holy Priesthood, but ye shall know when ye receive a fulness by reason of the anointing; For it is my will that, in time, ye should take unto you wives of the Lamanites and Nephites, that their posterity may become white, delightsome and just . . ." Phelps said that when he asked Joseph in private some three years later how this could be, since the brethren were already married, he replied, "In the same manner that Abraham took Hagar and Kuturah; and Jacob took Rachel, Bilhaha and Zilpah, by *revelation . . .*"[14]

Joseph F. Smith, son of Hyrum and later sixth president of the Utah church, said in a statement published in the *Deseret News* on May 20, 1886, that plural marriage was revealed to Joseph Smith in 1831, but having been forbidden to teach it or make it known in public, he confided in only a few of his trusted friends, among whom were Oliver Cowdery and Lyman E. Johnson. Lyman told Orson Pratt about it in 1832.

Joseph B. Noble said that Joseph told him the doctrine was made known to him while he was translating the Scriptures. This was about the same time that Joseph had the Saints in Kirtland begin work on their first temple, but, as one historian has mentioned, there was no suggestion at that time that temples were the place for the ordinance of celestial marriage.

Joseph was fully aware that not all of his beliefs could be made known to his followers at once. He said to Brigham Young in Kirtland; "if I were to reveal to this people what the Lord has revealed to me, there is not a man or a woman that would stay with me."[15] Nevertheless, as early as the Kirtland period, rumors had begun to spread that polygamy was practiced among the Mormons.

In answer, William W. Phelps read an "Article on Marriage" before the general assembly of the church at Kirtland, on August 17, 1835, which included the statement:

> Inasmuch as this church of Christ has been reproached with the crime of fornication, and polygamy, we declare that we believe that one man should have one wife, and one woman but one husband, except in case of death, when either is at liberty to marry again.[16]

This article was unanimously accepted by the assembly. As the Mormon historian B. H. Roberts points out, however, the article was written and adopted by the church in the absence of Joseph Smith, who was at that time visiting the Saints in Michigan. Testimony exists that Joseph not only considered polygamy during the Kirtland period, but began its practice. Johnson implied that Joseph married Fannie Alger in Kirtland in 1836.[17]

For several years, however, he would continue to disclaim the practice. In letters he wrote from Liberty jail in Missouri in 1838–39, Joseph denied practicing polygamy, which, oddly enough, as one recent study pointed out, his enemies at that time did not charge.[18] He continued to deny polygamy publicly until after the Saints moved to Nauvoo.

There is testimony that the prophet tried to introduce the subject of polygamy in a sermon in Nauvoo more than two years before the official revelation.

Helen Mar Kimball, daughter of apostle Heber C. Kimball, wrote that one Sabbath morning in 1841, before the apostles returned from their mission to England, Joseph astonished his congregation by preaching on the restoration of all things as they were in ancient times with Abraham, Isaac and Jacob. His meaning was so plain that the prophet's wife Emma, Helen's mother Vilate and many others became excited.[19] Men too were upset. Ebenezer Robinson wrote that the prophet's younger brother, Don Carlos, said about that time, "Any man who will teach and practice the doctrine of spiritual wifery will go to hell, I don't care if it is my brother Joseph."[20]

Helen Kimball said that seeing the effect of his sermon, Joseph told the people that the time might be further off than he had ancitipated, but in any event, the Lord would help them to understand and to do His will if they were faithful.[21]

Between January 1841 and July 1843, the prophet gave nine revelations laying the doctrinal background for celestial, or eternal, marriage. He established ordinances which "turned the hearts of the children to the fathers" in providing baptism for the dead with their living relatives as proxy and in "sealing" family members to each other for eternity. Further revelations declared that matter was eternal and that spirit was matter of a refined nature. Spirit existed before the body, had to be brought to earth to take a body and would exist after death of the body. The intelligence attained on earth would persist after the resurrection, since the hereafter would be a continuation of life on earth.[22] Joseph said, "the same sociality which exists among us here will exist among us there, only it will be coupled with eternal glory, which glory we do not now enjoy."[23]

The ordinance of sealing in eternal marriage was of the utmost significance in the plan of salvation as revealed by the prophet, and of great importance to him personally, since through it he would hold forever, on earth and in the hereafter, the wives, children, parents, brothers, sisters, relatives and, by family extension, the friends whom he ardently loved. That the extended family Joseph would acquire through his numerous wives was of such importance to him is manifested by the fact that first among the blessings to accrue to Joseph in the polygamous estate, as set forth in the official revelation, were "an hundred fold, in this world, of fathers and mothers, brothers and sisters, houses and lands," after which came "wives and children, and crowns in the eternal worlds."[24] Benjamin Johnson wrote that the prophet taught the brethren that dominion and power in the "great future" would be commensurate with the number of "wives, children and friends that we inherit here, and that our mission to the earth was to organize a nucleus of Heaven, to take with us, to the increase of which there would be no end."[25]

Joseph had experienced the painful loss of members of his own family and had shared Emma's suffering over the deaths of their children. To mothers he was especially sympathetic, and reassured them about the hereafter, "Yes, Mothers, you will have your children."

He spoke often about the time when the dead would rise and greet their loved ones. He wanted families and friends to be buried close to one another, so that at the resurrection, they could stand up and embrace at once, and friends could strike hands in joyful reunion. He believed in ties that would bind for eternity. On Sunday, April 16, 1843, in speaking of the death of a missionary abroad, he said that when the voice called for the dead to arise:

> what would be the first joy of my heart? To meet my father, my mother, my brother, my sister; and when they are by my side, I embrace them, and they me . . .
>
> The expectation of seeing my friends in the morning of the resurrection cheers my soul and makes me bear up against the evils of life. It is like their taking a long journey, and on their return we meet them with increased joy.
>
> God has revealed His Son from the heavens and the doctrine of the resurrection also; and we have a knowledge that those we bury here God will bring up again . . .[26]

If the prophet's teachings and the cohesiveness and comprehensiveness of his message are not ignored, it must be recognized that his drive to establish polygamy was complex. It cannot be dismissed, as some historians have tried to do, simply by the suggestion that he had excessive sexual needs. Neither is it sufficient to say that Emma was worn out and frequently ill from the hard life of pioneering and childbearing. Nor can it merely be called an aspect of his Old Testament orientation, nor be said to have relieved his strict Puritan conscience which would not allow extramarital sex, nor to have derived from a wish not to dishonor the women he loved, nor to have been a device to cloak his proclivities by making polygamy accepted by his community, although a case might be made to support each of these assumptions. Account must be taken also of his enormous capacity to love, which has been made manifest by scores of his contemporaries of both sexes and all ages, and of his wish to bind his loved ones to himself forever, in this life, in the millennium and throughout eternity. He interpreted the Lord's plan for the salvation of men as progression to the state of godhood, in an eternal family union.

He did not find his situation easy. He was particularly anguished to have friends turn against him. On June 11, 1843, he said:

It always has been when a man was sent of God with the Priesthood and he begins to preach the fulness of the gospel then was thrust out by his friends—and they are ready to butcher him if he teach things which they had imagined to be wrong. Jesus was crucified upon this principle.[27]

Joseph was further troubled by periods of doubt and anxiety, not about his role but about his actions. Sometimes his own revelations rebuked him for his shortcomings, and even his revelation on polygamy contained a request that Emma forgive his trespasses. John D. Lee reported that in 1840 he said publicly that he had his failings, passions and temptations to struggle against, just as had the greatest stranger to God, and that no man was justified in submitting to his sinful nature.

He did not want his followers to sanctify him. In a speech of May 21, 1843, he said, "I have not an idea that there has been a great many very good men since Adam . . . I do not want you to think I am very righteous for I am not very righteous."[28]

To keep his actions from being misconstrued, Joseph frequently pointed out the difference between his behavior as a man and as a prophet. On one occasion he told visitors to Nauvoo, "A prophet is only a prophet when he is acting as such."[29]

At other times he spoke for tolerance of human weakness and frankly asked for indulgence for his own. On Sunday, November 7, 1841, after one of the brethren had delivered a two-hour sermon reproving the Mormons for their lack of solemnity, temperance and holy living, Joseph rose and reproved him in turn. He said:

If you do not accuse each other, God will not accuse you. If you have no accuser, you will enter heaven, and if you will follow the revelations and instructions which God gives you through me, I will take you into heaven as my back load. If you will not accuse me, I will not accuse you. If you will throw a cloak of charity over my sins, I will over yours—for charity covereth a multitude of sins. What many people call sin is not sin; I do many things to break down superstition, and I will break it down.[30]

He believed that God was speaking to him through his thoughts by putting ideas and words into his mind, thus giving him inspiration. Yet he knew this process was not proof against error. Having no formal knowledge of the workings of the subconscious, he yet recognized that influences upon thought and feeling could have more than one source. David Whitmer said Joseph had mentioned early in the history of the church that revelations sometimes came from God, sometimes from Satan and sometimes from man.[31] It remained for the prophet to differentiate, and mistakes might be recognized only later, as had occurred, according to Whitmer, with the revelation to sell *The Book of Mormon* copyright in Canada.

There is evidence that he was troubled by conscience from an early date in his career. As has been noted in the letter he wrote to Emma, June 6, 1832, he had shed tears of remorse for his follies, although he does not there identify them.

At a later period, one of his contemporaries, Joseph Lee Robinson, brother of Ebenezer, ascribed to Joseph one specific matter of conscience:

God revealed unto him that any man that ever committed adultery in either of his probations that that man could never be raised to the highest exaltation in the celestial glory, and he felt anxious with regard to himself that he inquired of the Lord that the Lord told him that he Joseph had never committed adultery.[32]

In spite of his troubles of spirit, Joseph never in any way expressed doubt of his calling to establish the new dispensation. There is never the slightest suggestion of insincerity in his most private conversations, in his personal journal or in the letters he wrote in his own hand. On April 6, 1843, he said, "If I had not actually got into this work, and been called of God, I would back out. But I cannot back out, I have no doubt of the truth."[33]

Helen Mar Kimball wrote that Joseph so urgently felt the need to give the commandment of plural marriage to the apostles that he could hardly wait for them to get back from England. On the very day that seven of them arrived in Nauvoo, July 1, 1841, Joseph met with them until late, teaching celestial marriage. Helen said that according to her father, after delivering the keys of the kingdom to the apostles, Joseph jumped and clapped his hands like a schoolboy let out to play.[34]

As time passed, Joseph seemed more and more determined that the Saints accept the doctrine of celestial marriage as holy and necessary. William Clayton wrote:

During the last year of his life we were scarcely ever together, alone, but he was talking on the subject, and explaining that doctrine and principles connected with it . . . From him I learned that the doctrine of plural and celestial marriage is the most holy and important doctrine ever revealed to man on the earth, and that without obedience to that principle no man can ever attain to the fulness of exaltation in celestial glory.[35]

Joseph F. Smith confirmed this, saying that after Joseph had taught the doctrine to the other leaders of the church:

the subject, in connection with the great principles of baptism, redemption and sealings for the dead, became the great themes of his life, and, as the late President George A. Smith repeatedly said, to me and others, "The Prophet seemed irresistibly moved by the power of God to establish that principle, not only in theory, in the hearts and minds of his brethren, but in practice also, he himself having led the way."[36]

Joseph urged his closest friends in the church to follow his example at once. According to William Law, he said the Saints were ready for strong meat, not just milk any more.[37] He told John Taylor that the church could not go on until polygamy was established, and without it the highest glory could not be attained in heaven. Very soon polygamy became a test of his followers' loyalty and willingness to live by every word that issued from the mouth of the Lord, through His prophet.

THE
EARLY POLYGAMISTS

To many of Joseph's followers, most of whom were from a New England background in which sexual mores were strict, the commandment to practice plural marriage seemed bitterly hard. Several of his friends confessed that the new tenet brought them close to apostatizing. Brigham Young said that when he heard the revelation, "it was the first time in my life that I desired the grave."[1] Later, he also wrote, no doubt sincerely but choosing an unfortunate turn of phrase, "I foresaw, when Joseph first made known this doctrine, that it would be a trial, and a source of great care and anxiety to the brethren, and what of that. We are to gird up our loins and fulfill this, just as we would any other duty."[2]

Helen Mar Kimball wrote that when Joseph commanded her father to take another wife, "If it had been his death sentence he could not have felt worse, and there were others who felt similar; and if it could have been just as acceptable in the sight of God, they would have chosen death."[3]

Helen added that Joseph at first told her father not to confide in his wife Vilate for fear she would not acquiesce. Her father understood, and would not betray Joseph, but he began to be afraid he would apostatize. He became ill in mind and body and would walk the floor at night, wringing his hands and weeping. When Vilate grew worried about him, Heber prayed that the Lord would reveal the truth to her. Vilate had a revelation, Helen wrote, and was satisfied.

Heber at first thought of marrying two elderly sisters named Pitkin, friends of his wife, but this was not acceptable. He was told to take a convert recently arrived from England, a woman with two children whose husband had gone back home. At last, in 1842, after repeated commandments to him, Heber married Sarah Peeke Noon, and had a son by her a year later, about the time that Vilate also had a son.

Little by little, many of Joseph's other close friends were won to the principle of celestial marriage, including Orson Pratt. Although, according to testimony, Orson had been told about polygamy as early as 1832, he was so shocked by the story that Joseph had approached his wife while he was in England that his friends were afraid he would kill himself. Later, however, Orson said that if the doctrine of polygamy were not true: "I would not give a fig for all your other revelations that came through Joseph Smith the Prophet; I would renounce the whole lot of them, because it is utterly impossible . . . to believe a part of them to be divine—from God—and a part of them to be from the devil."[4]

The doctrine seemed less difficult for some of the young and unmarried men. Job Smith, a convert from Liverpool who came to Nauvoo in 1843 at the age of fifteen, displayed a youthful adaptability and faith. He wrote:

> I myself being a strong believer in the prophet could not suppose it possible that he could do or advocate anything wrong of a sexual nature . . . [I] asked Elder Browett [Daniel Browett, with whom he was then living] about it. He assured me that plural marriage was practiced by the patriarchs of old and that a revelation had been received authorizing the practice, and that it was in line of the restitution of all things . . . This satisfied my mind and I soon learned to say nothing about it if I wanted to avoid contention. Of course, at the time nothing in public was taught or referred to.[5]

Eliza R. Snow wrote that when her brother Lorenzo became convinced it was his duty, he had two wives sealed to him at once, explaining that since the ceremony was the same for all, none would have a higher status than the others, but that their marriage relations could not yet be revealed.[6]

As might be expected, one who found it extremely difficult to reconcile herself to polygamy was the prophet's first wife, Emma.

Emma had been dearly loved by the Saints from the earliest days of the church and through all its tribulations, including the move to fever-ridden Nauvoo, where she had revealed her courage and compassion in sheltering the homeless, feeding the hungry and ministering to the sick.

In an excellent position to judge her, although in common expectation she would have done so with a strict eye, was her mother-in-law, Lucy Mack Smith. Several years after Joseph's death, when Emma had become a controversial figure in the Utah church because of her opposition to Brigham Young and her final stand against polygamy, Lucy wrote of her early life with Joseph:

She was then young and being naturaly ambitious and her whole heart
was in the work of the Lord and she felt no interest ex [*sic*] for the
church and the cause of truth whatever Her hands found to do she
did with her might and did not ask the selfish question shall I be
benefited any more than any one else if Elders were sent away to
preach she was the first to volunteer her services to assist in clothing
them for their journey and let her own privations be what they might
like the son of Altnomak she scorned to complain.[7]

Of the later course of Emma's life, Lucy wrote:

I have never seen a woman in my life, who would endure every species of fatigue and hardship, from month to month, and from year to
year, with that unflinching courage, zeal, and patience, which she has
ever done; for I know that which she has had to endure—she has been
tossed upon the ocean of uncertainty—she has breasted the storms of
persecution, and buffeted the rage of men and devils, which would
have borne down almost any other woman.[8]

Very likely Emma had changed over the years. More talented and better
educated than most of her friends, she had always been known for dignity
and reserve. Lately, however, she had grown rather austere. No doubt to
some extent this came from being honored as "the Elect Lady," but it was
also perhaps defensive.[9] She had grown more severe in expression and it
seems that she was strict in governing her children. In his letter to her of
April 4, 1839, written while he was in Liberty jail, Joseph had admonished her to be gentle with them, saying, "don't be Fractious to them,
but listen to their wants . . ."[10] Her love for her husband, children and
home was fierce and proud, and she could be goaded out of her usual
reserve by the intensity of her anger or jealousy and perhaps also because
of her fatigue from constant overwork and frequent illness.

Polygamy caused Emma long and agonizing doubts. Her Puritan ethics
were affronted by plural marriage; she felt that her status was undermined
and her prerogatives as a wife were threatened. She wondered if Joseph
could be right in every other respect regarding the restored gospel and yet
be led astray by overpowering sexual desires. Or was polygamy, as he
insisted, a necessary part of God's plan, which she, as the Elect Lady,
must not only consent to but promote, and act as an example to her sisters
in the gospel? Her attitude fluctuated from day to day, sometimes from
moment to moment. At times certain that her husband was a common
philanderer, she raged at him, spied upon him, threw out the women
whom she thought temptation had put in his way, railed behind his back
and fought his efforts with every means she could command.

Samuel H. Smith's daughter, Mary Smith Norman, wrote that she
learned from George Albert Smith's wife that Emma announced to the Re-

lief Society that a great evil was creeping into the church, and that they should use every honorable means to combat it and protect the sanctity of their homes.[11] Mary Barzee Boyce, a contemporary of Emma's in Nauvoo, said that Emma went even further and told the sisters that if they knew of any such thing going on, to burst the doors open.

According to Mary Boyce, Aidah Clements, who worked for Joseph's family, said that she saw Emma jerk her husband by the collar one day as he was leaving the house and heard her give him a tongue-lashing about going after women. Aidah said that Emma pulled Eliza Snow downstairs by her hair. Rumor had it also that although Emma agreed to allow Joseph more wives, she got into such a rage about it on one occasion that she left home and went to Quincy, although she soon came back.[12]

One of Joseph's life guards, Allen J. Stout, Sr., said that while on duty at the Mansion House, with only a door between him and the family, he heard Emma and Joseph talking about plural marriage. Stout wrote:

This impulsive woman from moments of passionate denunciation would subside into tearful repentance and acknowledge that her violent opposition to that principle was instigated by the power of darkness; that Satan was doing his utmost to destroy her, etc. And solemnly came the prophet's inspired warning. "Yes, and he will accomplish your overthrow, if you do not heed my counsel."[13]

Orson Pratt also spoke of Emma's difficult and stormy feelings about polygamy:

She was embittered against Joseph, her husband, and at times fought against him with all her heart; and then again she would break down in her feelings, and humble herself before God and call upon His Holy name, and would then lead forth ladies and place their hands in the hands of Joseph, and they were married to him according to the law of God.[14]

Regardless of the fact that he took other wives, Joseph always seemed devoted to Emma. Benjamin Johnson wrote of one Sunday morning when he was in the Mansion House with Joseph:

two of Emma's children came to him, as just from their mother, all so nice, bright, and sweet, and calling to them my attention, he said, "Benjamin, look at these children, how could I help loving their mother; if necessary I would go to hell for such a woman." And although at the time he had in the Mansion other wives, younger and apparently more brilliant, yet Emma, the wife of his youth, to me, appeared the queen of his heart and of his home.[15]

Even Brigham Young, who had no sympathy for Emma, or she for him, used to speak of Joseph's devotion to her, and of his habit of saying that he would have Emma in the hereafter if he had to go to hell for her. Brigham liked to add that in his opinion, "he will have to go to hell for her as sure as he ever gets her."[16]

Apparently after he surrendered to Governor Ford at Carthage, and shortly before his martyrdom, Joseph sent a message to Emma telling her to write a blessing exactly as she would like it, and he would sign it when he returned. In that document, which exists in her own hand, Emma reveals her humility, piety and courage, and between the lines, her heartache:

> I desire the Spirit of God to know and understand myself, that I might be able to overcome whatever of the tradition or nature that would not tend to my exaltation in the eternal worlds. I desire a fruitful, active mind, that I may be able to comprehend the designs of God, when revealed through His servants without doubting . . . I particularly desire wisdom to bring up all the children that are, or may be committed to my charge, in such a manner that they will be useful ornaments in the Kingdom of God . . . I desire prudence that I may not through ambition abuse my body and cause it to become prematurely old and care-worn, but that I may wear a cheerful countenance . . . and be a blessing to all who may in any wise need aught at my hands.
>
> I desire with all my heart to honor and respect my husband as my head, ever to live in his confidence and by acting in unison with him retain the place which God has given me by his side, and I ask my Heavenly Father that through humility, I may be enabled to overcome the curse which was pronounced upon the daughters of Eve . . . that whatever may be my lot through life I may be enabled to acknowledge the hand of God in all things.
>
> These desires of my heart were called forth by Joseph sending me word . . . that he had not time to write as he would like, but I could write out the best blessing I could think of and he would sign the same on his return.[17]

Tradition has it that Emma never saw Joseph alive again.

Despite Emma's doubts and protests, and before the official revelation of 1843, Joseph married a number of women. Exactly how many is a subject of debate, but it may be significant that Joseph F. Smith wrote, "the prophet found no one any more willing to lead out in this matter in righteousness than he was . . . none excelled, or even matched the courage of the Prophet himself."[18]

Although there is evidence that Joseph had married in polygamy before Louisa Beaman, she is generally regarded by the Mormons as his first plural wife. Louisa was sealed to Joseph by her sister's husband, Joseph B. Noble, on April 5, 1841. Noble wrote that Joseph told him an angel of the

Lord had announced to him that the time for plural marriage had arrived. The prophet added, "In revealing this to you, I have placed my life in your hands, therefore do not in an evil hour betray me to my enemies."[19] Noble described Louisa as an irreproachable woman who accepted Joseph from deep conviction that plural marriage was God's law.

There is evidence that some undeclared polyandry existed in the early stages of Mormon plural marriage. Two sisters, Zina and Prescindia Huntington, married to the prophet by their brother Dimick in the latter part of 1841, both had living husbands. Zina had married Henry Baily Jacobs March 7, 1841, and was married to Joseph Smith that year on October 27.[20] She left Jacobs in 1846 to marry Brigham Young. Prescindia had married Norman Buell in 1827 and had two sons by him before she joined the church in 1836. She was married to Joseph Smith December 11, 1841.[21] In 1846, she left Buell to marry Heber C. Kimball.

Mary Elizabeth Rollins was the wife of Adam Lightner when she married Joseph. Mary had joined the church in 1830, and according to a biographical sketch written by her great-granddaughter, had married Adam Lightner in 1835.[22] About her marriage to Joseph Smith, Mary said in a sworn statement made in her old age, "In the spring of 1831, the Savior appeared and commanded him to seal me up to everlasting life, gave me to Joseph to be with him in his Kingdom . . . Joseph said I was his before I came here and he said all the Devils in Hell should never get me from him . . ."[23]

In a letter to "Sister Wells," Mary wrote that she was married to Joseph Smith in 1842, in a room over the red brick store in Nauvoo.[24]

Mary's great-granddaughter wrote that Adam Lightner was a good friend of Joseph's, but he did not accept the gospel until on his deathbed in Utah, where he had moved with Mary in 1863.

Probably best-known of Joseph's plural wives was Eliza Roxey Snow, poet and educator, whom he married June 29, 1842, when she was about Emma's age, a spinster of thirty-eight. Tall, slim and dignified, Eliza was noted for the exquisite cut of her features and for her distinct enunciation of every syllable.

Eliza had been baptized a Campbellite in Ohio, and had become interested in the ancient prophets through Sidney Rigdon, a friend of her father's. When she heard of Joseph Smith as a modern-day prophet who actually heard the Lord speak, she could hardly believe it, but when she met Joseph in 1831 she was utterly convinced. Baptized into his church in 1835 she experienced an "inexpressible happiness."

With the other Saints, the Snow family left Ohio for Missouri, were driven out and moved to Illinois. In Nauvoo, Eliza lived with Joseph and Emma and ran a school of sixty-five pupils. She became secretary in the Relief Society while Emma was president.

Eliza said that she had rejected other suitors without knowing why, but later was thankful because marriage to any of them would have prevented her from receiving the fullness of the gospel. She wrote:

> In Nauvoo I first understood that the practice of plurality was to be introduced into the church. The subject was very repugnant to my feelings—so directly was it in opposition to my educated prepossessions . . . But when I reflected that I was living in the Dispensation of the fulness of times, embracing all other Dispensations, surely Plural Marriage must necessarily be included . . . I increased in knowledge concerning the principle and . . . today esteem it a precious, sacred principle—necessary in the elevation and salvation of the human family—in redeeming women from the curse, and the world from corruptions.[25]

Eliza had married Joseph without Emma's knowledge, a fact which might have been especially painful to Emma when she discovered it, since she had worked with and trusted Eliza. There is a persistent story that Eliza conceived a child by Joseph in the spring of 1844 but had a miscarriage.[26]

On July 27, 1842, about a month after his marriage to Eliza, Joseph married Sarah Ann Whitney, the seventeen-year-old daughter of his friends Newel K. and Elizabeth Ann Whitney, in a ceremony performed by Newel, in response to Joseph's revelation, which said:

> These are the words which you shall pronounce upon my servant Joseph and your daughter S. A. Whitney. They shall take each other by the hand and you shall say, You both mutually agree, calling them by name, to be each other's companion so long as you both shall live, preserving yourselves for each other and from all others and also throughout eternity, reserving only those rights which have been given to my servant Joseph by revelation and commandment and by legal authority in times passed. If you both agree to covenant and do this, I then give you, S. A. Whitney, my daughter, to Joseph Smith, to be wife, to observe all the rights between you both that belong to that condition. I do it in my own name and in the name of my wife, your mother, and in the name of my holy progenitors, by the right of birth which is of priesthood . . . All these things I do in the name of the Lord Jesus Christ, that through this order he may be glorified . . .[27]

Six or more of Joseph's wives had lived under his roof for extended periods, some as youthful protégées or family helpers. Two of these were Emily and Eliza Partridge, daughters of the faithful Edward Partridge, who had died of fever not long after he had settled in Nauvoo. As Emily told it, the prophet approached her when she was eighteen and asked if she would burn his letter if he wrote to her. This greatly troubled Emily. She prayed about it and finally told the prophet that she would refuse a private letter from him, but she became more miserable than ever. A few days after her nineteenth birthday, she was told confidentially that the prophet wanted her to meet him that night at Heber C. Kimball's, to become his wife.

It was a Saturday, March 4, 1843. Emily wrote that she had been helping with the washing all day, but she did not change her wash dress for fear of rousing suspicion. She threw on a cloak and said she was going to see her mother, which she did briefly on the way to Kimball's. Heber's wife was not at home and he sent his children, Helen and William, off to the neighbors. In Heber's presence, Joseph told Emily that the Lord had given her to him in plural marriage, and although he realized she was frightened, he knew she would have him. Emily wrote that by this time she had suffered so much anxiety that she was prepared for that step. She and Joseph were married on the spot by Heber, after which Joseph went home one way and Emily another.

Years later, Emily wrote, "It was a rather peculiar wedding. I would be pleased to meet him again . . . but not exactly as I did that evening."

She also said:

Since I have had children of my own, I can realize some things what my mother must have suffered, for somebody got an inkling of what was going on and reported it to her, but when Joseph talked with her and explained the principles she was perfectly satisfied.[28]

Emily confided in her sister Eliza, who felt bad at first, according to Emily. However, the news prepared Eliza for the principle of celestial marriage and a few days later she too was married to Joseph by Heber C. Kimball.

Eliza wrote that a woman living in polygamy at that time did not dare let it be known:

I thought my trials were very severe in the line and I am often led to wonder how it was that a person of my temperament could get along with it and not rebel, but I know it was the Lord who kept me from opposing his plans although in my heart I felt that I could not submit to them, but I did and I am thankful to my Heavenly Father for the care he had over me in those troublous times.[29]

Emily too said it was hard:

Then even our own people seemed to think that the Lord had given men plural wives for stepping stones for them and their first wives to mount to glory on, and that we could never rise because of our inferiority.[30]

The two young women continued to live with the Smith family after their secret weddings to the prophet. Sometime in May, Emma consented to Joseph's taking two more wives if he would let her choose them. She selected the Partridge sisters, helped to explain the principles to them and on May 11, stood present while the girls went through another ceremony with her husband.

According to Emily, Emma regretted what she had done before the day was over and kept Joseph up very late talking to him. She maintained a close watch, and if either of the girls was missing while Joseph was out, she searched the house from top to bottom and if necessary, the neighborhood.

One day, Emma called the girls to her room, where Joseph waited, as Emily said, a picture of despair. Emma announced that Joseph must give the girls up or blood would flow. Apparently Emma had been trying to induce the girls to find other husbands, since, according to Emily, Joseph asked her to stop trying to persuade them to marry someone else. When Emma agreed, Joseph shook hands with Emily and Eliza in the understanding that everything was ended between them.

Emily wrote that Emma could not rest until she got her and Eliza out of the house. Afterward, Emily saw Joseph only once to speak to, and that was just before he started on his fateful trip to Carthage, where he would be assassinated. Emily wrote that afterward she called upon Emma to see her baby David, who was born five month's after the prophet's death. Emma was gracious, Emily said, since by that time there was no Joseph to rouse her jealousy. Much later, Emily wrote:

> After these many years, I can truly say; poor Emma, she could not stand polygamy but she was a good woman and I never wish to stand in her way of happiness and exaltation. I hope the Lord will be merciful to her, and I believe he will . . . Perhaps she had done no worse than any of us would have done in her place.[31]

Emma's feelings about Joseph's other wives have been better documented than their feelings about one another. One of the young plural wives did leave a comment, however. Lucy Walker, who after her mother died was taken with eight of her brothers and sisters into the Smith home and married Joseph in 1843 when she was seventeen, wrote that she knew Joseph had married the Partridge sisters and two others also living in the Smith household, the orphans from Canada, Sarah and Maria Lawrence. She wrote, "Instead of a feeling of jealousy, it was a source of comfort to us. We were as sisters to each other."[32]

It seemed that Joseph was sometimes testing the loyalty of his followers. His requirements in some cases were especially hard, as when he courted some women through their fathers or brothers. Benjamin Johnson wrote that in the spring of 1843 the prophet told him that the Lord had commanded him to take more wives and that he wanted Benjamin to teach the principles of celestial marriage to his sister Elmera on his behalf. Benjamin was shocked but he agreed. He approached Elmera trembling with anxiety, but as Joseph had predicted, his words soon began to flow freely, and he was convinced that he was telling her the truth.

Benjamin took Elmera to Nauvoo on April 5, 1843, where she was married to Joseph by Hyrum in the presence of Louisa Beaman.[33]

A severe test was given to Heber C. Kimball and his wife Vilate. Their daughter Helen wrote that in the summer of 1843, when she was fifteen, her father asked if she would believe it was right for a man to have other wives. Helen wrote: "I felt such a sense of personal injury and displeasure; for him to mention such a thing to me I thought altogether unworthy of my father."[34] Of her reactions when she learned that her father had offered her to Joseph, she wrote:

> My father had but one ewe lamb, but willingly laid her upon the alter. How cruel this seemed to the mother whose heart strings were already stretched until they were ready to snap asunder, for he had taken Sarah Noon to wife and she thought she had made sufficient sacrifice, but the Lord required more.

Helen added that Joseph came and taught the principle to her and her parents, after which he told her, "If you will take this step, it will insure your eternal salvation and exaltation and that of your father's household and all of your kindred." Helen wrote:

> This promise was so great that I willingly gave myself to purchase so glorious a reward. None but God and his angels could see my mother's bleeding heart when Joseph asked her if she was willing. She replied, "If Helen is willing I have nothing more to say."[35]

Helen became devoted to the principles of plural marriage, however, and later wrote at some length on the subject.[36]

Considering the prophet's emphasis upon the importance of a large family in the hereafter, some have been puzzled that there was no acknowledged issue from his polygamous marriages. Suggestion has been made that Joseph might have practiced birth control, which he could have learned from John C. Bennett, who had taught midwifery and, it was said, practiced abortion.[37] Lucy Walker had a simpler explanation: "Could they but realize the hazardous life he lived, after that revelation was given, they would comprehend the reason. He was harassed and hounded and lived in constant fear of being betrayed by those who ought to have been true to him."[38]

So far as is known, none of the women wrote about her physical relationship with the prophet, perhaps because of modesty and the repudiation at that time of female sexuality. Occasional statements were made that Joseph married the women "in all that sense implies" or that he occupied the same room and bed with them.[39] There was some attempt by Emma after the prophet's death to establish that he married other women for eternity, and not as wives on this earth. Lucy Smith, wife of George Albert Smith, wrote that after the prophet's death, Emma told her that Joseph had taught that such women were sealed in celestial marriage for the future in eternity, but that the Twelve had made "bogus" of the principle by living with their plural wives and having children. Lucy discussed this with George, who said, "Emma knows better."

Lucy wrote:

> He then related to me the circumstance of calling on the Prophet one evening about 11 o'clock, and he was out on the porch with a basin of water washing his hands, I said to him what is up, said Joseph one of my wives has just been confined and Emma was midwife and I have been assisting her . . . This word for word as I had it from br. G. A. Smith. Mrs. Lucy M. Smith.[40]

Lucy did not say who the wife was or what became of the child, but in contrast to the usual circumspection, her statement, which was made to abolish Emma's claim, is surprisingly candid. The wife in confinement was very likely one of those living in the Smith home, but there is no indication that any became pregnant, except for the miscarriage reportedly suffered by Eliza R. Snow.

From the testimony of Joseph's wives, it seems he was tender toward them and did not take nearly so hard a line as did Brigham Young, who told the women, "if you lift your heels against this revelation, and say that you would obliterate it, and put it out of existence if you had the power . . . you will go to hell, just as sure as you are living women."[41]

Of Joseph's attitude, Lucy Walker wrote that Joseph often said that a man's wives:

> should be his bosom companions, the nearest and dearest objects on earth in every sense of the word. He said men must beware how they treat their wives. They are given them for a holy purpose that the myriads of spirits waiting for tabernacles might have pure healthy bodies. He also said many would awake in the morning of the resurrection sadly disappointed; for they, by transgression would have neither wives or children, for they surely would be taken from them, and given to those who should prove themselves worthy.[42]

Women in the prophet's time who were not accustomed to taking offense if the word "object" was applied to them very likely saw this as solicitous. However, behind the prophet's solicitousness was an indomitable will, expressed in his address to the Relief Society as recorded by Eliza R. Snow, March 30, 1842, "all difficulties which might and would cross our way must be surmounted, though the soul be *tried,* the heart faint, and hands hang down . . . there must be decision of character aside from sympathy—that when instructed we must obey that voice, observe the Laws of the Kingdom of God . . . move according to the Ancient Priesthood . . ."43

Joseph would tolerate no gossip and no furtive undermining of the principles. In a sermon given October 15, 1843, he said, "set our women to work & stop their street yarn and talking about spiritual wives."44

Women in the church were expected to be subservient to their husbands. Orson Pratt spoke of the status of women among the Mormons, which status was of course common to many fundamentalist groups. "The husband is the head of the family, and it is his duty to govern his wife or wives, and the children, according to the law of righteousness; and it is the duty of his wife to be subject unto him in all things, even as the Church is subject unto Christ . . . Each wife should seek counsel from her husband, and obey the same with all meekness and patience in all things."45

That their situation was accepted by some women only with effort is made evident by Helen Mar Kimball, who wrote that her mother, Vilate, was naturally quick and frank, but she learned to respect the authority of the priesthood. Helen wrote:

Had it not been for her abiding faith in the principles that were advanced by the Prophet and Seer and the confidence which she felt in her husband as a man of God, she could never have borne up under all the trials with which her life's path was filled. She often testified to me that she never opposed my father, no matter how much cause she thought she had for doing so, without losing the Good Spirit and making herself tenfold more wretched than before; and he felt the same respect for the ones who held the Priesthood above himself.46

Some must have felt that this was subjugation of women, however benevolent, in an unanswerable way through their religious faith. In her journals, which she began in 1874 at age fifty after years of sacrifice and devotion to the church and marriages in polygamy to Joseph Smith and then to Brigham Young, Emily Partridge wrote, "Long live womans sufrage and equal rights. No need for four fifths of the inhabitants of the earth to grovel in the dust in order that the other fifth may stand a little higher."47

Joseph's difficulties in establishing polygamy were compounded by the fact that not everyone who learned of the revelation was pure in heart, as was seen in the case of John C. Bennett. Helen Mar Kimball wrote:

If some have become degraded in the practice of this celestial order it is because they were naturally low and depraved, and have occasionally dragged others with them into corruption. The prophet said this order would damn more than it would save because it was a holy principle that could not be trifled with.48

However, Joseph did his best to keep the system of plural marriage under control. Any practice beyond his jurisdiction was put down on pain of excommunication, as in the case of Elder Hyram Brown of Lapeer County, Michigan, who was reported to be preaching polygamy early in 1844. Joseph and Hyrum sent him notice that he was cut off from the church and required to appear at the next conference to answer charges. On March 8, 1844, Hyrum Smith wrote to the brethren at China Creek, Hancock County, that any man found advocating that doctrine would risk his membership in the church.[49]

For those who accepted the new doctrine, the course was not easy. The polygamists were not only defying the moral code but breaking the law. Of Joseph's friends to whom he confided the secret, Helen Mar Kimball wrote, "He charged them not to divulge it, as he was harassed by day and by night by his enemies, and on their secrecy depended his life."[50]

Even after he announced the principle to the apostles the great majority of Mormons knew nothing about it. If they heard anything, most believed that spiritual wifery was invented by the apostate John C. Bennett, and they were encouraged in this belief by the leaders of the church. More than a year after he had revealed the doctrine to the apostles, and less than a year before he put his revelation in writing and had it read to the church High Council, Joseph said in the *Times and Seasons,* Vol. 3, October 1, 1842, "Dr. J. C. Bennett's secret wife system is a matter of his own manufacture . . . a foul and infamous slander upon an innocent people."

In the same issue was a statement signed by a number of church leaders, "we give this certificate to show, that Dr. J. C. Bennett's secret wife system is a creature of his own make, as we know of no such society in this place, nor never did." Among the signatures was that of Newel K. Whitney, who had himself performed the plural marriage ceremony for Joseph and his daughter only a little more than two months before.

In that issue also was a statement to the same effect signed by nineteen members of the Relief Society, several of whom knew of polygamy firsthand. These included Emma Smith, Elizabeth Ann Whitney (the mother of Sarah Ann) and Eliza R. Snow.

Later, the denials were justified in the *Deseret News* in Salt Lake City, 1886:

> The almighty has revealed things on many occasions which were for his servants and not for the world. . . . when assailed by enemies and accused of practicing things which were really not countenanced in the church, they were justified in denying . . . and at the same time avoiding the avowal of such doctrines as were not intended for the world. This course which they have taken when necessary, by com-

mandment . . . is all the ground which their accusers have for charging them with falsehood.[51]

Despite official reticence about it and the social and legal hazards it presented, the practice of celestial marriage continued after Joseph's death. When the Nauvoo temple was opened for ordinances in the winter of 1845–46, plural marriages were an important part of the ceremonies performed, and in 1852, under Brigham Young, polygamy was publicly announced as a tenet of the Church of Jesus Christ of Latter-day Saints.

However, Emma and Joseph's followers who remained behind would never accept that tenet. The agonizing quandary was over for Emma and after the shock of Joseph's martyrdom had passed, she attained serenity. Of her own life, she wrote to her son, Joseph III, in 1869:

Joseph I have seen many, yes very many trying scenes in my life, in which I could not see any good in them, neither could I see any place where any good could grow out of them but yet I feel a divine trust in God, that all things shall work for good, perhaps not to me, but it may be to some one else . . .[52]

Apparently Emma was no longer troubled by Joseph's revelation that she would be destroyed unless she accepted polygamy, because after his death she repudiated that tenet. She made a happy marriage to Major Lewis Bidamon, who helped her raise Joseph's children. In another letter to Joseph III, she said that, looking back, she could not find anything she had done that was not simply her duty, which she did without anticipation of future reward, and she added that the happiness she currently felt was entirely new and unexpected.[53]

Emma insisted that polygamy was the institution of Brigham Young. In October 1879, the year she died, a published account appeared in which Emma is quoted as saying in answer to direct questions:

No such thing as polygamy, or spiritual wifery, was taught publicly or privately, before my husband's death, that I have now or ever had any knowledge of. He had no other wife but me nor did he to my knowledge ever have. He did not have improper relations with any woman that ever came to my knowledge.[54]

Eliza R. Snow found it difficult to accept that Emma could have made such a statement. Eliza said:

I once dearly loved "Sister Emma," and now, for me to believe that she, once honored woman, should have sunk so low . . . as to deny what she *knew* to be true, seems a palpable absurdity. If what purports to be her "last testimony," was really her testimony she died with a libel on her lips . . . Sister Emma, of her own free will and choice, gave her husband four wives, two of whom are now living, and ready to testify . . .[55]

However, Joseph III, who became president of the Reorganized Church, told one of his Utah cousins, Samuel H. Smith, in 1860 that he did not believe his father ever taught or practiced polygamy, and this has always been the stand of his church.[56]

Contrary to popular belief, most Mormons who went to Utah continued to live in monogamy. According to one official statement, no more than 3 per cent of Mormon families in Utah practiced polygamy. Although other calculations variously put the figure from 10 to about 20 per cent, even the highest figure reveals that most Utah Mormons were monogamous, while many other church groups based upon the teachings of Joseph Smith never practiced polygamy at all.[57]

Polygamy has been the subject of much levity, scorn and self-righteous indignation by non-Mormons. On the other hand, the later Utah Mormons often glorified polygamy beyond reality, praising the bond of sisterhood among polygamous women, the warm relationships between "aunts" (other wives) and children in the family, and the cooperation of members, which no doubt did exist but were by no means universal. The Mormons further justified the practice by saying that it relieved husbands of the desire for extramarital sex, abolished prostitution and adultery and made it possible for every woman to have a husband. It was said to solve the problem of a preponderance of women in the church and to populate the barren wilderness. It was also advanced as a way of redeeming women's status. According to Helen Mar Kimball, polygamy was believed to free a woman "from that bondage and curse which fell upon her through transgression . . . the ones who practice and advocate it will be the first to stand as man's equal, as did our first mother, Eve, in the garden of Eden."[58]

The Mormons were in fact comparatively free from prostitution and adultery, but this was also true of those of Joseph's followers who did not practice polygamy and was better accounted for by the mores than by the polygamy of a few. Neither did it enlarge the total population, since although it increased the children per father it decreased them per mother. As one scholar's examination of the statistics revealed, women bore an average of six children in polygamy and eight in monogamy.[59] The claim of surplus women is not valid, since the United States census from 1850 to 1940 and all available records of the Utah church show that men outnumbered women in the church and in Utah.[60]

The idea of polygamy as redeeming women from the curse of Eve, which process was never well explained, did not retain popularity and in any case was inconsistent with the Mormon axiom that man was responsible for his own sins and not for Adam's transgression and that the fall was part of the plan of salvation.

The most candid statements about polygamy were made by the early polygamists in their memoirs, diaries and letters, which revealed their ideals, their motivations and their problems in living a family life so different from all they and their Puritan antecedents had known. Their writings provide valuable information about that institution as a religious and sociological phenomenon.[61]

The ideal patriarchal attitude was exhibited by Benjamin Johnson, who wrote at the age of eighty-five after a long life close to the gospel, "while I can believe that to some plural marriage was a great cross, yet I cannot say so from my own experience, for although in times that tried men's hearts, I married seven wives, I was blessed with the gift to love them all; and although providing for so many was attended with great labor, care and anxiety, yet there was sympathy and love as my reward."[62]

The ideal woman might well have been represented by Heber C. Kimball's first wife Vilate. Lucy Walker, who married Heber in polygamy after the death of Joseph Smith and had nine children by him, had the highest praise for Vilate as "one of the noble women of the earth." Lucy wrote, "She was dearly beloved by his wives and children, as well as by all who intimately knew her. Too little has been said of her exemplary life. She was as a ministering angel to those in distress, ever ready to aid those who had not been so fortunate as herself in regards to the comforts of life. She never seemed so happy as while seeking to make others happy."[63]

In the words of one Mormon woman, who gave a just appraisal of the attitude of the devout polygamist:

> The principle of Celestial Marriage was considered the capstone of the Mormon religion. Only by practicing it would the highest exaltation in the Celestial Kingdom of God be obtained. According to the founders of the Mormon Church, the great purpose of this life is to prepare for the Celestial Kingdom in the world to come. The tremendous sacrifices of the Mormon people can be understood only if one keeps in mind this basic otherworld philosophy.[64]

CHAPTER

10

THE KINGDOM
OF GOD ON EARTH

While polygamy received greater notoriety than any other aspect of the Mormon Church, it was to Joseph Smith only part of the plan of salvation. Joseph believed that as the Lord's chosen people, the seed of Abraham in the last dispensation, the Mormons were to prepare the way for the millennium by establishing the kingdom of God on earth. To the Mormons, religion was not a practice for Sunday only but an everyday matter and they fully subscribed to the idea that it was right and wise for every aspect of their society—economic, political, military and religious —to be directed by inspiration of the Lord through His prophet. In such a belief they saw no conflict with the Constitution, to which they steadfastly proclaimed loyalty. As they pointed out, it was the Constitution that declared the citizens' right to order his religious life as he saw fit. Consistently failing to understand how some of their attitudes aroused the suspicions and the anger of their neighbors, the Mormons considered every display of hostility as the work of Satan in opposition to the will of God.

On the other hand, while the neighbors spoke against what they saw as the Mormon union of church and state in violation of the ideals of the founders of their country, the force that moved them to action was fear of finding themselves under Mormon domination. In Illinois, as in each area the Mormons had occupied, the neighbors were initially sympathetic toward them or at least tolerant, but the stronger the Mormons became the more their neighbors objected to their views. The neighbors always ended by behaving hysterically, as though their very survival required the elimination of these "peculiar" people.

The men who had tried in vain on August 12, 1843, to prevent Robert D. Foster from taking office as the new school commissioner held a rally in the courthouse at Carthage on August 19. A committee of six was appointed to draft resolutions and setting to work with a sense of urgency, they were ready to offer their results at another rally on September 6. Their opening paragraph stated:

> we are necessarily and irresistibly forced to the conclusion that a certain class of people have obtruded themselves upon us, calling themselves Mormons, or Latter-day Saints, and under the sacred garb of Christianity, assumed, as we honestly believe, that they may the more easily, under such a cloak, perpetrate the most lawless and diabolical deeds that have ever, in any age of the world, disgraced the human species.

The committee charged the Mormons with yielding implicit obedience to their prophet and under his "Heaven-daring assumption claiming to set aside, by his vile and blasphemous lies, all those moral and religious institutions which have been established by the Bible."

They accused Joseph Smith of acting in violence against an officer of the law, and said that he had passed laws in the Nauvoo City Council that were contrary to those of the state, had caused a writ of habeas corpus to be issued by the municipal court in a case beyond its jurisdiction and in that court had had himself tried and acquitted of charges made by a neighboring state. They also accused him of putting men in office who were under his control, and of maintaining a large army of "ragamuffin soldiers" and of sending them out against officers authorized to arrest him. The committee added:

> to crown all, he claims to merge all religion, all law, and both moral and political justice, in the knavish pretension that he receives fresh from heaven divine instructions in all matters pertaining to these things; thereby making his own depraved will the rule by which he would have all men governed.

Although the committee said they "would deprecate anything like lawless violence without justifiable cause, yet we pledge ourselves in the most solemn manner to resist all the wrongs which may be hereafter attempted to be imposed on this community by the Mormons, to the utmost of our ability,—peaceably, if we can, but forcibly, if we must."[1]

They pledged as well to refuse to support any man of either party who sought the Mormon vote. To further their ends committees were appointed from each election precinct of the county. The committee chairman from Warsaw was the well-known anti-Mormon agitator Thomas C. Sharp. Chosen to coordinate all efforts was a central committee from Carthage comprising a number of the most virulent anti-Mormons, among whom were Robert F. Smith, Harmon T. Wilson, Levi Williams and Frank A. Worrell.

It was resolved to ask the governor of Missouri to demand once more that authorities of Illinois deliver Joseph Smith for trial in Missouri, and to offer a posse to help arrest him. Proceedings of the meeting were sent to newspapers in Illinois, Missouri and Iowa Territory.

The Mormons were well aware of what had occurred at that meeting, but they refused to be intimidated. An editorial entitled, "Carthage V. Nauvoo" in the *Nauvoo Neighbor* of September 13, 1843, declared that if the Carthaginians came to make war on Rome (Nauvoo) they might be destroyed "like Hannibal of old."

No doubt the anti-Mormons would have thought they had even more reason for alarm if they had known the extent of Joseph Smith's plans for the kingdom of God.

To most people at that time, including the great majority of Mormons, the kingdom of God on earth implied the church. Joseph himself frequently used the phrase in that sense, but to him and a few of his very close followers it had assumed another and more literal meaning. The kingdom was to be worldwide and all-encompassing, and until the Lord Jesus Christ descended in His time to reign, it was to be under the leadership of the prophet, Joseph Smith.[2]

Just when Joseph began to plan for what has been called the "political kingdom of God," as distinct from the church, cannot be documented, but Sidney Rigdon suggested that a worldwide view existed in the early church. At the conference of April 1844, he announced that he had chosen a subject he had known "from its infancy," the history of the church, and would speak "with no ordinary degree of satisfaction . . . [since the] want of health and other circumstances have kept me in silence for nearly the last five years." He said:

I recollect in the year 1830 I met the whole Church of Christ in a little old log-house about 20 feet square, near Waterloo, N.Y., and we began to talk about the kingdom of God as if we had the world at our command . . .

We talked about the people coming as doves to the windows; and that nations should flock unto it; that they should come bending to the standard of Jesus . . . and of whole nations being born in one day. We talked such big things that men could not bear them, and they not only ridiculed us for what we did say in public, but threatened and inflicted much personal abuse; and if they had heard all we said, their violence would have been insupportable. . . . Would you not be astonished if even now we should tell the glories and privileges of the Saints of God to you and to the world? We should be ridiculed; and no wonder we shut it up in secret. . . . Do not be astonished, then, if we even yet have secret meetings, asking God for things for your benefit.

Do not be afraid . . . There was no evil concocted when we first held secret meetings, and it is the same now . . . Mankind have labored under one universal mistake about this—viz., salvation was distinct from government, i.e., that I can build a Church without government, and that thing have power to save me!

When God sets up a system of salvation, He sets up a system of government. When I speak of government, I mean what I say. I mean a government that shall rule over temporal and spiritual affairs.[3]

Soon after the church was founded, Joseph had begun to extend his influence from the religious to the temporal affairs of his people. Although it is difficult to establish that this was for any reason beyond the need to care for the poor who were always among them, opposition to that aspect of the prophet's dominance arose among some of his closest associates, including Oliver Cowdery, who said that Joseph was trying to "make the secular power subservient to church direction." To that, Oliver said, he could not in conscience subscribe.[4]

A few years later, in 1838, after the Saints were driven out of Far West, several Mormons who had turned against the church testified before Judge Austin A. King at the trial in Richmond that Joseph intended to establish an earthly kingdom of God which would subdue all other kingdoms, by force if necessary.

It was not Joseph's intention to use force, but it was certainly his purpose to bring the world under the influence of the restored gospel—he saw this as no more than his appointed mission in life.

On January 19, 1841, by which time the Saints were settled in Illinois, Joseph had a revelation that kings and other rulers of the earth were to receive an admonition from him to accept the gospel:

. . . you are now called immediately to make a solemn proclamation of my gospel . . . to all the kings of the world, to the four corners thereof, to the high honorable president-elect, and the high minded governors of the nation in which you live, and to all the nations of the earth scattered abroad. . . . fearing them not, for they are as grass, and all their glory as the flower thereof which soon falleth . . .[5]

The following draft entitled "A Religious Proclamation" is in the Church Historian's Office, among Joseph Smith's papers of 1842:

From Joseph Smith, President of the Church of Jesus Christ of Latter-Day Saints, the Prophet, Seer and Revelator of the Most High

God, to the President of the United States of North America—the Governors of the Several States—the Emperors, Kings, and Princes of the earth—the Executives of all nations—the Chiefs of all tribes—and all occupying high places in the administration of governments. . . .

Now in obedience to a revelation given January 19th, 1841, I proceed to call upon you to yield yourselves as obedient subjects to the requirements of heaven . . . to believe on the Lord Jesus Christ, repent of and abandon your sins, be immersed for the remission of your sins, receive the imposition of hands for the gift of the Holy Ghost, and, in fine, to embrace the gospel in its beauty and fulness . . . Hasten then to Zion! and contribute to the erection of temples, sanctuaries, and palaces, such as this world never saw—with their walls finished with the pencil of Raphael, decorated with gold, or pearls, and precious stones, beautified by the finger of God. Tho your minds are yet darkened, and your eyes yet dim of sight by the traditions, superstitions, and follies of the ages, imposed upon you by the Papal See, and hierarchy of Rome, the Patriarch and ecclesiastical council of Constantinople, and the priesthood of the Protestant sects, the God of heaven addresses you as intelligent beings, and directs you to come out from among them, that you may become the elite of the kingdom . . .[6]

In 1842, the *Millennial Star* announced that Nauvoo was "the nucleus . . . of that kingdom of Messiah which shall roll forth, from conquering and to conquer until it shall be said, that *'the kingdoms of this world are become the kingdoms of our Lord, and of His Christ.'* 'AND THE SAINTS OF THE MOST HIGH SHALL POSSESS THE GREATNESS OF THE KINGDOM UNDER THE WHOLE HEAVEN.' "[7]

Although Joseph's plans for what has been called the "political kingdom of God" had antecedents in the earliest days of the church, it was probably not until the Saints were firmly established in Nauvoo that he began to envision a council that would govern the kingdom and bring about the will of the Lord in temporal matters. The suggestion has been made that the organization rituals and practices of this council were similar to those in the Masonic order and that the Masonic oaths of secrecy and loyalty could have been useful to Joseph when he revealed polygamy and the plans for the political kingdom of God to the trusted few. In any case, it seems more than coincidental that some of the outstanding members of the Nauvoo Masonic Lodge were the first polygamists and later became members of Joseph's governing council when it was officially organized.[8] Among them were Joseph's brother Hyrum and his most trusted friends, William Clayton, Heber C. Kimball, Brigham Young and Newel K. Whitney.

The Nauvoo Lodge was instituted on March 15, 1842, by the Grand

Master of Illinois, after a dispensation was obtained by John C. Bennett, a master Mason himself. Joseph received the first degree on that same evening and the sublime degree the next day, and about three weeks later, on April 7, 1842, he had a revelation outlining the political kingdom of God.

Although the council, the governing body of the political kingdom of God, was not organized officially until two years later, from April 1842 until close to the time of his death Joseph made cryptic notes in his journal of occasional meetings of a "special council" at which it was apparent that matters not directly pertaining to religion were conducted.[9]

On September 28, 1843, Joseph wrote that he was unanimously chosen president of the special council. Joseph was careful to name everyone present and everyone became a member of the council when it was officially organized except William Law, who attended an evening meeting of the group on that same date.

It seems likely that the special council was responsible for an editorial that appeared in the *Times and Seasons* three days later, on October 1, advising the Saints in the coming presidential elections to choose the man most likely to redress their wrongs, and promising to search out that man. It is also likely that the council gave George J. Adams his special assignment to Russia at that time, since his commission, although designated as from the church presidency, was signed by Joseph but not by his two co-officials, Sidney Rigdon and William Law.

The purpose of Adams's mission, as described on October 1, 1843, in the *Times and Seasons,* was "to introduce the fullness of the Gospel to the people of that vast empire, and also to which is attached some of the most important things concerning the advancement and building up of the kingdom of God in the last days, which cannot be explained at this time."

It has been suggested that Adams was probably sent to ascertain what Russia's attitude would be toward an independent Mormon state.[10] Later, the council would send representatives to other nations.

Meanwhile, rumors and speculations about Joseph's secret meetings were spreading among Mormons and Gentiles alike and there was some fear that the Danites had been revived. No evidence can be found to sustain such a suggestion, although credence might have been given to it by the fact that some members of the council had belonged to the old Danite band, among whom were Reynolds Cahoon, Benjamin F. Johnson, John D. Lee, Amasa Lyman, Orrin Porter Rockwell and Lyman Wight.[11]

The Mormons' neighbors found further cause to be angry and suspicious when Joseph sent a petition to Congress, December 21, 1843, again recounting the grievances of the Saints in Missouri and asking as assurance against further outrage that Congress grant the city of Nauvoo "all the rights, powers, privileges, and immunities belonging to Territories, and not repugnant to the Constitution of the United States" and that Joseph be empowered to call United States forces to help him subdue mobs. He also asked that when involved in such action the Nauvoo Legion receive the same pay as the United States Army.[12]

With the spreading rumors of secret meetings, the incendiary stories of John C. Bennett and the visibly growing strength and demands of the Mormons, alarm about Joseph Smith's purpose was increasing. On January 10, 1844, Thomas Gregg said that Joseph's "black heart would exult in carnage and bloodshed, rather than yield one iota of what power he had obtained by his hellish knavery." On February 7, Gregg wrote, "Your career of infamy cannot continue but a little longer! Your days are numbered!"[13]

On March 11, 1844, Joseph began the formal organization of his special council. Benjamin F. Johnson wrote that the council was "a select circle of the Prophet's most trusted friends, including the Twelve [Apostles] but not all of the constituted authorities of the Church."[14] According to George Miller, who was an early member of the council and Presiding Bishop of the Church at the time of Joseph's death, the organization was accomplished over a period of time. Miller wrote:

> Joseph said to me . . . we will call together some of our wise men and proceed to set up the kingdom of God by organizing some of its officers. And from day to day he called some of the brethren about him, organizing them as princes in the kingdom of God, to preside over the chief cities of the Nation, until the number of fifty-three were called. In this council we ordained Joseph Smith as King on earth.[15]

That Joseph was crowned king was also reported by another contemporary, George Davis, who said that his information came from former members of the Council of Fifty. Davis wrote that Joseph declared that the authority he had from God took precedence over any other, and that he must be crowned. Davis added, "Joe was accordingly crowned KING under God, over the immediate house of Israel. This ceremony was performed in 1842 . . . He further impressed upon the council crowning him, that God's desire was, as revealed to him (Joe), that, for the time being, this was to remain *a perfect secret* until God should reveal to the contrary . . ."[16]

If any such ceremony as a coronation was performed, it was likely intended as symbolic; nevertheless rumors that Joseph had had himself crowned king on earth added to the neighbors' sense of outrage.

Governor Ford himself was persuaded that Joseph Smith had monarchial amibitions. Giving as the source of his information "the best men who had seceded from the Mormon Church," Ford wrote:

> He instituted a new and select order of the priesthood, the members of which were to be priests and kings temporally and spiritually. These were to be his nobility, who were to be the upholders of his

throne. He caused himself to be crowned the anointed king and priest, far above the rest; and he prescribed the form of an oath of allegiance to himself, which he administered to his principal followers. To uphold his pretensions to royalty, he deduced his descent by an unbroken chain from Joseph the son of Jacob, and that of his wife from some other renowned personage of Old Testament history. The Mormons openly denounced the government of the United States as utterly corrupt, and as being about to pass away, and to be replaced by the government of God, to be administered by his servant Joseph.[17]

The council's official name, as recorded by John D. Lee, was "The Kingdom of God and His Laws with the keys and powers thereof and judgment in the hands of his servants," but this was used only upon occasion in council meetings. The organization was also called the General Council, the Council of the Gods, the Living Constitution and the Council of the Kingdom. Joseph himself merely continued to refer to it as the "special council" or the "general council." It became best-known, however, as the Council of Fifty, from the approximate number of its members at the time of its official organization.[18]

Joseph's journal for March 11, 1844, states only that he spent the day in the lodge room over Henry Miller's house with twenty-three brethren, whose names he took care to record. He said that he organized them into a "special council" to consider two letters dated February 15 which he had received from Lyman Wight in behalf of the brethren in the pine woods lumber camp at Black River Falls, Wisconsin. The brethren were discontented with the operation there and asked permission to sell the mills and go to the tablelands of Texas to lumber and to make a gathering place for the Saints. As Joseph wrote, he and the special council also took under consideration:

. . . the best policy for this people to adopt to obtain their rights from the nation and insure protection for themselves and children; and to secure a resting place in the mountains, or some uninhabited region, where we can enjoy the liberty of conscience guaranteed to us by the Constitution of our country, rendered doubly sacred by the precious blood of our fathers, and denied to us by the present authorities, who have smuggled themselves into power in the States and Nation.[19]

In a meeting held March 13, Joseph named three new members of the council and recorded that Willard Richards was appointed historian and William Clayton, clerk.

On March 19, Joseph wrote that the council met again. He recorded the names of eight more brethren who attended, including William Marks, Orson Spencer, Orrin Porter Rockwell and Sidney Rigdon.[20]

At these and following meetings, the council studied the principles of the national government and discussed what they considered the true foundation of government should be.

Despite the fact that the leaders of the council were also the leaders of the church, and the two organizations had the same president (Joseph Smith and afterward Brigham Young and John Taylor) the council members considered their body separate from that of the church, with distinct functions.[21] Since the council was to represent the Gentiles as well as the Saints, in theory at least it was to have Gentile representation in its membership.

Brigham Young and John D. Lee both maintained that there were Gentiles on the council. The known membership lists do not include any Gentiles, although it has been suggested that Thomas L. Kane, friend and defender of the Mormons after their exodus from Nauvoo, might have been a member, since he participated in sessions of the Council of Fifty on the trek west. Another possible member was Daniel H. Wells, a justice of the peace in Nauvoo and an officer in the Nauvoo Legion. Wells might have been a Mormon at heart, however, since he was baptized into the church after the exodus.

The council had several alternative plans for establishing the kingdom, one of which was to find new territory for the Saints. Actually, Joseph had had this in mind for some time. Many others both in and out of the church had thought moving out of settled country was the best course for the Mormons. The citizens of Clay County, after sheltering them for as long as they could, urged the Saints to move to Wisconsin. James Arlington Bennet, among others, had recommended that they migrate to Oregon. In July 1843, Joseph had sent Jonathan Dunham to explore the west and in February 1844, he instructed the Twelve to send twenty-five men on an expedition to California and Oregon, asking for volunteers who could provide themselves with five hundred dollars, a good horse and mule and a double-barreled shotgun.

The council tried to gather information about unoccupied territory open to settlers. They sent Lucien Woodworth to negotiate with Sam Houston and the Congress of Texas for land in which the kingdom might be established as an independent nation. Since the republic of Texas was in financial difficulty, the council hoped that their leaders might be willing to grant the Mormons a great lawless tract that spread from the Nueces River south to the Rio Grande in return for help in defending Texas against the Mexicans.

The council also had other ideas about finding a refuge. On March 26, Joseph wrote Congress a petition to appoint him an officer of the United States Army with power to raise 100,000 armed volunteers to open unsettled regions and to protect the borders of the United States.[22]

On March 30, Joseph prepared a similar memorial to President John Tyler, in case his first to the Congress should fail.[23] Such a request did

not seem unreasonable to Joseph, since President Tyler had recently recommended that Congress establish military posts along the Oregon Trail
to protect pioneers against the Indians.

Joseph appointed Orson Hyde to carry the memorials to Congress and
at the same time to learn whether or not Congress would be likely to approve the annexation of Texas, an issue that had been warmly disputed in
Washington for several years. Expansionists and slaveholders who hoped
to gain strength in the legislature by the addition of Texas as another slave
state were opposed by Whigs and anti-slavery Democrats and by those
who feared that such a move would precipitate a war with Mexico. Orson
Hyde sent Joseph intelligent evaluations of the debates in Washington but
he concluded that annexation was not likely. He offered little hope for any
special legislation in behalf of the Mormons should they move to Oregon.
Joseph's petition was in fact put down in the House of Representatives on
May 25, without being read through on the floor.

On the other hand, according to George Miller, Woodworth reported
that he had good results from his mission to the republic of Texas. Although the exact nature of his negotiations with Texas is not known,
Woodworth returned on May 2 with a draft of a "treaty," and the next
day reported to the Council of Fifty that "it was altogether as we could
wish it."

Miller said that commissioners, including himself and Woodworth, were
appointed "to sanction or ratify the said treaty, partly entered into by our
minister and the Texan cabinet."[24]

Meanwhile, suspicions of the Mormons' neighbors grew, fed by Mormon denunciations of the federal government as corrupt. Rumors spread
that Nauvoo was the center of subversive activities, plots against the Constitution and plans to overthrow the country. It was not generally understood or believed that Joseph Smith's purpose was to establish the kingdom of God by converting the people to righteousness. This he openly
stated in a speech of May 12, 1844, in which he said:

> I calculate to be one of the instruments of setting up the kingdom of
> Daniel by the word of the Lord and intend to lay a foundation that
> will revolutionize the whole world . . . It will not be by sword or by
> gun that this kingdom will roll on: the power of truth is such that all
> nations will be under the necessity of obeying the Gospel.[25]

CHAPTER

11

CANDIDATE
FOR PRESIDENT

By 1843, the city Joseph Smith and his followers had built in a few brief seasons out of swampland was competing in size with Chicago, while the state capital, Springfield, was still a little prairie town without decent sidewalks. That year, 374 missionaries were ordained and converts continued to pour into Nauvoo.[1]

Nauvoo was the busiest city in the state. The day was begun every morning at seven by the ringing of a bell at the temple site, and the streets were soon bustling with workers setting out and with traffic—wagons, carriages and horsemen, and frequently an oxcart with a heavy load of stone for the temple site.

Nauvoo could now boast of an iron foundry, two steam grist and saw mills, a water mill, two stone quarries, a match and powder factory, a pottery and a wagon shop, as well as numerous smaller enterprises, blacksmiths, tailors, milliners, tanners, cobblers and storekeepers.

Two periodicals were published in the city, the semi-monthly *Times and Seasons,* which was both newspaper and official organ of the church, and the local gossip sheet, the *Nauvoo Neighbor,* which William Smith had first put out as *The Wasp.*[2]

Five riverboats docked on an average day at the landing at the bottom of Water Street, bringing freight and passengers—converts to the church, tourists, journalists, politicians and businessmen. Passengers whose destination was somewhere farther up the Mississippi usually stopped over in Nauvoo. Sight-seers liked to climb to the platform on the bluff, from which a sweeping view could be had to north and south of the Mississippi River Valley, west across the river to Iowa and east to a sea of grass-covered prairie broken by clumps of woods and patches of farm land.

Visitors liked to come too to take part in public holidays at Nauvoo, since there was nothing of Puritan solemnity among the Mormons. The prophet's love of good times was reflected by his people, who never missed an opportunity to gather for festivities. They loved music and dancing, and supported three bands, a brass band, a quadrille band with stringed instruments and the Nauvoo Legion Band. They held cornhusking parties, excursions on the riverboats with band music and dancing by moonlight, quilting parties, followed by supper to which the men were invited for dancing, singing and games until midnight. Cotillion parties, held sometimes as a benefit for widows or missionaries, became popular at the Mansion House. Singing groups often serenaded newlyweds or sang in the streets at Christmas and New Year's. Debating societies and amateur dramatics were popular, and the Mormons were always pleased to welcome a traveling circus or theatrical group.

In 1842, Joseph had built a handsome two-story frame house called the Mansion House and had moved in with his family sometime after 1843, leaving the log and frame "Homestead" on the riverbank in which they had lived since 1839. With his ever-present dangers in mind, Joseph had built a secret escape route into his new house. Behind a false back in one closet was space for a ladder to the second floor and a trap door to the roof, over which a tree hung, giving access to the ground.

Emma, the children and those who shared their home, including Joseph's mother, were much more comfortable in the new house, but Joseph soon found that so many of Nauvoo's visitors stopped to see him and crowded his table that he could no longer welcome all comers, as had been his habit since the early days of the church. Some of his friends suggested that since the completion of Nauvoo's inn (to be called Nauvoo House) seemed far in the future, Joseph should receive paying instead of non-paying guests at home. During the summer of 1843, Joseph added a spacious two-story wing to the back of the Mansion, with a dining room and kitchen on the ground floor and ten bedrooms upstairs. He built a stable large enough for seventy-five horses. Emma went to St. Louis to buy furniture, china, linens and utensils. A new red carpet from St. Louis, a chandelier of glittering prisms and marble-topped tables were installed in the Mansion.

In October the family raised a sign "Nauvoo Mansion" and turned the event into a cause for celebration. At the opening on October 3, 1843, they held a great party. Food was prepared all day—prairie chickens, wild turkey, hot breads, mashed rutabagas, pumpkin pies and cider. The Mansion was decked with flags and bunting, and Joseph in his best suit and a new white stock and Emma in a new dress greeted some two hundred guests.

Robert D. Foster rose to speak after dinner, saying, "Whether we view him as a Prophet at the head of the Church, a General at the head of the Legion, a Mayor at the head of the City Council, or as a landlord at the head of his table, if he has equals, he has no superiors." He ended with praises for the city, the Legion and for "Thomas Ford, Governor of Illinois, fearless and faithful in the discharge of all official duties, long may he live, and blessings attend his administration."[3]

Music and dancing went on until late.

The Mansion House became a popular hotel, and acquired a reputation for providing the best food on the Mississippi.

Not all was harmonious in Joseph's life, however. Lately he had grown more and more discontented with Sidney Rigdon and had deep suspicions of his loyalty. A few days after the party at the Mansion House, he called a special conference of the church and brought complaint against him, charging him with treacherous correspondence with John C. Bennett and ex-governor Carlin and of advising the Missourians to pursue Joseph in Dixon. He also accused Sidney of failing to discharge his duties as a counselor and of mismanaging the post office.

Sidney denied all charges and entered a long defense, which continued the next day with an appeal to the prophet, reminding him of their former friendship and the sufferings they had shared, and closing with a sorrowful offer to resign. The people were so moved that in a rare instance of siding against the prophet, they voted to retain Sidney as First Counselor in the Presidency.

Joseph would not be mollified. "I have thrown him off my shoulders," he said, "and you have again put him on me. You may carry him, but I will not."[4]

However, it seems that Sidney was able to appease the prophet somehow, since several months later he was chosen as his running mate in the biggest political campaign Joseph ever undertook.[5]

About a month after his editorial in the *Times and Seasons,* October 1, 1843, advising the Saints to elect that man most likely to obtain justice for them and promising to find him, Joseph met with Willard Richards and John Taylor at the Mansion House to write letters interviewing five possible candidates for the presidency, John C. Calhoun, Richard M. Johnson, Henry Clay, Lewis Cass and the incumbent, Martin Van Buren. The brethren reminded the candidates that the Mormons were now a sizable class of voters, and asked for "an immediate, specific, and candid reply to *What will be your rule of action relative to us as a people,* should fortune favor your ascension to the chief magistracy?"

In a postscript to Van Buren they asked whether his views had changed since 1841 when he had treated the Mormons "with coldness, indifference, and neglect, bordering on contempt."[6]

Calhoun replied that since the Constitution and the laws of the union made no distinction between citizens of different religious creeds, he would make none, but added that he felt the Mormons' case did not come within the jurisdiction of the federal government, which had limited and specific powers.[7]

Henry Clay wrote that although he viewed the sufferings of the Mormons with sympathy and thought they ought to have the security and protection of the Constitution, he would make no promises to any particular people, intending, if elected, to enter that high office "free and unfettered."[8]

Lewis Cass said that the "Mormonites," like everyone else, should be protected in their rights and punished when they violated the laws, but he could make no further declaration since he had been out of the country when the events Joseph described had occurred. He added, however, that if the state and Congress had failed to redress the Mormons' wrongs, he did not see what the President could do.[9]

Joseph answered the candidates scornfully and at length.

It seemed obvious that there was no one the Mormons could endorse for the presidency. Joseph met with the apostles on January 29, 1844, to consider a course they might propose for the coming elections. Willard Richards moved and the apostles voted unanimously to propose a ticket of their own with Joseph at the head. That this move was a part of the Council of Fifty's plan for the establishment of the kingdom of God on earth is attested to by George Miller, who said that if Joseph were elected to the presidency, "the Kingdom would be forever established in the United States, and if not successful, we would fall back on Texas, and be a kingdom not with standing. . . ."[10]

The prophet accepted the proposal, and told the brethren that they would have to send every man who could speak in public to advance the campaign, and at the same time preach the gospel. "Tell the people we have had Whig and Democratic Presidents long enough; we want a President of the United States." It was his opinion that he would not have to campaign in person. He said, "There is oratory enough in the Church to carry me into the presidential chair the first slide."[11]

At once Joseph began dictating ideas for his platform, and with the help of William Phelps completed his *Views of the Powers and Policy of the Government of the United States,* a pamphlet of some length which he published February 7, 1844, and mailed to about two hundred leaders of the country.[12]

Joseph made proposals which were likely to appeal to voters in both major parties. He wanted, he said, to revoke imprisonment for debt, turn prisons into seminaries of learning, put felons to work on roads or other public projects and economize in national and state governments as a means of lowering taxes. Some of his proposals, however idealistic, were not likely to succeed. He wanted to petition slave states to abolish slavery by 1850 and to reimburse slaveholders out of revenue from the sale of public lands, but he took insufficient account of the significance of slavery in the southern economy and seemed unaware that the sale of public lands could not have raised nearly the amount needed to pay for the slaves. He ignored the fact that earlier attempts by abolitionists to petition Southerners to free their slaves had only roused anger. The idea he suggested that a national bank be established with branches in each state had been advanced by the Whigs in 1842 and vetoed twice by President Tyler.

Joseph proposed that the country be expanded from coast to coast with the consent of the Indians and that Texas, Canada and Mexico be included in the Union, if they should so request. He also wanted to assure the President the power to send an army to suppress mobs without the formality of a request from the governor. This would later happen but in Joseph's day it was considered an infringement upon States' rights.

Clearly reflected in Joseph's platform were his feelings about the cruelties of imprisonment, which he knew from his own experience, his concern for the poor and unfortunate and his belief in the possibility of a utopia on earth through reform. His most important aim in running for office, although it was not unduly emphasized, was probably to gain redress for the wrongs suffered by the Mormons.[13]

The *Times and Seasons* of March 1 presented Joseph's name to the public as a candidate. On the seventh, he spoke with perfect candor about his feelings to an enormous assembly of Saints:

> We have as good a right to make a political party to gain power to defend ourselves, as for demagogues to make use of our religion to get power to destroy us—we will whip the mob by getting up a president.[14]

Of the prophet's manner in public speaking, Job Smith, a young convert then living in Nauvoo, wrote:

> The stand from which he spoke, was, I think, between twenty and thirty feet long, and it was his custom in addition to his arm gesture to walk the stand from one end to the other and sometimes call upon the audience for an expression of approval which was usually answered by a loud "Aye" from the congregation. I have never but once since heard a preacher or lecturer exercise the mental power and earnestness manifested by that great man. He was large in stature and powerful in invective, and occasionally sarcastic . . .

Job Smith mentioned that the apostles and elders had been out distributing General Smith's "Views" and presenting his name as a candidate for the coming presidential election. He added:

> The prophet in a discourse which I remember, referring to the attitude of some of the lawyer politicians on learning that "General Joseph Smith" was the Mormon prophet would roll up a big chew of tobacco around their mouths and exclaim with surprise, "Old Joe Smith, by G—d."[15]

On March 4, Joseph proposed James Arlington Bennet, who had been baptized into the church by Brigham Young, as his running mate. That same day Willard Richards wrote to him, "General Smith is the greatest statesman of the 19th century." Quoting Joseph as saying that if he must be President, James Arlington Bennet must be Vice-President, Willard asked Bennet to get up an electoral ticket in the east, and suggested that preaching Mormonism would help his cause. He wrote, "Open your mouth wide and God shall fill it . . ." and advised that he start at his own mansion, and travel by a popular route to Nauvoo, campaigning all the way:

> At every stage, tavern, boat and company, expose the wickedness of Martinism . . . uphold Joseph Smith against every aspersion & you shall triumph gloriously. . . . our Elders will go forth by hundreds or thousands and search the land, preaching religion & politics—and if God goes with them, who can withstand their influence?[16]

Bennet had earlier written to Joseph that he was considering running for governor of the state of Illinois, but Richards told him that would be mere child's sport, when the whole nation was "on the board."[17]

Bennet declined to serve, however, and in any event was not eligible, having been born outside of the country, in Ireland. Eventually, Sidney Rigdon was given his place on the ticket.

Some wondered about Joseph's motives in running since they could not see how he had any hope of being elected. James Arlington Bennet wrote to Willard Richards on April 14 that he was sure that if Joseph could be put in office by "supernatural means," he would govern in good faith, but he thought that by natural means the prophet had not the slightest chance to win even one state. However, he said that if the object of Joseph's friends in campaigning for him was to aid the cause of Mormonism, he thought they might succeed.[18]

To this Willard replied on June 20 that the Mormons would extend their influence through the campaign, but that was not all. They meant to elect their man "because we are satisfied, fully satisfied, that this is the best or only method of saving our free institutions from total overthrow."[19]

It has been said that there are some indications that Joseph and other leaders tried to prepare themselves and the Saints for his failure.[20] However, Ephraim Ingals, who visited Nauvoo that spring and spent about two weeks in Joseph's hotel, conversed with the prophet frequently, and wrote in his journal that Joseph expressed belief he would be elected. Told that nobody outside of Nauvoo would vote for him, Joseph replied, "The Lord will turn the hearts of the people."[21]

Joseph's followers campaigned with great energy. They planned a convention in New York for July 13, 1844, and Brigham Young put his great talent to work writing letters, visiting newspaper offices and organizing committees.

Willard Richards wrote to Hugh Clark, alderman at Philadelphia, May 24, to ask for his support, saying, "The Mormons and the Catholics . . . are the only two who have not persecuted each other & others in these United States, and the only two who have suffered from the cruel hand of *mobocracy* for their *religion* under the name of *foreigners*—And to stay this growing evil and establish 'Jeffersonian Democracy' . . . Help us to Elect this man and we will help you to secure those privileges which belong to *you,* and break every yoke."[22]

For the spring and summer of 1844, nearly fifty conferences were organized in some fourteen states and the District of Columbia, and to each elders were assigned to preach the gospel, present Joseph's views and campaign for his election. The Twelve Apostles were scheduled to attend as many conferences as possible. Missionaries went out to speak wherever opportunity arose, in large cities and small towns, in public squares, town halls, country stores and on steamboats.

On June 19, Lyman Wight wrote to Joseph from Philadelphia, where he was preaching and campaigning:

> We are and continue your most humble and obedient servants, and wherever we go they are not at a loss to know that you are the Prophet of God and that you are bound to be the President of the United States on the 4th March 1845, and that you are already president pro tem of the world and they can't help themselves . . .[23]

Whenever possible, the missionaries sent new converts out to campaign for Joseph. Adding to a letter by Heber C. Kimball from Philadelphia, Lyman Wight wrote to Joseph on June 26:

> We ordained ten as promising young Elders as we ever laid hands upon. They pledged themselves to start this week and go through the state of Delaware from house to house and proclaim that the Kingdom of heaven is at hand and to bear you up as the *only* suitable candidate for the next presidency . . .

Naming the five candidates now running as Joseph Smith, Bering, Clay, Polk and Tyler, Lyman said, "It is generally believed that there will be about an even race between the 5, but this is not our opinion."[24]

BLACKS
IN THE EARLY CHURCH

P art of Joseph's campaign for the presidency, which might seem inconsistent with views he had put forth previously, was his proposal to abolish
slavery.

At the outset of the church, Joseph had expressed no policy regarding
Blacks, other than to include them with all other peoples of the earth in
the eyes of the Lord. In *The Book of Mormon*, 2 Nephi 26:33, it was
written:

> (the Lord) inviteth them all to come unto him and partake of his
> goodness; and he denieth none that come unto him, black and white,
> bond and free, male and female; and he remembereth the heathen;
> and all are alike unto God, both Jew and Gentile.

There were no Black members of the church in New York, so far as is
known, but among the early converts in Ohio was a Negro called "Black
Pete," and Blacks played a part from the outset of the church in Missouri.
In July 1831, when William Phelps preached the first sermon in Missouri
on the edge of the wilderness, Joseph mentioned that among the little
gathering who heard him were representatives of all the families of the
earth, including "quite a respectable number of negroes."[1] In 1832, A
Black man, Elijah Abel, was baptized into the church in Kirtland.

During the next year, the Mormons moved into the slave state of Missouri in large numbers. Because they were not slaveholders, they soon
raised resentment and then fierce animosity among their neighbors. The

Missourians, who preferred to keep free Blacks out of their state on the theory that they would inspire slaves to revolt, were enraged when Phelps published instructions in his newspaper on how Black Mormons who wished to move with their brethren to Missouri might meet the state's legal requirements. What angered the Missourians even more was that Phelps had added, "In connection with the wonderful events of this age, much is doing towards abolishing slavery, and colonizing the blacks in Africa."[2] The Missourians rose in a furious mob and drove the Mormons out of Jackson County.

Not long afterward, in December 1833, Joseph had a revelation which said in part, "it is not right that any man should be in bondage one to another."[3] However, this was not cited by the church as a stand against slavery.

That same month, the American Anti-Slavery Society was organized in Philadelphia, with the help of Theodore D. Weld and the brothers Arthur and Lewis Tappan. These three men were followers of the revivalist Charles G. Finney, whose vigorous movement for temperance, women's rights and the abolition of slavery had begun in New York in 1824 and had spread rapidly throughout much of the North. The Anti-Slavery Society undertook a campaign to abolish slavery immediately as a moral evil. Members traveled widely, usually in the North, lecturing and establishing local branches from which thousands of petitions against slavery were sent to Congress. They poured so many letters, pamphlets, tracts and magazines upon the slave states that Congressmen from the South tried to ban their literature from the mails.

Slaveholders responded vehemently and produced an abundant literature of their own to justify their practice. They propounded the alleged racial inferiority and sexual corruption of Blacks, advocated the right of states to determine the issue of slavery for themselves, and as a scriptural defense of slavery, they cited Noah's curse on Canaan, "Cursed be Canaan; a servant of servants shall he be unto his brethren" (Gen. 9:25), which they maintained applied directly to Blacks of African origin who were supposedly Canaan's descendants.

Many Northerners, although opposed to slavery, declared the abolitionists fanatic or disruptive to society and likely to cause bloodshed. Among them were the Mormons, who, without condoning slavery as such, took a stand that where government allowed slavery, citizens should not intervene. In an official statement of August 1835, the Mormons said:

> we do not believe it right to interfere with bond-servants, neither preach the gospel to, nor baptize them contrary to the will and wish of their masters, nor to meddle with or influence them in the least to cause them to be dissatisfied with their situations in this life, thereby jeopardizing the lives of men; such interference we believe to be un-

lawful and unjust, and dangerous to the peace of every government allowing human beings to be held in servitude.[4]

Free Blacks were not rejected by the Mormons, however, and a few did join the church. In 1835, when Emma collected hymns for the church, she included one which said that the word was to be taken "to Afric's black legions."[5]

When in the spring of 1836, an abolitionist came to Kirtland and formed a society, Joseph grew worried. He did not want the Mormons to be identified with the movement, since he was mindful of the troubles they had endured in Jackson County over the question of the Blacks and concerned as well about his missionaries in the South. He had long been afraid of a national disaster over the issue of slavery, and in his prophecy of 1832 had said that a war would "shortly come to pass" between the North and the South, in which "slaves shall rise up against their masters."[6] In the *Messenger and Advocate* of April 1836, Joseph published his objections to the abolitionists. Allowing that "this must be a tender point," he said that the abolitionists were "calculated to . . . loose, upon the world a community of people who might peradventure overrun our country and violate the most sacred principles of human society—chastity and virtue."

Any evil attending slavery would be apparent to the pious men of the South, the prophet maintained, adding, "I do not believe that the people of the North have any more right to say that the South *shall not* hold slaves, than the South to say the North *shall* . . . what can divide our union sooner, God only knows."

He considered the signing of petitions among the Northerners to be a declaration of hostilities against the South. Citing precedents for slavery in the Bible, he said that the sons of Canaan were cursed with servitude by Jehovah's decree, which curse was not yet lifted, and that "God can do his work without the aid of those who are not dictated by his counsel."

As Joseph said, he was offering opinions as an individual. He did not propose them as doctrine. In fact, the ideas he expressed resembled those in the literature of slaveholders, whom Joseph and the Mormons were then trying not to antagonize further.

About this time, elders laboring in the South consulted Joseph about applications they had received from Blacks for membership in the church. Abraham O. Smoot made a statement later that as he understood it, Joseph replied that Negroes could be baptized with the consent of their masters but they "were not entitled to the Priesthood."[7] As has been pointed out, however, there is no indication of whether this restriction was made because the Negroes were Black or because they were slaves.[8] The latter seems likely, considering the situation, and also because on March 3, 1836, in Kirtland the Black convert Elijah Abel was ordained an elder under Joseph Smith's direction, received his patriarchal blessing from Joseph Smith, Sr., and on December 20 of that year was ordained a seventy by Zebedee Coltrin.[9]

Zebedee Coltrin claimed in later years that he had personal information from the prophet about the Negro and the priesthood. In May 1879, John Taylor, who was then president of the church, questioned Coltrin on that subject in person.

Coltrin told him that in the spring of 1834, when the brethren were gathering for Zion's Camp, he and J. P. Greene got into a dispute over whether or not Blacks could hold the priesthood, Coltrin maintaining that they could not. When Greene threatened to report Coltrin to the prophet for preaching false doctrine, they went to him together to pose the question. According to John Taylor, Coltrin said:

> Brother Joseph kind of dropt his head and rested it on his hand for a minute, and then said, "Brother Zebedee is right, for the Spirit of the Lord Saith the Negro has no right nor cannot hold the Priesthood."
> He made no reference to Scripture at all, but such was his decision.

What Coltrin revealed in the account he then made of washing and anointing Elijah Abel in the Kirtland temple was apparently his own racism. He said that he "never had such unpleasant feelings in my life— and I said I never would again Annoint another person who had Negro blood in him unless I was commanded by the Prophet to do so."

Coltrin said that Abel was ordained a seventy because he had worked on the temple, and added, "when the Prophet learned of his lineage he was dropped from the Quorum, and another was put in his place."[10]

John Taylor reported this interview at a council meeting the following week. Joseph F. Smith, who was Hyrum's son and would himself become president of the church in 1901, said he thought Zebedee's memory that Elijah had been dropped from the Seventies was incorrect, since he had seen Abel's certificate as renewed in Nauvoo in 1841, and another one given to him still later in Salt Lake City. He told the council that Abel maintained that the prophet had said he was entitled to the priesthood, and that it was not Coltrin who had washed and anointed him, but Coltrin had ordained him a seventy in 1841.[11]

It has been reported that Joseph F. Smith gave this information about Abel's ordination on several occasions. In a council meeting of 1908, however, Joseph F. Smith said that although Abel had been ordained a seventy, "this ordination was declared null and void by the Prophet himself." The reason for this change in the account remains conjectural. It has been suggested that Joseph F. Smith might have suffered a lapse of memory, since on that same day he made the mistake of reversing his earlier, and correct, statement that Coltrin had ordained Abel.[12]

Apparently Elijah Abel held a responsible social position in Kirtland, his name being among those who signed the agreement to form the Kirtland Safety Society Anti-Banking Company. In Nauvoo he proved himself a courageous and faithful brother in the church, and reportedly lived for a time in the prophet's home. On June 6, 1841, when news came that the prophet had been arrested by a posse shortly after visiting Governor Carlin at his home in Quincy, Abel and six others set out for Quincy from the Nauvoo landing in a skiff, fighting heavy winds on the river, ready to rescue the prophet if necessary.[13] In 1883, at the age of seventy-three, Abel left Salt Lake City to serve a mission in Canada and afterward in Ohio. There he suffered severe exposure, and died of resulting debility in 1884, two weeks after he returned to Utah. According to his biographer, he died with full faith in the gospel.[14]

For several years after his statement of 1836, Joseph and the Mormons said little about slavery. The gospel was still proclaimed as meant for all. Rules for the Kirtland temple, set forth in 1836, welcomed everyone, "male or female, bond or free, black or white, believer or unbeliever . . ."[15]

In Nauvoo in 1840, the first presidency spoke of "persons of all languages, and of every tongue, and of every color; who shall with us worship the Lord of Hosts in His holy temple."[16] However, the ordinances afterward denied to Blacks—sealing and endowments—were not revealed until 1841 and 1842, and not performed in the Nauvoo temple until 1846 and 1845, respectively, after the prophet's death.

In 1842, John C. Bennett, then mayor of Nauvoo, received a letter from Charles V. Dyer, an outstanding physician in Chicago, asking for support for three abolitionists held in prison in Missouri and expressing indignation as well at the behavior of Missourians toward the Mormons. Bennett replied that he was for universal liberty to every soul of man. Apparently hearing about their exchange, Joseph wrote Bennett a note saying that slavery and the treatment given the abolitionists made his "blood boil." He published the letters of Bennett and Dyer in the *Times and Seasons,* with an introduction advocating universal liberty.[17]

Thereafter, from 1842 until his death, Joseph persistently stated that he was opposed to slavery.

On December 30, 1842, at the home of Judge Adams, where Joseph and his party were received after having come to Springfield for Joseph's appearance before Judge Pope, Orson Hyde asked the prophet what advice he would give a man coming into the church with a hundred slaves. As recorded by Willard Richards in the journal he was then keeping for the prophet, Joseph said, "I have always advised such to bring their slaves into a free country & set them free—Educate them & give them equal Rights."[18]

Joseph's feelings were complex, however, and cannot be neatly classified as liberal. He did not seem to think it would be advisable for the slaves to be allowed to govern themselves. According to Richards, Joseph said, "should the slaves be organized into an independent government they would become quarrelsome it would not be wisdom."[19] A few days later, on January 2, while Joseph and his friends were at supper at the home of Sollars, Orson Hyde again questioned Joseph about the Blacks. Joseph said,

> They came into the world slaves, mentally and physically. Change their situation with the whites, and they would be like them. They have souls, and are subjects of salvation. Go into Cincinnati or any city, and find an educated negro, who rides in his carriage, and you will see a man who has risen by the powers of his own mind to his exalted state of respectability. The slaves in Washington are more refined than many in high places, and the black boys will take the shine off many of those they brush and wait on.
> Elder Hyde remarked, "Put them on the level, and they will rise above me." I replied, if I raised you to be my equal, and then attempted to oppress you, would you not be indignant and try to rise above me? . . . Had I anything to do with the negro, I would confine them by strict law to their own species, and put them on a national equalization.[20]

As evident in these statements, Joseph was not influenced by the opinion commonly held in his day that the Blacks were congenitally inferior. He recognized that their condition was the result of environment and lack of opportunity, an advanced opinion for his time. He did, however, exhibit the then current antipathy toward miscegenation.

In 1844, with the publication of his *Views of the Powers and Policy of the Government of the United States,* Joseph deplored the fact that two or three millions were held as slaves "because the spirit in them is covered with a darker skin that ours," and advocated that the slaves be freed within six years, with federal compensation to the slaveholders.[21]

It might be debated whether Joseph's anti-slavery reflected a change of spirit, whether at last it revealed his true attitude or whether it was merely expedient for political reasons. A case against the latter suggestion could be made from the fact that Joseph had changed his public statements about slavery some two years before his decision to run for the presidency. By that time the Mormons had moved to Illinois, which counted itself a free state, and slavery was no longer the dangerous issue it had been for them when they lived in Missouri. Again, Joseph's experience with oppression and persecution had made the concept of freedom important to him. After the safety of his own people was no longer an issue, Joseph said he had always advised that slaves be freed. If indeed he had always felt slavery to be wrong, the prophet might be censured for not having taken a strong moral stand against it from the outset, whatever the consequences.

However, that he had chosen not to do so in consideration of the danger he felt to his people and to the nation may be only an indication of his priorities. The evidence does not seem sufficient for a conclusion that he changed his public statements about slavery to suit the political winds of 1844.

Joseph did not suggest any specific plan for the slaves after their emancipation except to educate and equalize them, but apparently he entertained other ideas. In his address of March 7, 1844, he said that while some opposed the annexation of Texas because of slavery he would bring Texas into the Union for that very reason, to prevent the British from enlisting the slaves and the Indians in a war to "use us up." He proposed to free the Blacks, have them fight in the war against Mexico and eventually send them there, where "all colors are alike."[22]

While Joseph promoted "national equalization" for Blacks, his statements revealed the racist ideas common in his century. He wanted Blacks "confined by strict law to their own species," and as mayor of Nauvoo, went so far in January 1844 as to fine two Black men "for attempting to marry white women."[23]

No direct statement has come to light from Joseph that he would deny free Blacks the priesthood. On the contrary, he had the priesthood bestowed upon Elijah Abel. Evidence that restriction against the Blacks was not practiced by the prophet's brother William appears in a letter from the president of the church in the eastern and middle states, who wrote to Brigham Young from Batavia, New York, in 1847 that he had met a Black brother named Lewis whom William had ordained as an elder.[24]

Between the time Elijah Abel was ordained an elder at Kirtland and the time he received a renewed certificate as a seventy in Nauvoo, Joseph was at work on *The Book of Abraham,* which in later years would be cited as the scriptural basis for the church policy of denying the priesthood to Blacks.

According to his journal, Joseph began on July 5, 1835, to translate *The Book of Abraham* from the Egyptian papyri bought from Chandler. In Chapter 1:26 of that work it is written that Noah blessed Pharaoh "with the blessings of the earth, and with the blessings of wisdom, but cursed him as pertaining to the Priesthood." Verses 21 and 22 say:

Now this king of Egypt was a descendant from the loins of Ham, and was a partaker of the blood of the Canaanites by birth.

From this descent sprang all the Egyptians, and thus the blood of the Canaanites was preserved in the land.

Verse 27 described Pharaoh as "of that lineage by which he could not have the right of Priesthood." Nowhere in *The Book of Abraham* does it say that Pharaoh and his people were Negroes; rather it says they were Egyptians, although in Joseph's *The Book of Moses* (7:22), it is written that the seed of Cain were black.

No indisputable evidence has come to light that Joseph himself presented *The Pearl of Great Price* as authority for denying the priesthood to Blacks. However, it began to be used several decades after his death, and gradually became the standard church reference on the subject. In 1947, David O. McKay, who was to become ninth president of the church in 1951, said that *The Book of Abraham* 1:26 was the only scriptural basis he knew for that church policy.[25]

There is some evidence that after the prophet's death church denial of the priesthood to Blacks became formalized by his successors. Wilford Woodruff recorded in his journal that Brigham Young said in his gubernatorial address of 1852:

> . . . any man having one drop of the seed of [Cain] . . . in him cannot hold the priesthood and if no other Prophet ever spake it before I will say it now in the name of Jesus Christ I know it is true and others know it.[26]

The belief has been maintained by Mormons that the priesthood was denied Blacks because of the role they played in the pre-existence. Anson Call said that Joseph had told him and several others that some spirits had remained neutral during the council in heaven,[27] and because of that came to earth as Negroes, through the lineage of Cain, whose black skin was perpetuated after the flood through the seed of Ham and his son Canaan.[28]

In 1869, as recorded in the journal of Wilford Woodruff, Brigham declared that Joseph had said the posterity of Cain were black because God set His mark upon them after Cain had committed murder, but he said he would not believe anyone who claimed to have heard Joseph say the spirits of Blacks were neutral in heaven, because he had heard Joseph say to the contrary. Brigham, presumably quoting Joseph Smith's belief, added, "All spirits are pure that come from the presence of God."[29]

13

DISSENT IN NAUVOO

I t now seemed, in early 1844, that Joseph Smith was on a great tide of success. Besides being candidate for the highest office in the land, he was mayor, judge of the municipal court, lieutenant general of the Nauvoo Legion, trustee-in-trust of the church, steamboat owner, real estate agent, husband of a number of women and leader of the earthly kingdom of God.

In reality, however, his situation was precarious. He was faced with the rising hostility of non-Mormons in the area who were outraged by the spreading rumors of secret practices in the Holy City. Members and officers of the state militia were indignant over the size and independence of the Nauvoo Legion. Citizens of Warsaw and Carthage were fiercely resentful of Nauvoo's political power.

Though concerned, the prophet felt defiant. In a sermon on Sunday, October 15, he had said:

I prophesy in the name of the Lord God anguish [indecipherable word] & wrath & tribulation and the withdrawing of the spirit of God await this generation, until they are visited with utter desolation. this generation is as corrupt as the generation of Jews that crucified Christ & if he were here today, & should preach the same doctrine he did then they would [crucify?] him. I defy all the world & I prophecy they never will overthrow me till I get ready.[1]

Actually, Joseph was most worried about discontent among the Saints and said more than once that some people within the church were more dangerous to him personally than all his enemies without. On December 29 he appointed forty city policemen to patrol Nauvoo around the clock. Nominally their duties were to enforce city ordinances and maintain the peace, but from Joseph's speech to them after they were sworn in, it was apparent that they were also to protect him from his enemies within the church. He said, "My life is more in danger from some little dough-head of a fool in this city than from all my numerous and inveterate enemies abroad." His enemies could accomplish nothing, he said, unless some who had sat in council with him and called him brother turned false. He added, ". . . and *we have a Judas in our midst.*"[2]

Those who opposed some of Joseph's policies began to feel uneasy after the institution of the police. Among them was William Law, who had been Joseph's second counselor for the previous two years. Law, a well-to-do convert from Canada who had come to Nauvoo and invested in industry, land, farming and building, became displeased with Joseph's control of real estate and his threat to excommunicate any who bought land without his approval. Considering that Joseph was constantly raising money for it and selling stock in it, Law thought Nauvoo House ought to be making more progress. He came to believe that Joseph was using Nauvoo House donations to buy land and sell it to converts at a profit. In any case, Law advocated that work on Nauvoo House and even on the temple be postponed until all citizens were decently housed.

With Dr. Robert D. Foster, Law had begun to buy lumber brought from Wisconsin for the church buildings and to use it for houses and commercial property. The partners paid wages, which laborers naturally preferred to the goods and city scrip they received for labor on Nauvoo House and the temple. Joseph had protested against the competition and tried to persuade the brethren not to work for Foster and Law.

William Law told Hyrum that he suspected the police were secretly sworn in "to put him out of the way." On January 3, Law repeated his charge before the City Council saying that some of the police had told him they had sworn another oath to "take care of" the Judas who stood near the prophet, who was not only a dough-head and a traitor but an assassin. Joseph protested that he had given special instructions only to the chief policemen and they were to protect him against the Missourians. The council spent most of the day questioning the police, until Law was satisfied that he was not in danger.[3]

On January 4, 1844, a severely cold night, someone built a fire on the bank of the river, opposite William Marks's house. Marks was badly frightened, suspecting he was the "dough-head of a fool" whom the police meant to kill. At Marks's request, the police were questioned the next morning before another session of the City Council.[4]

Leonard Soby protested at the same session that he had been intimidated by an armed policeman and that he had been told by another policeman that he and Law were Joseph's enemies and they might be "popped over."[5]

Among the prophet's circle, in particular Leonard Soby, William Law, William Marks and Francis Higbee, there was excited talk about who the Brutus might be and where the prophet's suspicions lay.

In his journal for January 5 Joseph wrote, "What can be the matter with these men? Is it that the wicked flee when no man pursueth? . . . Can it be possible that the traitor whom Porter Rockwell reports to me as being in correspondence with my Missouri enemies, is one of my quorum?"[6]

Joseph could, however, still be facetious about his predicament. In a sermon on March 10, he said; "The Lord once told me that what I asked for I should have. I have been afraid to ask God to kill my enemies, lest some of them should, peradventure, repent."[7]

To William Law and the others, there was nothing humorous in the situation, which they saw as growing worse with passing time. Then Law claimed to have discovered that Joseph had made overtures to his wife, Jane. This seemed the final outrage. Law demanded that Joseph either confess and repent before the High Council or have his sins exposed to the world. As Law told it, Joseph replied that such a confession would mean the downfall of the church, and when Law said that was already inevitable, Joseph answered, "Then we can all go to Hell together and convert it into a heaven by casting the Devil out!" According to Law, Joseph added that contrary to the opinion of this world of fools, hell was quite an agreeable place.[8]

According to Alexander Neibaur, Joseph's version of the incident between himself and the Laws was that William wanted to be married to his wife Jane for eternity, but Joseph inquired of the Lord and said it could not be done because William was adulterous. When Jane asked why the ceremony could not be performed, Joseph refused to tell her, hoping to spare her feelings. As Joseph was passing her doorway several days later, Jane beckoned to him, drew him inside and embraced him, saying, "if you won't seal me to my husband seal myself unto you." Joseph said that he put her gently aside with a refusal and left. When William returned, Jane told him that Joseph had wanted her to marry him.[9]

Fundamentally, William Law believed that Joseph was not a false but a fallen prophet, and he was reluctant to act against Joseph until he became convinced that the "Destroying Angels" had been ordered out against him. William and his brother Wilson, major general in the Nauvoo Legion, began to exchange views with other disaffected Mormons, including William Marks, president of the church High Council, council members Austin Cowles and Leonard Soby, who were violently opposed to polygamy, and Francis and Chauncey Higbee (sons of Joseph's valued friend, the late Judge Elias Higbee), who had not been in good standing in the church since they had been known as associates of John C. Bennett.

In March, the Law brothers held a series of secret meetings. One M. G. Eaton made a sworn statement that on or about March 15 he was invited to a meeting in the back room of the Keystone Store in Nauvoo by Joseph H. Jackson. Jackson was a prepossessing, somewhat mysterious newcomer who had been friendly with Joseph but who would later publish a virulent anti-Mormon pamphlet in Warsaw. There Robert D. Foster, one of the Higbee brothers and the Law brothers started "talking about the spiritual wife system." Foster related that he had come home one day to find "a person" at dinner with his wife. Suspicious, Foster questioned his wife after her guest was gone, but she would not tell him what had occurred, and remained silent even when he put a pistol to her head. He thrust another into her hand, crying that she must talk, shoot him or be shot herself. She fainted. When Foster revived her, she confessed that her guest had been preaching the spiritual wife doctrine.

Foster, Higbee and Jackson said they proposed to stop such things. Robert Foster said he was afraid for his life and did not dare go out at night. One of the men suggested that the citizens of Carthage would help in case of an insurrection.[10]

William Clayton reported in his journal that he went with Joseph to face Mrs. Foster in the presence of her friend, a Mrs. Gillman. Joseph told her he had been informed that her husband accused him of making propositions to her "calculated to lead her astray from the path of virtue." Joseph asked her if she had ever known him to be guilty of an immoral act. She answered, "No." He then asked her if he had ever preached anything like the "plurality of wife" doctrine to her in private, or if he had ever proposed having illicit intercourse with her, especially when he had dinner with her during her husband's absence. Again she said, "No." Satisfied, Joseph left.[11]

On March 24, Sunday, Joseph addressed the people, saying that he had been informed that a conspiracy existed in Nauvoo against him, his family and all the heads of the church, and named the conspirators as Chauncey L. Higbee, Robert D. Foster, Joseph H. Jackson, William and Wilson Law.

> I ask, Did I ever exercise any compulsion over any man? Did I not give him the liberty of disbelieving any doctrine I have preached, if he saw fit? Why do not my enemies strike a blow at the doctrine? They cannot do it: it is truth, and I defy all men to upset it. I am the voice of one crying in the wilderness, "Repent ye of your sins and prepare the way for the coming of the Son of Man; for the kingdom of God has come unto you, and henceforth the ax is laid unto the root of the tree; and every tree that bringeth not forth good fruit, God Almighty (and not Joe Smith) shall hew it down and cast it into the fire.[12]

On Saturday, April 13, Joseph met with the municipal court, before whom he asked Foster, "Have I ever misused you any way?" Foster replied, "I do not feel at liberty to answer this question, under existing circumstances." Joseph repeated his question and got the same answer. Again Joseph asked the question. Foster said, "I do not feel at liberty to answer. I have treated you Christianly and friendly too, so far as I have had the ability." Joseph then told Foster to name the wrong done him and he would ask his forgiveness, saying, "For I want you to prove to this company by your testimony that I have treated you honorably." Foster said, "I shall testify no further at present."

Joseph preferred charges against Foster before the High Council "for unchristianlike conduct in general, for abusing my character privily, for throwing out slanderous insinuations against me, for conspiring against my peace and safety, for conspiring against my life, for conspiring against the peace of my family, and for lying."[13] According to later account in the *Nauvoo Expositor* Foster received notice on April 15 to appear before the church High Council on the following Saturday, April 20. While Foster was assembling his witnesses, who were forty-one in number, he was notified that his trial had already taken place. Members of the High Council had met on the eighteenth and by a unanimous decision excommunicated him along with William, Wilson and Jane Law, for "unchristianlike conduct."

Although news of their excommunication was published in the *Times and Seasons,* Foster and the Laws did not wish to abandon their strong business interests and leave Nauvoo.

Foster confronted Joseph. As Joseph put it, ". . . he charged me with many crimes, and said that Daniteism was in Nauvoo; and he used a great variety of vile and false epithets and charges."

Foster proposed to meet Joseph on the public stand for a settlement, and said he would publish the results in the Warsaw papers. Joseph wrote:

> I told him if he did not agree to be quiet, and not attempt to raise a mob, I would not meet him; if he would agree to be quiet, I would be willing to publish the settlement in the *Neighbor.* But Foster would not agree to be quiet. I then told him I had done my duty; the skirts of my garments were free from his blood; I had made the last overtures of peace to him; and then delivered him into the hands of God, and shook my garments against him as a testimony thereof.[14]

The next day, April 28, Foster met with the others who had been excommunicated and some sympathizers. As a group they professed belief that Joseph was a fallen prophet, and decided to set up a reformed church, with William Law in Joseph's place at the head. A committee, including Foster and the Law brothers, was appointed to visit and try to convert Mormon families to the new church. A press was ordered and plans were made to launch an opposition newspaper to be called the *Nauvoo Expositor.*

They were able to rally about three hundred of the Saints to their cause and began to hold regular meetings, at which they demanded that the Nauvoo charters be revoked.

On May 7, the press arrived by steamer from St. Louis and was hauled through the city and set up. According to Thomas Gregg, great excitement prevailed throughout the county when the press was landed, but no one interfered with its establishment. The new owners began work at once and three days later issued a prospectus in which they said they espoused "unmitigated DISOBEDIENCE TO POLITICAL REVELATIONS," and proposed to "censure and decry gross moral imperfections wherever found, either in plebeian, patrician or SELF-CONSTITUTED MONARCH."[15]

Meanwhile, Wilson Law was suspended as major general of the Legion, William was released as Joseph's second counselor and complaint was made against them both in the Masonic Lodge. On the day of the prospectus, Robert Foster was relieved of his office as surgeon general of the Nauvoo Legion.

Soon afterward, William Law got the grand jury in Carthage to indict Joseph for adultery and polygamy and Foster brought a charge against him for false swearing.

On Sunday, May 26, Joseph made a public defense against the allegations against him: "I, like Paul, have been in perils, and oftener than anyone in this generation. . . . I should be like a fish out of water, if I were out of persecutors. Perhaps my brethren think it requires all this to keep me humble. The Lord has constituted me so curiously that I glory in persecutions. . . ."

Joseph added that his persecutors would be unable to prove anything against him, since for the last three years he had had clerks follow him everywhere and record his every word and action. He went on:

It appears a holy prophet has arisen up, and he has testified against me: the reason is, he is so holy . . . God knows, then, that the charges against me are false. I had not been married scarcely five minutes, and made one proclamation of the Gospel, before it was reported that I had seven wives . . . This new holy prophet has gone to Carthage and swore that I had told him that I was guilty of adultery. This spiritual wifeism! Why, a man dares not speak or wink, for fear of being accused of this. . . . I am the same man, and as innocent as I was fourteen years ago; and I can prove them all perjurers. . . . As I grow older, my heart grows tenderer for you. I am at all times willing to give up everything that is wrong, for I wish this people to have a virtuous leader . . . I have nothing in my heart but good feelings.[16]

The next day Joseph and a party of friends rode to Carthage for his trial, but the case was deferred until the next term of the circuit court.

Joseph launched a campaign against the Higbees in the *Nauvoo Neighbor*. Francis was accused of seduction, adultery and perjury, and of contracting a venereal disease from prostitutes. Chauncey was confronted with old charges from the Bennett days of having seduced three women with the promise of making them his spiritual wives.

On June 7, the Law, Higbee and Foster brothers published the first, and as it happened, the only issue of the *Nauvoo Expositor*. The editor was Sylvester Emmons, a lawyer and a member of the City Council, although not a member of the church. In their newspaper the collaborators complained of Joseph's control of the land in and around Nauvoo and accused him of abusing the rights of the Nauvoo charters. They decried his political aspirations, saying that they did not believe God ever raised a prophet to Christianize the world by political intrigue. "We will not acknowledge any man as king or lawgiver to the church; for Christ is our only king and lawgiver."[17]

The paper condemned Joseph's "moral imperfections," meaning polygamy. No woman was specifically named, but a story was told of a hypothetical convert, a young girl from England arriving alone in Nauvoo, where she was taught the principles of the gospel by the prophet in person, including the shocking news of plural marriage. Austin Cowles and William and Jane Law published statements that they had seen, or heard read, Joseph's revelation allowing men to marry up to ten virgins.

Distributed throughout Nauvoo, the *Expositor* caused an immediate furor among the faithful who were practicing, or knew about, polygamy as well as among those who still believed that polygamy was a false rumor. Beyond Nauvoo, it also raised a frenzy over Joseph's ultimate political aims.

Joseph found himself in an alarming situation. His tolerance of such enemies in the midst of the Saints and the continued publication of their newspaper would disrupt the harmony of his religious community, endanger his candidacy for the highest office in the land, threaten the establishment of the political kingdom of God and in short dash all his dearest hopes. To suppress his enemies and their newspaper would be a violation of those principles of freedom on which he was now so vigorously campaigning for office. To sue the paper for libel over issues that were already charged with emotion would expose him to sensational publicity, even if he should win, which was not likely. To lose such a suit would endanger the city charter and might result in the dissolution of the city government, or its assumption by the dissenters. The terrors of the Missouri persecutions could well be reenacted.

In his dilemma, Joseph did not know which way to turn. William Marks, to whom the matter of gravest concern was the spread of polygamy, wrote that Joseph told him privately that unless it could be abolished polygamy would destroy the church. Marks said that Joseph asked him to bring all polygamists to trial before the High Council, offered to prefer charges himself and added that those who would not repent must be cut off from the church. He promised to stand before the church and preach against the practice. According to Marks, Joseph "was satisfied that it was a cursed doctrine, and that there must be every exertion made to put it down."[18]

What Joseph might have said to Marks was one thing, but what he decided to do was something else. On June 8 he called the City Council for an investigation of the *Expositor*. In a session which carried over until Monday, June 10, Joseph read aloud and denied the charges in the *Expositor*. He declared that the Constitution did not authorize the publication of libel. One after another council members rose and accused the publishers of theft, seduction, pandering and counterfeiting. Hyrum Smith pronounced the paper a nuisance. Another councilman defined nuisance as anything that disturbed the peace, and added that their whole community was disgraced by the lies in the *Expositor,* and that he favored suppression of all such publications. Another councilor found and cited a passage in Blackstone on public wrongs.

Hyrum suggested that the best solution would be to smash the press and pie the type. One councilor by the name of Warrington, a non-Mormon, proposed instead that the council levy a fine of $3,000 for every libel, but Joseph protested that no one would dare to go to Carthage to prosecute, and that his own life had been threatened there.

The council found the *Expositor* guilty of libel, declared it a nuisance and directed Joseph, as mayor, to have the nuisance removed. Joseph immediately ordered the marshal, with the aid of troops under Jonathan Dunham, acting major general of the Nauvoo Legion, to destroy the press.

THE
PROPHET SURRENDERS

At 8 p.m. on June 10, the same day as the City Council's decision that the *Expositor* was a public nuisance, the marshal and a contingent of the Legion marched out at Joseph's order and wrecked the press, broke down what had been set up (the inside part of number two of the *Expositor*), spilled the type into the street and burned every printed sheet in the office.

Followed by several hundred people, the marshal and the troops returned to the front of the Mansion, where Joseph made a speech saying that the men had done right in executing the City Council's orders and that he would never allow another libelous newspaper to be published in Nauvoo. This was received with cheers.

William Law, who was in Carthage when the *Expositor* was wrecked, said that in returning home he rode over his type scattered in the street and over his broken furniture. He maintained that the printing office, a new brick building, was absolutely gutted.

The publishers of the *Expositor* and some of their allies left Nauvoo at once. William and Wilson Law took their families up the Mississippi on a steamboat to Burlington, Iowa. Unable to sell the property they had been forced to leave, William said their losses in Nauvoo amounted to about $30,000, including their homes, farms, city lots, a large steam flour and saw mill and a store.[1]

Robert Foster gave a fiery complaint to Thomas Sharp for publication in the *Warsaw Signal*, which appeared June 12. He complained of the destruction of the press, saying, "I hasten to inform you of the unparalleled outrage perpetrated upon our rights & interests, by the ruthless, lawless, ruffian band of Mormon mobocrats, at the dictum of that unprincipled wretch Jo Smith . . . We made no resistence but . . . leave it for the Public to avenge this climax of insult & injury."

At once Sharp began a campaign in the *Warsaw Signal* to rouse the countryside against Joseph Smith and the Mormons.

In that same issue he wrote, "CITIZENS ARISE, ONE AND ALL!!!" On the eighteenth he put out an extra edition of his paper, in which he said, "To our friends at a distance we say come! We are too weak in this county, without aid, to effect our object. Come! You will be doing your God and your country service, in aiding us to rid earth of a most heaven-daring wretch."

The following day he continued, "Let there be no cowards in the camp . . . but upon every man's countenance let there be written, the desperate determination . . . to strike the tyrant to the dust . . . You, fellow Citizens, are justified before the world, and in the sight of Heaven. Strike then! for the time has fully come."

Public reaction was intense. Mass meetings were held at Warsaw and Carthage at which it was announced that Hyrum Smith had offered a reward for the destruction of the *Warsaw Signal* and had threatened the life of editor Sharp. (This, Hyrum later said, was "false as hell.")[2] The citizens declared:

> We must not only defend ourselves from danger, but we must resolutely carry the war into the enemy's camp . . . We will sustain our press and the editor at all hazards . . . we hold ourselves in readiness to co-operate with our fellow-citizens in this state, Missouri and Iowa, to exterminate, utterly exterminate the wicked and abominable Mormon leaders . . .[3]

Meanwhile, on June 14, Joseph wrote a justification of his actions to Governor Ford, saying that "after a long and patient investigation" the City Council determined that the *Expositor* had to be removed for the peace of the city and that the orders were carried out without riot or confusion. On the sixteenth, he wrote again to tell the governor that the Nauvoo Legion was at his service to put down any disturbance, and to invite him to visit Nauvoo with his staff and investigate the whole affair.[4]

Nevertheless, the prophet and some seventeen others were charged at Carthage with instigating a riot in destroying the *Expositor* and a sheriff was sent to arrest them, but Joseph had no faith in the impartiality of the law under those inflamed circumstances and refused to surrender. Instead he secured a writ from the Nauvoo court and he, Hyrum, John Taylor, William W. Phelps and several others were tried on those charges and acquitted on June 17 before Daniel H. Wells, a non-Mormon (although pro-Mormon) judge, in Nauvoo.[5]

When the sheriff returned to Carthage without his prisoners, some seven hundred old citizens rallied to a meeting with "such excitement I never witnessed in my life," said Samuel O. Williams, an officer of the Carthage Greys. "We all felt that the time had come when either the Mormons or old citizens had to leave."[6]

In Rushville, three thousand men enlisted, and hundreds more took up arms in McDonough County, Keokuk and Green Plains. Emissaries were sent to Governor Ford to ask for support from the state militia. Citizens cried they would take up arms and march on Nauvoo if the governor did not respond.[7]

On June 18, Joseph called out the Nauvoo Legion, which by now numbered some five thousand men (although many were away on missions), and put the city under martial law. In full military uniform, he stood on top of the framework of a new building going up near the Mansion and spoke to the Legion for over an hour. It was recorded by George Albert Smith that he said:

It is thought by some that our enemies would be satisfied with my destruction; but I tell you that as soon as they have shed my blood they will thirst for the blood of every man in whose heart dwells a single spark of the spirit of the fullness of the Gospel. . . . I call God, angels and all men to witness that we are innocent of the charges which are heralded forth through the public prints against us by our enemies . . . Will you all stand by me to the death, and sustain at the peril of your lives, the laws of our country, and the liberties and privileges which our fathers have transmitted unto us, sealed with their sacred blood? ("Aye!" shouted thousands.) He then said, It is well. If you had not done it, I would have gone out there (pointing to the west) and would have raised up a mightier people. . . . I call God and angels to witness that I have unsheathed my sword with a firm and unalterable determination that this people shall have their legal rights, and be protected from mob violence, or my blood shall be spilt upon the ground . . . I call upon all friends of truth and liberty to come to our assistance; and may the thunders of the Almighty and the forked lightnings of heaven and pestilence, and war and bloodshed come down on those ungodly men who seek to destroy my life and the lives of this innocent people.[8]

Messages were sent in every direction asking for Mormon volunteers. Apostles who were on missions in the east, including Brigham Young in Boston, Heber C. Kimball and Orson Pratt in Washington, Orson Hyde and the prophet's brother William in Philadelphia, and Parley P. Pratt in New York, were asked to come home at once, with arms. On June 20, Willard Richards wrote to James Arlington Bennet asking him to join the cause. He wrote:

we are already being surrounded by an armed mob; and, if we can believe a hundredth part of their statements we have no alternative but
to fight or die. All the horrors of Missouri's murders are crowding
thick upon us, and the citizens of this county declare in mass-meet-
ings, "No peace till the Mormons are utterly exterminated from the
earth." . . . Cannon, ammunition and men are passing over the Mississippi from Missouri to Illinois, and the mob is collected by hundreds at different points in the county swearing everlasting vengeance;
and when their oaths and writs will end, God knows . . . I write you
at this time at the request of the Prophet, and I invite you to come to
our assistance with as many volunteers as you can bring. And if the
mob cannot be dispersed and the government will not espouse our
righteous cause, you may soon, very soon, behold the second birth of
our nation's freedom . . . Will you come? . . . If you do not, your
turn may come next; and where will it cease?[9]

Meanwhile, Joseph was feverishly preparing for the defense of Nauvoo.
He commanded the Legion to dig trenches and to pitch tents and make
camp at the eastern section of the town. He gave orders for the manufacture of artillery, but at the same time he prophesied that no gun would be
fired by the Saints during this trouble. Nevertheless, he pleaded with
Hyrum to escape with his family on the next steamboat for Cincinnati.
Hyrum replied, "Joseph, I can't leave you."[10]

By this time, Governor Ford decided that he had better visit the scene
of the disturbance. Arriving in Carthage on the morning of June 21, he
found armed forces assembled by order of the county constables, drilling
four hours a day and standing guard at night. He said that militia had been
mustered at Warsaw under Colonel Levi Williams and that the general of
the brigade, Minor R. Deming, had called for troops en masse from
McDonough and Schuyler counties.[11] (Deming, however, wrote that it
was Ford who ordered out the troops from his brigade.)[12]

Ford later wrote in his *History of Illinois* that there was great activity to
stir up the people against the Mormons—public meetings, inflammatory
speeches, messengers riding day and night. Warsaw was especially fervid.
Anti-Mormon feelings were not unanimous, Ford said, but those who
wanted peaceful cohabitation, the "Jack Mormons," as they were called,
were threatened. Rumors were spread that the Mormons were burning,
looting, stealing horses and murdering but investigation consistently proved
the rumors false.

As Ford saw it, the intense animosity of the people toward the Mormons had many causes, which he named as the Mormons' violation of
freedom of the press, their religious views, their polygamy and their military strength. To these objections he said rumors were added that Hyrum
had offered a reward for the destruction of the *Warsaw Signal,* that the

Mormons had an alliance with the Indians, that Joseph Smith had been crowned king, that the Danites were revived and had sworn to obey him in everything except the shedding of innocent blood but only Mormon blood was considered innocent, and that the Mormons said God had consecrated all property to the Saints. The greatest popular outrage, Ford believed, was over the fact that the Mormons voted as a bloc, which prevented anyone from attaining office without their approval.[13]

On June 21, Ford wrote to Joseph Smith and the Nauvoo City Council to say that grave charges had been made against them and to ask that "one or more well informed and discreet persons" come to Carthage and give him the Mormon account of the affair.[14]

Joseph at once prepared affidavits, which he sent to Ford with John M. Bernhisel and John Taylor as his representatives. He also wrote to Ford to say that he was sure Ford recognized that it would not be safe for him or any of the City Council to come to Carthage, and to ask again that Ford come to Nauvoo to review the case.[15]

Joseph's representatives met with Ford on Saturday, June 22. Taylor reported that they were treated rudely, kept waiting an inordinately long time, and when finally admitted, they found the governor surrounded by Joseph's accusers, including the Law brothers, the Higbee brothers, Robert Foster and some fifteen others. When Joseph's delegates tried to present their case, they were frequently interrupted with, 'That's a lie! That's a God damned lie!'[16]

In his *History,* Ford said that at their meeting he came to the conclusion that the proceedings of the Nauvoo City Council, court and mayor had been illegal on many counts, though he thought there was some excuse for the court, which had been continually misinformed of its powers.[17]

Ford told the delegates that no matter how Joseph and the others felt about it, they should come to Carthage for trial to demonstrate their adherence to the law and to allay public excitement.[18]

After closing the interview, Ford kept the delegates waiting some five or six hours while he prepared a message for them to carry to Joseph and the City Council. In his message, which the delegates delivered at 10 P.M. that night, Ford said:

> I now express to you my opinion that your conduct in the destruction of the press was a very gross outrage upon the laws and the liberties of the people. It may have been full of libels, but this did not authorize you to destroy it.
>
> There are many newspapers in this state which have been wrongfully abusing me for more than a year, and yet such is my regard for the liberty of the press and the rights of a free people in a republican government that I would shed the last drop of my blood to protect those presses from any illegal violence.

Ford continued that the Mormons had violated at least four principles of the Constitution: that the presses should be free, that proprietors of a libelous press may be brought to trial but had the right to give evidence, that the people should not be subjected to search and seizure of their property without due process and that there should be no union of legislative and judicial powers in the same body. He said that if Joseph and the others refused to submit to the law:

I have great fears that your city will be destroyed, and your people many of them exterminated. . . . excitement is a matter which grows very fast upon men when assembled. The affair, I much fear, may assume a revolutionary character, and the men may disregard the authority of their officers.[19]

The Mormons protested the tone and substance of that message, especially from a former judge, a man of such avowed dedication to the law. To them it seemed more like a summation before passing sentence than a plea for the defendants to appear in a court of law where supposedly everyone is innocent until proved guilty.[20]

Ford later said that though convinced of the Mormons' guilt he was determined that they should have just legal process. Realizing that mob violence was a real danger, he addressed the militia and elicited their support. To later allegations that he should have called in neutral forces from another part of the state, Ford replied that he was afraid a famine would result if the men were taken off the farms, since recent floods had damaged mills and warehouses along the riverbanks and caused a shortage of meal.[21]

It was midnight before Joseph was ready to reply to the governor's message to surrender. Although it had been a long, trying day, Joseph sent Ford an accurate and poignant evaluation of his dilemma:

we would not hesitate to stand another trial according to your Excellency's wish, were it not that we are confident our lives would be in danger. We dare not come. Writs, we are assured, are issued against us in various parts of the country. For what? To drag us from place to place, from court to court, across the creeks and prairies, till some bloodthirsty villain could find his opportunity to shoot us. We dare not come, though your Excellency promises protection. Yet, at the same time, you have expressed fears that you could not control the mob, in which case we are left to the mercy of the merciless. Sir, we dare not come, for our lives would be in danger . . . Sir, you must not blame us, for "a burnt child dreads the fire."[22]

In a brief consultation with the delegates and his brother Hyrum, Joseph considered going to Washington to lay his case before President Tyler, but abandoned that idea. According to Abraham C. Hodge, who was with Joseph later when he was trying to decide what to do, Joseph told his friends that he saw no mercy in the governor's attitude. Hodge wrote:

All at once Joseph's countenance brightened up and he said, "The way is open. It is clear to my mind what to do. All they want is Hyrum and myself; . . . they will not harm you in person or property, and not even a hair of your head. We will cross the river tonight, and go away to the West."[23]

Joseph gave instructions for his and Hyrum's families and effects to be put on board the steamboat *Maid of Iowa* and carried down the Mississippi and up the Ohio River to safety.

About 2 A.M. on June 23, Joseph, Hyrum, Willard Richards and Porter Rockwell pushed off in a leaky skiff. The Mississippi was swollen from previous downpours and dangerous with debris and rocks washed down from the flooded banks. The night was so dense and black they could scarcely see one another. Porter Rockwell rowed while Joseph, Hyrum and Willard bailed hurriedly with their boots to keep the skiff afloat. It was daybreak before they made the opposite shore. Exhausted from strain and anxiety, they stumbled to the cabin of one of the faithful brethren. Joseph wrote Emma a note at once.

Do not despair. If god ever opens a door that is possible for me, I will see you again. I do not know when I shall go, or what I shall do, but shall if possible endeavor to get to the city of Washington . . . May god Almighty bless you and the children, and mother, all my friends My heart bleeds no more at present. If you conclude to go to Kirtland, Cincinnati or any other place, I wish you would . . . inform me . . .[24]

The tireless Porter Rockwell was sent back across the river with the message, and with instructions to get Joseph's best horses across the river to him somehow.

Rockwell found Nauvoo in chaos, divided as to whether they should scatter and flee or stand to defend the city. Leaderless, with Joseph gone and the apostles still in the east, the people quarreled and floundered.

Some of Joseph's friends accused him of cowardice, suggesting that he was saving his skin at their expense.[25] Excitement increased among the anti-Mormons when a story was spread that the governor favored allowing Joseph to escape. Although he did not admit it until afterward, Ford said that even then he thought that would have been the best solution.[26]

Vilate Kimball wrote to her husband, Heber, on June 24, that between three and four thousand of the brethren had been under arms for the whole week, expecting every day that the mob would fall upon the citizens of Nauvoo. Some of the Saints, she wrote, were "dreadfully tried in their faith to think that Joseph should leave them in the hour of danger. Hundreds have left the city, most of the merchants on the hill have left." The Whitneys were packing. She added that word had just reached Joseph's family to follow him, and that this made her heart sink.[27]

Instead of getting ready for flight, Emma gave Porter Rockwell a letter for Joseph pleading with him to come back and surrender to the governor. Reynolds Cahoon went back with Rockwell, carrying word to Joseph that the governor guaranteed him a fair trial and his personal protection. Joseph was led to believe that unless he returned, Nauvoo would be sacked, and was reminded of the fable about the shepherd who ran away when the wolves attacked and left his sheep to be devoured.[28]

According to one report, Joseph was told even more directly, "You always said if the Church would stick to you, you would stick to the Church, now trouble comes you are the first to run."[29]

"If my life is of no value to my friends, it is of none to myself," Joseph said. He turned to Rockwell. "What shall I do?"

Rockwell was not ready to renounce his faith in Joseph. "You are the oldest and ought to know best," said Rockwell. "As you make your bed, I will lie with you."

For perhaps the only time in his life, Joseph deferred to Hyrum. "Brother Hyrum, you are the oldest, what shall we do?"

Hyrum, always a man of strong and simple convictions, saw only one course. "Let us go back and give ourselves up."

"We shall be butchered," Joseph protested.

"The Lord is in it," Hyrum said. "If we live or die, we shall be reconciled to our fate."[30]

While waiting for a boat to take them back across the river, Joseph wrote the governor that he would come to Carthage the next day. He also began making preparations for his defense, sending messages to witnesses and lawyers.

The men returned to Nauvoo together. When Joseph expressed a wish to speak to the Saints once more, Rockwell suggested that he do so by starlight, but it was decided that there was not enough time. Joseph went home to Emma and his children, fully aware that it would probably be his last night with them in his own house.

At 6:30 A.M. on Monday, June 24, Joseph, Hyrum, John Taylor, Porter Rockwell, William W. Phelps and thirteen other members of the Nauvoo City Council charged with riot in destroying the *Expositor* set out on horseback for Carthage, accompanied by Willard Richards and a number of friends. The weather had cleared and it was a balmy, sunny day. A number of people wrote that Joseph told them as he passed that he was going like a lamb to the slaughter. According to Eliza R. Snow, he added, "but I am as calm as a summer's morning; I have a conscience void of offence towards God, and towards all men; I shall die innocent, and it shall yet be said of me—*he was murdered in cold blood.*"[31]

Another version of his parting words was carried in the Smith family. Joseph's niece Mary, daughter of the prophet's brother Samuel, wrote to her cousin Ina, daughter of Don Carlos, that when Joseph was leaving for Carthage, he told his mother that he would never return alive, and added, "I go as a lamb to the slaughter, but if my death will atone for any faults I have committed during my life time I am willing to die."[32]

Joseph's companions said that when they reached the hilltop, his eyes lingered on the temple and he paused to look out over the city, at the neat rows of houses and gardens and the spreading orchards in bloom. He said, "This is the loveliest place and the best people under the heavens. Little do they know the trials that await them." After they passed his farm, Joseph turned so many times to look at it, that his friends questioned him. He said, "If some of you had got such a farm and knew you would not see it any more, you would want to take a good look at it for the last time."[33]

About 10 A.M., four miles west of Carthage, they met Captain Dunn with a company of some sixty mounted militia of the Union Dragoons. Dunn gave Joseph an order from Governor Ford for all state arms held by the Navuoo Legion. Without hesitation, Joseph countersigned the order. At the same time he wrote to Major General Jonathan Dunham and all officers of the Legion "to comply strictly and without delay" to Governor Ford's order to disband.[34] At Dunn's request, Joseph agreed to go back with him to Nauvoo to forestall any resistance. Joseph sent a note to the governor explaining his delay in reaching Carthage.

The Mormons surrendered three small cannons and about two hundred firearms, which were all that had been issued to them, although rumor among the frightened Gentiles had enlarged these figures to thirty cannons and six thousand small arms.

The Nauvoo Legion thought the recall of the arms unjust, since they had mustered only in self-defense, and there was no corresponding order to disarm any of the other militia. The orders revived agonizing memories of the Mormon disarmament before the Missouri massacre. No doubt with this in mind, Joseph ordered that all personal arms be secretly stored in a warehouse, to be ready the moment they might be needed.

About 6 P.M., Joseph and his party started back for Carthage, although this time Porter Rockwell remained behind.

Passing through the woods near Nauvoo, they met Abraham Hodge coming back from Carthage, where he had been sent by Hyrum for news. Hodge said, "If it was my duty to council you, I would say do not go another foot, for they say they will kill you if you go to Carthage."[35] Nevertheless, Joseph and Hyrum had made their decision, and the group pressed on.

About four miles from Carthage where they stopped to rest and eat their provisions, they were overtaken by Captain Dunn and his militia, bearing the arms collected in Nauvoo. The captain expressed relief and gratitude that the Mormons had complied so peacefully with the governor's command. He told Joseph and his friends that he would protect them if it cost his life.

CHAPTER

15

MARTYRDOM

At five minutes before midnight on June 24, 1844, Captain Dunn and
his company of sixty mounted militia from the Union Dragoons rode into
Carthage with Joseph Smith, his brother Hyrum and fifteen other Mormon
leaders, including members of the Nauvoo City Council, as voluntary cap-
tives.

Having ridden hard and long, the horsemen were tired, but none more
than Joseph and Hyrum, who had been under stress for the previous seventeen days, and were exhausted from flight, hiding out and the fear of assassination. Nevertheless, the brothers were impressive. Handsome men in
their prime—Joseph the prophet, thirty-eight; Hyrum, forty-four; both
towering over the average man of their day—they rode in proudly, having
delivered themselves up by their own decision, convinced that they had
done no wrong.

Late though it was, the company of troops and prisoners rode into a
riot. Mobs of irate townsmen and farmers from miles around who had
been clamoring for days for the arrest of the Mormons were not to miss
this chance now of seeing them brought in by armed men. Among the mob
were more than fourteen hundred unruly militia, including a regiment
from McDonough, a battalion from Schuyler County and most vociferous
of all, the local Carthage Greys, a small independent company of about
thirty men, who had the apparently undeserved reputation of being very
well disciplined.[1]

Ugly crowds had been ranging the town all day, drinking and brawling, and now they pushed in around the mounted men, shouting threats. The public square was in ferment when Dunn and his party struggled through on their way to Hamilton's hotel and tavern, where it had been decided the prisoners would be lodged, and where the governor himself was staying. Shouts from the Carthage Greys rose above the din. Witnesses to the scene recorded that the mob was shouting: "God damn you, old Joe, we've got you now. He has seen the last of Nauvoo. Stand away, you McDonough boys, and let us shoot the damned Mormons. Kill all the damn Mormons."

The Greys, whooping and cursing, displayed a dangerous trick of tossing their rifles in an arc overhead and allowing them to fall to the ground with their bayonets imbedded in the turf.

Jockeying horses and Dragoons, Captain Dunn got the prisoners safely inside the tavern. The Greys swarmed under the windows demanding the prophet, and making such a clamor that the governor himself at last put his head out and signaled for quiet. Ford was very uneasy in this present trouble. He raised his thin voice above the shouts.

"I know your great anxiety to see Mr. Smith, which is natural enough," he told them, "but it is quite too late tonight. . . . I assure you, gentlemen, you shall have that privilege tomorrow morning as I will cause him to pass before the troops upon the square, and now I wish you to return to your quarters."

Without much enthusiasm, somebody cried, "Hurrah for Tom Ford." The crowd seemed satisfied for the moment and they began to disperse.

The next morning, June 25, the town was up and bustling early. By eight o'clock the Mormons had surrendered to the constable upon reiterated word of Governor Ford that they would be protected from violence and given trial without prejudice. At eight-thirty the governor ordered the troops to the public ground near the courthouse, where he climbed up on an old table and addressed them for half an hour.

He said that the prisoners were dangerous men, and guilty of all that might be charged against them, but they were now in the hands of the law, and the law must take its course. If this was meant to placate the mobs, the result was entirely otherwise. Although the people were now raging, the governor went to the hotel to get Joseph and Hyrum so that they could pass before the troops, as promised.[2]

The governor walked a few paces ahead as they went out on the street. Brigadier General Minor R. Deming took Joseph on his right and Hyrum on his left, while Willard Richards, William W. Phelps and John Taylor followed.

According to Samuel O. Williams, an officer in the Carthage Greys, the Mormons were first taken to General Deming's headquarters, where the Greys were stationed on guard. Although the Greys formed a three-sided square with muskets at charge, they had difficulty in keeping back the mobs, which were now in a frenzy of shouting and pushing. General Deming ordered the Greys to form a hollow square around his party and march them under protection three hundred yards to where the 57th Regiment was waiting.

There, with the governor in the lead, the Mormons and the general passed before the troops of the 57th Regiment, and, according to Mormon account, Joseph and Hyrum were introduced as generals by the governor about twenty times along the line. Williams wrote that it was General Deming, the "Jack Mormon," who introduced the brethren, saying, "Gentlemen officers of the 57th Regiment, I introduce you to Joseph and Hyrum Smith, Generals of the Nauvoo Legion." The troops were incensed at the use of those military titles for the two men. According to Williams, the officers of the Greys threw up their hats, drew swords and cried they would introduce themselves in a different style.[3]

Very likely the anger of the militia was out of proportion to its provocation because they had a long-standing grudge against the prophet. The military in Illinois, both United States army and the state militia, had resented Joseph and his Nauvoo Legion ever since its organization three years before. The charter for the city of Nauvoo had established the Legion as an independent militia, with power to make its own laws and responsibility to the governor but to no other military authority. Officers were outraged that this Joseph Smith, who was exempt from regular military duty because of his lame leg and his license to preach, should have been commissioned lieutenant general by the governor. Although officers of the Nauvoo Legion could not have ranked those of the regular army in a call to active service, this did not ease bitterness when Joseph made use of his title in correspondence and was often heard to jest that he outranked every officer in the land.

Samuel O. Williams went on that when the Smiths and General Deming passed on their way back, the Greys, though standing at order arms, "commenced hissing, groaning and making all sorts of hellish sounds," in outrage because they thought they had been ordered to escort the Smiths as an honor guard. Williams said, "I all the time tried my utmost to preserve silence but had no more command over them than I would have had over a pack of wild Indians. At this demonstration of feeling on the part of the Greys Jo actually fainted."[4]

Reports of what followed disagree. Williams said General Minor Deming, in command of the Hancock County militia, ordered the Greys put under arrest for their demonstration, whereupon one jumped on a wagon and made a speech to the troops, who loaded their muskets and swore they would not surrender arms. Without naming him, the *Warsaw Signal* said that it was the officer in command who addressed the Greys (this would have been Captain Robert F. Smith), demanding if they would submit to arrest.

"No!" they cried.

"Then load with ball cartridges!"

The Greys defied the general and were so "Wrought up . . . that the least notion to execute the order would in all probability have closed the career of the two prisoners."[5]

Governor Ford hurried to the scene and addressed the troops. He assured them that he had intended no honor to the prisoners but merely wanted to exhibit them and that it was not he who had directed the form of their introduction.

General Deming maintained that he had not given a command to disarm or arrest the Greys, but had merely ordered their officers to report to his quarters.

Whatever the provocation, the soldiers, especially the home town Carthage Greys, were furious at the idea that these upstart "generals" should be given military recognition. Williams wrote that after the governor had denied any honor to the prisoners was intended, "the shout of the multitude ascended to the heavens. We cheered the Governor for about 2 minutes and we made some noise."[6]

Rumor spread through the town that Joseph had fainted before the troops three times. The Mormons denied this, and it does hardly seem credible that a man who in his short career had already been mobbed, beaten, tarred and feathered, imprisoned and chained would be overcome by hissing noises, however "hellish." It is not unlikely, however, that he was shocked at the realization of how intense the hatred was against him. It is even conceivable, despite his repeated statement that he was going like a lamb to the slaughter, that this was his first strong premonition of death. As he later remarked, "I have had a good deal of anxiety about my safety since I left Nauvoo, which I never had before when I was under arrest. I could not help those feelings, and they have depressed me."[7]

Nevertheless, when the brethren returned to their hotel, Joseph wrote Emma a reassuring letter, saying that the governor was treating them kindly, and that "When the truth comes out we have nothing to fear. We all feel calm and composed . . . Governor Ford has just concluded to send some of his militia to Nauvoo to protect the citizens, and I wish that they may be kindly treated. They will cooperate with the police to keep the peace."[8]

The brethren were hopeful, or at least wanted to appear so to their families and friends.

John Taylor wrote to his wife that day, "I am well, we are all well except for a slight indisposition of Hyrum Smith, occassioned by over fatigue in travelling. Relative to our affairs here we can say little; There is however a strong disposition on the part of the Governor to sustain law & put down mobocracy . . . we shall have a fair hearing . . . we know that we are innocent of any crime & 'truth will prevail.'

"There are plenty of persons passing to & from Nauvoo & will be daily so that you will hear the news regularly."[9]

Joseph's message to Porter Rockwell, who had been named on the same writ that charged Joseph and the others, had rather a different tone. He told Porter to stay in Nauvoo and not let himself be taken prisoner by anyone.

About four o'clock, Joseph, Hyrum and the others had a preliminary hearing before Robert F. Smith, a justice of the peace who was also captain of the Carthage Greys and active in the anti-Mormon party. At that hearing they were charged with riot in destroying the *Nauvoo Expositor* and were released on bond of five hundred dollars each to appear at the next term of the circuit court. Most of the accused then left for Nauvoo, but Joseph and Hyrum went for a short interview with the governor and then returned to Hamilton's hotel.

At eight o'clock that night a constable appeared with a mittimus signed by Robert F. Smith to hold Joseph and Hyrum in jail until they could be tried for treason. Joseph and his lawyers, H. T. Reid and James W. Woods, protested that the mittimus was illegal, since no mention of that charge had been made at their hearing. Woods declared that there was no law in Illinois that would allow a justice to commit persons to jail on a criminal charge without a preliminary investigation of their possible guilt. He went to complain to Ford, who was in the adjoining room at the hotel, but Ford told him that he could not interrupt a civil officer in the discharge of his duty.

Robert Smith, as captain of the Greys, then sent his soldiers to carry out the mittimus he had issued as justice of the peace, and Joseph and Hyrum were hustled off to jail through a great rabble clamoring at the hotel door and in the streets. Another account has it that it was Captain Dunn and his men who accompanied Joseph and Hyrum to jail. Eight of their friends went with them, including Willard Richards and John Taylor. On either side of Joseph and Hyrum keeping off the drunken crowd were Dan Jones with a walking stick and Stephen Markham, with his great hickory cane he called "the rascal beater."

As it happened, the jail was probably the safest place in town. It was a small, solid building of stone, surrounded by a low fence. The front door opened upon a little entrance with a room on the right for the jailer and his wife and a narrow stairway leading to the second floor. Directly at the top of the stairs was a cell furnished only with mattresses. On the right was a somewhat larger room where debtors were held. Bright, airy and more comfortable, the debtors' room had two windows on the south and one on the east, a large fireplace on the north wall, and was furnished with a double bed and some chairs. The room was in no way secure, however. There were no bars on the windows and the door had neither a lock nor a workable latch.

The brothers were received courteously by the jailer, George W. Stigall, and his wife, and were given the debtors' room. Their friends were allowed to stay with them that night, and the ten men slept as they could, most of them on the floor.

The next morning at Joseph's request, Governor Ford came to see him in jail. According to reports of those present, their conversation was long, lively and mostly amiable, although they disagreed over Joseph's destruction of the *Nauvoo Expositor*. Ford said that act was looked upon by the people as subversion of freedom of the press. According to John Taylor, who wrote about the incident some ten years later, Joseph replied that the newspaper was "a flagrant violation of every principle of right, a nuisance, and it was abated on the same principle that any nuisance, stench or putrefied carcass would have been removed. Our first step, therefore, was to stop the foul, noisome, filthy sheet, and then the next, in our opinion, would have been to have prosecuted the men for a breech of public decency."

Joseph said he had heard that the Governor was going to Nauvoo and that without the governor he and Hyrum would not be safe in Carthage. Ford told Joseph that if he did go to Nauvoo he would take the brothers along.[10]

After the governor left, Joseph spent the afternoon dictating to Willard Richards, while Dan Jones and Stephen Markham whittled at the warped door with a penknife to make the latch workable and prepare the room against possible attack.

That night, five of their friends, including Willard Richards, John Taylor and Dan Jones, remained with the brothers in jail. They prayed together, read *The Book of Mormon,* and Joseph bore his testimony to the guards. It was late before they lay down to sleep, Joseph and Hyrum on the only bed, the others on the floor. Willard Richards sat up writing until the last candle went out.

Later a gunshot near the jail roused Joseph and he left the bed to lie on the floor with the other brethren. Joseph whispered to Dan, "Are you afraid to die?" "Has it come to that?" Dan asked, but added that in such a cause as theirs he did not think death would have many terrors. Joseph reassured him that he would see Wales and fulfill his appointed mission before he died.

Joseph believed that in surrendering he had shown obedience to the law and his faith in its sanctity. His enemies were to demonstrate that they did not share his principles.

The next morning, June 27, when Dan Jones went down at Joseph's request to find out what had caused the disturbance in the night, the officer on duty, Frank A. Worrell of the Carthage Greys, said to him, "We had too much trouble to bring old Joe here to let him ever escape alive, and unless you want to die with him you had better leave before sundown . . . you'll see that I can prophesy better than Old Joe."

Hastening to report this to the governor, Dan Jones overheard more. In the town square a soldier from Warsaw was proclaiming to a crowd of eager listeners, "Our troops will be discharged this morning . . . but when the Governor and the McDonough troops have left for Nauvoo . . . we will return and kill those men, if we have to tear the jail down." The crowd raised shouts and cheers.

To Dan Jones's report, Ford replied, "You are unnecessarily alarmed. The people are not that cruel."

Jones urged the replacement of the Greys with another guard. "If you don't," he said, "I have only one prayer—that I will live to testify that you have been warned."[11]

John P. Greene, marshal of Nauvoo, also told the governor that if he went to Nauvoo leaving the Greys alone to guard the jail, Joseph and Hyrum would be murdered, but Ford told him that he was too enthusiastic.

The governor was clearly in a grave dilemma and frightened by the threat of a full-scale war.[12] Apparently he did not know which side to fear more, the Mormons or their enemies, and it seems likely that he spoke the truth when he said that his first goal was to prevent a wholesale uprising. Mormons and some historians have maintained that although the governor said compliance with the law was uppermost in his mind, he failed to preserve the rights of the accused and to assure them the protection to which they were entitled. It has been said that he should have brought militia from downstate to sustain a neutral atmosphere. Although he was warned a number of times, even by one of his own aides, that a conspiracy existed to murder the Smiths, he failed to act.[13] When Cyrus Wheelock told him that even if the prisoners were safe in the hands of the law, they were not protected against midnight assassins, Ford answered, "I was never in such a dilemma in my life, but your friends shall be protected . . . I have the pledge of the whole army to sustain me.[14]

That morning Joseph dictated to Willard Richards another letter to Emma. He told her he wanted Jonathan Dunham to instruct the Saints to stay at home unless called out to hear the governor. Joseph said there was no danger of an "exterminating order," and in case of mutiny, he was sure that at least some of the troops would defend the right. He added, however, that in the extreme it was the duty of all men to protect themselves and their families. In a postscript in his own hand he wrote, "Dear Emma, I am very much resigned to my lot, knowing I am justified, and have done the best that could be done. Give my love to the children and all my friends . . . and as for treason, I know that I have not committed any, and they cannot prove anything of the kind . . ." At twenty minutes to ten, Joseph dictated to Willard a second postscript to his letter: "I just saw

that the Governor is about to disband his troops.—all but a guard to protect us and the peace,—and come himself to Nauvoo and deliver a speech
to the people. This is right, as I suppose."[15] Despite his reassuring words
to Emma, Joseph wrote a hurried note to Jonathan Dunham asking for
troops to come to his rescue. Horsemen were sent off at once with the
message, but for some unknown reason, Dunham never received, or in any
case never acted upon, the prophet's request.[16]

He also sent a letter to the well-known lawyer Orville H. Browning, who
had defended Joseph so eloquently when he had appeared before Stephen
A. Douglas seeking a writ of habeas corpus after his arrest for extradition
to Missouri in June of 1841. To Browning he wrote: "Myself and brother
Hyrum are in jail on charge of Treason,. To come up for Examination on
Saturday Morning. 29th inst and we request your professional Services. at
that time, on our expense without fail . . . There is no cause for action for
we have not been guilty of any crime; neither is there any just cause of
suspiecion against us. but certain circumstances make your attendance
very necessary"[17]

Soon afterward, the rest of Joseph's friends, except Willard Richards
and John Taylor, were forced to leave the jail.

Ford had, in fact, left for Nauvoo early that morning, taking as his escort Captain Dunn's Dragoons, the only troops that had shown neutrality
in the affair.

According to Ford the Hancock militia had wanted to march into
Nauvoo to search for counterfeit money and to display enough force to
discourage further Mormon "outrages." The governor later wrote that he
was inclined at first to permit this, and plans were made for the militia to
assemble at Golden's Point about halfway between Nauvoo and Warsaw.
When Ford heard threats of destruction and murder and saw that the excitement of the Hancock troops was increasing as they prepared to march
he became convinced that once inside the town the militia meant to find
some excuse to start a battle.

Ford wrote that although the outnumbered anti-Mormon militia could
not have won such a fight, the death of many innocent women and children
would have been inevitable. On the morning of June 27 he ordered the militia at Carthage and Warsaw to disband, except for troops to remain on
guard at Carthage and one company to go with him to Nauvoo.

He said he changed his mind about taking the Smith brothers along because he was advised that it would be too dangerous.[18] However, the
troops he left behind to guard the jail were the Carthage Greys, the prophet's most vociferous enemies, under command of Robert F. Smith.

According to Samuel O. Williams, the governor had been gone about
two hours when he sent word to Robert F. Smith that he feared violence
against the prisoners but expected the captain to do his duty. Captain
Smith sent back his assurance that he would.[19]

At Nauvoo, the governor made what the Mormons considered "one of the most infamous and insulting speeches that ever fell from the lips of an executive." He told them:

A great crime has been done by destroying the Expositor press and placing the city under martial law, and a severe atonement must be made . . . Depend upon it, a little more misbehavior from the citizens, and the torch, which is already lighted, will be applied, and the city may be reduced to ashes, and extermination would inevitably follow; and it gives me great pain to think that there is danger of so many innocent women and children being exterminated. If anything of a serious character should befall the lives or property of the persons who are prosecuting your leaders, you will be held responsible.[20]

Ford remained in Nauvoo until about six-thirty that evening. On the way out of town he marched through Main Street with his escort of militia, who made a display of sword exercises, passes, cuts and thrusts, for the purpose, as the Mormons believed, of intimidating the people.

Some of the troops from Warsaw had started out that morning toward Golden's Point, expecting to meet troops from Carthage for the march to Nauvoo. They had gone about eight miles in a light rain when they received the governor's orders to disband. Instead of commanding the officers to march their men home, Ford turned the men loose in the field.

William M. Daniels, a young member of Colonel Levi Williams' regiment who joined the Mormon Church after the martyrdom, later testified that after Colonel Williams read Ford's dispatch ordering the troops to disband, Thomas Sharp addressed the men and called for them to march east to Carthage. Shouts followed for volunteers to kill the Smiths.[21]

Some of the troops refused to participate. Thoroughly tired of the riotous affair, they set off for home to tend to their shops and farms. Others who still had a thirst for excitement daubed their faces with mud mixed with gunpowder and started out for Carthage.

One company of the Carthage Greys had been disbanded and the other was camped in the public square, almost half a mile from the jail, with six or eight soldiers posted at the jail to guard the prisoners. According to evidence uncovered later, it seems that the conspirators arranged with the guards to load their guns with blanks.[22]

Earlier that morning, the rain had given Cyrus Wheelock an excuse to wear an overcoat and in his pocket he was able to smuggle a loaded six-shooter into the jail for Joseph. Joseph handed Hyrum the single-barreled pistol which one of the other brethren had already given him. Hyrum took it under protest.

"I hate to use such things or see them used," Hyrum said.

"So do I," Joseph replied. "But we may have to defend ourselves."[23]

Joseph and Hyrum overwhelmed Wheelock with messages for Nauvoo, their friends and families. Joseph asked Wheelock to urge the Nauvoo Legion not to make any military display and to keep the city calm.

Later the day grew hot. The men sat in their shirt sleeves, gravely depressed. With Wheelock gone, there were now just four, Joseph and Hyrum and the two friends who refused to leave them no matter what the danger to themselves, John Taylor and the stout Willard Richards.

John Taylor, a tall man with a sweet, youthful face, was a composer of songs and had a voice of singular charm. His friends now asked him to sing a popular song that had lately been introduced in Nauvoo, "A Poor Wayfaring Man of Grief," about a suffering stranger who revealed himself at last as Jesus. Joseph asked Taylor to sing it again, which he did.

At 4 P.M., the guard was changed at the jail. In charge of the men who now came on duty was Franklin A. Worrell, who had that morning made a threat against the prophet's life to Dan Jones. Captain Robert Smith and the rest of the Greys remained encamped in the Carthage public square.

According to John Taylor, the brethren sent for some wine to revive their spirits and shared it with their guards. At 5 P.M., jailer Stigall came to suggest that the men would be safer in the cell. Joseph agreed that he and Hyrum would go in after supper, and his friends said they would go with them.

William Hamilton, young son of the hotelkeeper, had been sent with a companion that afternoon to the cupola of the courthouse to keep watch for the Greys with a large field glass. About four o'clock the boys discovered men assembling on the prairie about two miles from town. When one of the boys clambered down excitedly to report this to Captain Smith, he ordered the boys to remain on watch and to tell him and nobody else if the men came through the woods toward the jail. Forty-five minutes later, William saw men approaching the jail at a quick step, in single file, going along north of the old rail fence, out of sight of anyone on the ground, and trailing their guns, as though to keep them hidden. William says he ran to look for the captain but could not find him until the men had reached the jail.[24]

Eudocia Baldwin Marsh, a resident of Carthage, had two brothers in the Carthage Greys, in the company that had pitched their tents on the square. She had just returned home from town when her brother-in-law, an officer in the Greys, rushed in and said that men were coming to the jail to take Joe Smith and hang him in the square. His face was very white as he buckled on his sword and rushed back to his company. Eudocia ran to the door and saw men with frightened faces dashing about and gathering in troops. She heard another report that Mormons were coming to rescue the Smiths. Fearing for her older brother, who had just been sent to the jail on guard duty, she ran to the square.

Captain Smith, an impressive man of over six feet, seemed to be trying to get the men in line but some had been napping on their bunks and were still half asleep. Eudocia's younger brother Tom, however, was wide awake and very upset. Eudocia saw an officer take him by the arm several times and shove him roughly back into the ranks. At last he broke free and shouted, "Come on, you cowards, damn you, come on! those boys will all be killed!" Carrying his gun, he ran with all his might past his sister toward the jail.[25]

William Hamilton said that there were many delays before the Greys were assembled. At last they formed and marched to the jail with guns on their shoulders and their flag flying, as though on dress parade.

Samuel O. Williams, who was in camp with the Greys, told a different story. He said that their lookout thought the men creeping through the pasture were Mormons and shouted that about four hundred of them were coming along the fence toward the jail. According to Williams, the Greys formed at once and went to the jail in double quick time.[26]

A youth named Darnell, a member of the militia just disbanded, said in an account written years later that he had come to get his horse and was within a few steps of the pasture gate, which was east of the jail, when he saw a file of men in hunting shirts creeping up from the direction of the creek at the northwest corner of the pasture, stooping as they approached. Their faces were painted a brownish color. Darnell said that he knew something terrible was going to happen and felt transfixed to the spot. He was sure, from the behavior of the guard at the jail, that the men were expected.

William Hamilton said that the guards seemed to know very well what was happening. Although they fired at the attackers from twenty feet no one was injured.

The men with blackened faces jumped the low fence and surrounded the jail. One young guard who was not aware of the conspiracy made an objection, but he was told by the assailants not to resist.[27]

It was shortly after five o'clock when the prisoners heard a scuffle downstairs at the door followed by a shout for surrender and three or four shots. Willard Richards dashed to the window and saw the armed men surrounding the jail.

In a moment men were heard on the stairs. Joseph sprang for his six-shooter and Hyrum for his single-barreled pistol. Taylor grabbed Markham's great "rascal beater" which he had left for the prisoners. Richards snatched a hickory cane and the two men threw themselves against the door. Balls whistled up the stairway. The raiders tried to shove in. Richards, a great heavy man who weighed over three hundred pounds, braced himself against the door and he and Taylor tried to deflect the barrels of the muskets with their canes. Balls were fired into the room, lodging in the walls and ceiling. Swearing and shouting, more men crowded up the stairway and pushed against the door. When Hyrum stood back to aim his pistol, a shot through the panel of the door struck the left side of his nose and he fell moaning, "I am a dead man."

Joseph leaned over his brother and cried, "Oh, dear brother Hyrum!"[28] Seeing that he was dead, Joseph jumped up, threw open the door and emptied his six-shooter into the passageway. The gun missed fire once or twice, but reports had it that Joseph wounded three or four men and that he slipped his fist through the door and punched a young man from Warsaw in the neck.

An account written for the *Atlantic Monthly* some years later commented upon Joseph's courage, saying that he stood by the jamb of the door and fired four shots, bringing his man down every time. According to that report, he shot an Irishman named Wills in the arm; a Southerner from the Mississippi bottom named Gallagher (spelled Gallaher on the indictment) in the face, a gawky youth from Bear Creek named Voorhees (spelled Voras on the indictment) in the shoulder, and another man whom the reporter did not care to name because he was six feet two in moccasins (identified as Allen on the indictment). It was, said that account, "a handsome fight."[29]

The shots made the conspirators pause only a moment. John Taylor knocked aside the gun barrels as long as he could, but he had to give way at last and ran to jump out the window. A shot from the doorway pierced his left thigh to the bone. As he stumbled on the sill, a shot through the window from below knocked him back into the room, hitting the watch in his vest pocket and stopping it at five-sixteen. He fell to the floor and was hit on his left wrist and again below his left knee. Rolling under the bed, he was shot again from the stairway. One ball struck him on the left hip, tearing a ghastly wound and scattering his blood on the floor and wall.

Joseph threw down his empty gun. His friends said that he thought the others would be spared if he drew off the fire by leaping through the window. He sprang to the sill. He was shot from the door and through the window from outside. He swayed a moment on the window ledge with one arm and leg dangling. With a cry of "O Lord, my God!" he fell to the ground. Accounts do not agree about the precise moment of his death. One witness, Thomas Dixon, who was close enough to see blood on Joseph's trousers as he was hanging in the window, said he raised himself against the well curb and died instantly. Various accounts had it that Joseph's body was stabbed with a bayonet or otherwise molested but this was refuted by two close witnesses.[30]

Willard Richards maintained that the shots through the window must have come from the Greys at a distance of ten or twelve rods, because shots by the mob just below hit the ceiling.

Richards was merely grazed on the left ear. According to one account, Richards said that when the brethren braced themselves against the door he had been next to the hinges, and as the door was thrown open he was pushed back against the wall behind it, out of the line of fire. His escape was regarded as the fulfillment of Joseph's prophecy of a year before that Richards would one day be in a hail of bullets and see his friends fall to left and right, but there should not be one hole in his clothing.

When the prophet fell, someone cried, "He's leaped the window!" The men on the stairs ran out.

Willard Richards caught Taylor up and took him to the cell, where he stretched him on the floor and covered him with a mattress. "I'm sorry I can't do better for you," he said, "but maybe this will hide you. I want you to live to tell the story." Willard afterward wrote that he expected the mob to come back any moment and kill him.

The mob did rush up the stairs again but found only Hyrum's body. They were clattering down to search for the others when someone shouted, "The Mormons are coming!" At this the mob fled to the woods.

The whole affair took less than three minutes.[31]

By the time the rest of the Carthage Greys had marched to the jail, the mob was already in flight. The Greys made no pursuit. They posted a detail but the others put away their guns and got out of town.

When they heard the news, the citizens of Carthage fled in terror. Samuel O. Williams wrote that by daylight only six men remained in town and he was not one of them.

William Hamilton said only four families remained, including his father's family and one widow with a sick child. William and his friend were sent around to close the windows, doors and gates on the property of those who had fled.

The prophet was left alone for some time, until Richards ventured out to pick up his body and carry it back to the jail, to lay it beside that of his brother. Finally Artois Hamilton came with a wagon and team and took the bodies to his hotel, where they were kept until coffins could be made.

It was close to midnight before Willard Richards could get any food or medical attention for the suffering John Taylor.

The doctor, Thomas L. Barnes, who was eventually found to care for Taylor wrote that he was a pitiable sight. He had bled a great deal and his clothing and the straw from the mattress were stuck to his wounds by coagulated blood. Barnes wrote that he took the best care of Taylor that he could, but Taylor said the man was a surgical butcher, and cut the bullet out of his hand with a dull penknife and a carpenter's compass. The doctor later told a friend of Taylor's that he had "nerves like the devil" to stand such an operation.[32]

Taylor afterward wrote that his wounds were agonizing but the desolation of his spirit was even worse. The Saints had lost Joseph Smith. "In the midst of our difficulties he was always the first in motion . . . our guide for things spiritual and temporal . . . as our prophet he approached our God had obtained for us his will . . . now our prophet, our counselor, our general was gone. For all things pertaining to this world or the next, he had spoken for the last time on earth."[33]

16

THE SUCCESSOR CHOSEN, THE ACCUSED ASSASSINS TRIED

Ford was badly frightened by the news. After warning the people at Carthage that the Mormons would burn the town to the ground before morning, he left in the dead of night and rode south for nine miles before he stopped at an inn to rest and water his horses. There he was seen by Eudocia Baldwin Marsh and her family, who had also fled from Carthage. Ford ordered them to go on at once to Augusta, and was "storming scolding and impatient to be off."[1]

Governor Ford maintained that the Smiths were assassinated while he was at Nauvoo in the hope that the Mormons would kill him in retaliation and give the mobs an excuse to sack the Mormon town.[2]

Ford has been accused of weakness and cowardice by the Mormons and even by some historians who were not especially pro-Mormon. In justice to him, however, it should be acknowledged that he was in what was probably an impossible dilemma and that at times he showed considerable personal courage. An educated man who had more integrity than was common in that lawless frontier, his words and actions indicated that he followed the course that seemed to him most likely to secure the peace and allow the proper functioning of the law. Although he had no great personal ambition, he had been thrust into the highest office of his state when it was on the edge of disaster. With little support in the legislature from members of his own party, who had hoped, as he said, to make him a mere figurehead, he had struggled to save the state from financial ruin and to cope with a series of calamities, including floods, famine, social upheaval and the threat of civil war. Although perhaps misguided, it must have been an act of no small courage to dismiss most of the militia and go in person to Nauvoo with one company, and give the Mormons a speech of reprobation, when he knew their fear and anger and the reputation of their military. After the Smiths were assassinated and he heard rumors that the Mormons would ride out and destroy Carthage, Ford's return to that town to warn the people before fleeing for his own safety was a brave act since after the failure of his personal guarantee of safety for the Smiths, he believed that he would be a special target of Mormon revenge.

Ford wanted justice for the Mormons but he did not like them. He did not know the Mormon people well and was guilty of making unwarranted accusations, such as his statement that after the death of their prophet the Mormon leaders devoted their sermons to profanity, hate mongering and preaching revenge against their enemies, which any reading of the transcripts of their sermons and speeches will at once make evident as grossly untrue.

For days following the murders, excited talk continued about who might have committed them. Some speculated that Missourians had done it, others that the brothers were killed in an exchange of gunfire when Mormons raided the jail in a rescue attempt. It was soon learned, however, that the brothers had been killed by men of the Warsaw militia, under the instigation of Thomas Sharp.

For a while the citizens of Hancock County were subdued in shock and fear, and the Mormons were devastated by grief. However, if the assassins thought they would cause the disintegration of the Mormon Church by killing the leaders, they soon discovered their mistake. The Mormons now had a martyr to their cause. Instead of weakening, they grew stronger. Their faith was confirmed, their zeal increased and so did their numbers. Converts continued to pour into Nauvoo, which by now had a population of about 15,000, and there were members in nearby villages and settlements. The neighbors' fear and envy of the Mormons was only dormant, the lull in hostilities temporary.

In July 1844, a delegation went to Governor Ford to petition that he expel the Mormons. Of this, Ford wrote, "It seemed that it had never occurred to these gentlemen that I had no power to exile a citizen."[3]

Meanwhile, although the faith and ardor of the Mormons had not diminished, they were in disharmony over who was to assume the leadership of the church.

At the time of the assassination, the Twelve Apostles (except Willard Richards and John Taylor) and many other leaders of the church were off on preaching and campaigning tours around the country. They read the profoundly shocking news in letters from home or in local newspapers.

On June 30, Willard Richards wrote to Brigham Young, who was in Boston with Wilford Woodruff:

The effect of this Hellish butchery was like the bursting of a tornado on Carthage and Warsaw, their villages were without inhabitants.—as in an instant they ran for their lives lest the Mormons start to burn & kill them . . . The excitement has been great, but the indignation more terrible.—a reaction is taking place and men of influence are coming from abroad to learn the facts and going away satisfied. the *Mormons are not the aggressors* . . . The Saints have borne this trial with great fortitude and forbearance . . .

Willard suggested that if the Twelve approved, Brigham, Wilford, Heber C. Kimball, Orson Pratt and George Albert Smith should return to Nauvoo at once, but that William Smith, whose life was considered in danger, and the others remain in the east and continue to preach. At this time, the Saints did not seem to cast any especial blame upon Governor Ford. Willard added, "The Saints have entered into covenants of peace with the Governor & government officers, not to avenge the blood of the martyrs, but leave it with the Executive . . . at *present* we must conciliate, it is *for our salvation*. The Governor has appeared to aid with honest intention we bring no charge against him. . . ."[4]

A number of leaders contended for Joseph's role as head of the church. Several claimed to have been appointed by him as his successor.[5]

One faction, led by Emma Smith and Joseph's brother William, maintained that the rightful successor was Joseph's eldest son, and that his father had ordained him while he was in Liberty jail in 1839, and had confirmed the ordination in Nauvoo about a year before his death.[6] However, Joseph III was only twelve years old. At one point, William proposed to lead the church himself until Joseph III came of age.

James J. Strang had been a member of the church only a few months, but he claimed to have a letter from Joseph appointing him sucessor.[7] Brigham Young called the letter a "wicked forgery," and pointed out that it would have been very strange if Joseph had appointed a successor without telling the church authorities.[8]

Martin Harris and others testified that Joseph and his counselors had laid hands upon David Whitmer on July 8, 1834, and ordained him to lead the church in the event of his death.[9]

Others, in particular George Miller, believed that the Council of Fifty should reorganize the church, but the Council was not well known to the main body of Saints and in any event claimed to be a political rather than a religious group and to have Gentile members.

Still others maintained that the leadership should fall upon the officer next in line. This they said was William Marks, president of the High Council in Zion. Joseph's proper successor was not the Twelve, this faction said, because they had authority only among the branches of the world, and it was not Sidney Rigdon, since he was only Joseph's counselor.

Many remembered that Joseph had written to Brigham Young and Heber C. Kimball from Liberty jail in 1839, to say that the management of church affairs fell to the Twelve Apostles, adding, "Whether we live or die let the work of the Lord go on." To this letter, which had been signed by Joseph Smith, Hyrum Smith and Sidney Rigdon, a significant N.B. had been added, "appoint the oldest of those twelve who were first appointed, to be the President of your Quorum."[10] This, it was contended, laid the foundation for Brigham to succeed Joseph.

Brigham Young and Sidney Rigdon became the strongest contenders for the church leadership.

Sidney maintained that the role was properly his as the only remaining member of the church presidency, since Joseph was dead and the other counselor, William Law, had apostatized.

After the persecutions in Missouri, Sidney had suffered continual poor health and had dwindled to a shade of his former robust and imposing physique. His relationship with the prophet had lately been strained and his opponents put it about that he was unstable. However, Sidney had never denied the faith, and although not Joseph's first choice, he had been his running mate in the forthcoming elections for the presidency of the United States.

In Pittsburgh with his family when he heard of Joseph's death, Sidney hurried back to Nauvoo and arrived Saturday, August 3, ahead of the apostles. At services on the fourth he told a large gathering of Saints that on the day of Joseph's death the Lord had shown him a vision making it known that he should be guardian of the church until the rightful successor could be found. At Sidney's request, a conference was scheduled for the following Tuesday, then postponed until Thursday. On Tuesday evening, however, Brigham Young arrived, and on Wednesday he and Sidney spoke at a meeting of the authorities, Sidney again relating his vision.

Brigham said he did not care who led the church, but added, "one thing I must know and that is what God says about it. I have the keys and the means of obtaining the mind of God on the subject . . ."[11]

On Thursday, August 8, at the special conference Sidney had requested, Sidney stood on a wagon in the grove where meetings were held and talked for an hour and a half but failed to arouse much enthusiasm. Brigham called a reassembly for two o'clock that afternoon.

Describing that day's events in the journal kept in his own hand, Brigham said:

this day is long to be remembered by me, it is the first time I have met with the Church at Nauvoo since Brs Joseph and Hyram was kild— and the occasion on which the Church was caule somewhat painful to me, Br Rigdon had com from Pitsburge to see the Brothern and find out if they would sustain him as the Leador of the Saints. I perseved a Spirit to hurry business, to get a Trustee in Trust and a Presedecy over the Church Priesthood or no Priesthood right or wrong &c. this grieved my hart, now Joseph is gon it seed as though manny wanted to draw off a party and be leaders, but this cannot be, the Church must be one or they are not the Lords; the Saints looked as though they had lost a friend that was able and willing to councel them in all thin; in this time of Sorrow my hart was filed with compastion . . .[12]

By two o'clock that afternoon the Saints had assembled in the grove by the thousands. Rising to speak, Brigham told them that their prophet had gone from their midst, had sealed his testimony with his blood, and now for the first time they must walk by faith and not by sight.
He said:

You are like children without a father and sheep without a shepherd . . . You cannot take any man and put him at the head; you would scatter the saints to the four winds, you would sever the priesthood . . . I tell you in the name of the Lord that no man can put another between the Twelve and the Prophet Joseph. Why? Because Joseph was their file leader, and he has committed into their hands the keys of the kingdom in this last dispensation, for all the world . . .[13]

Brigham wrote in his journal for that day that he talked about two hours in blustering weather, putting before the people the order of the church and the power of the priesthood. He said that the Holy Ghost was with him and he was able to comfort them.

Letters and memoirs of a number of Saints who were present mentioned a strange phenomenon—that Brigham seemed to assume Joseph's voice, appearance and personality. The phenomenon was mentioned in retrospect, however. Although he did not mention it in the account of that day's events in his diary, Wilford Woodruff said in 1892 that he saw the transformation with his own eyes.[14]

Rigdon did not try to take the stand, but asked Phelps to speak for him. When he rose, however, Phelps told the assembly, "If you want to do right, uphold the Twelve."

Brigham said that Sidney asked that the vote for the Twelve be taken first.[15] One member who sat close to the proceedings told a different story, that Sidney tried to call the assembly to sustain him but Brigham put him down, saying, "I will manage the vote for Elder Rigdon. He does not preside here."[16] When the church sustained the Twelve with a show of hands, Brigham said, "This supersedes the other question."[17]

As president of the Quorum of the Twelve, Brigham took control of church affairs and from that moment, although some would not follow him, he never relinquished his position.

Sidney Rigdon would not be reconciled to Brigham as leader. According to Brigham, Sidney claimed higher authority than the Twelve and did not consider himself bound to their council. The Twelve met with Rigdon, tried in vain to change his opinion and then demanded his license, but he would not surrender it. Later he said he would go to Pittsburgh and publish the whole history of the evil in Nauvoo whether it involved the living or the dead.

On Sunday, September 8, Brigham accused Sidney before the church High Council of intending to rule or ruin the church. Although Sidney was absent, claiming to be ill, the council cut him off from the church.

Sidney returned to Pittsburgh, established a church and for a while published his version of the old Kirtland newspaper, the *Latter-day Saints' Messenger and Advocate,* in which he continued to oppose the apostles, calling them apostates and polygamists.

Sidney was not the only one to assume leadership of a splinter group. Lyman Wight led a small faction to settle on the Colorado River, not far from Austin, Texas, later moving several times, but they dispersed after Lyman's death.

James Strang formed a colony on Beaver Island, Michigan, published the *Voree Herald,* gave revelations, established polygamy, sent missionaries to England and for a while attracted some of Joseph's former followers, including John C. Bennett, Martin Harris and John E. Page. Strang, however, had difficulties with his neighbors, who resented the practice of polygamy and accused him of theft, and in 1850 became especially indignant when he had himself crowned king in Zion. Six years later he was murdered by two of his own followers, and his church declined.

William Smith, the prophet's only surviving brother, returned from the east where he had lived for three years, and was made patriarch, replacing Hyrum.

While William was like Joseph in his good looks and charm, his fiery temper often ruled. He soon quarreled with Brigham and the Twelve over his rights in the church.

On June 30, 1845, Brigham wrote to William:

As to your having the right to administer all ordinances, in the world and no one standing at your head we would not sanction because the president of the church stands at the head of all the officers in the church . . . but as to your right to officiate in the office of patriarch we say you have the right to officiate in all the world wherever your lot may be cast and no one to dictate or control you excepting the Twelve . . .[18]

William claimed that he was defending the rights of Joseph III. He wrote to a friend on October 5, "Brigham Young is a tirant and userper & he shall not prosper in his *fals clames* So help me God the man that Robbes the fatherless child God will curse . . . I shall not trouble Nauvoo myself very soon not at least until they can treat the Smith blood with more respect."[19]

William's niece Mary, daughter of Samuel, wrote that he had seats built in the grove for a big assembly, but the seats were strewn with refuse from outhouses and William was ordered to leave town.[20]

William published a blast against Brigham Young in the *Warsaw Signal*, October 29, 1845, calling him a tyrant surrounded by men who would commit almost any crime at his command.

The *Times and Seasons* of November 1 announced that William was cut off from the church.

In St. Louis, William organized a council of high priests and cut off Brigham. Later, in the winter of 1845–46, he formed a branch of the church in Cincinnati.

Despite the loss to various factions, by far the largest body of the Saints remained with Brigham, and he soon had enough to occupy his attention without undue concern over rivals.

During the summer of 1844, the Saints were so preoccupied with the death of their prophet and with choosing his successor that most of them paid little attention to the fact that local and national elections were due in August. Some were disgusted with politics and reluctant to vote. However, as election day approached, they were reminded of the importance for their own security of maintaining their political power, and a rally was called to determine how they should make that power felt at the polls. For sheriff, they gave support to General Minor Deming, the "Jack Mormon" whom they respected as a man of peace and justice; for coroner, Daniel H. Wells, who was very active in Nauvoo although he had not as yet joined the Mormon Church; and for state representative, Jacob B. Backenstos, who had been a friend of Joseph Smith's. On election day, the continuing political strength of the Mormons became apparent to their enemies, when Mormon favorites took every post in Hancock County. Franklin Worrell, officer of the Carthage Greys who had been in command at the jail when the Smiths were murdered, wrote to Thomas Gregg deploring the results, and reminding Gregg that Deming had promised to bring the murderers of the Smiths to justice. Worrell wrote, "I hope Deming will attempt to arrest some of the mob, if he does—we will then have some more Sport—& no mistake."[21]

Much has been written about the lawlessness of non-Mormons of Hancock County at that time, but little about non-Mormons who made heroic efforts to uphold justice. Among these was the new sheriff, Minor R. Deming. To release himself for his duties in Carthage, he rented his farm, as he

said, to a "highly respectable" Mormon family, and for this he and his
wife and two young sons were subjected to much abuse.[22] In spite of
threats, Deming, a man of religious convictions who believed in turning
the other cheek, would not carry a gun until it became essential in exercis-
ing his responsibilities.

Not long after Deming took office, a public advertisement was made by
anti-Mormons that a "Grand Military Encampment" would be held in
Warsaw from September 27 through October 2 for the purpose of "keeping up a proper military spirit among the several companies." Notices to
captains of the militia said that the muster was for a six-day "wolf hunt" in
Hancock County, and secret word identified Mormons and "Jack Mormons" as the wolves.[23]

Governor Ford thought that the intention was to harass the Mormons.
Later opinion has it that the real purpose was to intimidate the newly
elected sheriff and county commissioners, whose job it was to select the
grand jury that would issue the indictments and the petit jury that would
try those accused of the murder of the Smiths. This seems especially likely
in view of the fact that four of the ten leaders of the troops involved were
later indicted for the murders of the Smiths and another, Robert Smith,
captain of the Carthage Greys, was under suspicion.[24]

Deming afterward wrote to his parents:

> . . . there were about 200 directly or indirectly engaged in the
> murder and they are bound by common guilt & danger to commit al-
> most any act to save them from infamy and punishment. This number
> with their relatives & friends forms a bold, desperate and ferocious
> band, that expect by their perjury & violence to overawe the courts &
> evade justice. They have so long & often threatened me that I have
> become familiar with the *talk* of lynchings & death.[25]

Anti-Mormon newspapers tried to renew hatred of the Mormons by
publishing accounts of robberies and outrages supposedly perpetrated by
them, and the Whig press echoed the stories all over the country.

Although the men put into office by the Mormon vote were Democrats,
the party at large would take no part in their defense, not even in their
newspapers. This left the Mormons with no means to make known their
true situation except in papers published in Nauvoo, which had little
influence on the wider public. For this Ford held his party in the utmost
scorn, saying that they were anxious enough for Mormon votes but were
unwilling to risk popularity by supporting their governor in keeping the
peace or even in sustaining law and justice when it was on the side of the
Mormons.

Certain that trouble was ahead, Ford called for 2,500 volunteers to ride
with him to Warsaw on September 25 to ensure the peace in Hancock
County. For this Thomas Sharp publicly ridiculed him and denied that

"wolf hunt" circulars had been distributed. Sharp suspected that Ford, who was anxious to vindicate the honor of the state, was actually out to capture suspects for trial, and there was perhaps some justification for his belief, since Ford later wrote that as much as anything else, he had ordered the expedition "with a view to arrest the murderers."[26]

Ford was able to raise only 450 men in response to his call. However, it was enough to make the anti-Mormons abandon their plans. The leaders fled to Missouri. Among them, according to Ford, were almost the entire body of Carthage Greys and three of the men later indicted for the murder of the Smiths.

The grand jury, which met in October 1844, was given the names of about sixty suspects, but they found the evidence so inconclusive that they brought indictments against only nine, editor Thomas Sharp and eight others, three of whom were said to have been wounded by Joseph's pistol shots in jail. Four of the nine, including the wounded, escaped arrest, however, and were never brought to trial.

Even under indictment, the tireless Sharp continued his campaign against the Mormons. The *Illinois State Register* of November 8, 1844, quoted "an observer at Warsaw" who attributed the Mormons' continuing problems largely to Sharp:

He it is who invents and publishes all the lies about Mormon stealing, Mormon murders, Mormon adulteries, spiritual wives and Danites, for the purpose of exciting the people to riot and murder . . . He has . . . settled at Warsaw and made himself the organ of a gang of town lot speculators there, who are afraid that Nauvoo, is about to kill off their town, and render their speculations abortive.

The Mormons were dealt a further injustice in January 1845, when the state legislature abolished the Nauvoo charters despite a vigorous defense by Jacob B. Backenstos and efforts by the governor to have them amended rather than repealed.

Nauvoo was left with no legal government and no alternative to deal with lawlessness in their own city. Ford advised Brigham to incorporate part of Nauvoo as a town, but a town could be no larger than one square mile and could have no court, merely a justice of the peace. Twelve towns would have been needed to cover Nauvoo as then constituted. Nevertheless, one town was incorporated and for the rest, Brigham ingeniously adapted the church government to civil use, assigning bishops to maintain the peace in each ward, with the help of especially appointed deacons.

The Nauvoo Legion was now illegal, but it stood ready nonetheless for the Mormons' defense and was useful in maintaining order. Even the Boys Legion continued to drill once a week.

Despite their setbacks, the objectives of the Saints were intact, and their lives remained well disciplined, their faith undiminished. Most important to them, construction of the temple went on. Slowly the walls went up and were topped by thirty capitals, each composed of five enormous carved stones, the largest more than two tons, raised into place with rude cranes and ropes. Even rainstorms did not stop the workmen, who kept on until the first heavy snow of 1844, and started again as soon as the weather allowed.

A great multitude of Saints assembled early on the wet, cold morning of Saturday, May 24, 1845, for the laying of the final capstone on the southeast corner of the temple. At 6 A.M., in an absolute hush, the mortar was spread and the stone hoisted. Brigham Young stood on the stone and knocked it into place with a beetle. The band played "The Capstone March," composed for the occasion, and Brigham said, "The last stone is now laid upon the Temple and I pray the Almighty in the name of Jesus to defend us in this place and sustain us until the Temple is finished and we have all got our endowments."[27]

Three times the assembled Saints gave a mighty shout of joy, "Hosanna, hosanna, hosanna to God and the Lamb, amen, amen and amen!" When raised by thousands of voices in full throat, the great Mormon "Hosanna," given only on rare occasions, has been described as awe-inspiring. One Mormon wrote, "it is impossible to stand unmoved . . . It seems to fill the prairie or woodland, mountain wilderness or tabernacle, with mighty waves of sound . . . and is followed by a feeling of reverential awe—a sense of oneness with God."[28]

During the ceremonies, officers were standing by to take John Taylor and other Mormons as witnesses for the trial of Joseph Smith's murderers, which was to open that same day in Carthage. The Mormons had no expectation of justice from the state, however, and no intention of serving at the trial. John Taylor's memory of the past events at Carthage was so painful that he had no faith in the ability of the state to protect its witnesses. In an editorial in the *Nauvoo Neighbor* of April 23 that year he had said, "Until the blood of Joseph and Hyrum Smith have been atoned for . . . no Latter-day Saint should give himself up to the law."

That Ford was also anxious for the safety of the state's witnesses was apparent in the letter he had written to Sheriff Deming on May 13, in which he said it was rumored that certain people of Hancock County would try to prevent the witnesses from attending court. He told Deming that if necessary to protect the court he was authorized to call out the militia, including the men of Nauvoo.

Such a promising diversion as this trial brought hundreds of eager spectators from all over Hancock County. Many came with weapons, afraid that hostilities would break out. Some said they had heard the Mormons would destroy the new county courthouse if they did not like the verdict. William Clayton wrote that he believed such rumors were deliberately spread to bring the Mormons into conflict with the state and cause their expulsion or extermination.[29]

Separate trials were to be held for the two murders, that for the murder of Joseph Smith to be first. Of the nine men indicted, Sheriff Deming had been able to arrest only five, the well-known Thomas Sharp and four other prominent young men in the county, Levi Williams, Mark Aldrich, Jacob Cunningham Davis and William N. Grover. Williams was colonel of the 59th Regiment of militia, to which the battalion commanded by Mark Aldrich was attached. Aldrich had taken out bankruptcy when a scheme of his had failed to entice Mormon immigrants to settle permanently on land he and his partners owned in Warren. Davis was a member of the Illinois state senate and captain of a company in Aldrich's battalion. William N. Grover was captain of the other company in Aldrich's battalion and a justice of the peace in Warsaw.

Judge at the trial was Richard M. Young. Young was not regularly assigned to that circuit but he was well known as a justice of the state supreme court. Although a handsome and sociable man, a fiddler and a wit, Young was noted for keeping strict order in court. In this trial, however, he would be hard pressed to control the excited spectators.

The prosecutor was Josiah Lamborn, who walked with a bad limp because of a defective foot. He was considered an able and indefatigable criminal lawyer, but his reputation was not impeccable, and he was noted already for the heavy drinking that would soon, in 1847, bring on delirium tremens and death. Opposing the lone prosecutor were four capable lawyers for the defense, headed by Orville H. Browning, a sober man who would not break the Sabbath even to travel. Ironically, it was Browning to whom Joseph had written from Carthage on the day he was murdered to ask for help in his pending trial and Browning who had been commended by the Mormons for his spectacular defense of Joseph before Stephen A. Douglas when he had been arrested for extradition to Missouri in 1841.

It was known to all concerned that the murders had been committed by members of the Warsaw militia, of whom the defendants were officers, and that Thomas Sharp had publicly urged the murders, and had justified them afterward. No alibis were possible, since the defendants had been seen in

Nevertheless, prosecution would not be easy. No witness to the actual shooting could be found. It remained for the prosecutor to establish beyond a reasonable doubt that the accused men were guilty of conspiracy, in which case there would be no need to prove that any one of them had fired the shots, since under Illinois law at the time, anyone convicted of participating in a criminal act was responsible for all the consequences. However, the case for the prosecution depended upon the careful disclosure of evidence that a conspiracy did exist, that the defendants were party to it and that the murders were committed as a result.[30]

But one after the other, witnesses called for the state gave only vague statements, or details of little consequence.

They established that the defendants were members of the militia discharged at Golden's Point and that they had raised volunteers to go to Carthage, but the witnesses would not say what the purpose for going to Carthage was, or admit that anyone had talked about killing the Smiths. To the surprise of all, one witness testified that Davis had said he would be damned if he would kill men in jail, and had left in the opposite direction. However, the prosecution was unable to make anything more of this promising point. It was obvious that the witnesses knew far more than they would tell, but to the satisfaction of the noisy spectators, Lamborn could not draw out their testimony.

Unexpectedly, Lamborn called Franklin A. Worrell. Worrell was an unlikely witness for the prosecution, since his anti-Mormon attitude was well known. It was he who had been in command of the guards at the jail and had indicated to Dan Jones that the Smiths would be dead before sundown. All Lamborn could get from him were a few details that incriminated no one. Asked directly if he had seen any of the defendants at the time of the attack, Worrell solemnly swore that he had not, and in fact did not recognize anybody in the mob. When asked if he and his men on guard at the jail had loaded their guns with blank cartridges, he answered, prompted by the defense, that he would not respond to that question on the grounds that he might incriminate himself.

Lamborn's most important witness was a young man named William Daniels. Unlike his predecessors on the witness stand, Daniels spoke openly, courageously and in great detail about what he had seen and heard, giving the prosecution exactly what was needed for the case. He said that the accused had been at Golden's Point, that Sharp had made a speech to raise a mob to kill the Smiths, that Grover was the first to volunteer for action and that all of the others except Davis had participated. It began to look hopeful for the prosecution.

The youthful Daniels was not equal to the wiles of the defense, however, and he was led by cross-examination to make statements highly prejudicial to his testimony.

Browning concentrated on the fact that Daniels had published a sensational account of the murders in a little booklet that appeared for sale shortly before the trial. In that booklet, Daniels had said that after Joseph had fallen from the window of the jail, a ruffian had set him up against the well curb and raised his bowie knife to cut off his head. At that moment a blazing light had burst from heaven and passed like a chain between the mob and their victim. Terrified, the ruffian had stood like a statue unable to move until he was carried away. The booklet continued that Daniels had afterward seen Joseph in a vision and had received his blessing.[31]

Browning brought Daniels' testimony into disrepute on several points, including the fact that the light he had described was not within the realm of common experience, that the young man had made money from his booklet and that he had since joined the Mormon Church and was now living in Nauvoo without visible means of support.

Nine witnesses were called by the defense to try to discredit Daniels further, some with allegations that he had been offered money to testify, although it was not proved that Daniels had accepted.

In summation Lamborn astonished the court by repudiating his own best witness, saying that Daniels' book was ridiculous and his evidence unreliable. He conceded that the testimony of several other witnesses for the state had been successfully repudiated by the defense. In what amounted to a capitulation, he said that he had no case against two of the defendants and that the evidence against the others was circumstantial.

Suggestion has been made that Lamborn was frightened of the armed men in the courtroom, or that possibly he expected or had received favors from the opposition. No evidence has arisen to substantiate the latter supposition, but he had a reputation as not above taking a bribe.

The lawyers who spoke for the defense declared that the witnesses were incredible and the evidence inconclusive, but they also reminded the jury and the court how much the Smiths had been hated and feared by non-Mormons and they managed to imply that a verdict of guilty might well bring on a civil war.

The trial had lasted for less than a week and the jury deliberated for less than three hours, including time for lunch. They filed back with a verdict that surprised no one—not guilty.

It has been pointed out that the jury might have reached that conclusion because of the inefficiency or corruption of the prosecution or because they were determined not to convict no matter what the evidence. One study of the trial suggests that the most important reason for the acquittal of the defendants was that the community at large approved of the crime.[32] According to one opinion, "There was not a man on the jury, in the court, in the county, that did not know the defendants had done the murder. But it was not proven, and the verdict of NOT GUILTY was right in law. And you cannot find in this generation an original inhabitant of Hancock County who will not stoutly sustain that verdict."[33] The best that could be said for the trial was that it had ended without bloodshed.

In a scene of triumph for the mob, the defendants were released on bail and a special term of the circuit court to try them for the murder of Hyrum was set for June 24.

On June 24, however, the court waited in vain for Lamborn or some other prosecutor and for the states' witnesses. When the prosecution failed to appear again the next day, Judge Young dismissed the case.

That Lamborn stayed away on his own initiative is not thought likely.

He wrote to Ford on June 11 asking whether he should go to Carthage for that special term of the circuit court but Ford's reply is not known. It has been suggested that Ford might have thought the honor of the state had been sufficiently vindicated.[34]

AFTERMATH

On June 24, the day trial was supposed to be held for the murderers of Hyrum Smith, the county clerk, a noted anti-Mormon, quarreled with Sheriff Deming in the courthouse and got his powerful hands on Deming's throat. After warning him in vain, Deming shot the clerk in the abdomen and he died within fifteen minutes.

Deming's friends were convinced that the county clerk would have killed him if he had not defended himself, but Deming was indicted for willful, premeditated murder in the first degree. Heartbroken, Deming resigned from his post to await his trial, but before it came up, he died of a fever. His last request to his wife was that she teach her sons to defend the right, whether it made them friends or enemies. Of his death, Brigham Young wrote, "We feel to mourn the loss of such a man."[1]

The anti-Mormons seemed less content than ever to have the Mormons in their midst. Abigail, Minor Deming's wife, wrote to her sister that when the "Mobocrats" learned of Minor's death, they threw up their hats and shouted as if they had gained a political victory. She saw an immediate connection in the fact that depredations against the Mormons at Lima occurred the very day Minor died.[2]

The evening before, September 9, citizens of Green Plains and Lima had met at a schoolhouse to discuss how they could get rid of a little group of Mormons in Lima known as Morley Settlement (founded by Isaac Morley, who had had the communal society in Kirtland) on the prairie some twenty-five miles south of Nauvoo. During the meeting someone fired into the schoolhouse. The nature of the incident led Governor Ford and even the noted anti-Mormon Thomas Gregg to say that it must have been staged to provide an excuse to raid the Mormons. The next day the mob rode out and began burning Mormon houses, barns and fields of grain. Abigail Deming wrote, "They took the sick on their beds and laid them out in the sun, threw out their goods and then set fire to their houses before their eyes."[3]

Although many non-Mormons expressed outrage at this, not one would answer the call for a posse raised by the new sheriff, Jacob B. Backenstos, because it was said he had been put in office by the Mormons.

Mob action against the Mormons at Morley Settlement continued for a week, during which time some three hundred men burned 175 houses and farms, reduced the settlement to ashes and drove out the whole population.

On September 16, Backenstos dashed to Nauvoo with news that the mobocrats had driven him out of his house in Carthage, and that he had been chased by men on horseback. Called to help the sheriff, Porter Rockwell had shot the leader off his horse. He proved to be Frank Worrell of the Carthage Greys, who had been in command of the guard at the jail when the Smiths were killed. (Later, Backenstos and Rockwell were indicted and tried for Worrell's murder, but were acquitted.)

Unable to get help elsewhere, Backenstos raised a posse of several hundred Mormons who rode out with him and put down marauders wherever found. They drove the mobocrats out of Carthage and set up a guard at the courthouse.

Ford concluded that the upheavals in the state would end only if the Mormons could be persuaded to leave. He sent a commission of four, one of whom was Stephen A. Douglas, to Brigham Young. They extracted his promise that the Mormon leaders and a thousand families would leave Illinois in the spring, and that if means allowed, the whole church would follow. The commission said that if the Mormons failed to keep their promise "violent means will be resorted to, to compel your removal . . ."[4]

The Saints were divided into companies, under the leadership of captains. Among the needs listed for a family of five besides a strong, well-covered wagon, good oxen and other cattle, were a thousand pounds of flour, and supplies of sugar, salt and black pepper, bushels of beans, dried apples, peaches and pumpkins and twelve nutmegs. Arms and ammunition were specified, and a tent, fishhooks and lines, farm tools, nails and cooking utensils. In addition, each company was to take two ferryboats, pulley blocks and ropes, a fish seine and a keg of alcohol. Parley P. Pratt's estimate of the cost of supplies for each family was $250. Every worthy family that wanted to go, no matter how needy, would have means provided.

Some of the Saints looked forward to the exodus as an adventure, una-

Mansion House, Nauvoo, Illinois. COURTESY OF THE LIBRARY OF CONGRESS.

The Carthage (Illinois) jail, scene of the murders of Joseph and Hyrum Smith.
COURTESY OF THE LIBRARY OF CONGRESS.

The Mormon temple at Nauvoo, Illinois: two artists' renderings.

John Taylor, seriously wounded by the mob which assassinated Joseph and Hyrum Smith in Carthage, Illinois. UTAH STATE HISTORICAL SOCIETY.

Willard Richards, who escaped the Carthage mob and returned to Nauvoo with the tragic news. UTAH STATE HISTORICAL SOCIETY.

Brigham Young.

Thomas Ford, governor of Illinois in 1844, who pledged to protect Joseph Smith but failed.

ware of the terrible ordeal ahead. One young convert had just had a baby, but she wrote to her mother in September, 1845, trying to persuade her parents to come along, adding, "How can I go without you? Or how can you stay behind!" She suggested that her father would enjoy hunting all the way, and said, "What good times we will have journeying and pitching our tents like the Israelites."[5]

By November, every company had established one or more wagon shops. Blacksmiths were set to work night and day.

To the disappointment of the Saints, they received few offers for their property. Brigham began trying to sell Nauvoo as an entity. On December 2 he wrote to one prospective buyer in Iowa, offering city property and surrounding farm land at half the fair price. Some bishops of the Catholic Church were also interested, and on December 10, he offered them the same terms, saying that at a moderate estimate, the Mormon property in Hancock County was worth more than $2 million, but the Mormons would accept half. If all other property was purchased the Mormons would make the buyer a gift of the temple, otherwise it could be had for rent. The only condition, Brigham said, was that the temple be kept in good repair.[6]

The sale of the whole town did not materialize, however, and neither did many other sales.

Nevertheless the Saints were determined to fulfill the Lord's requirement that they finish their temple and perform their ordinances before they left. Although they knew that they would have to sacrifice it, their temple was to be the finest they could produce. The work went on despite poverty, anxiety, sickness and desperate efforts to prepare for their exodus. Toward the last, when harassments increased, laborers carried their weapons with their tools and worked under constant guard. They built an edifice of beautiful white sandstone, towering over the countryside and visible for miles up and down the Mississippi, a stunning achievement in frontier country, and a monument to their skill, courage and devotion.

At last, on December 10, 1845, Brigham Young and Heber C. Kimball began administering the temple ordinances. Day and night, the secret ceremonies were performed, as long as the Saints remained in Nauvoo.

Open only to full tithe payers, the ordinances included covenants and blessings, washing and anointing with consecrated oil, marriages and the "sealing" of family members for eternity and ceremonies of adoption (no longer performed) in which men and their families were sealed to a particular leader of the church as their own children. More than five thousand men and women went through the ceremonies in great urgency even as interior work on the temple went on plastering, laying the floor and putting up pulpits and seats.

Meanwhile, Brigham and the other leaders studied maps and read reports, in particular John C. Frémont's account of his recent exploration of the Great Salt Lake Valley.

Benjamin F. Johnson and Newel K. Whitney were sent by Brigham to see Emma to try to persuade her to join the exodus, but she refused, remained in Nauvoo and continued to run Mansion House as an inn. Brigham also attempted to persuade Lucy to go west, but she elected to stay in her little house in Nauvoo. She spent the last two years of her life with Emma, and died in the summer of 1856, just three years after the publication of her memoirs.

On February 5, 1846, the first company of Mormons started across the Mississippi with their wagons, teams and goods on a fleet of flatboats, skiffs and old lighters. The earliest to cross were considered among the most faithful in the church, and included the plural wives of apostles and some of the first children born in polygamy. The pioneers moved on and made camp at Sugar Creek, Iowa, to wait for Brigham, who crossed the river February 15 with George Albert Smith, Willard Richards and their families.

On Tuesday morning, February 25, a severe snowstorm blew in from the northwest. The thermometer fell to twelve below zero and the Mississippi River froze solid above Montrose. The cold proved a benefit for several days to some of the emigrating Mormons, who were able to ride across the river in their wagons on a bridge of ice. But many were without adequate shelter and suffered intensely.

During February, more than a thousand wagons crossed the river to Iowa, remaining on the banks in great hardship, until they could push on to Sugar Creek. Some Mormons were already ill and without food and a number soon died.

On March 1 the Saints at Sugar Creek began their push west, their first objective being Council Bluffs on the Missouri River in Iowa, about four hundred miles away, where they would remain until they could gather strength for the great trek of over a thousand miles to Salt Lake Valley. By mid-May, some sixteen thousand Mormons were in wagon trains moving toward Council Bluffs.

Meanwhile, about a thousand Mormons remained in Nauvoo, among whom were business agents, the feeble, poor and ill and those who refused to follow Brigham. Now there was also a group known as the "new citizens," several hundred laborers, and a few merchants, doctors and lawyers. Among these was Major Lewis Bidamon, who met and later married Emma Smith.

The mobocrats became impatient to be rid of the last few Mormons and found a pretext to resume hostilities. Incidents and retaliations roused anger on both sides. One Thomas Brockman, whom Ford characterized as "a large, awkward, uncouth, ignorant semi-barbarian, ambitious of office, and bent upon acquiring notoriety," got seven or eight hundred men under his command and some small artillery and on September 11 attacked Nauvoo. The next day he demanded surrender of the town.

The Mormons resisted with what forces they had, reportedly 150 men. In the battle that followed, several men and one boy were killed and a number wounded. When Brockman got more ammunition from Quincy, the Mormons realized their position was hopeless, and agreed that Brockman could have the city September 17.

Ford's agent Brayman, in Nauvoo at the time, reported to him that the Mormons began a desperate exodus during the night of September 16. He wrote.

they fled . . . without means of conveyance . . . without tents, money, or a day's provision, with as much of their household stuff as they could carry in their hands. Sick men and women were carried upon their beds—weary mothers, with helpless babes . . . The ferry boats were crowded, and the river bank was lined with anxious fugitives . . .[7]

Brockman and his army entered Nauvoo followed by hordes of curious people and set himself up as war lord. Remaining residents, including the "new citizens," were brought before him and he determined who should be allowed to stay and who should go. Most were told they had to leave within an hour or two. His edict was cruelly enforced, as Brayman reported, by bands of armed men who broke into houses, confiscated arms and threw the residents and their goods into the street.

On Wednesday, September 23, a torrent of rain fell on the wretched Mormons camped across the river, some 640 refugees. At last, on October 5, the pioneers who had gone ahead, impoverished though they were, sent back wagons for the relief of the last refugees, the most destitute of all.

Six months later, in April 1847, a company of 143 men, three women and two children led by Brigham Young set out from Council Bluffs to open the route through unknown hazards for the great migration that followed in what has been called "a sublime spectacle of devotion which the most sceptical cannot regard without profound admiration."[8]

The plight of the Mormons raised little national sympathy, but here and there a champion came to their defense. Perhaps most noteworthy was the young Thomas Kane, a law clerk in his father's office in Philadelphia. Kane was present when a Mormon on his way to Washington to try to get help stopped to visit his father. After hearing the Mormon's story, Kane traveled to Nauvoo and the camp of refugees on the Mississippi, and even farther to Council Bluffs, to see conditions for himself.

In Nauvoo he made note of the neat brick houses and garden plots, which he thought remarkable for that rude frontier and the equal of the best New England villages. He wrote:

I never saw more abundant proofs of intelligent industry and quiet domestic thrift . . . Ropewalks, boat yards, smith shops, tanneries, all the marks of mechanical skill and enterprize were in the town. The farms were large and well enclosed, well cultivated, beyond any, that I had met in that portion of the West: and when I saw them they were absolutely groaning under the weight of their neglected harvests . . . A no less saddening spectacle than the blighted country is the city which has shared the same fate. Its streets are as quiet as the fields, and its gardens as fast running to waste . . . the marks of recent life are along them as everywhere; the blocks of stone half carved, the planks half shaped by the carpenter, the water horn in the black-smith's shop, the fresh tan in the vat . . .

Kane found drunken men in the temple, "carousing in the porch of the splendid marble building . . . beastly intoxicated, who had much defiled it with their vomit & filth." Armed men prowled the streets and required visitors to get passports from their leader.

Kane wrote hotly indignant letters to public figures in defense of the Saints. In a draft of one letter of 1847, he said:

the Mormons have been as grievous sufferers by slander as by any other wrong, and that so far from being the creatures they have been represented by their enemies and as I myself once believed them, they are a people of *singular* virtue in every sense of the word. Pious though not austere—honest, frugal—self sacrificing, humane, decorous; such are the Mormons as I have known them; and I am confident that I should hunt in vain through our Eastern States for any community of equal size, better entitled no matter how great its pretensions, to the name of Christian.[9]

On November 19, 1848, the temple was burned by an arsonist, and in 1850, a tornado struck what was left of it. Little by little the stones were carted away until nothing remained. To the Mormons, this seemed the Lord's will, to prevent its defilement.

In June of 1852, those who believed that the prophet's rightful successor was his son, Joseph III, formed the Reorganized Church of Jesus Christ of Latter Day Saints, which renounced certain tenets such as polygamy and disclaimed all fellowship with the Utah church.

Brigham Young had wanted to take the bodies of Hyrum and Joseph west with the Mormons, but Emma would not agree. When their followers left, the brothers remained buried in the last city they had founded, the nearly deserted Nauvoo.

For well over half a century after the death of Joseph Smith, the Mormons as a religious and social institution were considered not merely atypical of Americans, but were suspected of being subversive in purpose and at times were even accused of being traitors to their country. Most alarming to others was the Mormons' seeming reversal of the cherished American ideals of separation of church and state, monogamous family life and individualized as opposed to communal society.

Gradually, however, as the functions of church and state became distinct among the Mormons, attempts at communal living were deferred and the practice of polygamy was discontinued, they began to acquire a more favorable national image.

During the First World War, the Mormons were frequently lauded in the national press for their endeavors in behalf of their country, in the Liberty Bond drive, in providing wheat during the national emergency, and for similar efforts. By 1949, the Mormons were called "Americanism in miniature," in particular for combining devotion to religious cause with worldly aspirations, for holding a sense of destiny, for resourcefulness, enterprise and organization.[10]

The followers of Joseph Smith in various denominations have continued to increase in membership, works and influence and have spread over the globe.

In Salt Lake City, on Temple Square, stand two life-sized statues of Joseph Smith and Hyrum, bearing commemorative tablets. On the base of Joseph's statue are excerpts from his teachings which have become maxims of his followers everywhere:

> The glory of God is intelligence,
> This is the work and the glory of God; to bring to pass
>   the immortality and eternal life of man.
> Adam fell that man might be; and men are that they
>   might have joy.
> The intelligence of spirits had no beginning, neither
>   will it have an end.

APPENDIX

JOSEPH SMITH'S
CONTEMPORARIES

The following biographies, which use dates derived mainly from secondary sources, are intended as an aid to the reader in identifying characters in this work.

Unless otherwise indicated, references to religious activities pertain to the church founded by Joseph Smith.

ABEL, ELIJAH ca. 1810–84. First Black to hold the Mormon priesthood. Baptized 1832. Helped establish the Kirtland bank and build the temple. In 1836 ordained an elder and then a seventy. His priesthood opposed by Zebedee Coltrin because of his race, but his certificate of ordination was renewed in Nauvoo in 1841 and again in Salt Lake City. In 1883, he served a mission in Canada and Ohio, but suffered exposure and died of resulting debility soon after returning to Utah.

BENNET, JAMES ARLINGTON (fl. 1820–52). Born in Ireland, emigrated to the United States. Proprietor and principal of Arlington House, an educational institution on Long Island. Author of a classic manual on bookkeeping. A friendly correspondent of Joseph Smith's. Proposed as candidate for Vice-President, as Joseph's running mate, 1844, but not a native, he was ineligible.

BENNETT, JAMES GORDON 1795–1872. Born in Scotland, emigrated to Canada and then to the United States. In 1831 he made a personal investigation in Palmyra of the origins of *The Book of Mormon,* and wrote articles for the *Morning Courier and New York Enquirer* which contributed to early prejudice against the Mormons. Began the *New York Herald* in 1835 and made it an enormously successful enterprise. After a visit to Nauvoo, he wrote frequently about Joseph Smith and helped make him a figure of national interest.

BENNETT, JOHN COOK 1804–58. Physician, educator and military leader. Joined the church in 1840, helped put the Nauvoo charters through the state legislature, Illinois. Became mayor of Nauvoo and major general of the Nauvoo Legion. Excommunicated in 1842 for immoral conduct. Published a series of anti-Mormon letters in the *Sangamo Journal* which were brought out in book form as *The History of the Saints; or an Exposé of Joe Smith and Mormonism,* 1842.

BOGGS, LILBURN W. 1798–1861. Born in Kentucky. Elected lieutenant governor of Missouri in 1832 and became governor upon resignation of Daniel Dunklin, 1836. Elected governor 1836. Considered the Mormons at fault in the troubles in Missouri and issued order to exile or exterminate them, 1838. Furious after Joseph Smith made his complaints against Missouri before Congress, he tried to have Joseph Smith extradited to Missouri on old charge of treason. When he was wounded in an attempt on his life in 1842, Porter Rockwell was accused and Joseph Smith named as conspirator but neither was convicted.

COWDERY, OLIVER 1806–50. Scribe to Joseph Smith while he was working on *The Book of Mormon.* He and Joseph baptized each other and ordained each other to the Aaronic Priesthood, 1829. One of the three witnesses to *The Book of Mormon.* Was ordained second elder in the church, preached the first public discourse, 1830. Excommunicated 1838. He continued to declare that he knew *The Book of Mormon* to be true, was rebaptized in 1848 and was said to be on his way to join the Saints in Utah when he died.

DONIPHAN, ALEXANDER WILLIAM 1808–87. Born in Kentucky. Moved to Liberty, Clay County, Missouri, in 1833, where he practiced law and acted for the Mormons as counsel on several occasions. Brigadier general in command of the 1st Brigade of state militia in 1838, he was ordered out against the Mormons at Far West. Refused to obey his superior's command to execute Joseph and other Mormon leaders on the grounds that it was "murder." Became a colonel in the Mexican War and served with distinction at Chihuahua.

DUNKLIN, DANIEL 1790–1844. Born in South Carolina. Moved to Missouri in 1810. Elected governor of Missouri in 1833. Investigated mob action against the Mormons in Jackson County and offered to send militia to escort the exiled Mormons back to their homes but said he could not maintain a guard there to protect them. Ordered the Mormon arms restored to them, but his order was defied. At last said he was unable to reinstate the Mormons—that there were times when public sentiment was paramount to law. Resigned three months before the end of his term to accept post offered him by President Jackson as surveyor general of Missouri, Illinois and Arkansas.

FORD, THOMAS 1800–50. Born in Pennsylvania. When his father died, his mother moved with her eight children to a farm in Illinois. Ford passed the bar, 1823, and was named to the state supreme court, 1840. Although he did not seek the nomination, he was called to replace the deceased Democratic gubernatorial candidate, 1842, and elected. His term was beset with great problems, including famine, floods, social uprisings and fiscal disaster. Despite the promise of his personal protection, Joseph and Hyrum Smith were murdered in Carthage jail by a mob in 1844. Personally bankrupt upon his retirement from office, he devoted his remaining years to writing his *History of Illinois* . . . , which was published posthumously in 1854 for the benefit of his five orphaned children.

HARRIS, MARTIN 1783–1875. Well-to-do farmer in Palmyra. Took a copy of characters from *The Book of Mormon* plates to Professor Charles Anthon in New York, 1828, and was satisfied that the professor thought them authentic, although Anthon denied it. Became Joseph Smith's scribe, lost the first 116 pages of his manuscript. Was one of the three witnesses to *The Book of Mormon*, later mortgaged his farm to help finance its publication. Baptized soon after the church was organized. Had some relapse of faith, but moved to Utah in 1870 and from that time on bore frequent testimony to his belief in *The Book of Mormon*.

HIGBEE, ELIAS 1795–1843. Joined the church in 1832. Appointed county judge, Caldwell County, 1836. Accompanied Joseph Smith to Washington, D.C., in 1839 to plead the Mormon cause against Missouri. His sons, Chauncey L. and Francis, joined the Law brothers in publishing the dissident *Nauvoo Expositor*, 1844.

HYDE, ORSON 1805–78. Baptized 1831. In 1832, served a mission to the eastern states without purse or scrip, walking two thousand miles. Was ordained one of the original Twelve Apostles in 1835. Served a mission to England, 1837. At the trial of Mormon leaders at Richmond, Missouri, he denounced the Danites, but later repented and was reinstated in the church at Nauvoo. In 1840, he went alone on a mission to Jerusalem when his companion, John E. Page, withdrew. Sent by Joseph Smith as an envoy to Washington, D.C., in 1844.

KIMBALL, HEBER CHASE 1801–68. Joined the church in 1832. Marched with Zion's Camp, 1834. Was ordained one of the original apostles in 1835. Appointed head of the first mission to England, 1837, and made several thousand converts on that and subsequent missions. Gave his fifteen-year-old daughter, Helen Mar, in plural marriage to Joseph Smith, 1843. After Joseph's death, was made first counselor to Brigham Young.

KNIGHT, NEWEL 1800–47. Son of Joseph Knight, Sr., and his wife Polly, old friends of the Smiths in New York. In 1830, suffered a seizure which Joseph alleviated by commanding the devil to depart from his body, and this was accepted as the first miracle in the church. Led the Colesville Saints to Ohio and then to Missouri, 1831, where his mother was the first member to die in Zion. After death of his wife Sally he married Lydia Goldthwait in the first ceremony performed by Joseph Smith, 1835.

LAW, WILLIAM 1809–92. A convert from Canada, he moved to Nauvoo in 1839, became a member of the municipal council, a captain in the Nauvoo Legion and second counselor to Joseph Smith. Served a mission to the eastern states with Hyrum Smith, 1842. Rode with his brother Wilson and party to rescue Joseph from capture at Dixon, 1843. Opposed Joseph over his control of real estate sales in Nauvoo and on other matters, had a final break with him when he believed Joseph had made advances to his wife, Jane. Excommunicated 1844. Convinced that Joseph was a fallen prophet, he formed a new church with himself as president. With his brother Wilson and other dissenters, published the *Nauvoo Expositor*.

NOBLE, JOSEPH BATES 1810–1901. Joined the church in 1832, became one of the first Quorum of Seventy at Kirtland. A member of Zion's Camp, 1834, he was commended by Joseph Smith for helping to care for the sick and bury the dead when the Camp was struck by cholera. Severely ill himself. In 1841, he performed what is considered (erroneously) to be the first plural marriage in the church, when he married his sister-in-law, Louisa Beaman, to Joseph Smith.

PAGE, HIRAM 1800–52. Born in Vermont. Studied medicine. Settled in Seneca County, New York, where he met the Whitmer family and married Katharine Whitmer. Was one of the eight witnesses to *The Book of Mormon*. Baptized 1830. Gave revelations not in keeping with Joseph Smith's teachings, but renounced them at church conference 1830. Moved to Kirtland 1831, and to Missouri 1832. Although he left the church in 1838, it was said that he sustained his testimony of the divinity of *The Book of Mormon* to the end.

PAGE, JOHN E. 1799–1867. Born in New York, baptized 1833, moved to Kirtland 1835. Began mission to Canada in 1836, traveled more than five thousand miles in two years, mostly on foot. Became an apostle in 1838. Did not go to England with the other apostles as commanded and neither did he go with Orson Hyde on his appointed mission to Jerusalem, but stopped at Philadelphia. Excommunicated 1846.

PARTRIDGE, EDWARD 1793–1840. A well-to-do hatter in Kirtland, went with Sidney Rigdon to New York to meet Joseph Smith and was baptized by him in 1830. Became first presiding bishop of the church. Moved to Independence, Missouri (Zion), 1831. Was tarred and feathered by mob 1833 and expelled with his family and other Saints from Jackson County. In 1836, went with William Phelps to explore western Missouri as possible home for the exiles. After fall of Far West, was marched as a prisoner to Richmond. Appointed bishop in Nauvoo. When he died of fever, his daughters Emily and Eliza were taken into the home of Joseph Smith and later became his wives in polygamy.

PHELPS, WILLIAM WINE 1792–1872. Baptized in 1831. He published *The Evening and the Morning Star* in Independence, Missouri, 1832. His press demolished by a mob, 1833, in protest against his article advising free blacks on how to emigrate to Missouri. Went with Edward Partridge in 1836 to explore western Missouri as a possible home for exiled Saints. In 1838 he objected to activities of the Danites at Far West and was excommunicated. Was reinstated by special request of Joseph Smith, 1841. Became a member of the Nauvoo City Council and the Council of Fifty. Composed hymns still used in Mormon services.

PRATT, ORSON 1811–81. Converted by his brother Parley, 1830. Crossed the Atlantic sixteen times on missions for the church. Member of Zion's Camp. Was ordained one of the original apostles, 1835. Member of the Council of Fifty. Was temporarily disillusioned with Joseph Smith when he heard the story that Joseph had approached his wife Sarah with an offer of plural marriage while he was in England, but later reconciled. In addition to religious pamphlets, he published works on mathematics, astrology and calculus.

PRATT, PARLEY PARKER 1807–57. Joined the church in 1830 and converted his younger brother Orson. On his way to a mission to the Indians in 1830, stopped in Kirtland, Ohio, and helped convert Sidney Rigdon and his followers. Member Zion's Camp. Became one of the original apostles, 1835. During the disturbances at Far West, was imprisoned without trial for eight months, escaped 1839. Served mission to England, 1840. Author of numerous church pamphlets and hymns which are still sung in Mormon congregations. While returning from a mission, he was assassinated in Arkansas by a non-Mormon whose wife had joined the church and married Parley in polygamy.

RICHARDS, WILLARD 1804–54. Joined the church in 1837 and was sent on a mission to England, where he was made an apostle in 1840. Upon his return in 1841, became a member of the Nauvoo City Council, historian for the church and private secretary to Joseph Smith, keeping his journal. Was with Joseph, Hyrum and John Taylor in Carthage jail when the

Smiths were murdered and Taylor injured, but he escaped with a mere scratch. After death of Joseph, became second counselor and secretary to Brigham Young.

RIGDON, SIDNEY 1793–1876. Licensed as Baptist preacher in 1819, later helped establish the Campbellite sect and preached in Ohio, where he founded a communal society on Isaac Morley's farm in Kirtland. Converted with his followers to Joseph Smith's church by Parley P. Pratt, 1830. Went to New York to meet Joseph and with him returned to Kirtland, followed by the church. Served as first counselor to Joseph 1833–44. Fled with him to Missouri after the Kirtland bank fiasco. During trouble at Far West, he was imprisoned in Liberty jail. Opposed polygamy. Joseph tried to have him dismissed as first counselor, 1843, but he was sustained by the church. Chosen as Joseph's running mate in presidential election of 1844. Upon death of Joseph he contended with Brigham Young for leadership of the church. Excommunicated, he founded a church of his own in Pennsylvania.

ROCKWELL, ORRIN PORTER 1813–78. The son of neighbors of the Smiths in Palmyra. Joined the church in 1830. Became Joseph's friend and bodyguard. Accompanied him to Washington, D.C., to plead cause of the Saints against Missouri. Member of the Danites at Far West and of the first Council of Fifty at Nauvoo. Accused of shooting ex-governor Boggs, was imprisoned nine months, 1842–43. Tried for the murder of Franklin A. Worrell of the Carthage Greys, but exonerated. After death of Joseph Smith, became bodyguard of Brigham Young, later a sheriff and marshal in Utah.

SHARP, THOMAS COKE 1818–94. Born in New Jersey, moved to Illinois in 1840 and practiced law, but hard of hearing, he gave it up and began publication of the *Warsaw Signal*. Conducted a journalistic campaign against Joseph Smith and the Mormons and a feud with William Smith's paper, *The Wasp*. After dismissal of the militia by Governor Ford in 1844, he urged them to "render justice" to the Smiths held in Carthage jail. Tried for the murder of the Smiths, he was acquitted, 1845. Elected first mayor of Warsaw, 1853.

SMITH, DON CARLOS 1816–41. Youngest brother of the prophet. Ordained to the ministry at age fourteen. Learned printing from Oliver Cowdery in Kirtland, 1833, later became editor of the *Elders' Journal*. President of High Priests' quorum. Served several missions. While on a mission in 1838 his wife Agnes and two babies were driven off their farm in Daviess County, Missouri, and had to walk three miles in snow to Far West. Member of the Nauvoo City Council and a brigadier general of the Nauvoo Legion. Editor of the *Times and Seasons*, caught fever in dank basement office, died, age twenty-five.

SMITH, EMMA (HALE) 1804–79. A schoolteacher, known for a lovely singing voice. Married Joseph Smith in 1827 against the wishes of her father, Isaac Hale. Baptized 1830. Selected hymns for the first Mormon hymnal. Lost several children in infancy. Adopted Julia Murdock and reared her and four sons, Joseph III, Frederick Granger Williams, Alexander Hale and David Hyrum, to maturity. Went with her husband to Ohio, Missouri and Illinois, enduring much hardship with the other Saints. Became first president of the Female Relief Society, 1842. After the death of her husband and the exodus of the Saints to Utah under Brigham Young, she remained in Nauvoo and married Major Lewis Bidamon, 1847. Helped establish the Reorganized Church, of which her son, Joseph III, became president in 1860.

SMITH, GEORGE ALBERT 1817–75. Son of the prophet Joseph's uncle John. Moved with parents by covered wagon from New York to Kirtland 1833. Hauled first load of stone for the temple. Marched as a youth with Zion's Camp, became Joseph's armor-bearer. Served several missions to the eastern states without purse or scrip. Was made an apostle at the age of twenty-two. In Nauvoo, became a member of the Council of Fifty. Was made first counselor to Brigham Young in Utah, 1868.

SMITH, HYRUM 1800–44. Elder brother of Joseph Smith. Baptized 1829. One of the eight witnesses to *The Book of Mormon*. Led a contingent of Zion's Camp from Michigan to Salt River, Missouri, where he joined Joseph. Taken prisoner at Far West, was confined to Liberty jail. Appointed to the committee to establish Nauvoo, 1839. Became a major general in the Nauvoo Legion. Second counselor to Joseph Smith until released and appointed patriarch to the church, 1840, succeeding his father. Murdered in Carthage jail, with Joseph.

SMITH, JOSEPH, SR. 1771–1840. Father of the prophet. Born in Massachusetts, son of Asael and Mary (Duty) Smith. In 1791, moved with his parents to Tunbridge, Vermont. Married Lucy Mack, 1796, and took up farming. About 1802, lost everything in a ginseng investment. Moved to Palmyra, 1816. Was one of the eight witnesses to *The Book of Mormon*. Baptized 1830. With his wife and children followed Joseph to Ohio, Missouri and Illinois, enduring hardships and persecutions with the Saints. Served a mission with son Don Carlos in 1830 to upstate New York and Canada, and converted several of his brothers and sisters. Ordained patriarch and president of the High Priests in Kirtland, 1833, and a member of the first High Council, 1834. In 1836, traveled over two thousand miles with his brother John to visit branches of the church and confer patriarchal blessings. After Boggs's "extermination order," fled from Missouri to Illinois in midwinter 1839, suffered severe exposure and died in Nauvoo.

SMITH, LUCY (MACK) 1775–1856. Mother of the prophet. Born in New Hampshire, youngest child of Solomon and Lydia (Gates) Mack. Married Joseph Smith, Sr., in 1796. Had ten children. Baptized in 1830. With her husband and children followed her son Joseph to Ohio, Missouri and Illinois, suffering privations and persecutions with the Saints. Survived the death of her husband and all of her sons except William. In her old age, with the help of scribes, she wrote *Biographical Sketches of Joseph Smith the Prophet* . . . , 1853. Declining to go west with Brigham Young, she remained in Nauvoo and lived her last years with her daughter-in-law, Emma.

SMITH, SAMUEL HARRISON 1808–44. The prophet's younger brother. Baptized in 1829. One of the eight witnesses to *The Book of Mormon* and one of the first missionaries in the church. Went with the Saints to Ohio, Missouri and then Illinois, where he had a farm in Hancock County. Became alderman in the first city election of Nauvoo, 1841. Hearing of his brothers' imprisonment at Carthage, he rode to try to help them, was pursued by a mob, arrived after his brothers were murdered, carried their bodies to Nauvoo. Contracted a fever during that ordeal and survived his brothers by only a few weeks.

SMITH, WILLIAM 1811–93. Younger brother of the prophet. Baptized 1831. Was ordained one of the original Twelve Apostles, 1835. Quarreled with Joseph and church authorities more than once. Member of the Illinois state legislature 1842–43. In Nauvoo, 1842, began fiery little newspaper called *The Wasp* (later called *Nauvoo Neighbor*) in which he carried on a feud with editor Thomas C. Sharp of the *Warsaw Signal*. Made church patriarch after the death of his brother Hyrum. Refused to support Brigham Young as head of the church after Joseph's death, claiming succession belonged to the Smith family. Excommunicated.

SNOW, ELIZA ROXEY 1804–87. Born in Massachusetts, joined the church in 1835 with several of her family, including her younger brother Lorenzo, who later became the fifth president of the Mormon Church. Well known among the Saints as an educator, poet and author of hymns still sung in their congregations. Ran a school in Nauvoo. Became the first secretary of the Female Relief Society. Married Joseph Smith in polygamy, 1842. After death of Joseph, married Brigham Young, and was among the early pioneers to Utah.

TAYLOR, JOHN 1808–87. Born in England, emigrated to Canada, where he was converted in 1836. Moved to Kirtland, Ohio, then to Missouri. Made an apostle at Far West in 1838. Served missions to England. Was grievously wounded in Carthage jail 1844 when Joseph and Hyrum Smith were murdered. On a mission to France, he learned beet sugar process and introduced it in Utah. In 1877, he became third president of the church in Utah.

WHITMER, DAVID 1805–88. Son of Peter Whitmer, Sr., who gave shelter to Joseph Smith part of the time he was working on *The Book of Mormon*. Baptized 1829. Was one of the original three witnesses to *The Book of Mormon* and one of six who helped organize the church. Ordained a High Priest in 1831. Moved to Jackson County, Missouri, driven out with the rest of the Saints. Excommunicated at Far West, 1838, but gave a deathbed testimony to his belief in *The Book of Mormon*. His brothers Christian, Jacob, John and Peter Jr. were four of the later group of eight witnesses to *The Book of Mormon*.

WHITNEY, NEWEL KIMBALL 1795–1850. Partner of Algernon Sidney Gilbert in Kirtland store. Joined the church in 1831. Took Joseph and Emma into his home when they arrived in Kirtland, 1831. Appointed second presiding bishop of the church. Broke his leg on the way home from Missouri 1832 and was tended by Joseph Smith. Went with Joseph to New York to buy goods and arrange loans for the church, 1832. In Nauvoo, became a member of the Council of Fifty. Performed polygamous marriage of his daughter Sarah Ann to Joseph Smith, 1842, after Joseph gave him a special revelation to do so.

WIGHT, LYMAN 1796–1858. A member of Isaac Morley's communal society in Kirtland, was baptized 1830. Appointed second-in-command of Zion's Camp, was angered when no military action occurred. Made one of the church High Council. Taken hostage at Far West 1839 and imprisoned in Liberty jail. Went to Wisconsin 1843 to supervise lumber operations for Nauvoo temple. Recommended in 1844 that the church move to Texas, and led a group of dissidents there himself after Brigham Young became president of the church. Disfellowshipped 1848.

WOODRUFF, WILFORD 1807–98. Converted in 1833, moved to Kirtland in 1834. Marched with Zion's Camp. Moved to Missouri 1838 and to Illinois 1839. Made an apostle 1839. Served mission to England 1840–41, and again 1844–46. In Utah, 1889, became fourth president of the church. In compliance with federal law, issued manifesto in 1890 discontinuing practice of polygamy.

YOUNG, BRIGHAM 1801–77. Was a carpenter and joiner, painter and glazier. Baptized 1832, at once served a mission, converted many, including his older brother Joseph. Member of Zion's Camp. Was ordained one of the original Twelve Apostles, 1835. Supervised the painting and finishing of the Kirtland temple, 1836. Organized the exodus of the Saints expelled from Far West, 1839. Served a mission to England with the other apostles 1839–41, and directed the emigration to Nauvoo of several thousand converts. Made president of the Quorum of Twelve Apostles. Became a member of the Nauvoo City Council and Council of Fifty. After the death of Joseph Smith, was sustained as president of the church, 1844. Led the epic crossing of the plains to Utah, beginning 1846.

ABBREVIATIONS USED IN NOTES

BYU	Brigham Young University, or Brigham Young University Library, Provo, Utah.
Dialogue	*Dialogue: A Journal of Mormon Thought* (Los Angeles, California).
Doctrine and Covenants	*The Doctrine and Covenants of the Church of Jesus Christ of Latter-day Saints, containing Revelations Given to Joseph Smith, the Prophet.* Salt Lake City, 1952.
Era	*The Improvement Era* (Salt Lake City, Utah).
HDC	Historical Department of the Church of Jesus Christ of Latter-day Saints, Salt Lake City, Utah.
Historical Record	*The Historical Record. Devoted Exclusively to Historical, Biographical, Chronological and Statistical Matters* (Salt Lake City, Utah).
History of the Church	*History of the Church of Jesus Christ of Latter-day Saints, Period I. History of Joseph Smith, the Prophet, by Himself,* Vols. I–VI. *Period II. From the Manuscript History of Brigham Young and Other Original Documents,* Vol. VII. Introduction and notes by B. H. Roberts. Salt Lake City: The Deseret Book Company, 1965–68.
Huntington	The Huntington Library and Art Gallery, San Marino, California.
Journal History	Journal History of the Church of Jesus Christ of Latter-day Saints. [A chronological collection of typescripts of diaries, letters, clippings and other documents relating to the church, 1830 to date.] Historical Department of the Church of Jesus Christ of Latter-day Saints, Salt Lake City, Utah.
Journal of Discourses	*The Journal of Discourses. Reports of Addresses by Brigham Young and Others.* 26

	Vols. Liverpool and London: F. D. and S. W. Richards, 1853–86.
LDS	Church of Jesus Christ of Latter-day Saints.
NYPL	The New York Public Library.
RLDS	Library and Archives, Reorganized Church of Jesus Christ of Latter Day Saints, The Auditorium, Independence, Missouri.
TS	Typescript, or typed copy.

NOTES

Prologue: BURIAL OF A MARTYR

1. Description of the return of the martyrs' bodies to Nauvoo and their burial can be found in *History of the Church*, VI, 626–28; VII, 134.

2. Ibid., VI, 627.

3. Ursula B. Hascall to Colonel Wilson Andrews, May 2, 1846, "Letters of a Proselyte," *Utah Historical Quarterly* 25 (April 1957), 146.

4. Job Smith, a young English convert who arrived in Nauvoo in 1840, wrote that he had been allowed to see where the prophet's body was hidden to prevent the head from being carried to Missouri for rewards. *Diary of Job Smith, a Pioneer of Nauvoo, Illinois and Utah* (Arcadia, Calif.: Printed by Louise Smith Willard, 1956?), p. 8. A copy of this is in Huntington.

5. Joseph Smith's journal as kept by Willard Richards, October 15, 1843. HDC. This quotation differs slightly in *History of the Church*, VI, 58, where it is given as, "I defy all the world to destroy the work of God; and I prophesy they never will have power to kill me till my work is accomplished, and I am ready to die."

6. John Taylor wrote that John M. Bernhisel told him Joseph made that statement to him, "looking him full in the face, and as solemn as eternity." *History of the Church*, VII, 120.

7. Emily Dow Partridge Young's statement is in her "What I Remember," June 27, 1897. Emily Dow Partridge Young Papers, HDC. Taylor's quote can be found in *History of the Church*, VII, 106.

8. Ibid., VI, 630.

9. *New York Herald*, April 3, 1842, as quoted in *Deseret News*, "Church News Section," March 2, 1946, p. 5.

10. As quoted in *History of the Church*, VII, 35–36.

11. Orson Spencer, *Letters Exhibiting the Most Prominent Doctrines of the Church of Jesus Christ of Latter-day Saints* (Salt Lake City: Deseret News Co., 1889), pp. 30, 47.

12. Angus M. Cannon, as quoted in *Young Woman's Journal*, XVII, 546, and repeated in Hyrum Andrus, *Joseph Smith Man and Seer* (Salt Lake City: Deseret Book Co., 1960) p. 4.

13. As quoted in Andrus, p. 10.

14. From a talk given by Jesse N. Smith to the Church History class of Professor John Henry Evans in the L.D.S. College, Salt Lake City, April 11, 1905 as recorded in *Journal of Jesse Nathaniel Smith, the Life Story of a Mor-*

mon Pioneer, 1834-1906 (Salt Lake City: Jesse N. Smith Family Association, 1953), pp. 454–55. Original MS is in HDC.

15. *Journal of Discourses*, XVII, 92, as quoted in Andrus, p. 5.

16. Emma Smith letter to Joseph Smith III is dated only August 1, but since she mentions in it that her son David was leaving for Salt Lake, it may be 1869. Used by permission of the Library and Archives, Reorganized Church of Jesus Christ of Latter Day Saints, The Auditorium, Independence, Missouri.

17. No. 7, November 21, in *Painesville Telegraph,* December 6, 1831, p. 1.

18. *Journal of Discourses,* IV, 78.

19. *Juvenile Instructor,* XXVII, 129, as quoted in Andrus, p. 61.

20. "Journal of Newel Knight," *Scraps of Biography: Tenth Book of the Faith Promoting Series* (Salt Lake City, Juvenile Instructor's Office, 1883), p. 47.

21. Benjamin F. Johnson to George S. Gibbs, 1903, p. 4, TS, Mormon File, Box 7, Huntington. BYU also has a copy.

22. Peter H. Burnett, *An Old California Pioneer* (Oakland: Biobooks, 1946), p. 40. Burnett was an editor and lawyer in Liberty, Missouri; later he became first governor of California.

23. Burnett, p. 34.

24. *History of the Church,* V, 218.

25. From a lecture by Newhall reported in the Salem, Mass., *Advertiser and Argus,* as reproduced in *Nauvoo Neighbor,* June 21, 1843. Newhall maintained that this was from a conversation with Joseph Smith.

26. Letter of June 6, 1832, written from Greenville, Indiana. Original is in the Mormon Collection, Chicago Historical Society, and is quoted by permission.

27. *Doctrine and Covenants* 3.6.

28. Ibid., 5.21.

29. Ibid., 93.47.

30. Ibid., 124.1

31. Quoted from the original in the Mormon Collection, Chicago Historical Society, by permission. For an account of Joseph's circumstances when he wrote this letter see *History of the Church,* I, 271–72.

32. The prophet's remark is recorded in *History of the Church,* V, 553–56.

Part One: New England

Chapter 1: JOSEPH SMITH'S ANCESTORS

1. Joseph's comment that his parents were in a miserable situation is in his letter to his brother William, December 18, 1835, *History of the Church,* II, 343. That they were indigent is in Joseph Smith Jr. Letter Books 1829–1835 (MS, HDC), p. 1.

2. Mary Audentia Smith Anderson, *Ancestry and Posterity of Joseph Smith and Emma Hale . . .* (Independence, Missouri, 1929), p. 52.

3. For a study of early Topsfield see George Francis Dow, *History of Topsfield Massachusetts* (Topsfield, Mass.: The Topsfield Historical Society, 1940).

4. Mary Anderson, p. 54. She says the average estate in Robert Smith's day was under fifty pounds.

5. Mary Anderson, p. 56. She gives an impressive list of offices held by Samuel the second.

6. Mary Anderson, p. 58. See also Richard Lloyd Anderson, *Joseph Smith's New England Heritage* (Salt Lake City: Deseret Book Co., 1971) p. 195, n. 144. That Priscilla Gould was descended from Zaccheus Gould, the founder of Topsfield, was confirmed for me through the Vital Records of Topsfield by kind effort of Mary E. Bradstreet, of The Topsfield Historical Society.

7. Asael and Mary had eleven children, Jesse 1768, Priscilla 1769, Joseph 1771, Asael 1773, Mary 1775, Samuel 1777, Silas 1779, John 1781, Susanna 1783, Stephen 1785 and Sarah 1789. Lucy Smith, *Biographical Sketches of Joseph Smith the Prophet, and his Progenitors for Many Generations* (Liverpool, England, 1853), p. 39.

8. The statement that some regarded Asael's views as more distorted than his neck was made by Nehemiah Cleaveland, a physician of Topsfield who was acquainted with Asael. *An Address Delivered at Topsfield, in Massachusetts, August 28, 1850: The Two Hundredth Anniversary of the Incorporation of the Town* (New York, 1851), p. xxv, as quoted in Richard Anderson, p. 206, n. 182. The statement that he would not yield to bigotry is quoted by Mary Anderson, p. 60. The baptismal record is in George Francis Dow, "Baptismal Records of the Church in Topsfield," *Historical Collections of . . . Topsfield,* Vol. 1 (1895), pp. 37–38; the covenant acceptance is in "Records of the Congregational Church" (cit. n. 120), p. 58, as quoted by Richard Anderson, p. 191, n. 129.

9. The Journal of John Smith, (MS, HDC), entry for July 20, 1839.

10. Samuel Smith's obituary is reproduced in Mary Anderson, p. 58.

11. John says Asael undertook this despite the fact that he was in poor health. Journal of John Smith, entry for July 20, 1839.

12. Hillsborough County, N.H., Land Records, Vol. 19, pp. 47–48, and Essex County, Mass., Land Records, Vol. 145, p. 192, as quoted in Richard Anderson, p. 195, n. 147.

13. For a description of Topsfield in that day see Donald Q. Cannon, "Topsfield, Massachusetts: Ancestral Home of the Prophet Joseph Smith," *BYU Studies,* Autumn 1973, pp. 56–76.

14. For the rest of the jingle see Mary Anderson, p. 65. Richard Anderson has revised the spelling and lost some of the charm, but adds some facts and dates it ca. 1786–91. See his pp. 98–99, 199–200, n. 156.

15. Mary Anderson, pp. 60–62. Richard Anderson publishes the text with a facsimile of the letter, pp. 118–23.

16. Richard Anderson, p. 106.

17. Richard Anderson, p. 105.

18. Mary Anderson, pp. 62–64; for a photocopy of the original, see Richard Anderson, pp. 124–40.

19. George Albert Smith, "History of George Albert Smith," MS, HDC. BYU has two copies. Pagination differs.

20. Solomon Mack, *A Narraitve* [sic] *of the Life of Solomon Mack, Con-*

taining an Account of the Many Severe Accidents He Met with During a Long Series of years, together with the Extraordinary Manner in which He Was Converted to the Christian Faith (Windsor, Vt., n.d.). Date of its publication is usually given as 1810, but Richard Anderson makes a convincing case for the date as the spring of 1811. Anderson, p. 161, n. 3. A copy of this rare book is in NYPL.

21. See Richard Anderson, Chapter 2 and footnotes, for his verification of Solomon's holdings and the events in his life.

22. Marcus Wilson Jernegan, *Laboring and Dependent Classes in Colonial America 1607–1783: Studies of the Economic, Educational, and Social Significance of Slaves, Servants, Apprentices, and Poor Folk,* Social Service Monographs, No. 17 (Chicago: University of Chicago Press, [1931]), p. 104–5. See also Mack, pp. 4–5.

23. Richard Anderson, pp. 9, 163, n. 22.

24. Mack, p. 14.

25. Ibid., p. 24.

26. Ibid., p. 25. These excerpts are edited for spelling and punctuation.

Chapter 2: EARLY LIFE OF JOSEPH'S PARENTS.

1. Lucy Smith's book was suppressed by Brigham Young in 1865 on the grounds that it was "transmitting lies to posterity" (*The Latter-day Saints' Millennial Star* 27 [1865], pp. 657–58). It has since been published in several editions in revised form. Recently Modern Microfilm Co., Salt Lake City, issued a photomechanical reprint of the 1853 edition, with an introduction discussing alterations made in later editions. References in this work are to the 1853 edition.

2. Lucy Smith, p. 48.

3. Ibid., p. 54.

4. As quoted by Richard Anderson, p. 207, n. 183.

5. Richard Anderson gives background information on Joseph's illness in his "The Trustworthiness of Young Joseph Smith," *Era,* October 1970, pp. 86–88. See also Lucy Smith, pp. 62–65.

6. Source for Joseph's claim that he refused to have the operation but later consented to the "experiment" of removing bone is in Manuscript History of the Church, opening narrative, Note A, pp. 291, 294, HDC, as quoted by Anderson, "Trustworthiness," p. 87. For Lucy's statement see her p. 64.

7. A Dr. Buckley in *Christian Advocate,* November 29, 1906, expressed the opinion that Joseph's mother provided his motivation. The writer of an article in the New York *Daily Advertiser* of 1856 said that he talked with an old neighbor of the Smiths who told him that Joseph's mother "had the intellect," and spurred her son on with visions of his greatness. This article can be found in First Half Century of Mormonism; Papers, engravings, photography and autographed letters collected and arranged by Charles Woodward, 1880, NYPL.

8. James Gordon Bennett gave this description of Joseph Smith, Sr., probably based upon gossip he heard when he visited Palmyra in 1831, after the Smiths had moved on. "Mormonism—Religious Fanaticism—Church and State Party," New York *Morning Courier and Enquirer,* August 31, 1831, as

reprinted in Leonard J. Arrington, "James Gordon Bennett's 1831 Report on 'The Mormonites,'" *BYU Studies,* Spring 1970, p. 357.

Part Two: New York

Chapter 1: JOSEPH'S FIRST VISION

1. William Smith, "William B. Smith's Last Statement." [Interview by J. W. Peterson], *Zion's Ensign* 5, No. 3 (1894), p. 6.

2. Lucy Smith's preliminary MS, HDC.

3. Ibid.

4. William Smith, op. cit.

5. Lucy Smith, op. cit.

6. Lorenzo Dow, *The Dealings of God, Man and the Devil, as Exemplified in the Life, Experience and Travels of Lorenzo Dow, In a Period of More than Half a Century* (Norwich: William Faulkner, 1833), pp. 10–11.

7. Lucy Smith, *History,* pp. 58–59.

8. The quote about Lucy is from *William Smith on Mormonism* (Lamoni, Iowa: Herald Steam Book & Job Office, 1883), p. 6. William tells about the religious practices of their home in "Notes written on 'Chambers' Life of Joseph Smith,'" [*Chambers' Miscellany*] TS, p. 18, HDC.

9. *History of the Church,* VII, 470.

10. Joseph Smith Letter Books, p. 1. However, the educational attainments of the Smith family should be viewed in the context of their times. In 1870, when the U. S. Office of Education began issuing reports, 20 per cent of the population over age ten were illiterate; the average number of days spent in school per year was only 78.4 and only 2 per cent of those over age seventeen graduated from high school. U. S. Bureau of the Census. *Historical Statistics of the United States, Colonial Times to 1970.* Bicentennial Edition, Part I. (Washington, D.C., 1975), pp. 376, 379, 382.

11. William H. Kelley, "The Hill Cumorah, and the Book of Mormon; The Smith Family . . . from Late Interviews," *The Saints Herald,* June 1, 1881, p. 167.

12. Quoted by Marvin S. Hill, "The Role of Christian Primitivism in the Origin and Development of the Mormon Kingdom 1830–1845," Diss. Univ. of Chicago 1968, p. 53.

13. *Deseret Evening News,* January 20, 1894, p. 11.

14. Kelley, p. 165.

15. Ibid., p. 166.

16. Ibid., p. 167.

17. Ibid., p. 167.

18. Lucy Smith, *History,* p. 84. Her actual statement was that he "had never read the Bible through in his life." Later Joseph acquired an impressive knowledge of the Bible. It was reported of Josiah Quincy, who visited Nauvoo in 1844, that, "Mr. Quincy speaks of Joe having an extraordinary acquaintance with the Bible & that he was very ready in reply, & clever in supporting his notions by quotations and reasonings— . . ." Henry Halkett, Notes on Mr. Quincy's visit to Joseph Smith [May 1844]. Miscellaneous Manuscripts. Clements Library, Univ. of Michigan. Quoted by permission.

19. Joseph Smith Letter Books, pp. 1–2. I am grateful to Dean C. Jessee, of the Historical Department of the Church of Jesus Christ of Latter-day Saints, for informing me that it has been established that parts of Joseph's 1832 autobiography, including the account of his first vision, are in his own hand.

20. Sandford Fleming, *Children and Puritanism; the Place of Children in the Life and Thought of the New England Churches 1620–1847* (New Haven: Yale Univ. Press, 1933).

21. *History of the Church*, I, 2–3.

22. Lucy Smith, *History*, pp. 37, 48, 54.

23. Milton V. Backman, Jr., and James B. Allen, "Membership of Certain of Joseph Smith's Family in the Western Presbyterian Church of Palmyra," *BYU Studies*, Summer 1970, p. 482.

24. A Short Sketch of the Life of Solomon Chamberlain, p. 1. A photocopy of a typed copy is in the Mormon Collection, Huntington.

25. History and Journal of Jesse W. Crosby, pp. 1–2. Typed copy in the Mormon Collection, Huntington.

26. Diary of Joel Hills Johnson 1802–1882, p. 2. Typed copy, BYU.

27. William Bacon, *Regeneration: The New Birth* (Waterloo, N.Y., 1818), as cited in Milton V. Backman, Jr., *Joseph Smith's First Vision* (Salt Lake City: Bookcraft, 1971), pp. 109–10.

28. Charles G. Finney gave this name to the whole region of central and western New York, saying that seeing so much revivalist excitement had caused many to consider religion a delusion. *Memoirs of Rev. Charles G. Finney by Himself* (N.Y.: A. S. Barnes & Co., 1876), p. 78, as noted by Hill, p. 55, n. 3. For a study of that revivalist phenomenon see Whitney R. Cross, *The Burned-over District: The Social and Intellectual History of Enthusiastic Religion in Western New York, 1800–1850* (N.Y.: Cornell Univ. Press, 1950).

29. Milton V. Backman, Jr., "Awakenings in the Burned-over District: New Light on the Historical Setting of the First Vision," *BYU Studies*, Spring 1969, p. 317.

30. *Palmyra Register*, June 7, August 16, September 13, 1820, as reported by Backman, p. 316. Backman, p. 309, says Methodist camp meetings were held so often in Joseph's neighborhood that newspapers did not report them unless something unusual happened, as in the case of one Irishman who died from intoxicating beverages bought at a grog shop near a Palmyra camp grounds. *Palmyra Register*, June 28, 1820.

31. Backman's article refutes the argument that there was no great religious revival during the time Joseph maintained, as advanced by Wesley P. Walters, "New Light on Mormon Origins from Palmyra (N.Y.) Revival," *Bulletin of the Evangelical Theological Society* 10 (Fall 1967), 227–44.

32. Backman, p. 307.

33. Ibid., p. 307–8.

34. Alexander Neibaur Journal, May 24, 1844, HDC.

35. Charles W. Brown, "Manchester in the Early Days," *Shortsville Enterprise Press*. Exact date not known. This is in the Shortsville Free Press MS file, BYU. Turner said that Joseph "caught the spark of Methodism in a camp meeting, was an exhorter in the evening meetings." O. Turner, *History of the*

Pioneer Settlement of Phelps and Gorham's Purchase and Morris' Reserve (Rochester: William Allington, 1851), p. 213.

36. *History of the Church,* I, 3.

37. Joseph Smith Letter Books, pp. 2–3. This and other accounts of the first vision are transcribed and some pages from early MSS are reproduced in Dean C. Jessee, "The Early Accounts of Joseph Smith's First Vision." *BYU Studies,* Spring 1969, pp. 275–94.

38. *History of the Church,* I, 4–6. This varies slightly from the MS, mainly in leaving out a parenthetical phrase, "(for at this time it had never entered into my heart that all were wrong)," that in the MS followed "which of all the sects was right." See transcript of the Mulholland MS in Jessee, pp. 287–91. The first part of the MS of Joseph's history was written in 1838 and copied by Mulholland in 1839 when he and Joseph took up the work together.

39. *History of the Church,* I, 6. Lucy Smith, p. 90. Joseph wrote in his history, 1838, that about the time of his first vision his mother, Hyrum, Samuel and Sophronia joined the Presbyterian Church. There was thought to be little to support this until Presbyterian Church records in Palmyra were found. These showed that at least three of the Smiths were members of that church in 1828, although not active by that time. On March 10, 1830, a committee sent to visit Lucy, Hyrum and Samuel reported that they admitted that they had neglected church ordinances for the previous year and a half and no longer wished to sustain membership. Contrary to rumor, there were no other charges made against them. They were suspended on March 29. *Records of the Session of the Presbyterian Church in Palmyra* (N.Y.), Vol. 2.

40. *History of the Church,* I, 6–7.

41. Ibid., I, 1.

42. See James B. Allen, "The Significance of Joseph Smith's 'First Vision' in Mormon Thought," *Dialogue* (Autumn 1966), 29–45.

43. Joshua Bradley, *Accounts of Religious Revivals in Many Parts of the United States from 1815 to 1818* (Albany, N.Y.: G. J. Loomis & Co., 1819).

44. Dow, pp. 10–11. Asa Wild is quoted in Hill pp. 57–58. John Samuel Thompson's vision is from his *Christian Guide* (Utica, N.Y., 1826), p. 71, as quoted in Fawn Brodie, *No Man Knows My History: The Life of Joseph Smith, the Mormon Prophet* (New York: Knopf, 1945), p. 22.

45. Brodie, pp. 25, 285.

Chapter 2: VISITATION OF MORONI

1. Lucy's account of the attack on Joseph is in her *History,* p. 73. Her statement about the house they were building is on p. 87. The suggestion that the materials were probably acquired as needed was made by Carter E. Grant, "The Joseph Smith Home," *Era,* December 1959, p. 899.

2. *History of the Church,* I, 9.

3. Ezra Pierce as told by Kelley, p. 163. According to one historian, it was a common belief among early Americans that those working outdoors in the heat needed a tonic of liquor and water as a guard against sunstroke. Catherine D. Bowen, *Miracle at Philadelphia* (Boston: Little, Brown, 1966). My thanks to Dean C. Jessee for pointing this out.

4. Reminiscences of Joseph Smith by Cragun Cox, MS, Utah State Historical Society.

5. Benjamin F. Johnson to George S. Gibbs, 1903, p. 4, TS, Mormon File, Box 7, Huntington. This is a facsimile.

6. Joseph Smith to Oliver Cowdery, *Messenger and Advocate* 1 (December 1834).

7. *History of the Church*, I, 11–14.

8. When first published in the *Times and Seasons* at Nauvoo, Joseph's history gave the name of the angel as Nephi, and this name was retained in an account published later in the *Millennial Star*. B. H. Roberts, editor of the *History of the Church*, says, "That it is an error is evident, and it is so noted in the manuscripts to which access has been had in the preparation of this work." *History of the Church* I, 11 n. Of this error, Orson Pratt wrote in response to one inquiry, "The discrepancy in the history to which you refer may have occurred through the ignorance of the historian or transcriber. It is true, that the history reads as though the Prophet himself was writing; but the Prophet was a slow and awkward writer; and many events recorded were written by his scribes who undoubtedly trusted too much to their memories, and the items probably were not sufficiently scanned by Bro. Joseph, before they got into print." Orson Pratt to John Christensen, March 11, 1876. Orson Pratt Letter Book, HDC.

9. Joseph Smith Letter Books, p. 4.

10. *Letters by Oliver Cowdery, to W. W. Phelps, on the Origin of the Book of Mormon, and the Rise of the Church of Jesus Christ of Latter-day Saints* (Liverpool: Thomas Ward, 1844), p. 33.

11. Lucy Smith, *History*, pp. 83, 35–36.

12. See note 39, chapter 1, Part II.

13. Lucy Smith, *History*, p. 84.

14. Joseph Smith's Journal as kept by Willard Richards, January 9, 1843, HDC, as quoted in Richard Lloyd Anderson, "The Trustworthiness of Young Joseph Smith," *Era*, October 1970, p. 85.

15. *History of the Church*, V, 247.

16. C. M. Stafford, a neighbor of the Smiths' in Palmyra, said this, as reported by A. B. Deming in his newspaper, *Naked Truths About Mormonism* I (Oakland, California), April 1888. BYU.

17. William Smith quoted in an interview by E. C. Briggs, *Deseret News* (Salt Lake City, Utah), January 20, 1894.

18. Text of this notice is quoted in Brodie, p. 28.

Chapter 3: COURTSHIP, MONEY-DIGGING, MARRIAGE

1. As cited by Carter E. Grant, "The Joseph Smith Home," *Era*, December 1959, p. 978.

2. For a facsimile of the discovered bill and a discussion of its significance and a comparison of various accounts of the trial see Marvin S. Hill, "Joseph Smith and the 1826 Trial: New Evidence and New Difficulties," *BYU Studies*, Winter 1972, pp. 223–33.

3. New Series (London, February 1873), p. 225.

4. W. D. Purple, *Chenango Union*, May 3, 1877.

5. *Messenger and Advocate*, October 1835, p. 201.

6. *Evangelical Magazine and Gospel Advocate* 2 (April 9, 1831).

7. *Journal of Discourses* 19 (1878), 37.

8. *Millennial Star* 26 (1864), 118–19.

9. Martin Harris told this to Ole A. Jensen in an interview in July 1875, as recorded in Grant Ivins, "Notes on the 1826 Trial of Joseph Smith," MS, HDC.

10. James Colin Brewster, *Very Important to the Mormon Money Diggers* (Springfield: n.p., March 20, 1843). Utah State Hist. Soc. has a photo duplicate of this pamphlet.

11. Purple, op. cit.

12. Martha L. Campbell to Joseph Smith, December 19, 1843. HDC.

13. Statement by Mrs. M. C. R. Smith, *Naked Truths About Mormonism*, Vol. I, April 1888.

14. Barnes Frisbie, *The History of Middletown, Vermont in Three Discourses* (Rutland, Vt.: Tuttle & Co., 1867) pp. 44–46. Frisbie said that Oliver Cowdery's father was a member of the cult.

15. *A Book of Commandments for the Government of the Church of Christ* (Zion [Independence, Mo.]: W. W. Phelps, 1833; rpt. Church of Christ (Temple Lot), Independence, Missouri, 1960), 7.3, p. 15.

Chapter 4: THE GOLD PLATES

1. The brief (five pages on both sides) manuscript by Joseph Knight, Sr., is undated and unsigned, but was apparently written sometime between 1833 and Knight's death in 1847. Some punctuation has been added in this and the following quotations. The MS is in HDC. I am grateful to Dean Jessee for drawing it to my attention.

2. Lucy Smith, *History*, pp. 101, 107. She said, "The whole plate was worth at least five hundred dollars," p. 107. This was deleted in later editions.

3. *The Saints Herald* 31 (1884), 643–44.

4. Ibid. 28 (1881), 167.

5. William W. Campbell, *The Life and Writings of De Witt Clinton* (New York: Baker and Scribner, 1849), p. 150.

6. Joseph Knight, Sr., MS. HDC.

7. Journal of Joseph Bates Noble. BYU TS, p. 10.

8. Lucy Smith, p. 109.

9. *Rochester Advertizer and Telegraph*, August 31, 1829, reported that *The Book of Mormon* was said to have a doctrine "far superior to the book of life." *Rochester Gem*, September 5, 1829, wrote that it claimed to be "an ancient record of divine origin." Marvin S. Hill makes these points in his "Secular or Sectarian History? A Critique of *No Man Knows My History*," *Church History* 43 (March 1974), 87.

10. Emma's description of the stone is in her letter to Mrs. Pilgrim, March 27, 1870. Emma Bidamon letters, Reorganized Church Library. Her account of his translating is in "Last Testimony of Sister Emma," *Saints Advocate*, October 1879, pp. 49–52, 290.

11. Joseph's statement was made in his letter to John Wentworth, published in *Times and Seasons*, March 1, 1842. It is reproduced in *History of the*

Church, IV, 535–41. See also Preston Nibley, "The Wentworth Letter," *Era*, February 1962, pp. 96–118.

12. Joseph Knight, Sr., MS. HDC.

13. Lucy Smith, pp. 110, 114.

14. Joseph Smith Letter Books, p. 5.

15. John A. Clark, *Gleanings by the Way* (Philadelphia, 1842), pp. 222, 229.

16. For a discussion of Harris's possible sources of information see Stanley B. Kimball, "The Anthon Transcript: People, Primary Sources, and Problems," *BYU Studies*, Spring 1970, pp. 328–30.

17. *History of the Church*, I, 20.

18. Reprinted in Thomas Gregg, *The Prophet of Palmyra* (New York: John B. Alden, 1890), pp. 57–59.

19. This observation is made by Brodie, p. 51. She reproduces the characters said to have been copied from the plates.

20. Gregg, pp. 60–62. See also *Church Record*, Vol 1, No. 22, p. 231.

21. Kimball, pp. 335–36.

22. Champollion had worked out the principles for deciphering hieroglyphics with the aid of the Rosetta stone, and had published several works on that subject, but his Egyptian grammar would not be published until 1836 and his Egyptian dictionary not until 1841

23. Joseph Smith Letter Books, p. 5.

24. Clark, p. 229.

25. Memorandum of John Gilbert, Esq., September 8, 1892. TS copy, p. 4, HDC.

26. For contemporary newspaper and other accounts, see Kimball, "Anthon Transcript," pp. 342–46.

27. Lucy Smith, p. 115.

28. Kimball, pp. 346–47.

Chapter 5: JOSEPH TRANSLATES

1. Lucy Smith, pp. 116–17.

2. Joseph Smith Letter Books, p. 5.

3. Lucy Smith, p. 121.

4. Joseph Smith Letter Books, pp. 5, 6.

5. *History of the Church*, I, 22–23.

6. *Doctrine and Covenants* 10.30ff.; *History of the Church, I*, 22–28.

7. George Albert Smith, History. Only the quotations from these letters by Joseph and his father, as given by George Albert, are extant.

8. *Doctrine and Covenants* 5.11, 25, 29, 34.

9. Joseph Knight, Sr., MS.

10. *Doctrine and Covenants* 6.18–23.

11. Ibid. 6.25; 8.1–3, 11.

12. Ibid. 9.7–8, 10.

13. *History of the Church*, I, 39–41.

14. Ibid., 42.

15. *Messenger and Advocate* 1 (October 1834), pp. 15–16.

16. See B. H. Roberts's editorial comment in *History of the Church*, I, 40–43 n.

17. MS by Joseph Knight, Jr., HDC.

18. David Whitmer, *An Address to All Believers in Christ* (Richmond, Missouri, 1887. Rpt. Concord, Calif.: Pacific Publishing Co., 1959), p. 30.

Chapter 6: THE MANUSCRIPT PUBLISHED

1. *Doctrine and Covenants* 17.5.

2. Whitmer told this to Kelley during the winter of 1881–82. "Letter from Elder W. H. Kelley," *The Saints Herald* 29 (March 1, 1882), 68–69.

3. *History of the Church*, I, 55.

4. Lucy Smith, p. 139.

5. *Messenger and Advocate* 2 (February 1836), 236–37.

6. *The Ensign of Liberty of the Church of Christ* (Kirtland, Ohio), I, January 1848.

7. Gregg, p. 99.

8. Thomas Ford, *A History of Illinois* (Chicago: S. C. Griggs & Co., 1854), p. 257.

9. S. Burnett to Br. Johnson, April 15, 1838. Joseph Smith Letter Books.

10. George A. Smith to Josiah Fleming, March 29, 1838. George A. Smith Letters, HDC.

11. Gregg, p. 37.

12. Huntington has a collection of Cowdery's letters.

13. For a well-documented discussion of Cowdery's testimonies from the Mormon point of view see Richard Lloyd Anderson, "The Second Witness of Priesthood Restoration," *Era*, September 1968, pp. 15–24. Cowdery's deathbed testimony is in *The Saints Herald* 35 (October 13, 1888).

14. Whitmer, p. 75.

15. Ibid., p. 31.

16. For an account of the fate of the original MS and facsimiles of some pages, see Dean C. Jessee, "The Original Book of Mormon Manuscript," *BYU Studies*, Spring 1970, pp. 259–78.

17. Lucy Smith, pp. 148–50.

18. Gregg, pp. 39–43.

19. *Doctrine and Covenants* 19.

20. A photo-reprint of the original 1830 edition of *The Book of Mormon* has been published under title of *Joseph Smith Begins His Work*, Vol. 1 (Salt Lake City: Modern Microfilm Company). A replica is also available from Herald House, Independence, Mo.

21. The signed agreement is in the Joseph Smith Senior file, HDC.

Chapter 7: THE BOOK OF MORMON

1. Richard Bushman made this point in a lecture at Brigham Young University in 1970.

2. *Painesville Telegraph*, March 15, 1831, p. 2, as quoted by Hill in "The Role of Christian Primitivism," p. 112.

3. Reed A. Stout (ed.), "Autobiography of Hosea Stout, 1810–1835," *Utah Historical Quarterly* 30 (Summer 1962), 243.

4. Journal of Jared Carter, MS, HDC, pp. 1–2. History of Zerah Pulsipher, MS, BYU Special Collections, pp. 5–7.

5. Parley Parker Pratt, ed., *Autobiography of Parley Parker Pratt* (1874; 3rd ed. Salt Lake City: Deseret Book Co., 1938), p. 37.

6. "Journal of Newel Knight," *Scraps of Biography, Tenth Book of the Faith Promoting Series* (Salt Lake City: Juvenile Instructor Office, 1883), p. 48.

7. Autobiography and Sketch of the life of Anson Call, MS, BYU Special Collections.

8. Jason Whitman, "The Book of Mormon," *The Unitarian*, January 1, 1834, pp. 40–50.

9. Brown cites "the author of the 'Phelps and Gorham Purchase.'" "Manchester in the Early Days," *Shortsville Enterprise Press*, March 11, 1904. MS file, BYU.

10. Walter Franklin Prince, "Psychological Tests for the Authorship of the Book of Mormon," *American Journal of Psychology* 28 (1917), 373–89.

11. Brodie, pp. 46–47.

12. For a brief discussion of the history of this belief see Frederick W. Hodge (ed.), *Handbook of American Indians North of Mexico* (1906; rpt. New York: Rowman and Littlefield, Inc., 1965), p. 775.

13. *Messenger and Advocate* 2 (December 1835), 229.

14. *History of the Church*, IV, 461.

15. *Gospel Reflector* 1 (March 1, 1841), 101.

16. Brown, loc. cit.

Chapter 8: THE EARLY CHURCH

1. In May 1834 the name was changed to "The Church of the Latter-day Saints." *History of the Church*, II, 62–63. In April 1838 it became "The Church of Jesus Christ of Latter-day Saints." *History of the Church*, III, 23–24 n.

2. Lucy Smith, p. 151.

3. Joseph Knight Sr., MS, HDC.

4. *Doctrine and Covenants* 21.1–5.

5. Whitmer, *Address*, p. 4.

6. Missionaries of the Church of Jesus Christ of L.D.S. set apart since 1830. Film, HDC.

7. Joseph Smith Letter Books, HDC.

8. Newel Knight, "Journal," p. 48.

9. *History of the Church*, I, 83.

10. Newel Knight, p. 54.

11. The Rev. John Sherer to the American Home Missionary Society, November, 1830. Collection of the Chicago Theological Seminary, Chicago, Illinois.

12. *History of the Church*, I, 94–95 n.

13. Ibid., 88–96. Also Newel Knight, pp. 55–61.

14. "A. W. B." letter to the editors, *Evangelical Magazine and Gospel Advocate* 2 (April 9, 1831).

15. *History of the Church*, I, 97; Newel Knight, p. 61.

16. *Doctrine and Covenants* 25.

17. Newel Knight, pp. 62–63.

18. *History of the Church*, I, 108.

Chapter 9: CONVERSION OF SIDNEY RIGDON

1. *History of the Church*, I, 105.

2. Whitmer, *Address*, p. 32.

3. *Doctrine and Covenants* 28.3, 6, 7.

4. Ibid. 29.8, 11.

5. Ibid. 28.9.

6. Newel Knight, p. 65.

7. *History of the Church*, I, 118.

8. John Wickliffe Rigdon, "The Life and Testimony of Sidney Rigdon," ed. Karl Keller, *Dialogue* 1 (Winter 1966), 23–24.

9. Ibid., p. 24.

10. Cowdery's speech to the Delawares and the chief's reply are in Pratt, *Autobiography*, pp. 54–56.

11. Joseph Smith Letter Books, letter 7, HDC.

12. *Messenger and Advocate*, 2 (October 1835).

13. Joseph's comment re Partridge is in *History of the Church*, I, 128. Emily Partridge's statement is from her MS, "What I Remember," Emily Dow Partridge Young papers, HDC, p. 5.

14. *History of the Church*, I, 129, 131.

15. Whitmer, *Address*, p. 35.

16. Ibid., p. 71.

Part Three: Ohio

Chapter 1: THE CHURCH IN TWO MAIN SETTLEMENTS

1. *History of the Church*, I, 154.

2. *Doctrine and Covenants* 42.30–36.

3. B. H. Roberts makes this observation, pointing out that Joseph Smith did not at any time pretend to the knowledge of ancient languages necessary to a translator of the Scriptures. *History of the Church*, I, 215 n.

4. Leonard J. Arrington, "James Gordon Bennett's 1831 Report on 'The Mormonites,' " *BYU Studies*, Spring 1970, pp. 353–64.

5. *History of the Church*, I, 189.

6. Joseph Knight, Sr., MS, HDC. Knight dates his wife's death as August 7 and her funeral as August 8.

7. Emily Partridge papers, pp. 7–8.

8. *Doctrine and Covenants* 72.11–13.

Chapter 2: TAR AND FEATHERS

1. Zebedee said this at a meeting of High Priests in Utah, February 5, 1878, as recorded by Thomas Matley, Ward Clerk. Papers of Zebedee Coltrin, journal call no. MS D747, HDC.

2. *History of the Church,* I, 226.

3. Ibid., 235.

4. Ibid., 270. Joseph's letter to Phelps is in HDC.

5. "Recollections of Joseph Smith," *Juvenile Instructor,* May 15, 1892, pp. 303–4.

6. *History of the Church,* I, 247.

7. Ibid., 245–53.

8. *Doctrine and Covenants* 78.

9. Hayden, *Early History of the Disciples' Church in the Western Reserve,* p. 221, as quoted by William Alexander Linn, *The Story of the Mormons* (New York: Macmillan, 1923), pp. 134–35.

10. S. F. Whitney, Newel's brother, said the Johnson boys were angry because Joseph and Sidney urged their father to "let them have his property." *Naked Truths About Mormonism,* Vol. I, January 1888. Luke Johnson told about the intention to castrate Joseph in his "History of Luke Johnson," *Deseret News,* Vol. 8. Brodie reports the story about Eli, p. 119.

11. Genealogical Archives, Salt Lake City, record that Nancy was sealed to Joseph by Orson, July 31, 1857. Brodie, p. 440.

12. "Orson Pratt's Testimony," *Historical Review* 6 (July 1887), 230.

13. Lucy Smith. Preliminary MS, HDC.

14. *Doctrine and Covenants* 82.11–12, 17.

15. Joseph's letter is in the Mormon Collection, Chicago Historical Society. Quoted by permission.

Chapter 3: PROGRESS AND PERIL IN KIRTLAND

1. Used by permission of the Library and Archives, Reorganized Church of Jesus Christ of Latter Day Saints, The Auditorium, Independence, Missouri.

2. Brigham Young, *Journal of Discourses,* I, 215, as quoted by Linn, p. 143.

3. *Millennial Star* 25 (1863), 439.

4. Ibid.

5. *Deseret News,* June 6, 1877.

6. *Doctrine and Covenants* 87.

7. *History of the Church,* I, 324, and Joseph Smith to the Brethren in Zion, April 21, 1833, Ibid., 340–41.

8. The Utah church has always used the King James Bible with the reservation, "insofar as it has been translated correctly." The Reorganized Church has published Joseph's revision and uses it regularly in congregations.

9. *Doctrine and Covenants* 89.

10. Eber D. Howe, *Mormonism Unvailed* (Painesville, Ohio, 1834), pp. 232–68, as reproduced in Brodie, pp. 410–18.

Chapter 4: CONFLICT IN ZION

1. *History of the Church,* I, 372–73 and nn.; 392.

2. Emily Partridge papers.

3. Phelps's articles and the manifesto are published in *History of the Church,* I, 374–79.

4. That Boggs had contended with Mormons for land in Jackson County is stated by William Earl Parrish, "The Life of David Rice Atchison," Diss. Univ.

of Missouri 1955, p. 18. The quote by Boggs is in *History of the Church,* I, 391–92.

5. Lucy Smith, p. 198.

6. *Ensign of Liberty of the Church of Christ* (Kirtland, Ohio) I (March 1847), 4.

7. "no overt acts of transgression [by the Mormons against the non-Mormons in Jackson County] were being committed . . ." *History of Jackson County, Missouri* (Kansas City: Union Historical Company, 1881) as quoted in *History of the Church,* I, 392 n.

8. "Joseph Smith Jr.'s Book for Record," November 13, 1833. HDC.

9. *History of the Church,* I, 448–51.

10. Ibid., 457–58.

11. *Doctrine and Covenants* 101.

12. U. S. (Courts) Circuit Court. Missouri. Legal Proceedings . . . Edward Partridge Vs. Samuel D. Lucas & Others, p. 5

Chapter 5: THE SAINTS RECRUITED

1 *Doctrine and Covenants* 103.15–19.

2. The Saints' petition to the President and the War Department's reply are reproduced in *History of the Church,* I, 483–85, 493.

3. A copy of the brochure is with the Letters of Sidney Rigdon, HDC.

4. *Ensign of Liberty* I (March 1847), 4.

5. Oliver Cowdery to W. W. Phelps, March 30, 1834, Huntington.

6. The roster of those who marched in Zion's Camp, men, women and children, is in *History of the Church,* II, 183–85.

7. This and other information about George A. Smith in this chapter are from his History of George Albert Smith, MS, HDC. BYU has two copies. Pagination differs.

8. *Times and Seasons,* 6, p. 788, as quoted in *History of the Church,* II, 80 n.

9. George A. Smith, History.

Chapter 6: DISASTER IN ZION'S CAMP

1. *The Evening and Morning Star,* 2, pp. 333, 334, as reproduced in *History of the Church,* II, 92–83, n.

2. The account of hired men and the flag is in *History of the Church,* II, 121. The letter is John Chauncey to Francis Dallam, "A Clay Countian's Letters of 1834," *Missouri Historical Review* 45 (July 1951), 353.

3. Dunklin's letter and most of the following account of Zion's Camp and events in Missouri are from *History of the Church,* II, 84–126.

4. *Doctrine and Covenants* 105.

5. Reed Peck Manuscript, September 18, 1839, p. 82, Mormon File, Box 10, Huntington.

6. Sketch of the Life of James Henry Rollins, dictated by himself, 1898. Utah Historical Society.

7. George A. Smith, History.

8. Primitive Mormonism, Personal Narrative by Mr. Benjamin Winchester,

in "First Half Century of Mormonism," papers compiled by Charles L. Woodward, 1880. NYPL Manuscript Division.

9. McLellin to Joseph Smith III, July 1872. RLDS.

10. *Ensign of Liberty* I (March 1847), p. 5.

11. Joseph Young, Sen., *History of the Organization of the Seventies* (Salt Lake: Deseret News Steam Printing Establishment, 1878), p. 1. Huntington has a copy.

12. *History of the Church*, II, xxiv.

Chapter 7: LIFE IN KIRTLAND

1. *History of the Church*, II, 142–60.

2. *Doctrine and Covenants* 104.

3. Journal History, HDC.

4. Benjamin F. Johnson to George S. Gibbs, 1903, pp. 11, 13–14, TS, Mormon File, Box 7, Huntington. This is a facsimile.

5. The Cowdery letters, Huntington.

6. Primitive Mormonism, Personal Narrative by Mr. Benjamin Winchester, in "First Half Century of Mormonism," papers compiled by Charles L. Woodward, 1880, p. 195. NYPL Manuscript Division.

7. Johnson to Gibbs, p. 11.

8. Ibid., p. 14.

9. *History of the Church*, II, 245–47.

10. Testimony given in Temple Lot Case, p. 309, as quoted in The Book of Mormon and Plural Marriage, facsimile of a TS, Mormon File, Box 3, Huntington.

11. Ibid., pp. 320–21.

12. Kirtland Council Minute Book, Sept. 7, 1837, p. 239. HDC.

13. *History of the Church*, II, 320.

14. Ibid., 377.

15. Ibid., 301.

16. The foregoing quotes are from Ibid., 368, 385ff., 390, 397. For an account in detail of Joseph's studies in Hebrew and results, see Louis C. Zucker, "Joseph Smith as a Student of Hebrew," *Dialogue* 3 (Summer 1968), 41–55.

17. *History of the Church*, II, 236.

18. Ibid., 238. John Whitmer said that Joseph translated the records "by the revelation of Jesus Christ." "The Book of John Whitmer Kept by Commandment." MS, p. 76, as quoted in Richard P. Howard, "A Tentative Approach to the Book of Abraham," *Dialogue* 3 (Summer 1968), 89 n. 1.

19. *History of the Church*, II, 388.

20. Richard A. Parker, "The Joseph Smith Papyri: A Preliminary Report," *Dialogue* 3 (Summer 1968), 86.

21. John A. Wilson, "The Joseph Smith Egyptian Papyri; A Summary Report," *Dialogue* 3 (Summer 1968), 70.

22. Howard, p. 92.

23. Hugh Nibley, "Phase One," *Dialogue* 3 (Summer 1968), 99, 101. For a preliminary investigation of the subject of the papyri, with photocopies, see John A. Wilson et al., "The Joseph Smith Egyptian Papyri; Translations and Interpretations," *Dialgue* 3 (Summer 1968), 67–105.

Chapter 8: PROGRESS IN KIRTLAND; PROBLEMS IN CLAY

1. Joseph made occasional references to enjoying wine at weddings. See *History of the Church*, II, 369, 378. He was quick, however, to speak out against intemperance, saying, "How long, O Lord, will this monster intemperance find its victims on the earth!" Ibid., 406.

2. *Doctrine and Covenants* 110.2–9.

3. *History of the Church*, II, 444–45.

4. Durward T. Stokes (ed.), "The Wilson Letters 1835–1849," *Missouri Historical Review* 60 (July 1966), 505.

5. *History of the Church*, II, 449–52.

6. Stokes, pp. 506, 508–9.

7. *History of the Church*, II, 455–46.

8. Ibid., 456–61.

9. Ibid., 461–62.

10. *The History of Daviess County Missouri* (Kansas City, Mo: Birdsall & Dean, 1882).

Chapter 9: THE ANTI-BANKING COMPANY

1. August C. Bolino, *The Development of the American Economy* (Columbus, Ohio: Charles E. Merrill Books, 1961), p. 188, as quoted in Scott H. Partridge, "The Failure of the Kirtland Safety Society," *BYU Studies*, Summer 1972, p. 443.

2. Paul Studenski and Herman E. Krooss, *Financial History of the United States* (New York: McGraw-Hill Book Company, 1963), p. 107, as quoted in Partridge, p. 443.

3. *Ensign of Liberty* I (March 1847), 7–8.

4. John Wickliffe Rigdon, p. 28.

5. Minutes of the meeting are in *History of the Church*, II, 470–72.

6. For an analysis of the Kirtland bank in the economic context of its times, see Partridge, pp. 437–54.

7. The records of the Kirtland bank were thought to have been destroyed in the fire which occurred in the office, but the stock ledger was recently discovered in the Mormon collection of the Chicago Historical Society. The handwriting has been verified by Dean C. Jessee as that of Warren Parrish. For an analysis of the ledger and some photocopies of its pages, see D. Paul Sampson and Larry T. Wimmer, "The Kirtland Safety Society: The Stock Ledger Book and the Bank Failure," *BYU Studies*, Summer 1972, pp. 427–36.

8. Wilford Woodruff Journal. The Third Book of Willford [sic] for 1837. HDC.

9. Book of John Whitmer, typewritten copy, HDC, p. 39.

10. John Jay Knox, *A History of Banking in the United States* (New York: Bradford Rhodes & Company, 1903), p. 315, as cited by Partridge, p. 445.

11. Knox, p. 677, as cited by Partridge, p. 448.

12. *History of the Church*, II, 479.

13. Woodruff, April 6, 1837.

14. *History of the Church*, II, 480.

15. Willard Richards to Hepsy, January 20, 1837. Willard Richards letters 1821–43. HDC.

16. Woodruff, April 9, 1837.

17. *History of the Church*, II, 486, 448 n. According to Brodie, pp. 202, 203, 203 n., Warren Parrish took from Joseph's files a letter by Parley to Joseph of May 23, 1837, asking him to take back three lots Joseph had sold him for $2,000, which had not cost the prophet one tenth of that amount. Parley asked to be reimbursed the $75 he had paid and to be relieved of his note for the rest, which he said Joseph had turned over to the bank for collection. Sidney Rigdon was now demanding not only the three lots but Parley's house as well. Parley accused Joseph of "taking advantage of your brother by an undue religious influence." The letter was sent to *Zion's Watchman* by Parrish, and published there March 24, 1838. Parley said in the *Elders' Journal*, August 1838, that that letter was not a perfect copy, but he confessed that he had written to Joseph "in great severity."

18. Pratt, *Autobiography*, p. 168.

19. *History of the Church*, II, 488.

20. Woodruff, April 2, 1837.

21. *History of the Church*, II, 489.

22. Heber C. Kimball journal, as quoted in Edward W. Tullidge (ed.), *The Women of Mormondom* (New York: Tullidge & Crandall, 1877), pp. 112–13.

23. Vilate Kimball, in Tullidge, pp. 114–15.

24. Oliver Cowdery Docket Book, Kirtland, Geauga Co., Ohio, p. 16. Huntington.

25. George Albert Smith is quoted by Sampson and Wimmer, p. 432.

26. Benjamin F. Johnson, *My Life's Review* (Independence, Mo.: Zion's Printing and Publishing Co., 1947), p. 29.

27. Leonard J. Arrington, *Great Basin Kingdom* (1958; rpt. Lincoln, Nebraska: Univ. of Nebraska Press, 1966), pp. 427–28, n. 43.

28. Sampson and Wimmer, p. 436.

29. Brodie, p. 198, and Arrington, p. 427, n. 43.

30. Nathan Tanner Biographical History, 1831–1846, pp. 23–24. MS, BYU.

31. Warren Parrish, letter of February 5, 1838, in *Painesville Republican*, February 15, 1838.

32. Newel K. Whitney to his brother, S. F., September 9, 1843. Whitney Collection, BYU.

33. Lucy Smith, pp. 212–13.

34. *History of the Church*, II, 515–18.

35. John Smith letter file, HDC.

36. *History of the Church*, III, 1.

37. *Fort Madison Patriot*, Vol. I, No. 2, April 4, 1838, p. 1, repeats a story from the Cleveland *Gazette* about the disintegration of Mormon society in Kirtland, with "Reformers" left in possession of the town.

38. John Smith and Don C. Smith to George A. Smith, January 15, 1838, John Smith letter file, HDC.

39. *Elders' Journal*, July 1838, p. 24.

40. Parrish, loc. cit., and Brodie, p. 207.

41. Johnson, p. 29.

42. John Smith and Don C. Smith, loc. cit.

43. George A. Smith Letters, HDC.

44. For an account of the decline of Kirtland after the departure of the Kirtland Camp see Davis Bitton, "The Waning of Mormon Kirtland," *BYU Studies*, Summer 1972, pp. 455–64.

45. Joseph Smith papers, HDC. Joseph probably hoped to regain possession of the temple, which was in the hands of the dissenters. In this letter Joseph asked Granger, who was gravely ill, to turn over the affairs to Isaac Galland, who would be in Kirtland shortly. Granger died soon afterward and Galland proved dishonest.

Part Four: Missouri

Chapter 1: MORE TROUBLE IN MISSOURI

1. *History of the Church*, III, 35.

2. Book of John Whitmer, p. 39.

3. *History of the Church*, III, 180–82.

4. "Remainder of Dr. Avard's testimony," Notes from *Missouri Intelligencer and Boon's Lick Advertiser*, 1831–34, James O. Broadhead papers, Missouri Historical Society, St. Louis.

5. *Document Containing the . . . Evidence Given Before the Hon. Austin A. King . . . 1838* (Fayette, Mo: By Order of the General Assembly, 1841), pp. 57–59.

6. John Corrill, *A Brief History of the Church of Christ of Latter Day Saints . . .* (St. Louis: By the author, 1839), p. 31.

7. Lyman Wight quoted in Rollin J. Britton, *Early Days on the Grand River and the Mormon War* (Columbia, Mo.: By the State Historical Society, 1920), p. 86.

8. *History of the Church*, III, 181–82.

9. Reed Peck and John Cleminson maintained that they were present at the meeting when Joseph said this. *Document Containing the . . . Evidence Given Before the Hon. Austin A. King*, pp. 114–20.

10. Quoted by Brodie, p. 216.

11. Reed Peck MS, pp. 88–89. Mormon File, Box 10, Huntington.

12. Ibid., p. 92.

13. Ibid., p. 100.

14. *Oration Delivered by Mr. S. Rigdon on the 4th of July, 1838, at Far West, Missouri* (Far West, Mo.: The Journal Office, 1838). Chicago Historical Society has a copy. See also John Wickliffe Rigdon, pp. 30–31.

15. Ebenezer Robinson, *The Return* (Davis City, Iowa), I (1889), 170.

16. *Missouri Republican*, November 13, 1838, and *Missouri Argus*, September 27, 1838.

17. House of Representatives, 25th Congress, 3d Session, Doc. No. 42 "Memorial of Ephraim Owens Jr. . . . Asking of Congress to afford protection to the people called Mormons," pp. 1–2.

18. *An Appeal to the American People*, 2nd Ed. (Cincinnati: Shepard & Stearns, 1840), p. 16. This purports to be "by an Authority of the Church." Linn, p. 214, says it is by Sidney Rigdon.

19. Journal History, August 6, 1838. HDC.

20. John Taylor, *A short account of the MURDERS, ROBERIES, BURN-INGS . . . by the MOB and MILITIA of the State of Missouri, upon the LAT-TER DAY SAINTS* (Springfield [?], Ill., 1839), p. 2. The same text with slightly different spelling and punctuation is in *History of the Church*, III, 59–60.

21. September 22, 1838.

22. Reminiscences of Zadoc Knapp Judd, p. 6. Photo of TS, Mormon Collection, Huntington.

23. *History of the Church*, III, 150.

24. Ibid., 157.

25. Judd, p. 7.

26. Testimony of Hyrum Smith before the municipal court at Nauvoo, June 30, 1843, published in Lucy Smith, pp. 229–30.

27. For Joseph's state of mind see John Corrill's testimony in *Senate Document No. 189*, 26th Congress, 2nd Session, 1841 (photocopy, Salt Lake City: Modern Microfilm Co.), p. 13. This pamphlet, an excerpt from *Document Containing the . . . Evidence Given Before the Hon. Austin A. King,* is more accessible than the original. Joseph's speech is quoted in the Reed Peck Ms, pp. 109–10. Peck's quote of it is reproduced also in L. B. Cake, *Peepstone Joe and the Peck Manuscript* (New York: By the Author, 1899), p. 109. It does not appear in *History of the Church*.

28. *Missouri Republican,* November 9, 1838. See also testimony of William W. Phelps in *Senate Document 189,* p. 45.

29. Joseph and Hyrum were both wary of the charges that they had made war on the state and were careful to record that Wight had been ordered by Parks to go out against the mob. Hyrum, in Lucy Smith, p. 230, and *History of the Church*, III, 163.

30. Reed Peck MS, p. 111.

31. Parley P. Pratt, *Late Persecution of the Church of Jesus Christ of Latter Day Saints* (New York: J. W. Harrison, printer, 1840), p. 65. Huntington has a copy. See also James Henry Rollins, p. 5.

32. Albert P. Rockwood, October 29, 1838. Yale Univ. Library.

33. Testimony of George Hinkle, *Senate Document 189,* p. 24. Testimony of Thomas B. Marsh, *Document Containing the . . . Evidence Given Before the Hon. Austin A. King,* p. 59. William Swartzell, *Mormonism Exposed* (Pekin, Ohio: By the author, 1840), p. 23.

34. Peter H. Burnett, *An Old California Pioneer* (Oakland: Biobooks, 1946), pp. 34–35, and Leland Gentry, "A History of the Latter-day Saints in Northern Missouri from 1836 to 1839," Diss. Brigham Young Univ., 1965, pp. 279–83.

35. John Wickliffe Rigdon, p. 32. See also *History of the Church*, III, 169–71.

36. Joseph Thorp, *Early Days in the West Along the Missouri One Hundred Years Ago* (Liberty, Mo.: Irving Gilmer, rpt. 1924), pp. 85–86.

37. *History of the Church*, III, 175.

38. Ibid., 175.

Chapter 2: THE FALL OF FAR WEST

1. James Henry Rollins, pp. 5–6.

2. According to Major Reburn S. Holcombe, quoted by Rollin J. Britton, *Early Days on the Grand River and the Mormon War* (Columbia, Mo.: The State Historical Society, 1920), p. 39. Joseph Young said that according to the raiders' own count, they were 240 in number. *History of the Church,* III, 184. Holcombe said there were 200. Britton, p. 38.

3. Amanda Smith's personal narrative of these events, dated April 18, 1839, is in *History of the Church,* III, 323–25. The report about Isaac Laney is in Journal History, May 6, 1839.

4. Names of the Mormon dead and wounded are in *History of the Church,* III, 186 and 325–36, n. Account of the wounded raiders is in the same place. Joseph Young said the number of shots was the raiders' own count. Ibid., 186.

5. Ibid., 325.

6. John Wickliffe Rigdon, p. 34.

7. Ibid., p. 187. Corrill, p. 42, and Gentry, p. 473.

8. Corrill, p. 40.

9. Rollins, p. 6.

10. Biographical Sketch of Luman Andros Shurtliff, 1807–64, p. 35. BYU.

11. Mrs. Joseph Horne. Migration and Settlement of the Latter Day Saints (Bancroft Collection on Mormonism, Univ. of California at Berkeley), p. 7.

12. Corrill, p. 44.

13. Ibid., p. 42.

14. Judd, p. 9.

15. John Wickliffe Rigdon, p. 35.

16. Pratt, *Autobiography,* pp. 186–88.

17. *History of Caldwell and Livingston Counties Missouri* (St. Louis: National Historical Co., 1886), p. 137. Peter H. Burnett, with others of Clay County, told Doniphan that the troops from Clay County would support him in his stand against Lucas. Burnett believed that since the prisoners were not members of any legal military organization they were not accountable to military law. He wrote that he was sure, nevertheless, that if it had not been for Doniphan and the others from Clay County, the prisoners would have been executed. Burnett, pp. 37–38.

18. Rollins, pp. 6–7.

19. Horne, p. 7.

20. Corrill, p. 44.

21. *History of the Church,* VI, 128.

22. Report of General S. D. Lucas to Governor Boggs. *History of the Church,* III, 195–99.

23. Joseph Smith's Journal as kept by Willard Richards, December 30, 1842, HDC. Joseph told this, recalling events in Far West, while he was in Springfield to await trial before Judge Pope.

24. Lucy Smith, pp. 250–51.

25. *History of the Church,* III, 202–4.

Chapter 3: IN JAIL AT LIBERTY

1. Pratt, *Autobiography,* pp. 191–92.

2. *History of the Church,* III, 200–1.

3. Joseph Smith to Emma, November 4, 1838. Used by permission of the Library and Archives, Reorganized Church of Jesus Christ of Latter Day Saints, The Auditorium, Independence, Missouri.

4. Burnett, *An Old California Pioneer,* pp. 39–40.

5. *Journal of Discourses,* XVII, p. 92, as quoted in Hyrum Andrus, *Joseph Smith Man and Seer* (Salt Lake City: Deseret Book Co., 1960), p. 5.

6. *History of the Church,* III, 328.

7. Hyrum's statement is in Lucy Smith, p. 240.

8. Clark's report to Governor Boggs is in *History of the Church,* III, 206–7.

9. Joseph Smith to Emma, November 12, 1838. Used by permission of the Library and Archives, Reorganized Church of Jesus Christ of Latter Day Saints, The Auditorium, Independence, Missouri.

10. Pratt, *Autobiography,* pp. 210–11.

11. Lucy Smith, p. 241.

12. Burnett, pp. 47–48. He added that King grew more mellow in later life.

13. *Missouri Republican,* January 15, 1839, p. 2.

14. Ibid., January 23, 1839, p. 2.

15. *Nauvoo Neighbor,* June 12, 1844, p. 255.

16. Journal History, June 2, 1839.

17. *History of the Church,* III, 212 n.

18. Ibid., 209–11, 418–19; also Lucy Smith, pp. 241–42.

19. *History of the Church,* III, 213.

20. See the apology in the introduction to the official state publication of the hearing, *Document Containing the . . . Evidence Given Before the Hon. Austin A. King.*

21. December 24, 1838, and subsequent issues through January 1839.

22. *History of the Church,* III, 213–14.

23. The committee said that they considered it injudicious to predicate a report upon the documents purporting to be copies of the evidence taken before the court in Richmond, which evidence they considered "not of the character which should be desired" for a fair investigation, and the documents had not been satisfactorily certified. The report also said that the evidence was to be used in further trials of the Mormons in circuit court, and if the committee examined it, the two branches of government "may be brought into collision"; and that if the committee concluded and published a report that the accused were guilty, their right to an impartial trial would be placed in jeopardy. *Document Containing the . . . Evidence Given Before the Hon. Austin A. King,* pp. 1–4. The report is reproduced in full in *History of the Church,* III, 235–38.

24. The Mormons' petition appears in *History of the Church,* III, 217–24. For account of its reception, see Ibid., 238–40.

25. Ibid., 330.

26. Prescindia's comment and Joseph's letter are reproduced in Tullidge, pp. 210–12. Joseph's letter is also in *History of the Church,* III, 285–86.

27. *History of the Church*, III, 294, 304. See also other letters to and from the prophet during this time, Ibid., 272–305.

28. Joseph Smith papers, HDC.

29. "Memoirs of President Joseph Smith, 1832–1914," *The Saints Herald* 81 (Nov. 6, 1934), 1414.

30. Joseph Smith papers, HDC.

31. *History of the Church*, III, 321 n.

32. Wilford Woodruff Journal, April 26, 1839. HDC. The minutes of the meeting of the apostles are published in *History of the Church*, III, 336–39.

33. May 1, 1839. W. W. Phelps Papers, HDC.

34. Lucy Smith, p. 248.

35. *History of the Church*, III, 329–30.

Part Five: Illinois

Chapter 1: A NEW START IN ILLINOIS

1. Clyde E. Buckingham, "Mormonism in Illinois," *Journal of the Illinois State Historical Society* 32 (June 1939), 175.

2. D. B. Huntington's Statement of Joseph's Landing at Quincy, April 22, 1839. MS. Vol. 12415. HDC.

3. *History of the Church*, III, 265.

4. Ibid., 298.

5. For an account of life in early Commerce as reflected in the letters of the youthful Daniel H. Wells, see Maureen Ursenbach Beecher, "Letters from the Frontier: Commerce, Nauvoo, and Salt Lake City," *Journal of Mormon History* 2 (1975), 35–51.

6. "Latter-Day-ism, No. 2," *Hawk-Eye and Iowa Patriot* (Burlington, Iowa), October 7, 1841, p. 2.

7. *History of the Church*, III, 342.

8. Ibid., 378.

9. John Wickliffe Rigdon, p. 39. There has been debate over whether or not "Nauvoo" is actually a Hebrew word. Zucker says it is in the Hebrew manual that Joseph's Hebrew teacher, Seixus, published in 1834, in his list of anomalous forms used in the Hebrew Bible, p. 111. A verb meaning "are beautiful," it can be used of a person, place or thing. Louis C. Zucker, "Joseph Smith As a Student of Hebrew," *Dialogue* 3 (Summer 1968), 48.

10. History and Journal of Jesse W. Crosby, TS, p. 7. Huntington.

11. E. H. Ackerknecht, *Malaria in the Upper Mississippi Valley, 1760–1900* (Baltimore, 1945), as cited by Robert Bruce Flanders, *Nauvoo: Kingdom on the Mississippi* (Urbana: Univ. of Illinois Press, 1965), p. 53 n. The disease was known to be endemic to swampy areas, but its carrier, the anopheles mosquito, was not yet identified. Quinine was not yet generally used. Flanders suggests that typhoid and typhus might have been prevalent also, but not cholera, which was not known in that area between 1834 and 1849. T. Edgar Lyon, historian of Nauvoo Restoration, Inc., believes that the settlers in that area might have been affected also with dengue fever, undulant fever and typhoid fever, any of which they might have described as "chills and fever." Beecher, p. 41, n. 14.

12. Wilford Woodruff, *Leaves from my Journal*, ch. xix, as quoted in *History of the Church*, IV, 4 n.

13. Wilford Woodruff Journal. The Second Book of Willford [sic] for 1839. HDC.

14. Ibid.

15. Joseph Smith to Emma, November 9, 1839. Used by permission of the Library and Archives, Reorganized Church of Jesus Christ of Latter Day Saints, The Auditorium, Independence, Missouri.

16. *History of the Church*, IV, 23–24, 41–42.

17. Ibid., 39–41.

18. Ibid., 41.

19. Ibid., 78–79. Davis's middle initial was "L" rather than "S," as there published. Joseph mistook Davis for a congressman, but Richard Anderson has discovered that he was a reporter for an eastern newspaper. My thanks to Dean C. Jessee for this information.

20. Ibid., 80.

21. Ibid., 89, and "A Glance at the Mormons" (from the *Alexandra Gazette*), the Alton *Telegraph*, Nov. 14, 1840, p. 2.

Chapter 2: THE RISE OF NAUVOO

1. Hyrum's statement, dated November 26, 1841, is in *History of the Church*, IV, 460–61.

2. John and Clarissa Smith to George A., June 17, 1840. John Smith file, HDC.

3. Statements by the kidnapped men, the protest of Nauvoo citizens and the memorial to Governor Carlin are in *History of the Church*, IV, 154–60; 180–81. A statement sent to Governor Boggs by citizens of Tully, July 24, 1840, setting forth their account of the affair, is in the Missouri Historical Society, St. Louis. An account of the affair in some detail, although not well documented, is given by Samuel W. Taylor in his *Nightfall at Nauvoo* (New York: Macmillan, 1971), pp. 56–58, 61–63.

4. Lucy Smith, pp. 265–70.

5. *History of the Church*, IV, 191–97.

6. Ibid., 190.

7. "Narrative of James Greenhalgh, Cotton Spinner, Egerton, near Bolton-le-Moors," *The Struggle*, No. 36 (1842), n.p. HDC.

8. Milo M. Quaife (ed.), *An English Settler in Pioneer Wisconsin; the Letters of Edwin Bottomly, 1844–1850. Publications of the State Historical Society of Wisconsin: Collections* (Madison), 25 (1918), 90–91, as quoted in Flanders, pp. 88–89.

9. *History of the Church*, IV, 272–73.

10. Journal of Howard Coray, TS, 1961, p. 7. BYU.

11. *History of the Church*, V, xix.

12. *Doctrine and Covenants* 124.17.

13. *History of the Church*, IV, 249.

14. "An Act to Incorporate the City of Nauvoo," is published in *History of the Church*, IV, 239–45.

15. Flanders, pp. 96–98. In naming the powers of the City Council, the

Nauvoo charter, Section 13, said that the council was "to exercise such other legislative powers as are conferred on the city council of the city of Springfield." See Springfield charter Article 1, Sections 4, 5; Article II, Sections 1, 2, 12; Article V, Section 36; Article VI, Section 8; and Nauvoo charter, Sections 2, 3, 4, 5, 13 and 17.

16. Laws of the State of Illinois passed by the Eleventh General Assembly, Special Sessions of 1839, pp. 6–15, and Laws . . . Twelfth General Assembly, pp. 52–57.

17. Bennett's inaugural address, published in *Times and Seasons,* 2, No. 8, p. 316, is also in *History of the Church,* IV, 288–92.

18. Ralph V. Chamberlin, *The University of Utah: A History of Its First Hundred Years 1850 to 1950* (Salt Lake City: Univ. of Utah Press, 1960), pp. 3–4.

19. The writer is anonymous, but describes himself as from Montrose, Iowa. His article, printed in the Alton *Telegraph,* November 14, 1840, was from the *Alexandra Gazette,* n.d.

20. Buckingham, pp. 182–83.

21. The organization and character of the Legion are described in *History of the Church,* IV, 353–56. See also *The Revised Laws of the Nauvoo Legion, from the Constitution of the United States.* By authority. (Nauvoo, Ill.: John Taylor, printer, 1844).

22. The boys' corps is described briefly in Jesse Nathaniel Smith, *Six Decades in the Early West* (Provo: Jesse N. Smith Family Assn., 1970), p. 8.

23. *History of the Church,* V, 383–84.

24. Daniel J. Boorstin, *The Americans: The Colonial Experience* (New York: Random House, 1958), pp. 345–52.

25. John Corrill quoted the prophet to that effect. See *Senate Document 189,* p. 12.

26. John C. Bennett, *The History of the Saints: Or An Exposé of Joe Smith and Mormonism* (Boston: Leland & Whiting, 1842), p. 212.

27. Letter of John Nevius, May 2, 1841, Stanley Kimball Collection, Southern Illinois Univ.

Chapter 3: NAUVOO FLOURISHES

1. *In Memoriam: Thomas Coke Sharp.* [Carthage, Illinois? 1894?] Huntington.

2. The Record of Norton Jacobs [or Jacob]. Mormon Collection, Huntington.

3. William recorded his impression a year later in *The Wasp,* April 23, 1842, p. 2.

4. *History of the Church,* IV, 331.

5. Ibid., 332.

6. George R. Gayler, "The Attempts of the State of Missouri to Extradite Joseph Smith, 1841–1843," *Northwest Missouri State College Studies,* 19 (June 1, 1955), 3–18.

7. *History of the Church,* IV, 366–71.

8. Flanders, p. 71.

9. Flanders, p. 42.

10. Hotchkiss's letter and Joseph's reply are in *History of the Church,* IV, 405–7.

11. Joseph's postscript is not included in the letter as published in the preceding reference. The original letter is in the Illionis State Library. Huntington has a photocopy.

12. *History of the Church,* IV, 430–33.

13. Joseph's note and Galland's reply are in the Joseph Smith papers, HDC.

14. James Arlington Bennet to Lieut. Gen. Smith, February 20, 1843. Used by permission of the Library and Archives, Reorganized Church of Jesus Christ of Latter Day Saints, The Auditorium, Independence, Missouri.

15. March 17 (?), 1843. Historical Society of Pennsylvania. HDC has a copy.

16. *History of the Church,* IV, 449.

17. James M. Adams to Joseph Smith, November 16, 1842. Whitney Collection, BYU.

18. "Baptism for the Dead," editorial in *Times and Seasons,* as reprinted in *History of the Church,* IV, 595–99. The quotations are on pp. 598, 599.

19. "The Temple," in Ibid., 608–10.

Chapter 4: THE FRIEND TURNED ENEMY

1. *History of the Church,* V, 4.

2. Ibid., 71–73.

3. The original statement from Joseph Smith to James Sloan is in the Joseph Smith papers, HDC. It is reproduced in Bennett, p. 40. A copy of Sloan's notice about Bennett's withdrawal, dated May 17, 1842, is also in the Joseph Smith papers, HDC. The original was given to Bennett.

4. Bennett's resignation, dated May 17, 1842, is in the John C. Bennett file, HDC.

5. *History of the Church,* V, 13.

6. Ibid., 18–19, 32.

7. Ibid., 35–40.

8. Bennett, p. 40.

9. *History of the Church,* V, 74.

10. Wilhelm Wyl, *Mormon Portraits* (Salt Lake City, 1886), p. 61. According to Joseph III, however, Sarah denied to him that his father had ever said an improper word to her. "Memoirs of President Joseph Smith," *The Saints Herald,* January 22, 1935, p. 109, as quoted by Brodie, p. 316 n.

11. *History of the Church,* V, 138.

12. Reva Stanley, *A Biography of Parley P. Pratt; the Archer of Paradise* (Caldwell, Idaho: Caxton Printers, Ltd., 1937), p. 158.

13. Minutes of the Council of Twelve, in box labeled "High Council Meetings, etc., Conference and Public Meetings," HDC.

14. Parley P. Pratt to "Dear Cousin" [John Van Cott in New York], May 7, 1843. Orson Pratt papers, HDC. Orson's comments were attached to Parley's letter.

15. John Wickliffe Rigdon, p. 39, n. 57.

16. Bennet's letter is in the Reorganized Church Library.

17. Journal History, HDC.

18. John E. Page papers, HDC.
19. Ibid.

Chapter 5: THE PROPHET IN HIDING

1. Thomas Gregg, *The Prophet of Palmyra* (New York: John B. Alden, Publisher, 1890), pp. 165–66.
2. *History of the Church*, IV, 479.
3. *Times and Seasons* 3 (March 15, 1842).
4. Thomas Ford, *A History of Illinois from Its Commencement as a State in 1814 to 1847* (Chicago: S. C. Griggs & Co., 1854), pp. 271–78.
5. *Reports Made to Senate and House of Representatives of the State of Illinois at their Session Begun at Springfield, December 5, 1842*, Vol. I (Springfield: Wm. Walters, printer, 1842), pp. 127–28.
6. James Elder Armstrong, *Life of a Woman Pioneer . . . Elsie Strawn Armstrong . . .* (Chicago [John F. Higgins Ptg. Co.], 1931), pp. 59–60.
7. William M. Boggs, "A Short Biographical Sketch of Lilburn W. Boggs, by His Son," *Missouri Historical Review* 4 (1910) 108, as quoted in George R. Gayler, "The Attempts of the State of Missouri to Extradite Joseph Smith, 1841–1843," *Northwest Missouri State College Studies* 19 (June 1, 1955), 8.
8. Perry McCandless, *A History of Missouri*, Vol. II, 1820–1860 (Columbia: Univ. of Missouri Press, 1972), p. 121.
9. *Hawk-Eye and Iowa Patriot*, July 21, 1842.
10. Bennett, p. 283.
11. Joseph's statement to the municipal court and a copy of Carlin's writ are in Joseph Smith papers, HDC.
12. The ordinance is reproduced in *History of the Church*, V, 87–88.
13. Ibid., 92, 167.
14. Ibid., 106–9.
15. Ibid., 103–5.
16. Ibid, 110.
17. See Chapter 9, Part Five, in this work for text of this revelation.
18. Joseph Smith papers, HDC.
19. *History of the Church*, V, 108.
20. William Taylor's account is reproduced in "Joseph Smith the Prophet," *Young Woman's Journal* 17 (December 1906), 547.
21. *Doctrine and Covenants* 233.1, 5, 6, 8, 15, 18, 19, 24.
22. The letters are reproduced in *History of the Church* V, 115–17; 153–55.
23. *Niles National Register*, October 1, 1842, and *Warsaw Signal*, September 17, 1842, both as quoted in Gayler, p. 11 and p. 11, n. 41.

Chapter 6: TWO AFFAIRS IN SPRINGFIELD

1. *History of the Church*, IV, 594–98.
2. An itemized list of Joseph's Nauvoo debts, totaling $73,066.38, is given by Brodie, p. 266 n.
3. For a study of Joseph's attempts to obtain bankruptcy and related litigation, in particular U.S. efforts to secure payment for the note, see Dallin H. Oaks and Joseph I. Bentley, "Joseph Smith and Legal Process: In the Wake

of the Steamboat Nauvoo," *Brigham Young University Law Review,* 3 (1976), 735–82.

4. Butterfield to Penrose, August 2, 1842. Solicitor of the Treasury, National Archives, Washington, D.C. Record Group 206—Records relating to attempts by the United States Government to obtain payment on a promissory note ($4,866.38) made by the government by Peter Haws, H. W. Miller, George Miller, Joseph Smith, and Hyrum Smith (brother of Joseph Smith), 1841–1852. This letter, extracts from the *Sangamo Journal* and other documents relating to Joseph's bankruptcy proceedings are published in M. Hamlin Cannon (ed.), "Documents: Bankruptcy Proceedings Against Joseph Smith in Illinois," *The Pacific Historical Review* 14 (December 1945), 425–33.

5. Flanders, pp. 170–71. Also Oaks and Bentley, pp. 745–50.

6. Butterfield to Penrose, October 13, 1842, National Archives, loc. cit.

7. Oaks and Bentley, pp. 750–52, say that although news of the bankruptcy law was carried in non-Mormon papers in western Illinois, no mention was made in the Mormon press until two months after the law became effective, when *The Wasp* carried notice of it in its first issue, April 16. So far as Oaks and Bentley could discover, no mention of the law was made previous to that time in any other Mormon sources, such as diaries and minutes of meetings. Joseph's inventory of property is in HDC.

8. *History of the Church,* V, 205,

9. National Archives. See Oaks and Bentley, pp. 773–79.

10. Bernhisel's letter is in the Reorganized Church Library.

11. Bennett, p. 7.

12. This broadside is in the John C. Bennett file, HDC.

13. Galland's letter is in Journal History; original on file in the HDC.

14. J. A. Bennet to Joseph Smith, April 10, 1843. RLDS.

15. RLDS.

16. The letters by Ford, Butterfield and Adams are published in *History of the Church,* V, 205–6.

17. Ibid., 214.

18. Ibid., 215.

19. Inez Smith Davis, *The Story of the Church* (Independence, 1948), p. 319, as quoted in Gayler, "The Attempts," p. 13, n. 52.

20. President Joseph Smith's Journal 1843, as kept by Willard Richards, HDC.

21. The course of the hearing is in Joseph Smith's Journal 1843, as kept by Richards, and *History of the Church,* V, 220–31.

22. Documents related to Joseph's hearing are published in *History of the Church,* V, 233–44.

23. Joseph Smith to Butterfield, March 18, 1843. Joseph Smith papers, HDC.

24. Butterfield to Joseph Smith, March 27, 1843. RLDS.

Chapter 7: THE PROPHET KIDNAPPED

1. *History of the Church,* V, 439.

2. Ibid., 439–41.

3. Gregg, pp. 220–22.

4. *Nauvoo Neighbor,* November 8, 1843, published the testimony of the citizens of Dixon that Joseph was held under protest at least an hour.

5. *History of the Church,* V, 444.

6. Ibid., 444–45.

7. Ibid., 474.

8. From the synopsis of Joseph's speech as reported by Willard Richards and Wilford Woodruff, Ibid., 465–73.

9. *Nauvoo Neighbor,* December 13, 27, 1843; also *History of the Church,* VI, 105–6, 124, 212.

10. *Nauvoo Neighbor,* November 8, 1843.

11. *History of the Church,* V, 489–90.

12. Ibid., 490.

13. M. Brayman to Joseph, July 29, 1843. RLDS. Used by permission.

14. Ford's letter is reproduced in *Nauvoo Neighbor,* August 30, 1843.

15. Ford, p. 271.

16. Ibid., p. 319.

17. Ibid., p. 318.

18. Joseph Smith's Journal by Richards. HDC. This differs in slight details in *History of the Church,* V, 526.

19. Ford, p. 319.

20. Ibid.

Chapter 8: THE ROOTS OF CELESTIAL MARRIAGE

1. *History of the Church,* V, 500–1.

2. *Historical Record* 6 (July 1887), 225.

3. *History of the Church,* V, 500–7. *Doctrine and Covenants* 132.

4. *History of the Church,* V, 509.

5. *Historical Record* 6 (July 1887), 226.

6. William Law interview with Wyl, March 30, 1887, as published in Gregg, p. 510. See also Charles L. Woodward, First Half Century of Mormonism, papers, etc., 1880, pp. 286–87. NYPL.

7. *Historical Record* 6 (July 1887), 226.

8. *Journal of Discourses,* XVII, 159.

9. McLellin to Joseph Smith, III, July 1872. RLDS.

10. Thomas Grover's testimony, pp. 226–27, David Fullmer's testimony, p. 227, in *Historical Record* 6 (July 1887).

11. Helen Mar Whitney, *Plural Marriage as Taught by the Prophet Joseph* (Salt Lake City: *Juvenile Instructor Office,* 1882), pp. 16–17.

12. *Millennial Star* 21 (1859), 19.

13. *Doctrine and Covenants* 49.15–16.

14. William W. Phelps to Brigham Young, August 12, 1861. HDC.

15. *Journal of Discourses,* IX, 294.

16. *History of the Church,* II, 246–47.

17. Benjamin F. Johnson to George S. Gibbs, April–October 1903, TS, p. 11. Huntington.

18. Thomas O'Dea, *The Mormons* (Chicago: Univ. of Chicago Press, 1957), p. 61.

19. H. M. Whitney, p. 11.

20. *The Return* II (1890), 287.

21. H. M. Whitney, p. 11.

22. *Doctrine and Covenants* 124–32.

23. *History of the Church,* V, 323.

24. Ibid., 506.

25. Benjamin F. Johnson, *My Life's Review* (Independence, Mo.: Zion's Printing and Publishing Co., 1947), p. 10.

26. *History of the Church,* V, 362.

27. Joseph's Journal by Richards, HDC.

28. Ibid. Varies slightly in *History of the Church,* V, 401.

29. *History of the Church,* V, 265.

30. Ibid., IV, 445.

31. David Whitmer, p. 31.

32. Joseph Lee Robinson, Journal and autobiography, as quoted in The Book of Mormon and Plural Marriage, facsimile of TS, Mormon File, Box 3. Huntington.

33. Joseph's Journal by Richards.

34. H. M. Whitney, p. 12.

35. *Historical Record* 6 (July 1887), 226.

36. *Deseret News,* May 20, 1886 as quoted in *Historical Record* 6 (July 1887), 219.

37. Law as told to Wyl, in Gregg, p. 515. See also Woodward, pp. 286–87.

Chapter 9: THE EARLY POLYGAMISTS

1. *Journal of Discourses,* III, 266.

2. Ibid., 265.

3. Helen Mar Whitney, "Life Incidents," *Woman's Exponent* 10 (August 15, 1881), 85–86.

4. *Journal of Discourses,* XVII, 224–25.

5. *Diary of Job Smith, a Pioneer of Nauvoo, Illinois and Utah* [Arcadia, Calif.: Printed by Louise Smith Willard, 1956?], pp. 5–6. Huntington Library has a copy.

6. Eliza R. Snow, *Biography and Family Record of Lorenzo Snow* (Salt Lake City: Deseret News Co., 1884), p. 84.

7. Lucy Smith, Preliminary MS, HDC.

8. Lucy Smith, in her work as published, p. 169.

9. This idea is suggested by Harry M. Beardsley, *Joseph Smith and His Mormon Empire* (Boston and New York: Houghton Mifflin Co., 1931), p. 286.

10. Joseph Smith papers, HDC.

11. Mary B. Smith Norman to Ina Smith Coolbrith, February 3, 1911. Reorganized Church Library.

12. Diary of Mrs. Mary N. Barzee Boyce, p. 40. Church Manuscripts compiled by Alan H. Gerber, Vol. I. Seven reels at BYU.

13. From a letter published in the *Deseret Evening News,* January 20, 1885, as quoted in *Historical Record* 6 (July 1887), 231.

14. *Journal of Discourses,* XIII, 194.

15. Johnson to Gibbs, p. 4.

16. *Journal of Discourses*, XVII, 159.

17. Emma Smith Blessing [1844?]. Emma Smith file, HDC.

18. *Journal of Discourses*, XX, 28–31. "Plural Marriage," *Historical Record* 6 (July 1887), 233–34, names twenty-seven women who were sealed to Joseph Smith during the last three years of his life, gives testimonies and some biographies, and adds that there were a few more about whom information was incomplete. Fawn Brodie says Andrew Jenson, former historian of the Utah church, named twenty-seven wives. After an intensive study, Brodie named forty-eight wives, and gives brief biographies (Brodie, pp. 435–65). She admits, however, that evidence is slim for a number of them. Stanley S. Ivins said that Joseph was probably "the most married" of the polygamists, and added that the number of his wives could only be guessed, but that it might have been more than sixty. However, he does not document his statement. See his "Notes on Mormon Polygamy," *Western Humanities Review* 10 (Summer 1956), rpt. *Utah Historical Quarterly* 35 (Fall 1967), 313. Marvin S. Hill believes that there might have been eleven or twelve, perhaps fewer, that Joseph actually lived with as wives. "Secular or Sectarian History? A Critique of *No Man Knows My History*," *Church History* 43 (March 1974), 78–96.

19. *Historical Record* 6 (July 1887), 221.

20. Zina's marriage to Jacobs is in Record of Marriages, Hancock County, Book A, p. 40, as cited by Brodie, p. 442 n. Her marriage to Joseph is noted in *Historical Record* 6 (July 1887), 233.

21. Brodie, p. 438, and *Historical Record*, loc. cit. Brodie believes that Prescindia's son Norman could have been by Joseph.

22. Sketch of the Life of Mary Elizabeth Rollins Lightner by her great-granddaughter Hollie Osbourne Murdock, BYU.

23. Brodie, p. 444.

24. Mary E. Rollins Lightner to Sister Wells [Emmaline B. Wells?], n.d., BYU.

25. Eliza R. Snow, "Sketch of My Life," MS, P-F 57, pp. 12–14, Bancroft Library, Berkeley. These pages, which were omitted from Eliza's sketch as published in *The Relief Society Magazine* 31 (March–October 1944).

26. Brodie (pp. 345–46, 447–48) says tradition in the Snow family has it that Emma struck Eliza in a jealous rage, causing her to fall downstairs and have a miscarriage. In a letter to me of March 16, 1976, Maureen Ursenbach Beecher, who has done intensive study of Eliza R. Snow, says that Brodie's source, Eliza's nephew LeRoi C. Snow, was a very young boy when Eliza died (in 1887), and it seems highly unlikely that Eliza would have confided in him. Beecher has examined Brodie's supporting evidence, a letter from John R. Young, and gives it far less credence than Brodie did, since Young was quoting a report he had heard after a lapse of forty years. Beecher also says that her investigations indicate that the Smiths were in the Homestead when Eliza was living with them, and not in the Mansion House, where the story is usually placed.

27. Revelation to Newel K. Whitney through Joseph the Seer, at Nauvoo, Illinois, July 27, 1842. HDC.

28. Diary of Emily Dow Partridge Young. TS, pp. 106, 118. BYU.

29. Autobiography and Diary of Eliza Marie Partridge (Smith) Lyman 1820–1885, p. 8. Copied by BYU, 1945.

30. Emily Dow Partridge Young, p. 103.

31. Ibid., p. 120.

32. Statement of Mrs. L. W. Kimball—A Brief but Intensely Interesting Sketch of Her Experience Written by Herself . . . TS, p. 7. Kimball Young Collection, Huntington.

33. Johnson to Gibbs, pp. 12–13. Also *Historical Record* 6 (July 1887), 221–22.

34. Helen Mar Whitney, "Life Incidents," *Woman's Exponent* 11 (August 1, 1882), 39.

35. Statement written and signed by Helen in Salt Lake City, March 30, 1881. Helen Mar Whitney papers, HDC.

36. See Helen Mar Whitney, *Plural Marriage as Taught by the Prophet Joseph, A Reply to Joseph Smith, Editor of the Lamoni (Iowa) Herald* (Salt Lake City: Juvenile Instructor Office, 1882). Also her *Why We Practice Plural Marriage* (Salt Lake City: Juvenile Instructor Office, 1884).

37. Brodie, p. 346.

38. Statement of Mrs. L. W. Kimball, p. 8.

39. Johnson to Gibbs, p. 13.

40. Statement by Lucy M. Smith on Polygamy. MS, BYU.

41. *Journal of Discourses,* XVII, 159.

42. Statement of Mrs. L. W. Kimball, p. 5.

43. Brief Sketch [of Joseph Smith's instructions to the Relief Society] reported by Miss E. R. Snow. Joseph Smith Letters, HDC.

44. Joseph's Journal by Richards, HDC.

45. Orson Pratt, *The Bible and Polygamy,* 2nd ed. (Salt Lake City: Deseret News Steam Printing Establishment, 1877), p. 96.

46. H. M. Whitney, *Plural Marriage,* p. 16. Traditionally, the Mormon priesthood has been reserved for males, but there may be reason to speculate whether some form of it was intended for females. Heber C. Kimball, in his journal entry for February 1, 1844, said that he and Vilate were anointed priest and priestess "unto our god under the hands of B Young and by the ways of the Holy Order." The significance of the ordination is not made known. Benjamin Winchester in his Personal Narrative wrote that Joseph promised his sister Lucy Smith that he would make her a priestess and the highest woman in the church if she would accept polygamy, but she refused. See Winchester in the collection of Charles Woodward, First Half Century of Mormonism, NYPL. I do not know of any corroboration of Winchester's statement.

47. Emily Dow Partridge Young, p. 48.

48. H. M. Whitney, *Plural Marriage,* p. 27.

49. Both accounts are in Alexander H. Smith, *Polygamy: Was It an Original Tenet of the Church of Jesus Christ of Latter Day Saints?* (Lamoni, Iowa: RLDS, n.d.), pp. 6, 7.

50. H. M. Whitney, *Plural Marriage,* p. 16.

51. As quoted by W. Wyl, *Mormon Portraits* (Salt Lake City: Tribune Publishing Co., 1886), p. 87.

52. Emma to Joseph III, no month, 17, 1869. RLDS. Used by permission.

53. February 2, 1866 [or 1867]. RLDS.

54. "Last Testimony of Sister Emma," *Saints Advocate,* October 1879, p. 50.

55. Eliza's statement is in *Woman's Exponent,* November 1, 1879, p. 85. I am grateful to Maureen Ursenbach Beecher for pointing this out to me.

56. Samuel H. B. Smith to George A. Smith, July 10, 1860. BYU.

57. Ivins, pp. 310–11.

58. H. M Whitney, "Life Incidents," *Woman's Exponent,* October 15, 1883, p. 74.

59. Ivins, p. 318.

60. John A. Widtsoe, *Evidences and Reconciliations,* pp. 307, 309, 310, as cited in The Book of Mormon and Plural Marriage, p. 11.

61. Despite limitations, the most comprehensive sociological study of later polygamy is Kimball Young, *Isn't One Wife Enough?* (New York: Henry Holt and Company, 1954).

62. Johnson to Gibbs, p. 15.

63. Statement of Mrs. L. W. Kimball, p. 9.

64. Annie Turner Clark, *A Mormon Mother: An Autobiography* (Salt Lake City: Univ. of Utah Press, 1969), pp. 1, 116.

Chapter 10: THE KINGDOM OF GOD ON EARTH

1. *History of the Church,* VI, 4–8.

2. See Klaus J. Hansen, *Quest for Empire: The Political Kingdom of God and the Council of Fifty in Mormon History* (East Lansing: Michigan State Univ. Press, 1967).

3. *History of the Church,* VI, 288–92.

4. Quoted by Hansen, p. 151.

5. *Doctrine and Covenants* 124.2, 3, 7.

6. A Religious Proclamation from Joseph Smith, about 1842. Joseph Smith papers, 1842. HDC.

7. *Millennial Star* 3 (1842), 69, as quoted in Hansen, p. 51.

8. Hansen, pp. 55–56.

9. Hansen points this out, p. 59. Examples are in *History of the Church,* IV, 500; VI, 39, 45.

10. Hansen, p. 60.

11. Ibid., p. 199, n. 45.

12. *History of the Church,* VI, 125–32.

13. Quoted from the *Warsaw Message* and the *Warsaw Signal,* by Brodie, pp. 357–58.

14. Johnson to Gibbs, p. 9.

15. The Miller letter was written at St. James, Michigan, June 1855. This quotation is from a copy of the letter made by John Zahnd, and included in the Zahnd Manuscript on Mormons, Manuscript and Archives Division, The New York Public Library, Astor, Lenox and Tilden Foundations.

16. George T. M. Davis, *An Authentic Account of the Massacre of Joseph Smith, the Mormon Prophet, and Hyrum Smith, His Brother*   (St. Louis, 1844), p. 7, as quoted by Hansen, p. 155.

17. Ford, pp. 321–22.

18. Hansen, pp. 65–66.

19. *History of the Church,* VI, 261.

20. Johnson to Gibbs, p. 9, says that Rigdon, Law and Marks were not members of the council. Hansen, p. 60, says Rigdon and Law were not members. However, I have it from the Historical Department of The Church of Jesus Christ of Latter-day Saints that Rigdon was made a member of the council on March 19, 1844.

21. James R. Clark, "The Kingdom of God, the Council of Fifty and the State of Deseret," *Utah Historical Quarterly* 26 (April 1958), 131–48.

22. HDC has two copies of Joseph's memorial to Congress, one by Orson Hyde and one by Thomas Bullock. The copy by Hyde omits Section 4, which states that Joseph's forces are not to be construed as part of the U. S. Army, and that Joseph shall not break the faith of treaties, violate laws or endanger the peace of the United States. The memorial, including Section 4, is published in *History of the Church,* VI, 275–77.

23. Ibid., 282–83.

24. Quoted by Klaus J. Hansen, "Joseph Smith & the Political Kingdom of God," *The American West,* 5 (Sept. 1968), 23.

25. *History of the Church,* VI, 365.

Chapter 11: CANDIDATE FOR PRESIDENT

1. The Missionaries of the Church of Jesus Christ of L.D.S. Set Apart Since 1830. Film, HDC.

2. William had resigned as editor of *The Wasp* on December 10, 1842, the year he was elected representative to the Illinois General Assembly. He was succeeded as editor by John Taylor. *History of the Church,* V, 204. On March 15, 1843, *The Wasp* was superseded by *Nauvoo Neighbor,* a larger paper with wider coverage. Ibid., 304–5.

3. *Nauvoo Neighbor,* October 3, 1843, as quoted in *History of the Church,* VI, 42–43.

4. *History of the Church,* VI, 49.

5. For discussion of Mormon politics in Illinois, see George R. Gayler, "The Mormons and Politics in Illinois: 1839–1844," *Journal of the Illinois State Historical Society* 49 (Spring 1956), 48–65. See also Robert Bruce Flanders, "The Kingdom of God in Illinois: Politics in Utopia," *Dialogue* 5 (Spring 1970), 26–36.

6. *History of the Church,* VI, 49.

7. Calhoun to Joseph Smith, Dec. 2, 1843, and Joseph's reply, Jan. 2, 1844, are in *The Voice of Truth, Containing General Joseph Smith's Correspondence* [etc.] (Nauvoo, Ill.: Printed by John Taylor, 1844), pp. 21–26.

8. Clay to Joseph Smith, Nov. 15, 1843, is in *History of the Church,* VI, 376.

9. Cass to Joseph Smith Dec. 9, 1843. Journal History, HDC.

10. George Miller, June 1855, loc. cit.

11. *History of the Church,* VI, 188.

12. *Views . . .* was also published in *Times and Seasons,* May 15, 1844; in *The Voice of Truth,* pp. 26–38.

13. Joseph summarized the priorities of his campaign in reply to inquiry made by the Central Committee of the National Reform Association; see *Workingman's Advocate,* July 30, 1844.

14. Joseph Smith's Journal by Richards, HDC. See also Wilford Woodruff's Daily Journal, 1843–1844, HDC. The speech is published in *History of the Church*, V, 243.

15. *Diary of Job Smith, a Pioneer of Nauvoo, Illinois and Utah* [Arcadia, Calif.: Printed by Louise Smith Willard, 1956?], pp. 6–7. Huntington has a copy.

16. W. Richards file, HDC, has a copy of this letter. See also *History of the Church*, VI, 231–33.

17. Ibid. Bennet's letter about his hopes to become governor, written October 24, 1843, appeared in *Nauvoo Neighbor*, Dec. 6, 1843, and is reproduced in *History of the Church*, VI, 71–73.

18. HDC.

19. W. Richards file, HDC.

20. Flanders, "Politics in Utopia," p. 35.

21. "Autobiography of Dr. Ephraim Ingals," *Journal of the Illinois State Historical Society* 29 (January 1936), 295.

22. W. Richards file, HDC.

23. HDC.

24. HDC.

Chapter 12: BLACKS IN THE EARLY CHURCH

1. *History of the Church*, I, 191.

2. Ibid., 379.

3. *Doctrine and Covenants* 101.79.

4. Ibid., 134.12.

5. "There's a Feast of Fat Things for &c," Hymn number 8, *A Collection of Sacred Hymns for the Church of the Latter Day Saints* (Kirtland, 1835). This is pointed out by Lester E. Bush, Jr., "Mormonism's Negro Doctrine: an Historical Overview," *Dialogue* 8 (Spring 1973), 17. This article has excellent documentation.

6. *Doctrine and Covenants* 87.1, 4.

7. Statement signed by A. O. Smoot, in the file labeled Negroes, HDC.

8. Armand L. Mauss, "Mormonism and the Negro: Faith, Folklore, and Civil Rights," *Dialogue* 2 (Winter 1967), 21, n. 4.

9. Andrew Jenson, L.D.S. *Biographical Encyclopedia*, 3, 577. Also History of the 3rd Quorum of Seventy—Kirtland, Tuesday evening, Dec. 20, 1836. Jenson says that Abel's certificate shows that Abel was ordained a seventy [for the second time?] on April 4, 1841. Joseph F. Smith said at a meeting of authorities on August 22, 1895, that Abel was ordained a seventy and afterward a high priest under the direction of Joseph Smith. Third Quorum of Seventy Minute and Roll Book 1898–1907, p. 22. HDC.

10. Statement signed by Coltrin, in the file labeled Negroes, HDC. Also Bush, p. 59, n. 113, says this is in the Journal of John Nuttal, I (1876–1884): 290–93, TS, BYU, and that a corrected copy is in the minutes of the Council Meeting, June 4, 1879, in the Adam S. Bennion papers, BYU.

11. Bush, pp. 31–32.

12. Ibid., p. 34.

13. *History of the Church*, IV, 365.

14. Jenson, loc. cit.

15. *History of the Church*, II, 368–69.

16. Ibid., IV, 213.

17. The letters are reproduced in *History of the Church*, IV, 544–48.

18. Joseph Smith's Journal kept by Willard Richards, HDC.

19. Ibid.

20. *History of the Church*, V, 217. Original in Joseph Smith's Journal by Richards varies slightly.

21. *History of the Church*, VI, 197, 205.

22. Ibid., VI, 244.

23. Ibid., VI, 210.

24. William I. Appleby to Young, June 2, 1847. Journal History. HDC.

25. Llewelyn R. McKay, *Home Memories of President David O. McKay* (Salt Lake City, 1956), pp. 226–31, as cited in Bush, pp. 46, 68, n. 214. For an anti-Mormon view on the role of Blacks in the church see Jerald and Sandra Tanner, *The Negro in Mormon Theology* (Salt Lake City: Modern Microfilm Co., [1967]).

26. Wilford Woodruff Journal, January 16, 1852, as quoted by Bush, p. 26.

27. Before life on earth, Lucifer and the Beloved Son presented plans for man's salvation at a council in heaven. When the Beloved Son was chosen Redeemer, Lucifer and a third of the hosts rebelled, while the majority either opposed him, led by Michael in the war in heaven, or remained neutral, thus keeping their "first estate" and earning the right to come to earth and assume bodies, while Lucifer and his hosts were cast out. For an explanation of this in Mormon belief, see James E. Talmage, *Jesus the Christ; A Study of the Messiah and His Mission according to Holy Scriptures both Ancient and Modern*, 24th ed. (Salt Lake City: Deseret Book Company, 1956), pp. 6–16.

28. Anson Call, statement of 1877, to Thomas Wm. Whitaker. Utah Hist. Society.

29. Journal History, December 25, 1869.

Chapter 13: DISSENT IN NAUVOO

1. Joseph Smith's Journal by Richards, HDC. Differs slightly in *History of the Church*, VI, 58.

2. "Address of the Mayor to the Nauvoo Police," *History of the Church*, VI, 152.

3. The minutes of the Nauvoo City Council special session of January 3, 1844, are published in *History of the Church*, VI, 162–65.

4. Synopsis of the minutes of the special City Council session of January 5, 1844, Ibid., 166–70.

5. Ibid., 167.

6. Ibid., 170.

7. Ibid., 253.

8. *Nauvoo Expositor*, I, No. 1 (June 7, 1844), p. 2. BYU has a copy.

9. Alexander Neibaur Diary, May 24, 1844. MS, HDC. I am grateful to Dean Jessee for drawing this to my attention.

10. Eaton's affidavit is reproduced in *History of the Church*, VI, 279–80.

Two others, Dennison L. Harris and Robert Scott, informed Joseph that there was a plot to kill him, Hyrum and other leaders of the church. Ibid., 280 n.

11. For this extract from Clayton's journal, see Ibid., 271.

12. Outline of Joseph's speech from the journal of Wilford Woodruff. *History of the Church,* VI, 272–74.

13. Ibid., 332–33.

14. Ibid., 345.

15. As quoted by Klaus J. Hansen, "Joseph Smith & the Political Kingdom of God," in *The American West* 5 (September 1968), 24.

16. As reported by Thomas Bullock, who was clerk of the steamer *Maid of Iowa, History of the Church,* V, 408–12.

17. *Nauvoo Expositor,* p. 2.

18. William Marks's statement in *The True Latter Day Saints' Herald,* January 1860, as reproduced in Joseph Smith [III], *One Wife, or Many* (Lamoni, Iowa: Reorganized Church of Jesus Christ of Latter Day Saints, n.d.), p. 12.

Chapter 14: THE PROPHET SURRENDERS

1. William Law interview with Dr. Wyl, March 30, 1887, *Salt Lake Tribune,* as published in Gregg, p. 513.

2. *History of the Church,* VI, 500.

3. Ibid., 463–64.

4. Ibid., 466–67, 480.

5. Evidence of the violence of non-Mormon reaction to the destruction of the *Expositor* is in *Warsaw Signal,* June 12, 1844: *Alton Telegraph and Democratic Review,* June 15, 1844; *Quincy Whig,* June 19, 1844; and *Lee County Democrat,* June 22, 1844. Account of Joseph's arrest and minutes of the trial at Nauvoo are in *History of the Church,* VI, 487–91.

6. Letter of Samuel O. Williams to John A. Prickett, July 10, 1844, is in the collection of Mormon manuscripts, Chicago Historical Society.

7. *Warsaw Signal,* June 19, 1844.

8. "The Last Speech of President Smith to the Legion," as compiled by George Albert Smith from the reports of Joseph G. Hovey, William G. Sterrett and others who heard it. *History of the Church,* VI, 498–500.

9. Ibid., 516–18.

10. Ibid., 520.

11. Thomas Ford, *A History of Illinois from its Commencement as a State in 1814 to 1847* (Chicago: S. C. Griggs & Co., 1854), p. 324.

12. Minor Deming to his parents, June 26, 1844. Minor Deming papers, Illinois Historical Survey, Univ. of Illinois Library, Urbana.

13. Ford, pp. 324–29.

14. *History of the Church,* VI, 521.

15. Ibid., 525.

16. Ibid., 543–45.

17. Ford, p. 324.

18. *History of the Church,* VI, 544.

19. Ibid., 533–37.

20. Ibid., 542. For a review of the legal considerations of the action against the *Expositor,* see Dallin Oaks, "The suppression of the *Nauvoo Expositor,*"

Utah Law Review 9 (Winter 1965), 890–91. Oaks says there was some legal justification for the City Council to declare the paper a public nuisance, but none for the destruction of the press.

21. Ford, p. 333.

22. *History of the Church,* VI, 538–41.

23. Ibid., 545–46.

24. A copy of this letter is in the Joseph Smith papers, HDC.

25. "Interview between Emma Smith and Edmund C. Briggs," *The Journal of History* 9 (October 1916), 453–54. See also *Quincy Whig,* June 19, 1844.

26. Ford, p. 339.

27. Quoted by Helen Mar Whitney in "Life Incidents," *Woman's Exponent,* December 15, 1882, p. 106.

28. *History of the Church,* VI, 549.

29. Journal of Wandle Mace, p. 144. TS, BYU, as quoted by Dallin H. Oaks and Marvin S. Hill, *Carthage Conspiracy: The Trial of the Accused Assassins of Joseph Smith* (Urbana, Ill.: Univ. of Illinois Press, 1975), p. 17.

30. Most of the account of the last days of Joseph and Hyrum is based upon statements by participants in the action, Willard Richards, John Taylor, Dan Jones, Cyrus H. Wheelock, Stephen Markham, the prophet's lawyer John S. Reid and others, as compiled by George Albert Smith, who was church historian 1854–75. *History of the Church,* VI and VII.

31. Eliza R. Snow, *Biography and Family Record of Lorenzo Snow . . .* (Salt Lake City: Deseret News Co., 1844), p. 157.

32. Mary B. Smith Norman to Ina Smith Coolbrith, March 27, 1908. RLDS.

33. *History of the Church,* VI, 558.

34. *Manuscripts from Goodspeed's,* Catalogue 545, February 1968, has on its cover a reproduction of Joseph Smith's order to Dunham. The catalog is in Joseph Smith papers, HDC.

35. *History of the Church,* VI, 558.

Chapter 15: MARTYRDOM

1. Names of the officers and men belonging to the Carthage Greys in June 1844 are listed in *History of the Church,* VII, 142–43.

2. Ibid., VI, 559–64.

3. Williams, loc. cit.

4. Ibid.

5. *Warsaw Signal,* June 29, 1844.

6. Williams, loc. cit.

7. *History of the Church,* VI, 592.

8. Ibid., 565.

9. John Taylor file, HDC.

10. *History of the Church,* VI, 585.

11. Ibid., 601–4.

12. For an evaluation of Ford's difficult situation, see Keith Huntress, "Governor Thomas Ford and the Murderers of Joseph Smith," *Dialogue* 4 (Summer 1969), 41–52.

13. For John Taylor's summary of the Mormon opinion about Ford's guilt see *History of the Church,* VII, 113–16.

14. Ibid., VI, 607.

15. Joseph to Emma, June 27, 1844. Joseph Smith papers, HDC. Differs slightly in published version, *History of the Church*, VI, 605, and the second postscript is omitted.

16. Allen J. Stout's journal, p. 13. Transcript in the Utah State Historical Society Library, as cited by Brodie, p. 392, n.

17. Joseph Smith papers, HDC. Ironically, Browning would later defend and secure the acquittal of Joseph's accused murderers.

18. Ford, pp. 339ff.

19. Williams, loc. cit.

20. *History of the Church*, VI, 623.

21. Minutes of Trial of Members of Mob Who Helped Kill Joseph Smith, the Prophet, 45. TS of the manuscript in HDC is unpaged. The TS of trial proceedings page numbers are in original, as cited by Oaks and Hill. See their Bibliographical Note, pp. 227–28, for a description of the original and a discussion of its authenticity.

22. Minor Deming made this statement in a letter to Ford, *Warsaw Signal*, Sept. 24, 1844. When directly questioned about this at the trial, Frank Worrell, who was in command of the guards at the jail, refused to testify on the grounds that he might incriminate himself. Minutes of Trial, 44, as quoted by Oaks and Hill, pp. 124–25.

23. *History of the Church*, VI, 607–8.

24. "The Statement of William B. Hamilton," *History of McDonough County* (Chicago: Munsell Publishing Co.), as quoted by Charles J. Scofield, *History of Hancock County* (Chicago, 1921), pp. 845–46.

25. "Statement of Mrs. Eudocia Baldwin Marsh," Scofield, pp. 848–50.

26. Williams, loc. cit.

27. "The Statement of J.H.S.," Scofield, p. 847. Gregg also quotes the statement, p. 279.

28. *History of the Church*, VI, 617–18.

29. John Hay, in the *Atlantic Monthly*, December 1869, as recorded in *History of the Church*, VI, xli, n.

30. Oaks and Hill, p. 21.

31. Willard Richards in *Times and Seasons*, as published in *History of the Church*, VI, 619–21.

32. John Taylor's account in *History of the Church*, VII, 107.

33. Ibid., 106.

Chapter 16: THE SUCCESSOR CHOSEN, THE ACCUSED ASSASSINS TRIED

1. Oaks and Hill, p. 30.

2. Ford, p. 349.

3. Ibid., pp. 361–410.

4. Underscoring as in original. Willard Richards papers, HDC. Varies slightly as published in *History of the Church*, VII, 147–48.

5. One well-documented study of the difficult situation that arose over who was to be Joseph's successor identifies and discusses eight types of possible claims to that role, the foundations for which were laid by the prophet himself: 1) by a counselor in the first presidency (Sidney Rigdon), 2) by secret appoint-

ment (James J. Strang, Lyman Wight and Alpheus Cutler), 3) by the associate president (Oliver Cowdery), 4) by the presiding patriarch (William Smith), 5) by the Council of Fifty, 6) by the Quorum of Twelve, 7) by various priesthood councils, including the first Quorum of Seventy and the Nauvoo High Council under President William Marks, and 8) by a descendant of the prophet. D. Michael Quinn, "The Mormon Succession Crisis of 1844," *BYU Studies*, 16 (Winter 1976), 187–233.

6. W. W. Blair, "The Ministry of Joseph's Sons," *One Wife or Many* (Lamoni, Iowa: Reorganized Church of Jesus Christ of Latter Day Saints, n.d.), pp. 14–16. See also Flanders, p. 312.

7. The purported letter from Joseph Smith to Strang is No. 4 in the James J. Strang papers, Yale University Library. It has been pronounced a forgery by several people, as cited by Quinn, p. 195. Milo Quaife, who found the letter, was uncertain of its authenticity. See his biography of Strang, *The Kingdom of Saint James, A Narrative of the Mormons* (New Haven: Yale Univ. Press, 1930).

8. Brigham Young to the churches in Ottawa, Illinois, Jan. 24, 1846. James J. Strang papers, Yale.

9. *Ensign of Liberty of the Church of Christ*, I, 17 (Dec. 1847), 43.

10. January [?] 16, 1839, Joseph Smith papers, HDC.

11. *History of the Church*, VII, 224, 231–35.

12. Brigham Young's Journal, August 8, 1844. HDC.

13. *History of the Church*, VII, 231–36. See also Thomas Bullock's report of Brigham's speech, HDC.

14. Wilford's recollection of the event is in *Deseret Evening News*, March 12, 1892, as quoted in *History of the Church*, VII, 236 n. See also the entry for August 8, 1844, Wilford Woodruff Journal, HDC. Among others who mentioned it in retrospect were Job Smith, Sarah Leavitt quoting her husband, Benjamin F. Johnson and Zadoc Knapp Judd. However, the comment of William C. Staines in his diary, that Brigham spoke in a voice like Joseph's, is cited in *History of the Church*, VII, 236 n., as having been made on that day.

15. *History of the Church*, VII, 237–38.

16. Jacob Hamblin told this, as quoted by Flanders, p. 315.

17. *History of the Church*, VII, 240.

18. Brigham Young file, HDC.

19. William to Bro Robbins, William Smith papers, HDC.

20. Mary B. Smith Norman to Ina Smith Coolbirth, April 24, 1908, Reorganized Church Library.

21. August 8, 1844, Yale Univ. Library, as quoted in Oaks and Hill, pp. 34–35.

22. See the Minor Deming letters to his parents, 1844–1845, Minor Deming papers, Illinois Historical Survey, Univ. of Illinois Library, Urbana.

23. *Warsaw Signal*, Sept. 25, 1844.

24. Oaks and Hill, pp. 35–36.

25. Dec. 22, 1844. Minor Deming papers.

26. Ford, p. 367.

27. *History of the Church*, VII, 417–18.

28. B. H. Roberts, Ibid., 624 n.

29. Journal of William Clayton, May 6, 1845, HDC, as quoted by Oaks and Hill, p. 72.

30. For the actions that led to the selection of the jury, the legal aspects and course of the trial and its implications, with excellent documentation, see Oaks and Hill.

31. William M. Daniels, *Correct Account of the Murder of Generals Joseph and Hyrum Smith, at Carthage on the 27th Day of June, 1844* (Nauvoo: By John Taylor, 1845). HDC has a copy.

32. Oaks and Hill, p. 185.

33. John Hay, as quoted in Ibid., pp. 185–86.

34. Ibid., p. 192.

Epilogue: AFTERMATH

1. Brigham Young to Jacob Backenstos, September 11, 1845. Brigham Young file, HDC.

2. September 29 [1845]. Minor Deming papers.

3. Ibid.

4. *History of the Church*, VII, 450.

5. "Letters of a Proselyte," *Utah Historical Quarterly* 25 (April 1957), 135.

6. Brigham Young to Reverends Tucker and Hamilton, of the Catholic Church (no location), December 10, 1845. HDC has a copy in the Brigham Young file.

7. *Warsaw Signal*, October 20, 1846, as quoted in Linn, p. 350.

8. T. B. H. Stenhouse, *The Rocky Mountain Saints* (New York: D. Appleton and Co., 1873), p. 223.

9. Oscar Osburn Winther (ed.) *The Private Papers and Diary of Thomas Leiper Kane: A Friend of the Mormons* (San Francisco: Gelber-Lilienthal, Inc., 1937), pp. 7–8, 34. The Kane letters and manuscripts are in Stanford University Library.

10. Ralph Barton Perry, *Characteristically American* (New York: Alfred A. Knopf, 1949), p. 97.

BIBLIOGRAPHY

The literature on Joseph Smith and his followers is so extensive that a comprehensive bibliography might well fill volumes. Great numbers of original diaries, journals, letters, contemporary newspaper accounts and other documents exist in collections throughout the country. The number of secondary sources is also enormous, but few of the early works are of use to scholarship for any purpose other than to trace the development of opinion about Joseph Smith and his followers and the course of church apology. In recent years, however, a flowering of scholarship has occurred which has brought about much understanding to difficult areas of this discipline. The publication of important monographs is increasing, and studies of significant and controversial aspects of the theology and history of Joseph Smith and his followers are appearing with almost bewildering frequency in journals such as *Brigham Young University Studies; Church History; Dialogue: A Journal of Mormon Thought; Journal of Mormon History; Utah Historical Quarterly;* and *Western Humanities Review.*

Collections of original materials that have been important to research for this work may be roughly classified into church libraries, university libraries, collections of historical societies, and national, state, public and private libraries.

Church Libraries

The Historical Department of the Church of Jesus Christ of Latter-day Saints, Salt Lake City, Utah, has the most extensive holdings of manuscripts and published works on Joseph Smith, the early Mormons and related subjects. Of great value for this work has been the collection of several hundred diaries, in particular the journals kept by Joseph Smith and those kept for him by scribes, and other diaries as noted below. Of much use also were the collections of letters and papers by and relating to Joseph Smith and his contemporaries, especially those of John C. Bennett, Thomas Ford, Joseph L. Heywood, John E. Page, Edward Partridge, William Wine Phelps, Orson Pratt, Parley P. Pratt, Willard Richards, Sidney Rigdon, Don C. Smith, Emma Smith, John Smith, William Smith, Orson Spencer, John Taylor, Newel K. Whitney, Wilford Woodruff and Brigham Young.

Also of particular value were the diaries and memoirs of Lorenzo Barnes, Gideon H. Carter, Jared Carter, William Clayton, Zebedee Coltrin, Howard Coray, Heber C. Kimball, Joseph Knight, Jr., Joseph Knight, Sr., Newel Knight, Alexander Neibaur, Edward Partridge, David W. Patten, William W. Phelps, Orson Pratt, Willard Richards, George Albert Smith, John Smith, John Lyman Smith and Joseph Smith (those kept by himself and those kept by others for him).

Of much help also has been the work called "Journal History of the Church," a collection of some 750 volumes of typed copies of diaries, letters, clippings and other documents from 1830 to date, compiled by the late Andrew Jenson, former Church Historian, and arranged chronologically to provide in effect an excellent daily history of events relating to the church.

Materials in the Library and Archives, Reorganized Church of Jesus Christ of Latter Day Saints, Independence, Missouri, have also been very useful, in particular the McLellin letters, the Joseph Smith letters and the Emma Bidamon letters.

University Libraries

Collections in the Brigham Young University Library, Provo, Utah, have been of much importance in this work, especially the Howard Coray papers; the Sidney Rigdon papers; the Newel K. Whitney collection; the Diedrick Willers "papers on Mormonism," filmed at the Historical Society, Seneca Falls, New York; the collection of Xerox copies of manuscripts from the U. S. Archives regarding the Mormon difficulties in Missouri, 1833–39; and the Alan H. Gerber compilation of church manuscripts on seven reels of film. Individual items used included the diaries and memoirs of Mary N. Barzee Boyce, Lorenzo Brown, John Lowe Butler, Anson Call, Oliver Boardman Huntington, Joel Hills Johnson, Joseph Bates Noble, John Nuttal, Zerah Pulsipher, Luman Andros Shurtliff and Hyrum Smith.

At Yale University, New Haven, Connecticut, materials in the William Robertson Coe collection have been of much use, in particular the James Jesse Strang papers and the Thomas C. Sharp papers.

Also valuable have been materials in the Stanley B. Kimball Collection at Southern Illinois University Library, Edwardsville; the collection at Stanford University Library, California, especially the Thomas Leiper Kane papers and diaries; the Illinois Historical Survey, University of Illinois Library, Urbana, in particular the Minor Deming papers; materials in the University of Utah Library; and collections at Bancroft Library, University of California, Berkeley.

Historical Societies

Of value for this work have been the collections in the Illinois State Historical Society, Springfield; the Missouri Historical Society, St. Louis, including the

James O. Broadhead papers; the Utah State Historical Society, Salt Lake City, in particular the Whittemore family papers, copied from originals in the Michigan Historical Collection, and the diaries of James Henry Rollins and Allen J. Stout. Useful also has been material in the Chicago Historical Society collection, which has a large holding of anti-Mormon manuscripts.

National, State, Public and Private Libraries

Of great use in research for this work has been the Mormon Collection of the Henry E. Huntington Library, San Marino, California, in particular the Oliver Cowdery letters, the Richards family correspondence, the Lewis Crum Bidamon and Emma Smith Bidamon papers, which number 208 letters and documents, 1830–91, and other materials, including the diaries of George Washington Bean, Henry G. Boyle, Jesse W. Crosby, Isaac C. Haight, Norton Jacob, Zadoc Knapp Judd, Sarah Leavitt, John Doyle Lee and Erastus Snow.

Of much use also has been the collection of Mormon materials, including manuscripts, rare books and newspaper clippings, in The New York Public Library; and the collections in the Library of Congress, Washington, D.C., notably typed copies of diaries and memoirs by Mormons. Documents relating to the early Mormons in the National Archives, Washington, D.C., have also been of use. Also important were the materials in the Illinois State Archives, especially those relating to the political history of the Mormons in Nauvoo, including the executive records of Governor Ford. Of value also were the materials in the New York State Library at Albany, and in the King's Daughters Free Public Library and Historical Branch, Palmyra, New York.

Selected Works of Joseph Smith

A Book of Commandments for the Government of the Church of Christ, Organized According to Law, on the 6th of April, 1830. Zion [Independence, Missouri]: W. W. Phelps & Co., 1833; rpt. Independence, Missouri: Board of Publication, Church of Christ Temple Lot, 1960.

The Book of Mormon. Palmyra, New York: Egbert B. Grandin, 1830; photorpt. as *Joseph Smith Begins His Work*. Salt Lake City: Modern Microfilm Co., n.d.

The Book of Mormon . . . Translated by Joseph Smith, Jun. Salt Lake City, Utah: The Church of Jesus Christ of Latter-day Saints, 1950. This edition is the one to which references are made in this work.

Correspondence between Joseph Smith, the Prophet, and Col. John Wentworth . . . Gen. James Arlington Bennet . . . and the Hon. John C. Calhoun. . . . In which is given a Sketch of the Life of Joseph Smith, The Rise and Progress of the Church of Latter Day Saints, . . . New York: John E. Page and L. R. Foster, 1844.

Discourses Delivered by Presidents Joseph Smith and Brigham Young on the Relation of the "Mormons" to the Government of the United States. Great Salt Lake City: Printed at the Office of the *Deseret News*, 1855.

The Doctrine and Covenants of the Church of Jesus Christ of Latter-day Saints, Containing Revelations given to Joseph Smith, the Prophet . . . Kirtland, Ohio: 1835; rpt. Salt Lake City: the Church of Jesus Christ of Latter-day Saints, 1952.

General Joseph Smith's Appeal to the Green Mountain Boys, December 1843. Nauvoo, Illinois, 1843.

General Smith's Views of the Powers and Policy of the Government of the United States, Nauvoo, by John Taylor, 1844.

The Holy Scriptures, translated and corrected by the spirit of revelation. Plano, Illinois: Reorganized Church of Jesus Christ of Latter Day Saints, 1867.

The Pearl of Great Price: a Selection from the Revelations, Translations and Narrations of Joseph Smith . . . Liverpool, England: F. D. Richards, 1851; rpt. Salt Lake City: The Church of Jesus Christ of Latter-day Saints, 1952.

"Reply to the Central Committee of the National Reform Association, who inquired of the candidates for the Presidency where they stood on subject of making the public lands free to all American citizens who desired to cultivate them." *Workingman's Advocate,* July 30, 1844.

The Voice of Truth, Containing General Joseph Smith's Correspondence with Gen. James Arlington Bennet; Appeal to the Green Mountain Boys; Correspondence with John C. Calhoun, Esq.; Views of the Powers and Policy of the Government of the United States; Pacific Innuendo, and Gov. Ford's Letter; A Friendly Hint to Missouri, and a Few Words of Consolation for the "Globe"; also, correspondence with the Hon. Henry Clay. Nauvoo, Illinois: Printed by John Taylor, 1844. (Also published as individual pamphlets, 1844.)

BOOKS AND PAMPHLETS

Ackerknecht, E. H. *Malaria in the Upper Mississippi Valley, 1760–1900.* Baltimore, 1945.

Adams, G. J. *A Letter to His Excellency John Tyler, President of the United States, Touching the Signs of the Times, and the Political Destiny of the World.* New York: Printed by C. A. Calhoun, 1844.

An Appeal to the American People. 2nd ed. Cincinnati: Shepard & Stearns, 1840.

Anderson, Mary Audentia Smith. *Ancestry and Posterity of Joseph Smith and Emma Hale.* Independence, Missouri: Herald Publishing House, 1929.

Information in great detail, based upon research in genealogical archives.

Anderson, Richard Lloyd. *Joseph Smith's New England Heritage: Influences of Grandfathers Solomon Mack and Asael Smith.* Salt Lake City: Deseret Book Co., 1971.

Valuable for its careful research in government, military, maritime, land office and other official records. Verifies much about Joseph's ancestors that has heretofore been known only from family writings and traditions.

Andrus, Hyrum. *Joseph Smith Man and Seer.* Salt Lake City: Deseret Book Co., 1960.

Arbaugh, George B. *Revelation in Mormonism.* Chicago: University of Chicago Press, 1932.

Makes some attempt to place the church in its social context, but in the Hurlbut-Howe approach.

Armstrong, James Elder. *Life of a Woman Pioneer, as illustrated in the life of*

Elsie Strawn Armstrong 1789–1871 . . . Chicago: [John F. Higgins Ptg. Co.], 1931.

Arrington, Leonard J. *Great Basin Kingdom: An Economic History of the Latter-day Saints 1830–1900*. 1958; rpt. Lincoln, Nebraska: University of Nebraska Press, 1966.

A study in depth and a landmark in Mormon scholarship.

Austin, Emily M. *Mormonism: or Life Among the Mormons*. Madison, Wisconsin: M. J. Cantwell, 1882.

Bacon, Leonard. *The Christian Doctrine of Stewardship in Respect to Property*. New Haven, Connecticut: Nathan Whiting, 1832.

Bacon, William. *Regeneration: The New Birth*. Waterloo, New York, 1818.

Bailey, Elijah. *Primitive Trinitarianism Examined and Defended*. Bennington: Darius Clark, 1826.

Bailey, Paul. *The Armies of God*. Garden City, New York: Doubleday, 1968.

Beardsley, Harry M. *Joseph Smith and his Mormon Empire*. Boston and New York: Houghton Mifflin Co., The Riverside Press, Cambridge, 1931.

Presents Joseph Smith as an illiterate who perpetrated a hoax in *The Book of Mormon* with Sidney Rigdon. In the popular anti-Mormon idiom.

Bennett, John C. *The History of the Saints: Or An Exposé of Joe Smith and Mormonism*. Boston: Leland & Whiting, 1842.

Lurid tirade by a man who had a short term in high office in the Mormon Church at Nauvoo and who left after the exposure of his immoral conduct.

Berrett, William E., and Alma D. Burton, eds. *Readings in L.D.S. Church History*. 3 vols. Salt Lake City, 1953–58.

Reprints from original manuscripts.

Bethune, George Washington. *The Faults of the Age in its religious Character; an address of the Rev. Geo. W. Bethune, before the Association of Alumni and Friends of Hamilton Literary and Theological Institution*. Utica, June 5, 1833.

Huntington Library has a copy.

Blackman, Emily C. *History of Susquehanna County, Pennsylvania*. Philadelphia, 1873.

Blair, W. W. "The Ministry of Joseph's Sons." *One Wife or Many*. Lamoni, Iowa: Reorganized Church of Jesus Christ of Latter Day Saints, n.d.

Bolino, August C. *The Development of the American Economy*. Columbus, Ohio: Charles E. Merrill Books, 1961.

Boorstin, Daniel J. *The Americans: The Colonial Experience*. New York: Random House, 1958.

Bottomly, Edwin. *An English Settler in Pioneer Wisconsin: the Letters of Edwin Bottomly, 1844–1850*. Ed. by Milo M. Quaife. Publications of the State Historical Society of Wisconsin 25. Madison, 1918.

Boudinot, Elias. *A Star in the West: or a Humble Attempt to Discover the Long Lost Tribes of Israel*. Trenton, New Jersey: D. Fenton, S. Hutchinson and J. Dunham, 1816.

Bradley, Joshua. *Accounts of Religious Revivals in Many Parts of the United States from 1815 to 1818*. Albany, New York: G. J. Loomis & Co., 1819.

Brewster, James Colin. *Very Important to the Mormon Money Diggers.* Springfield: n.p., 1843.
At Utah State Historical Society. Photo dup.

Briggs, Jason W. *The Basis of Brighamite Polygamy: A Criticism upon the (so called) Revelation of July 12th, 1843.* True Latter Day Saints Tract No. 28. Lamoni, Iowa. Reorganized Church of Jesus Christ of Latter Day Saints, 1875.

Britton, Rollin J. *Early Days on the Grand River and the Mormon War.* Columbia, Missouri: The State Historical Society, 1920.

Brodie, Fawn. *No Man Knows My History: The Life of Joseph Smith, the Mormon Prophet.* New York: Knopf, 1945.
Best-known of twentieth-century biographies of Joseph Smith. Well documented, although based largely upon anti-Mormon sources; is in the long tradition of the Mormon exposé.

Brooks, Juanita. *John Doyle Lee, Zealot—Pioneer Builder—Scapegoat.* Glendale, California: Arthur H. Clark Co., 1962.

Burnett, Peter H. *An Old California Pioneer.* New York: D. Appleton and Co., 1880; rpt. Oakland: Biobooks, 1946.

Burrows, J. M. D. *Fifty Years in Iowa.* Davenport: Glass & Co. printers, 1888.

Cake, L. B. *Peepstone Joe and the Peck Manuscript.* New York: By the editor, 1899.

Call, Anson. "A Busy Life." *Gems of Reminiscence.* Seventeenth Book of the Faith Promoting Series. Salt Lake City: Geo. C. Lambert, 1915.

Campbell, William W. *The Life and Writings of De Witt Clinton.* New York: Baker and Scribner, 1849.

Carter, Kate B. *Denominations that Base their Beliefs on the Teachings of Joseph Smith.* 2nd ed. [Salt Lake City]: Daughters of Utah Pioneers, 1969.

Caswall, Henry. *The City of the Mormons; Or, Three Days at Nauvoo, in 1842.* London: J. G. F. & J. Rivington, 1842.

Chamberlin, Ralph V. *The University of Utah: A History of Its First Hundred Years 1850 to 1950.* Salt Lake City: University of Utah Press, 1960.

Cheever, George B. *The Removal of the Indians.* Boston: Peirce and Williams, 1830.

Clark, Annie Turner. *A Mormon Mother: An Autobiography.* Salt Lake City: University of Utah Press, 1969.

Clark, John A. *Gleanings by the Way.* Philadelphia: Simon Bros., 1842.

A Collection of Sacred Hymns for the Church of the Latter Day Saints. Kirtland, 1835.

Cook, Thomas L. *Palmyra & Vicinity.* n.p. 1930.

Corbett, Pearson H. *Hyrum Smith, Patriarch.* Salt Lake City: Deseret Book Co., 1963.

Corrill, John. *A Brief History of the Church of Christ of Latter Day Saints, (Commonly Called Mormons); Including an Account of their Doctrines and Discipline; . . .* St. Louis: By the author, 1839.

Cowdery, Oliver. *Defence in a Rehearsal of My Grounds for Separating Myself from the Latter-day Saints.* Norton, Ohio; Pressley's Job Office, 1839.

Some doubt about the authenticity of this work has been cast by Richard L. Anderson.

———. *Letters by Oliver Cowdery, to W. W. Phelps, on the Origin of the Book of Mormon, and the Rise of the Church of Jesus Christ of Latter-day Saints.* Liverpool: Thomas Ward, 1844.

Cowley, Matthias F. *Wilford Woodruff.* Salt Lake City: Deseret Book Co., 1909.

Crary, Christopher G. *Pioneer and Personal Reminiscences.* Marshalltown, Iowa: n.p., 1893.

Cross, Whitney R. *The Burned-over District: The Social and Intellectual History of Enthusiastic Religion in Western New York, 1800–1850.* New York: Cornell University Press, 1950.

A discussion of the social and philosophical aspects of the early Mormon Church in a broad context of the times. Has had a strong influence on Mormon scholarship.

Daniels, William M. *Correct Account of the Murder of Generals Joseph and Hyrum Smith, at Carthage on the 27th Day of June, 1844.* Nauvoo: John Taylor, 1845.

Rare. Brigham Young University Library has a copy.

Davis, George T. M. *An Authentic Account of the Massacre of Joseph Smith, the Mormon Prophet, and Hyrum Smith, His Brother . . .* St. Louis: Chambers and Knapp, 1844.

Dow, George Francis. *History of Topsfield, Massachusetts.* Topsfield, Massachusetts: The Topsfield Historical Society, 1940.

Dow, Lorenzo. *Biography and Miscellany.* Norwich, Connecticut: William Faulkner, 1834.

———. *The Dealings of God, Man and the Devil, As Exemplified in the Life, Experience and Travels of Lorenzo Dow, In a Period of More than Half a Century.* Norwich, Connecticut: William Faulkner, 1833.

Evans, John Henry. *Joseph Smith: An American Prophet.* New York: Macmillan, 1933.

A popular biography from the Mormon point of view; ignores many controversial issues.

Farnham, Eliza W. *Life in Prairie Land.* New York: Harper and Brothers, 1846.

Finney, Charles G. *Memoirs of Rev. Charles G. Finney by Himself.* New York: A. S. Barnes & Co., 1876.

Flanders, Robert Bruce. *Nauvoo: Kingdom on the Mississippi.* Urbana: University of Illinois Press, 1965.

Considers the political and social aspects of the Mormons in Illinois, when Joseph Smith was doing his utmost to further his plans for a utopian society.

Fleming, Sandford. *Children and Puritanism: The Place of Children in the Life and Thought of the New England Churches 1620–1847.* New Haven: Yale University Press, 1933.

Flint, B. C. *An Outline History of the Church of Christ (Temple Lot).* Revised and Prepared for Publication by the Revising Committee. 2nd ed. Independence, Missouri: The Board of Publications, The Church of Christ (Temple Lot), 1953.

Ford, Thomas. *A History of Illinois from Its Commencement as a State in 1814 to 1847*. Chicago: S. C. Griggs & Co., 1854.

Frisbie, Barnes. *The History of Middletown, Vermont in Three Discourses*. Rutland, Vermont: Tuttle & Co., 1867.

Goodwin, S. H. *Mormonism and Masonry: A Utah Point of View*. Salt Lake City: Grand Lodge F. & A. M. of Utah, 1925.

Greene, John P. *Facts Relative to the Expulsion of the Mormons or Latter Day Saints, from the State of Missouri*. Cincinnati: R. P. Brooks, 1839.

Gregg, Thomas. *The Prophet of Palmyra*. New York: John B. Allen, 1890.

An anti-Mormon work by an Illinois journalist during the Mormon period in Nauvoo. Espouses the Spaulding theory.

————. *History of Hancock County Illinois*. Chicago: Charles C. Chapman & Co., 1880.

Gunn, Stanley R. *Oliver Cowdery*. Salt Lake City: Bookcraft, Inc., 1962.

Hansen, Klaus J. *Quest for Empire: The Political Kingdom of God and the Council of Fifty in Mormon History*. East Lansing: Michigan State University Press, 1967.

Discusses a once little-known but very significant aspect of the early Mormon hope to establish a worldwide government by the church.

Harris, William. *Mormonism Portrayed*. Warsaw, Illinois: Sharp & Gamble, 1841.

Hart, Albert Bushnell, ed. *American History told by Contemporaries:* Vol. I. *Era of Colonization 1492–1689*. New York: Macmillan, 1929.

Hill, Marvin S., and James B. Allen, eds. *Mormonism and American Culture*. New York: Harper & Row, 1972.

A collection of outstanding recent articles on Mormonism and its relationship to the larger American society, with introduction and commentary by the editors.

The Historical Collections of the Topsfield Historical Society. Vol. X. Topsfield, Massachusetts: By the Society, 1905.

History of Caldwell and Livingston Counties Missouri. St. Louis: National Historical Co., 1886.

The History of Daviess County Missouri. Kansas City, Missouri: Birdsall & Dean, 1882.

History of Jackson County, Missouri. Kansas City, Missouri: Union Historical Co., 1881.

History of the Church of Jesus Christ of Latter-day Saints. Period I. History of Joseph Smith, the Prophet, by Himself. Vols. I–VI. *Period II. From the Manuscript History of Brigham Young and Other Original Documents*. Vol. VII. Introduction and notes by B. H. Roberts. Salt Lake City: The Deseret Book Co., 1965–68.

Has been produced in various editions. Reprints many letters, memorials, extracts from diaries, newspaper accounts and other documents. The first six volumes were long purported to be by Joseph Smith, and a good deal of the material is taken from his journals. However, some was compiled from the diaries of other church leaders and put into the first person as though by Joseph Smith. Comparison with originals in the Historical Department of the

Church of Jesus Christ of Latter-day Saints discloses that some minor changes have been made, but the accusations of gross falsifying that have been levied by anti-Mormons are not justified.

History of Wayne County. New York: Everts, Ensign & Everts, 1877.

Hodge, Frederick W., ed. *Handbook of American Indians North of Mexico.* Bureau of American Ethnology Bulletin No. 30. 2 vols. Washington, D.C.: Smithsonian Institution, 1906; rpt. New York: Rowman and Littlefield, Inc., 1965.

Hotchkin, James H. *A History of the Purchase and Settlement of Western New York.* New York: M. W. Dodd, 1848.

Howe, Eber D. *Autobiography and Recollections of a Pioneer Printer.* Painesville, Ohio: Telegraph Steam Printing House, 1878.

————. *Mormonism Unvailed.* Painesville, Ohio, 1834.

   Advances the theory that *The Book of Mormon* was Solomon Spaulding's MS, as modified by Sidney Rigdon. Formed the basis for almost every anti-Mormon work written since. About half of the text is comprised of affidavits against the character of Joseph Smith and his family as collected by Philastus Hurlbut. Also includes Ezra Booth's letters, 1831.

Hudson, Winthrop S. *Religion in America: An Historical Account of the Development of American Religious Life.* 2nd ed. New York: Scribner's, 1973.

Hyde, Orson. *Speech of Elder Orson Hyde, Delivered Before the High Priests' Quorum in Nauvoo, April 27th, 1845, Upon the Course and Conduct of Mr. Sidney Rigdon and Upon His Claims to the Presidency . . .* Liverpool: James & Woodburn, 1845.

————. *A Voice from Jerusalem, or a Sketch of the Travels and Ministry of Elder Orson Hyde, Missionary of the Church of Jesus Christ of Latter Day Saints . . .* Liverpool: P. P. Pratt, Star Office, Printed by James & Woodburn, n.d.

An Illustrated Historical Atlas of Caldwell County, Missouri. Philadelphia: Edwards Brothers, 1876.

In Memoriam: Thomas Coke Sharp. [Carthage, Illinois: n.p., 1894?]

   Rare. Huntington Library has a copy.

Jenson, Andrew. *Church Chronology. A Record of Important Events Pertaining to the History of the Church of Jesus Christ of Latter-day Saints.* 2nd ed. Salt Lake City: Deseret News, 1899.

   Compiled by the former Church Historian from the Journal History, a collection of diaries, letters, memoirs, clippings and other documents in the Historical Department of the Church.

————. *Latter-day Saint Biographical Encyclopedia.* 4 vols. Salt Lake City: Andrew Jenson History Company, 1902, 1914, 1920, 1936.

Jernegan, Marcus Wilson. *Laboring and Dependent Classes in Colonial America 1607–1783.* Social Service Monographs, No. 17. Chicago: University of Chicago Press, 1931.

Johnson, Benjamin F. *"Mormonism as an Issue" An Open Letter to the Editor of the Arizona Republican.* Tempe, 1890.

————. *My Life's Review.* Independence, Missouri: Zion's Printing and Publishing Co., 1947.

The Journal of Discourses. Reports of Addresses by Brigham Young and Others. 26 vols. Liverpool and London: F. D. and S. W. Richards, 1853–86.

    A collection of the writings and sermons of many nineteenth-century leaders of the church.

Kane, Thomas Leiper. *The Private Papers and Diary of Thomas Leiper Kane: A Friend of the Mormons,* with an introduction and edited by Oscar Osburn Winther. San Francisco: Gelber-Lilienthal, Inc., 1937.

Kelley, William H. *A Defense of Monogamic Marriage.* n.p. [Reorganized Church of Jesus Christ of Latter Day Saints?] n.d.

Kennedy, James Harrison. *Early Days of Mormonism.* New York: Scribner's, 1888.

Kent, George. *The Characteristics and Claims of the Age in which we live, an oration pronounced at Dartmouth College before the New Hampshire Alpha of PBK Society.* Concord: Moses G. Atwood, 1832.

    Rare. Huntington Library has a copy.

Kett, Joseph F. "Growing Up In Rural New England, 1800–1840. in *Anonymous Americans,* Tamara K. Hareven, ed. Englewood Cliffs, New Jersey: Prentice-Hall, 1971.

Kirkham, Francis W. *A New Witness for Christ in America.* 3rd ed. 2 vols. Independence, Missouri: Zion's Printing and Publishing Co., 1951.

Knight, Newel. "Journal." *Scraps of Biography.* Salt Lake City, 1883.

Lathrop, Joseph. *Christ's Warning to the Churches, To Beware of False Prophets, Who Come as Wolves in Sheep's Clothing: And the MARKS by which they are known: Illustrated in TWO DISCOURSES.* Springfield, Massachusetts: Ezra W. Weld, 1789.

————. *Sermons by the Late Rev. Joseph Lathrop, D.D., Pastor of the First Church in West Springfield, Mass. New Series. with a Memoir of the Author's Life, written by Himself.* Springfield: A. G. Tannatt & Co., 1821.

Lee, John Doyle. *A Mormon Chronicle: The Diaries of John D. Lee, 1848–1876.* 2 vols. Edited by Robert Glass Cleland and Juanita Brooks. San Marino, California: Huntington Library, 1955.

————. *The Mormon Menace: Being the Confessions of John Doyle Lee DANITE . . .* Introduction by Alfred Henry Lewis. New York: Home Protection Publishing Co., 1905.

————. *Mormonism Unvailed.* St. Louis: Bryan, Brand & Co., 1877.

The life and labors of Eliza R. Snow Smith; with a full account of her funeral services. Salt Lake City: Juvenile Instructor Office, 1888.

Linn, William Alexander. *The Story of the Mormons from the Date of their Origin to the Year 1901.* 1902; rpt. New York: Macmillan, 1923.

    A detailed general study of the Mormon movement as a whole to 1900. Linn took a greater interest in the origins of Mormonism than had any writer before him, and his work is better documented, but most of his material came from early anti-Mormon writers and from the largely anti-Mormon Berrian Collection at the New York Public Library.

Lyne, T. A. *A True and Descriptive Account of the Assassination of Joseph and Hiram Smith, The Mormon Prophet and Patriarch.* New York: C. A. Calhoun, 1844.

Mack, Solomon. *A Narraitve* [sic] *of the Life of Solomon Mack, Containing an Account of the Many Severe Accidents He Met with During a Long Series of years, together with the Extraordinary Manner in which He Was Converted to the Christian Faith.* Windsor, Vermont: By the author, [1811?].
  Rare. New York Public Library has a copy.

Marks, David. *Life of David Marks to the 26th Year of His Age.* Chapter XXII. "Particulars of My travels and labours from November, 1829, to September, 1830." Limerick, Maine: Office of the Morning Star, 1831.

McCandless, Perry. *A History of Missouri. Vol. II. 1820 to 1860.* Columbia: University of Missouri Press, 1972.

M'chesney, James. *An Antidote to Mormonism: A Warning Voice to the Church and Nation.* New York: By the author, 1838.

Macgregor, Daniel *Changing of the Revelations.* Independence, Missouri: Board of Publications, Church of Christ Temple Lot, rpt. 1973.

McKay, Llewelyn R. *Home Memories of President David O. McKay.* Salt Lake City, 1956.

McNiff, William. *Heaven on Earth: A Planned Mormon Society.* Oxford, Ohio: The Mississippi Valley Press, 1940.

Mattison, Hiram. *An Essay on the Doctrine of the Trinity; or a Check to Modern Arianism, As Taught by Campbellites, Hicksites, New Lights, Universalists, and Mormons; And Especially by a Sect Calling themselves 'Christians.'* Watertown: N. W. Fuller, 1843.
  Rare. Huntington Library has a copy.

Milliken, Charles F. *A History of Ontario Co. N. Y. and Its People.* Vol. I. New York: Lewis Historical Publishing Co., 1911.

Mills, Samuel J., and Daniel Smith. *Report of a Missionary Tour Through That Part of the U.S. which lies West of the Appalachian Mts.* Andover: Flagg and Gould, 1815.

Mormonism Dissected, Or, Knavery "On Two Sticks," Exposed. By One Who hates imposture. Printed by Reuben Chambers. Bethania, Lancaster County, Pennsylvania, 1841.

The Mormons, or, Knavery Exposed. Giving an Account of the Discovery of the Golden Plates; The translation, and various tricks resorted to . . . Frankford Pennsylvania: E. G. Lee 1841.

Morrish, William John. *The Latter-Day Saints and the Book of Mormon.* Ledbury, England: J. Gibbs, Jun., printer, [1840].
  Huntington Library has a copy.

Mulder, William, and A. Russell Mortensen, eds. *Among the Mormons: Historic Accounts by Contemporary Observers.* New York: Knopf, 1958.

Mullen, Robert. *The Latter-day Saints: The Mormons Yesterday and Today.* New York: Doubleday, 1966.

Nibley, Hugh. *The Myth Makers.* Salt Lake City: Bookcraft, 1961.

Oaks, Dallin H., and Marvin S. Hill. *Carthage Conspiracy: The Trial of the Accused Assassins of Joseph Smith.* Urbana, Illinois: University of Illinois Press, 1975.
  A study of events preceding and the legal and sociological aspects of the trial of the accused assassins of Joseph and Hyrum Smith. Well documented.

O'Dea, Thomas F. *The Mormons.* Chicago: University of Chicago Press, 1957.
    A penetrating and disinterested study of Mormons and Mormonism in the context of the American social structure.
Paine, Thomas. *The Age of Reason.* New York: rpt. Matt & Lyon for Fellows & Adam & J. Reid, 1796.
Palmyra: Wayne County, New York. Compiled by The Woman's Society of the Western Presbyterian Church, 1907.
Parsons, Tyler. *Mormon Fanaticism Exposed. A Compendium of the Book of Mormon, or Joseph Smith's Golden Bible. Also, The Examination of its Internal and External evidences; with the argument to refute its pretences to a revelation from God: Argued before the Free Discussion Society in the City of Boston, July, 1841. Between Elder Freeman Nickerson, a Mormon and the author, Tyler Parsons.* Boston, 1842.
    Huntington Library has a copy.
Perry, Ralph Barton. *Characteristically American.* New York: Knopf, 1949.
Pratt, Orson. *The Bible and Polygamy.* 2nd ed. Salt Lake City: Deseret News Steam Printing Establishment, 1877.
———. *Divine Authenticity of the Book of Mormon.* Liverpool: Franklin D. Richards, 1851.
———. *An Interesting Account of Several Remarkable Visions.* New York: Joseph W. Harrison, 1841.
Pratt, Parley P. *An address By a Minister of the Church of Jesus Christ of Latter Day Saints, to the People of England.* Manchester: James Jones, n.d.
———. *Autobiography of Parley Parker Pratt: One of the Twelve Apostles of the Church of Jesus Christ of Latter-day Saints, Embracing His Life, Ministry and Travels, with Extracts, in Prose and Verse, from His Miscellaneous Writings.* 1874; 3rd ed. Salt Lake City: Deseret Book Co., 1938.
———. *History of the Late Persecution Inflicted by the State of Missouri Upon the Mormons.* Mexico, New York: Reprinted at the Office of the *Oswego County Democrat,* 1840.
———. *Late Persecution of the Church of Jesus Christ, of Latter Day Saints. Ten thousand American Citizens Robbed, Plundered, and Banished . . .* Written in prison. New York: J. W. Harrison, 1840.
———. *Mormonism Unvailed.* 2nd ed. New York: O. Pratt & E. Fordham, 1838.
———. *A Voice of Warning.* London: F. D. Richards, 1854.
Quaife, Milo. *The Kingdom of Saint James, A Narrative of the Mormons.* New Haven: Yale University Press, 1930.
Redmond, Pat H. *History of Quincy and Its Men of Mark.* Quincy, Illinois, 1869.
Remy, Jules A., and Julius Brenchly. *A Journey to Great Salt Lake City.* 2 vols. London: W. Jeffs, 1861.
Rich, Ben E. *Are the Mormons Loyal to the Government?* New York, 1910.
Rigdon, Sidney. *Oration Delivered by Mr. S. Rigdon on the 4th of July, 1838, at Far West, Missouri.* Far West, Missouri: The Journal Office, 1838.
    Chicago Historical Society has a copy.
———. to Messrs. Bartlett and Sullivan, May 27, 1839, *in Plain Facts Show-*

ing the Falsehood and Folly of Rev. C. S. Bush. [Manchester? W. R. Thomas? 1839?], pp. 14–16.

Rare. Huntington Library has a copy.

Riley, Isaac Woodbridge. *The Founder of Mormonism: A Psychological Study of Joseph Smith, Jr.* New York: Dodd, Mead & Co., 1902.

Describes Joseph as an epileptic who had seizures during which he saw visions.

Roberts, B. H. *Mormonism, Its Origin and History.* Independence, Missouri: Press of Zion's Printing & Publishing Co., 1923.

Scofield, Charles J., ed. *History of Illinois & History of Hancock County.* Chicago, 1921.

Simon, Barbara Anne. *The Ten Tribes of Israel Historically Identified with the Aborigines of the Western Hemisphere.* London: R. B. Seely and W. Burnside, 1836.

Smith, Alexander H. *Polygamy: Was It An Original Tenet of The Church of Jesus Christ of Latter Day Saints?* Lamoni, Iowa: Reorganized Church of Jesus Christ of Latter Day Saints, n.d.

Smith, David H. *The Bible Versus Polygamy.* Plano, Illinois: Reorganized Church of Jesus Christ of Latter Day Saints, n.d.

Smith, Emma, comp. *A Collection of Sacred Hymns, for the Church of Jesus Christ of Latter Day Saints.* Nauvoo, Illinois: E. Robinson, 1841.

Smith, Ethan. *View of the Hebrews.* 2nd ed. Poultney, Vermont: Smith & Shute, 1825.

Smith, James H. *History of Chenango and Madison Counties, New York.* Syracuse, 1880.

Smith, Jesse Nathaniel. *Six Decades in the Early West: The Journal of Jesse Nathaniel Smith; Diaries and Papers of a Mormon Pioneer, 1834–1906.* 3rd ed. Edited by Oliver R. Smith. Provo, Utah: Jesse N. Smith Family Association, 1970.

Smith, Job. *Diary of Job Smith, a Pioneer of Nauvoo, Illinois and Utah.* Arcadia, California: Printed by Louise Smith Willard, [1956?].

Smith, Joseph III. *One Wife, or Many.* Lamoni, Iowa: Reorganized Church of Jesus Christ of Latter Day Saints, n.d.

————. *Reply to Orson Pratt, By Joseph Smith, President of the Reorganized Church of Jesus Christ of Latter Day Saints.* Plano, Illinois, 1870.

Smith, Joseph III, and Heman C. Smith. *The History of the Reorganized Church of Jesus Christ of Latter Day Saints.* 4 vols. Lamoni, Iowa: 1896–1903.

Smith, Joseph F., Jr. *Asahel Smith, of Topsfield, Massachusetts, with some Account of the Smith Family.* Topsfield, Massachusetts: The Topsfield Historical Society, 1902.

Smith, Joseph Fielding. *Essentials in Church History.* 13th ed. Salt Lake City, 1953.

Emphasizes religious aspects of the history of the Utah church.

Smith, Lucy. *Biographical Sketches of Joseph Smith the Prophet and His Progenitors for Many Generations.* Liverpool: S. W. Richards, 1853; photo rpt. Salt Lake City: Modern Microfilm Co., n.d.

Smith, William. *Defence of Elder William Smith, Against The Slanders of*

Abraham Burtis, and Others. Philadelphia, Pennsylvania: Brown, Bicking & Guilbert, Printers, 1844.

In which are included several Certificates and the duties of Members in the Church of Christ, in settling difficulties one with another, according to the Law of God.

————. *William Smith on Mormonism.* Lamoni, Iowa: Herald Steam Book & Job Office, 1883.

Snow, Eliza R. *Biography and Family Record of Lorenzo Snow . . . written and compiled by his sister, Eliza R. Snow Smith.* Salt Lake City: Deseret News Co., 1884.

————. *Eliza R. Snow, an immortal. Selected writings of Eliza R. Snow.* Nicholas G. Morgan, Sr., Foundation, 1957.

Spafford, Horatio Gates. *Gazetteer of the State of New York.* Albany: Packard and Benthuysen, 1824.

Spencer, Orson. *Letters Exhibiting the Most Prominent Doctrines of the Church of Jesus Christ of Latter-day Saints.* Salt Lake City: Deseret News Co., 1889.

Stanley, Reva. *A Biography of Parley P. Pratt; the Archer of Paradise.* Caldwell, Idaho: Caxton Printers, Ltd., 1937.

Stenhouse, Fanny. *Expose of polygamy in Utah: A Lady's life among the Mormons . . .* New York: American News Company, 1872.

Stenhouse, T. B. H. *The Rocky Mountain Saints.* New York: D. Appleton and Co., 1873.

An able writer and journalist. He left the church and here presents his view that Joseph Smith was sincere but misguided.

Stout, Hosea. *On the Mormon Frontier; the Diary of Hosea Stout, 1844–1861.* Ed. by Juanita Brooks. 2 vols. Salt Lake City: University of Utah Press, 1964.

Swartzell, William. *Mormonism Exposed.* Pekin, Ohio: By the author, 1840.

Taggart, Stephen G. *Mormonism's Negro Policy: Social and Historical Origins.* Salt Lake City: University of Utah Press, 1970.

Tanner, Jerald and Sandra. *The Negro in Mormon Theology.* Salt Lake City: Modern Microfilm Co., [1967].

Taylor, John. *A short account of the MURDERS, ROBERIES, BURNINGS, THEFTS, and other outrages committed by the MOB and MILITIA of the State of Missouri, upon the LATTER DAY SAINTS. The Persecutions they have endured for their Religion, and their Banishment from that State by the Authorities Thereof.* Springfield? Illinois, 1839.

————. *Three Night's Public Discussion Between the Revds. C. W. Cleeve, James Robertson, and Philip Cater and Elder John Taylor, of the Church of Jesus Christ of Latter-day Saints, at Boulogne-Sur-mer France.* Liverpool: John Taylor, 1850.

Taylor, Samuel W. *Nightfall at Nauvoo.* New York: Macmillan, 1971.

Thompson, John Samuel. *Christian Guide.* Utica, New York, 1826.

Thorp, Joseph. *Early Days in the West Along the Missouri One Hundred Years Ago.* Liberty, Missouri: Irving Gilmer Publisher; rpt. 1924.

Towle, Nancy. *Vicissitudes Illustrated, in the Experience of Nancy Towle, in*

Europe and America . . . 2nd ed. Preface by Lorenzo Dow. Portsmouth: John Caldwell, 1833.

Tucker, Pomeroy. *Origin, Rise and Progress of Mormonism.* New York: D. Appleton & Co., 1867.

    A very influential work by an anti-Mormon resident of Palmyra who had worked in the shop where *The Book of Mormon* was printed. Used much from Howe and Hurlbut, but added material of his own.

Tullidge, Edward W., ed. *The Women of Mormondom.* New York: Tullidge & Crandall, 1877; rpt. Salt Lake City, 1957.

Turner, J. B. *Mormonism In All Ages.* New York: Platt & Peters, 1842.

Turner, O. *History of the Pioneer Settlement of Phelps and Gorham's Purchase, and Morris' Reserve.* Rochester: William Allington, 1851.

Tyler, Alice Felt. *Freedom's Ferment: Phases of American Social History to 1860.* 1944; rpt. New York: Harper Torchbooks, 1962.

West, Ray B., Jr. *Kingdom of the Saints: The Story of Brigham Young and the Mormons.* New York: Viking Press, 1957.

Whitmer, David. *An Address to All Believers in Christ, by A Witness to the Divine Authenticity of The Book of Mormon.* Richmond, Missouri: David Whitmer, 1887; photo rpt. Concord, California: Pacific Publishing Co., 1959.

Whitney, Helen Mar. *Plural Marriage as Taught by the Prophet Joseph, A Reply to Joseph Smith, Editor of the Lamoni (Iowa) Herald.* Salt Lake City: Juvenile Instructor Office, 1882.

————. *Why We Practice Plural Marriage.* Salt Lake City: Juvenile Instructor Office, 1884.

Winchester, B. *A History of the Priesthood.* Philadelphia: Brown, Bicking & Guilbert, 1843.

Wislizenus, F. A. *A Journey to the Rocky Mountains in the year 1839.* St. Louis: Missouri Historical Society, 1912.

Wyl, Wilhelm. *Mormon Portraits. Joseph Smith the Prophet, His Family and His Friends.* Salt Lake City: Tribune Publishing Co., 1886.

Young, Joseph. *History of the Organization of the Seventies.* Salt Lake City: Deseret News Steam Printing Establishment, 1878.

Young, Kimball. *Isn't One Wife Enough?* New York: Henry Holt and Company, 1954.

    Sociological aspects of polygamy, based upon case studies of polygamous families mainly in Utah.

DISSERTATIONS AND THESES

Dahl, Paul E. "William Clayton, Missionary, Pioneer, and Public Servant." M.A. thesis, Brigham Young University, 1959.

Fielding, Robert Kent. "The Growth of the Mormon Church in Kirtland, Ohio." Ph.D. dissertation, Indiana University, 1957.

Gentry, Leland. "A History of the Latter-day Saints in Northern Missouri from 1836 to 1839." Ph.D. dissertation, Brigham Young University, 1965.

Guthrie, Gary Dean. "Joseph Smith as an Administrator." M.S. thesis, Brigham Young University, 1969.

Hill, Marvin S. "The Role of Christian Primitivism in the Origin and Development of the Mormon Kingdom, 1830–1845." Ph.D. dissertation, University of Chicago, 1968.

Jennings, Warren Abner. "Zion is Fled: The Expulsion of the Mormons from Jackson County, Missouri." M.A. thesis, University of Florida, 1962.

McCarl, William B. "The Visual Image of Joseph Smith." M.A. thesis, Brigham Young University, 1962.

Parrish, William Earl. "The Life of David Rice Atchison: A Study in the Politics of a Border State." Ph.D. dissertation, University of Missouri, 1955.

Patrick, John R. "The School of the Prophets: Its Development and Influence in Utah Territory." M.A. thesis, Brigham Young University, 1969.

Shipps, JoAnn Barnett. "The Mormons in Politics: The First Hundred Years." Ph.D. dissertation, University of Chicago, 1965.

Swensen, Russel Brown. "The Influence of the New Testament upon Latter-day Saint Eschatology from 1830–1846." M.A. thesis, University of Chicago, 1931.

Yorgason, Laurence M. "Preview on A Study of the Social and Geographical Origins of Early Mormon Converts, 1830–1845." M.A. thesis, Brigham Young University, 1974.

MISCELLANEOUS MANUSCRIPTS

Blakeslee, M. P. "Notes for a History of Methodism in Phelps." 1886. Typescript. Brigham Young University Library, Provo, Utah.

"The Book of Mormon and Plural Marriage." Facsimile of a typescript. Mormon Collection, Huntington Library, San Marino, California.

Call, Anson. Statement of 1877 to Thomas Wm. Whitaker. Utah State Historical Society, Salt Lake City.

Coltrin, Zebedee. Address at a meeting of the High Priests, Spanish Fork, Utah, February 5, 1878. Recorded by Thomas Matley, ward clerk. MS D747, Zebedee Coltrin papers, Historical Department of the Church of Jesus Christ of Latter-day Saints, Salt Lake City.

————. Statement. File labeled Negroes. Historical Department of the Church of Jesus Christ of Latter-day Saints, Salt Lake City.

Cowdery, Oliver. "Oliver Cowdery Docket Book." Kirtland, Geauga County, Ohio. Mormon Collection, Huntington Library, San Marino, California.

Cox, Cragun. "Reminiscences of Joseph Smith." Utah State Historical Society, Salt Lake City.

Halkett, Henry. "Notes on Mr. Quincy's Visit to Joseph Smith." May 1844. Miscellaneous Manuscripts, Clements Library, University of Michigan. Ann Arbor, Michigan.

Harris, Martin. "The Last Testimony of Martin Harris." Typewritten, notarized account by William H. Homer, dated April 9, 1927. Brigham Young University Library, Provo, Utah.

Herrick, Lemual. Sworn affidavit, January 8, 1840. Document No. 9, United States Archives Manuscripts, Xerox Copy. Brigham Young University Library, Provo, Utah.

High Council Minutes, Far West, Missouri. 1838. Historical Department of the Church of Jesus Christ of Latter-day Saints, Salt Lake City.

High Council Minutes. Nauvoo, Illinois. 1839–45. Q1428R. Historical Department of the Church of Jesus Christ of Latter-day Saints, Salt Lake City.

Horne, Mrs. Joseph. "Migration and Settlement of the Latter Day Saints." Bancroft Collection, University of California, Berkeley.

Huntington, Dimick B. "D. B. Huntington's Statement of Joseph's Landing at Quincy, April 22, 1839." Historical Department of the Church of Jesus Christ of Latter-day Saints, Salt Lake City.

"Indenture made this the twenty third day of January in the year . . . one thousand eight hundred and forty four between Joseph Smith . . . of the one part; and Ebenezer Robinson . . . of the other part. Witnesseth that the said Joseph Smith . . . doth lease unto said Ebenezer Robinson . . . the 'mansion House' . . ." Copy. Whitney Collection, Brigham Young University Library, Provo, Utah.

Ivins, Grant. "Notes on the 1826 Trial of Joseph Smith." Historical Department of the Church of Jesus Christ of Latter-day Saints, Salt Lake City.

Kimball, Lucy Walker (Smith). "Statement of Mrs. L. W. Kimball—A Brief but Intensely Interesting Sketch of Her Experience Written by Herself—Her Marriage with Joseph Smith the Prophet . . ." Typed copy. Kimball Young Collection. Mormon Collection, Huntington Library, San Marino, California.

Kirtland Council Minute Book. Historical Department of the Church of Jesus Christ of Latter-day Saints, Salt Lake City.

Kirtland Revelations. Record Book 1830–34. Historical Department of the Church of Jesus Christ of Latter-day Saints, Salt Lake City.

"Kirtland Stake High Council Minutes 1834–1837, High Priests, Elders, Conference, Bishop Council, United Firm, Court Trials & Ordinations 1832–37." 02431R. Historical Department of the Church of Jesus Christ of Latter-day Saints, Salt Lake City.

Lee, John D., and Levi Stewar. Account of the Gallatin affair, August 6, 1838. Journal History. Historical Department of the Church of Jesus Christ of Latter-day Saints, Salt Lake City.

"Manuscript History of the Anti-Mormon Disturbances in Illinois, 1845, from the Anti-Mormon Viewpoint." Thomas C. Sharp papers, Yale University Library, New Haven, Connecticut.

Manuscript Revelations. Historical Department of the Church of Jesus Christ of Latter-day Saints, Salt Lake City.

Minutes of the Council of Twelve. In box labeled "High Council Meetings, etc., Conference and Public Meetings." Historical Department of the Church of Jesus Christ of Latter-day Saints, Salt Lake City.

"Missionaries of the Church of Jesus Christ of L. D. S. Set apart since 1830." Missionary Record. Film. Historical Department of the Church of Jesus Christ of Latter-day Saints, Salt Lake City.

Murdock, Hollie Osbourne. "Sketch of the Life of Mary Elizabeth Rollins Lightner by her great grand daughter Hollie Osbourne Murdock." Mary E. Lightner MS Collection, Brigham Young University Library, Provo, Utah.

Nauvoo House Day Book, 1842–45. Historical Department of the Church of Jesus Christ of Latter-day Saints, Salt Lake City.

Nauvoo House Ledger, 1841–45. Historical Department of the Church of Jesus Christ of Latter-day Saints, Salt Lake City.

Peck, Reed. "Reed Peck Manuscript." Mormon File Box 10. Huntington Library, San Marino, California.

Powell, Mary (Bennion), to George R. Stewart. MS in the form of letters on polygamy. Typescript. Mormon File Box 11. Huntington Library, San Marino, California.

Pratt, Parley P. Testimony before the municipal court, Nauvoo. [July 1, 1843.] Parley Pratt papers, Historical Department of the Church of Jesus Christ of Latter-day Saints, Salt Lake City.

Richards, Willard. "List of Mobocrats, June 29, 1844." Historical Department of the Church of Jesus Christ of Latter-day Saints, Salt Lake City.

Rigdon, John W. "Lecture Written By John W. Rigdon on the Early History of the Mormon Church." Typed copy. Brigham Young University Library, Provo, Utah.

Rockwell, Orrin Porter. Sworn affidavit, February 3, 1840. Document No. 9, United States Archives Manuscripts, Xerox copy. Brigham Young University Library, Provo, Utah.

Smith, Emma. Blessing. [1844?] Emma Smith file, Historical Department of the Church of Jesus Christ of Latter-day Saints, Salt Lake City.

Smith, Joseph. "Joseph Smith Jr.'s Book for Record." Historical Department of the Church of Jesus Christ of Latter-day Saints, Salt Lake City.

————. King Follet Sermon. [April 7, 1842.] MS in unidentified hand, with corrections by Thomas Bullock. Joseph Smith papers, Historical Department of the Church of Jesus Christ of Latter-day Saints, Salt Lake City.

————. Letter Book. Historical Department of the Church of Jesus Christ of Latter-day Saints, Salt Lake City.

————. "A Religious Proclamation from Joseph Smith, about 1842." Joseph Smith papers, Historical Department of the Church of Jesus Christ of Latter-day Saints, Salt Lake City.

————. Revelation to Newel K. Whitney, Nauvoo, Illinois, July 27, 1842. Historical Department of the Church of Jesus Christ of Latter-day Saints, Salt Lake City.

————. Sermon on the Godhead, June 16, 1844. Copy by Thomas Bullock. Joseph Smith papers, Historical Department of the Church of Jesus Christ of Latter-day Saints, Salt Lake City.

Smith, Lucy Mack. "The History of Lucy Smith Mother of the Prophet." MS in the hand of Howard Coray. Historical Department of the Church of Jesus Christ of Latter-day Saints, Salt Lake City.

Smith, William. Notes written on "Chambers Life of Joseph Smith" [Chambers' Miscellany]. Typed copy. Historical Department of the Church of Jesus Christ of Latter-day Saints, Salt Lake City.

Snow, E.[liza] R. "Brief Sketch of some instructions which Joseph Smith gave the female Relief Society." Joseph Smith papers, Historical Department of the Church of Jesus Christ of Latter-day Saints, Salt Lake City.

————. "Meeting of the Female Relief Society at the Grove August 31, 1842, reported by E. R. Snow" Joseph Smith papers, Historical Department of the Church of Jesus Christ of Latter-day Saints, Salt Lake City.

"Statements regarding a funeral sermon preached by Joseph Smith at the funeral of Seymour Brunson, August 15, 1840." Joseph Smith papers, Historical Department of the Church of Jesus Christ of Latter-day Saints, Salt Lake City.

Third Quorum of Seventy Minute and Roll Book 1898–1907. Historical Department of the Church of Jesus Christ of Latter-day Saints, Salt Lake City.

Whitney, Helen Mar. Statement on Celestial Marriage, written and signed at Salt Lake, March 30, 1881. Helen Mar Whitney papers, Historical Department of the Church of Jesus Christ of Latter-day Saints, Salt Lake City.

Woods, J. W. "The Mormon Prophet; A true Version of the Story of his Martyrdom; Reminiscences of an old timer, who was Joe Smith's attorney." Journal History, June 27, 1844, Historical Department of the Church of Jesus Christ of Latter-day Saints, Salt Lake City.

Woodward, Charles L. "First Half Century of Mormonism. Papers, engravings, photographs and autographed letters collected and arranged by Charles Woodward, 1880." Manuscripts Division. New York Public Library.

Zahnd, John. Manuscript on Mormons. Typescript. Manuscripts Division. New York Public Library.

INDEX

Joseph Smith Country

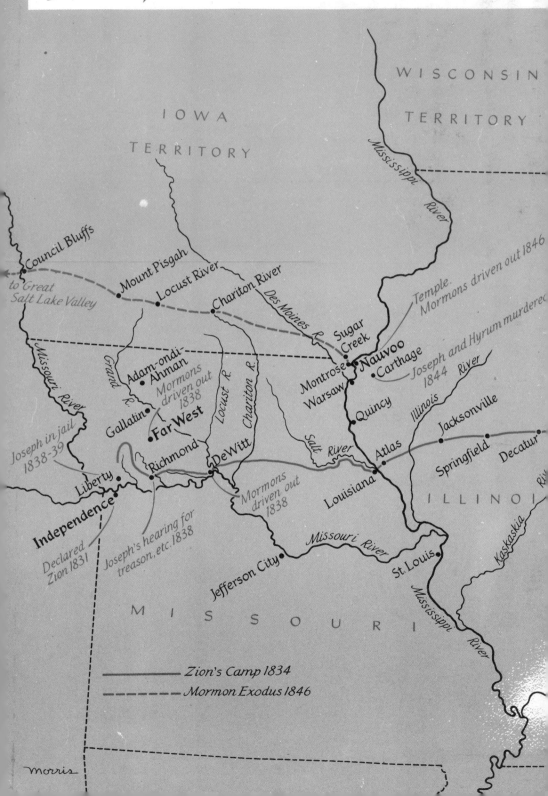

WISCONSIN TERRITORY

IOWA TERRITORY

Mississippi River

Council Bluffs

to Great
Salt Lake Valley

Mount Pisgah

Locust River

Chariton River

Des Moines R.

Sugar
Creek

Temple.
Mormons driven out 1846

Montrose

Nauvoo

Carthage

Joseph and Hyrum murdered
1844

Missouri River

Grand R.

Adam-ondi-
Ahman

Mormons
driven out
1838

Locust R.

Chariton R.

Warsaw

Quincy

Illinois River

Jacksonville

Gallatin

Far West

Springfield

Decatur

Joseph in jail
1838-39

Richmond

DeWitt

Atlas

Liberty

Independence

Declared
Zion 1831

Joseph's hearing for
treason, etc. 1838

Mormons
driven out
1838

Salt River

Louisiana

ILLINOI

Kaskaskia Riv

Missouri River

MISSOURI

Jefferson City

St. Louis

Mississippi River

—————— Zion's Camp 1834
— — — — Mormon Exodus 1846

morris